REGISTER OF SHIPS
OF THE U.S. NAVY,
1775–1990

REGISTER OF SHIPS OF THE U.S. NAVY, 1775–1990

Major Combatants

K. JACK BAUER
and
STEPHEN S. ROBERTS

GREENWOOD PRESS
New York • Westport, Connecticut • London

Library of Congress Cataloging-in-Publication Data

Bauer, K. Jack (Karl).
    Register of ships of the U.S. Navy, 1775-1990 : major combatants /
K. Jack Bauer and Stephen S. Roberts.
      p. cm.
    Includes bibliographical references and index.
    ISBN 0-313-26202-0 (alk. paper)
    1. United States. Navy—Lists of vessels. 2. Warships—United
States—History. 3. United States. Navy—History. I. Roberts,
Stephen S. II. Title.
    VA61.B36 1991
    359.3'25'0973—dc20   91-25241

British Library Cataloguing in Publication Data is available.

Library of Congress Catalog Card Number: 91-25241
ISBN: 0-313-26202-0

First published in 1991

Greenwood Press, 88 Post Road West, Westport, CT 06881
An imprint of Greenwood Publishing Group, Inc.

Printed in the United States of America

The paper used in this book complies with the
Permanent Paper Standard issued by the National
Information Standards Organization (Z39.48-1984).

10 9 8 7 6 5 4 3 2 1

Contents

Illustrations..vii
Preface...xi
Standard Abbreviations..xv
Ship and Engine Builders..xvii

1. The Sail Navy, 1775-1853

    Ships of the Line...1
    Ships of the Line (Lake)...4
    Frigates...5
    Frigates (Lake)...15
    Sloops of War...16
    Sloops of War (Lake)...23
    Brigs...24
    Brigs (Lake)..27
    Schooners...29
    Schooners (Lake)..32
    Sloops..32
    Blockships..32
    Armed Merchantmen (Sail)..33

2. The Old Steam Navy, 1814-1876

    Ironclads..39
    Ironclads (River)...47
    Steam Floating Batteries..53
    Steam Frigates and Large Sloops (1st rates)...53
    Steam Sloops (2nd and 3rd rates)..60
    Small Steam Sloops and Gunboats (4th rates)...71
    Double-Ended Gunboats (3rd rates)...78
    Steamers (Lake)...82
    Spar Torpedo Boats..83
    Armed Merchantmen (Steam)...86

3. The New Navy, 1883-1990

    Monitors (BM)...99
    Battleships (BB)...102
    Battle Cruisers (CC)...114

    Aircraft Carriers (CV)...115
    Small Aircraft Carriers (CVL)..120
    Large Aircraft Carriers (CVB)..121
    Attack Aircraft Carriers (CVA)...123
    Nuclear Powered Attack Aircraft Carriers (CVAN)..124
    Aircraft Escort Vessels (AVG)..125
    Auxiliary Aircraft Carriers (ACV)..126
    Escort Aircraft Carriers (CVE)...131

    Armored Cruisers (CA)..133
    Large Cruisers (CB)..135
    Heavy Cruisers (CA)..136
    Protected and Unprotected Cruisers...141
    Dynamite Cruisers..146
    Torpedo Cruisers...147
    Scout Cruisers...147
    Light Cruisers (CL)..148
    Tactical Command Ships (CLC)...153
    Guided Missile Heavy Cruisers (CAG)..153
    Guided Missile Light Cruisers (CLG)..154

vi   CONTENTS

Nuclear Powered Guided Missile Cruisers (CGN)......................................154
Guided Missile Cruisers (CG)..155
Gunboats (Seagoing) (PG)..155
Dispatch Vessels..161
Armored Rams..162

Torpedo Boats...162
Destroyers (DD)...168
Guided Missile Destroyers (DDG)...211
Destroyer Leaders (DL)..213
Guided Missile Frigates (DLG)...213
Nuclear Powered Guided Missile Frigates (DLGN)....................................215
Nuclear Powered Guided Missile Cruisers (CGN, ex DLGN)............................217
Guided Missile Cruisers (CG, ex DDG)..217

Escort Vessels (DE)...219
Escort Research Ships (AGDE)..244
Guided Missile Escort Ships (DEG)...245
Corvettes (Twin Screw) (PG)...245
Frigates (PF)...246
Guided Missile Frigates (FFG)...251

Submarines (SS)...253
Anti-Submarine Submarines (SSK)...284
Nuclear Powered Submarines (SSN)..284
Radar Picket Submarines (SSR)...291
Nuclear Powered Radar Picket Submarines (SSRN)....................................291
Guided Missile Submarines (SSG)...291
Nuclear Powered Guided Missile Submarines (SSGN)..................................292
Nuclear Powered Fleet Ballistic Missile Submarines (SSBN).........................292
Auxiliary Submarines (AGSS)...296
Target and Training Submarines (SST)..296

Armed Merchantmen (New Navy)..297

Bibliography..299
Hull Number Index...303
Index...309

Illustrations

The ship of the line Vermont as a receiving ship at New York after the Civil War. (NH 93915)........3

The frigate Constitution at the Boston Navy Yard on 18 August 1914 as rebuilt in 1907. The scout cruiser Chester is in the background. (NH 55907)............13

The frigate Sabine ca. 1869. (NH 91722)............13

The sloop of war Vandalia as drawn by Frank Muller. Her main battery was in the open. (NH 43851).. 22

The sloop of war St. Mary's as a training ship after the Civil War. Her main battery was covered by a complete spardeck. (NH 55474)............22

The schooner Enterprise in 1812 after being rerigged as a brigantine. From a contemporary etching by the French artist Baugean. (NH 63535)............30

The monitor Nahant ca. 1898. The hurricane deck was added after the Civil War and the roof over the turret was added when she was put in reserve. (NH 69787)............41

The double-turret monitor Agamenticus after receiving a hurricane deck between the turrets in 1865. (NH 47016)............41

The river ironclads Baron de Kalb, Cincinnati, and Mound City off Cairo, Ill., in 1863. (NH 56663).48

The paddle frigate Powhatan. (NH 2738)............48

The screw frigate Minnesota at the New York Navy Yard soon after the Civil War. (NH 92)............56

The large screw sloop Florida (ex-Wampanoag) in drydock at the New York Navy Yard ca. 1869. (NH 54159)............56

A Wyoming-class screw sloop during the Civil War. (NH 45368)............65

The screw sloop Ticonderoga at Venice between 1866 and 1869. (NH 45373)............65

The 90-day gunboat Marblehead. (NH 46630)............74

The small screw sloop Adams off Mare Island. (NH 57279)............74

The double-ended gunboat Conemaugh. (NH 49989)............84

The torpedo ram Alarm in drydock at the New York Navy Yard ca. 1874. (NH 57291)............84

The "rebuilt" double-turret monitor Miantonomoh (BM-5) ca. 1907. (NH 60649)............100

The battleship Kentucky (BB-6). (NH 61959)............100

The battleship Georgia (BB-15) in 1907. (NH 73911)............105

The battleship Florida (BB-30) ca. 1918. (NH 54174)............105

The battleship Arizona (BB-39) during gunnery practice ca. 1917. Her forward 5" guns have not yet been removed. (NH 95244)............110

The battleship Wisconsin (BB-64) alongside the hulk of the Oklahoma (BB-37) at Pearl Harbor on 11 November 1944. (NH 78940)............110

The aircraft carrier Lexington (CV-2) on 31 May 1934. (NARA 80-G-415861)............116

The ASW support aircraft carrier Tarawa (CVS-40) on 13 August 1958, in a configuration typical of unmodified Essex-class carriers. (NARA 80-G-1046503)............116

The large aircraft carrier Midway (CVB-41) near Norfolk on 4 April 1947. (NH 49826)............122

The nuclear powered aircraft carrier Dwight D. Eisenhower (CVN-69) during sea trials on 23 August 1977. (USN 1170824)...122

The escort aircraft carrier Altamaha (CVE-18) off San Francisco on 16 July 1943 with a deck load of P-51 fighters. (NARA 80-G-74453)..127

The escort aircraft carrier Badoeng Strait (CVE-116). (NH 67541).................................127

The armored cruiser Brooklyn (CA-3) in 1898 just after the Spanish American War. (NH 61501).......134

The large cruiser Guam (CB-2) near Trinidad in January 1945. (NARA 80-G-290578)..................134

The heavy cruiser Louisville (CA-28) in the early 1930s. (NH 51903)..............................137

The heavy cruiser Rochester (CA-124) off the east coast of Korea on 16 March 1954. (NARA 80-G-644206)...137

The protected cruiser Atlanta ca. 1886. (NH 57444)..142

The "semi-armored" cruiser Charleston (No. 22) alongside the receiving ship Philadelphia (formerly protected cruiser No. 4) at Puget Sound before World War I. (NH 92172)...............142

The light cruiser St. Louis (CL-49) on trials off Rockland, Maine, on 28 April 1939. Her 5"/38 gun mounts have not yet been installed. (NH 48998)...149

The nuclear powered guided missile cruiser Long Beach (CGN-9) on sea trials on 7 July 1961. (USN 1056853)..149

The gunboat Bennington (PG-4) ca. 1891. (NH 63248)..156

The gunboat Erie (PG-50) photographed by the New York Navy Yard on 19 October 1936. (NH 54262)....156

The torpedo boat Cushing (No. 1). (NH 69186)..163

The destroyer Stewart (DD-13) with the Preble (DD-12) at Guaymas, Mexico, on 26 December 1915. (NH 92183)..163

The destroyer Preston (DD-19) soon after completion. (NH 44198).................................173

A World War I destroyer, probably Gilmer (DD-233) or Kane (DD-235), on sea trials. She has 5"/51 instead of the usual 4"/50 guns. (NH 43771)..173

The destroyer Cassin (DD-372) on 2 February 1937. (NARA 19-N-17931)..............................185

The destroyer Anderson (DD-411) at high speed, probably on sea trials. Her fifth 5"/38 gun has not yet been removed and her Mk. 37 gun director has not yet been fitted. (NH 96119)............185

The Fletcher-class destroyer Anthony (DD-515) on 8 December 1944. (NARA 80-G-77161)...............197

The Gearing-class destroyer Rich (DD-820) photographed by the New York Navy Yard on 17 September 1947. She is in her original configuration except that Mount 52 has been removed to make room for a training hedgehog. (NH 86114)...197

The destroyer David R. Ray (DD-971) off southern California ca. 1979. (NARA KN-27644).............209

The guided missile destroyer Henry B. Wilson (DDG-7) underway in October 1969. (USN 1142937)......209

The guided missile frigate Mahan (DLG-11) preparing to refuel from the carrier Kitty Hawk on 14 November 1965. (USN 1115255)...216

The nuclear powered guided missile cruiser Mississippi (CGN-40) in Hampton Roads on 28 June 1978. (USN 1172840)..216

The Buckley-class escort vessel England (DE-635) off San Francisco on 9 February 1944. (NARA 19-N-60938)..229

The John C. Butler-class escort vessel Walter C. Wann (DE-412) in 1944. (NH 90602)................229

The escort ship Bradley (DE-1041) in 1965. (NH 96714)................................242

The escort ship Gray (DE-1054) ca. 1970. (USN 1143228)...............................242

The frigate Albuquerque (PF-7) ca. 1943. (NH 81377)..................................249

The guided missile frigate Wadsworth (FFG-9) on 1 January 1979. (DOD DN-SC-83-11901)..............249

The submarine Tarpon (SS-14) in 1909. She was soon renamed C-3. (NH 43600).......................255

The submarine AA-1 (SS-52) off Provincetown, Mass., ca. 1920. She became the fleet submarine
T-1 (SF-1) later in 1920. (NH 43762)...255

The cruiser submarine V-6 (SC-2) on sea trials in San Francisco Bay on 8 October 1930. She
became USS Nautilus (SS-168) in 1931. (NH 63446)..................................266

The submarine Grampus (SS-207) off Groton, Conn., on 26 March 1941. (NARA 19-N-23816).............266

The Gato-class submarine Croaker (SS-246) on 16 July 1952, in a configuration typical of
war-built submarines in 1945. (NARA 80-G-445899)..................................274

The submarine Trout (SS-566) on 13 May 1952. (NARA 80-G-443363)..................................274

The nuclear powered submarine Skate (SSN-578) on 6 December 1957. (NARA 80-G-1037389).............285

The nuclear powered submarine San Francisco (SSN-711) on sea trials in the James River on
31 March 1981. (USN 1180787)..285

The nuclear powered guided missile submarine Halibut (SSGN-587) in early 1960. (USN 1046796)......294

The nuclear powered fleet ballistic missile submarine Henry L. Stimson (SSBN-655) on 14 August
1966. (USN 1117530)...294

Preface

At the time of his death, Jack Bauer was at work on this volume, the first of three designed to update and expand his Ships of the Navy 1775-1969, published in 1969 by Rensselaer Polytechnic Institute. His revision of the preface was virtually complete. Therefore, as appropriate and with a minimum of change, the original author speaks for himself.

During the summer and fall of 1775, George Washington organized a squadron of converted fishermen and coasters to harass the British garrison in Boston. Later in the year, the Continental Congress established a more permanent force with an equally ill-assorted collection of vessels at Philadelphia. From these inauspicious beginnings has sprung the world's greatest navy. During its existence over 10,000 vessels, large and small, have flown the commission pennant of the United States Navy.

Students of American naval history cannot find detailed information on those vessels in any single source. This work attempts to fill that lack by bringing together in one place the surviving statistical information on those vessels which have been commissioned into naval service or were intended for it. Insofar as possible, this volume rests on official sources, but those are sometimes incomplete and often contradictory. Where feasible, the omissions in the official record have been filled from other sources. Yet, major gaps in our knowledge of the ships of the navy still persist. The author hopes that this work will lead others to fill in some of the blank spaces.

The inability of sources, even official ones, to agree is little short of amazing. For instance, research for this study located nine different figures for the beam of the frigate Constitution and six for the displacement of the Civil War period Contoocook class of screw sloops. Where conflicts have arisen, the criteria for selection have been, first, genealogy, and, second, apparent inherent validity. To those readers whose favorite figures have not been used, the author offer his regrets and assures them that those used appeared even more valid.

Any work of this nature presents problems of organization. No arrangement will meet the needs of all researchers, but the one selected appears best to blend both accuracy and utility. This volume covers major combatants; left for later coverage are minor combatants, auxiliaries, and large commissioned amphibious craft. Entries are arranged by type and chronologically within type by date of authorization. Vessels not specifically authorized by an act of Congress (a not uncommon nineteenth century occurrence) or captured are inserted at the chronologically appropriate point in the development of a type.

Since the United States Navy has possessed too many vessels to permit their inclusion in a single volume, arbitrary criteria have been established to govern placement. For inclusion as a major combatant, a vessel must meet one of the following requirements:

Old Navy (Prior to 1883)
1. Sailing vessels mounting 10 or more guns;
2. Armored vessels;
3. Steam vessels mounting 4 or more guns;

New Navy (Since 1883)
1. Armored vessels;
2. Aircraft carriers;
3. Large unarmored vessels, i.e. unprotected cruisers and gunboats of over 1,000 tons or mounting four or more guns of 4" or greater caliber;
4. Torpedo craft and large escorts, i.e. torpedo boats, destroyers, destroyer escorts, frigates, and submarines, including their specialized sub-types.

Data have been selected for its utility to the general student rather than to the specialist in naval architecture or marine engineering. Therefore, the maximum dimensions (overall length, extreme beam, maximum draft) have been used when known. An exception has been made for vessels having bowsprits. Since their overall length would give a false impression of their size, length between perpendiculars has been substituted. The following information has been given, when available:

1. Displacement or tonnage. Normal displacement has been preferred; other types of displacement such as standard and light are specified when known. Tonnage, which signifies burden or measurement tonnage, should be used with caution since the rules governing its calculation varied widely.

2. <u>Dimensions</u>. The form is length x beam x draft. When known, the type of measurement, i.e. length overall or between perpendiculars, molded or extreme beam, maximum or mean draft, has been specified.

3. <u>Armament</u>. The original armament and any permanent changes have been shown along with the date of change. Guns intended primarily for use away from the vessel like boat howitzers and field guns have not been included. Neither have been secondary batteries of guns lighter than 3" because of the frequency of their alteration.

4. <u>Armor</u>. The maximum thickness of the armor belt, turrets, gun shields, decks and conning towers have been shown.

5. <u>Propulsion</u>. The rig has been shown for all rigged craft prior to 1883. It has been dropped for later vessels because of their nearly total reliance on steam for movement. The horsepower, engine type, and means of propulsion are shown for steamers.

6. <u>Complement</u>. Where possible, the authorized complement at the time of commissioning has been shown. Where that could not be determined, the earliest known figure has been used. No attempt has been made to record the frequent later changes in authorized complement or to indicate the actual crew carried at any date.

7. <u>Ship Names</u>. Ships are generally listed under the final U.S. name assigned during construction. Earlier and later U.S. names are given in the notes. Names in parentheses are foreign names given to ships that never got U.S. names. Such ships were mostly built under the World War II Lend Lease and the postwar Offshore Procurement programs.

8. <u>Construction data for each vessel</u>. Where known, the builders of both the hull and the machinery, the keel laying, launching, and first commissioning dates of each vessel have been shown. In some cases, the machinery builder is indicated instead in the propulsion listing.

9. <u>Disposition of each vessel</u>. Information is supplied on losses, sales, transfers, and (except for losses) the dates ships were stricken from the Naval Vessel Register. For a brief period in 1919-22 strikes were not used, and the nearest equivalent dates are given here. Where possible, sale dates are those of awards to the buyers--after the bids were opened and before the ships were delivered to the purchasers. Award dates are generally available after about 1960; many sale dates in the late 1940s and early 1950s are probably delivery dates. The initial foreign names of transferred ships are given unless they are shown in parentheses in the name column.

10. <u>Notes</u>. These include changes in name, reclassifications, rebuildings, and other pertinent information. Shipbuilding program information--authorizations, order dates, or fiscal years--is also given. Authorization dates before 1860 are from two works by Jack Bauer, fiscal years are primarily from the <u>Navy Yearbook</u> and works by Roberts and Alden, all cited in the bibliography.

Few historians plow untilled fields. Most must make frequent and rewarding use of the work of those who preceded them, and the present author is no exception. The researches of George F. Emmons, Frank M. Bennett, Robert W. Neeser, and Howard I. Chapelle have not only eased the preparation of this study but have served as an inspiration. The author has not always agreed with their conclusions but was tremendously impressed by the magnitude and value of their work. Nor can anyone who researches the vessels of the United States Navy ignore the contributions of the often anonymous authors of the Naval Historical Center's <u>Dictionary of American Naval Fighting Ships</u>, especially Dean C. Allard, Larry R. Smart, James L. Mooney, and John C. Reilly.

One of the pleasures in preparing this study has been the opportunity to conduct research in many libraries and repositories, notably Widener Memorial Library of Harvard University, Sterling Memorial Library of Yale University, Rensselaer Polytechnic Institute Library, Indiana University Library, New York Public Library, the Library of Congress, Navy Department Library, Library of the Marine Corps Historical Center, the National Archives, and the Franklin D. Roosevelt Library at Hyde Park. It has been the kind and efficient service rendered by their staffs which made this study possible.

As might be expected from a project which has spanned over forty years, many friends, far too numerous to permit mention here by name, gave support and counsel at critical moments. Three, however, stand out and must be mentioned: W. Jacques Steeple, Jesse Burgess Thomas, and Ronald A. Mueller.

On a personal note, the undersigned wishes to thank Mildred Vasan at Greenwood Press for her infinite patience and understanding, gentle prodding and encouragement during difficult times. It was fortuitous indeed that Stephen S. Roberts undertook to guide this work to fruition. There could be no steadier hand on the tiller. I am especially grateful to Dean C. Allard, Director of Naval History, for his assistance, advice, and support so swiftly and unstintingly offered and so unsparingly and gratefully taken.

The research material, ledgers, and updated manuscript, which form the basis for this book, are in the Archives at Rensselaer Polytechnic Institute, John F. Dojka, archivist.

Dorothy S. Bauer

* * *

In completing the revision of this volume, the undersigned has attempted to remain faithful to the original scope and format of the work while incorporating the results of an additional twenty years of research by Dr. Bauer and others. The indispensable starting point was Dr. Bauer's updated copy of the 1969 edition, which contained many of the changes that have occurred since then such as the deletion from the fleet of nearly all World War II era ships and the addition of many new vessels. Dr. Bauer also produced a new draft of the sail navy section, which appears here largely as he wrote it. His format for this section was also used as a pattern for the format of the remainder of the revised volume.

During the revision, information on ship dispositions was expanded to include the dates ships were stricken from the Naval Vessel Register. Information on shipbuilding programs (authorizations or fiscal years if available) was added to the notes, and information on renamings and reclassifications was moved to separate sections at the end of the notes. Finally, the notes for many classes were expanded in an effort to explain why the ships were built. Such information is now available in an impressive series of books by Norman Friedman and in important volumes by other authors, including John D. Alden, Donald L. Canney, Robert O. Dulin, Jr., William H. Garzke, Jr., Ivan Musicant, John C. Reilly, Jr., Robert L. Scheina, Paul H. Silverstone, and Robert F. Sumrall.

Photographs have been added to this edition. Their sources are indicated by the prefixes of the negative numbers at the end of the captions. "NH" photographs are from the collection of the Naval Historical Center, "NARA" photographs are from the National Archives and Records Administration, "USN" photographs are Navy photographs recently transferred to the National Archives and added to their 80-G series, and "DN" photographs are from the Department of Defense, Still Media Records Center. For information on obtaining copies of these photographs, contact the appropriate repository:

Naval Historical Center, Navy Yard, Washington, DC 20374-0571
Still Picture Branch, National Archives (NNSP), Washington, DC 20408
Department of Defense, Still Media Records Center, Code SSRC, Washington, DC 20374-1681.

In collecting information on the subject of this volume, I also have benefited from the work of friends and fellow researchers too numerous to mention. Work carried out over many years by Samuel Loring Morison is the basis of much of the information available today on U.S. Navy ship disposals. More recently, I owe special thanks to Charles R. Haberlein, Christopher C. Wright, Norman Friedman, John C. Reilly, Jr., Donald L. Canney, and Michael D. Roberts for their advice and comments during the preparation of this volume and to Sue G. Ross for her patient support.

Stephen S. Roberts

Standard Abbreviations

AA	Anti-aircraft gun(s)
AB	Crane Ship
ACV	Auxiliary, Aircraft Carrier
AG	Miscellaneous Auxiliary
AGDE	Escort Research Ship
AGER	Escort Research Ship; Environmental Research Ship (1967)
AGFF	Frigate Research Ship
AGMR	Major Communications Relay Ship
AGSS	Auxiliary Submarine
AHP	Actual Horsepower
AKV	Cargo Ship and Aircraft Ferry
AO	Oiler
AOSS	Submarine Oiler
APD	High Speed Transport
APS	Transport, Submarine
APSS	Transport, Submarine
AS	Submarine Tender
ASSA	Cargo Submarine
ASSP	Transport Submarine
ASW	Antisubmarine Warfare
AV	Seaplane Tender
AVD	Seaplane Tender (Destroyer)
AVG	Aircraft Escort Vessel
AVP	Small Seaplane Tender
AVT	Auxiliary Aircraft Transport; Training Aircraft Carrier (AVT-16)
BACV	Auxiliary, Aircraft Carrier for Britain
BAVG	Aircraft Escort Vessel for Britain
BB	Battleship
BBG	Guided Missile Capital Ship
b.d.	Berth Deck
BDE	Escort Vessel for Britain
BHP	Brake Horsepower
BLR	Breech Loading Rifle
BM	Monitor
b.p.	Between Perpendiculars
c	Carronade
CA	Armored Cruiser; Heavy Cruiser (1931)
CAG	Guided Missile Heavy Cruiser
CB	Large Cruiser
CBC	Large Tactical Command Ship
CC	Battle Cruiser; Command Ship (1961)
CG	Guided Missile Cruiser
CGN	Nuclear Powered Guided Missile Cruiser
CL	Light Cruiser
CLAA	Anti-Aircraft Light Cruiser
CLC	Tactical Command Ship
CLG	Guided Missile Light Cruiser
CLGN	Nuclear Powered Guided Missile Light Cruiser
CLK	Cruiser-Hunter Killer Ship
CM	Mine Layer
col	Columbiad
Commiss'd	Commissioned
CSS	Confederate States Ship

CV	Aircraft Carrier
CVA	Attack Aircraft Carrier
CVAN	Nuclear Powered Attack Aircraft Carrier
CVB	Large Aircraft Carrier
CVE	Escort Aircraft Carrier
CVHA	Assault Helicopter Aircraft Carrier
CVHE	Escort Helicopter Aircraft Carrier
CVL	Small Aircraft Carrier
CVN	Nuclear Powered Aircraft Carrier
CVS	ASW Support Aircraft Carrier; ASW Aircraft Carrier
CVT	Training Aircraft Carrier
CVU	Utility Aircraft Carrier
d	Deck
DASH	Destroyer Antisubmarine Warfare Helicopter
DD	Destroyer
DDE	Escort Destroyer; Anti-Submarine Destroyer
DDG	Guided Missile Destroyer
DDK	Hunter Killer Destroyer
DDR	Radar Picket Destroyer
DE	Escort Vessel; Escort Ship (1961)
DEC	Control Escort Vessel
DEG	Guided Missile Escort Ship
DER	Radar Picket Escort Vessel; Radar Picket Escort Ship (1961)
DL	Destroyer Leader; Frigate (1955)
DLG	Guided Missile Frigate
DLGN	Nuclear Powered Guided Missile Frigate
DM	Light Mine Layer; Destroyer Minelayer (1955)
DMS	High Speed Mine Sweeper; Destroyer Minesweeper (1955)
e	Extreme
f.d.	Flight Deck
FF	Frigate
FFG	Guided Missile Frigate
FFR	Radar Picket Frigate
FRAM	Fleet Rehabilitation and Modernization
g.d.	Gun Deck
h	Depth of Hold
HIJMS	His Imperial Japanese Majesty's Ship
HMS	His Majesty's Ship (Great Britain)
HP	Horsepower
IHP	Indicated Horsepower
IX	Unclassified Miscellaneous Vessel
IXSS	Unclassified Miscellaneous Submarine

k	Keel		SF	Fleet Submarine
kts.	Knots		SHP	Shaft Horsepower
			SM	Mine-Laying Submarine
			SS	Submarine
LPH	Amphibious Assault Ship		SSA	Submarine Cargo
LPR	Amphibious Transport (Small)		SSAG	Auxiliary Submarine
LPSS	Amphibious Transport Submarine		SSBN	Nuclear Powered Fleet Ballistic Missile Submarine
			SSG	Guided Missile Submarine
m	Molded		SSGN	Nuclear Powered Guided Missile Submarine
M	Mortar		SSK	Anti-Submarine Submarine
max	Maximum		SSKN	Nuclear Powered Anti-Submarine Submarine
MC	Maritime Commission (U.S.)		SSN	Nuclear Powered Submarine
MDAP	Mutual Defense Assistance Program		SSO	Submarine Oiler
Mk.	Mark		SSP	Submarine Transport
MMD	Destroyer Minelayer		SSR	Radar Picket Submarine
MTB	Motor Torpedo Boat(s)		SSRN	Nuclear Powered Radar Picket Submarine
			SST	Target and Training Submarine
			Stk.	Stricken from the Naval Vessel Register
NHP	Nominal Horsepower			
			T	Torpedo Tube(s)
oa.	Overall Length			
o.g.	Over Guards		u.d.	Upper Deck
			USM	Underwater to Surface Missile
			UUM	Underwater to Underwater Missile
PF	Frigate; Patrol Escort (1955); Patrol Frigate (1973)			
PG	Gunboat		WSA	War Shipping Administration
pur.	Purchased		wl.	Waterline
			YFB	Ferry Boat
R	Muzzle Loading Rifle		YW	Water Barge
SAM	Surface to Air Missile		#	Pounder
SC	Fleet Submarine, Cruiser Type; Submarine Chaser, 110' (1943)		*	Date given is not commissioning
SCB	Ship Characteristics Board		( )	Name given is not USN
s.d.	Spar Deck			

Ship and Engine Builders

A. C.	Allis Chalmers Manufacturing Co.	Milwaukee, Wisc.
A. C. Loire	Ateliers et Chantiers de la Loire	St. Nazaire, Fr.
A. Denny	Archibald Denny	Dumbarton, England
Abrahams	J. J. Abrahams	Baltimore, Md.
Adams	Aquilla Adams	Boston, Mass.
Aitken & Mansel	Aitken & Mansel	Greenock, Scotland
Alameda	Bethlehem Steel Corp.	Alameda, Calif.
Alco	American Locomotive Co.	Auburn, N. Y.
Allain	Allain Works	New York, N. Y.
Allaire	Allaire Iron Works	New York, N. Y.
Allen	G. B. Allen & Co.	St. Louis, Mo.
Ash	James Ash	Millwall, London, England
Atlantic	Atlantic Works	Boston, Mass.
Avondale	Avondale Marine Ways, Inc.	Avondale, La.
Barclay Curle	Barclay Curle & Co.	Glasgow, Scotland
Barker	Josiah Barker	Charlestown, Mass.
Bath	Bath Iron Works	Bath, Me.
Bazan	Factoria de Bazan	Ferrol, Spain
Beloit	Beloit Iron Works	(Unknown)
Bestor	George C. Bestor	Mound City, Ill.
Beth-SF	Bethlehem Steel Corp.	San Francisco, Calif.
Birely	Jacob Birely	Philadelphia, Pa.
Birely & Lynn	Jacob Birely & John W. Lynn	Philadelphia, Pa.
Borys	M. Borys	Amsterdam, Neth.
Boston	Boston Navy Yard	Charlestown, Mass.
Boston Loco	Boston Locomotive Works	Boston, Mass.
Bowers	Sylvester Bowers	Providence, R. I.
Box	Alfred Box & Co.	New York, N. Y.
Briggs	Enos Briggs	Salem, Mass.
Brown	Adam & Noah Brown	New York, N. Y.
Brown, Cincinnati	Joseph Brown	Cincinnati, Ohio
Brown, Erie	Adam & Noah Brown	Presque Ille, Pa.
Brown, New Albany	Joseph Brown	New Albany, Ind.
Brown, Philadelphia	William & Abraham Brown	Philadelphia, Pa.
Brown, Sackets Hbr.	Adam & Noah Brown	Sackets Harbor, N. Y.
Brown, Storrs Hbr.	Adam & Noah Brown	Storrs Harbor, N. Y.
Brown, Vergennes	Adam & Noah Brown	Vergennes, Vt.
Burtis	Devine Burtis	Brooklyn, N. Y.
Buffalo	Bethlehem Shipbuilding Corp.	Buffalo, N. Y.
Burling	Lancaster Burling	Poughkeepsie, N. Y.
Busch-Sulzer	Busch-Sulzer Bros. Diesel Engine Co.	St. Louis, Mo.
Butler	Walter Butler	Superior, Wisc.
C. B.	Cooper-Bessemer Corp.	Grove City, Pa.
Caird	Caird & Co., Ltd.	Greenock, Scotland
California	California Shipbuilding Co.	Los Angeles, Calif.
Canadian Vickers	Canadian Vickers, Ltd.	Montreal, Que.
Cant. Nav. di Taranto	Cantieri Navali di Taranto	Taranto, Italy
Capes & Allison	Capes & Allison	Hoboken, N. J.
Carr	Caleb Carr	Warren, R. I.
Carraca Dockyard	La Carraca Dockyard	Cartagena, Spain
Cartagena Dockyard	Cartagena Naval Dockyard	Cartagena, Spain
Carter	Columbus P. Carter	Belfast, Me.
Caverly	Joseph Caverly	Baltimore, Md.
Ch. de la Med.	Chantiers de la Mediterranee	La Seyne, France
Charleston	Charleston Navy Yard	Charleston, S. C.
Cheeseman	Foreman Cheeseman	New York, N. Y.

Churchill	C. & D. Churchill	Portland, Conn.
City Pt.	City Point Works (Harrison Loring)	East Boston, Mass.
Claghorn	George Claghorn (at Hartt's Shipyard)	Boston, Mass.
Cleveland	American Shipbuilding Co.	Cleveland, Ohio
Coats	Warwick Coats	Southwark, Pa.
Columbian	Columbian Iron Works & Drydock Co.	Baltimore, Md.
Colwell	Joseph Colwell	Jersey City, N. J.
Coney	Jabez Coney	Boston, Mass.
Consolid.	Consolidated Steel	Los Angeles, Cal.
Cont'l Bklyn.	Continental Works (T. F. Rowland)	Brooklyn, N. Y.
Continental	Continental Iron Works	Greenport, N. Y.
Continental, Vallejo	Continental Iron Works & Secor & Co.	Vallejo, Calif.
Conway	Richard Conway	Alexandria, Va.
Copeland	Charles W. Copeland	New York, N. Y.
Corliss	Corliss Steam Engine Co.	Providence, R. I.
Cotton	John Cotton	Portland, Conn.
Craig	Craig Shipbuilding Co.	Long Beach, Calif.
Cramp	William Cramp & Sons Ship & Engine Building Co.	Philadelphia, Pa.
Crescent	Crescent Shipyard	Elizabethport, N. J.
Cross	Stephen & Ralph Cross	Newburyport, Mass.
Cross & Clark	William Cross & Thomas M. Clark	Newburyport, Mass.
Cross & Merrill	Cross & Merrill	Newburyport, Mass.
Culley	Langley B. Culley	Baltimore, Md.
Curtis, Boston	Paul Curtis	Boston, Mass
Curtis, Medford	J. O. Curtis	Medford, Mass.
Curtis, Melrose	Paul Curtis	Melrose, Mass.
Curtis & Tilden	Curtis and Tilden	Boston, Mass.
Defoe	Defoe Shipbuilding Co.	Bay City, Mich.
Delamater	C. H. Delamater Iron Works	New York, N. Y.
DeLaval	DeLaval Steam Turbine Co.	Trenton, N. J.
Delaware River	Delaware River Iron Shipbuilding & Engine Works (N. F. Palmer)	Chester, Pa.
Denmead	A. & W. Denmead & Son	Baltimore, Md.
Denny	William Denny & Bros., Ltd.	Dumbarton, Scotland
DeRochbrune	DeRochbrune	Baltimore, Md.
Dialogue	J. H. Dialogue & Son	Camden, N. J.
Diamond	Diamond Iron Works	(Unknown)
Diehl	Diehl Manufacturing Co.	Bridgeport, Conn.
Dolan & Farron	Dolan & Farron	Williamsburgh, N. Y.
Donahue, Ryan, & Secor	Donahue, Ryan, & Secor	San Francisco, Calif.
Dravo, Pittsburgh	Dravo Corp.	Pittsburgh, Pa.
Dravo, Wilmington	Dravo Corp.	Wilmington, Del.
Dudgeon	J. & W. Dudgeon	Millwall, London, England
Dunham	R. H. Dunham	New York, N. Y.
Dyer	J. W. Dyer	Portland, Me.
EB-Quincy	Electric Boat Div., General Dynamics Corp.	Quincy, Mass.
E. D.	Electro-Dynamic Co.	Bayonne, N. J.
Eads, Carondelet	James B. Eads	Carondelet, Mo.
Eads, Mound City	James B. Eads	Mound City, Ill.
Eads, St. Louis	James B. Eads	St. Louis, Mo.
Eckford, Sackets Hbr.	Henry Eckford	Sackets Harbor, N. Y.
Eckford & Bergh	Henry Eckford & Christian Bergh	Oswego, N. Y.
Eckford Webb	Eckford Webb	Greenpoint, N. Y.
Eggleston	Moses Eggleston	Vergennes, Vt.
Elliott	Elliott Motor Co.	Jeannette, Pa.
Ellis	William M. Ellis	Washington, D. C.
Elswick	Armstrong, Mitchell & Co.	Newcastle-on-Tyne, England
Englis	John Englis	New York, N. Y.
Esler	Henry Esler & Co.	New York, N. Y.

Etna	Etna Iron Works	New York, N. Y.
Eyre	Manuel, Jehu, & Benjamin Eyre	Kensington, Pa.
F. M.	Fairbanks, Morse & Co.	Beloit, Wisc.
Fiat	Fiat-San Giorgio Ltd.	Turin, Italy
Flannigan & Parsons	Flannigan & Parsons	Baltimore, Md.
Fletcher	Fletcher Harrison & Co.	New York, N. Y.
Fore River	Fore River Ship & Engine Co.	Quincy, Mass.
Fox	Josiah Fox	Norfolk, Va.
Froemming	Froemming Bros. Inc.	Milwaukee, Wisc.
Fulton	Robert Fulton	New York, N. Y.
Fulton Fdry.	Fulton Foundry	Jersey City, N. J.
Fulton IrWks	Fulton Iron Works (Pease & Murphy)	New York, N. Y.
G. E.	General Electric Co.	Lynn, Mass., & Schenectady, N. Y.
G. M.	General Motors Corp.	Cleveland, Ohio
Gas Engine	Gas Engine & Power Co. & Charles L. Seabury & Co. Consolidated	Morris Heights, N. Y.
Gatz, McClune	Gatz, McClune & Co.	St. Louis, Mo.
Gaylord	Thomas G. Gaylord	St. Louis, Mo.
Germania	Friederich Krupp Germaniawerft A. G.	Kiel, Germany
Gildersleeve	Gildersleeve & Sons	East Haddam, Conn.
Globe	Globe Iron Works	Boston, Mass.
Globe SB	Globe Shipbuilding Corp.	Superior, Wisc.
Goodspeed	E. G. & W. H. Goodspeed	East Haddam, Conn.
Greenleaf	Jonathan Greenleaf	Newburyport, Mass.
Greenman	George Greenman & Co.	Mystic, Conn.
Greenwood	Miles Greenwood	Cincinnati, Ohio
Grice	Joseph & Thomas Grice	Southwark, Pa.
Groton	Electric Boat Co.	Groton, Conn.
Gulf	Gulf Shipbuilding Corp.	Chickasaw, Ala.
H. O. R.	Hooven, Owens, Rentschler Co.	Hamilton, Ohio
Hackett, Paul & Hill	James Hackett, Stephen Paul, & James Hill	Portsmouth, N. H.
Hall	Samuel Hall	Boston, Mass.
Hall, Renfrew	Lawrence Hall	Renfrew, Scotland
Hambleton	S. T. Hambleton & Co.	Cincinnati, Ohio
Hambleton, Collier	Hambleton, Collier	Peoria, Ill.
Harlan & Hollingsworth	Harlan & Hollingsworth Corp.	Wilmington, Del.
Hartt	Edmund Hartt	Boston, Mass.
Hartt & Badger	Edmund Hartt & William Badger	Portsmouth, N. H.
Hartt & Barker	Edmund Hartt & Josiah Barker	Boston, Mass.
Harvey, Hayle	Harvey & Son	Hayle, England
Hawthorne, Leslie	R. & A. Hawthorne, Leslie & Co., Ltd.	Newcastle-on-Tyne, England
Hazlehurst & Wiegard	Hazlehurst & Wiegard	Baltimore, Md.
Hendry	J. Hendry Iron Works	(Unknown)
Herreshoff	Herreshoff Manufacturing Co.	Bristol, R. I.
Hews & Philips	Hews & Philips	Belfast, Ireland
Hickson	Robert Hickson & Co.	Belfast, Ireland
Highland	Highland Iron Works	Newburgh, N. Y.
Hillman	Charles Hillman Co.	Philadelphia, Pa.
Hillman & Streaker	Hillman & Streaker	Philadelphia, Pa.
Hilt	John Hilt	Thomaston, Me.
Hingham	Bethlehem-Hingham Shipyards, Inc.	Hingham, Mass.
Houston	Brown Shipbuilding Co.	Houston, Tex.
Howaldt	Gesellshaft Howaldtwerke	Kiel, Germany
Humphreys	Joshua Humphreys	Southwark, Pa.
Humphreys, Hutton & Delavane	Samuel Humphreys, Nathaniel Hutton, & John Delavane	Philadelphia, Pa.

Humphreys & Penrose	Humphreys & Penrose	Philadelphia, Pa.
Humphreys & Tennant	Humphreys & Tennant, Ltd.	London, England
Huntington	Joshua Huntington	Chatham, Conn.
Hutton	Benjamin Hutton	Philadelphia, Pa.
Ingalls	Ingalls Shipbuilding Corp.	Pascagoula, Miss.
Iowa	Iowa Iron Works	Dubuque, Iowa
J. & F. Grice	Joseph & Francis Grice	Southwark, Pa.
J. A. & D. D. Westervelt	John A. & Daniel D. Westervelt	New York, N. Y.
J. K. Hackett	James K. Hackett	Portsmouth, N. H.
Jackman	George W. Jackman, Jr.	Newburyport, Mass.
Jackson & Sheffield	John Jackson & William Sheffield	Brooklyn, N. Y.
Jackson & Watkins	Jackson & Watkins	London, England
Jenks	Jenks Shipbuilding Co.	Port Huron, Mich.
Jewett	James C. Jewett & Co.	Brooklyn, N. Y.
Jones Quiggin	Jones Quiggin & Co.	Liverpool, England
Kaiser	Kaiser Cargo Inc.	Richmond, Cal.
Kearny	Federal Shipbuilding & Dry Dock Co.	Kearny, N. J.
Kemp	Thomas Kemp	Baltimore, Md.
Kirkpatrick	Kirkpatrick & McIntyre	Glasgow, Scotland
Koppers	Koppers Co.	(Unknown)
L. Arman	L. Arman	Bordeaux, France
L. Smith	Leathem D. Smith Shipbuilding Co.	Sturgeon Bay, Wisc.
Laing	Sir James Laing & Sons, Ltd.	Sunderland, England
Lake	Lake Torpedo Boat Co.	Bridgeport, Conn.
Larrabee & Allen	Larrabee & Allen	Bath, Me.
Lawley	George Lawley & Sons, Corp.	South Boston, Mass.
Lawrence, Portland	George W. Lawrence	Portland, Me.
Lawrence, Thomaston	George W. Lawrence	Thomaston, Me.
Lawrence & Foulkes	Lawrence & Foulkes	Brooklyn, N. Y.
Levingston	Levingston Shipbuilding Co.	Orange, Tex.
Lisnave	Estaleiros Navais Lisnave	Lisbon, Portugal
Litherbury	J. Litherbury	Cincinnati, Ohio
Lockheed	Lockheed Shipbuilding & Construction Co.	Seattle, Wash.
Lorain	American Shipbuilding Co.	Lorain, Ohio
Lorient	Lorient Naval Dockyard	Lorient, France
Loring	Harrison Loring	Boston, Mass
Lupton	Edward Lupton	Brooklyn, N. Y.
Lynn	John W. Lynn	Philadelphia, Pa.
McCord	Charles W. McCord	St. Louis, Mo.
McCord & Junger	McCord & Junger	New Albany, Ind.
McKay	Donald McKay	East Boston, Mass.
McKay & Aldus	Nathaniel McKay & Aldus	East Boston, Mass.
McKnight	John L. McKnight	Bordentown, N. J.
McLeod	Daniel M. McLeod	Brooklyn, N. J.
Maizuru	Maizuru Naval Dockyard	Maizuru, Japan
Mallory	Charles Mallory	Mystic, Conn.
Manitowoc	Manitowoc Shipbuilding Corp.	Manitowoc, Wisc.
Mare I.	Mare Island Navy Yard	Vallejo, Calif.
Marsh	James Marsh	Charleston, S. C.
Maryland Steel	Maryland Steel Co.	Spsrrows Pt., Md.
Maxon, Fish	Maxon, Fish, & Co.	Mystic River, Conn.
Mazeline	Mazeline	Le Havre, France
Mehaffey	A. Mehaffey & Co.	Portsmouth, Va.

Merrick & Sons	Merrick & Sons	Philadelphia, Pa.
Merrick & Towne	Merrick & Towne	Philadelphia, Pa.
Merrill	Nathan & Orlando B. Merrill	Newburyport, Mass.
Mershon	D. S. Mershon, Jr.	Bordentown, N. J.
Mitsubishi, Kobe	Shin-Mitsubishi Jyuko Co.	Kobe, Japan
Mitsubishi, Nagasaki	Mitsubishi Zosen	Nagasaki, Japan
Moore	Moore Shipbuilding Co.	Elizabethport, N. J.
Moore & Richardson	Moore & Richardson (Cincinnati Locomotive Works)	Cincinnati, Ohio
Moran	Moran Brothers Co.	Seattle, Wash.
Morgan	Morgan Iron Works	New York, N. Y.
Morris	I. P. Morris & Co.	Philadelphia, Pa.
Morris, Towne	Morris, Towne, & Co.	Philadelphia, Pa.
Murphy	James Murphy	New York, N. Y.
Murray & Hazlehurst	Murray & Hazlehurst	Baltimore, Md.
Mystic	Mystic Iron Works	Mystic, Conn.
Napier	R. Napier & Sons, Ltd.	Glasgow, Scotland
Nash & Herbert	Nash & Herbert	Norfolk, Va.
Navalmecc. Castellammare	Navalmeccanica Castellammare di Stabia	Castellammare di Stabia, Italy
Neafie & Levy	Neafie & Levy Ship & Engine Building Co.	Philadelphia, Pa.
Neilson	Neilson & Co.	Glasgow, Scotland
Nelseco	New London Ship & Engine Co.	Groton, Conn.
Neptune	Neptune Works	New York, N. Y.
New York	New York Navy Yard	Brooklyn, N. Y.
New York SB	New York Shipbuilding Corp.	Camden, N. J.
Newport News	Newport News Shipbuilding & Dry Dock Co.	Newport News, Va.
Niles	Niles Tool Works	Niles, Ohio
Nixon	Lewis Nixon (Crescent Shipyard)	Elizabethport, N. J.
Norfolk	Norfolk Navy Yard	Gosport, Va.
Norfolk SB	Norfolk Shipbuilding & Drydock	Norfolk, Va.
Novelty	Novelty Iron Works	New York, N. Y.
Orange	Consolidated Steel Corp., Ltd.	Orange, Tex.
Oswald	T. R. Oswald & Co.	Sunderland, England
Otto	Schleicher, Schumm, & Co. (Otto Gas Engine Works)	Philadelphia, Pa.
Overton	Seth Overton	Chatham, Conn.
Pacific	Pacific Iron Works	Bridgeport, Conn.
Pechon	M. Pechon	Chefuncte, La.
Peck & Carpenter	Peck & Carpenter	New York, N. Y.
Penhoet	Chantiers et Ateliers de St. Nazaire (Penhoet) S. A.	St. Nazaire, France
Penrose	Thomas Penrose	Philadelphia, Pa.
Pensacola	Pensacola Navy Yard	Warrington, Fla.
Perrine	William Perrine	Williamsburg, N. Y.
Perrine, Patterson & Stack	Perrine, Patterson, & Stack	Williamsburg, N. Y.
Philadelphia	Philadelphia Navy Yard	Philadelphia, Pa.
Pile	W. Pile & Co.	Sunderland, England
Poillon	C. & R. Poillon	New York, N. Y.
Pook	S. H. Pook Iron Works	Mystic, Conn.
Pook, Fairhaven	S. H. Pook	Fairhaven, Conn.
Poole & Hunt	Poole & Hunt	Baltimore, Md.
Port Newark	Federal Shipbuilding & Dry Dock Co.	Port Newark, N. J.
Portland	Portland Locomotive Works	Portland, Me.
Portsmouth	Portsmouth Navy Yard	Kittery, Me.
Price	William Price	Fells Point, Md.
Pritchard	Paul Pritchard	Charleston, S. C.
Providence	Providence Steam Engine Works	Providence, R. I.

Puget Sd.	Puget Sound Navy Yard	Bremerton, Wash.
Puget Sd. Br.	Puget Sound Bridge & Dredging Co.	Seattle, Wash.
Pusey & Jones	Pusey & Jones Corp.	Wilmington, Del.
Quincy	Bethlehem Steel Corp.	Quincy, Mass.
Quintard	Quintard Iron Works	New York, N. Y.
Randall & Eldridge	Randall & Eldridge	Belfast, Ireland
Reaney	Reaney, Son, and Archbold	Chester, Pa.
Reaney & Neafie	Reaney & Neafie	Chester, Pa.
Reeder	Charles Reeder	Baltimore, Md.
Reliance	Reliance Machine Co.	Mystic, Conn.
Richmond	Richmond Locomotive Works	Richmond, Va.
Ridgeway	Ridgeway Dynamo & Engine Co.	Ridgeway, Pa.
Roach	John Roach & Son	Chester, Pa.
Robb	John A. Robb	Baltimore, Md.
Roosevelt	Roosevelt, Joyce & Co.	New York, N. Y.
S. Brooklyn	South Brooklyn Engine Works	South Brooklyn, N. Y.
S. Smith	Sylvanus Smith	Boston, Mass.
Sampson	A. & G. T. Sampson	Boston, Mass.
Samuelson	Martin Samuelson & Co.	Hull, England
San Francisco	San Francisco Naval Shipyard	San Francisco, Calif.
San Pedro	Bethlehem Steel Corp.	San Pedro, Calif.
Schichau	F. Schichau G. m. b. H.	Elbing, Germany
Schott & Whitney	Schott & Whitney	Baltimore, Md.
Sea-Tac, Seattle	Seattle-Tacoma Shipbuilding Corp.	Seattle, Wash.
Sea-Tac, Tacoma	Seattle-Tacoma Shipbuilding Corp.	Tacoma, Wash.
Seattle	Seattle Shipbuilding & Dry Dock Co.	Seattle, Wash.
Secor & Co.	T. F. Secor & Co.	New York, N. Y.
Sequin	William Sequin	Philadelphia, Pa.
Sherman	Jahaziel Sherman	Vergennes, Vt.
Ship Owners	Ship Owners' Dry Dock Co.	Chicago, Ill.
Simonson	Jeremiah Simonson	New York, N. Y.
Smith & Dimon	Smith & Dimon	New York, N. Y.
Sneeden	Samuel Sneeden	New York, N. Y.
Snowden	Snowden & Mason	South Pittsburgh, Pa.
Spencer	Henry Spencer	Baltimore, Md.
Squantum	Bethlehem Shipbuilding Co.	Squantum, Mass.
Stack	Thomas Stack	New York, N. Y.
Stack & Joyce	Stack & Joyce	New York, N. Y.
Stackhouse & Tomlinson	Stackhouse & Tomlinson	Pittsburgh, Pa.
Staten I.	Bethlehem Steel Co.	Staten I., N. Y.
Steers	Henry Steers	Greenpoint, N. Y.
Stevens	Robert L. Stevens	Hoboken, N. J.
Stodder	David Stodder	Baltimore, Md.
Stodder, Norfolk	David Stodder	Norfolk, Va.
Stover	Stover Machine Co.	New York, N. Y.
Sun	Sun Shipbuilding & Dry Dock Co.	Chester, Pa.
Sutton	James T. Sutton & Co.	Philadelphia, Pa.
Swift	Alexander Swift & Co.	Cincinnati, Ohio
Swift, Evans	Swift, Evans, & Co.	Cincinnati, Ohio
Talman	Benjamin Talman	Warren, R. I.
Talman & de Wolf	Benjamin Talman & James de Wolf	Warren, R. I.
Tampa	Tampa Shipbuilding & Engineering Co.	Tampa, Fla.
Taunton	Taunton Locomotive Works	Taunton, Mass.
Teas & Birely	Teas & Birely	Philadelphia, Pa.
Thatcher	W. & A. Thatcher	Wilmington, Del.
Thompson	Nathaniel W. Thompson	Kennebunk, Me.
Thomson	J. & G. Thomson	Glasgow, Scotland

Thornycroft	John I. Thornycroft & Co., Ltd.	Woolston, England
Tod & McGregor	Tod & McGregor	Glasgow, Scotland
Todd, San Pedro	Todd-Pacific Shipyards, Inc.	San Pedro, Calif.
Todd, Seattle	Todd-Pacific Shipyards, Inc.	Seattle, Wash.
Todd, Tacoma	Todd-Pacific Shipyards, Inc.	Tacoma, Wash.
Tomlinson	Joseph Tomlinson	Pittsburgh, Pa.
Tomlinson, Hartupee	Tomlinson, Hartupee, & Co.	Pittsburgh, Pa.
Tredegar	Tredegar Iron Works	Richmond, Va.
Trigg	William R. Trigg Co.	Richmond, Va.
Tucker	F. Z. Tucker	Brooklyn, N. Y.
Underhill	J. S. Underhill Dry Dock & Iron Works	New York, N. Y.
Union	Union Iron Works	San Francisco, Calif.
Union, Carondelet	Union Iron Works	Carondelet, Mo.
United	United Shipyards Inc.	Staten I., N. Y.
Valley	Valley Iron Works	(Unknown)
Vancouver	Henry J. Kaiser Co., Inc.	Vancouver, Wash.
Van Deusen	J. B. & J. D. Van Deusen	New York, N. Y.
Van Deusen & Birely	Van Deusen & Birely	Kensington, Pa.
Vaughn & Lynn	Vaughn & Lynn	Philadelphia, Pa.
Viana	Estaleiros Navais de Viana do Costelo	Viana do Costelo, Port.
Vulcan	Vulcan Iron Works	New York, N. Y.
W & J Hackett	William & James M. Hackett	Salisbury, Mass.
Walsh	Walsh-Kaiser Co., Inc.	Providence, R. I.
Washington	Washington Navy Yard	Washington, D. C.
Washington IrWks	Washington Iron Works	Newburgh, N. Y.
Webb	William H. Webb	New York, N. Y.
Webb & Bell	Webb & Bell	New York, N. Y.
Webster	Daniel Webster	Salisbury, Mass.
Wells	George Wells	Fells Point, Md.
West Pt.	West Point Foundry	Newburgh, N. Y.
Western Pipe	Western Pipe & Steel Co.	San Francisco, Calif.
Westervelt	Jacob A. Westervelt	New York, N. Y.
Westinghouse	Westinghouse Electric Co.	Pittsburgh, Pa.
Wharton & Humphreys	John Wharton & Joshua Humphreys	Kensington, Pa.
White & Middleton	White & Middleton Co.	Springfield, Ohio
Whitlock	E. S. Whitlock	Greenpoint, N. Y.
Wilcox & Whiting	Wilcox & Whiting	Camden, N. J.
Wilhelmshaven	Wilhelmshaven Naval Dockyard	Wilhemshaven, Germany
Willamette	Willamette Iron & Steel Corp.	Portland, Ore.
William Hackett	William Hackett	Newburyport, Mass.
William Pritchard	William Pritchard	Charleston, S. C.
Williams	E. F. Williams	Greenpoint, N. Y.
Winton	Winton Engine Corp.	Cleveland, Ohio
Wolf & Zwicker	Wolf & Zwicker Iron Works	Portland, Ore.
Woodruff	Woodruff Iron Works	New York, N. Y.
Woodruff & Beach	Woodruff & Beach	Hartford, Conn.
Wright	William Wright & Co.	Newburgh, N. Y.
Yarrow	Yarrow & Co., Ltd.	Glasgow, Scotland
York Ice	York Ice Machine Corp.	(Unknown)
Zeno, Secor	Zeno, Secor & Co	Jersey City, N. J.

The Sail Navy, 1775–1853

Ships of the Line

1776

AMERICA (74)

Tonnage: 1982 tons
Dimensions: 182'6"(u.d.) x 59'6"(e) x 23'(h)
Armament: 30-18# 32-12# 14-9# (designed)

Rig: Ship
Speed: Unknown
Complement: 626

	Builder	Laid down	Launched	Commiss'd	Disposition
AMERICA	J.K. Hackett	May 77	5 Nov 82	No	To France 3 Sep 82 as America.

Notes: Authorized 20 Nov 76. Rate reduced to 56 guns on 29 May 78; restored to 74 on 28 Dec 79.
Probably designed by William Hackett. The designed armament was too heavy for her displacement with
the result that her lower deck gunports were too close to the water. On 3 Sep 82 Congress offered her
to France to replace the French 74 Magnifique, wrecked at Boston in 1782. Although considered to be
well built by American standards she lasted only three years in French service.

Unnamed (74)

Tonnage: Unknown
Dimensions: Unknown
Armament: Unknown

Rig: Ship
Speed: Unknown
Complement: Unknown

	Builder	Laid down	Launched	Commiss'd	Disposition
Unknown	Unknown, Boston	1777	No	No	Construction abandoned 1778
Unknown	Unknown, Philadelphia	No	No	No	Probably never begun.

Notes: Authorized 20 Nov 76. Their construction was abandoned because of shortages of money and
material. There is also mention in 1777 of a 74 projected to be built at Poughkeepsie, N. Y.

1799

COLUMBUS class (74)

Tonnage: 1859 tons
Dimensions: 183'(b.p.) x 48'6"(m) x 19'6"(h)
Armament: 28-32# 28-18# 18-9# (designed)

Rig: Ship
Speed: Unknown
Complement: Unknown

	Builder	Laid down	Launched	Commiss'd	Disposition
COLUMBUS	Portsmouth	No	No	No	Cancelled 1800
Unknown	Boston	No	No	No	Cancelled 1800
Unknown	New York	No	No	No	Cancelled 1800
FRANKLIN	Philadelphia	10 Jun 00	No	No	Cancelled 1800
Unknown	Washington	No	No	No	Cancelled 1800
Unknown	Norfolk	No	No	No	Cancelled 1800.

Notes: Authorized 25 Feb 99. Designed by Joshua Humphreys with an armament heavier than their
European contemporaries.

1813

INDEPENDENCE class (74)

Tonnage: 2259 tons
Dimensions: 188'(b.p.) x 51'6"(e) x 24'4"(max)
Armament: Independence--63-32# 24-32#c; 60-32# (1836); 4-8"
  56-32# (1842); 8-8" 48-32# (1846); 10-8" 46-32# (1854);
  22-32# (1876); 1-60#R 6-32# (1888); 6-32# (1889); 3-20#BLR
  (1898); 2-6# (1900); 1-12# (1910)
Washington--63-32# 24-32#c; 62-32# 20-32#c (ca. 1820)

Rig: Ship
Speed: Unknown
Complement: 750

	Builder	Laid down	Launched	Commiss'd	Disposition
INDEPENDENCE	Hartt & Barker	18 Aug 13	20 Jun 14	by 3 Jul 1815	Sold 23 Nov 1914
WASHINGTON	Hartt & Badger	Mar 14	1 Oct 14	28 Aug 15	Broken up 1843.

Notes: Authorized 2 Jan 13. Built to a modified version of the 1799 design, with changes probably by Edmund Hartt. Although well built, they floated their lower batteries too close to the water. The Independence was razeed at Boston Navy Yard in 1846. As rebuilt her tonnage dropped to 1891 tons but retention of the original sail plan permitted her to reach 13 kts. Her displacement as a razee was 3270 tons. She served as the Mare Island receiving ship between 1857 and 1914.

FRANKLIN (74)

Tonnage: 2257 tons
Dimensions: 187'11"(b.p.) x 50'(e) x 26'6"(max)
Armament: 63-32# 24-32#c; 58-32# 24-32#c (ca. 1820)

Rig: Ship
Speed: Unknown
Complement: 786

	Builder	Laid down	Launched	Commiss'd	Disposition
FRANKLIN	Humphreys & Penrose	1815	25 Aug 15	1815	Broken up 1853.

Notes: Authorized 2 Jan 13. (This act also authorized a fourth 74, but the money for her was spent instead on ships for Lake Ontario.) Samuel Humphreys's design differed only slightly from the Independence class. The Franklin served as a receiving ship 1843-1852.

1816

PENNSYLVANIA (120)

Tonnage: 3241 tons
Dimensions: 210'(b.p.) x 59'6"(e) x 26'6"
Armament: 16-8" 90-32#; 12-8" 92-32# 24-32#c (1845)

Rig: Ship
Speed: Unknown
Complement: 1100

	Builder	Laid down	Launched	Commiss'd	Disposition
PENNSYLVANIA	Philadelphia	Nov 22	18 Jul 37	by 30 Nov 1837	Burned to avoid capture, Norfolk, 20 Apr 61.

Notes: Authorized 29 Apr 16. A graceful design by Samuel Humphreys, she was the largest ship of the line built for the United States and probably the most powerful vessel in the world when completed. She had a poor reputation as a sailer which probably resulted from her commanders' inexperience with a vessel of her size. She spent most of her life as the Norfolk receiving ship.

DELAWARE class (74)

Tonnage: 2633 tons
Dimensions: 196'3"(b.p.) x 54'4"(e) x 26'2"
Armament: Delaware--32-42# 32-32# 28-42#c (1833); 8-8" 28-42# 30-32# 22-42#c (1841);
  Vermont--4-8" 20-32#; 10-8" 8-32# (1864); 12-11" 2-8" 1-100#R 1-60#R (1876); none (1891); 1-6"BLR (1893); none (1897);
  New Hampshire--4-100#R 6-9"; 15-32# (1876); none (1892); 6-32# (1897); 2-20#BLR (1898); none (1901); 1-4"/40 (1912);
  Virginia and New York--Never mounted;
  North Carolina--34-42# 36-32# 24-42#c; 32-42# 34-32# 24-42#c (1841); 8-8" 32-42# 26-32# 24-42#c (1845); 4-9" 1-30#R (1862)

Rig: Ship
Speed: 11 kts.
Complement: 820

	Builder	Laid down	Launched	Commiss'd	Disposition
DELAWARE	Norfolk	Aug 17	21 Oct 20	by 10 Feb 1828	Burned to avoid capture, Norfolk, 20 Apr 61
VERMONT	Boston	Sep 18	14 Sep 48	30 Jan 62	Sold 15 Apr. 1902
NEW HAMPSHIRE	Portsmouth	1 Jun 19	23 Jan 64	11 May 64	Burned 23 May 1921
VIRGINIA	Boston	May 22	No	No	Broken up on ways 1884
NEW YORK	Norfolk	May 20	No	No	Burned to avoid capture, Norfolk, 20 Apr 61
NORTH CAROLINA	Philadelphia	Jun 16	7 Sep 20	by 18 Dec 1824	Sold 1 Oct 67.

Notes: Authorized 29 Apr 16. William Doughty designed this highly successful class. The Vermont remained in ordinary until fitted as a storeship in 1861. She served as a receiving ship 1864-1876 and 1879-1901. The New Hampshire was completed as a storeship and served as such, as a training vessel, or as a receiving ship throughout her career. Her wreck was sold on 19 Aug 21. The North Carolina was completed by Norfolk Navy Yard and served as the New York receiving ship after 1839. 4150 tons displacement.

The ship of the line *Vermont* as a receiving ship at New York after the Civil War. (NH 93915)

Renamings: Vermont ex Virginia 27 Apr 27. Virginia ex Vermont 27 Apr 27 and ex Massachusetts prior to construction. New Hampshire ex Alabama 28 Oct 63, to Granite State 30 Nov 1904.
Reclassification: The Granite State (ex New Hampshire) was designated "unclassified" on 17 Jul 20.

OHIO (74)

Tonnage: 2757 tons

Rig: Ship

Dimensions: 197'2"(b.p.) x 53'10"(e) x 26'6"(max)

Speed: 13 kts.

Armament: 32-42# 34-32# 24-42#c; 12-8" 28-42# 16-32# (1846);
  12-8" 28-42# 44-32# (1847); 4-100#R 1-8" 12-32# (1863); 4-
  100#R 1-50#R (1876)

Complement: 820

	Builder	Laid down	Launched	Commiss'd	Disposition
OHIO	New York	Nov 17	30 May 20	11 Oct 38	Sold 27 Sep 83.

Notes: Authorized 29 Apr 16. The design by Henry Eckford produced one of the finest 74's in the world. She was fast, a good sea boat, and carried her guns high. The last active ship of the line in the United States Navy, she served as a receiving ship 1842-1846 and 1851-1876. 4250 tons displacement.

COLUMBUS (74)

Tonnage: 2480 tons

Rig: Ship

Dimensions: 191'10"(b.p.) x 53'6"(e) x 25'6"(max)

Speed: 12.5 kts.

Armament: 68-32# 24-42#c; 8-8" 56-32# 22-32#c (1842)

Complement: 780

	Builder	Laid down	Launched	Commiss'd	Disposition
COLUMBUS	Washington	Jun 16	1 Mar 19	7 Sep 19	Burned to avoid capture, Norfolk, 20 Apr 61.

Notes: Authorized 29 Apr 16. One of William Doughty's early designs, she handled well but was a poor sea boat. She served as a receiving ship 1839-1842. Her hulk was raised 22 Apr 68 and sold 6 May 68.

Ships of the Line (Lake)

1813

CHIPPEWA (74)

Tonnage: 2805 tons

Rig: Ship

Dimensions: 204'(k) x 56'(e) x unknown

Speed: Unknown

Armament: 63-32# 24-32#c (designed)

Complement: Unknown

	Builder	Laid down	Launched	Commiss'd	Disposition
CHIPPEWA	Brown, Storrs Harbor	5 Oct 14	No	No	Sold on ways 1 Nov 23.

Notes: Authorized 3 Mar 13. Construction halted at end of the War of 1812.

NEW ORLEANS (74)

Tonnage: 2805 tons

Rig: Ship

Dimensions: 204'(b.p.) x 56'(e) x 26'6"

Speed: Unknown

Armament: 63-32# 24-32#c (designed)

Complement: Unknown

	Builder	Laid down	Launched	Commiss'd	Disposition
NEW ORLEANS	Brown, Sackets Harbor	5 Oct 14	No	No	Sold on ways 24 Sep 83.

Notes: Authorized 3 Mar 13. Although construction ceased at the end of the War of 1812 she was kept under cover and was reported in good condition as late as 1861. 4200 tons displacement.

Frigates

1775

HANCOCK (32)

Tonnage: 763 tons
Dimensions: 136'7"(g.d.) x 35'6"(e) x 15'10"
Armament: 26-12# 10-6#

Rig: Ship
Speed: 12 kts.
Complement: 290

	Builder	Laid down	Launched	Commiss'd	Disposition
HANCOCK	Greenleaf	1776	10 Jul 76	by 23 Jun 1777	Captured off Nova Scotia by HMS Rainbow 8 Jul 77.

Notes: Authorized 13 Dec 75. A large, fast, and well built vessel probably designed by Joshua Humphreys. She served in the Royal Navy as HMS Iris.

RANDOLPH class (32)

Tonnage: Unknown
Dimensions: 132'9"(b.p.) x 34'6"(e) x 18'
Armament: Randolph--26-12# 10-6#
   Washington--26-12# 6-6# (designed)

Rig: Ship
Speed: Unknown
Complement: 315

	Builder	Laid down	Launched	Commiss'd	Disposition
RANDOLPH	Wharton & Humphreys	1775	10 Jul 76	1776	Blown up in action with HMS Yarmouth 7 Mar 78
WASHINGTON	Eyre	1776	7 Aug 76	No	Scuttled Whitehall, N. J., 2 Nov 77.

Notes: Authorized 13 Dec 75. Very large vessels for their rate, they were probably designed by Joshua Humphreys. The Washington's hulk was burned by a British boat expedition 8 May 78.

WARREN (32)

Tonnage: Unknown
Dimensions: 132'1"(g.d.) x 34'6" x 11'(h)
Armament: 12-18# 14-12# 8-9#

Rig: Ship
Speed: Unknown
Complement: 250

	Builder	Laid down	Launched	Commiss'd	Disposition
WARREN	Talman	1776	15 May 76	by Dec 76	Burned to avoid capture near Frankfort, Me., 14 Aug 79.

Notes: Authorized 13 Dec 75. Despite its extremely heavy battery, this Sylvester Bowers design was the least successful of the 32's.

RALEIGH (32)

Tonnage: 697 tons
Dimensions: 131'5"(b.p.) x 35'5"(e) x 11'(h)
Armament: 26-12# 6-6#

Rig: Ship
Speed: 11 kts.
Complement: 180

	Builder	Laid down	Launched	Commiss'd	Disposition
RALEIGH	Hackett, Paul, & Hill	21 Mar 76	21 May 76	by Aug 77	Captured by British squadron while aground on Wooden Ball I., Me., 28 Sep 78.

Notes: Authorized 13 Dec 75. This well built, white oak vessel was probably designed by William Hackett. She also served in the Royal Navy.
Renaming: Unofficially called New Hampshire prior to her launching.

VIRGINIA (28)

Tonnage: 682 tons
Dimensions: 126'4"(g.d.) x 34'10"(e) x 18'
Armament: 24-12# 2-6#

Rig: Ship
Speed: Unknown
Complement: 305

	Builder	Laid down	Launched	Commiss'd	Disposition
VIRGINIA	Geo. Welles, Fells Pt., Md.	1776	12 Aug 76	1777	Captured by British squadron while aground off Hampden, Va., 31 Mar 78.

Notes: Authorized 13 Dec 75. Probably another Joshua Humphreys design, she was taken into the Royal Navy as HMS Virginia.

CONGRESS (28)

Tonnage: 681 tons
Dimensions: ca. 126'(b.p.) x 34'10" x 10'6"
Armament: 26-12# 2-6# (designed)

Rig: Ship
Speed: Unknown
Complement: Unknown

	Builder	Laid down	Launched	Commiss'd	Disposition
CONGRESS	Burling	ca. 7 Mar 1776	ca. 29 Oct 1776	No	Burned to avoid capture, Ft. Montgomery, N.Y., 7 Oct 77.

Notes: Authorized 13 Dec 75. Probably another Joshua Humphreys design.

PROVIDENCE (28)

Tonnage: 632 tons
Dimensions: 126'7"(g.d.) x 33'10" x 10'8"(h)
Armament: 26-12# 6-4#

Rig: Ship
Speed: Unknown
Complement: 170

	Builder	Laid down	Launched	Commiss'd	Disposition
PROVIDENCE	Bowers	1776	18 May 76	by Dec 76	Captured by British with Charleston, S.C., 12 May 80.

Notes: Authorized 13 Dec 75. Designed by Sylvester Bowers and considered the least successful of the 28's. She served in the Royal Navy as HMS Providence.

TRUMBULL (28)

Tonnage: Unknown
Dimensions: Unknown
Armament: 24-12# 6-6#

Rig: Ship
Speed: Unknown
Complement: 191

	Builder	Laid down	Launched	Commiss'd	Disposition
TRUMBULL	John Cotton, Portland, Ct.	1776	5 Sep 76	by May 80	Captured by HMS Iris and General Monk off Delaware Capes 9 Aug 81.

Notes: Authorized 13 Dec 75. She is believed to have been a Joshua Humphreys design. The delay in her completion was caused by difficulties in getting her across the bar at the mouth of the Connecticut River. She was not taken into British service.

EFFINGHAM (28)

Tonnage: Unknown
Dimensions: ca. 124'(k) x unknown x unknown
Armament: 26-12# 2-6# (designed)

Rig: Ship
Speed: Unknown
Complement: Unknown

	Builder	Laid down	Launched	Commiss'd	Disposition
EFFINGHAM	Grice	1776	31 Oct 76	No	Scuttled at Whitehall, N. J., 2 Nov 77.

Notes: Authorized 13 Dec 75. Believed to be another Joshua Humphreys design, her hulk was burned by a British boat expedition 8 May 78.

DELAWARE (24)

Tonnage: 563 tons
Dimensions: 119'(b.p.) x 32'11" x 9'9"(h)
Armament: 22-12# 6-6#

Rig: Ship
Speed: Unknown
Complement: Unknown

	Builder	Laid down	Launched	Commiss'd	Disposition
DELAWARE	Coats	1776	ca. 12 Jul 1776	by 30 Mar 1777	Captured by British battery in Delaware R. 27 Sep 77.

Notes: Authorized 13 Dec 75. Another probable Joshua Humphreys design, she was taken into British service as HMS Delaware.

BOSTON (24)

Tonnage: 514 tons
Dimensions: 114'3"(b.d.) x 32' x 10'3"(h)
Armament: 5-12# 19-9# 2-6# 4-4#

Rig: Ship
Speed: 10 kts.
Complement: Unknown

	Builder	Laid down	Launched	Commiss'd	Disposition
BOSTON	Cross	1776	3 Jun 76	1777	Captured by British with Charleston, S. C., 12 May 80.

Notes: Authorized 13 Dec 75. Probably designed by Joshua Humphreys and considered well built.

MONTGOMERY (24)

Tonnage: Unknown
Dimensions: Unknown
Armament: Unknown

Rig: Ship
Speed: Unknown
Complement: Unknown

	Builder	Laid down	Launched	Commiss'd	Disposition
MONTGOMERY	Burling	ca. 7 Mar 1776	4 Nov 76	No	Burned to avoid capture, Ft. Montgomery, N. Y., 7 Oct 77.

Notes: Authorized 13 Dec 75. Probably built to Joshua Humphreys's standard design for the 24-gun frigates which called for a vessel 120'6"(g.d.) x 32'6" x 10'6"(h) mounting 24-9#.

1776

ALLIANCE (36)

Tonnage: 900 tons
Dimensions: 151'(b.p.) x 36' x 12'6"
Armament: 26-12# 10-9#; 28-12# 8-9# (1779); 28-18# 12-9# (1780); 28-12# 8-9# (1781)

Rig: Ship
Speed: 12 kts.
Complement: 300

	Builder	Laid down	Launched	Commiss'd	Disposition
ALLIANCE	W. & J. Hackett	1777	28 Apr 78	1778	Sold 3 Jun 85.

Notes: Authorized 20 Nov 76. A William Hackett design, she was reputedly the fastest vessel in the Continental Navy.
Renaming: Originally named Hancock, renamed shortly before launching.

Unnamed

Tonnage: Unknown
Dimensions: Unknown
Armament: Unknown

Rig: Probably ship
Speed: Unknown
Complement: Unknown

	Builder	Laid down	Launched	Commiss'd	Disposition
Unnamed	David Stodder, Norfolk	by 27 Aug 1777	No	No	Burned on ways by British May 79
Unnamed	David Stodder, Norfolk	by 27 Aug 1777	No	No	Burned on ways by British May 79
Unnamed	Unknown, Baltimore, Md.	No	No	No	Probably never begun
Unnamed	Unknown, Baltimore, Md.	No	No	No	Probably never begun.

Notes: Authorized 20 Nov 76. The two Virginia vessels were intended as a 36 and a 28. Work on both was ordered halted on 11 Apr 78 but construction of one (probably the 28) subsequently resumed.

L'INDIEN (40)

Tonnage: 1300 tons
Dimensions: 172'6"(b.p.) x 43'3"(e) x 16'6"(h)
Armament: 28-36# 12-12#

Rig: Ship
Speed: Unknown
Complement: 550

	Builder	Laid down	Launched	Commiss'd	Disposition
L'INDIEN	M. Borys, Amsterdam, Netherlands.	1777	Unknown	No	Sold to France ca. 30 Nov 77.

Notes: Authorized 23 Dec 76 with three other ships which were not acquired. Built to a French design in a Dutch yard, she incorporated the keel and sides of a two decker. Even so, she appears to have been too weak for her armament. British pressure forced her sale to France. The King of France loaned her to the Duke of Luxembourg who hired her to the South Carolina State Navy. As South Carolina she was captured by the British 20 Dec 82 but not taken into the Royal Navy.

DEANE (32)

Tonnage: 517 tons
Dimensions: 96'(k) x 32' x unknown
Armament: 24-12# 2-6# 8-4#

Rig: Ship
Speed: Unknown
Complement: 215

	Builder	Laid down	Launched	Commiss'd	Disposition
DEANE	Unknown, Nantes, Fr.	1777	1777	1777	Sold 2 Oct 83.

Notes: Probably authorized 23 Dec 76.
Renaming: To Hague Sep 82.

1777

CONFEDERACY (36)

Tonnage: 971 tons   Rig: Ship
Dimensions: 154'9"(b.p.) x 37'(e) x 16'   Speed: Unknown
Armament: 28-12# 8-6#   Complement: 260

	Builder	Laid down	Launched	Commiss'd	Disposition
CONFEDERACY	Joshua Huntington, Chatham, Ct.	1777	8 Nov 78	by Apr 79	Captured by HMS Roebuck and Orpheus off Virginia Capes 15 Apr 81.

Notes: Authorized 23 Jan 77. Fast and fitted with sweeps, she became HMS Confederate.

BOURBON (28)

Tonnage: ca. 900 tons   Rig: Ship
Dimensions: Unknown   Speed: Unknown
Armament: Unknown   Complement: Unknown

	Builder	Laid down	Launched	Commiss'd	Disposition
BOURBON	John Cotton, Portland, Ct.	1779	31 Jul 83	No	Sold unfinished Sep 83.

Notes: Authorized 23 Jan 77. Found to be too deep draft to cross the bar at the mouth of the Connecticut River, she was never completed.

FOX (28)

Tonnage: 585 tons   Rig: Ship
Dimensions: 121'(d) x 34' x 15'   Speed: Unknown
Armament: 24-9# 4-3#   Complement: Unknown

	Builder	Launched	Acquired	Commiss'd	Disposition
FOX	Thos. Calhoun, Northam, England	2 Sep 73	7 Jun 77	Jun 77	Recaptured by HMS Flora off Nova Scotia 7 Jul 77.

Notes: Formerly the British Fox, she was taken by Hancock and Boston off Newfoundland Banks.

1779

SERAPIS (44)

Tonnage: 886 tons   Rig: Ship
Dimensions: 140' x 38' x unknown   Speed: Unknown
Armament: 20-18# 20-9# 10-6#   Complement: 320

	Builder	Launched	Acquired	Commiss'd	Disposition
SERAPIS	Randall, Rotherhithe, England	4 Mar 79	23 Sep 79	24 Sep 79	Seized by Dutch authorities, Texel, Oct 79.

Notes: Formerly the British Serapis, she was captured by Bon Homme Richard off Flamborough Head, England.

1794

UNITED STATES class (44)

Tonnage: 1576 tons   Rig: Ship
Dimensions: 175'(b.p.) x 44'2"(e) x 23'6"   Speed: 13.5 kts.
Armament: United States--30-24# 14-12#; 32-24# 22-42#c   Complement: 420
  (1812); 32-24# 16-42#c (1820); 32-24# 20-32#c (1841); 4-8"
  28-32# 22-42#c (1845); 4-8" 46-32# (1848);
  Constitution--30-24# 22-12#; 30-24# 14-12# 8-32#c (1804);
  30-24# 1-18# 24-32#c (1812); 32-24# 22-42#c (1812); 31-24#
  20-32#c (1814); 30-24# 20-32#c (1820); 32-24# 20-32#c
  (1840); 4-8" 28-32# 22-42#c (1845); 4-8" 46-32# (1848);
  8-8" 42-32# (1849); 4-8" 46-32# (1852); 8-32# (1860); 6-32#
  (1876); 4-32# (1888); none (1901);
  President--30-24# 22-12#; 32-24# 1-18# 22-42#c (1813)

	Builder	Laid down	Launched	Commiss'd	Disposition
UNITED STATES	Humphreys	Dec 94	10 May 97	11 Jul 98	Broken up 1865
CONSTITUTION	Claghorn	Nov 94	21 Oct 97	22 Jul 98	USN 1990
PRESIDENT	Cheeseman	Unknown	10 Apr 00	by 5 Sep 1800	Captured by British squadron in Long I. Sd. 15 Jan 15.

Notes: Authorized 27 Mar 94 and re-authorized 20 Apr 95 (first two) and 16 Jul 98 (President). The precedent-setting design of Joshua Humphreys produced fast, weatherly, and seaworthy vessels. They were very heavily armed and large for the period, approximating the size of contemporary 74's. Construction was delayed initially because of alterations in the plans. Work on the President was suspended between 1796 and 1798. As completed by Christian Bergh she was slightly lighter than the others. She served as HMS President 1815-18. The United States was captured by the Confederates with the Norfolk Navy Yard 20 Apr 61 and used by them as a receiving ship. She was retaken with the yard 25 May 62 and her scrapping was authorized by the President on 26 Feb 64. The Constitution served as a training vessel 1860-1881 and has been maintained since as a relic. 2200 tons displacement (Constitution).
Renamings: The Constitution was renamed Old Constitution 1 Jan 1917 but regained her original name 24 Jul 1920.
Reclassifications: The Constitution was designated "unclassified" (IX-21) 17 Jul 1920. The IX hull number was dropped effective 1 Sep 1975.

CHESAPEAKE (36)

Tonnage: 1244 tons
Dimensions: 153'10"(b.p.) x 40'11"(e) x 13'9"(h)
Armament: 28-18# 16-9#; 30-18# 12-32#c (1800); 28-18# 12-32#c (1807); 28-18# 20-32#c (1813)

Rig: Ship
Speed: Unknown
Complement: 340

	Builder	Laid down	Launched	Commiss'd	Disposition
CHESAPEAKE	Josiah Fox, Norfolk, Va.	10 Dec 98	2 Dec 99	by 22 May 1800	Captured by HMS Shannon off Boston 1 Jun 13.

Notes: Authorized 27 Mar 94 (as a 44) and 16 Jul 98 (as a 36). The particulars given are those of Josiah Fox's fast, handsome, 36-gun design. Her lines as a 44 were probably similar to the United States class.

CONSTELLATION class (36)

Tonnage: 1265 tons
Dimensions: 163'3"(b.p.) x 41'(e) x 20'
Armament: Constellation--28-24# 10-12#; 28-24# 10-24#c (1799); 2-32# 24-18# 18-32#c (1812); 2-32# 28-18# 18-32#c (1815); 30-18# 16-32#c (1840);
Congress--28-18# 12-9#; 24-18# 12-12# (1800); 24-18# 20-32#c (1812)

Rig: Ship
Speed: 12.5 kts.
Complement: 340

	Builder	Laid down	Launched	Commiss'd	Disposition
CONSTELLATION	Stodder, Baltimore	1795	7 Sep 97	by 26 Jun 1798	Broken up 1854.
CONGRESS	J.K. Hackett	Unknown	15 Aug 99	by Dec 99	Broken up 1836.

Notes: Authorized 27 Mar 94 and re-authorized 20 Apr 95 (Constellation) and 16 Jul 98 (Congress). The design probably originated with Joshua Humphreys. The original armament was too heavy for the displacement but the Constellation overcame this when her beam was increased to 42'2" during her 1812 rebuilding. Construction of the Congress was suspended 1796-1798. After the War of 1812 they were classified as 2d class frigates. There was an abortive 1845 plan to convert the Constellation to a screw sloop, and she was instead rebuilt as a corvette in 1854.

1798

GENERAL GREENE (28)

Tonnage: 655 tons
Dimensions: 139'(b.p.) x 34'8" x 17'4"(h)
Armament: 24-12# 6-6#

Rig: Ship
Speed: Unknown
Complement: 267

	Builder	Laid down	Launched	Commiss'd	Disposition
GENERAL GREENE	Talman & de Wolf	1798	21 Jan 99	by 2 Jun 1799	Burned to avoid capture, Washington, 24 Aug 14.

Notes: Authorized 27 Apr 98. Probably designed by Benjamin Talman; she was reduced to a sheer hulk in 1805.

ADAMS (28)

Tonnage: 530 tons
Dimensions: 113'(b.p.) x 34' x 10'9"(h)
Armament: 24-12# 4-9#

Rig: Ship
Speed: Unknown
Complement: 258

	Builder	Laid down	Launched	Commiss'd	Disposition
ADAMS	Jackson & Sheffield	30 Jul 98	8 Jun 99	by 23 Sep 1799	Rebuilt as sloop of war 1807.

Notes: Authorized 27 Apr 98. Designed by William Sheffield, she was fast but had a deep draft.

PHILADELPHIA (36)

Tonnage: 1240 tons
Dimensions: 157'(b.p.) x 39'(m) x 13'6"(h)
Armament: 28-18# 10-9#; 28-18# 16-32#c (1803)

Rig: Ship
Speed: Unknown
Complement: 307

	Builder	Laid down	Launched	Commiss'd	Disposition
PHILADELPHIA	Humphreys, Hutton, & Delavane	ca. 11 Nov 1798	28 Nov 99	by 5 Apr 1800	Captured by Tripolitan gunboats while aground off Tripoli 31 Oct 04.

Notes: Authorized 30 Jun 98 and built by public subscription in Philadelphia to a design of Josiah Fox. She was well built and fast although the 14 kts. with which she is sometimes credited is unlikely.
Renaming: Initially called the City of Philadelphia.

NEW YORK (36)

Tonnage: 1130 tons
Dimensions: 144'2"(b.p.) x 37'(m) x 11'9"(h)
Armament: 26-18# 14-9#

Rig: Ship
Speed: Unknown
Complement: 351

	Builder	Laid down	Launched	Commiss'd	Disposition
NEW YORK	Peck & Carpenter	Aug 98	24 Apr 00	by 20 Oct 1800	Uncertain.

Notes: Authorized 30 Jun 98 and built by public subscription in New York. A beautiful and well built vessel, she was not worth repairing in 1812. Her hulk was apparently not consumed with the Washington Navy Yard when it was burned in 1814.

ESSEX (32)

Tonnage: 850 tons
Dimensions: 140'(b.p.) x 37'(e) x 12'3"(h)
Armament: 26-12# 10-6#; 6-12# 40-32#c (1810); 6-18# 36-32#c (1811)

Rig: Ship
Speed: 12 kts.
Complement: 258

	Builder	Laid down	Launched	Commiss'd	Disposition
ESSEX	Enos Briggs, Salem, Mass.	13 Apr 99	30 Sep 99	by 17 Dec 1799	Captured by HMS Phoebe & Cherub off Valparaiso, Chile, 28 Mar 14.

Notes: Authorized 30 Jun 98 and built by public subscription in Salem, Mass. William Hackett's design was large for the rate. She proved fast until rearmed in 1810 with carronades. This refit hampered her sailing qualities and reduced her combat effectiveness.

BOSTON (28)

Tonnage: 700 tons
Dimensions: 134'(b.p.) x 35'6"(e) x 11'6"
Armament: 24-12# 8-9#; 26-12# 12-32#c (1801)

Rig: Ship
Speed: Unknown
Complement: 250

	Builder	Laid down	Launched	Commiss'd	Disposition
BOSTON	Hartt	22 Aug 98	20 May 99	by 12 Jun 1799	Burned to avoid capture, Washington, 24 Aug 14.

Notes: Authorized 30 Jun 98 and built by public subscription in Boston. Designed by Edmund Hartt, she was a well built, fast vessel and the first in the Navy to have her bottom coppered. She was reported "unworthy of repair" in 1812.

JOHN ADAMS (28)

Tonnage: 544 tons
Dimensions: 139'(b.p.) x 32'(e) x 16'4"(h)
Armament: 24-12# 2-9# 6-24#c; 24-12# 8-24#c (1804); 4-18#
  20-32#c (1820)

Rig: Ship
Speed: Unknown
Complement: 258

	Builder	Laid down	Launched	Commiss'd	Disposition
JOHN ADAMS	Pritchard	Unknown	5 Jun 99	by 1 Oct 1799	Broken up 1829.

Notes: Authorized 30 Jun 98 and built by public subscription in Charleston, S. C. She was well built to a Josiah Fox design but was cut down to a 24-gun sloop-of-war or corvette about 1808.

PORTSMOUTH (24)

Tonnage: 593 tons
Dimensions: Unknown
Armament: Unknown

Rig: Ship
Speed: Unknown
Complement: 220

	Builder	Laid down	Launched	Commiss'd	Disposition
PORTSMOUTH	J.K. Hackett	1798	11 Oct 98	1798	Sold 1801.

Notes: Authorized 30 Jun 98. Designed by Josiah Fox.

CONNECTICUT (24)

Tonnage: 492 tons
Dimensions: 93'(k) x 31' x 13'6"(h) (designed)
Armament: 26-12#

Rig: Ship
Speed: Unknown
Complement: 220

	Builder	Laid down	Launched	Commiss'd	Disposition
CONNECTICUT	Seth Overton, Chatham, Ct.	1798	7 Jun 99	by 15 Oct 1799	Sold 1801.

Notes: Authorized 30 Jun 98. She was reported to be very fast but whether she was built according to the plan furnished by the Navy Department is not certain.

MERRIMACK (24)

Tonnage: 467 tons
Dimensions: Unknown
Armament: 20-9# 8-6#

Rig: Ship
Speed: Unknown
Complement: 220

	Builder	Laid down	Launched	Commiss'd	Disposition
MERRIMACK	Cross & Clark	9 Jul 98	12 Oct 98	by 1 Jan 1799	Sold 1801.

Notes: Authorized 30 Jun 98 and built by public subscription in Newburyport, Mass. She was reputed to be the best of the small frigates.

1799

INSURGENTE (36)

Tonnage: 950 tons
Dimensions: 148'(g.d.) x 37'5" x 16'2"
Armament: 2-18# 24-12# 8-6# 4-32#c 2-24#c (when captured);
  26-18# 10-12# 4-32#c (1799)

Rig: Ship
Speed: Unknown
Complement: 340

	Builder	Launched	Acquired	Commiss'd	Disposition
INSURGENTE	Lorient	27 Apr 93	9 Feb 99	Feb 99	Lost at sea after 8 Aug 00.

Notes: Formerly the French 12-pdr. frigate L'Insurgente, captured by the Constellation off Nevis.

1812

MACEDONIAN (36)

Tonnage: 1325 tons
Dimensions: 156'2"(b.p.) x 40'(e) x 21'
Armament: 28-18# 2-12# 2-9# 16-32#c 1-18#c (when captured);
  26-18# 2-9# 10-32#c (1820)

Rig: Ship
Speed: Unknown
Complement: 362

	Builder	Launched	Acquired	Commiss'd	Disposition
MACEDONIAN	Woolwich Dockyard	2 Jun 10	25 Oct 12	Apr 13	Broken up 1829.

Notes: Formerly the British Macedonian, captured by the United States west of the Canary Is.

1813

GUERRIERE class (44)

Tonnage: 1511 tons
Dimensions: 175'(b.p.) x 45'(e) x 14'2"(h)
Armament: 33-32# 20-42#c; 32-32# 24-42#c (1820)

Rig: Ship
Speed: Unknown
Complement: 400

	Builder	Laid down	Launched	Commiss'd	Disposition
GUERRIERE	J. & F. Grice	1813	20 Jun 14	by 20 May 1815	Broken up 1841
COLUMBIA	Washington	1813	No	No	Burned to avoid capture, Washington, 24 Aug 14
JAVA	Flannigan & Parsons	1813	1 Aug 14	by 5 Aug 1815	Broken up 1842.

Notes: Authorized 2 Jan 13. (This act also authorized three other 44s, but the money for these was spent instead on ships for Lake Ontario.) Designed by William Doughty. They deteriorated rapidly because of poorly seasoned timber and hasty construction. The act of 10 Jul 32 authorized assembling timber for the reconstruction of the Java, but she was not rebuilt and instead served as a receiving ship 1831-1842.
Renamings: The Guerriere was originally named Continental and was renamed while building, but the reported change of the Columbia to Essex apparently never officially occurred.

1815

CYANE (28)

Tonnage: 643 tons
Dimensions: 120'4"(b.p.) x 31'6"(e) x 17'3"
Armament: 2-12# 22-32#c 8-18#c 2-12#c (when captured); 2-12# 2-9# 22-32#c 6-18#c 2-12#c (1818); 4-12# 20-32#c 8-18#c (1820)

Rig: Ship
Speed: Unknown
Complement: 185

	Builder	Launched	Acquired	Commiss'd	Disposition
CYANE	Bass, Topsham, England	14 Oct 06	20 Feb 15	1815	Broken up 1836.

Notes: Formerly the British 22-gun sixth rate Cyane (renamed from Columbine in 1805), captured by the Constitution off Madeira. She was carried on the Navy List as a 24-gun corvette after 1822.

1816

POTOMAC class (44)

Tonnage: 1708 tons
Dimensions: 175'(b.p.) x 45'(m) x 22'4"(max)
Armament: Brandywine--30-32# 24-32#c; 4-8" 28-32# 22-32#c (1840); 8-8" 42-32# (1847);
Potomac--4-8" 28-32# 20-32#c (1840); 4-8" 26-32# 20-32#c (1846); 4-8" 42-32# (1847); 10-8" 40-32# (1855); 10-8" 22-32# (1861); 4-8" 20-32# 1-30#R 1-20#R (1864); 2-8" 18-32# (1876);
Columbia--4-8" 28-32# 22-42#c; 8-8" 42-32# (1847); 10-8" 40-32# (1853);
Santee--10-8" 36-32#; 12-8" 36-32# (1861); 12-8" 34-32# 1-30#R (1862); 1-100#R 1-11" 10-32# (1862); 24-8" 24-32# (1871)
Savannah--4-8" 28-32# 22-42#c; 8-8" 42-32# (1849); 10-8" 40-32# (1853); 2-10" 8-8" 14-32# (1858); 2-10" 6-8" 12-32# (1862); 1-11" 2-9" 4-32# (1862); 1-11" 2-9" 6-32# 2-20#R (1865);
Sabine--12-8" 36-32#; 2-10" 10-8" 38-32# (1862); 1-100#R 2-10" 10-9" 38-32# (1862); 2-100#R 10-9" 34-32# 2-20#R (1863); 2-100#R 10-9" 22-32# (1864); 18-9" 4-32# (1876);
Raritan--4-8" 28-32# 22-42#c; 8-8" 42-32# (1848);
Cumberland--4-8" 28-32# 20-42#c; 8-8" 42-32# (1847); 2-10" 6-8" 16-32# (1857); 1-10" 22-9" (1860); 1-10" 22-9" 1-70#R (1862);
St. Lawrence--8-8" 42-32#; 10-8" 40-32# (1856); 10-8" 34-32# 2-50#R (1863); 8-9" 2-32# 1-30#R (1864)

Rig: Ship
Speed: 13 kts.
Complement: 480

The frigate *Constitution* at the Boston Navy Yard on 18 August 1914 as rebuilt in 1907. The scout cruiser *Chester* is in the background. (NH 55907)

The frigate *Sabine* ca. 1869. (NH 91722)

	Builder	Laid down	Launched	Commiss'd	Disposition
BRANDYWINE	Washington	20 Sep 21	16 Jun 25	25 Aug 25	Burned accidentally, Norfolk, 3 Sep 64
POTOMAC	Washington	9 Aug 19	22 Mar 22	15 Jun 31	Sold 24 May 77
COLUMBIA	Washington	Nov 25	9 Mar 36	by 6 May 1838	Scuttled, Norfolk, 20 Apr 61
SANTEE	Portsmouth	Aug 21	16 Feb 55	8 Jun 61	Sold 29 Jul 1912
SAVANNAH	New York	Jul 20	24 May 42	15 Oct 43	Sold 27 Sep 83
SABINE	New York	Feb 23	12 Feb 55	23 Aug 58	Sold 23 Sep 83
RARITAN	Philadelphia	Sep 20	13 Jun 43	1 Dec 43	Scuttled, Norfolk, 20 Apr 61
CUMBERLAND	Boston	1825	24 May 42	by 20 Nov 1843	Sunk by CSS Virginia in Hampton Roads, Va., 8 Mar 62
ST. LAWRENCE	Norfolk	1826	25 Mar 47	17 Aug 48	Sold 31 Dec 75.

Notes: Authorized 29 Apr 16. These well built, handy, fast, and graceful craft were designed by William Doughty as improved Javas. They formed the backbone of the active navy during the 1840's and 1850's. The completion of the last two, Sabine and Santee, was authorized 6 Apr 54. These two were lengthened to 190'(b.p.) on the ways which increased their tonnage to 1726 tons. The Cumberland and Savannah were razeed in 1856 and 1857 respectively. The Brandywine served as a storeship 1861-1864. Her wreck was raised and sold 26 Mar 67. The Potomac acted as a store ship 1862-1865 and a receiving ship 1867-1877. The Santee served as a training vessel 1861-1870. The Savannah also acted as one 1861-1870 as did the Sabine 1864-1871 before becoming a receiving ship 1872-1883. The St. Lawrence served as an ordnance store ship 1863-1865 and a barracks or receiving ship 1866-1875. The Cumberland's wreck was sold in 1867 and the Columbia's wreck was sold 10 Oct 67 after being raised.
Displacements: 2330 (Potomac, Savannah, St. Lawrence), 2430 (Santee), 2450 (Sabine) tons.
Renaming: The Brandywine was originally named Susquehannah and was renamed in 1825.

1825

HUDSON (44)

Tonnage: 1728 tons
Dimensions: 176'4"(b.p.) x 45'(m) x 13'8"(h)
Armament: 32-32# 30-42#c

Rig: Ship
Speed: Unknown
Complement: Unknown

	Builder	Laid down	Launched	Commiss'd	Disposition
HUDSON	Smith & Dimon	1825	18 Nov 25	by 27 Sep 1828	Sold 4 Jun 44.

Notes: Her purchase was authorized 27 Jun 25 in lieu of one of the twelve frigates in the Act of 29 Apr 16. She was begun as the Liberator for Greek revolutionaries who could not pay for her and was taken over 23 Aug 26. Considered poorly built and only a fair sailer, she was designed by her builders with the lines of a packet. A sister, Hellas, was delivered to the Greeks in 1826 and burned 1 Aug 31 during a rebellion.

1832

MACEDONIAN (36)

Tonnage: 1341 tons
Dimensions: 164'(b.p.) x 42'(e) x 21'8"(max)
Armament: 30-18# 16-32#c; 2-10" 16-8" 4-32# (1853); 1-10" 4-8" (1862); 2-100#R 8-8" 4-32# (1863); 2-100#R 2-9" 6-8" 4-32# (1864); 2-100#R 2-9" 8-8" 2-32# (1864)

Rig: Ship
Speed: 11 kts.
Complement: 380

	Builder	Laid down	Launched	Commiss'd	Disposition
MACEDONIAN	Norfolk	1832	1 Nov 36	by 11 Oct 1837	Sold 31 Dec 75.

Notes: Authorized 10 Jul 32 as a reconstruction of the old frigate. Designed by Samuel Humphreys on a clipper model. Although fast she was not considered successful because she could not carry her intended armament of 32-32# 24-32#c. Razeed by New York in 1853, she served as a training vessel 1862-1870. Displacement as such 1856 tons.

1834

CONGRESS (44)

Tonnage: 1867 tons
Dimensions: 179'(b.p.) x 47'8"(m) x 22'6"
Armament: 4-8" 48-32#; 4-8" 46-32# (1845); 8-8" 42-32# (1850); 10-8" 40-32# (1855)

Rig: Ship
Speed: Unknown
Complement: 480.

	Builder	Laid down	Launched	Commiss'd	Disposition
CONGRESS	Portsmouth	1 Jun 39	16 Aug 41	7 May 42	Sunk by CSS Virginia in Hampton Roads, Va., 8 Mar 62.

Notes: Authorized 30 Jun 34 as a reconstruction of the old frigate. A big, fast, and successful design by Samuel Humphreys, she was the highest development of the frigate in the United States. Her wreck was raised 29 Sep 66 and sold.

PAUL JONES (?)

Tonnage: Unknown
Dimensions: Unknown
Armament: Unknown

Rig: Probably ship
Speed: Unknown
Complement: Unknown

	Builder	Laid down	Launched	Commiss'd	Disposition
PAUL JONES	Portsmouth	1835 ?	No	No	Broken up on ways 1843.

Notes: Authorized 30 Jun 34. The contracts for her frame and timbers were let in December 1834.

Frigates (Lake)

1813

PLATTSBURG (44)

Tonnage: 1749 tons
Dimensions: 185'(k) x 46'(e) x unknown
Armament: 32-24# 20-42#c (designed)

Rig: Ship
Speed: Unknown
Complement: Unknown

	Builder	Laid down	Launched	Commiss'd	Disposition
PLATTSBURG	Brown, Sackets Harbor	1814	No	No	Sold on ways 23 Mar 25.

Notes: Authorized 3 Mar 13. Construction halted at the end of the War of 1812.

SUPERIOR (44)

Tonnage: 1580 tons
Dimensions: 180'(b.p.) x 43'(m) x unknown
Armament: 30-32# 2-24# 26-42#c

Rig: Ship
Speed: Unknown
Complement: 500

	Builder	Laid down	Launched	Commiss'd	Disposition
SUPERIOR	Eckford, Sackets Harbor	11 Feb 14	1 May 14	1814	Sold 30 Apr 25.

Notes: Authorized 3 Mar 13. Designed by Henry Eckford and lengthened 20 feet during construction. She was reported sunk and decayed in 1823.

MOHAWK (32)

Tonnage: 1350 tons
Dimensions: 155'(b.p.) x 37'6"(m) x 15'6"(h)
Armament: 26-24# 16-32#c

Rig: Ship
Speed: Unknown
Complement: 350

	Builder	Laid down	Launched	Commiss'd	Disposition
MOHAWK	Eckford, Sackets Harbor	7 Apr 14	11 Jun 14	1814	Sold 30 Apr 25.

Notes: Authorized 3 Mar 13. A heavily built vessel designed by Henry Eckford, she was reported sunk and decayed in 1823.

1814

CONFIANCE (36)

Tonnage: 1200 tons
Dimensions: 147'5"(d) x 37'2" x 7'(h)
Armament: 27-24# 2-18# 4-32#c 6-24#c

Rig: Ship
Speed: Unknown
Complement: 325

	Builder	Launched	Acquired	Commiss'd	Disposition
CONFIANCE	Royal Navy, Isle aux Noix, P.Q.	1814	11 Sep 14	Unknown	Unknown.

Notes: Formerly the British Confiance, captured in the Battle of Lake Champlain. She was reported sunk and badly decayed near Whitehall, N.Y. in 1823.

Sloops of War

1776

RANGER (18)

Tonnage: 308 tons
Dimensions: 116'(g.d.) x 28' x 13'6"(h)
Armament: 18-9#

Rig: Ship
Speed: Unknown
Complement: 150

	Builder	Laid down	Launched	Commiss'd	Disposition
RANGER	J.K. Hackett	1777	10 May 77	by 1 Nov 1777	Captured by British with Charleston, S. C., 12 May 80.

Notes: Another William Hackett design, she was considered oversparred as built. She was known as Halifax in British service.
Renaming: Called Hampshire before launching.

SARATOGA (18)

Tonnage: 150 tons
Dimensions: 68'(k) x 25'4" x 12'(h)
Armament: 16-9# 2-4#

Rig: Ship
Speed: Unknown
Complement: 86

	Builder	Laid down	Launched	Commiss'd	Disposition
SARATOGA	Wharton & Humphreys	Dec 79	10 Apr 80	by 13 Aug 1780	Foundered off Bahamas 18 Mar 81.

Notes: Authorized 20 Nov 76. Construction delayed because of lack of funds.

1780

ARIEL (20)

Tonnage: 435 tons
Dimensions: 108' x 30' x unknown
Armament: 26-9#

Rig: Ship
Speed: Unknown
Complement: Unknown

	Builder	Launched	Acquired	Commiss'd	Disposition
ARIEL	Perry, Blackwall, England	7 Jul 77	1780	1780	Returned to France 1781.

Notes: Formerly the British Ariel, she was taken by the French frigate Amazone on 10 Sep 79 and loaned to the United States in 1780.

1798

TRUMBULL (18)

Tonnage: 400 tons
Dimensions: Unknown
Armament: 18-12#

Rig: Ship
Speed: Unknown
Complement: 220

	Builder	Laid down	Launched	Commiss'd	Disposition
TRUMBULL	Jos. Howland, Norwich, Ct.	1799	1799	1800	Sold 1801.

Notes: Authorized 30 Jun 98 and built by public subscription in Norwich, Ct.

WARREN (20)

Tonnage: 385 tons
Dimensions: Unknown
Armament: Unknown

Rig: Ship
Speed: Unknown
Complement: 160

	Builder	Laid down	Launched	Commiss'd	Disposition
WARREN	Webster	Unknown	26 Sep 99	1799	Sold by 1 Jun 01.

Notes: Authorized 30 Jun 98.

MARYLAND class (20)

Tonnage: 380 tons
Dimensions: 87'(k) x 29' x 12'(h)
Armament: 20-9# 6-6#

Rig: Ship
Speed: Unknown
Complement: 157

	Builder	Laid down	Launched	Commiss'd	Disposition
MARYLAND	Price	1799	3 Jun 99	by 12 Sep 1799	Sold 2 Oct 01
PATAPSCO	DeRochbrune	1799	20 Jun 99	1799	Sold 23 Apr 01.

Notes: Authorized 30 Jun 98 and built by public subscription in Baltimore. The particulars are for the Patapsco but those of the Maryland were probably similar. They were considered good sailers.
Renaming: The Patapsco was originally named Chesapeake and was renamed 10 Oct 99.

1799

Unnamed (18)

Tonnage: Unknown
Dimensions: Unknown
Armament: 18 guns

Rig: Ship
Speed: Unknown
Complement: Unknown

	Builder	Laid down	Launched	Commiss'd	Disposition
Unknown	Portsmouth	No	No	No	Cancelled ca. 1800
Unknown	Boston	No	No	No	Cancelled ca. 1800
Unknown	New York	No	No	No	Cancelled ca. 1800
Unknown	Philadelphia	No	No	No	Cancelled ca. 1800
Unknown	Washington	No	No	No	Cancelled ca. 1800
Unknown	Norfolk	No	No	No	Cancelled ca. 1800.

Notes: Authorized 25 Feb 99 with the Columbus-class ships of the line. They may never have been ordered.

1800

BERCEAU (24)

Tonnage: Unknown
Dimensions: Unknown
Armament: 2-12# 22-9#

Rig: Ship
Speed: Unknown
Complement: 220

	Builder	Launched	Acquired	Commiss'd	Disposition
BERCEAU	Unknown	1794	12 Oct 00	Unknown	Returned to France under Treaty of 30 Sep 00.

Notes: Formerly the French Le Berceau captured by Boston NE of Guadeloupe.

1812

ADAMS (24)

Tonnage: Unknown
Dimensions: 128'(b.p.) x 34' x 10'9"
Armament: 1-12# 26-18#

Rig: Ship
Speed: Unknown
Complement: Unknown

	Builder	Laid down	Launched	Commiss'd	Disposition
ADAMS	Washington	Jun 12	24 Dec 12	1813	Burned to avoid capture near Hampden, Me., 3 Sep 14.

Notes: Rebuilt from the frigate Adams to a new design by Josiah Fox. The 18# guns were Columbiads.

1813

ONTARIO class (18)

Tonnage: 559 tons
Dimensions: 117'11"(b.p.) x 32'3"(e) x 16'(max)
Armament: 2-18# 20-32#c

Rig: Ship
Speed: Unknown
Complement: 150

	Builder	Laid down	Launched	Commiss'd	Disposition
ONTARIO	Thos. Kemp, Baltimore, Md.	1813	1813	*25 Oct 13	Sold 15 Jul 56
ERIE	Thos. Kemp, Baltimore, Md.	1813	3 Nov 13	by 20 Mar 1814	Rebuilt 1821
ARGUS	Washington	1813	29 Jan 14	No	Burned to avoid capture, Washington, 24 Aug 14.

* Completed
Notes: Authorized 3 Mar 13. Designed by William Doughty on an extreme clipper model. They were fast but difficult to steer. The Ontario was a receiving ship 1840-1852.

WASP class (18)

Tonnage: 509 tons
Dimensions: 117'11"(Wasp), 119'(Peacock), 119'6"(Frolic) (all
  b.p.) x 31'6"(m) x 14'2"(Frolic, h), 14'6"(others, h)
Armament: Wasp--3-12# 19-32#c;
  Peacock--2-12# 20-32#c 1-12#c; 2-12# 18-32#c (1815);
  Frolic--2-12# 20-32#c

Rig: Ship
Speed: Unknown
Complement: 140

	Builder	Laid down	Launched	Commiss'd	Disposition
WASP	Cross & Merrill	1813	21 Sep 13	by 1 May 1814	Disappeared in North Atlantic after 10 Oct 14
PEACOCK	Brown, N.Y.	26 Jul 13	27 Sep 13	by 12 Mar 1814	Broken up 1828
FROLIC	Barker	1813	11 Sep 13	by 18 Feb 1814	Captured by HMS Orpheus off Matanzas, Cuba, 20 Apr 14.

Notes: Authorized 3 Mar 13. Designed by William Doughty to a more conservative plan than the Ontario class but were considered fast in heavy winds. The Frolic was taken into British service as HMS Florida.

1821

ERIE (18)

Tonnage: 611 tons
Dimensions: 121'11"(b.p.) x 32'6" x 14'9"(h)
Armament: 2-18# 20-42#c

Rig: Ship
Speed: Unknown
Complement: 150

	Builder	Laid down	Launched	Commiss'd	Disposition
ERIE	New York	1821	Unknown	1822	Broken up 1840.

Notes: Officially the old sloop Erie rebuilt. She apparently followed a new design.

1825

FALMOUTH (18)

Tonnage: 703 tons
Dimensions: 127'6"(b.p.) x 35'11"(e) x 16'(max)
Armament: 24-24#; 22-24# (1846); 4-8" 16-32# (1849); 4-8"
  14-32# (1857); 2-32# (1861)

Rig: Ship
Speed: 12 kts.
Complement: 190; 26 as storeship

	Builder	Laid down	Launched	Commiss'd	Disposition
FALMOUTH	Boston	5 Dec 26	3 Nov 27	by 20 Jan 1828	Sold 7 Nov 63.

Notes: Authorized 3 Mar 25. Designed by Josiah Barker, she was handy and a good sailer. She served as a storeship 1858-1863.

BOSTON class (18)

Tonnage: 700 tons
Dimensions: 127'(b.p.) x 34'9"(e) x 16'6"(max)
Armament: Boston--24-24#; 2-24# 20-42#c (1840); 4-8" 16-32#
  (1846);
  Vincennes--24-24#; 8-24# 2-9# (1838); 24-24# (1842); 22-24#
  (1846); 4-8" 16-32# (1849); 4-8" 4-32# (1852); 4-8" 16-32#
  (1857); 4-8" 14-32# (1861); 2-9" 4-8" (1861); 2-9" 4-8"
  1-20#R (1863);
  Vandalia--24-24#; 4-8" 16-32# (1849); 4-8" 16-32# 1-30#R (1863);
  Fairfield, Concord--24-24#;
  St. Louis--24-24#; 4-8" 16-32# (1848); 4-8" 14-32# (1859); 4-8" 12-32# 2-20#R (1862); none (1888);
  John Adams--24-24#; 2-18# 22-32#c (1842); 22-24# (1846); 4-8" 16-32# (1849); 4-8" 14-32# (1851);
  2-8" 4-32# 2-20#R (1862); 2-8" 1-50#R 4-32# 1-30#R (1864); 2-8" 4-32# 2-30#R 2-20#R (1864)

Rig: Ship
Speed: 12 kts.
Complement: 190

	Builder	Laid down	Launched	Commiss'd	Disposition
BOSTON	Boston	13 May 25	15 Oct 26	1826	Wrecked on Eleuthera I. 13 Nov 46
VINCENNES	New York	1825	27 Apr 26	27 Aug 26	Sold 5 Oct 67
VANDALIA	Philadelphia	1828	26 Aug 28	6 Nov 28	Broken up 1872
FAIRFIELD	New York	1828	28 Jun 28	by 20 Aug 1828	Broken up 1853
CONCORD	Portsmouth	19 Mar 27	24 Sep 27	7 May 30	Wrecked in Loango R., East Africa, 2 Oct 43
ST. LOUIS	Washington	12 Feb 27	16 Aug 28	20 Dec 28	Sold 5 Jun 1907
JOHN ADAMS	Norfolk	1829	16 Nov 30	by 8 May 1831	Sold 5 Oct 67.

Notes: Authorized 3 Mar 25 except for the John Adams, which was officially the old frigate rebuilt. Designed by Samuel Humphreys, they were good sea boats but not particularly fast. The original 24-gun armament proved to be too heavy for their hulls. The John Adams operated as a training vessel in 1861-1863. The Vandalia was lengthened 30' by Norfolk in 1848 and served as a receiving ship after 1863. The Vincennes acted as a store ship 1865-1867 while the St. Louis, lengthened 13' at New York in 1838-39, was a receiving ship in 1867-1894 and a training vessel thereafter. Displacements: 830 (St. Louis), 920 (Vandalia) tons.

Renaming: The St. Louis was renamed Keystone State on 30 Nov 1904.

LEXINGTON class (18)

Tonnage: 691 tons
Dimensions: 127'(b.p.) x 34'7"(e) x 16'6"(max)
Armament: Lexington--24-24#; 6-32# (1843); 4-9# 4-32#c (1844); 4-9" 2-32#c (1845); 4-32# (1853);
  Warren--24-24#; none (1853);
  Natchez--24-24#

Rig: Ship
Speed: 11.5 kts.
Complement: 190

	Builder	Laid down	Launched	Commiss'd	Disposition
LEXINGTON	New York	1825	9 Mar 26	12 Jun 26	Sold 1860
WARREN	Boston	1 Jun 25	29 Nov 26	14 Jan 27	Sold 1 Jan 63
NATCHEZ	Norfolk	1827	8 Mar 27	by 9 Jul 1827	Broken up 1840.

Notes: Authorized 3 Mar 25. A William Doughty design, they proved to be poor sailers. The Lexington was converted into a storeship by New York in 1843. The Warren served as a receiving ship 1857-1859 and a storeship thereafter.

1828

PEACOCK (18)

Tonnage: 559 tons
Dimensions: 118'(b.p.) x 31'6"(m) x 15'7"
Armament: 6-18#; 2-12# 20-32#c (1831); 8-24# 2-9# (1838)

Rig: Ship
Speed: Unknown
Complement: 190

	Builder	Laid down	Launched	Commiss'd	Disposition
PEACOCK	New York	1828	30 Sep 28	1 Nov 28	Wrecked Cape Disappointment, Wash., 18 Jul 41.

Notes: Officially the old sloop rebuilt. Designed by Samuel Humphreys specifically for exploring.

1837

CYANE class (22)

Tonnage: 792 tons
Dimensions: 132'4"(Cyane, b.p.), 132'3"(Levant, b.p.) x 36'3"(e) x 16'6"(max)
Armament: Cyane--4-24# 18-32#c; 20-32# (1840); 4-8" 16-32# (1851); 4-8" 14-32# (1856); 1-8" 1-32# (1863); 4-8" 14-32# (1864); 2-32# (1870);
  Levant--4-24# 18-32#c; 20-32# (1840); 4-8" 18-32# (1843); 4-8" 16-32# (1852); 4-8" 14-32# (1856)

Rig: Ship
Speed: 12 kts.
Complement: 190

	Builder	Laid down	Launched	Commiss'd	Disposition
CYANE	Boston	1837	2 Dec 37	by 24 Jun 1838	Sold 30 Jul 87
LEVANT	New York	1837	28 Dec 37	17 Mar 38	Disappeared off Hawaii after 18 Sep 60.

Notes: Authorized 3 Mar 37 using timber collected under the Acts of 10 Jul 32 (Cyane) and 30 Jun 34 (Levant). Designed by Samuel Humphreys as improved versions of the 1825 sloops but proved to be unhandy and poor sea boats. The Cyane was converted into a store ship at Mare Island in 1867. 950 tons displacement (Cyane).

DALE class (16)

Tonnage: 566 tons
Dimensions: 117'(b.p.) x 32'(m) x 15'8"
Armament: Dale--2-12# 14-32#c; 16-32# (1846); 14-32# (1853); 2-32# 1-30#R (1863); 8-32# (1876); none (1889);
  Decatur--2-12# 14-32#c; 16-32# (1847); 14-32# (1853); 4-8" 4-32# (1863); 16-32# (1865);
  Yorktown--2-12# 14-32#c; 2-32# 2-18# 12-32#c (1844); 16-32# (1848);
  Preble--2-12# 14-32#c; 2-32# 14-32#c (1844); 16-32# (1846); 10-32# (1851); 8-32# (1853); 10-32# (1858); 2-9" 8-32# (1859); 2-8" 7-32# (1861); 4-8" 12-32# 2-20#R (1864);
  Marion--2-12# 14-32#c; 16-32# (1845); 14-32# (1858); 10-32# 1-20#R (1862); 6-32# 1-20#R (1862)

Rig: Ship
Speed: 13 kts.
Complement: 150

	Builder	Laid down	Launched	Commiss'd	Disposition
DALE	Philadelphia	1839	8 Nov 39	11 Dec 40	To Treasury Dept. 23 Jul 1906
DECATUR	New York	1838	9 Apr 39	by 16 Mar 1840	Sold 17 Aug 65
YORKTOWN	Norfolk	1838	17 Jun 39	by 13 Dec 1840	Wrecked in Cape Verde Is. 6 Sep 50
PREBLE	Portsmouth	Apr 38	13 Jun 39	by 2 Jun 1840	Burned Pensacola 27 Apr 63
MARION	Boston	1838	24 Apr 39	4 Oct 39	Broken up 1871.

Notes: Authorized 3 Mar 37. A successful class of small sloops similar to the Peacock designed by John Lenthall. The Dale served as a school ship after 1868. Returned by the Coast Guard 19 Sep 1921, she was sold 20 Dec 1921. The Decatur acted as a floating battery 1861-1865; the Preble as a school ship 1851-1856; and the Marion as a training vessel 1861-1871. 675 tons displacement (Dale).
Renaming: The Dale was renamed Oriole 30 Nov. 1904

1841

SARATOGA (20)

Tonnage: 882 tons
Dimensions: 146'4"(b.p.) x 36'1"(e) x 16'8"(max)
Armament: 4-8" 16-32#; 4-8" 18-32# (1846); 6-8" 16-32# (1855); 6-8" 14-32# (1856); 6-8" 12-32# (1857); 6-8" 12-32# 1-30#R (1863); 16-32# 1-20#R (1864); 6-8" 12-32# 1-30#R (1864); 4-8" (1876); 11-8" 1-60#BLR (1887); none (1889)

Rig: Ship
Speed: 13 kts.
Complement: 275

	Builder	Laid down	Launched	Commiss'd	Disposition
SARATOGA	Portsmouth	Aug 41	26 Jul 42	7 Jan 43	To State of Pennsylvania 14 Aug 1907.

Notes: Like the other sloops and brigs laid down in 1841-1843 she was built without specific Congressional authorization. She was a weatherly and fast craft designed by Samuel Pook and Samuel Humphreys as an improved Cyane and served as a quarantine or training vessel after 1866. She was loaned in 1889 to the state of Pennsylvania and the city of Philadelphia as a seagoing nautical school ship. 1025 tons displacement.

1843

ALBANY (20)

Tonnage: 1042 tons
Dimensions: 147'11"(b.p.) x 38'6"(m) x 17'6"(max)
Armament: 4-8" 18-32#

Rig: Ship
Speed: 13 kts.
Complement: 210

	Builder	Laid down	Launched	Commiss'd	Disposition
ALBANY	New York	1843	27 Jun 46	6 Nov 46	Disappeared in West Indies after 29 Sep 54.

Notes: No authorization. A handsome, well built vessel, designed by Francis Grice on the Baltimore clipper model, she was fast and easily handled.

PORTSMOUTH (20)

Tonnage: 1022 tons
Dimensions: 153'1"(b.p.) x 38'1"(e) x 17'(max)
Armament: 4-8" 18-32#; 6-8" 16-32# (1852); 16-8" (1856);
  16-8" 1-20#R (1861); 18-8" 1-20#R (1863); 18-8" (1864);
  1-100#R 18-8" 1-20#R (1864); 16-8" 1-20#R (1865); 14-8"
  1-30#R (1869); 4-8" 1-30#R (1872); 12-8" 2-20#R (1874);
  10-8" 2-20#R (1875); 11-8" 2-20#R (1879); 1-8" 1-60#BLR
  (1884); 11-8" 1-60#R 2-20#R (1887); 9-8"R 1-60#R (1894);
  11-8"R 1-60#BLR (1895); none (1901)

Rig: Ship
Speed: 14 kts.
Complement: 210

	Builder	Laid down	Launched	Commiss'd	Disposition
PORTSMOUTH	Portsmouth	15 Jun 43	23 Oct 43	10 Nov 44	Sold 12 Jul 1915.

Notes: No authorization. This design by Josiah Barker produced probably the best of the 1841-1843 sloops. She spent 1867-1870 and 1879-1911 as a training vessel before serving 1911-1915 with the Marine Hospital Service. 1125 tons displacement.

JAMESTOWN (20)

Tonnage: 988 tons
Dimensions: 163'5"(b.p.) x 36'2"(e) x 18'(max)
Armament: 4-8" 18-32#; 6-8" 16-32# (1851); 6-8" 14-32#
  (1861); 14-32# 2-30#R (1869); 10-8" 4-32# 2-30#R (1870);
  6-8" 1-30#R (1876); 12-8" 2-20#BLR (1887); 12-8" 1-60#BLR
  (1890); none (1892)

Rig: Ship
Speed: 13 kts.
Complement: 210

	Builder	Laid down	Launched	Commiss'd	Disposition
JAMESTOWN	Norfolk	1843	16 Sep 44	25 Jan 45	Sold 7 Oct 1912.

Notes: No authorization. Designed by Foster Rhodes and considered fast but difficult to trim properly. She was converted to a storeship at Mare Island in 1865 and served as a training vessel 1877-1879 and 1883-1892. After 1892 she was on loan to the Marine Hospital Service. 1125 tons displacement.

GERMANTOWN (20)

Tonnage: 982 tons
Dimensions: 150'(b.p.) x 36'(e) x 17'3"(max)
Armament: 4-8" 18-32#; 6-8" 16-32# (1854); 8-8" 12-32# (1857)

Rig: Ship
Speed: 14 kts.
Complement: 210

	Builder	Laid down	Launched	Commiss'd	Disposition
GERMANTOWN	Philadelphia	7 Sep 43	21 Aug 46	9 Mar 47	Burned to avoid capture, Norfolk, 20 Apr 61.

Notes: No authorization. A good sailer, particularly in light winds, she was designed by John Lenthall.

PLYMOUTH (20)

Tonnage: 974 tons
Dimensions: 147'6"(b.p.) x 38'1"(e) x 18'(max)
Armament: 4-8" 18-32#; 4-8" 8-32# (1856); 1-11" 4-9" (1857);
  1-11" 4-9" 4-8" (1858); 2-8" 6-32# (1859)

Rig: Ship
Speed: 12 kts.
Complement: 210

	Builder	Laid down	Launched	Commiss'd	Disposition
PLYMOUTH	Boston	1843	11 Oct 43	by 3 Apr 1844	Captured by Confederates, Norfolk, 20 Apr 61.

Notes: No authorization. Samuel Pook's design produced a stiff, dry, and fast vessel. She served as a training vessel 1859-1860. The Confederates scuttled her at Norfolk 10 May 62.

ST. MARY'S (20)

Tonnage: 958 tons
Dimensions: 150'(b.p.) x 37'4"(e) x 17'3"(max)
Armament: 4-8" 18-32#; none (1874); 8-8" (1876); none (1893)

Rig: Ship
Speed: Unknown
Complement: 210

	Builder	Laid down	Launched	Commiss'd	Disposition
ST. MARY'S	Washington	1843	24 Nov 44	13 Dec 44	Sold Aug 1908.

Notes: No authorization. A fast and weatherly design by Charles B. Brodie, she served as a training ship after 1874. 1025 tons displacement.

The sloop of war *Vandalia* as drawn by Frank Muller. Her main battery was in the open. (NH 43851)

The sloop of war *St. Mary's* as a training ship after the Civil War. Her main battery was covered by a complete spardeck. (NH 55474)

1846

AUSTIN (18)

Tonnage: 589 tons
Dimensions: 130'2"(b.p.) x 31'9" x 11'
Armament: Unknown; mounted 2-18# 18-24#c in 1840

Rig: Ship
Speed: Unknown
Complement: Unknown

	Builder	Launched	Acquired	Commiss'd	Disposition
AUSTIN	Schott & Whitney	1839	11 May 46	No	Broken up 1848.

Notes: Transferred from the Texas Navy at Galveston but found to be rotten and never used. She acted as the Pensacola receiving ship 1846-1848.

1853

CONSTELLATION (24)

Tonnage: 1265 tons
Dimensions: 176'(b.p.) x 42'(e) x 19'3"
Armament: 2-10" 16-8" 4-32#; 16-8" 4-32# (1859); 16-8" 4-32#
 1-30#R 1-20#R (1862); 1-100#R 10-10" (1871); 1-100#R 1-11"
 8-10" 1-20#R (1872); 1-100#R 1-11" 8-9" (1876); 10-9"
 2-20#R (1880); 10-8" 2-20#R (1888); 10-8" 1-60#BLR 1-20#BLR
 (1891); 6-6# (1900); 2-6# (1916)

Rig: Ship
Speed: 14 kts.
Complement: 227

	Builder	Laid down	Launched	Commiss'd	Disposition
CONSTELLATION	Norfolk	1853	26 Aug 54	28 Jul 55	Museum at Baltimore, Md.,
					7 Aug 1955, stk. 15 Aug 1955.

Notes: Officially the old frigate razeed and rebuilt. The new vessel sailed and steered well. After 1865 she served as a training and receiving ship. 1886 tons displacement.
Renamings: She was renamed Old Constellation on 1 Dec 1917 but regained her original name on 24 Jul 1920.
Reclassification: Designated "unclassified" (IX-20) 17 Jul 1920.

Sloops of War (Lake)

1813

MADISON (20)

Tonnage: 593 tons
Dimensions: 112'(k) x 32'6" x 11'6"(h)
Armament: 4-12# 20-32#c; 14-18# 8-32#c (1814)

Rig: Ship
Speed: Unknown
Complement: 274

	Builder	Laid down	Launched	Commiss'd	Disposition
MADISON	Eckford, Sackets Harbor	11 Sep 12	26 Nov 12	by 25 Apr 1813	Sold 30 Apr 25.

Notes: Authorized 3 Mar 13. Designed by Henry Eckford; reported sunk and decayed in 1823.

GENERAL PIKE (24)

Tonnage: 875 tons
Dimensions: 145'(b.p.) x 37'(m) x 15'(h)
Armament: 28-24#

Rig: Ship
Speed: Unknown
Complement: 300

	Builder	Laid down	Launched	Commiss'd	Disposition
GENERAL PIKE	Eckford, Sackets Harbor	9 Apr 13	12 Jun 13	by 21 Jul 1813	Sold 30 Apr 25.

Notes: Authorized 3 Mar 13. Designed by Henry Eckford; reported sunk and decayed in 1823.

DETROIT (18)

Tonnage: 400 tons
Dimensions: Unknown
Armament: 2-24# 1-18# 6-12# 8-9# 1-24#c 1-18#c (when
 captured); 1-24# 18-12# 2-18#c (1814)

Rig: Ship
Speed: Unknown
Complement: 150

	Builder	Launched	Acquired	Commiss'd	Disposition
DETROIT	Malden, Ont. Navy Yard	1813	10 Sep 13	Unknown	Sold 12 Jul 25.

Notes: Formerly the British Detroit, taken in the battle of Put-in-Bay. She sank at her moorings in 1815 but was not removed until 1835.

QUEEN CHARLOTTE (18)

Tonnage: 300 tons
Dimensions: 96'(d) x 25' x 12'(h)
Armament: 1-12# 2-9# 14-24#c (when captured); 14-24# 3-12# (1814)

Rig: Ship
Speed: Unknown
Complement: 126

	Builder	Launched	Acquired	Commiss'd	Disposition
QUEEN CHARLOTTE	Malden, Ont. Navy Yard	1809	10 Sep 13	Unknown	Sold 12 Jul 25.

Notes: Formerly the British Queen Charlotte, captured in the battle of Put-In-Bay. She sank at her moorings in 1815.

1814

SARATOGA (26)

Tonnage: 734 tons
Dimensions: 143'(b.p.) x 36'6"(m) x 12'6"(h)
Armament: 8-24# 6-42#c 12-32#c

Rig: Ship
Speed: Unknown
Complement: 240

	Builder	Laid down	Launched	Commiss'd	Disposition
SARATOGA	Brown, Vergennes	7 Mar 14	11 Apr 14	1814	Sold 1824.

Notes: May have been acquired. Designed by Noah Brown to carry 6-24# 20-32#c, she was considered a successful vessel which sailed and handled well. She was reported "very much decayed" in 1823.

Brigs

1779

DILIGENT (14)

Tonnage: 236 tons
Dimensions: 88'6"(d) x 24'8" x 10'10"(h)
Armament: 14-4#

Rig: Brig
Speed: Unknown
Complement: 50

	Builder	Launched	Acquired	Commiss'd	Disposition
DILIGENT	Unknown, America	Unknown	7 May 79	Unknown	Burned to avoid capture, Penobscot R., Me., 14 Aug 79.

Notes: Formerly the British Diligent, purchased by the British in America in 1776 and taken by Providence off Sandy Hook, N. Y.

1798

Unknown (18)

Tonnage: "Not to exceed" 360 tons
Dimensions: Unknown x unknown x 14'
Armament: 18-9# (designed)

Rig: Brig
Speed: Unknown
Complement: ca. 110

	Builder	Laid down	Launched	Commiss'd	Disposition
Unknown	Unknown, Newburyport	No	No	No	Cancelled 1799
Unknown	Rich. Conway, Alexandria, Va.	No	No	No	Cancelled 30 Apr 99.

PINCKNEY (18)

Tonnage: 195 tons
Dimensions: 62'(k) x 23' x 10'6"(h)
Armament: Unknown

Rig: Brig
Speed: Unknown
Complement: 140

	Builder	Launched	Acquired	Commiss'd	Disposition
PINCKNEY	Wm. Pritchard, Charleston, S.C.	13 Oct 98	1798	1798	Sold 18 Apr 00.

Notes: Transferred from the Revenue Cutter Service while under construction; converted to a galley 11 Dec 98.

PICKERING (14)

Tonnage: 187 tons
Dimensions: 58'(k) x 20' x 9'(h)
Armament: 14-4#

Rig: Brig
Speed: Unknown
Complement: 105

	Builder	Launched	Acquired	Commiss'd	Disposition
PICKERING	Merrill	1798	11 Jul 98	1798	Disappeared in West Indies after 20 Aug 00.

Notes: Transferred from Revenue Cutter Service. Hull duplicated the Diligence class schooners.

1803

ARGUS (16)

Tonnage: 299 tons
Dimensions: 94'6"(b.p.) x 28'2"(e) x 12'8"(h)
Armament: 2-12# 16-24#c; 1-12# 12-24#c (1804)

Rig: Brig
Speed: Unknown
Complement: 142

	Builder	Laid down	Launched	Commiss'd	Disposition
ARGUS	Hartt	12 May 03	21 Aug 03	by 6 Sep 1803	Captured by HMS Pelican in English Channel 14 Aug 13.

Notes: Authorized 28 Feb 03. Designed by Joseph Hartt with very fine lines for North African operations.
Renaming: Originally named Merrimack, renamed during construction.

SYREN (16)

Tonnage: 250 tons
Dimensions: 93'4"(b.p.) x 27'9"(e) x 12'6"(h)
Armament: 2-12# 16-24#c; 1-12# 16-24#c (1804); 2-12# 16-24#c (1813); 2-9# 2-42#c 12-24#c (1814)

Rig: Brig
Speed: Unknown
Complement: 137

	Builder	Laid down	Launched	Commiss'd	Disposition
SYREN	Benj. Hutton, Philadelphia	1803	6 Aug 03	by 27 Aug 1803	Captured by HMS Medway off West Africa 12 Jul 14.

Notes: Authorized 28 Feb 03. Designed by Benjamin Hutton, Jr., for North African service, she was a light weather vessel. Her name is sometimes given as Siren.

1804

WASP (18)

Tonnage: 450 tons
Dimensions: 105'7"(b.p.) x 30'11"(e) x 14'2"(h)
Armament: 2-12# 16-32#c; 2-12# 18-32#c (1812)

Rig: Brig
Speed: Unknown
Complement: 140

	Builder	Laid down	Launched	Commiss'd	Disposition
WASP	Washington	1805	21 Apr 06	by 1 May 1807	Captured by HMS Poictiers off North Carolina 18 Oct 12.

Notes: Authorized 26 Mar 04. Designed by Josiah Fox as a brig but altered to a ship while building. Fast, steady, and weatherly, she served in the Royal Navy as HMS Peacock.

HORNET (18)

Tonnage: 441 tons
Dimensions: 106'9"(d) x 31'5"(e) x 14'11"
Armament: 2-12# 14-9#; 2-12# 18-32#c (1811); 2-18# 18-32# (1813)

Rig: Brig
Speed: Unknown
Complement: 140

	Builder	Laid down	Launched	Commiss'd	Disposition
HORNET	Wm. Price, Fells Pt., Md.	Unknown	28 Jun 05	18 Oct 05	Wrecked off Tampico, Mex., 10 Sep 29.

Notes: Authorized 26 Mar 04. Designed by Josiah Fox, she was considered a fast vessel and was converted to a ship-rigged sloop-of-war at Washington Navy Yard in 1811.

1814

EPERVIER (18)

Tonnage: 447 tons
Dimensions: 100'(b.p.) x 30'6"(e) x 12'9"(h)
Armament: 2-18# 16-32#c

Rig: Brigantine
Speed: Unknown
Complement: 128

	Builder	Launched	Acquired	Commiss'd	Disposition
EPERVIER	Mary Ross, Rochester, Eng.	2 Dec 12	29 Apr 14	Unknown	Disappeared in North Atlantic after 14 Jul 15.

Notes: Formerly the British Epervier, taken by Peacock off Indian River Inlet, Fla.

CHIPPEWA (14)

Tonnage: 390 tons
Dimensions: 107'(b.p.) x 29'11"(e) x 16'9"
Armament: 2-18# 14-32#c

Rig: Brig
Speed: Unknown
Complement: 90

	Builder	Laid down	Launched	Commiss'd	Disposition
CHIPPEWA	Caleb Carr, Warren, R. I.	1814	Apr 15	by 3 Jul 1815	Wrecked on Caicos I. 12 Dec 16.

Notes: Authorized 15 Nov 14. Designed by William Doughty; sometimes has name spelled Chippeway.

BOXER class (14)

Tonnage: 370 tons (Boxer), 360 tons (Saranac)
Dimensions: 114'11"(b.p.) x 28'7"(e) x 14'2" (Boxer),
  94'(k) x 28'7"(e) x 14' (Saranac)
Armament: Boxer--2-9# 14-24#c;
  Saranac--2-18# 14-24#c

Rig: Brig
Speed: Unknown
Complement: 90

	Builder	Laid down	Launched	Commiss'd	Disposition
BOXER	Churchill	1814	May 15	1815	Foundered off Belize, British Honduras, 25 Oct 17
SARANAC	Churchill	1814	1815	by 23 Dec 1815	Sold 1818.

Notes: Authorized 15 Nov 14. Designed by William Doughty.

1834

DOLPHIN class (10)

Tonnage: 224 tons
Dimensions: 88'(b.p.) x 25'(m) x 13'
Armament: Dolphin--2-9# 8-24#c; 2-32# (1851); 6-32# (1855);
  4-32# (1858);
    Porpoise--2-9# 2-24#c; 2-9# 10-24#c (1843); 2-9# 8-24#c
  (1846); 2-32# 6-24#c (1848); 2-32# (1852)

Rig: Brig (Dolphin), Brigantine
(Porpoise)
Speed: 10.5 kts.
Complement: 80

	Builder	Laid down	Launched	Commiss'd	Disposition
DOLPHIN	New York	1836	17 Jun 36	6 Sep 36	Burned to avoid capture, Norfolk, 20 Apr 61
PORPOISE	Boston	1836	31 May 36	25 Aug 36	Disappeared in S. China Sea after 21 Sep 54.

Notes: Authorized 30 Jun 34. They were fast, improved versions of the Boxer class of schooners designed by Samuel Humphreys. The Porpoise was rerigged as a brig in 1840.

1841

TRUXTUN (10)

Tonnage: 331 tons
Dimensions: 102'6"(b.p.) x 28'2"(e) x 12'3"(mean)
Armament: 10-32#c

Rig: Brig
Speed: Unknown
Complement: 80

	Builder	Laid down	Launched	Commiss'd	Disposition
TRUXTUN	Norfolk	Dec 41	16 Apr 42	18 Feb 43	Wrecked on Tuxpan Bar, Mex., 14 Aug 46.

Notes: No authorization. Designed by Francis Grice and considered fast as well as weatherly.

BAINBRIDGE class (10)

Tonnage: 259 tons
Dimensions: 100'(b.p.) x 25'(m) x 13'6"(max)
Armament: 10-32#c; 6-32# (Bainbridge, 1850)

Rig: Brig
Speed: 11 kts.
Complement: 80

	Builder	Laid down	Launched	Commiss'd	Disposition
BAINBRIDGE	Boston	1842	26 Apr 42	16 Dec 42	Foundered off Cape Hatteras 21 Aug 63
SOMERS	New York	1842	16 Apr 42	12 May 42	Foundered off Veracruz, Mex., 8 Dec 46.

Notes: No authorization. Fast and weatherly, but oversparred, they were designed by Samuel Humphreys.

1843

LAWRENCE (10)

Tonnage: 364 tons
Dimensions: 109'9"(b.p.) x 26'2"(m) x 16'6"
Armament: 2-32# 8-32#c

Rig: Brig
Speed: Unknown
Complement: 80

	Builder	Laid down	Launched	Commiss'd	Disposition
LAWRENCE	Culley	1843	1 Aug 43	19 Sep 43	Sold 1846.

Notes: No authorization. An unsuccessful design by her builder, she drew too much water and carried too few stores to be a useful warship.

PERRY (10)

Tonnage: 280 tons
Dimensions: 105'(b.p.) x 25'6"(m) x 13'2"(max)
Armament: 10-32#c; 2-32# 6-32#c (1846); 6-32# (1858); 6-32#
   2-20#R (1863)

Rig: Brig
Speed: 11 kts.
Complement: 80

	Builder	Laid down	Launched	Commiss'd	Disposition
PERRY	Norfolk	18 Feb 43	9 May 43	13 Oct 43	Sold 10 Aug 65.

Notes: No authorization. Reputedly the fastest vessel in the navy when built, she was designed by Francis Grice on the Baltimore clipper model.

1846

WHARTON class (18)

Tonnage: 419 tons
Dimensions: 112' x 29' x 11'(h)
Armament: Unknown

Rig: Brig
Speed: Unknown
Complement: Unknown

	Builder	Launched	Acquired	Commiss'd	Disposition
WHARTON	Schott & Whitney	1838	11 May 46	No	Sold 30 Nov 46.
ARCHER	Schott & Whitney	1838	11 May 46	No	Sold 30 Nov 46.

Notes: Transferred from the Republic of Texas at Galveston but found to be rotten and never used. In Texas service they were initially called Colorado and Galveston respectively.

Brigs (Lake)

1807

ONEIDA (14)

Tonnage: 243 tons
Dimensions: 85'6"(b.p.) x 23'(e) x 8'(h)
Armament: 1-32# 16-24#c; 2-6# 16-24#c (1813); 2-12# 14-24#c
   (1814); 14-12# (1815)

Rig: Brig
Speed: Unknown
Complement: 115

	Builder	Laid down	Launched	Commiss'd	Disposition
ONEIDA	Eckford & Bergh	1808	31 Mar 09	1809	Sold May 25.

Notes: Built under the gunboat authorization of 18 Dec 07 for use on Lake Ontario. Heavily built to a design of Christian Bergh, she was considered a dull sailer. She was sold in May 1815 but was quickly reacquired. She was not worth repairing in 1821.

1813

JEFFERSON class (18)

Tonnage: 500 tons
Dimensions: 121'6"(b.p.) x 31'6"(m) x 14'6"(h)
Armament: Jefferson--2-12# 16-42#c;
   Jones--2-12# 20-32#c; 2-24# 18-42#c (1815)

Rig: Brig
Speed: Unknown
Complement: 160

	Builder	Laid down	Launched	Commiss'd	Disposition
JEFFERSON	Eckford, Sackets Harbor	Feb 14	7 Apr 14	1814	Sold 30 Apr 25
JONES	Eckford, Sackets Harbor	Feb 14	10 Apr 14	1814	Sold 30 Apr 25.

Notes: Authorized 3 Mar 13. Designed by Henry Eckford using the moulds of the Peacock. Both were reported sunk and in a decayed condition in 1823. The Jefferson was not removed following her sale.

NIAGARA class (18)

Tonnage: 493 tons
Dimensions: 110'(b.p.) x 30'(e) x 9'
Armament: 2-12# 18-32#c

Rig: Brig
Speed: Unknown
Complement: 136

	Builder	Laid down	Launched	Commiss'd	Disposition
NIAGARA	Brown, Erie	Mar 13	May 13	4 Aug 13	Sold 12 Jul 25
LAWRENCE	Brown, Erie	Mar 13	24 May 13	5 Aug 13	Sold 12 Jul 25.

Notes: Probably authorized 3 Mar 13. Designed by Noah Brown and built of green wood like the other lake vessels. They were sunk in Misery Bay, Erie, Pa., in 1818 and 1815 respectively for preservation. Neither was removed after sale. The hulk of the Lawrence was raised in 1876 and that of the Niagara in 1913.

HUNTER (10)

Tonnage: 180 tons
Dimensions: Unknown
Armament: 4-6# 2-4# 2-2# 2-12# (when captured)

Rig: Brig
Speed: Unknown
Complement: 45

	Builder	Launched	Acquired	Commiss'd	Disposition
HUNTER	Malden, Ont. Navy Yard	1806	10 Sep 13	Unknown	Probably sold 1816.

Notes: Ex-British Hunter taken in battle of Put-in-Bay. She may never have been taken into service.

1814

EAGLE (20)

Tonnage: 500 tons
Dimensions: 128' x 32' x unknown
Armament: 8-18# 12-32#c

Rig: Brig
Speed: Unknown
Complement: 150

	Builder	Laid down	Launched	Commiss'd	Disposition
EAGLE	Brown, Vergennes	29 Jul 14	11 Aug 14	6 Sep 14	Sold 1825.

Notes: May have been acquired. Unofficially called Surprize before launching.

LINNET (16)

Tonnage: 350 tons
Dimensions: 82'6"(d) x 27'(e) x 6'8"(h)
Armament: 16-12#

Rig: Brig
Speed: Unknown
Complement: 125

	Builder	Launched	Acquired	Commiss'd	Disposition
LINNET	Royal Navy, Isle aux Noix, P.Q.	1814	11 Sep 14	Unknown	Sold 1825.

Notes: Ex British Linnet (ex Niagara) captured in the Battle of Lake Champlain. She was unfit for repairs in 1821.

Schooners

1798

DILIGENCE class (18)

Tonnage: 187 tons
Dimensions: 58'(k) x 20' x 9'(h)
Armament: 14-6# (except Diligence & South Carolina, 12-6#)

Rig: Schooner
Speed: Unknown
Complement: 105

	Builder	Launched	Acquired	Commiss'd	Disposition
DILIGENCE	Humphreys	1797	1798	1798	Returned 4 Jun 99
EAGLE	Brown, Philadelphia	3 Aug 98	1798	1798	Sold 17 Jun 01
GOVERNOR JAY	Unknown, New York	27 Jun 98	1798	1798	Returned ca. May 99
SOUTH CAROLINA	Unknown, Charleston, S.C.	27 Nov 98	1798	1798	Returned 20 Aug 99
SCAMMEL	J.K. Hackett	11 Aug 98	20 May 99	1799	Sold Dec 01.

Notes: Transferred from the Revenue Cutter Service.

VIRGINIA (14)

Tonnage: 187 (?) tons
Dimensions: 70'(k) x 18'10" x 8'6"(h)
Armament: 6-6# 8-4#

Rig: Brig
Speed: Unknown
Complement: 451

	Builder	Launched	Acquired	Commiss'd	Disposition
VIRGINIA	Unknown, Hampton, Va.	1797	1798	1798	Returned 3 Jun 99.

Notes: Transferred from the Revenue Cutter Service.

ENTERPRISE class (12)

Tonnage: 135 tons
Dimensions: 84'7"(d) x 22'6" x 9'6"(Experiment, h), 10' (Enterprise, h)
Armament: 12-6#; 14-6# (1801); 2-9# 14-18#c (1811); 1-9# 6-18#c 1-13"mortar (1821)

Rig: Schooner
Speed: Unknown
Complement: 70

	Builder	Laid down	Launched	Commiss'd	Disposition
ENTERPRISE	Henry Spencer, Baltimore	Unknown	1799	by 17 Dec 1799	Wrecked on Little Curacoa I. 9 Jul 23
EXPERIMENT	Unknown, Baltimore	Unknown	1799	by Nov 99	Sold 1801.

Notes: Authorized 27 Apr 98. Successful vessels, they were fast and handy. The Enterprise was almost completely rebuilt in Venice during 1805 with new dimensions of 80'6"(b.p.) x 23'9"(e) x 10'10"(h). She was rerigged as a brig at Washington Navy Yard in 1811 but as such was sluggish and unhandy.

1803

VIXEN (12)

Tonnage: 170 tons
Dimensions: 84'7"(b.p.) x 22'6"(m) x 9'6"(h)
Armament: 2-9# 12-18#c; 16-6# (1804)

Rig: Schooner
Speed: Unknown
Complement: 111

	Builder	Laid down	Launched	Commiss'd	Disposition
VIXEN	Price	1803	25 Jun 03	by 3 Aug 1803	Captured by HMS Southampton in West Indies 22 Nov 12.

Notes: Authorized 28 Feb 03. Designed by Benjamin Hutton, Jr. to be similar to the Enterprise. She was slow and crank after rerigging as a brig at Washington Navy Yard in 1811.

1804

FERRET (12)

Tonnage: 148 tons
Dimensions: 73'(d) x 23'8" x 7'6"(h)
Armament: 12-12# 2-6# (1812)

Rig: Schooner
Speed: Unknown
Complement: 64

The schooner *Enterprise* in 1812 after being rerigged as a brigantine. From a contemporary etching by the French artist Baugean. (NH 63535)

	Builder	Laid down	Launched	Commiss'd	Disposition
FERRET	Norfolk	Unknown	Unknown	18 Apr 09	Captured by HMS Narcissus 17 Jan 13.

Notes: Designed by Josiah Fox, she may have been purchased rather than built. After being rerigged as a brig in 1810 she was slow, overcrowded, and unseaworthy.
Renaming: Renamed Viper when converted to a brig in 1810.

1820

PORPOISE class (12)

Tonnage: 198 tons
Dimensions: 86'(b.p.) x 24'7"(m) x 12'4"(max)
Armament: 12-6#; 2-18# 10-6# (1825); 2-9# 8-24#c (Shark, 1840); 2-9# 10-24#c (Shark, 1842)

Rig: Schooner
Speed: Unknown
Complement: 70

	Builder	Laid down	Launched	Commiss'd	Disposition
PORPOISE	Portsmouth	16 Aug 20	2 Dec 20	30 Mar 21	Wrecked on Sacrificios I., Mex., 2 Nov 33
DOLPHIN	Philadelphia	1820	23 Jun 21	7 Oct 21	Sold 2 Dec 35
ALLIGATOR	Boston	1820	2 Nov 20	by Apr 21	Wrecked on Craysfort Reef, Fla., 23 Nov 23
SHARK	Washington	1820	17 May 21	17 May 21	Wrecked in Columbia R. 10 Sep 46.

Notes: Authorized 15 May 20. Fast, handy vessels designed by William Doughty, they were constructed of timber accumulated under the 1816 Act for the Increase of the Navy. The Dolphin was completed by New York.

GRAMPUS (12)

Tonnage: 172 tons
Dimensions: 92'6"(b.p.) x 24'6"(m) x 11'9"
Armament: 1-18# 10-12#c; 2-9# 10-12#c (1825); 2-9# 8-24#c (1840)

Rig: Schooner
Speed: Unknown
Complement: 64

	Builder	Laid down	Launched	Commiss'd	Disposition
GRAMPUS	Washington	1820	2 Aug 21	1821	Disappeared off Charleston, S. C., after 14 Mar 43.

Notes: Authorized 15 May 20. Designed by Henry Eckford and considered one of the fastest schooners of her day.

1831

BOXER class (10)

Tonnage: 194 tons
Dimensions: 88'(b.p.) x 23'6"(m) x 12'
Armament: 2-9# 8-24#c

Rig: Schooner
Speed: Unknown
Complement: 72

	Builder	Laid down	Launched	Commiss'd	Disposition
BOXER	Boston	1831	22 Nov 31	1832	Sold 7 Aug 48
ENTERPRISE	New York	1831	26 Oct 31	15 Dec 31	Sold 28 Oct 44.

Notes: Authorized 3 Feb 31. Designed by Samuel Humphreys, they were fast but tender. After rerigging as a brig by New York in 1842 the Boxer sailed well but was crank.

EXPERIMENT (10)

Tonnage: 176 tons
Dimensions: 88'6"(b.p.) x 23'6"(m) x 9'
Armament: 2-9# 8-24#c

Rig: Schooner
Speed: Unknown
Complement: Unknown

	Builder	Laid down	Launched	Commiss'd	Disposition
EXPERIMENT	Washington	1831	14 Mar 32	1832	Sold 16 May 48.

Notes: Authorized 3 Feb 31. Built without interior framing to a plan of William Annesley. Her hull consisted of five courses of planking laid on alternately transversely and longitudinally.

Schooners (Lake)

1777

Unnamed

Two schooners, 66'(k) x 20' x 6', were ordered built at Fort George, on Lake George, N. Y. They were never completed, if ever begun.

1813

SYLPH (16)

Tonnage: 300 tons   Rig: Schooner
Dimensions: Unknown   Speed: Unknown
Armament: 4-32# 12-6#; 2-9# 16-24#c (1814)   Complement: 70

	Builder	Laid down	Launched	Commiss'd	Disposition
SYLPH	Eckford, Sackets Harbor	26 Jul 13	18 Aug 13	by 21 Aug 1813	Sold 30 Apr 25.

Notes: Authorized 3 Mar 13. A fast and weatherly vessel designed by Eckford, she was rerigged as an 18-gun brig in 1814. In 1823 she was reported sunk and decayed.

LADY PREVOST (10)

Tonnage: 230 tons   Rig: Schooner
Dimensions: 83' X 21' X 9'   Speed: Unknown
Armament: 1-9# 2-6# 10-12#c (when captured)   Complement: 86

	Builder	Launched	Acquired	Commiss'd	Disposition
LADY PREVOST	Malden, Ont. Navy Yard	1810	10 Sep 13	Unknown	Sold 1815.

Notes: Formerly the British Lady Prevost, captured in the battle of Put-in-Bay.

Sloops

1798

GENERAL GREENE (10)

Tonnage: 150 tons   Rig: Sloop
Dimensions: Unknown   Speed: Unknown
Armament: 10-4#   Complement: 45

	Builder	Launched	Acquired	Commiss'd	Disposition
GENERAL GREENE	Wm. Price Fells Pt., Md.	1797	1798	1798	Returned 20 May 99.

Notes: Transferred from the Revenue Cutter Service.

Blockships

1814

TCHIFONTA (22)

Tonnage: 1500 tons   Rig: Schooner
Dimensions: 152'9"(d), 145'(b.p.) x 43'(m) x 8'6"   Speed: Unknown
Armament: 26-32# 16-42#c (designed)   Complement: Unknown

	Builder	Laid down	Launched	Commiss'd	Disposition
TCHIFONTA	M. Pechon, Chefuncte, La.	1814	No	No	Sold on ways 29 Jan 20.

Notes: An interesting shallow draft design, broad of beam and flat bottomed. Her construction stopped in 1815. Her completion was authorized 29 Apr 16 but was not carried out.

Armed Merchantmen (Sail)

1. Ships

1775

ALFRED (ex-Black Prince). 24-gun ship. 300 tons. Armament: 20-9# 10-6#; 20-9# (1778). Complement: 220. Built by Wharton & Humphreys 1774. Purchased Philadelphia 4 Nov 75. Converted by Wharton & Humphreys. Commissioned 3 Dec 75. Captured by HMS Ariadne and Ceres E of Antigua 9 Mar 78.

COLUMBUS (ex-Sally). 24-gun ship. ca. 200 tons. Armament: 18-9# 10-6#. Complement: 220. Built Philadelphia 1774. Purchased Philadelphia Nov 75. Converted by Wharton & Humphreys. Commissioned by 4 Jan 76. Run aground to avoid capture, Point Judith, R. I., 28 Mar 78.

1777

QUEEN OF FRANCE (ex-La Brune). 28-gun ship. ca. 581 tons. Armament: 24-6#. Purchased Brest, Fr., 1777. Scuttled off Shutes Folly I., S. C., Mar 80.

1779

BON HOMME RICHARD (ex-Duc de Duras). 42-gun ship. 998 tons. 152' x 40' x 19'(h). Armament: 6-18# 28-12# 6-9#. Complement: 320. Built in France 1766. Loaned by France 4 Feb 79. Commissioned May 79. Foundered in North Sea 25 Sep 79.

1782

DUC DE LAUZUN. 20-gun ship. Probably taken over at Havana Oct 82. Sold in France 1783.

GENERAL WASHINGTON (ex-HMS General Monk, ex-American privateer Congress). 20-gun sloop-of-war.   130'9" x 32'8". Armament: 18-9# 2-6#. Captured by privateer Hyder Ally off Cape May, N. J., 8 Apr 82. Sold Baltimore 1784. Used chiefly as a packet.

1798

BALTIMORE (ex-Adriana). 20-gun ship. 422 tons. 103'9"(b.p.) x 30'8". Armament: 18-9# 6-4#. Complement: 180. Built by Joseph Caverly, Baltimore, Md., 1798. Purchased Baltimore 23 May 98. Sold Philadelphia 1801.

DELAWARE (ex-Hamburg Packet). 20-gun ship. 321 tons. 94'9"(g.d.) x 28' x 14'(h). Armament: 16-9# 6-4#. Complement: 180. Built Philadelphia 1794. Purchased Philadelphia 5 May 98. Commissioned by 26 Jun 98. Sold Baltimore 1801.

GANGES (ex-Ganges). 24-gun ship. 504 tons. 116'4" x 31'4" x 15'8"(h). Armament: 26-9#. Complement: 220. Built by Thomas Penrose, Philadelphia, 1795. Purchased Philadelphia 3 May 98. Commissioned by 22 May 98. Sold Philadelphia by 8 Dec 01.

GEORGE WASHINGTON (ex-George Washington). 24-gun ship. 624 tons. 108'(k) x 32'6" x 14'(h). Armament: 24-9# 8-6#; 15-9# (1801). Complement: 220. Built Providence, R. I., 1794. Purchased Providence, R. I., 12 Oct 98. Commissioned ca. 20 Dec 98. Sold Philadelphia May 04.

HERALD (ex-Herald). 20-gun ship. 280 tons. 92'8" x 26'4" x 13'2"(h). Armament: 16-6# 6-4#. Complement: 128. Built Newburyport, Mass., 1798. Purchased Boston 15 Jun 98. Sold Boston 1801.

MONTEZUMA (ex-Montezuma). 20-gun ship. 347 tons. 16' draft. Armament: 20-9#. Built Virginia 1795. Purchased Baltimore 26 Jun 98. Commissioned Aug 98. Sold Baltimore 30 Dec 99.

1812

ALERT (ex-HMS Alert, ex Oxford). 20-gun ship. 325 tons. 105'(b.p.) x 29' x 11'. Armament: 2-12# 18-32#c. Complement: 100. Built Howdenpoint, Eng., 1803. Captured by Essex in North Atlantic 13 Aug 12. Used as a storeship 1816-18 and receiving ship thereafter. Broken up Norfolk 1835.

LOUISIANA (ex-Remittance). 16-gun ship. 341 tons. 99'6"(b.p.) x 23'(e) x 14'(h). Armament: 4-24# 8-12# 4-6#. Complement: 160. Built Athens, N.Y. 1805. Purchased New Orleans Aug 12. Receiving ship 1820-21. Broken up New Orleans 1821.

1813

ESSEX JUNIOR (ex-Atlantic). 20-gun ship. 355 tons. Armament: 10-6# 10-18#c. Complement: 60. Captured by Essex off Galapagos Is. 29 May 13. Commissioned Jun 13. Sold New York 26 Aug 14.

GEORGIANA (ex-Georgiana). 16-gun ship. 280 tons. Armament: 10-6# 6-18#c. Complement: 41. Captured by Essex off Galapagos Is. 29 Apr 13. Commissioned 8 May 13. Captured by HMS Boreas off Georges Bank 1814.

GREENWICH (ex-Greenwich). 16-gun ship. 351 tons. Complement: 25. Captured by Essex off Galapagos Is. 28 May 13. Burned to avoid capture in Marqueses Is. 1814.

2. Brigs

1775

ANDREW DORIA (ex-Defiance). 16-gun brig. Armament: 16-6#. Complement: 104. Purchased Philadelphia Nov 75. Converted by Wharton & Humphreys. Commissioned by 4 Jan 76. Burned to avoid capture in Delaware Bay Nov 77.

CABOT (ex-Sally). 14-gun brigantine. ca. 189 tons. 74'10"(d) x 24'8" x 11'4"(h). Armament: 14-6#; 16-6# (1777). Complement: 90. Purchased Philadelphia Nov 75. Converted by Wharton & Humphreys. Captured by HMS Milford after running aground to avoid capture off Cheboque Point, Nova Scotia, 25 Mar 77. Taken into British service.

PROVIDENCE (ex-Katy). 12-gun brig. Length ca. 70'. Armament: 12-4#; 12-6# (1776); 6-6# 6-4# 2-2# (1779). Complement: 90. Purchased Providence, R. I., Dec 75. Commissioned Jan 76. Burned to avoid capture in Penobscot Bay, Me., 14 Aug 79.

WASHINGTON (ex-Eagle, ex-Endeavour). 10-gun brig. 160 tons. Armament: 6-6# 4-4#. Complement: 74. Chartered Plymouth, Mass., 3 Nov 75. Captured by HMS Fowley off Cape Ann, Mass., 4 Dec 75.

1776

HAMPDEN. 14-gun brigantine. Purchased 1776. Converted New Haven, Conn. Sold Providence, R. I., "late" 1777.

LEXINGTON (ex-Wild Duck). 16-gun brig. ca. 210 tons. 86'(d) x 24'2" x 9'(h). Armament: 16-4#; 2-6# 14-4# (1777). Complement: 95. Built Bermuda. Purchased Philadelphia 13 Mar 76. Converted by Wharton & Humphreys. Commissioned by 22 Mar 76. Captured by HMS Alert off Ushant, Fr., 19 Sep 77.

REPRISAL (ex-Molly). 16-gun brig. 100' x 30' x unknown. Armament: 16-6#. Complement: 130. Built Philadelphia. Purchased Philadelphia 28 Mar 76. Foundered off Newfoundland 1 Oct 77.

1777

GENERAL GATES (ex-Industrious Bee). 16-gun brigantine. 160 tons. Armament: 16-4#. Complement: 100. Built Liverpool, Eng., 1777. Captured by Lee 29 Aug 77. Commissioned by 24 May 78. Sold Boston ca. Apr 79.

RESISTENCE. 10-gun brigantine. Armament: 10-4#. Purchased Stonington, Conn., 24 Apr 77. Commissioned by Aug 77. Captured by British squadron off Cape Cod 27 Aug 78.

1779

VENGEANCE. 12-gun brigantine. Armament: 12-6#. Loaned by France 1779. Returned 1783.

1798

NORFOLK. 18-gun brig. 200 tons. Armament: 18-6#. Complement: 140. Built by Nash & Herbert, Norfolk, launched 1 Sep 98. Purchased Norfolk 1798. Commissioned by 9 Sep 98. Sold Baltimore 1800.

RICHMOND (ex-Augusta). 18-gun brig. 200 tons. Armament: 18-6#. Complement: 123. Built at Norfolk, Va. Purchased Norfolk 1798. Sold New York 12 May 01.

1799

AUGUSTA (ex-Augusta). 14-gun brig. 344 tons. Armament: 10-6# 4-4#. Complement: 100. Built Norfolk. Purchased Norfolk 30 Jun 99. Sold Norfolk 1801.

CONQUEST OF ITALY (ex-French privateer L'Italie Conquise). 12-gun brig. Captured by Connecticut off Guadeloupe 29 Oct 99. Disposition unknown.

1804

SCOURGE (ex-Transfer). 16-gun brig. Armament: 16-6#. Complement: 36. Built in Great Britain. Captured by Syren off Tripoli 18 Mar 04. Commissioned by 17 Apr 04. Sold Norfolk 12 Jul 05.

1812

TROUP (ex-Georgia, ex-Princess Amelia). 16-gun brig. 180 tons. Armament: 4-18#c 4-12#c 4-6#c; 2-12# 16-9# 2-18#c (1812). Built in England ca. 1807. Captured by privateer Rossie. Purchased from Savannah, Ga., Prize Court 1812. Sold Savannah 1815.

1813

RATTLESNAKE (ex-Rambler). 14-gun brig. 278 tons. Complement: 110. Built by Calvin Turner, Medford, Mass., 1813. Purchased Medford 1813. Commissioned by 10 Jan 14. Captured by HMS Leander off Cape Sable, Nova Scotia, 22 Jul 14.

VIXEN. 14-gun brig. Never armed. Purchased Savannah, Ga., 1813. Captured by HMS Belvidera in Atlantic 25 Dec 13.

1814

FIREFLY (ex-Volent). 14-gun brig. 333 tons. 109'(b.p.) x 29'4" x 12'10". Armament: 4-18# 10-18#c; 4-12# 12-18#c (1816). Complement: 90. Purchased New York 8 Dec 14. Sold New York 3 Apr 16.

FLAMBEAU (ex-Leader). 14-gun brig. 300 tons. 107'(b.p.) x 26'2"(e) x 12'5". Armament: 2-18# 10-18#c. Complement: 90. Built by Enoch Burrows, Mystic, Conn. Purchased Baltimore 3 Dec 14. Sold New York 3 Apr 16. Also reported to have been purchased in New York.

SPARK. 14-gun brig. 287 tons. 103'3"(b.p.) x 26'(e) x 13'9". Armament: 2-18# 10-18#c. Complement: 67. Built Sag Harbor, N. Y., 1814. Purchased New York 1814. Commissioned by 20 May 15. Sold New York 1826.

1846

MALEK ADHEL (ex-Mexican Malek Adhel). 10-gun brig. 114 tons. 80'(d) x 20'7"(m) x 7'9"(h). Armament: 2-9# 10-6#. Built by Webb 1840. Captured by Warren at Mazatlan, Mex., 7 Sep 46. Sold San Francisco Sep 47.

3. Schooners

1798

RETALIATION (ex-French privateer Le Croyable). 14-gun schooner. 107 tons. Armament: 4-6# 10-4#. Captured off Egg Harbor, N. J., 7 Jul 98 by Delaware. Purchased from prize court 30 Jul 98. Recaptured by French L'Insurgente and Volontaire off Guadeloupe 20 Nov 98. Retaken by Merrimack 28 Jun 99 but not returned to service.

1803

NAUTILUS. 12-gun schooner. 105 tons. 87'6"(d) x 23'8" x 9'10"(h). Armament: 14-12#; 12-6# (1804); 2-9# 12-18#c (1810). Complement: 103. Probably built by Henry Spencer, Baltimore, 1799. Purchased Baltimore May 03. Commissioned 5 May 03. Rerigged as a brig 1810. Captured by British squadron 16 Jul 12.

1806

REVENGE. 12-gun schooner. Length ca. 70'(d). Armament: 10-6#. Complement: 43. Purchased New Orleans Dec 06. Wrecked near Watch Hill, R. I., 2 Feb 11.

1812

CAROLINA. 14-gun schooner. 230 tons. 89'6"(b.p.) x 24'4" x 11'4"(h). Armament: 3-9# 12-12#c. Complement: 100. Built by James Marsh, Charleston, S. C., launched 14 Nov 12. Purchased on ways at Charleston Nov 12. Commissioned 4 Jun 13. Sunk by British batteries below New Orleans 27 Dec 14.

NONSUCH (ex-Nonsuch). 14-gun schooner. 148 tons. 86'(b.p.) x 21'(e) x 8'(h). Armament: 1-6# 12-12#c; 1-12# 5-12#c (1816). Complement: 61. Built Baltimore. Purchased Charleston, S. C., Dec 12. Broken up 1826.

1813

COMET (ex-Comet). 14-gun schooner. 187 tons. 90'6"(b.p.) x 23'3" x 10'(h). Armament: 14-9#. Complement: 120. Built by Thomas Kemp, Baltimore, 1810. Chartered Baltimore Mar 13. Returned to owners Sep 13.

ISAAC HULL. 10-gun schooner. Chartered 1813. Returned to owners 1813.

PATAPSCO (ex-Patapsco). 16-gun schooner. 259 tons. 101'(b.p.) x 25' x 11'5"(h). Built by Thomas Kemp, Baltimore, 1812. Chartered Baltimore Mar 13. Returned to owners Sep 13.

REVENGE. 16-gun schooner. 102' x 23' x 10'(h). Armament: 1-18# 2-12# 14-12#c. Built Baltimore 1812. Chartered Mar 13. Returned to owners Sep 13.

1814

EAGLE. 12-gun schooner. 270 tons. Complement: 60. May have been built on Chesapeake Bay. Purchased New Orleans 1814. Sold 1816.

PROMETHEUS (ex-Escape). 12-gun schooner. 273 tons. 99'9"(b.p.) x 27'6"(e) x 11'4"(h). Armament: 2-32# 4-9# 6-32#c; 1-32# 4-9# 4-18#c (1816); 1-18# 6-9# 4-18#c (1818). Complement: 60. Built by William Sequin, Philadelphia, 1814. Purchased Philadelphia 1814. Sold New Orleans 1819.

SPITFIRE (ex-Grampus). 12-gun schooner. 278 tons. 102'(b.p.) x 25'8"(e) x 14'. Armament: 1-18# 2-9# 8-18#c. Complement: 60. Built by Thomas Kemp, Baltimore, 1812. Purchased Baltimore 1814. Sold 1816.

TORCH. 12-gun schooner. 252 tons. 106'(b.p.) x 26'6"(e) x 12'6". Armament: 1-18# 1-4# 10-18#c. Complement: 60. Purchased Baltimore 1814. Sold 3 Apr 16.

4. Schooners (Lake)

1775

ROYAL SAVAGE. 12-gun schooner, Lake Champlain. 70 tons. Armament: 4-6# 8-4#. Complement: 50. Captured St. John's, P. Q., 1775. Blown up to avoid capture, Cumberland Bay, Lake Champlain, 11 Oct 76.

1814

TICONDEROGA. 14-gun schooner, Lake Champlain. 350 tons. Length 120'. Armament: 4-18# 8-12# 5-32#c. Complement: 112. Built by Jahaziel Sherman, Vergennes, Vt. as steamer. Purchased, unfinished, 1814. Completed by Noah Brown, Vergennes. Commissioned 1814. Sold Whitehall, N. Y., 19 Jul 25 but not removed. The engine proved defective and was never fitted.

5. Sloops and Cutters

1775

HORNET (ex-Falcon). 10-gun sloop. 100 tons. Armament: 8-4#; 10-4# (1777). Complement: 35. Built Baltimore. Chartered Baltimore 1775. Blown up in Delaware River 15 Nov 77. Also reported captured by HMS Porcupine off Cape Florida, Fla., 27 Apr 77.

INDEPENDENCE. 10-gun sloop (rerigged brig 1777). Armament: 10-9#. Complement: ca. 30. Purchased 1775. Wrecked on Ocracoke Inlet Bar, N. C., 24 Apr 78.

1776

RACEHORSE (ex-HMS Racehorse). 10-gun sloop. Armament: 10-9#. Captured by Andrew Doria off Puerto Rico Dec 76. Burned to avoid capture at Philadelphia 15 Nov 77.

SACHEM (ex-HMS Edward). 10-gun sloop. 60 tons. Armament: 10-9#. Captured by Lexington off Virginia Capes 7 Apr 76. Burned to avoid capture in Delaware Bay 1777.

1777

DOLPHIN. 10-gun cutter. ca. 90 tons. Armament: 8-3# 4-2#. Purchased Dover, Eng., Feb 77. Seized by French authorities, Nantes, Fr., Sep 77.

INDEPENDENCE. 10-gun sloop. Armament: 10-4#. Complement: 30. Purchased 1777. Sold Edenton, N. C., 1779.

REVENGE (ex-Greyhound). 14-gun cutter. 150 tons. Armament: 14-6#. Complement: 106. Purchased Dunkerque, Fr., May 77. Commissioned by 16 Jul 77. Sold Philadelphia 12 Mar 79.

1778

MORRIS (ex-British Rebecca). 24-gun sloop. Armament: 16-6# 8-4#. Complement: 150. Captured by armed rowboat Rattletrap, Manchac, Mississippi R., 23 Feb 78. Commissioned Feb 79. Foundered at New Orleans 18 Aug 79.

1804

HORNET (ex-Traveller). 10-gun sloop. 71 tons. Built Amesbury, Mass., 1802. Purchased Malta 1804. Sold Philadelphia 3 Sep 09. May have been 86 tons, 64'6" x 19'8" x 8'(h).

6. Sloops (Lake)

1775

ENTERPRISE (ex-George). 12-gun sloop, Lake Champlain. 70 tons. Armament: 12-4# (1776); 8-4# 4-2# (1777). Complement: 50. Captured St. John's. P. Q. 18 May 75. Burned to avoid capture, Whitehall, N. Y., 6 Jul 77.

1812

EAGLE (ex-Bull Dog). 11-gun sloop, Lake Champlain. 110 tons. 64'(d) x 20'4"(e) x 5'8"(h). Armament: 1-18# 6-6#; 1-6# 10-18#c (1814). Complement: 112. Transferred from War Dept. 1812. Rebuilt by Eggleston. Captured by British battery on Isle au Noix 3 Jun 13. Retaken in Battle of Lake Champlain 11 Sep 14 as HMS Chubb. Sold Whitehall, N. Y., 28 Jun 15.

GROWLER (ex-Hunter). 11-gun sloop, Lake Champlain. 112 tons. 60'(d) x 19' x 5'8"(h). Armament: 1-18# 2-12# 4-6#; 1-6# 10-18#c (1814). Complement: 112. Transferred from War Dept. 1812. Rebuilt by Eggleston. Captured by British battery on Isle aux Noix 3 Jun 13. Retaken in Battle of Lake Champlain 11 Sep 14 as HMS Finch. Sold Whitehall, N. Y., 28 Jun 15.

2

The Old Steam Navy, 1814–1876

Ironclads

1842

"STEVENS BATTERY"

Tonnage: 5000 tons
Dimensions: 420'(oa.) x 52'(e) x 20'6"
Armament: 2-10"R 5-15" (designed)
Armor: 6 3/4" casemate, 3 1/2" sides, 1 1/2" deck
Rig: Unknown

Machinery: 8600 IHP; 8 vertical, overhead beam engines, 2 screws
Speed: 20 kts. (designed)
Complement: Unknown

	Hull	Machinery	Laid down	Launched	Commiss'd	Disposition
Unnamed	Stevens	Delamater	1854	No	No	Sold on ways 1874-75.

Notes: Authorized 14 Apr 42. She was the first ironclad steamer authorized for any navy but was never completed or named. She was designed by Robert L. Stevens and redesigned prior to the start of construction. The figures above are for the second (1854) design. The original design called for a 4683 ton vessel; 250' x 40' x 28'(h) powered by 900 HP from 4 condensing engines and 1 screw. It featured vertical sides armored with 4 1/2" plates and an unspecified armament. The second design had sloping armor protecting guns in an open redoubt. The Navy regarded the steam pressure used to obtain the 20-knot speed of the 1854 design as excessive and expected only 17 knots. The ship was nearly complete when construction was stopped by R. L. Stevens' death in 1856. Official interest in the vessel then waned and she was not completed. In 1861 Edwin A. Stevens built a 110' ship with 1-100#R to demonstrate the armor and armament scheme of the battery; this craft served as a revenue cutter under the names E. A. Stevens and Naugatuck from 1862 to 1890. On the death of Edwin A. Stevens in 1868 the title to the battery passed to the State of New Jersey, which sold the vessel in parts after Congress refused to appropriate money to purchase it. At that time the design, as modified by George B. McClellan and Isaac Newton, called for a single turret monitor of 6006 tons displacement; 401'(oa.) x 54'(e) x 22'(max); 6500 HP; twin screws; and a designed speed of 16.5 kts. The proposed armament was 2-20" smoothbores. Side armor was to be 10", the deck 1 1/2", and the turret 18".

1861

MONITOR

Displacement: 987 tons
Dimensions: 172'(oa.) x 41'6"(e) x 10'6"
Armament: 2-11"
Armor: 8" turret, 4 1/2" sides, 2"deck, 9" pilot house
Rig: None

Machinery: 320 IHP; 2 vibrating-lever engines, 36" diameter cylinders x 26" stroke, 1 screw
Speed: 9 kts. (designed), 6 kts. (service)
Complement: 49

	Hull	Machinery	Laid down	Launched	Commiss'd	Disposition
MONITOR	Continental	Delamater	25 Oct 61	30 Jan 62	25 Feb 62	Foundered off Cape Hatteras, N. C., 31 Dec 62.

Notes: Ordered 4 Oct 61. John Ericsson's famed brainchild for which he was the prime contractor. She had laminated armor.

NEW IRONSIDES

Displacement: 4120 tons
Dimensions: 232'(oa.) x 57'6" x 15'8"(max)
Armament: 2-150#R 14-11" 2-50#R; 2-150#R 14-11" 2-60#R (1864)
Armor: 4 1/2" sides, 1" deck, 10" conning tower
Rig: Bark

Machinery: 700 HP; 2 horizontal, direct-acting engines, 50" x 30", 1 screw
Speed: 9.5 kts. (designed), 6.5 kts. (trials)
Complement: 460

	Hull	Machinery	Laid down	Launched	Commiss'd	Disposition
NEW IRONSIDES	Cramp	Merr..ck & Sons	1862	10 May 62	21 Aug 62	Burned 15 Dec 66.

Notes: Ordered 15 Oct 61. Built by Cramp to the design of B. H. Bartol of Merrick and Sons who held the contract. She had a complete waterline belt and a 170-foot long armored battery with armored bulkheads at the ends. Despite her lack of speed, she was the strongest and best of the Civil War ironclads.

GALENA

Tonnage: 738 tons
Dimensions: 210'(oa.), 180'(b.p.) x 36'(e) x 11'
Armament: 2-100#R 4-9"; 1-100#R 8-9" 1-30#R (1864); 8-9"
  1-60#R 1-30#R (1865); 6-9" 1-60#R 2-20#R (1869)
Armor: 3 1/4" sides

Rig: Schooner (2 masts)
Machinery: 800 HP; 2 vibrating-lever
  engines, 48" x 36", 1 screw
Speed: 8 kts.
Complement: 150

	Hull	Machinery	Laid down	Launched	Commiss'd	Disposition
GALENA	Maxon,Fish	Delamater	1861	14 Feb 62	21 Apr 62	Broken up 1871.

Notes: Ordered ca. Oct 61. She was designed by Samuel H. Pook with sides having a considerable tumble
home and armor built of interlocking iron bars. C. S. Bushnell & Co. held the prime contract. The
armor proved to be inadequate and Philadelphia Navy Yard was ordered on 13 May 63 to remove it. She
recommissioned on 15 Feb 64 as a wood cruiser with a full 3-masted bark rig.

1862

ROANOKE

Displacement: 4700 tons
Dimensions: 265'(oa.) x 52'6"(e) x 24'3"
Armament: 2-150#R 2-15" 2-11"
Armor: 11" turrets, 4 1/2" sides, 2 1/4" deck, 9" pilot house
Rig: None

Machinery: 997 HP; 2 horizontal,
  direct-acting, trunk engines, 79.5"
  x 36", 1 screw
Speed: 10 kts. (designed), 6 kts.
  (service)
Complement: 350

	Conversion yard	Conversion begun	Recommissioned	Disposition
ROANOKE	Novelty	25 Mar 62	29 Jun 63	Sold 27 Sep 83.

Notes: Conversion ordered 21 Mar 62. The Navy's only triple turreted monitor, she was converted from
the screw frigate Roanoke. Although she had solid side armor, she was not successful since she drew
too much water for coastal use and rolled heavily even in moderate seas. Her hull was also too weak
to support the weight of her three turrets. Each of these had a different armament: 1-15" 1-150#R
(forward), 1-15" 1-11" (middle), and 1-11" 1-150#R (aft).

KEOKUK

Tonnage: 677 tons
Dimensions: 159'6"(oa.) x 36' x 8'6"
Armament: 2-11"
Armor: 4" hull
Rig: None

Machinery: ca. 500 IHP; 2 vertical,
  bell-crank engines, 23" x 20", 2
  screws
Speed: 9 kts.
Complement: 92

	Hull	Machinery	Laid down	Launched	Commiss'd	Disposition
KEOKUK	Underhill	Underhill	19 Apr 62	6 Dec 62	*24 Feb 63	Foundered after action with Confederate batteries, Charleston, S. C., 8 Apr 63.

* Delivered.
Notes: Ordered 25 Mar 62. Designed by Charles W. Whitney and built under a contract with him.
Armored by 4" flat iron clamped on edgeways and an inch apart with the intervening space filled with
wood. The arrangement proved to be extremely vulnerable to Confederate shells. She was hit over 90
times during the bombardment of the Charleston forts on 7 Apr 63 and foundered the next day. She had
two stationary gun towers each having three gun ports. She was fitted with a five-foot ram.
Renaming: Originally the Moodna, she was renamed prior to launching.

PASSAIC class

Displacement: 1875 tons
Dimensions: 200'(oa.) x 46'(e) x 10'6"(Lehigh, max),
  11'(Camanche, max), 11'9"(Montauk, Nahant, max),
  12'(Conestoga, Passaic, Patapsco, max), 11'6"(others, max)
Armament: Camanche--2-15";
  Lehigh, Passaic--1-15" 1-11"; 1-150#R 1-15" (1864); 2-15"
  (1875);
  Patapsco--1-150#R 1-15"; 2-15" (1888);
  Weehawken--1-15" 1-11";
  others--1-15" 1-11"; 2-15" (1873)

Armor: 11" turret, 5" sides, 1" deck,
  8" pilot house
Rig: None
Machinery: 320 IHP; 2 vibrating-lever
  engines, 40" x 22", 1 screw
Speed: 7 kts. (designed), 5 kts.
  (service)
Complement: 75

The monitor *Nahant* ca. 1898. The hurricane deck was added after the Civil War and the roof over the turret was added when she was put in reserve. (NH 69787)

The double-turret monitor *Agamenticus* after receiving a hurricane deck between the turrets in 1865. (NH 47016)

	Hull	Machinery	Laid down	Launched	Commiss'd	Disposition
CAMANCHE	Colwell	Fulton Fdry.	1862	14 Nov 64	24 May 65	Sold 22 Mar 99
CATSKILL	Continental	Delamater	1862	6 Dec 62	24 Feb 63	Sold 8 Jan 02
LEHIGH	Reaney	Morris, Towne	1862	17 Jan 63	15 Apr 63	Sold 16 Apr 04
MONTAUK	Continental	Delamater	1862	9 Oct 62	14 Dec 62	Sold 16 Apr 04
NAHANT	Loring	Loring	1862	7 Oct 62	29 Dec 62	Sold 16 Apr 04
NANTUCKET	Atlantic	Atlantic	1862	6 Dec 62	26 Feb 63	Sold 14 Nov 00
PASSAIC	Continental	Delamater	1862	30 Aug 62	25 Nov 62	Sold 10 Oct 99
PATAPSCO	Harlan & Hollingsworth		1862	27 Sep 62	2 Jan 63	Mined off Charleston, S.C., 16 Jan 65
SANGAMON	Reaney	Morris, Towne	1862	27 Oct 62	9 Feb 63	Sold 16 Apr 04
WEEHAWKEN	Colwell	Fulton Fdry.	17 Jun 62	5 Nov 62	18 Jan 63	Foundered off Charleston, S.C., 6 Dec 63.

Notes: Ordered Mar-Jun 1862. John Ericsson designed this highly successful class of single turret monitors. Since 15" guns were not expected to be available for this class the turrets were built with gunports for 11" ordnance. When 15" guns were fitted the gunports were too small and the guns had to be fired with their muzzles inside the turret. Ericsson was the prime contractor for the Lehigh, Montauk, Patapsco, Catskill, Passaic, and Sangamon. The Weehawken was built under a sub-contract from Zeno, Secor & Co and the Camanche was built under one from Donahue, Ryan, and Secor. The others were ordered directly from their builders. The Camanche was assembled at Secor's yard in Jersey City; disassembled and shipped to San Francisco; and reassembled there by the Union Iron Works. All surviving units of the class were rebuilt in 1871-75. The Passaic served as a training or receiving ship 1878-99; the Lehigh as a training vessel 1874-76; the Nantucket as a training vessel 1877-83 and 1896-99; and the Camanche as a training vessel 1896-99.
Renamings: The Sangamon was renamed from Conestoga on 9 Sep 62 and became the Jason on 15 Jun 69. The Catskill, Nantucket, and Nahant became the Goliath, Medusa, and Atlas on 15 Jun 69 but regained their original names 10 Aug 69.

ONONDAGA

Displacement: 2592 tons
Dimensions: 228'7"(oa.) x 51'2" x 13'2"
Armament: 2-150#R 2-15"
Armor: 11" turrets, 5 1/2" sides, 2" deck
Rig: None

Machinery: 642 IHP; 4 horizontal, back-acting engines, 2 screws
Speed: 9 kts. (designed), 7 kts. (service)
Complement: 130

	Hull	Machinery	Laid down	Launched	Commiss'd	Disposition
ONONDAGA	Continental	Morgan	1862	29 Jul 63	24 Mar 64	Returned to contractor 12 Jul 67.

Notes: Ordered 26 May 62. Built under a contract with George W. Quintard, she was a double-turreted monitor with an iron hull. She was returned to Quintard under an Act of Congress of 2 Mar 67. He sold her to France, and despite claims that she was a weak vessel unfit for sea duty she served the French under her American name until stricken 2 Dec 1904.

DUNDERBERG

Displacement: 7060 tons
Dimensions: 377'4"(oa.) x 72'10"(e) x 21'(max)
Armament: 2-15" 8-11" (contract); 2-15" 4-11" (trials, 1867)
Armor: 3 1/2" sides, 4 1/2" casemate, 1 1/2" deck
Rig: Brigantine

Machinery: 4500 IHP; 2 horizontal, back-acting engines, 100" x 45", 1 screw
Speed: 15 kts. (designed), 11.5 kts. (trials)
Complement: Unknown

	Hull	Machinery	Laid down	Launched	Commiss'd	Disposition
DUNDERBERG	Webb	Etna	4 Oct 62	22 Jul 65	No	Returned to builder 1867.

Notes: Ordered 3 Jul 62. An ironclad ram designed by John Lenthall, she had a 50-foot long solid oak ram. Her original design called for a casemate and two turrets but the latter were eliminated in the final plans. Her engines were designed by Erastus Smith and Thomas Main. At the time of her launch her armament was reported in the press as 4-15" and 12-11" or more. On 25 Sep 66 a portion of her armament was ordered installed for trials: 1-15" and 1-11" on each broadside and 1-11" at each end. She ran gunnery and machinery trials on 22-23 February 1867. She was returned to Webb under an Act of Congress of 2 Mar 67. Webb sold her in June 1867 to the French, who placed her in service as the Rochambeau. The French found her to be very wet at sea and she was stricken on 15 Apr 72.

MIANTONOMOH

Displacement: 3401 tons
Dimensions: 250'(b.p.) x 53'8"(e) x 14'9"(h)
Armament: 4-15"
Armor: 11" turrets, 5" sides, 1 1/2" deck, 8" pilot house
Rig: None

Machinery: 800 NHP; 2 horizontal, back-acting engines, 30" x 27", 2 screws
Speed: 9 kts.
Complement: 150

	Hull	Machinery	Laid down	Launched	Commiss'd	Disposition
MIANTONOMOH	New York	Novelty	1862	15 Aug 63	18 Sep 65	Broken up 1874.

Notes: Probably ordered 9 Jul 62. She was a double-turreted monitor with a wooden hull designed at New York by B. F. Delano under John Lenthall's direction. Her machinery came from the drafting board of Benjamin F. Isherwood. She proved her sea keeping abilities during an 1866 voyage to Europe.

TONAWANDA

Displacement: 3400 tons
Dimensions: 256'(b.p.) x 53'8"(e) x 13'5"(max)
Armament: 4-15"
Armor: 11" turrets, 5" sides, 1 1/2" deck, 8" pilot house
Rig: None

Machinery: 2 horizontal, back-acting engines, 30" x 21", 2 screws
Speed: Unknown
Complement: 150

	Hull	Machinery	Laid down	Launched	Commiss'd	Disposition
TONAWANDA	Philadelphia	Merrick & Sons	1863	6 May 64	12 Oct 65	Broken up 1874.

Notes: Ordered 9 Jul 62. Her wooden hull was probably designed at Philadelphia by H. Hoover under Lenthall's direction and her engines were an Isherwood product. She was longer than her three half-sisters and her turrets were closer together. She served as a training vessel 1866-72.
Renaming: She became the Amphitrite on 15 Jun 69.

MONADNOCK class

Displacement: 3295 tons
Dimensions: 259'6"(oa.), 250'(b.p.) x 52'6"(e) x 12'6"(max) (Monadnock); 261'(oa.), 251'(b.p.) x 52'(e) (Agamenticus)
Armament: 4-15"
Armor: 11" turrets, 5" sides, 1 1/2" deck, 8" pilot house
Rig: None

Machinery: 1426 IHP; 2 vibrating-lever engines, 32" x 20", 2 screws
Speed: 9 kts. (service)
Complement: 167

	Hull	Machinery	Laid down	Launched	Commiss'd	Disposition
AGAMENTICUS	Portsmouth	Morris, Towne	1862	19 Mar 63	5 May 65	Broken up 1874
MONADNOCK	Boston	Morris, Towne	1862	23 Mar 64	4 Oct 64	Sold 20 Nov 83.

Notes: Probably ordered 9 Jul 62. These two ships had engines designed by John Ericsson, in contrast to the Isherwood engines of their two half-sisters. The Monadnock was designed at Boston by W. L. Hanscom and the Agamenticus was designed at Portsmouth by Isaiah Hanscom, both under Lenthall's direction. Both ships were reported to be good sea boats and well built. The Monadnock made the long sea voyage from Norfolk to San Francisco in 1865-66.
Renaming: Agamenticus to Terror 15 Jun 69.

DICTATOR

Displacement: 4438 tons
Dimensions: 312'(oa.) x 50'(e) x 20'6"
Armament: 2-15"
Armor: 15" turret, 6" sides, 1 1/2" deck, 12" pilot house
Rig: None

Machinery: 1849 IHP; 2 vibrating-lever engines, 100" x 48", 1 screw
Speed: 15 kts. (designed), 9.26 kts. (trials)
Complement: 174

	Hull	Machinery	Laid down	Launched	Commiss'd	Disposition
DICTATOR	Delamater	Delamater	16 Aug 62	26 Dec 63	11 Nov 64	Sold 27 Sep 83.

Notes: Ordered 28 Jul 62. Built under a sub-contract from John Ericsson who designed her to incorporate the lessons learned in the earlier monitors. The Dictator had a single turret and a reputation as a good sea boat. Like all of the monitors, however, she suffered from small bunker capacity and low speed. Her turret had an unique construction. An inner cylinder of four layers of 1" plates was separated by 5" from the outer one of six layers of 1" plates. Curved segments of iron were fitted into the space between.

PURITAN

Displacement: 4912 tons
Dimensions: 340'(oa.) x 50'(e) x 20'
Armament: 2-20" (designed)
Armor: 15" turret, 6" sides, 2" deck, 12" pilot house
Rig: None

Machinery: 2 vibrating-lever engines, 100" x 48", 2 screws
Speed: 15 kts. (designed)
Complement: Unknown

	Hull	Machinery	Laid down	Launched	Commiss'd	Disposition
PURITAN	Continental	Allaire	1863	2 Jul 64	No	Broken up 1874.

Notes: Ordered 28 Jul 62. Ericsson, the prime contractor, preferred single-turret monitors and was allowed to substitute a single turret for the two specified by the Navy for this ship. Delays in producing the 20" Dahlgren smoothbores were among the factors which prevented her completion. She was delivered incomplete to the New York Navy Yard on 5 Jan 66.

CANONICUS class

Displacement: 2100 tons
Dimensions: 225'(Catawba, Oneota, oa.), 224'(Tippecanoe, oa.), 223'(Mahopac, Manhattan, Tecumseh, oa.), 225'(others, oa.) x 43'4"(Mahopac, Manhattan, Tecumseh, e), 43'3"(Catawba, Oneota, e), 43'(Tippecanoe, e), 43'3"(others, e) x 11'6"
Armament: 2-15"

Armor: 11" turret, 5" sides, 1 1/2" deck
Rig: None
Machinery: 320 IHP; 2 vibrating-lever engines, 48" x 24", 1 screw
Speed: 13 kts. (designed), 8 kts. (service)
Complement: 85

	Hull	Machinery	Laid down	Launched	Commiss'd	Disposition
CANONICUS	Loring	Loring	1862	1 Aug 63	16 Apr 64	Sold 19 Feb 08
CATAWBA	Swift,Evans	Niles	1862	13 Apr 64	**10 Jun 65	Sold 2 Apr 68 to builder
MAHOPAC	Colwell	Fulton Fd.	1862	17 May 64	22 Sep 64	Sold 25 Mar 02
MANAYUNK	Snowden	Snowden	1862	18 Dec 64	**27 Sep 65	Sold 10 Oct 99
MANHATTAN	Colwell	Fulton Fd.	1862	14 Oct 63	6 Jun 64	Sold 24 Mar 02
ONEOTA	Swift,Evans	Niles	1862	21 May 64	**10 Jun 65	Sold 2 Apr 68 to builder
SAUGUS	Harlan&Hollingsworth		1862	16 Dec 63	7 Apr 64	Sold 25 Mar 91
TECUMSEH	Colwell	Fulton Fd.	1862	12 Sep 63	19 Apr 64	Mined Mobile Bay 5 Aug 64
TIPPECANOE	Litherbury	Greenwood	28 Sep 62	22 Dec 64	*15 Feb 66	Sold 17 Jan 99.

  * Delivered.
 ** Completed.

Notes: Ordered Sep-Oct 62. Good sea boats, they handled well and were strongly built. Compared to the Passaic class, these had a protective glacis 5" thick and 15" high on deck around the turret, additional stiffening for the side armor, better ventilation, and finer lines aft. The engines were of a John Ericsson design. The Mahopac and Tecumseh were built under sub-contracts from Secor & Co. and the Manhattan under one from Perine, Secor & Co. Greenwood held the contract for the Tippecanoe. The Catawba and Oneota became the Peruvian Atahualpa and Manco Capac under a sale dated 2 Apr 68. The Ajax (ex-Manayunk) was first commissioned on 1 Jan 71. The Wyandotte (ex-Tippecanoe) served as a training vessel 1895-99 as did the Ajax (ex-Manayunk). The Canonicus and Wyandotte (ex-Tippecanoe) were rebuilt in 1872-74 at which time their decks were raised 15 inches.
Renamings: The Canonicus, Mahopac, Manayunk, Manhattan, Saugus, and Tippecanoe were renamed Scylla, Castor, Ajax, Neptune, Centaur, and Vesuvius on 15 Jun 69. The Canonicus, Mahopac, Manhattan, and Saugus regained their original names on 10 Aug 69 while the Vesuvius (ex-Tippecanoe) became the Wyandotte.

1863

CASCO class

Displacement: 1175 tons
Dimensions: 225'8"(Etlah), 225'5"(Squando), 225'(others, oa.) x 45'6"(Etlah, e), 45'3"(Naubuc, e), 45'2"(Squando, e), 45'1" (Modoc, e), 45'(others, e) x 8'3"(max)
Armament: Casco, Napa, Naubuc--1-11" 1-Spar Torpedo; Cohoes, Shawnee, Squando, Wassuc--2-11"; Chimo--1-150#R 1-Spar Torpedo; Modoc--1-Spar Torpedo; Etlah, Tunxis--1-150#R 1-11"; others--2-11"

Armor: 8" turret, 3" side, 10" pilot house
Machinery: 600 IHP; 2 inclined, direct-acting engines, 22" x 30", 2 screws
Speed: 9 kts. (designed), 5 kts. (service)
Complement: 69

	Hull	Machinery	Laid down	Launched	Commiss'd	Disposition
CASCO	Atlantic	Atlantic	1863	7 May 64	4 Dec 64	Scrapped 1875
CHIMO	Adams	Adams	1863	5 May 64	20 Jan 65	Scrapped 1875
COHOES	Continental	Hews&Philips	1863	31 May 65	*19 Jan 66	Scrapped 1874
ETLAH	McCord	McCord	1863	3 Jul 65	*12 Mar 66	Sold 12 Sep 74
KLAMATH	Hambleton	Moore & Richardson	1863	20 Apr 65	*6 May 66	Sold 12 Sep 74
KOKA	Wilcox & Whiting		1863	18 May 65	*28 Nov 65	Scrapped 1874
MODOC	Underhill	Underhill	1863	21 Mar 65	**23 Jun 65	Scrapped 1874
NAPA	Harlan & Hollingsworth		1863	26 Nov 64	**4 May 65	Scrapped 1874
NAUBUC	Perine	Dolan & Farron	1863	19 Oct 64	27 Mar 65	Scrapped 1874
NAUSETT	McKay	McKay & Aldus	1863	26 Apr 65	10 Aug 65	Scrapped 1874
SHAWNEE	Curtis & Tilden		1863	13 Mar 65	18 Aug 65	Scrapped 1875
SHILOH	McCord	McCord	1863	14 Jul 65	*12 Mar 66	Sold late 1874
SQUANDO	McKay	McKay & Aldus	1863	31 Dec 64	6 Jun 65	Scrapped 1874
SUNCOOK	Globe	Globe	1863	1 Feb 65	27 Jul 65	Scrapped 1874
TUNXIS	Reaney	Reaney	1863	4 Jun 64	12 Jul 64	Scrapped 1874
UMPQUA	Snowden	Snowden	Mar 63	21 Dec 65	**7 May 66	Sold 12 Sep 74
WASSUC	Lawrence	Lawrence	1863	25 Jul 65	**28 Oct 65	Scrapped 1875
WAXSAW	Denmead	Denmead	1863	4 May 65	**21 Oct 65	Scrapped 1874
YAZOO	Cramp	Merrick & Sons	1863	8 May 65	**15 Dec 65	Sold 5 Sep 74
YUMA	Hambleton	Moore & Richardson	1863	30 May 65	*6 May 66	Sold 12 Sep 74.

* Delivered.
** Completed.

Notes: Ordered Mar-Jun 63. This class was built in response to a need for armored gunboats to ascend the rivers and penetrate the sounds and bays along the Confederate coast in support of Union army operations. They were designed by Alan Stimers as light draft, single turret monitors with a turtleback deck and a draft of 6'5". They were failures because a mistake in calculating their displacement left them with insufficient freeboard. The Tunxis was completed to the original design with minor modifications but was unsuccessful and was deepened by Cramp during the winter of 1864-65. The Casco, Chimo, Napa, and Naubuc had their turrets replaced during construction by a single open gun and a spar torpedo while the Modoc received the spar alone. The others had their decks raised 22" during construction to increase their freeboard and allow them to carry their turrets. Their designed displacement increased by 130 tons, and the actual displacement of the Squando reached 1618 tons. Several ships were built under subcontracts: Cohoes under one from M. F. Merritt, Klamath and Yuma from Swift, Shiloh from Bestor, and Yazoo from Merrick. Much of the class was scrapped by or for three shipbuilders as payment for work on the "reconstruction" of the large monitors of the Miantonomoh and Puritan types: Hero (ex-Casco), Piscataqua (ex-Chimo), Cohoes, Modoc, Napa, Nausett, and Niobe (ex-Waxsaw) for John Roach; Shawnee, Algoma (ex-Squando), Otsego (ex-Tunxis), and Wassuc for Cramp; and Koka, Minnetonka (ex-Naubuc), and possibly Suncook and Yazoo for Harlan & Hollingsworth. The other five were disposed of at New Orleans.

Renamings: The members of the class were renamed as follows:
Casco to Hero 15 Jun 69;
Chimo to Orion 15 Jun 69; Piscataqua 10 Aug 69;
Cohoes to Charybdis 15 Jun 69; Cohoes 10 Aug 69;
Etlah to Hecate 15 Jun 69; Etlah 10 Aug 69;
Klamath to Harpy 15 Jun 69; Klamath 10 Aug 69;
Koka to Argus 15 Jun 69; Koka 10 Aug 69;
Modoc to Achilles 15 Jun 69; Modoc 10 Aug 69;
Napa to Nemesis 15 Jun 69; Napa 10 Aug 69;
Naubuc to Gorgon 15 Jun 69; Minnetonka 10 Aug 69;
Nausett to Aetna 15 Jun 69; Nausett 10 Aug 69;
Shawnee to Eolus 15 Jun 69; Shawnee 10 Aug 69;
Shiloh to Iris 15 Jun 69;
Squando to Erebus 15 Jun 69; Algoma 10 Aug 69;
Suncook to Spitfire 15 Jun 69; Suncook 10 Aug 69;
Tunxis to Hydra 15 Jun 69; Otsego 10 Aug 69;
Umpqua to Fury 15 Jun 69; Umpqua 10 Aug 69;
Wassuc to Stromboli 15 Jun 69; Wassuc 10 Aug 69;
Waxsaw to Niobe 15 Jun 69;
Yazoo to Tartar 15 Jun 69; Yazoo 10 Aug 69;
Yuma to Tempest 15 Jun 69; Yuma 10 Aug 69.

KALAMAZOO class

Displacement: 5660 tons
Dimensions: 345'(oa.), 332'6"(b.p.) x 56'8" x 17'6"
Armament: 4-15" (designed)
Armor: 15" turrets, 6" sides, 3" deck
Rig: None

Machinery: 4 horizontal, direct-acting engines, 46.5" x 50", 2 screws
Speed: 10 kts. (designed)
Complement: Unknown

	Hull	Machinery	Laid down	Launched	Commiss'd	Disposition
KALAMAZOO	New York	Delamater	Dec 63	No	No	Broken up on ways 1884
SHACKAMAXON	Philadelphia	Pusey & Jones	1863	No	No	Broken up on ways 1875
PASSACONAWAY	Portsmouth	Delamater	18 Nov 63	No	No	Broken up on ways 1884
QUINSIGAMOND	Boston	Atlantic	15 Apr 64	No	No	Broken up on ways 1884.

Notes: The Shackamaxon and probably the others were ordered 4 Nov 63. These double turret monitors, designed for ocean cruising, had composite (wood and iron) hulls designed by Benjamin F. Delano and machinery of John Baird's design. Construction was suspended on 30 Nov 65. Their machinery was completed and put in storage, but their hulls, built of unseasoned timber, deteriorated on the ways.
Renamings: On 15 Jun 69 they became Colossus, Hecla, Thunderer, and Hercules respectively. The last three became Nebraska, Massachusetts, and Oregon respectively on 10 Aug 69.

ATLANTA

Tonnage: 1006 tons
Dimensions: 204'(est.) x 41' x 15'9"
Armament: 2-7"R 2-6.4"R
Armor: 4" casemate, 1/2" deck
Rig: None

Machinery: Direct-acting engines, 1 screw
Speed: 7 kts.
Complement: 162

	Builder	Launched	Acquired	Commiss'd	Disposition
ATLANTA	Thomson, U.K.	9 May 61	17 Jun 63	1864	Sold at Philadelphia 4 May 69.

Notes: Formerly the Confederate casemate ironclad Atlanta. She was converted by N. and A. Tift at Savannah, Ga., from the iron-hulled British-built blockade runner Fingal. She was captured by the monitors Weehawken and Nahant in Wassaw Sd., Ga. Her buyer resold her to Haiti and she disappeared off Cape Hatteras as the Haitian Triumph on her delivery voyage in December 1869. Her guns were 150# and 100# Confederate rifles.

1864

TENNESSEE

Tonnage: 1273 tons
Dimensions: 209'(d) x 48'(e) x 14'(mean)
Armament: 2-7"R (pivots) 4-6.4"R
Armor: 6" casemate, 2" deck
Rig: None

Machinery: 2 geared non-condensing engines, 1 screw
Speed: 8 kts.
Complement: 133

	Builder	Launched	Acquired	Commiss'd	Disposition
TENNESSEE	Bassett, Selma Naval Station	15 Feb 63	5 Aug 64	5 Aug 64	Sold at New Orleans 22 Nov 67.

Notes: Formerly the Confederate casemate ironclad Tennessee, captured in the Battle of Mobile Bay. She was of a modified Columbia type, differing primarily in the casemate design and gun arrangement, and her engines came from the sidewheel steamer Alonzo Child.

1865

COLUMBIA class

Tonnage: 1456 tons
Dimensions: 216' x 51'4" x 13'6" (Columbia), 217'(oa.) x 50'4" x 13'6" (Texas)
Armament: Columbia--6 guns (4 pivots, 2 broadside); Texas--4 guns (2 pivots, 2 broadside, never mounted)
Armor: 6" casemate
Rig: None

Machinery: Non-condensing engines, 1 screw (Columbia), 2 horizontal direct-acting engines, 2 screws (Texas)
Speed: 6 kts.
Complement: 50

	Builder	Launched	Acquired	Commiss'd	Disposition
COLUMBIA	F.M. Jones, Charleston, S.C.	10 Mar 64	18 Feb 65	26 Apr 65	Sold at Norfolk 10 Oct 67
TEXAS	Richmond, Va. Naval Station	15 Jan 65	4 Apr 65	No	Sold at Norfolk 15 Oct 67.

Notes: Formerly Confederate casemate ironclads of the same names. The Columbia ran on a sunken wreck at Charleston on 12 Jan 65 and was captured with the port. She was raised on 26 Apr 65 and arrived at Norfolk under tow on 25 May 65. The Texas was captured incomplete at Richmond. Her casemate was shorter than that of the Columbia due to materiel shortages.

ALBEMARLE

Tonnage: Unknown
Dimensions: 158'(oa.) x 35'3"(e) x 9'
Armament: 2-8"R
Armor: 4" casemate
Rig: None

Machinery: 2 horizontal condensing engines, 2 screws
Speed: 5 kts.
Complement: 94

	Builder	Launched	Acquired	Commiss'd	Disposition
ALBEMARLE	Gilbert Elliott, Edward's Ferry, Va.	1 Jul 63	12 Apr 65	No	Sold at Norfolk 15 Oct 67.

Notes: Formerly the Confederate casemate ironclad Albemarle. She was sunk by a torpedo launch at Plymouth, N.C. on 27 Oct 64 and was captured with that town in April 1865. She was raised and taken to Norfolk, where she arrived on 27 Apr 65. Her armament is also reported as 2-6.4"/100#R

NASHVILLE

Tonnage: 1221 tons
Dimensions: 271' x 62'6" (95'6" o.g.) x 10'6"
Armament: 3-7"R 1-24#
Armor: 6" fwd. and pilot house, 2" aft

Rig: None
Machinery: Side wheels
Speed: Unknown
Complement: 112

	Builder	Launched	Acquired	Commiss'd	Disposition
NASHVILLE	Montgomery, Ala.	Aug 64	10 May 65	No	Sold at New Orleans 22 Nov 67.

Notes: Formerly the Confederate casemate ironclad Nashville. She was taken to Mobile for completion. She participated in several engagements in April 1865 and surrendered to the USS Cincinnati at Hanna Hubba Bluff, Ala. She was reported to be hogged when surrendered and not strong enough to carry the weight of all of her armor. Her designed armament was 7 guns.

STONEWALL

Displacement: 1400 tons
Dimensions: 171'10"(b.p.) x 32'8" x 14'4"
Armament: 1-9"R (fwd.) 2-6.4"R
Armor: 4 3/4" sides, 4 1/2" casemates

Rig: Brig
Machinery: 300 NHP, 1200 IHP; 2 screws
Speed: 10 kts.
Complement: 130

	Hull	Machinery	Launched	Acquired	Commiss'd	Disposition
STONEWALL	L. Arman, Bordeaux	Mazeline, Le Havre	21 Jun 64	Jul 65	2 Nov 65	Sold to Japan 5 Aug 67 as Kotetsu, then Azuma.

Notes: Formerly the Confederate ironclad ram Stonewall. She was built in France under the code name Sphinx, was embargoed by the French in February 1864, and was sold to Denmark as the Staerkodder in July 1864. She was refused by the Danes and was resold to the Confederates in December 1864. She sailed from Copenhagen under the name Olinde and was commissioned at sea by the Confederates in January 1865. She surrendered to Spanish authorities at Havana on 11 May 65, was turned over to the U.S. in July, and was taken to the Washington Navy Yard in November. Her guns were 300# and 70# Armstrong rifles.

Ironclads (River)

1861

CAIRO class

Tonnage: 512 tons
Dimensions: 175' x 51'2" x 6'(max)
Armament: Cairo--3-8" 4-42#R 6-32#; 3-8" 3-42#R 6-32# 1-30#R (1862);
Carondelet--3-8" 4-42#R 6-32#; 4-8" 1-50#R 1-42#R 6-32# 1-30#R (1862); 3-9" 4-8" 1-50#R 1-42#R 1-32# 1-30#R (1863); 2-100#R 3-9" 4-8" 1-50#R 1-30#R (1864); 2-100#R 3-9" 1-50#R 1-30#R (1864);
Cincinnati--3-8" 4-42#R 6-32#; 3-8" 2-42#R 6-32# 2-30#R (1862); 3-9" 2-8" 6-32# 2-30#R (1862); 2-100#R 2-9" 2-30#R (1864); 2-100#R 3-9" 2-30#R (1865);

Armor: 2 1/2" casemate, 1 1/4" pilot house
Rig: None
Machinery: 2 horizontal, high-pressure engines, 22" x 6', center wheel
Speed: 9 mph.
Complement: 251

The river ironclads *Baron de Kalb*, *Cincinnati*, and *Mound City* off Cairo, Ill., in 1863. (NH 56663)

The paddle frigate *Powhatan*. (NH 2738)

Louisville--3-8" 4-42#R 6-32#; 3-8" 2-42#R 6-32# 2-30#R (1862); 3-9" 2-8" 6-32# 2-30#R (1862);
1-100#R 4-9" 6-32# 2-30#R (1864); 1-100#R 4-9" 2-30#R (1864);
Mound City--3-8" 4-42#R 6-32#; 3-8" 1-50#R 2-42#R 6-32# 1-30#R (1862); 3-9" 3-8" 1-50#R 2-42#R 3-32#
1-30#R (1863); 4-9" 3-8" 1-50#R 2-42#R 2-32# 1-30#R (1863); 1-100#R 4-9" 3-8" 1-50#R 2-32# 1-30#R
(1864); 2-100#R 4-9" 2-8" 1-50#R 2-32# 1-30#R (1864); 2-100#R 3-9" 4-8" 1-50#R 2-32# 1-30#R (1864);
2-100#R 4-9" 1-50#R 1-30#R (1864);
Pittsburgh--3-8" 4-42#R 6-32#; 3-8" 2-42#R 6-32# 2-30#R (1862); 2-9" 2-8" 2-42#R 4-32# 2-30#R
(1863); 2-9" 3-8" 2-42#R 4-32# 2-30#R (1863); 1-100#R 4-9" 2-8" 4-32# 2-30#R (1864); 1-100#R 4-9"
2-30#R (1864);
St. Louis--2-8" 4-42#R 7-32#; 2-8" 2-42#R 6-32# 2-30#R (1862); 3-8" 2-42#R 6-32# 2-30#R (1862);
2-10" 3-8" 6-32# 2-30#R (1862); 1-10" 2-9" 2-8" 6-32# 2-30#R (1863)

	Hull	Laid down	Launched	Commiss'd	Disposition
CAIRO	Eads, Mound City	1861	1861	25 Jan 62	Mined Yazoo R. 12 Dec 62
CARONDELET	Eads, Carondelet	1861	22 Oct 61	15 Jan 62	Sold 29 Nov 65
CINCINNATI	Eads, Mound City	1861	1861	16 Jan 62	Sold 28 Mar 66
LOUISVILLE	Eads, Carondelet	1861	1861	16 Jan 62	Sold 29 Nov 65
MOUND CITY	Eads, Mound City	1861	1861	16 Jan 62	Sold 29 Nov 65
PITTSBURGH	Eads, Carondelet	1861	1861	16 Jan 62	Sold 29 Nov 65
ST. LOUIS	Eads, Carondelet	27 Sep 61	12 Oct 61	31 Jan 62	Mined Yazoo City, Miss., 13 Jul 63.

Notes: Ordered by the Army 7 Aug 61. Wood hulls. Their plan followed a design of John Lenthall which
was modified by Naval Constructor S. M. Pook and James B. Eads. They were known informally as "Pook
Turtles." A. Thomas Merritt prepared the engine design; the engine builder is unknown. All were
built under an Army contract but were transferred to the Navy 1 Oct 62 along with the other vessels in
the Mississippi Squadron. The Cincinnati returned to service after sinkings on 10 May 62 and 27 May
63. The wreck of the Cairo remained under water until the summer of 1965.
Renaming: The St. Louis became the Baron De Kalb on 8 Sep 62.

BENTON

Tonnage: 1033 tons
Dimensions: 202' x 72' x 9'
Armament: 2-9" 7-42#R 7-32#; 2-9" 2-50#R 4-42#R 8-32# (1862);
  4-9" 2-50#R 4-42#R 6-32# (1863); 2-100#R 8-9" 2-50#R 4-32#
  (1863)
Armor: 2 1/2" casemate, 2 1/2" pilot house

Rig: None
Machinery: 2 high-pressure inclined
  engines, 20" x 7', stern wheel
Speed: 5.5 kts.
Complement: 176

	Converted	Machinery	Started	Launched	Commiss'd	Disposition
BENTON	Eads, Carondelet	Unknown	Aug 61	Nov 61	24 Feb 62	Sold 29 Nov 65.

Notes: Formerly a catamaran snagboat Submarine No. 7, one of five purchased by James B. Eads' wrecking
company from the U.S. Government in 1855. (Her Government name may have been Benton.) The Army
purchased her in August 1861 and Eads rebuilt her into an ironclad to his own design. Although slow
and unwieldy she was the most powerful of the early river ironclads. The dates above refer to her
Army service--she was transferred to the Navy with most of the other Army ironclads on 1 Oct 62.

ESSEX

Tonnage: 614 tons
Dimensions: 159' x 47'6" x 6'(max)
Armament: 5-9"; 1-10" 3-9" 1-32# (1862); 1-10" 3-9" 2-50#R
  1-32# (1862); 1-100#R 4-9" 2-50#R 1-32# (1863); 2-100#R
  6-9" (1864)
Armor: 3" casemate

Rig: None
Machinery: 2 high-pressure engines,
  18" x 6', center wheel
Speed: 5.5 kts.
Complement: 134

	Converted	Machinery	Started	Launched	Commiss'd	Disposition
ESSEX	Eads, Carondelet	Gatz, McClune	1861	1861	by 15 Oct 1861	Sold 29 Nov 65.

Notes: Built at St. Louis in 1856 as the merchant ferryboat New Era and purchased there by the Army on
20 Sep 61. She was initially fitted out as a timberclad following a plan of Eads. The armor was
added in November 1861 by Theodore Adams at St. Louis under the direction of W. D. Porter and she was
renamed Essex. After being badly damaged in the Fort Henry attack of February 1862, she was
lengthened 40 feet and her forward casemate was refaced with 1" of iron over 1" of rubber. She also
received new engines, and her tonnage rose to 614 tons. Her new dimensions were 198'6" x 58' x 6'9".
She recommissioned on 28 Jun 62 and was transferred from the Army to the Navy on 1 Oct 62.

1862

EASTPORT

Tonnage: 800 tons
Dimensions: 280' x 43'(hull) x 6'3"
Armament: 4-32# 2-50#R 2-30#R; 2-100#R 6-9" (1863); 2-100#R
  4-9" 2-50#R (1863)
Armor: Unknown

Rig: None
Machinery: 2 high-pressure engines,
  26" x 9', side wheels
Speed: Unknown
Complement: 150

	Builder	Launched	Acquired	Commiss'd	Disposition
EASTPORT	New Albany, Ind.	1852	1 Oct 62	9 Jan 63	Destroyed in Red River 26 Apr 64.

Notes: Formerly the Confederate casemate ironclad Eastport, formerly a fast river steamer (possibly the C.E. Hillman) acquired by the Confederates in January 1862 and converted. She was captured on 7 Feb 62 while under conversion at Cerro Gordo, Tenn., by the timberclad gunboats Conestoga, Tyler, and Lexington. She was completed by the Army at Cairo, Ill., and was transferred to the Navy on 1 Oct 62. Mined in the Red River on 15 April 1864, she was raised but was blown up to avoid capture.

CHOCTAW

Tonnage: 1004 tons
Dimensions: 260' x 45' x 8'
Armament: 1-100#R 1-9" 2-30#R; 1-100#R 2-30#R 2-24# (1863);
  3-9" 2-30#R 2-24# (1863); 1-100#R 3-9" 2-30#R 2-24# (1863)
Armor: 2" + 1" rubber casemate

Rig: None
Machinery: 2 engines, 23" x 8', side
  wheels
Speed: 2 kts. (upstream)
Complement: 106

	Converted	Machinery	Started	Launched	Commiss'd	Disposition
CHOCTAW	Eads, Carondelet	Unknown	1862	27 Sep 62	23 Mar 63	Sold 28 Mar 66.

Notes: Formerly the merchant steamer Choctaw (built at New Albany, Ind., 1855), purchased by the Army in the spring of 1862 and converted to an ironclad according to a plan of W. D. Porter. The plans called for heavier armor and armament than the hull could safely carry. The two forward casemates were covered by iron plates fitted over India rubber while the third, abaft the wheels was unarmored. She had a platform for a pair of 12" mortars amidships but these were never mounted. She was fitted with a ram bow. She was transferred from the War Department 1 Oct 62.

LAFAYETTE

Tonnage: 1000 tons
Dimensions: 292'(oa.) x 45' x 8'(max)
Armament: 2-100#R 2-11" 4-9"; 2-100#R 2-11" 2-9" (1864)
Armor: 2 1/2" + 2" rubber
Rig: None

Machinery: 2 engines, 26" x 10', side
  wheels
Speed: 4 kts. (upstream)
Complement: 210

	Converted	Machinery	Started	Launched	Commiss'd	Disposition
LAFAYETTE	Eads, Carondelet	Unknown	1862	24 Sep 62	27 Feb 63	Sold 28 Mar 66.

Notes: Formerly the Quartermaster steamer Fort Henry (ex-Alick Scott, built at New Albany, Ind., 1858), ordered converted to an ironclad in the spring of 1862 according to another plan of W. D. Porter. She also had provisions for mounting 12" mortars. She had a single casemate and a ram bow.

CHILLICOTHE

Tonnage: 203 tons
Dimensions: 162' x 50' x 4'
Armament: 2-11"
Armor: 2" sides, 1" deck, 3" pilot house
Rig: None

Machinery: 2 engines, 22" x 4', side
  wheels
Speed: 7 kts.
Complement: Unknown

	Hull	Machinery	Laid down	Launched	Commiss'd	Disposition
CHILLICOTHE	Brown, Cincinnati	McCord & Junger	1862	1862	5 Sep 62	Sold 29 Nov 65.

Notes: Ordered 30 Apr 62. Wood hull. Designed by Samuel Hartt. Her bulwarks were not strong enough to support her armor adequately.

INDIANOLA

Tonnage: 442 tons
Dimensions: 175' x 52' x 5'

Machinery: 2 engines, 24" x 6', side
  wheels; 2 engines, 18" x 28", 2

Armament: 2-11" 2-9"
Armor: 3" casemate, 1" deck
Rig: None

screws
Speed: 6 kts.
Complement: 144

	Hull	Machinery	Laid down	Launched	Commiss'd	Disposition
INDIANOLA	Brown, Cincinnati	McCord & Junger	1862	4 Sep 62	by 14 Jan 1863	Captured by Confederate squadron near Vicksburg, Miss., 24 Feb 63.

Notes: Ordered 30 Apr 62. Wood hull. Designed and built by Joseph Brown. She was a powerful but hastily and poorly built vessel. She was placed in service on 27 Sep 62 before completion. The Confederates scuttled her 4 Mar 63 but she was raised on 5 Jan 65 and sold at Mound City, Ill., 29 Nov 65.

TUSCUMBIA

Tonnage: 565 tons
Dimensions: 178' x 75' x 7'
Armament: 3-11" 2-9"; 3-11" (1863); 3-11" 2-9" (1864)
Armor: 6" casemates
Rig: None

Machinery: 2 engines, 30" x 6', side wheels; 2 engines, 20" x 20", 2 screws
Speed: 10 mph. (upstream)
Complement: Unknown

	Hull	Machinery	Laid down	Launched	Commiss'd	Disposition
TUSCUMBIA	Unknown, New Albany	McCord	1862	12 Dec 62	12 Mar 63	Sold 29 Nov 65.

Notes: Ordered 30 Apr 62. Wood hull. Designed by Samuel Hartt. Joseph Brown was the contractor and sublet the contract for the hull to a unidentified builder in New Albany, Ind. (possibly McCord and Junger). She was poorly built. The 11" guns were in the forward casemate and the 9" in the after one.

OZARK

Tonnage: 578 tons
Dimensions: 180'(oa.) x 50'(e) x 5'
Armament: 2-11"; 2-11" 1-10" 3-9" (1864)
Armor: 6" turret, 2 1/2" sides, 1 1/4" deck
Rig: None

Machinery: 4 engines, 15" x 24", 4 screws
Speed: 9 mph. (designed), 2.5 kts (service)
Complement: 120

	Hull	Machinery	Laid down	Launched	Commiss'd	Disposition
OZARK	Hambleton, Collier	McCord	1862	18 Feb 63	18 Feb 64	Sold 29 Nov 65.

Notes: Ordered 14 May 62. The earliest of the Western river monitor designs, she was a cross between the salt water type and the early river gunboats. She had a wooden hull. She was lightly built and underpowered, but had the reputation of being the most voracious coal eater in the Navy. The 11" guns were in a turret, the others exposed. An attempt to fit her with an underwater torpedo was abandoned before launching. George C. Bestor held the prime contract.

MARIETTA class

Tonnage: 479 tons
Dimensions: 173'11"(oa.) x 52'1"(e) x 5'
Armament: 2-11"
Armor: 6" turret, 1 1/4" sides
Rig: None

Machinery: 4 high-pressure engines, 15" x 24", 4 screws
Speed: 9 mph. (designed)
Complement: 100

	Hull	Machinery	Laid down	Launched	Completed	Disposition
MARIETTA	Tomlinson,	Hartupee	1862	4 Jan 65	**16 Dec 65	Sold 17 Apr 73
SANDUSKY	Tomlinson,	Hartupee	1862	17 Jan 65	**26 Dec 65	Sold 17 Apr 73.

Notes: Ordered 16 May 62. Probably designed by their builders, they were flat bottomed iron hulled river boats mounting a turret. Neither was ever commissioned as they were finished after the end of fighting. Both were delivered on 25 Apr 66.
Renamings: They became the Circe and Minerva respectively on 15 Jun 69 but regained their original names 10 Aug 69.

NEOSHO class

Tonnage: 523 tons
Dimensions: 180'(oa.) x 45'(e) x 4'6"
Armament: 2-11"
Armor: 6" turret, 2 1/2" sides, 1 1/4" deck
Rig: None

Machinery: 2 horizontal high-pressure engines, 22" x 6', stern wheel
Speed: 12 mph; 7.5 mph (service)
Complement: 100

	Hull	Laid down	Launched	Commiss'd	Disposition
NEOSHO	Union, Carondelet	1862	18 Feb 63	13 May 63	Sold 17 Apr 73
OSAGE	Union, Carondelet	1862	13 Jan 63	10 Jul 63	Mined Blakely R., Ala., 29 Mar 65.

Notes: Ordered 21 May 62. Iron-hulled, single-turret monitors with stern wheels, they were designed by and ordered from James B. Eads, who owned the Union Iron Works at Carondelet, Mo. The Fulton Iron Works at St. Louis probably built the machinery. The ships were considered slow and underpowered. The wreck of the Osage was raised in 1865, sold at New Orleans 22 Nov 67, and converted to a merchant ship.
Renamings: The Neosho was renamed Vixen 15 Jun 69 and Osceola 10 Aug 69.

MILWAUKEE class

Displacement: 1300 tons
Dimensions: 229'(oa.) x 56'(e) x 6'
Armament: 4-11"
Armor: 8" turrets, 3" sides, 1 1/2" deck
Rig: None

Machinery: 4 horizontal high-pressure engines, 26" x 24", 4 screws
Speed: 9 kts. (designed & service)
Complement: 120

	Hull	Laid down	Launched	Commiss'd	Disposition
CHICKASAW	Union, Carondelet	1862	10 Feb 64	14 May 64	Sold 12 Sep 74
KICKAPOO	Union, Carondelet	1862	12 Mar 64	8 Jul 64	Sold 12 Sep 74
MILWAUKEE	Union, Carondelet	1862	4 Feb 64	27 Aug 64	Mined Blakely R., Ala., 28 Mar 65
WINNEBAGO	Union, Carondelet	1862	4 Jul 63	27 Apr 64	Sold 12 Sep 74.

Notes: Ordered 27 May 62. Designed by James B. Eads, these iron hulled twin turret monitors had one Eads and one Ericsson turret each. The machinery was undoubtedly built by a regular engine building concern, probably the Fulton Iron Works of St. Louis. The contractors were T. G. Gaylord (Chickasaw). G. B. Allen & Co. (Kickapoo). and Eads (Milwaukee and Winnebago).
Renamings: The Chickasaw, Kickapoo, and Winnebago were renamed Samson, Cyclops, and Tornado respectively 15 Jun 69. The Chickasaw and Winnebago recovered their original names 10 Aug 69 at which time the Cyclops (ex-Kickapoo) became the Kewaydin.

1863

BARATARIA

Tonnage: 400 tons
Dimensions: 125' x (unknown) x 3'6"
Armament: 2 guns
Armor: 1"

Rig: Unknown
Machinery: Stern wheel
Speed: Unknown
Complement: Unknown

	Builder	Launched	Acquired	Commiss'd	Disposition
BARATARIA	Barataria, La.	1857	1 Jan 63	1863	Destroyed in Lake Maurepas, La., 7 Apr 63.

Notes: Formerly the Confederate ironclad gunboat Barataria, converted at New Orleans from a merchant ship of the same name. She was captured at New Orleans in April 1862 and taken over by the Army, who transferred her to the Navy on 1 Jan 63. She struck a snag and was burned to avoid capture. Her tonnage is also reported as 52 tons.

1865

MISSOURI

Tonnage: 546 tons
Dimensions: 183' x 53'8" x 8'6"
Armament: 2-11" 4-9" 2-32#
Armor: 4 1/2" casemate, 4 1/2" deck fore and aft

Rig: None
Machinery: Stern wheel
Speed: Unknown
Complement: Unknown

	Builder	Launched	Acquired	Commiss'd	Disposition
MISSOURI	Shreveport, La.	14 Apr 63	3 Jun 65	No	Sold at Mound City 29 Nov 65.

Notes: Formerly the Confederate ironclad river ram Missouri. She was designed to carry two guns forward and three on each beam; the top part of her centerwheel aft was unprotected. She surrendered to a Union squadron at Alexandria, La.

Steam Floating Batteries

1814

FULTON

Displacement: 1450 tons
Dimensions: 153'2"(oa.) x 58'(e) x 13'
Armament: 26-32# (1815)
Rig: 2-masted lateen

Machinery: 120 HP; 1 vertical side-
lever engine, center wheel
Speed: 5.5 kts.
Complement: 200

	Hull	Machinery	Laid down	Launched	Commiss'd	Disposition
FULTON	Brown, New York	Fulton	20 Jun 14	29 Oct 14	18 Jun 17	Blew up 4 Jun 29.

Notes: Authorized 9 Mar 14. The first steam warship, she was proposed by Robert Fulton in December 1813 for the defense of New York and designed by him with a catamaran hull, or, more specifically, two half-hulls separated by a 14'10" wide race for a centerline paddle wheel. The boilers were in one hull and the engines in the other. Her sides were 58" thick and she carried a hot shot furnace. Four 100# columbiads were included in the design (to be fired underwater!) but were never mounted. Her engine was also described as 1 inclined cylinder, 48" diameter x 5' stroke, generating 73 NHP. The ship ran trials between June and December 1815 and was delivered to the Navy in June 1816. She was put in service for one day in 1817 to take President Monroe on a harbor cruise. Her guns and machinery were removed in 1821 and she spent 1825-29 as a receiving ship. She was destroyed by a powder magazine explosion. She had no official name. Fulton called her the Demologos (Voice of the People) but she was also called the Steam Battery, the Fulton Steam Frigate, the Fulton, and the Fulton the First.

Unnamed

Tonnage: Unknown
Dimensions: Unknown
Armament: Unknown
Rig: Unknown

Machinery: Unknown
Speed: Unknown
Complement: Unknown

	Hull	Machinery	Laid down	Launched	Commiss'd	Disposition
Unnamed	Unknown, Baltimore		1814	No	No	Sold 1815.

Notes: Authorized 9 Mar 14. Proposed by Captain Stiles, a Baltimore merchant, and designed by Uriah Brown with iron-sheathed, shot-proof inclined wooden sides. Funds were raised in Baltimore and "considerable progress" reputedly had been made on her before work was suspended after the War of 1812. A third battery was reportedly planned at Philadelphia but was not proceeded with.

1816

Notes: On 29 Apr 16 Congress authorized the Navy to accumulate materials for three steam batteries. In 1818 Henry Eckford produced plans for a steam battery which measured 147'8" x 36', was pierced for 10 guns per side, and was arranged as a conventional side wheel steamer except for a flat bottom. On 21 Oct 18 the Navy Commissioners ordered the machinery of an ocean-going steam frigate from the Columbian Foundry of Robert McQueen and Company in Baltimore. In 1822 the frames for two steam batteries were in storage at Washington Navy Yard while those for a third and a pair of engines were at New York Navy Yard.

Steam Frigates and Large Sloops
(Civil War classification: 1st rates)

1839

MISSISSIPPI class

Displacement: 3220 tons
Dimensions: 220'(b.p.) x 39', 66'6"(o.g.) x 21'9"(max)
Armament: 2-10" 8-8"; 1-10" 10-8" (1857); 1-9" 10-8" (1861);
    1-10" 19-8" 1-20#R (1862)

Machinery: Mississippi--458 NHP, 650 AHP; 2 side lever engines, 75" diameter cylinders x 7' stroke, side wheels;

Rig: Bark.
Complement: 257

Missouri--515 NHP; 2 inclined, direct-acting, condensing engines, 62" x 10', side wheels
Speed: 10 kts.

	Hull	Machinery	Laid down	Launched	Commiss'd	Disposition
MISSISSIPPI	Phila-delphia	Merrick & Towne	10 Aug 39	5 May 41	22 Dec 41	Sunk by Confederate batteries, Port Hudson, La., 14 Mar 63
MISSOURI	New York	West Pt.	1839	7 Jan 41	Feb 42	Burned at Gibraltar 26 Aug 43.

Notes: Authorized 3 Mar 39. Samuel Hartt, Samuel Humphreys, and John Lenthall collaborated on the hull design for these "sea steamers." Charles W. Copeland designed the Missouri's engines while the engines of the Mississippi were designed by Copeland in accordance with a standard British pattern. These ships were very successful and powerful steamers but were dull sailers. The Mississippi was listed as a 2nd rate in 1862.

1847

SUSQUEHANNA

Displacement: 3824 tons
Dimensions: 250'(b.p.) x 45'(e), 69'(o.g.) x 20'6"
Armament: 9-8"; 15-8" (1856); 2-150#R 12-9" (1863); 2-100#R 12-9" (1865); 2-11" 12-9" 1-30#R (1865) 1-11" 12-9" 1-30#R (1866)
Rig: Bark

Machinery: 448 NHP, 795 AHP, 2 inclined, direct-acting, condensing engines, 70" x 10', side wheels
Speed: 11 kts.
Complement: 300

	Hull	Machinery	Laid down	Launched	Commiss'd	Disposition
SUSQUEHANNA	Phila-delphia	Murray & Hazelhurst	8 Sep 47	6 Apr 50	24 Dec 50	Sold 27 Sep 83.

Notes: Authorized 3 Mar 47. Her hull was designed by John Lenthall along the lines of the Mississippi class and her engines by Charles W. Copeland. She was considered, along with the Powhatan, the most efficient naval vessel afloat when built. Her engines were removed in 1870 but plans to convert her into a screw steamer with 60" x 36" engines and an armament of 2-11" 2-100#R 18-9" 1-60#R were abandoned because of the cost.

POWHATAN

Displacement: 3765 tons
Dimensions: 250'(b.p.) x 45'(e), 69'6"(o.g.) x 20'9'(max)
Armament: 9-8"; 1-11" 10-9" (1857); 1-11" 1-100#R 7-9" (1863); 1-11" 2-100#R 15-9" (1863); 1-11" 3-100#R 14-9" (1863); 1-11" 3-100#R 16-9" (1865); 1-11" 2-100#R 14-9" (1869)
Rig: Bark

Machinery: 448 NHP, 795 IHP; 2 inclined, direct-acting, condensing engines, 70" x 10', side wheels
Speed: 11 kts.
Complement: 300

	Hull	Machinery	Laid down	Launched	Commiss'd	Disposition
POWHATAN	Norfolk	Mehaffy	14 Jul 47	14 Feb 50	2 Sep 52	Sold 30 Jul 87.

Notes: Authorized 3 Mar 47. Francis Grice designed the hull along new lines with a finer entry and Charles H. Haswell designed the engines. A highly successful vessel, she remained a dependable cruiser for over thirty years.

1853

FRANKLIN

Displacement: 5298 tons
Dimensions: 265'(wl.) x 53'8"(e) x 24'3"
Armament: 1-11" 4-100#R 34-9"; 1-11" 4-100#R 38-9" (1874); 22-9" 2-20#BLR (1887); 4-9" 2-20#BLR (1889); 4-9" (1894); 2-3# (1900)
Rig: Ship

Machinery: 2065 IHP; 2 horizontal, back-acting engines, 68" x 42", 1 screw
Speed: 10 kts.
Complement: 228

	Hull	Machinery	Laid down	Launched	Commiss'd	Disposition
FRANKLIN	Ports-mouth	Atlantic	May 54	17 Sep 64	3 Jun 67	Sold 29 May 1916.

Notes: Officially considered to be the old ship of the line razeed and rebuilt. In August 1853 a technical committee recommended replacing the old 74 with a frigate with, "in addition to her sails, an auxiliary steam power" and an armament made up entirely of shell guns. The new ship was ordered on 1 Sep 53. John Lenthall completed the plans for her lines in February 1854, but work progressed slowly because it was funded by limited repair appropriations. The machinery, designed by Isherwood, was not ordered until 16 Nov 63. The Franklin served as a training vessel or receiving ship after 1877.

1854

ROANOKE class

Displacement: 4772 tons
Dimensions: 263'8"(wl.) x 52'6"(wl.) x 23'9"(max)
Armament: Roanoke--2-10" 24-9" 14-8"; 2-10" 28-9" 14-8"
   (1861);
   Colorado--2-10" 24-9" 14-8"; 2-10" 28-9" 14-8" (1861);
   1-11" 1-10" 28-9" 14-8" (1861); 1-11" 1-10" 23-9" 1-30#R
   (1862); 1-200#R 1-11" 44-9" (1862); 1-200#R 1-11" 46-9"
   (1863), 1-150#R 1-11" 46-9" (1863); 1-11" 40-9" 1-60#R
   (1865); 32-9" 1-60#R (1865); 1-11" 2-100#R 42-9" 2-20#R
   (1870); 2-11" 2-100#R 42-9" (1873)

Rig: Ship
Machinery: 997 IHP; 2 horizontal,
   direct-acting, trunk engines, 79.5"
   x 36", 1 screw
Speed: 9 kts.
Complement: 674

	Hull	Machinery	Laid down	Launched	Commiss'd	Disposition
ROANOKE	Norfolk	Tredegar	May 54	13 Dec 55	4 May 57	Converted to monitor 1862
COLORADO	Norfolk	Tredegar	May 54	19 Jun 56	13 Mar 58	Sold 14 Feb 85.

Notes: Authorized 6 Apr 54. These ships and their three near sisters, below, were auxiliary screw frigates whose modest steam power was intended primarily for use in emergencies or when becalmed. Their propellers could be hoisted clear of the water when under sail. They also had an armament consisting entirely of large shell guns, greatly increasing their weight of broadside and destructive power. Their hull size was determined in part by the decision to use frames cut for additional ships of the 1839 Congress class which had never been ordered. The two Roanokes had hull lines almost identical to the Franklin and very similar dimensions, suggesting that the "rebuilt" ship was the prototype for the group. The hull plans for the Roanokes were by John Lenthall and the engines were designed by Daniel B. Martin. Strong and well built, both vessels sailed well when properly trimmed. The Colorado served as a receiving ship after 1876.

MINNESOTA

Displacement: 4833 tons
Dimensions: 264'9"(wl.) x 51'4"(wl.) x 23'10"
Armament: 1-10" 26-9" 14-8"; 1-10" 28-9" 14-8" (1861);
   1-200#R 1-11" 4-100#R 36-9" (1862); 1-150#R 1-11" 2-100#R
   21-9" (1863); 1-150#R 1-11" 4-100#R 38-9" (1863); 1-150#R
   1-11" 4-100#R 42-9" (1863); 1-150#R 1-11" 4-100#R 38-9"
   (1864); 1-11" 40-9" 2-60#R (1867); 2-11" 2-100#R 42-9"
   (1873); 1-11" 26-9" 4-32# (1875); 1-11" 38-9" 4-32# 2-20#R
   (1878); 24-9" 16-32# 2-20#BLR (1879); 24-9" 1-60#BLR
   2-20#BLR (1882); 18-9" 1-60#BLR 2-20#BLR (1887); 8-9"
   1-60#BLR 2-20#BLR (1890)

Rig: Ship
Machinery: 973 IHP; 2 horizontal,
   direct-acting, trunk engines, 79.5"
   x 36", 1 screw
Speed: 9 kts.
Complement: 646

	Hull	Machinery	Laid down	Launched	Commiss'd	Disposition
MINNESOTA	Washington		May 54	1 Dec 55	21 May 57	Sold 12 Aug 1901.

Notes: Authorized 6 Apr 54. The remaining three frigates of the 1854 group was built to separate John Lenthall plans which differed slightly in dimensions. All three had fuller lines fore and aft than the Roanoke and Franklin. The Minnesota's machinery was built to the same design as that of the Roanoke. She was a fast sailer and could make about 9 knots under steam alone. She served as a training vessel 1876-1901.

WABASH

Displacement: 4774 tons
Dimensions: 262'4"(wl.) x 51'4"(wl.) x 23'
Armament: 2-10" 24-9" 14-8"; 2-10" 28-9" 14-8" (1861); 2-10"
   42-9" (1862); 1-150#R 1-10" 42-9" 1-30#R (1863); 1-150#R
   1-10" 2-100#R 38-9" 1-30#R (1864); 1-150#R 1-10" 42-9"
   4-32# 1-30#R (1865); 1-150#R 1-11" 2-100#R 42-9" (1868);
   1-11" 2-100#R 42-9" (1871); 18-9" 2-20#BLR (1887); 2-20#BLR
   (1893); none (1897)

Rig: Ship.
Machinery: 950 IHP; 2 horizontal,
   direct-acting, steeple engines, 72"
   x 36", 1 screw
Speed: 9 kts.
Complement: 642

	Hull	Machinery	Laid down	Launched	Commiss'd	Disposition
WABASH	Phila-delphia	Merrick & Sons	16 May 54	24 Oct 55	18 Aug 56	Sold 30 Dec 1912.

The screw frigate *Minnesota* at the New York Navy Yard soon after the Civil War. (NH 92)

The large screw sloop *Florida* (ex-*Wampanoag*) in drydock at the New York Navy Yard ca. 1869. (NH 54159)

Notes: Authorized 6 Apr 54. The hull was designed by John Lenthall and the machinery by its builder. She was considered a fast and sure vessel. After 1875 she acted as a receiving ship.

MERRIMACK

Displacement: 4636 tons
Dimensions: 256'9"(wl.) x 51'4"(wl.) x 24'3"
Armament: 2-10" 24-9" 14-8"
Rig: Ship.

Machinery: 869 HP; 2 horizontal, double piston-rod engines, 72" x 36", 1 screw
Speed: 9 kts.
Complement: 519

	Hull	Machinery	Laid down	Launched	Commiss'd	Disposition
MERRIMACK	Boston	West Pt.	11 Jul 54	15 Jun 55	20 Feb 56	Burned to avoid capture at Norfolk 20 Apr 61.

Notes: Authorized 6 Apr 54. The hull was designed by John Lenthall and the machinery by its builder. The Merrimack sailed well but was underpowered as a steamer, and her machinery suffered from design defects. Her name is often mistakenly rendered as Merrimac. After salvage by the Confederates she was rebuilt as the casemate ironclad Virginia. She was blown up by her crew on 11 May 62 to keep her out of Union hands.

NIAGARA

Displacement: 5540 tons
Dimensions: 345'(oa.), 328'10" (b.p.) x 55'3" x 24'8"
Armament: 4-32#; 12-11" (1860); 11-11" 1-100#R (1862); 12-150#R 20-11" (1863); 12-150#R (1864)
Rig: Ship

Machinery: 1955 HP; 3 horizontal, direct-acting engines, 72" x 36", 1 screw
Speed: 10.9 kts.
Complement: 657

	Hull	Machinery	Laid down	Launched	Commiss'd	Disposition
NIAGARA	New York	Fulton IrWks	Oct 54	23 Feb 56	6 Apr 57	Sold 6 May 85.

Notes: Authorized 6 Apr 54. Although sometimes referred to as a frigate because of her great size, she was configured as a sloop with all her guns on a single deck. The hull was designed by George Steers, a specialist in fast sailing ships, and the engines were designed by James Murphy & Co. The largest vessel yet built in the United States when launched, she combined extreme clipper lines with a relatively large auxiliary steam engine and a hoisting screw. She was very fast and steady under sail but underpowered under steam. Before receiving her designed armament in May 1860 she helped lay the first transatlantic cable. Her engines were overhauled at Boston in 1862-63. At the same time, ports were cut in her hull and 20-11" guns were installed on her main deck, making her a true frigate. Her new 32-gun armament was too heavy for her, however, and the main deck guns were removed in 1864. In 1870 a refit was begun which involved iron plating her sides near the waterline, changing the line of her gun and berth decks, and fitting new engines, boilers, and a battery of 20-11". The refit was stopped because of the cost. Her engines, which had been removed, were scrapped in 1872.

1863

WAMPANOAG class

Displacement: 4215 (Wampanoag), 4105 (Madawasca) tons
Dimensions: 342'8"(s.d.), 335'(b.p.) x 45'2"(e) x 19'10"
Armament: Wampanoag--10-9" 3-60#R;
   Madawasca--2-100#R 10-8" 1-60#R; 2-11" 2-100#R 18-9" 1-60#R 2-20#R (1871); 2-11" 2-100#R 18-9" 1-60#R (1876); 2-8"R 16-9" 4-80#BLR 2-20#BLR (1879)
Rig: Bark

Machinery: Wampanoag--4049 HP; 2 horizontal, geared engines, 100" x 48", 1 screw;
   Madawasca--2143 HP; 2 vibrating-lever engines, 100" x 48", 1 screw
Speed: 17.25 kts. (Wampanoag), 15.25 kts. (Madawasca) (trials)
Complement: 375

	Hull	Machinery	Laid down	Launched	Commiss'd	Disposition
WAMPANOAG	New York	Novelty	3 Aug 63	15 Dec 64	17 Sep 67	Sold 27 Feb 85
MADAWASKA	New York	Allaire	1863	8 Jul 65	27 Jun 66	Sold 15 Sep 87.

Notes: Ordered ca. Jul 63, engines ordered 24 Sep 63 (Wampanoag) and 5 Nov 63 (Madawasca). These "screw sloops of great speed" belonged to the first of three groups of ocean-cruising ships ordered in 1863, the others being the Guerriere and Contoocook classes. Compared to the others, the Wampanoags were described as vessels with the most powerful engines "on which some sacrifice of armament has been made to obtain speed." They were designed to maintain 16 knots and "sweep the ocean and chase and hunt down the vessels of an enemy." With a hull designed by Benjamin F. Delano and engines by Isherwood, the Wampanoag was one of the landmarks of American marine engineering. Her hull lines closely resembled those of the Guerriere, Contoocook, Nipsic, and Swatara classes--below the waterline she was essentially a Guerriere lengthened 35' without increasing the beam. Her engines and boilers took up 166' of the ship's length (the design was lengthened 10' in September 1863 to fit them in). Isherwood adopted a large wooden reduction gear to reduce wear on the engines during prolonged high speed operations. On trials in February 1868 she averaged 16.6 knots on a 38-hour trial run and maintained 17.25 knots for a six hour period, making her the fastest steamer then afloat. She was criticised for inadequate space for crew accomodations and stores and was laid up soon after her trials.

The Madawasca was built with a hull identical to that of the Wampanoag to permit trials of competitive engine designs. (Both were built of live oak and were more durable than the other 1863 ships, in which unseasoned white oak was used.) Her engines were a John Ericsson design which used a vibrating lever arrangement instead of reduction gearing to connect the cylinders to the propeller shaft. They were identical in dimensions and type to the engines of the monitor Dictator. On trials in January 1867 she sustained a speed of 12.73 knots for 41 hours, well under her contract speed of 15 knots, and reached 15.25 knots for five hours. In 1869-70 she was modified along lines recommended by a Navy board for the entire Wampanoag group: half of her boilers and two funnels were removed and a complete spar deck and a full ship rig were fitted. Her remaining boiler power proved to be insufficient to operate the engines. In 1871-75 John Roach removed Ericsson's machinery and installed new 4-cylinder 3200 IHP horizontal back-acting compound engines made at the Morgan Iron Works and ten cylindrical boilers. Her displacement as rebuilt was 4840 tons and her draft 22'6"(max).
Renamings: To Florida and Tennessee respectively 15 May 69.

AMMONOOSUC class

Displacement: 3850 tons
Dimensions: 335'(b.p.) x 44'4" x 16'6"
Armament: 10-9" 3-60#R (Ammonoosuc); 2-100#R 10-8" 1-60#R
  (Neshaminy, designed)
Rig: Bark

Machinery: 4480 IHP; 2 horizontal, geared engines, 100" x 48", 1 screw
Speed: 17.11 kts. (Ammonoosuc, trials)
Complement: Unknown

	Hull	Machinery	Laid down	Launched	Commiss'd	Disposition
AMMONOOSUC	Boston	Morgan	1863	21 Jul 64	15 Jun 68	Sold 27 Sep 83
NESHAMINY	Philadelphia	Etna	1863	5 Oct 65	No	Sold Jun 74.

Notes: The Neshaminy was ordered on 10 Jul 63 and the other was probably ordered around the same time. Their engines were ordered on 24 Sep 63. The machinery duplicated that of the Wampanoag, and the hulls, built on plans by B. F. Delano, were also duplicates of the New York ship except for slightly fuller hull lines forward and somewhat lighter construction. They were built of unseasoned white oak which quickly decayed. On trials in June 1868 the Ammonoosuc averaged 17.11 knots over a distance of 49.8 miles. The engines of the Neshaminy were fitted at New York in 1866-68, but her hull was found to be twisted and she was not completed.
Renamings: Neshaminy (sometimes spelled Neshaming) to Arizona 15 May 69 and to Nevada 10 Aug 69; Ammonoosuc to Iowa 15 May 69.

POMPONOOSUC class

Displacement: 4446 tons
Dimensions: 335'(b.p.) x 48' x unknown
Armament: 2-100#R 12-9" 2-60#R (Pompanoosuc, designed)
Rig: Bark

Machinery: 4100 HP; 2 horizontal, geared engines, 1 screw
Speed: Unknown
Complement: 330

	Hull	Machinery	Laid down	Launched	Commiss'd	Disposition
POMPONOOSUC	Boston	Corliss	2 Jan 64	No	No	Broken up on ways 1884.
BON HOMME RICHARD	Not ord.	Washington	No	No	No	Cancelled 1866.

Notes: Engines ordered 26 Oct 63 (Pompanoosuc) and 2 Oct 64. Except for an additional four feet of beam, the Pomponoosuc was probably very similar to the Ammonoosuc class. Her hull plans (which have not been located) were attributed to John Lenthall. Her engines, duplicates of the Isherwood engines of the Wampanoag, were delivered incomplete in 1869. The Bon Homme Richard was named when her engines were placed on order on 2 Oct 64 but the hull was never ordered. She was listed with the same measurement tonnage (3713 tons) as the Pomponoosuc. Her engines, also copies of those of the Wampanoag, were completed and put in storage.
Renaming: Pomponoosuc to Connecticut 15 May 69.

IDAHO

Displacement: 3241 tons
Dimensions: 310'(oa.), 298'(b.p.) x 44'6" x 17'1"(mean)
Armament: 6-32# 1-30#R
Rig: Bark

Machinery: 645 HP; direct-acting engines, 30" x 8', 2 screws
Speed: 8.27 kts. (trials)
Complement: 400

	Hull	Machinery	Laid down	Launched	Commiss'd	Disposition
IDAHO	Steers	Morgan	1863	8 Oct 64	2 Apr 66	Sold Apr 74.

Notes: Ordered 22 May 63. Built under subcontracts from Paul S. Forbes. Her hull was designed by Henry Steers, the brother of the designer of the Niagara, and her engines were designed by Edward N. Dickerson, the politically-connected lawyer who had already produced one failure, the engines for the Pensacola. On trials in May 1866 Dickerson's engines could manage only 8.27 knots instead of the 15 in the contract. The ship was rejected by the Navy on 25 May 66. Ordered acquired by Congressional resolution, the Idaho was accepted in 1867, her engines were ordered removed on 7 Mar 67, and she was commissioned on 3 Oct 67 as a sailing store and hospital ship with a full ship rig. As such she was probably the fastest vessel afloat, having logged over 18.5 knots. She was badly battered in a typhoon on 21 Sep 69 and served thereafter as a hulk in Japan.

CHATTANOOGA

Displacement: 3043 tons (trial)
Dimensions: 336'(oa.), 315'(b.p.) x 46'(e) x 14'11"(mean)
Armament: 2-100#R 10-8" 1-60#R
Rig: Bark

Machinery: 1737 IHP; 2 horizontal, back-acting engines, 84" x 42", 1 screw
Speed: 13.37 kts. (trials)
Complement: Unknown

	Hull	Machinery	Laid down	Launched	Commiss'd	Disposition
CHATTANOOGA	Cramp	Merrick & Sons	1863	13 Oct 64	16 May 66	Sold 27 Jan 72.

Notes: Ordered 3 Sep 63, engines ordered 23 Oct 63. The hull and the machinery were each designed by their builders. The machinery was reportedly identical to a successful set built for the large Russian frigate General Admiral. A bowsprit was ordered fitted on 27 Feb 66. She made an average of 13.2 knots on a 24-hour trial run in August 1866, short of the contract speed. She was accepted in August 1867 and was sunk by floating ice while laid up at League Island Navy Yard in December 1871.

GUERRIERE class

Displacement: 3954 tons
Dimensions: 312'6"(b.p.) x 46'(e) x 21'5"(max)
Armament: 2-100#R 16-9" 1-60#R 4-20#R (Guerriere and
  Piscataqua, 1867); 2-100#R 18-9" 1-60#R 2-20#R (Guerriere, California, 1870); none (Antietam)
Rig: Ship

Machinery: 1010 IHP; 2 horizontal, back-acting engines, 60" x 36", 1 screw
Speed: 12 kts.
Complement: 325

	Hull	Machinery	Laid down	Launched	Commiss'd	Disposition
GUERRIERE	Boston	Globe	1864	9 Sep 65	21 May 67	Sold 12 Dec 72
KEWAYDIN	Boston	Loring	1865	No	No	Broken up on ways 1884
PISCATAQUA	Portsmouth	Woodruff & Beach	1864	11 Jun 66	21 Oct 67	Sold Feb 77
MINNETONKA	Portsmouth	Woodruff & Beach	1865	3 Jul 67	12 Dec 70	Sold May 75
ILLINOIS	Portsmouth	Corliss	1865	No	No	Broken up on ways Feb 72
ANTIETAM	Philadelphia	Morris, Towne	1865	13 Nov 75	No	Sold 8 Sep 88
ONTARIO	New York	Etna	Jan 65	No	No	Sold 31 May 88
JAVA	New York	Etna	1865	No	No	Broken up on ways 1884.

Notes: Twenty engines for this and the Hassalo and Contoocook classes were ordered between 25 Oct 63 and 13 Nov 63 and all twenty ships were named on 5 Nov 63. Sixteen hulls were funded and twelve (including all the Guerrieres) were ordered (Antietam on 28 Jun 64). These "screw sloops with spar decks" were the second of three types of ocean-cruising ships ordered in 1863, the others being the Wampanoag and Contoocook types. Compared to the Wampanoags, these were described as "vessels with steam machinery of rather less power, but . . . much more heavily armed." Their armament and beam were similar to those of the large 1857 sloops (Lancaster, etc.) but their length and displacement were greatly increased in an effort to reach higher speeds. The design was further lengthened 12 1/2 feet in September 1864 to increase the armament. All were designed with vertical bows but had clipper bows fitted during construction. The engines were designed by Isherwood and the hulls by Delano. Work on all incomplete ships was suspended on 30 Nov 65. The engines of the Kewaydin and Antietam were completed and put in storage and those of the Illinois, Ontario, and Java were delivered incomplete in 1869. The unseasoned white oak and hackmatack hulls quickly deteriorated. The Delaware (ex Piscataqua) served as a quarantine vessel in 1872-73 and sank at her pier at New York in 1877. The Antietam was launched to clear her slip and was used as a store hulk 1876-82 without machinery or armament. The Ontario had a frame of live oak and was proposed for completion as late as 1884.
Renamings: Kewaydin, Piscataqua, Minnetonka, and Ontario to Pennsylvania, Delaware, California, and New York 15 May 69.

HASSALO class

Tonnage: 3365 tons
Dimensions: Unknown
Armament: Unknown
Rig: Unknown

Machinery: Unknown
Speed: Unknown
Complement: Unknown

	Hull	Machinery	Laid down	Launched	Commiss'd	Disposition
HASSALO	Not ord.	S.Brooklyn	No	No	No	Cancelled 1866
WATAUGA	Not ord.	S.Brooklyn	No	No	No	Cancelled 1866.

Notes: The engines were ordered for these Guerriere-class ships on 25 Oct 63. The ships were named on 5 Nov 63 but the hulls were never ordered. During 1864 it was decided that two ships of the Guerriere class (probably these two) should be "in the space occupied by the guns, covered with a thin iron armor to resist shells, but not of sufficient weight to interfere with the nautical qualities of the vessels." This apparently raised their measurement tonnage to 3365 tons from the 3177 tons of the Guerriere class. These and other Civil War ships for which hulls had not been ordered were dropped from the Navy Register after funds requested for them failed to materialize in 1866. The engines of one, probably the Watauga, were delivered incomplete in 1869 and the engines for the other were completed and put in storage.

Steam Sloops (2nd and 3rd rates)

1835

FULTON

Displacement: 1011 tons
Dimensions: 181'6"(b.p.) x 34'10" x 13'(max)
Armament: 8-42# 1-24#; 4-32# (1837); 4-8" 2-32# (1840); 1-8" 4-32# (1852); 4-32# (1854); 2-9" (1858); 1-11" 4-9" (1859)
Rig: Schooner

Machinery: 221 NHP, 600 IHP; 2 horizontal, condensing engines, 50" x 9', side wheels
Speed: 12 kts.
Complement: 130

	Hull	Machinery	Laid down	Launched	Commiss'd	Disposition
FULTON	New York	West Pt.	1835	18 May 37	13 Dec 37	Captured by Confederates with Pensacola Navy Yard 12 Jan 61.

Notes: In 1835 the Secretary of the Navy used the unrepealed authorization of 29 Apr 16 for steam batteries to build a steamer "of a form and size best calculated for the defense of our ports and harbors." The hull plans closely followed a design for a 430-ton steam battery drafted by Samuel Humphreys in September 1831 except that they were lengthened 55'. The freeboard at the ends was low to allow strong end-on gunfire. The engines, mounted horizontally on deck, were designed by Charles H. Haswell, who soon became the Navy's first chief engineer. They produced high speeds (up to 16 knots being reported). The ship was satisfactory in coastal waters but had insufficient seakeeping qualities and coal endurance for ocean work and was too small for her original armament. She was laid up in 1842.
    The Fulton was rebuilt at New York in 1851, being relaunched on 30 Aug 51 and commissioned on 25 Jan 52. Samuel Humphreys' old hull was retained but was completely reshaped with a conventional sheer and a knee bow. The heavy bulwarks of the original ship were razeed. New 50" x 10'4" single-cylinder inclined condensing engines of 117 NHP and 500 AHP were designed by Charles B. Stuart and built by Dunham. The ship remained fast and handled well. She ran aground near Pensacola in 1859 and was being repaired when she was captured. She was never used by the Confederates and was destroyed by them prior to the evacuation of the Pensacola Yard 10 May 62.

1837

PRINCETON

Displacement: 954 tons
Dimensions: 156'6"(b.p.) x 30'6" x 19'11"(max)
Armament: 6-42#c; 2-12" 12-42#c (1844); 1-12" 4-32#c (1844); 1-8" 12-42#c (1845); 1-8" 8-42#c (1847)
Rig: Ship.

Machinery: 204 NHP, 195 IHP; 2 semi-cylinder engines with vibrating pistons, 57.5" x 36", 1 screw
Speed: 10 kts.
Complement: 166

	Hull	Machinery	Laid down	Launched	Commiss'd	Disposition
PRINCETON	Phila-delphia	Merrick & Towne	20 Oct 42	7 Sep 43	16 Oct 43	Broken up Oct 49.

Notes: Built as one of the six sloops of war authorized on 3 Mar 37, the others being sailing ships of the Dale class. She was the first screw warship and the first warship to burn anthracite coal. John Ericsson designed the machinery. He and Robert F. Stockton provided the specifications for the hull and John Lenthall produced the detailed plans. One of the two 12" shell guns was built in England for Ericsson and named "Oregon," the other was built in America for Stockton and named "Peacemaker." The "Peacemaker" exploded on 28 Feb 44 with heavy loss of life. Designed as a sailing ship with auxiliary steam power, she was fast under sail but averaged only 7.6 knots under steam alone. Her machinery was reliable but she had boiler problems and in 1849 her white oak hull was found to be too rotten to repair.

1839

UNION

Tonnage: 956 tons
Dimensions: 184'6"(d) x 33'6" x 12'6"
Armament: 4-8"
Rig: 3-masted schooner

Machinery: 159 NHP, 300 AHP; 2 horizontal high-pressure non-condensing engines, 28" x 48", 2 Hunter wheels
Speed: 5 kts.
Complement: 120

	Hull	Machinery	Laid down	Launched	Commiss'd	Disposition
UNION	Norfolk	Washington	1841	12 May 42	28 Nov 42	Sold 1858.

Notes: Authorized 3 Mar 39. The hull was designed by Francis Grice and Lt. William W. Hunter, USN; the machinery and its horizontal paddle wheels by Hunter and William M. Ellis. The Hunter wheels proved an abject failure even after reengining in 1846 with 108 NHP horizontal low-pressure condensing engines. In 1848 the engines were removed and in 1849 the hull was put into use as a receiving ship.

1844

ALLEGHANY

Tonnage: 989 tons
Dimensions: 185'(d) x 33'4" x 14'8"
Armament: 2-8"; 2-8" 8-32# (1852); 6-32# (1863)
Rig: Bark

Machinery: 243 NHP, 560 IHP; 2 horizontal, low-pressure, condensing engines, 60" x 48", 2 Hunter wheels
Speed: 6 kts.
Complement: 190

	Hull	Machinery	Laid down	Launched	Commiss'd	Disposition
ALLEGHANY	Stackhouse & Tomlinson		1844	22 Feb 47	22 Feb 47	Sold 15 May 69.

Notes: Authorized 15 Jun 44. William W. Hunter designed the hull and he and C. H. Haswell designed the engines. The ship left Pittsburgh one day after launch and completed fitting out at the Memphis navy yard on 4 Jun 47. She was a failure because of the Hunter wheels and the weakness of her iron hull, which was built to the standards of western river boats. She was rebuilt at the Washington Navy Yard in 1852 as a screw steamer using the old engines converted to a back-acting model by Mehaffy on plans by Benjamin F. Isherwood. She again failed because of boiler problems and the weakness of the hull and engine foundations. She served as a receiving ship 1856-68.

1847

SARANAC

Displacement: 2100 tons
Dimensions: 210'(b.p.) x 37'9"(e), 60'(o.g.) x 17'4"(max)
Armament: 6-8"; 9-8" (1854); 9-8" 2-20#R (1862); 1-11" 8-8" 2-20#R (1864); 1-11" 8-8" 2-30#R (1865); 1-11" 10-8" (1871)
Rig: Bark.

Machinery: 318 NHP, 570 IHP; 2 inclined, direct-acting, condensing engines, 60" x 9', side wheels
Speed: 10 kts.
Complement: 228

	Hull	Machinery	Laid down	Launched	Commiss'd	Disposition
SARANAC	Portsmouth	Coney	May 47	14 Nov 48	12 Oct 50	Wrecked in Seymour Narrows, B.C., 18 Jun 75.

Notes: Authorized 3 Mar 47. 2nd rate during Civil War. Her hull was designed by Samuel Hartt and her engines were designed by Charles W. Copeland as smaller versions of those of the Susquehanna. She was a very graceful vessel and her machinery was very reliable. She began her first trial trip on 10 Apr 50.

SAN JACINTO

Displacement: 2150 tons
Dimensions: 210'(b.p.) x 37'9"(e) x 17'3"
Armament: 6-8"; 10-8" (1854); 11-8" 2-32# (1855); 15-8"
  (1859); 1-11" 10-9" (1862); 1-100#R 10-9" 1-20#R (1863)
Rig: Bark

Machinery: 268 NHP, 500 AHP; 2
  horizontal "square" engines, 62.5"
  x 4.2', 1 screw
Speed: 10 kts.
Complement: 235

	Hull	Machinery	Laid down	Launched	Commiss'd	Disposition
SAN JACINTO	New York	Merrick & Sons	Aug 47	16 Apr 50	16 Dec 51	Wrecked in Bahama Is. 1 Jan 65.

Notes: Authorized 3 Mar 47. 2nd rate during Civil War. Samuel Hartt's hull plans for the Saranac were also used for the San Jacinto in order to test the relative merits of side wheel and screw propulsion. Charles H. Haswell designed the original engines. The San Jacinto did not prove as successful as her paddle sister since the space allotted for machinery was too restructed to permit the fitting of an adequate engine. As built, the off-center propeller shaft projected past the rudder, which divided into two parts to clear the shaft. The shaft was repositioned closer to the sternpost and a more normal rudder was installed before the ship entered service. In 1854 she received a centerline propeller shaft and new horizontal geared 70" x 48" condensing engines designed and built by Merrick. Her wreck was sold 17 May 71 at Nassau.

1851

PRINCETON

Displacement: 1370 tons
Dimensions: 177'6"(wl.) x 32'6" x 19'2"
Armament: 4-8" 6-32#
Rig: Bark

Machinery: 204 NHP, 195 AHP; 2 semi-
  cylinder, condensing engines, 57.5"
  x 36", 1 screw
Speed: 10 kts.
Complement: 190

	Hull	Machinery	Laid down	Launched	Commiss'd	Disposition
PRINCETON	Boston	Murray & Hazlehurst	Jun 51	29 Oct 51	18 May 52	Sold 9 Oct 66.

Notes: Officially considered the old Princeton rebuilt. Although the Ericsson engines of the old ship were retained and rebuilt by Murray, she had a new hull designed by Samuel Pook. She was plagued with boiler trouble and spent 1857-1866 as a receiving ship.

1857

LANCASTER

Displacement: 3290 tons
Dimensions: 235'8"(b.p.) x 46' x 18'6"
Armament: 2-11" 20-9"; 2-11" 24-9" 2-30#R (1863); 2-11" 20-9"
  (1869); 10-8"R 2-20#BLR (1881); 10-8"R (1888); 10-5"/40 BLR
  2-5"/30BLR (1895); 10-5"BLR (1899); 9-5"BLR (1905);
  10-5"BLR (1908)

Rig: Ship
Machinery: 810 IHP; 2 direct-acting,
  double piston-rod engines, 61" x
  33", 1 screw
Speed: 9.5 kts.
Complement: 300

	Hull	Machinery	Laid down	Launched	Commiss'd	Disposition
LANCASTER	Phila-delphia	Reaney & Neafie	Dec 57	20 Oct 58	12 May 59	Transferred to Treasury Dept. 29 May 1933.

Notes: Authorized 3 Mar 57. 2nd rate. The five ships in this program were successors to the large sail spar-deck corvettes converted from small frigates (the Cumberland, Macedonian, and Constellation), which had their batteries on a single deck except for pivoted shell guns on the forecastle and quarterdeck. The new ships were also a response to similar foreign ships, notably the British Cadmus and Pearl classes. The Lancaster was the only one of the five designed with a complete spar deck, although three of the others received them in postwar refits. As built she was not considered weatherly and steered poorly. In 1879-80 she was completely rebuilt at Portsmouth Navy Yard with a ram bow and with the 60" x 36" engines originally built for the Antietam. In this guise she resembled the newer Trenton, whose design had been based on her lines. She was to have been fitted in 1890 as a gunnery ship with 1-8"BLR 2-6"BLR 2-4"BLR but this project was cancelled. In 1896 she was fitted with a torpedo tube. From 1900 to 1904 she served as a training vessel and from 1904 to 1913 as a receiving ship. She was loaned to the Marine Hospital Service on 1 Feb 13 and served as a quarantine ship with them 1913-15 and with the Public Health Service 1915-30. In June 1933 the Public Health Service had her towed to sea and sunk.

PENSACOLA

Displacement: 3000 tons
Dimensions: 230'8"(b.p.) x 44'5" x 18'7"(mean)
Armament: 1-11" 18-9"; 1-11" 16-9" (1861); 22-9" 1-42#R
  (1861); 1-11" 1-100#R 22-9" (1862); 1-11" 1-100#R 20-9"
  (1863); 18-9" 2-60#R (1866); 2-11" 18-9" 2-60#R (1871);
  12-9" 2-80#BLR 2-60#BLR 2-20#BLR (1885); none (1893);
  1-4"BLR (1901)

Rig: Ship
Machinery: 1165 HP; 4-cylinder
  Dickerson engine, 62" x 34", 1
  screw
Speed: 9.5 kts.
Complement: 269

	Hull	Machinery	Laid down	Launched	Commiss'd	Disposition
PENSACOLA	Pensacola	Washington	Mar 58	15 Aug 59	16 Sep 61	Sold 19 Feb 1912.

Notes: Authorized 3 Mar 57. 2nd rate. John Lenthall designed the hull. She was in commission
between 5 Dec 59 and 31 Jan 60 for the transit to the Washington Navy Yard where her engines were
installed. These, designed by Edward N. Dickerson (a lawyer with political connections) and Frederick
E. Sickels, were a complete failure, and on 24 Sep 64 the Secretary of the Navy ordered the
horizontal, back-acting, 60" x 36" Isherwood engines intended for the Wanaloset to be installed in
their place. The Pensacola worked well under sail but was a weaker vessel than her sisters. In 1871
she received a complete spar deck, and in 1878 she received boilers and twin funnels from the Benicia.
She served as a receiving ship 1898-1911.

BROOKLYN

Displacement: 2686 tons
Dimensions: 233'(wl.) x 43' x 16'3"
Armament: 1-10" 20-9"; 22-9" (1861); 2-100#R 20-9" 2-60#R
  (1863); 18-9" 2-60#R (1865); 2-11" 2-100#R 16-9" (1870);
  2-100#R 16-9" 1-20#R (1874); 1-8"R 12-9" 1-60#BLR 2-20#BLR
  (1881)

Rig: Ship
Machinery: 705 HP; 2 horizontal,
  direct-acting, cross-head engines,
  61" x 33", 1 screw
Speed: 9.5 kts.
Complement: 335

	Hull	Machinery	Laid down	Launched	Commiss'd	Disposition
BROOKLYN	Wester-velt	Fulton IrWks	1857	27 Jul 58	26 Jan 59	Sold 25 Mar 91.

Notes: Authorized 3 Mar 57. 2nd rate. She was a good sailer and considered the best of the group
although lightly built. She was fitted with a complete spar deck in 1869-70 on orders from Admiral
Porter, but this was removed in 1879-81.

HARTFORD

Displacement: 2550 tons
Dimensions: 225'(b.p.) x 44'(e) x 17'2"
Armament: 16-9"; 20-9" 2-20#R (1862); 22-9" 2-20#R (1862);
  24-9" 1-45#R 2-30#R (1863); 2-100#R 18-9" 1-30#R (1864);
  2-11" 16-9" 2-20#R (1872); 1-8"R 12-9" 1-60#BLR 2-20#BLR
  (1882); 13-5"BLR (1894); 9-5"BLR (1905)

Rig: Ship
Machinery: 696 NHP; 2 horizontal,
  double piston-rod engines, 62" x
  34", 1 screw
Speed: 9.5 kts.
Complement: 310

	Hull	Machinery	Laid down	Launched	Commiss'd	Disposition
HARTFORD	Boston	Loring	1 Jan 58	22 Nov 58	27 May 59	Foundered at Norfolk 20 Nov 1956.

Notes: Authorized 3 Mar 57. 2nd rate. B. F. Delano designed the hull. The Hartford was considered a
strong ship which steered easily. She was fitted with a complete spar deck in 1871-72, but this was
removed in 1880-82. In 1880 she was fitted with new compound engines converted from the 60" x 36"
engines originally built for the Kewaydin. In 1887 she was rerigged as a bark and fitted as a
training vessel. In 1894-99 she underwent a complete reconstruction at Mare Island in which she was
reengined for a second time with 2000 HP compound machinery. She served as a training ship until 1912
and as a receiving and station ship between 1912 and 1926. Her remains were sold in July 1957.
Reclassification: She was designated "unclassified" (IX-13) on 17 Jul 20.

RICHMOND

Displacement: 2604 tons
Dimensions: 225'(b.p.) x 42'6" x 17'5"
Armament: 16-9"; 20-9" 1-100#R 1-30#R (1862); 1-100#R 18-9"
  1-30#R (1863); 1-100#R 18-9" 2-30#R (1864); 2-100#R 12-9"
  1-30#R (1869); 2-100#R 12-9" 1-20#R (1872); 1-8"R 12-9"
  1-60#BLR 2-20#BLR (1878); none (1897)

Rig: Ship
Machinery: 1078 HP; 2 horizontal,
  back-acting engines, 58" x 36", 1
  screw
Speed: 9.5 kts.
Complement: 260

	Hull	Machinery	Laid down	Launched	Commiss'd	Disposition
RICHMOND	Norfolk	Washington	27 Jul 58	26 Jan 60	by 13 Oct 1860	Sold 23 Jul 1919.

Notes: Authorized 3 Mar 57. 2nd rate. Samuel T. Hartt designed the hull. The original engines, designed by Samuel Archbold, did not prove a success because of their Sickels valve gear mechanism, and on 22 Aug 65 the Secretary of the Navy ordered their replacement by a set of 60" x 36" Isherwood engines built at the Washington Navy Yard in 1864-65. The Richmond served as a training vessel 1891-93 and a receiving ship 1895-1919.

1858

MOHICAN class

Displacement: 1461 tons
Dimensions: 198'6"(b.p.) x 33'10"(e) x 15'9"(max)
Armament: Mohican--2-11" 4-32#; 2-11" 1-100#R 4-32# (1862);
  1-100#R 4-9" 2-32# 2-30#R (1864); 1-100#R 6-9" 2-30#R
  (1864); 4-9" 1-60#R 2-30#R (1866); 1-11" 4-9" 1-60#R 1-20#R
  (1869);
  Kearsarge--2-11" 4-32# 1-28#R; 2-11" 4-32# 1-30#R (1862);
  2-11" 4-9" 2-20#R (1873); 2-8"R 4-9" 1-60#BLR (1879); 2-8"R
  4-9" 1-60#BLR 2-20#BLR (1890)

Rig: Bark
Machinery: 842 IHP; 2 horizontal, back-acting engines, 54" x 30", 1 screw
Speed: 11 kts.
Complement: 160

	Hull	Machinery	Laid down	Launched	Commiss'd	Disposition
MOHICAN	Portsmouth	Woodruff & Beach	Aug 58	15 Feb 59	29 Nov 59	Broken up 1873
KEARSARGE	Portsmouth	Woodruff & Beach	May 61	11 Sep 61	24 Jan 62	Wrecked on Roncador Reef, Caribbean, 2 Feb 94.

Notes: Authorized 12 Jun 58 (Mohican) and 21 Feb 61 (Kearsarge). The 1858 act provided for eight ships: four screw sloops with a 13-foot draft, three with a 10-foot draft, and one side-wheel steamer (the Saginaw). Sisters for three of the 13-foot draft ships were ordered in 1861. All seven screw ships featured an armament of one or two large shell guns on pivots in the waist with a broadside armament limited to a few 32# guns. They also had full steam power for high speed and a reduced sail rig. To carry the heavy guns and machinery on a limited draft, the hulls had to be relatively large. The Mohican class was designed by William L. Hanscom. The repeat ship, the famous Kearsarge, was laid down on a marine railway, transferred to a drydock 11 Sep 61, and put afloat 5 Oct 61. She was reengined in 1887 with 750 HP engines taken out of the Nantasket. The Mohican sank at her moorings at Mare Island in 1872.

IROQUOIS class

Displacement: 1488 tons
Dimensions: 198'10"(b.p.) x 33'10"(e) x 13'
Armament: Iroquois--2-11" 4-32#; 2-11" 1-50#R 4-32# (1862);
  1-100#R 2-9" 1-60#R 4-32# (1864); 1-100#R 1-9" 1-60#R 2-32#
  (1864); 1-100#R 4-9" 1-60#R (1867); 2-11" 4-9" 3-20#R
  (1871); 1-11" 1-8"R 4-8" 1-30#R (1882); 2-8"R 1-60#BLR
  4-60#R (1889); none (1893);
  Wachusett--2-11" 4-32# 2-30#R 1-20#R; 3-100#R 4-32# 2-30#R
  (1864); 2-11" 4-9" 3-20#R (1871); 2-11" 4-9" 1-60#R (1879);
  Oneida--2-9" 4-32# 3-30#R; 2-11" 6-8" 1-30#R (1864); 1-11"
  6-32# 1-30#R (1867)

Rig: Bark (Iroquois), Schooner (others)
Machinery: Wachusett--2 horizontal, back-acting steeple engines, 50" x 30", 1 screw;
  others--813 IHP; 2 horizontal, back-acting engines, 54" x 28", 1 screw
Speed: 11 kts.
Complement: 123

	Hull	Machinery	Laid down	Launched	Commiss'd	Disposition
IROQUOIS	New York	Fulton IrWks	Aug 58	12 Apr 59	24 Nov 59	Sold 5 Oct 1910
WACHUSETT	Boston	Morgan	Jun 61	10 Oct 61	3 Mar 62	Sold 30 Jul 87
ONEIDA	New York	Murphy	10 Jun 61	20 Nov 61	28 Feb 62	Sunk in collision off Yokohama, Japan, 24 Jan 70.

Notes: Authorized 12 Jun 58 (Iroquois) and 21 Feb 61 (Wachusett). The Oneida was ordered 6 Jun 61. The hulls were designed by B. F. Delano and the machinery of the Iroquois by Thomas Main. The Oneida was an exact copy of the Iroquois but the Wachusett had engines which duplicated those of the Seminole. The Iroquois originally had a hoisting screw, unlike the other 13-foot draft sloops which had uncoupling propellers. The Oneida may originally have had a vertical stem and a schooner rig. The Iroquois was transferred to the Marine Hospital Service in May 1892, returned in 1898, and transferred again in 1899. She was wrecked at Port Townshend, Wash., 26 Aug 10. The wreck of the Oneida was sold 9 Oct 72.
Renaming: Iroquois to Ionie 30 Nov 04.

A *Wyoming*-class screw sloop during the Civil War. (NH 45368)

The screw sloop *Ticonderoga* at Venice between 1866 and 1869. (NH 45373)

WYOMING class

Displacement: 1457 tons
Dimensions: 198'6"(b.p.) x 33'2" x 14'10"(max)
Armament: Wyoming--2-11" 4-32#; 2-11" 1-60#R 3-32# (1865);
    2-11" 4-9" 1-60#R 2-20#R (1871); 2-8"R 4-9" 1-60#R (1878);
    1-8"R 1-80#BLR 1-60#BLR 8-32# 2-20#R (1884);
    Tuscarora--1-11" 2-32#; 2-11" 6-32# 1-30#R (1861); 1-11"
    1-100#R 4-8" 2-30#R (1863); 1-11" 1-100#R 6-8" 2-30#R
    (1863); 2-11" 4-9" 2-20#R (1872); 4-9" 1-60#R (1878);
    1-60#R (1880)

Rig: Bark.
Machinery: 717 IHP; 2 horizontal,
    direct-acting engines, 50" x 30", 1
    screw
Speed: 11 kts.
Complement: 198

	Hull	Machinery	Laid down	Launched	Commiss'd	Disposition
WYOMING	Phila-delphia	Merrick & Sons	Jul 58	19 Jan 59	Oct 59	Sold 9 May 92
TUSCARORA	Phila-delphia	Merrick & Sons	27 Jun 61	24 Aug 61	5 Dec 61	Sold 20 Nov 83.

Notes: Authorized 12 Jun 58 (Wyoming) and 21 Feb 61 (Tuscarora). The hull design was by Francis Grice. Good sea boats which were considered strongly built and easy to steer. The Wyoming served as a training vessel 1882-91.

DACOTAH

Displacement: 1369 tons
Dimensions: 198'5"(b.p.) x 32'9" x 14'8"
Armament: 2-11" 4-32#; 1-10" 1-100#R 4-32# (1862); 1-10"
    1-100#R 4-32# 1-30#R (1863)
Rig: Bark

Machinery: 873 NHP; 2 horizontal,
    cross-head, geared engines, 63" x
    36", 1 screw
Speed: 11 kts.
Complement: 147

	Hull	Machinery	Laid down	Launched	Commiss'd	Disposition
DACOTAH	Norfolk	Murray & Hazlehurst	1858	23 Mar 59	1 May 60	Sold 30 May 73.

Notes: Authorized 12 Jun 58. She was designed by S. T. Hartt. She rolled badly until fitted with bilge keels in 1862. In 1870 her engines were removed and three years later she foundered while at her mooring. Her name was sometimes spelled Dakota or Dakotah.

PAWNEE

Displacement: 1533 tons
Dimensions: 233'(oa.), 221'6"(b.p.) x 47' x 11'(mean)
Armament: 4-11"; 8-9" (1860); 1-100#R 8-9" 1-50#R (1863);
    1-100#R 10-9" 1-50#R (1864); 1-100#R 12-9" 1-50#R (1864);
    10-9" 2-60#R (1867)
Rig: Bark

Machinery: 590 IHP; 2 horizontal,
    direct-acting, geared engines, 65"
    x 36", 2 screws
Speed: 10 kts.
Complement: 151

	Hull	Machinery	Laid down	Launched	Commiss'd	Disposition
PAWNEE	Phila-delphia	Reaney & Neafie	Oct 58	8 Oct 59	11 Jun 60	Sold 3 May 84.

Notes: Authorized 12 Jun 58, the largest of the three ships in this act which were to have a 10-foot draft. 2nd rate. She was designed by John W. Griffiths, a famed clipper ship designer who also created innovative shallow-draft merchant ships. He undertook to design a screw steamer carrying 4-11" pivot guns on a 10' draft. To carry the weight of the guns, he produced a hull with a greater length and beam than any of the other 1858 sloops and filled with other unusual design features, including twin screws. The ship had a much reduced rig and no bowsprit. She was a notable sea boat but her machinery was poorly built. In 1870 the cost of repairing her engines was considered excessive and they were removed. The hull was used as a hospital and receiving ship 1871-82.

NARRAGANSETT

Displacement: 1235 tons
Dimensions: 188' x 30'2" x 11'6"
Armament: 1-11" 4-32#; 1-60#R 4-32# (1869); 1-9" 4-32# 2-20#R
    (1870)
Rig: Bark

Machinery: 250 HP; 2 horizontal,
    direct-acting engines, 48" x 28", 1
    screw
Speed: 11 kts.
Complement: 120

	Hull	Machinery	Laid down	Launched	Commiss'd	Disposition
NARRAGANSETT	Boston	Boston Loco	Jul 58	15 Feb 59	29 Oct 59	Sold 20 Nov 83.

Notes: Authorized 12 Jun 58 as one of three sloops with a 10-foot draft. She was built to a conventional design by E. H. Delano with hull lines similar to those of the Iroquois.

SEMINOLE

Displacement: 1230 tons
Dimensions: 188' x 30'6" x ca. 11'
Armament: 1-11" 4-32#; 1-11" 6-32# 1-30#R (1863); 1-11" 6-32#
  1-20#R (1869)
Rig: Bark

Machinery: 2 horizontal, back-acting
  steeple engines, 50" x 30", 1 screw
Speed: 11 kts.
Complement: 120

	Hull	Machinery	Laid down	Launched	Commiss'd	Disposition
SEMINOLE	Pensacola	Morgan	Jul 58	25 Jun 59	25 Apr 60	Sold 20 Jul 70.

Notes: Authorized 12 Jun 58 as one of three sloops with a 10-foot draft. Her hull was designed by John L. Porter and her machinery was designed by T. F. Rowland. Her white oak hull was built of poor timber. She was rebuilt as a merchant ship in 1871.

1861

OSSIPEE class

Displacement: 1934 tons
Dimensions: 205'(b.p.) x 38'(e) x 16'7"(max)
Armament: Ossipee--1-11" 1-100#R 6-32# 3-30#R; 1-11" 2-9"
  1-60#R (1866); 1-11" 6-9" 1-60#R (1870); 1-8"R 6-9"
  1-60#BLR (1884);
  Juniata--1-11" 1-100#R 4-30#R; 1-100#R 6-8" 2-30#R (1864);
  1-100#R 10-8" 2-30#R (1864); 2-9" 10-8" 2-30#R (1865);
  1-11" 6-9" 1-60#R (1869); 1-8"R 6-9" 1-60#BLR 2-20#BLR
  (1882);
  Adirondack--2-11" 4-32#
  Housatonic--1-11" 1-100#R 2-32# 3-30#R; 1-11" 1-100#R
  4-32#R 3-30#R (1863)

Rig: Bark
Machinery: 1304 IHP; 2 horizontal,
  back-acting engines, 42" x 30", 1
  screw
Speed: 11.5 kts.
Complement: 160

	Hull	Machinery	Laid down	Launched	Commiss'd	Disposition
OSSIPEE	Portsmouth	Reliance	6 Jun 61	16 Nov 61	6 Nov 62	Sold 25 Mar 91
JUNIATA	Philadelphia	Pusey & Jones	Jun 61	20 Mar 62	4 Dec 62	Sold 25 Mar 91
ADIRONDACK	New York	Novelty	1861	22 Feb 62	Jun 62	Wrecked on Man of War Cay, Bahamas, 23 Aug 62
HOUSATONIC	Boston	Globe	1861	20 Nov 61	29 Aug 62	Torpedoed by CSS H. L. Hunley off Charleston, S.C., 17 Feb 64.

Notes: Authorized 21 Feb 61. 2nd rates. This act included seven "steam screw sloops of war of the 2nd class of not over 14' draft" for ocean service. To expedite construction, three were built as repeats of the Mohican, Iroquois, and Wyoming. The others were given increased tonnage, beam, and draft. John Lenthall's hull plans and Benjamin F. Isherwood's machinery design were used for all four ships. The wreck of the Housatonic was raised and sold in 1891.

LACKAWANNA class

Displacement: 2526 tons
Dimensions: 237'(s.d.), 232'(b.p.) x 38'2"(e) x 16'6"(max)
Armament: Lackawanna--1-200#R 2-11" 4-9" 1-50#R; 1-150#R
  2-11" 4-9" 1-50#R (1863); 1-150#R 2-11" 4-9" 1-60#R (1865);
  2-11" 2-9" 1-60#R (1866); 2-11" 8-9" 2-20#R (1872); 2-11"
  8-9" 1-60#R (1875); 2-11" 6-9" 1-60#R 2-20#R (1879);
  Ticonderoga: 1-150#R 6-9" 1-60#R; 1-150#R 6-9" 1-50#R
  (1863); 1-150#R 2-11" 4-9" 1-50#R (1863); 1-100#R 12-9"
  1-30#R (1863); 1-100#R 10-9" 1-30#R (1864); 10-9" 1-30#R
  (1865); 12-9" 1-50#R (1865); 2-11" 2-9" 1-60#R (1865);
  2-11" 8-9" 1-60#R 2-20#R (1871); 2-8"R 6-9" 1-60#BLR
  2-20#BLR (1878)

Rig: Barkentine
Machinery: 1304 IHP; 2 horizontal,
  back-acting engines, 42" x 30", 1
  screw
Speed: 11.5 kts.
Complement: 205

	Hull	Machinery	Laid down	Launched	Commiss'd	Disposition
LACKAWANNA	New York	Allaire	1862	9 Aug 62	8 Jan 63	Sold 30 Jul 87
TICONDEROGA	New York	Morgan	1862	16 Oct 62	12 May 63	Sold 5 Aug 87.

Notes: Ordered ca. Oct 61. 2nd rates. In August 1861 a board examined plans for "fast screw steamers." It decided on an Ossipee type ship lengthened to carry a third large pivot gun. The ships were to have no broadside guns. The engines in all six were designed by Benjamin F. Isherwood and were identical to those in the Ossipee. The hulls of the Lackawanna pair differed only slightly from each other; their plans were drawn by B. F. Delano under Lenthall's direction. The two ships received bowsprits in 1865-66 and clipper bows in their 1869-72 refits.

SACRAMENTO

Displacement: 2100 tons
Dimensions: 229'6"(b.p.) x 38' x 8'10"(light)
Armament: 1-150#R 2-11" 1-30#R; 2-11" 2-9" 1-60#R (1864);
  3-100#R 6-8" 1-30#R (1864); 2-11" 2-9" 1-60#R (1865)

Rig: Barkentine
Machinery: 1304 IHP; 2 horizontal,
  back-acting engines, 42" x 30", 1
  screw
Speed: 11.5 kts.
Complement: 161

	Hull	Machinery	Laid down	Launched	Commiss'd	Disposition
SACRAMENTO	Ports-mouth	Taunton	1861	28 Apr 62	7 Jan 63	Wrecked in Godaveri R., India, 19 Jun 67.

Notes: Ordered ca. Oct 61. 2nd rates. John Lenthall designed the hull and Benjamin F. Isherwood the engines.

MONONGAHELA class

Displacement: 2078 (Monongahela), 2030 (Shenandoah) tons
Dimensions: 225'(b.p.) x 38'(Monongahela, e),
  38'4"(Shenandoah, e) x 15'1"
Armament: Monongahela--1-200#R 2-11"; 1-150#R 2-11" 5-32#
  (1863); 2-11" 2-9" 1-60#R (1865); 2-11" 8-9" 1-60#R (1873);
  2-8"R 8-9" 1-60#R 2-20#R (1877); 2-8" (1883); 10-8" (1890);
  6-8" (1893); 4-8" (1895); 6-4"BLR (1900);
  Shenandoah--1-150#R 2-11" 1-30#R; 2-11" 2-9" 1-60#R (1865);
  2-11" 8-9" 1-60#R 2-20#R (1870); 2-8"R 6-9" 1-60#R 2-20#R
  (1879)

Rig: Barkentine
Machinery: 1304 IHP; 2 horizontal,
  back-acting engines, 42" x 30", 1
  screw
Speed: 11.5 kts.
Complement: 176

	Hull	Machinery	Laid down	Launched	Commiss'd	Disposition
MONONGAHELA	Phila-delphia	Merrick & Sons	Dec 61	10 Jul 62	15 Jan 63	Burned, Guantanamo Bay, Cuba, 17 Mar 1908
SHENANDOAH	Phila-delphia	Merrick & Sons	1862	8 Dec 62	20 Jun 63	Sold 30 Jul 87.

Notes: Ordered 30 Oct 61. 2nd rates. The hull plans for these two ships, both drawn by H. Hoover under Lenthall's direction, were very similar, the Monongahela having slightly fuller lines amidships and more rake to the stern. The two ships had the same measurement tonnage, 1378 tons. Their hulls were strong and well built. The two ships received bowsprits in 1865 and clipper bows in refits between 1869 and 1873. The Shenandoah was reported to handle poorly under sails alone. The Monongahela was washed ashore in a tidal wave at St. Croix on 18 Nov 67 and was refloated on 11 May 68. Her machinery was removed in 1884 during conversion to a bark-rigged storeship at Mare Island Navy Yard. She later served as a ship-rigged training vessel 1892-1904 and thereafter as the Guantanamo station ship.

CANANDAIGUA

Displacement: 2030 tons
Dimensions: 226'(b.p.) x 38'9"(e) x 15'
Armament: 2-11" 1-8" 3-20#R; 1-150#R 2-11" 3-20#R (1862);
  1-150#R 2-11" 1-30#R 2-20#R (1864); 2-11" 2-9" 1-60#R
  (1865); 2-11" 8-9" 2-20#R (1872)

Rig: Ship
Machinery: 1304 IHP; 2 horizontal,
  back-acting engines, 42" x 30", 1
  screw
Speed: 11.5 kts.
Complement: 191

	Hull	Machinery	Laid down	Launched	Commiss'd	Disposition
CANANDAIGUA	Boston	Atlantic	Dec 61	28 Mar 62	1 Aug 62	Broken up 1884 at Norfolk.

Notes: Ordered ca. Oct 61. 2nd rate. She had the same Isherwood engines as the rest of the 1861 sloops. She was designed by W. L. Hanscom under Lenthall's direction. As built she had her forward pivot gun on a long forecastle deck and lacked the pivot port forward. She received a bowsprit in 1865 and a clipper bow in her 1869-72 refit.
Renamings: To Detroit 15 May 69 and back to Canandaigua 10 Aug 69.

1863

CONTOOCOOK class

Displacement: 3003 tons
Dimensions: 290'(b.p.) x 41'1"(e) x 17'6"(max)
Armament: 16-9" 1-60#R 2-20#R (design, 1864); 8-9" 1-60#R
  2-20#R (Contoocook, 1868); 14-9" 1-60#R (Albany ex
  Contoocook, Severn, Worcester, 1869-71); 14-9" 2-60#R
  (Congress, 1870)
Rig: Bark, later ship

Machinery: 1220 IHP; 2 horizontal,
  back-acting engines, 60" x 36", 1
  screw
Speed: 13 kts.
Complement: 250

	Hull	Machinery	Laid down	Launched	Commiss'd	Disposition
CONTOOCOOK	Ports-mouth	Provi-dence	1864	3 Dec 64	14 Mar 68	Sold 12 Dec 72
MANITOU	Boston	Woodruff & Beach	1864	25 Aug 66	27 Feb 71	Sold 27 Sep 83
MOSHOLU	New York	South Brooklyn	Oct 64	22 Dec 67	27 Aug 69	Sold 2 Mar 77
PUSHMATAHA	Phila-delphia	Morris, Towne	1865	17 Jul 68	4 Mar 70	Sold 27 Sep 83
ARAPAHO	Not ord.	Providence	No	No	No	Cancelled 1866
KEOSAUQUA	Not ord.	Etna	No	No	No	Cancelled 1866
MONDAMIN	Not ord.	Washington IrWks	No	No	No	Cancelled 1866
TAHGAYUTA	Not ord.	Washington IrWks	No	No	No	Cancelled 1866
WANALOSET	Not ord.	Hazlehurst & Wiegard	No	No	No	Cancelled 1866
WILLAMETTE	Not ord.	Poole & Hunt	No	No	No	Cancelled 1866.

Notes: The engines for this class were ordered between 25 Oct 63 and 13 Nov 63 and all ten ships were
named on 5 Nov 63. Four hulls were ordered later (Pushmataha on 23 Jun 64); the other hulls were
never ordered. 2nd rates. These "clipper screw sloops" were the third type of ocean-cruising ships
ordered in 1863, the others being the Wampanoag and Guerriere types. Compared to the Guerrieres,
these were described as vessels "of less size but with equal machinery and intended for greater
speed." Their hulls were designed by John Lenthall and their engines were identical to those of the
Guerriere class. The Albany (ex Contoocook) and Severn (ex Mosholu) were completed as designed
without spar decks, while the Congress (ex Pushmataha) and Worcester (ex Manotou) received them during
construction. The Severn and Worcester had quarter galleries; the Congress did not. All were
designed with vertical bows but received clipper bows before completion. They proved fast and handy
in service but decayed quickly because of the use of unseasoned white oak timbers. The Albany was
loaned to New York State 1870-72 for use as a hospital ship, and the Worcester served as a receiving
ship 1876-77. All of the engines were completed except those of the Keosauqua, which were delivered
incomplete in 1869. The engines of the Arapaho, Mondamin, and Tahgayuta were probably reassigned to
the Illinois, Java, and Ontario and put in storage.
Renamings: Contoocook, Manitou and Mosholu to Albany, Worcester and Severn respectively 15 May 69.
Pushmataha to Cambridge 15 May 69 and to Congress 10 Aug 69.

1864

ALGOMA class (1)

Tonnage: 1380 tons
Dimensions: Unknown
Armament: 12 guns
Rig: Unknown

Machinery: 2 horizontal, back-acting
  engines, 50" x 42", 1 screw
Speed: 12.5 kts. (designed)
Complement: Unknown

	Hull	Machinery	Laid down	Launched	Commiss'd	Disposition
ALGOMA	Not ord.	Boston	No	No	No	Cancelled 1866
MEREDOSIA	Not ord.	Boston	No	No	No	Cancelled 1866
TAGHKANIC	Not ord.	New York	No	No	No	Cancelled 1866
TALLADEGA	Not ord.	New York	No	No	No	Cancelled 1866
SERAPIS	Not ord.	Boston	No	No	No	Cancelled 1866
CONFIANCE	Not ord.	Boston	No	No	No	Cancelled 1866
PEACOCK	Not ord.	New York	No	No	No	Cancelled 1866
DETROIT	Not ord.	New York	No	No	No	Cancelled 1866.

Notes: Two engines for "fast vessels of a small class" were ordered from the Boston Navy Yard on 13 Jun 64, two more were ordered from the New York Navy Yard at about the same time, and two repeat engines were ordered from each yard on 2 Oct 64. The first four ships were given Indian names on 29 Jul 64 and the last four were named on 2 Oct 64 after ships defeated by American ships. 2nd rates. The ships would have been follow-ons for the smaller sloops serving on blockade duty. The engines were completed, but no hulls were ordered and no plans dated before 1867 have been located. All of the names disappeared from the Navy Register after funds requested for them failed to materialize in 1866. Four of the engines were used in the new Algoma class and four were converted to compound engines in the 1870s and used in Vandalia and Galena class sloops.

1867

ALGOMA class (2)

Displacement: 2394 tons. Tonnage: 1740 tons
Dimensions: 250'6"(b.p.) x 38'(e) x 17'5"(max)
Armament: Benicia (ex-Algoma)--1-11" 10-9" 1-60#R 2-20#R;
 Alaska--1-11" 10-9" 1-60#R 2-20#R; 1-8"R 10-9" 1-60#BLR
 2-20#BLR (1876);
 Plymouth (ex-Kenosha)--1-11" 6-8" 1-60#R; 1-11 8-9" 1-60#R
 2-20#R (1874);
 Omaha--1-11" 10-9" 1-60#R 2-20#R; 1-8"R 10-9" 1-60#BLR
 2-20#BLR (1885); none (1891)

Rig: Ship (Alaska); Bark (others)
Machinery: 1165 IHP; 2 horizontal,
 back-acting engines, 50" x 42", 1
 screw
Speed: 11.5 kts. (designed)
Complement: 291

	Hull	Machinery	Laid down	Launched	Commiss'd	Disposition
ALGOMA	Portsmouth	Boston	May 67	18 Aug 68	1 Dec 69	Sold 3 May 84
ALASKA	Boston	Boston	1867	31 Oct 68	7 Dec 69	Sold 20 Nov 83
KENOSHA	New York	New York	27 Jun 67	8 Aug 68	20 Jan 69	Broken up 1884 at Portsmouth
OMAHA	Philadelphia	New York	1867	10 Jun 69	12 Sep 72	Sold 17 Apr 1915.

Notes: Hulls ordered 29 Apr 67 (Algoma, Kenosha, Omaha, and probably Alaska). In November 1866 the Chief of the Bureau of Construction and Repair noted that the screw gunboats Resaca and Swatara had been found very efficient and recommended that the somewhat larger Algoma class for which engines were being built be commenced. He noted that they would be very efficient for foreign service in time of peace, "performing with greater economy all the services that could be rendered by larger vessels." In 1867 the Secretary of the Navy decided to build four of them to replace larger ships. Four of the Isherwood engines for the first Algoma class were used, but tonnage figures suggest that Lenthall's '1867 hull design was larger than the one envisioned in 1864. As built, the ships were longer than the Shenandoah group, had the same beam, and were slightly lighter because of finer lines and lighter construction. Their armament of one pivot and ten broadside guns reflected a shift away from the wartime reliance on small numbers of large pivot guns. The Omaha was fitted with torpedoes in 1872, rebuilt in 1880-84, and loaned to the Marine Hospital Service in 1893. The Benicia (ex Algoma) was rerigged as a ship in 1869.
Renamings: Algoma and Kenosha to Benicia and Plymouth respectively 15 May 69; Omaha to Astoria 15 May 69 and back to Omaha 10 Aug 69.

1872

VANDALIA

Displacement: 2033 tons
Dimensions: 216'(b.p.) x 39'(e) x 17'3"(mean)
Armament: 1-11" 6-9" 1-60#R; 1-8"R 6-9" 1-60#BLR (1881)
Rig: Bark

Machinery: 1132 IHP; 2 back-acting
 compound engines, 1 screw
Speed: 12 kts.
Complement: 215

	Hull	Machinery	Laid down	Launched	Commiss'd	Disposition
VANDALIA	Boston	Boston	1872	23 Oct 74	10 Jan 76	Wrecked at Apia, Samoa, 16 Mar 89.

Notes: Officially considered to be the earlier Vandalia rebuilt. The hull was designed by W. L. Hanscom and the engines were converted from ones built for a cancelled Algoma class sloop. Compared to Civil War cruising ships, the ones built in the 1870s had more beam in proportion to length to carry heavier broadside armaments and to stand up well under canvas on long cruises.

SWATARA class

Displacement: 1900 tons
Dimensions: 216'(b.p.) x 37'(e) x 18'(max)
Armament: Swatara--1-60#R; 1-11" 6-9" 1-60#R (1875); 1-8"R
  6-9" 1-60#R (1879); 1-8"R 6-9" 1-60#BLR 2-20#BLR (1886);
  Marion--1-11" 6-9" 1-60#R 1-50#R; 1-8"R 6-9" 1-60#BLR
  2-20#BLR (1884); 1-8"R 6-9" 1-60#BLR (1887); 1-8"R 6-9"
  1-60#BLR 2-20#BLR (1891); none (1900);
  Quinnebaug--1-8"R 6-9" 1-60#BLR;
  Galena--1-8"R 6-9" 1-60#BLR 2-20#BLR; 1-8"R 6-9" 1-60#BLR
  (1890);
  Mohican--1-8"R 6-9" 1-60#BLR; 1-8"R 8-9" 1-60#BLR 2-20#BLR
  (1888); 8-9" 1-60#BLR (1898); 6-4"BLR (1899); 4-6# (1912)

Rig: Bark (Marion, Mohican), ship
  (others)
Machinery: 1132 IHP; 2 back-acting
  compound engines, 1 screw
Speed: 12 kts.
Complement: 230

	Hull	Machinery	Laid down	Launched	Commiss'd	Disposition
SWATARA	New York	New York	1872	17 Sep 73	11 May 74	Sold 2 Nov 96
MARION	Portsmouth	Boston	1872	22 Dec 73	12 Jan 76	Sold 24 Jul 1907
QUINNEBAUG	Philadelphia	New York	1872	28 Sep 75	2 Oct 78	Sold 25 Mar 91
GALENA	Norfolk	Norfolk	1872	13 Mar 79	26 Aug 80	Sold 9 May 92
MOHICAN	Mare I.	Mare I.	4 Sep 72	27 Dec 83	25 May 85	Sold 4 Mar 1922.

Notes: All were officially considered to be the earlier vessels of those names rebuilt. The live oak
hulls were designed by Isaiah Hanscom. The Marion, Quinnebaug, and Swatara had compound engines
converted from 50" x 42" engines originally built for Algoma class sloops. Similar engines were built
for the Galena and Mohican. The engines of the Quinnebaug were installed by Neafie and Levy. The
Mohican served as a training vessel 1899-1904, a station ship 1905-10, a submarine tender 1910-15, and
a receiving ship thereafter. The Marion was a training vessel in 1898-1907.
Reclassification: The Mohican was designated "unclassified" on 17 Jul 20.

1873

TRENTON

Displacement: 3900 tons
Dimensions: 253'(b.p.) x 48'(e) x 20'6"(mean)
Armament: 11-8"R 2-20#BLR; 10-8"R 2-20#BLR (1883); 10-8"R
  (1889)
Rig: Ship.

Machinery: 3500 IHP; 3 horizontal,
  back-acting, compound engines, 1
  screw
Speed: 13 kts.
Complement: 477

	Hull	Machinery	Laid down	Launched	Commiss'd	Disposition
TRENTON	New York	Morgan	28 Oct 73	1 Jan 76	14 Feb 77	Wrecked at Apia, Samoa, 16 Mar 89.

Notes: Authorized 10 Feb 73. She was designed as an enlarged copy of the Lancaster with one-sixth
more displacement. Her live oak hull was designed by Isaiah Hanscom and her engines by the Bureau of
Steam Engineering. She had an 8-foot ram. In 1883 she became the first warship to be fitted with
electric lights.

Small Steam Sloops and Gunboats (4th rates)

1841

SOUTHAMPTON class

Tonnage: 500 tons
Dimensions: 152'6"(b.p.) x 27'(m) x 16'(h)
Armament: 2-8" 6-32#
Rig: Unknown

Machinery: Side wheels
Speed: Unknown
Complement: Unknown

	Hull	Machinery	Laid down	Launched	Commiss'd	Disposition
SOUTHAMPTON	Norfolk	Unknown	Oct 41	22 Jan 45	27 May 45	Sold ca. 1855
Unnamed	New York	Unknown	No?	No	No	Probably never begun
TRENTON (?)	Philadelphia	Unknown	1841?	No	No	May never have been begun.

Notes: Authorized 3 Mar 41 as steamers "of medium size." The Norfolk ship was to have "English marine
engines" with side levers (220 HP), the New York ship inclined engines, and the Philadelphia ship

Notes: Authorized 3 Mar 41 as steamers "of medium size." The Norfolk ship was to have "English marine engines" with side levers (220 HP), the New York ship inclined engines, and the Philadelphia ship "Norris vertical direct action" engines. The lake steamer Michigan, begun at the same time, was to have had the same length and beam but a shallower draft. The last document to refer to these three ships as steamers was dated 2 Jun 42. The Southampton emerged as a sailing storeship with the same hull dimensions as the proposed steamers.

1852

WATER WITCH

Tonnage: 378 tons
Dimensions: 150'(d) x 23' x 9'
Armament: 3 howitzers; 4-32# (1861); 1-30#R (1863)
Rig: Schooner

Machinery: 54 NHP, 180 AHP; 1 inclined, low pressure, condensing engine, 37.5" x 6', feathering side wheels
Speed: 10 kts.
Complement: 93

	Hull	Machinery	Laid down	Launched	Commiss'd	Disposition
WATER WITCH	Washington	Ellis	1852	1852	12 Jan 53	Captured by Confederate battery, Ossabow Sd., Ga., 3 Jun 64.

Notes: Officially considered a reconstruction of the old Water Witch, an iron-hulled yard craft built in 1843 and fitted initially with Hunter wheels, then with twin screws, and finally with paddle wheels. The old ship originally measured 100' x 21' and was later lengthened to about 130'. The wooden hull of the new ship was designed by John Lenthall and the engines by Benjamin F. Isherwood. She was burned by the Confederates in December 1864 near Savannah, Ga., to prevent recapture.

1858

SAGINAW

Displacement: 508 tons
Dimensions: 155' x 26' x 4'5"(light)
Armament: 1-32#; 1-50#R 1-32# 2-24#R (1863); 2-30#R (1869)
Rig: Brig

Machinery: 2 inclined, oscillating engines, 39" x 49", side wheels
Speed: 9 kts.
Complement: 59

	Hull	Machinery	Laid down	Launched	Commiss'd	Disposition
SAGINAW	Mare I.	Union	16 Sep 58	3 Mar 59	5 Jan 60	Wrecked on Ocean I., 29 Oct 70.

Notes: Authorized 12 Jun 58. She was intended for the suppression of piracy on the China coast and was the first naval vessel built on the U. S. West Coast. Her machinery was designed by Peter Donahue of Union Iron Works. Her hull, built of laurelwood, was reportedly too weak to withstand the firing of her guns and was found to be quite rotten in January 1862.
Renaming: Launched as Toucey and renamed before commissioning.

1859

POCAHONTAS

Tonnage: 694 tons
Dimensions: 154' x 30'4"(e) x 12'
Armament: 1-10" 4-32#; 1-100#R 4-32# 1-20#R (1863)
Rig: Brig

Machinery: 60 NHP; 2 vertical, direct acting engines, 33" x 30", 1 screw
Speed: 8 kts.
Complement: 173

	Hull	Machinery	Laid down	Launched	Commiss'd	Disposition
POCAHONTAS	Norfolk	Loring	1859	Jan 60	19 Mar 60	Sold 30 Nov 65.

Notes: Rebuilt from the armed merchantman Despatch, which had been acquired in 1855 as a tender for Pensacola. Her new hull was designed by S. M. Pook and she received new engines.
Renaming: Ex Despatch 27 Jan 60.

1861

HARRIET LANE

Tonnage: 674 tons
Dimensions: 180' x 30' x 10'
Armament: 2-32#; 1-8" 4-32# (1861); 3-9" 1-30#R (1862)
Rig: Bark

Machinery: 2 inclined engines, side wheels
Speed: 12 kts.
Complement: 95

	Hull	Machinery	Launched	Acquired	Commiss'd	Disposition
HARRIET LANE	Webb	Allaire	20 Nov 57	11 Sep 61	1861	Captured by Confederate squadron off Galveston 1 Jan 63.

Notes: Designed by William H. Webb and built for the Revenue Cutter Service, this ship was taken into the Navy temporarily in July 1858 for an expedition to Paraguay. Returned in 1859, she was again temporarily assigned to the Navy on 5 April 1861 for the attempted relief of Fort Sumter. She was sold to the Navy in September and was fitted out at the Philadelphia Navy Yard. The Confederates converted her into a blockade runner in 1864. She was recovered at Havana at the end of the war and sold.

UNADILLA or "90 Day Gunboat" class

Displacement: 691 tons
Dimensions: 158'(wl.) x 28'(e) x 9'6"(max)
Armament: Aroostook--1-11" 1-20#R; 1-60#R (1868);
  Cayuga--1-11" 1-20#R; 1-11" (1862); 1-11" 1-30#R 1-20#R (1863);
  Chippewa--1-11" 1-20#R; 1-11" 2-30#R 1-20#R (1863); 1-11" 1-20#R (1864);
  Chocura--1-11" 1-20#R; 1-100#R 1-20#R (1863);
  Huron--1-11" 1-20#R; 1-11" 1-30#R (1864); 1-60#R 1-30#R (1867);
  Itasca--1-10" 2-32# 1-20#R; 1-11" 2-32# 1-20#R (1863);
  Kanawha--1-11" 1-20#R; 1-11" 1-9" 1-20#R (1863);
  Katahdin--1-11" 1-20#R; 1-11" 2-20#R (1862);
  Kennebec--1-11" 1-20#R; 1-11" 1-30#R (1864);
  Kineo--1-11" 1-20#R; 1-11" 2-32# 1-20#R (1862);
  Marblehead--1-11" 1-20#R; 2-8" 3-30#R (1863); 6-32# 1-30#R (1866);
  Ottawa--1-11" 2-20#R; 1-150#R 1-30#R (1863); 1-150#R 1-50#R (1864);
  Pembina--1-11" 1-20#R; 1-30#R (1865);
  Penobscot--1-11" 1-20#R; 1-60#R 6-32# (1868);
  Sciota--1-20#R; 1-11" 1-20#R (1863);
  Tahoma--1-10" 1-20#R; 1-150#R 1-20#R (1862);
  Winona--1-11" 1-20#R; 1-11" 2-32# 1-20#R (1863); 1-11" 1-32# 1-20#R (1863); 1-11" 1-30#R (1864);
  Wissahickon--1-11" 1-20#R; 1-150#R 1-20#R (1863);
  others--1-11" 1-20#R

Rig: Schooner
Machinery: 400 IHP; 2 horizontal, back-acting engines, 30" x 18", 1 screw
Speed: 10 kts.
Complement: 114

	Hull	Machinery	Laid down	Launched	Commiss'd	Disposition
AROOSTOOK	Thompson	Novelty	1861	Nov 61	20 Feb 62	Sold 18 Sep 69
CAYUGA	Gildersleeve	Woodruff & Beach	1861	21 Oct 61	21 Feb 62	Sold 25 Oct 65
CHIPPEWA	Webb & Bell	Morgan	1861	14 Sep 61	13 Dec 61	Sold 30 Nov 65
CHOCURA	Curtis & Tilden	Loring	1861	5 Oct 61	15 Feb 62	Sold 13 Jul 67
HURON	Curtis, Boston	Loring	1861	21 Sep 61	8 Jan 62	Sold 14 Jun 69
ITASCA	Hillman, Streaker	Morris, Towne	1861	1 Oct 61	28 Nov 61	Sold 30 Nov 65
KANAWHA	Goodspeed	Pacific	1861	21 Oct 61	21 Jan 62	Sold 13 Jun 66
KATAHDIN	Larrabee & Allen	Morgan	1861	12 Oct 61	17 Feb 62	Sold 30 Nov 65
KENNEBEC	Hilt	Novelty	1861	5 Oct 61	8 Feb 62	Sold 30 Nov 65
KINEO	Dyer	Morgan	29 Jul 61	9 Oct 61	8 Feb 62	Sold 9 Oct 66
MARBLEHEAD	Jackman	Highland	1861	16 Oct 61	8 Mar 62	Sold 30 Sep 68
OTTAWA	Westervelt	Novelty	1861	22 Aug 61	7 Oct 61	Sold 25 Oct 65
OWASCO	Mallory	Novelty	1861	5 Oct 61	23 Jan 62	Sold 25 Oct 65
PEMBINA	Stack	Novelty	1861	28 Aug 61	16 Oct 61	Sold 30 Nov 65
PENOBSCOT	Carter	Allaire	1861	19 Nov 61	*16 Jan 62	Sold 19 Oct 69
PINOLA	Abrahams	Reeder	1861	1861	29 Jan 62	Sold 30 Nov 65
SAGAMORE	Sampson	Atlantic	20 Jul 61	18 Sep 61	7 Dec 61	Sold 13 Jun 66

The 90-day gunboat *Marblehead*. (NH 46630)

The small screw sloop *Adams* off Mare Island. (NH 57279)

	Hull	Machinery	Laid down	Launched	Commiss'd	Disposition
SCIOTA	Birely	Morris, Towne	1861	15 Oct 61	15 Dec 61	Mined in Mobile Bay 14 Apr 65
SENECA	Simonson	Novelty	1861	27 Aug 61	14 Oct 61	Sold 5 Sep 68
TAHOMA	Thatcher	Reaney	1861	2 Oct 61	20 Dec 61	Sold 1 Oct 67
UNADILLA	Englis	Novelty	3 Aug 61	17 Aug 61	30 Sep 61	Sold 9 Nov 69
WINONA	Poillon	Allaire	1861	14 Sep 61	11 Dec 61	Sold 30 Nov 65
WISSAHICKON	Lynn	Merrick & Sons	1861	2 Oct 61	25 Nov 61	Sold 25 Oct 65.

* Delivered

Notes: All were ordered by the Navy Department between 29 Jun 61 and 10 Jul 61 without Congressional authorization as an emergency measure. They filled a need for small, heavily-armed screw vessels to serve as blockaders at the mouths of the lesser Southern rivers and harbors. The hulls were designed by S. H. Pook under John Lenthall's direction. Lenthall probably based the design on the rebuilt Pocahontas, a similar ship designed by Pook's father. Isherwood based the engine design on plans he had prepared for machinery built at Novelty for two 691-ton Russian Amur River gunboats. Four sets of engines were ordered immediately to the Russian plans and put in the Unadilla, Pembina, Ottawa, and Seneca. The machinery for the others was ordered to modified plans with 60 percent more boiler power. The Kennebec was built under a subcontract from George W. Lawrence and the Owasco under one from Maxon, Fish. All of the class appear to have been well built in spite of their rapid construction and the use of poorly seasoned wood. The ships sailed well in a strong wind and handled easily but rolled badly. The Marblehead served as a training vessel 1864-67. The Sciota's wreck was raised, taken to New York, and sold there 25 Oct 65. The Unadilla was sold at Hong Kong to the government of Annam as a warship and was sunk in a collision in 1870. The Sagamore became the Japanese warship Yoshun.

1862

NIPSIC class

Displacement: 836 tons
Dimensions: 179'6"(b.p.) x 30' x 12'(max)
Armament: Nipsic--1-150#R 2-9" 1-30#R; 1-100#R 2-8" 1-30#R (1865); 1-11" 2-8" 1-30#R (1868); 1-11" 2-9" 1-30#R (1869); Shawmut--1-100#R 2-9" 1-30#R 2-20#R; 1-11" 2-9" 1-20#R (1871); Yantic--1-100#R 2-9" 1-30#R; 4-9" 1-30#R (1865); 4-9" 1-20#R (1870); 1-11" 2-9" 2-20#R (1872); 1-8"R 2-9" 1-60#BLR (1880); none (1897); 1-4"BLR (1920) Nyack--1-100#R 2-9" 1-20#R; Saco--1-100#R 6-32# 1-30#R; 1-60#R 6-32# 1-30#R (1866); 1-11" 2-9" 2-20#R (1870); Kansas--1-150#R 2-9" 1-30#R 2-20#R; 1-100#R 2-9" 1-30#R 2-20#R (1864); 1-11" 2-9" 1-30#R 2-20#R (1865); 1-11" 2-9" 1-20#R (1870)

Rig: Brigantine
Machinery: Yantic--225 IHP; 2 horizontal, direct-acting engines, 32" x 18", 1 screw; Saco--335 IHP; 2 horizontal, vibrating lever engines, 28" x 24", 1 screw; Kansas--327 IHP; horizontal, direct-acting engines, 42" x 24", 1 screw; Others--670 IHP; 2 horizontal, back-acting engines, 30" x 21", 1 screw
Speed: 10 kts. (Yantic), 9.5 kts. (Saco), 11.5 kts. (others)
Complement: 134

	Hull	Machinery	Laid down	Launched	Commiss'd	Disposition
NIPSIC	Portsmouth	Woodruff & Beach	24 Dec 62	15 Jun 63	3 Sep 63	Broken up 1875
YANTIC	Philadelphia	Merrick & Sons	1862	19 Mar 64	12 Aug 64	Foundered, Detroit, Mich., 22 Oct 29
SHAWMUT	Portsmouth	South Brooklyn	2 Feb 63	17 Jun 63	1 Nov 64	Sold 27 Sep 83
SACO	Boston	Corliss	1862	28 Aug 63	11 Jul 64	Sold 20 Nov 83
NYACK	New York	South Brooklyn	1862	6 Oct 63	28 Sep 64	Sold 30 Nov 83
KANSAS	Philadelphia	Unknown	1863	29 Sep 63	21 Dec 63	Sold 27 Sep 83.

Notes: Orders: Yantic 16 Aug 62, Nipsic ca. Aug 62, the next three ca. Dec 62, and Kansas 2 Apr 63. Experience with the 90-day gunboats on the blockade showed a need for greater speed, and this follow-on class was described as "fast cruising gunboats." They were designed for an armament of 1-10" 300# Parrott rifle and 2 howitzers but the 300#R never materialized. The hull design was attributed to John Lenthall and the ships had a reputation for being well and strongly built. The six ships had four different types of engines. The engines of the Nipsic, Shawmut, and Nyack were designed by Benjamin F. Isherwood and those of the Saco and Yantic by their builders. The Kansas was added to the class to make use of English-made engines captured in the blockade runner Princess Royal. The Saco had two funnels and fourteen fire-tube boilers. Her engines proved so unsatisfactory that she was refitted with Isherwood back-acting engines and four boilers at the Washington Navy Yard in 1865-66.

All but the Nyack were given clipper bows, bowsprits, and ship rigs in 1869-71. The Yantic served as a training ship on the Great Lakes 1898-1929.
Reclassification: The Yantic was designated "unclassified" (IX-32) on 17 Jul 20.

PEQUOT class

Displacement: ca. 800 tons
Dimensions: 171'6"(b.p.) x 29'(e) x 12'
Armament: Pequot--1-150#R 6-32# 1-30#R;
  Maumee--1-100#R 1-30#R; 1-100#R 2-32# 1-30#R (1864);
  1-100#R 2-30#R (1865); 1-100#R 2-32# (1865); 1-11" 2-32#
  1-30#R (1865); 1-60#R 1-20#R (1867)
Rig: Brigantine

Machinery: Pequot--2 segmental
  cylinder, direct-acting engines,
  30" x 21", 1 screw;
  Maumee--2 horizontal, vibrating-
  lever engines, 40" x 22", 1 screw
Speed: 11.5 kts.
Complement: 134

	Hull	Machinery	Laid down	Launched	Commiss'd	Disposition
PEQUOT	Boston	Woodruff & Beach	1862	4 Jun 63	15 Jan 64	Sold 6 May 69
MAUMEE	New York	Stover	1862	2 Jul 63	29 Sep 64	Sold 15 Dec 69.

Notes: Ordered ca. Aug 62. Their hull plans are identical to William H. Webb's plans for an unidentified Russian government steamer except that the U.S. ships lacked a bowsprit. They had a raked stem, in contrast to the vertical stem of the Nipsic class as originally built. The engines of the Pequot were designed by their builder's engineer, William Wright, and those of the Maumee by John Ericsson. Unlike the Nipsic class, both were sold out of service after the Civil War. The Pequot was sold to the Haitian navy as Terreur.

1864

RESACA class

Displacement: 1129 tons
Dimensions: 216'(b.p.) x 31' x 12'10"
Armament: Resaca--1-100#R 6-8" 1-20#R;
  Nantasket--1-60#R 6-32# 2-20#R
Rig: Bark

Machinery: 750 HP, 2 horizontal,
  back-acting engines, 36" x 36", 1
  screw
Speed: 12 kts.
Complement: 213

	Hull	Machinery	Laid down	Launched	Commiss'd	Disposition
RESACA	Ports-mouth	Washing-ton	1864	18 Nov 65	11 Oct 66	Sold 18 Feb 73
NANTASKET	Boston	Ports-mouth	1865	15 Aug 67	22 Oct 69	Stk. 22 Jul 75, broken up 1876.

Notes: The engines for this class were ordered from Washington on 25 Mar 64. The Nantasket and Epervier (below) later traded engines. The Resaca and Swatara classes were follow-ons to the Nipsic class, with the same beam and internal layout but 36' more length for increased speed. Their extra tonnage led them to be classed third rates, although they had been designed as fast gunboats. The Resaca class had finer lines forward than the Swatara class and a rounder midsection. The Resaca was in commission 9-20 Jul 66 for the transit from Washington to Portsmouth after receiving her engines. She was completed with a vertical bow as designed while the Nantasket had a clipper bow fitted during construction. Their hulls were built of unseasoned wood which rapidly decayed. The Resaca was wrecked as the merchantman Ventura in 1875.

SWATARA class

Displacement: 1113 tons.
Dimensions: 216'(b.p.) x 30'(e) x 12'10"
Armament: Swatara--1-60#R 6-32# 3-20#R; 1-11" 6-32# 2-20#R
  (1869);
  Quinnebaug--1-60#R 4-32# 1-20#R
Rig: Bark
Complement: 213

Machinery: Swatara--750 HP, 2
  horizontal, back-acting engines,
  36" x 36", 1 screw;
  Quinnebaug--4 high-expansion
  engines, 38" x 21", 2 screws
Speed: 12 kts. (Swatara), 7 kts.
  (Quinnebaug)

	Hull	Machinery	Laid down	Launched	Commiss'd	Disposition
SWATARA	Phila-delphia	Washing-ton	1864	23 May 65	15 Nov 65	Broken up 1872
QUINNEBAUG	New York	Jackson & Watkins	Oct 64	31 Mar 66	17 Jul 67	Broken up 1871
ALERT	Ports-mouth	Ports-mouth	No	No	No	Cancelled 1866
EPERVIER	Ports-mouth	Washing-ton	No	No	No	Cancelled 1866.

Notes: The engines for the _Swatara_ were ordered on 25 Mar 64 and the hull was ordered on 6 Aug 64. The _Quinnebaug_ was ordered for comparative trials of machinery ordered in England. The engines and probably the hulls for the two Portsmouth ships were ordered on 21 Nov 64. The _Nantasket_ (above) and _Epervier_ later traded engines. The tonnage of all four was 831 tons. Like their half-sisters of the _Resaca_ class, they were initially described as fast gunboats and were third-rate follow-ons to the _Nipsic_ class. The _Swatara_ and _Quinnebaug_ were completed as designed with a vertical bow, and the _Swatara_ was refitted with a clipper bow in 1869. Their unseasoned white oak hulls rapidly decayed in service. The engines of the _Alert_ and _Epervier_ were completed and put in storage. The _Quinnebaug_'s engines proved unsatisfactory and were removed in 1870. They were to have been replaced by the _Epervier_'s engines (described as 36" x 48"), but the ship was scrapped and rebuilt to a new design instead.

1873

ADAMS class

Displacement: 1375 tons
Dimensions: 185'(b.p.) x 35'(e) x 16'4"
Armament: Adams--1-11" 4-9" 1-60#R; 1-8"R 4-9" 1-60#BLR
   (1880); 6-4"BLR (1898); none (1910); 4-4"/40BLR (1916);
   Alliance--1-11" 4-9" 1-60#R; 1-8"R 4-9" 1-60#BLR (1880);
   8-4"BLR (1894); 6-4"BLR (1895); none (1910);
   Enterprise--1-11" 4-9" 1-60#R; 1-8"R 4-9" 1-60#BLR (1881);
   4-32# (1892); none (1897);
   Essex--1-11" 4-9" 1-60#R; 1-8"R 4-9" 1-60#BLR (1881);
   8-4"BLR (1893); 6-4"BLR (1895); 2-6# (1910); 6-3# (1916);
   3-4"BLR (1921); 2-4"BLR (1924);
   Nipsic--1-8"R 4-9" 1-60#BLR; none (1890); 4-9" (1895); none
   (1900)

Rig: Bark
Machinery: 800 IHP; 2 back-acting
   compound engines, 1 screw
Speed: 11 kts.
Complement: 190

	Hull	Machinery	Laid down	Launched	Commiss'd	Disposition
ADAMS	McKay at Boston	Atlantic	Feb 74	24 Oct 74	21 Jul 76	Sold 5 Aug 1920
ALLIANCE	Norfolk	Quintard	1873	8 Mar 75	8 Jan 77	Sold 13 Nov 1911
ENTERPRISE	Griffiths at Portsmouth	Woodruff	1873	13 Jun 74	16 Mar 77	Sold 1 Oct 1909
ESSEX	McKay at Portsmouth	Atlantic	1873	26 Oct 74	3 Oct 76	Sold 23 Dec 1930
NIPSIC	Washington	Wright	1873	6 Jun 78	11 Oct 79	Sold 13 Feb 1913.

Notes: Authorized 10 Feb 73 except for the _Nipsic_, officially considered the old ship rebuilt. The _Adams_, _Enterprise_, and _Essex_ were built by leading private contractors (John W. Griffiths and Donald McKay) at the Navy Yards indicated. Intended for general overseas cruising, primarily under sail, these gunboats had a greater beam and draft and fuller lines than their Civil War predecessors. The new compound engines designed by the Bureau of Steam Engineering were more economical to operate than Civil War era machinery. The _Nipsic_ was badly damaged in the 16 Mar 89 Apia hurricane and never again cruised. She acted as a receiving ship 1892-99 and 1901-03 and then as a prison hulk. The _Alliance_ served as a training vessel 1894-1903 and a station ship 1904-11. The _Essex_ was used as a training vessel after 1893 and was reengined with a 1200 IHP triple-expansion engine around 1910. The _Enterprise_ served as a training ship after 1891 as did the _Adams_ in 1899-1904 and 1907-17.
Renaming: _Alliance_ ex _Huron_ 1 Nov 75.
Reclassification: The _Essex_ was designated "unclassified" (IX-10) on 17 Jul 20.

ALERT class

Displacement: 1020 tons
Dimensions: 175'(b.p.) x 32'(e) x 13'(mean)
Armament: Alert--1-11" 2-9" 1-60#R; 1-11" 2-9" 1-60#BLR
   (1887); 2-9" 1-60#BLR (1895); 6-4"/40BLR (1899); none
   (1910); 4-6# (1916); 1-6# (1918);
   Huron--1-11" 2-9" 1-60#R;
   Ranger--1-11" 2-9" 1-60#R; 1-11" 2-9" 1-60#BLR (1879);
   1-8"R 2-9" 1-60#BLR (1892); 6-4"BLR (1897); none (1910);
   1-4"/40BLR 2-3"/50BLR (1918); 4-4"BLR (1921)

Rig: Bark (Alert), schooner (others)
Machinery: 560 IHP; 2 back-acting,
   compound engines, 1 screw
Speed: 10 kts.
Complement: 202

	Hull	Machinery	Laid down	Launched	Commiss'd	Disposition
ALERT	Roach	Roach	Sep 73	18 Sep 74	27 May 75	Sold 29 Jul 1922
HURON	Roach	Roach	1873	2 Sep 74	15 Nov 75	Foundered off Nag's Head, N.C., 24 Nov 77
RANGER	Harlan & Hollingsworth	Roach	1873	10 May 76	27 Nov 76	Transferred to Maritime Commission 11 Apr 1940.

Notes: Authorized 10 Feb 73. Because of political pressure they were built with iron hulls. The Alert was fitted with spar torpedoes on commissioning. She served as a training vessel 1902-10 and was converted to a submarine tender in 1911 by the Mare Island Navy Yard. The Ranger was used as a training ship after 1909. As Emery Rice she served at the U.S. Maritime Academy as training vessel and museum until scrapped at Baltimore in 1958.
Renamings: Huron ex Alliance 1 Nov 75; Ranger to Rockport 30 Oct 17 and to Nantucket 20 Feb 18.
Reclassifications: On 17 Jul 20 the Alert was designated AS-4 and the Nantucket (ex Ranger) was designated PG-23. The Nantucket was redesignated "unclassified" (IX-18) on 1 Jul 21.

Double-Ended Gunboats (3rd rates)

1861

PAUL JONES

Displacement: 1210 tons
Dimensions: 216'10" x 35'4" x 8'
Armament: 1-11" 1-100#R 2-9" 2-50#R; 1-11" 1-100#R 4-9" (1863)
Rig: Schooner

Machinery: 630 IHP; 1 inclined, direct-acting engine, 48" x 7', side wheels
Speed: 11 kts.
Complement: 148

	Hull	Machinery	Laid down	Launched	Commiss'd	Disposition
PAUL JONES	Abrahams	Reaney	1861	30 Jan 62	9 Jun 62	Sold 13 Jul 67.

Notes: In 1861 the Navy ordered 12 "double-bowed" side-wheel steamers for use in the shallow sounds and rivers of the southeast. The distinctive feature of this type was that each end was shaped like a bow and fitted with a rudder. This, combined with the amidships location of the side wheels, permitted the ships to reverse direction in restricted waters without turning around. They were designed with one big gun at each end, although more were later added. This initial group of 12 ships was built to nine different designs prepared under the direction of John Lenthall, presumably by different Navy and civilian engineers. The engines of all except the Miami were built on plans by Benjamin F. Isherwood and were designed to produce 11 knots. The Paul Jones had the greatest displacement in this initial group. She was also one of three in the group known to have been true double-enders, with identical bows and sterns and with side wheels exactly amidships.

PORT ROYAL

Displacement: 1163 tons
Dimensions: 209' x 35' x 7'8"
Armament: 1-10" 1-100#R; 1-10" 1-100#R 2-9" 2-50#R (1863)
Rig: Schooner

Machinery: 630 IHP; 1 inclined, direct-acting engine, 48" x 7', side wheels
Speed: 11 kts.
Complement: 131

	Hull	Machinery	Laid down	Launched	Commiss'd	Disposition
PORT ROYAL	Stack	Novelty	1861	17 Jan 62	26 Apr 62	Sold 3 Oct 66.

Notes: One of the three true double-enders in the initial group of twelve, she apparently came the closest to matching the criteria for the type. Lenthall and Isherwood proposed her plans to prospective contractors as an example to be followed for the next group of double-enders, the Sassacus class.

GENESEE class

Displacement: 1120 tons
Dimensions: 209' x 34'11" x 10'6"
Armament: Genesee--1-10" 1-100#R; 1-100#R 5-9" (1863); 1-10" 1-100#R 4-9";
  Tioga--1-10" 1-100#R; 1-10" 1-100#R 4-32# (1863); 1-10" 1-100#R 6-32# (1864)

Rig: Schooner
Machinery: 630 IHP; 1 inclined, direct-acting engine, 48" x 7', side wheels
Speed: 10.9 kts.
Complement: 113

	Hull	Machinery	Laid down	Launched	Commiss'd	Disposition
GENESEE	Boston	Neptune	1861	2 Apr 62	3 Jul 62	Sold 3 Oct 67
TIOGA	Boston	Morgan	1861	18 Apr 62	30 Jun 62	Sold 17 Oct 67.

Notes: Designed by W. L. Hanscom. These two were double enders in name only, with conventional cruiser sterns and side wheels well aft of amidships. They had small triangular bow rudders.

SONOMA class

Displacement: 1105 tons
Dimensions: 233'9"(oa.) x 34'10" x 8'7"
Armament: Sonoma--1-11" 1-100#R; 1-11" 1-100#R 4-9" (1864);
  Conemaugh--1-11" 1-100#R; 1-11" 1-100#R 4-9" (1863); 1-11"
  1-100#R 6-9" (1864), 1-100#R 6-9" (1865); 4-8" 2-60#R
  (1865)

Rig: Schooner
Machinery: 630 IHP; 1 inclined,
  direct-acting engine, 48" x 7',
  side wheels
Speed: 11.3 kts.
Complement: 165

	Hull	Machinery	Laid down	Launched	Commiss'd	Disposition
SONOMA	Ports-mouth	Novelty	1861	15 Apr 62	8 Jul 62	Sold 1 Oct 67
CONEMAUGH	Ports-mouth	Novelty	1861	1 May 62	16 Jul 62	Sold 1 Oct 67.

Notes: These two double-enders appear to have had only minor differences between their bows and sterns, but their side wheels were well aft of amidships.
Renaming: Conemaugh to Cinemaugh 5 Dec 61, back to Conemaugh 26 Dec 61.

SEBAGO class

Displacement: 1070 tons
Dimensions: 228'2" x 33'10" x 9'3"
Armament: Sebago--1-100#R 1-9"; 1-100#R 5-9" (1862);
  Mahaska--1-100#R 1-9"; 1-100#R 5-9" (1862); 1-100#R 6-9"
  (1863); 1-100#R 5-9" (1864)

Rig: Schooner
Machinery: 590 IHP; 1 inclined,
  direct-acting engine, 44" x 7',
  side wheels
Speed: 11 kts.
Complement: 148

	Hull	Machinery	Laid down	Launched	Commiss'd	Disposition
SEBAGO	Ports-mouth	Novelty	May 61	30 Nov 61	26 Mar 62	Sold 19 Jan 67
MAHASKA	Ports-mouth	Morgan	1861	10 Dec 61	5 May 62	Sold 12 Oct 68.

Notes: This class met the criteria for double-enders only approximately, their sterns being of a conventional shape and their side wheels being aft of amidships.

CIMARRON

Displacement: 993 tons
Dimensions: 217'6"(wl.), 205'(b.p.) x 35' x 9'
Armament: 1-100#R 1-9"; 1-100#R 3-9" (1863); 1-150#R 3-9"
  (1864); 1-150#R 1-9" (1864); 1-150#R 3-9" (1865)

Rig: Schooner
Machinery: 630 IHP; 1 inclined,
  direct-acting engine, side wheels
Speed: 11.6 kts.
Complement: 122

	Hull	Machinery	Laid down	Launched	Commiss'd	Disposition
CIMARRON	Mershon	McKnight	1861	16 Mar 62	5 Jul 62	Sold 5 Nov 66.

Notes: This double-ender suffered from particularly shoddy construction.
Renaming: Her name was initially spelled Cimmerone.

OCTORARA

Displacement: 981 tons
Dimensions: 205'(wl.), 193'2"(b.p.) x 34'6" x 4'10"(light)
Armament: 1-100#R 1-9"; 1-100#R 3-9" 2-32# (1863); 2-32#
  (1865)

Rig: Schooner
Machinery: 590 IHP; 1 inclined,
  direct-acting engine, 44" x 7',
  side wheels
Speed: 11.3 kts.
Complement: 118

	Hull	Machinery	Laid down	Launched	Commiss'd	Disposition
OCTORARA	New York	Neptune	1861	7 Dec 61	28 Feb 62	Sold 9 Nov 66.

Notes: Designed by B. F. Delano. The shortest of the first group of double-enders, this ship was strongly built but considered under-powered. Her ends were identical but her side wheels were somewhat aft of amidships.

MARATANZA

Tonnage: 786 tons
Dimensions: 209' x 32'11" x 10'
Armament: 1-100#R 1-9"; 1-100#R 3-9" (1863); 1-100#R 1-9"
  (1864); 1-11" 3-9" (1865)

Rig: Schooner
Machinery: 590 IHP; 1 inclined,
  direct-acting engine, 44" x 7',
  side wheels
Speed: 10 kts.
Complement: 111

	Hull	Machinery	Laid down	Launched	Commiss'd	Disposition
MARATANZA	Boston	Loring	1861	26 Nov 61	12 Apr 62	Sold 26 Aug 68.

Notes: Designed by W. L. Hanscom. The distinctive feature of this early double-ender was a stern that was rounded above the waterline. She was considered strongly built. She became a Haitian gunboat in 1868, initially named Salnave and later Union.

MIAMI

Tonnage: 730 tons
Dimensions: 208'2"(u.d.) x 33'2" x 8'6"
Armament: 1-100#R 1-9"; 1-100#R 2-9" (1862); 1-100#R 6-9"
  (1863)

Rig: Schooner
Machinery: 1 inclined, direct-acting
  engine, 44" x 7', side wheels
Speed: 8 kts.
Complement: 134

	Hull	Machinery	Laid down	Launched	Commiss'd	Disposition
MIAMI	Phila-delphia	Merrick & Sons	1861	16 Nov 61	29 Jan 62	Sold 10 Aug 65.

Notes: One of three true double-enders in the initial group of twelve, this ship was reported as strongly built. Her machinery was designed by its builder.

1862

SASSACUS class

Displacement: 1173 tons
Dimensions: 240'(wl.) x 35' x 9'6"
Armament: Algonquin--never mounted;
  Chenango, Chicopee, Eutaw, Lenawee, Mingoe, Tallahoma, and
  Winooski--2-100#R 4-9" 2-20#R;
  Iosco, Osceola--2-100#R 4-9"; 1-11" 1-100#R 4-9" (1865);
  Mackinaw--2-100#R 4-9"; 6-9" (1865); 1-11" 1-100#R 4-9"
  (1865);
  Massasoit--2-100#R 4-9"; 2-100#R 3-9" (1865); 2-100#R 2-9"
  (1865);
  Mendota--2-100#R 4-9" 2-20#R; 2-100#R 4-9" 1-20#R (1864);
  Pawtuxet, Pontoosuc--2-100#R 4-9" 2-20#R; 1-11" 1-100#R
  2-20#R (1865);
  Sassacus--2-100#R 4-9"; 2-100#R 4-9" 2-20#R (1864); 2-100#R
  4-9" (1864);
  Shamrock--2-100#R 4-9" 2-20#R; 2-100#R 6-9" 2-20#R (1864);
  Tacony--2-100#R 4-9"; 2-11" 4-9" (1864); 2-11" 3-9" (1864);
  4-8" 2-60#R (1865);
  Tallapoosa--2-100#R 4-9" 2-20#R; 1-8"R 5-60#R (1887);
  others--2-100#R 4-9"

Rig: Schooner
Machinery: Algonquin--Dickerson
  engine, 48" x 10';
  others--712 IHP; 1 inclined,
  direct-acting engine, 58" x 8'9",
  side wheels
Speed: 13 kts.
Complement: 200

	Hull	Machinery	Laid down	Launched	Commiss'd	Disposition
AGAWAM	Lawrence, Portland	Portland	Oct 62	21 Apr 63	9 Mar 64	Sold 10 Oct 67
ALGONQUIN	New York	Providence	Mar 63	21 Dec 63	*Mar 66	Sold 21 Oct 69
ASCUTNEY	Jackman	Morgan	1862	4 Apr 63	28 Jul 64	Sold 28 Oct 68
CHENANGO	Simonson	Morgan	1862	19 Mar 63	29 Feb 64	Sold 28 Oct 68
CHICOPEE	Curtis, Boston	Neptune	1862	4 Mar 63	7 May 64	Sold 8 Oct 67
EUTAW	Abrahams	Vulcan	1862	Feb 63	2 Jul 63	Sold 15 Oct 67
IOSCO	Larrabee & Allen	Globe	Sep 62	20 Mar 63	26 Apr 64	Hulked Feb 68
LENAPEE	Lupton	Washington IrWks	1862	28 May 63	30 Dec 64	Sold 26 Aug 68
MACKINAW	New York	Allaire	1862	22 Apr 63	23 Apr 64	Sold 3 Oct 67

	Hull	Machinery	Laid down	Launched	Commiss'd	Disposition
MASSASOIT	Curtis & Tilden	Globe	1862	8 Mar 63	8 Mar 64	Sold 15 Oct 67
MATTABESETT	Sampson	Allaire	1862	1863	7 Apr 64	Sold 15 Oct 67
MENDOTA	Tucker	South Brooklyn	1862	13 Jan 63	2 May 64	Sold 7 Dec 67
METACOMET	Stack	South Brooklyn	1862	7 Mar 63	4 Jan 64	Sold 28 Oct 68
MINGOE	Mershon	Pusey & Jones	1862	6 Aug 63	29 Jul 64	Sold 3 Oct 67
OSCEOLA	Curtis & Tilden	Atlantic	1862	29 May 63	10 Feb 64	Sold 1 Oct 67
OTSEGO	J.A.&D.D. Westervelt	Fulton Fdry	1862	31 Mar 63	16 May 64	Mined Jamesville, N.C., 9 Dec 64
PAWTUXET	Portsmouth	Providence	3 Nov 62	19 Mar 63	26 Aug 64	Sold 15 Oct 67
PEORIA	New York	Etna	1862	29 Oct 63	26 Dec 66	Sold 26 Aug 68
PONTIAC	Hillman & Streaker	Neafie & Levy	1862	1863	7 Jul 64	Sold 15 Oct 67
PONTOOSUC	Lawrence, Portland	Portland	Oct 62	May 63	10 May 64	Sold 3 Oct 66
SASSACUS	Portsmouth	Atlantic	11 Sep 62	23 Dec 62	5 Oct 63	Sold 28 Oct 68
SHAMROCK	New York	Poole & Hunt	1862	17 Mar 63	13 Jun 64	Sold 1 Sep 68
TACONY	Philadelphia	Morris, Towne	1862	7 May 63	12 Feb 64	Sold 26 Aug 68
TALLAHOMA	New York	Stover	1863	28 Nov 63	*27 Dec 65	Sold 29 Aug 68
TALLAPOOSA	Boston	Neptune	1862	17 Feb 63	13 Sep 64	Sold 23 Feb 92
WINOOSKI	Boston	Providence	1862	30 Jul 63	27 Jun 65	Sold 26 Aug 68
WYALUSING	Cramp	Pusey & Jones	1862	12 May 63	8 Feb 64	Sold 15 Oct 67.

* Delivered

Notes: The contract-built ships were ordered 9 Sep 62 except Massasoit, 10 Sep 62, and Osceola, 5 Oct 62. In contrast to the first group of 12 double-enders, the ships in this group were built to a single standard plan and were true double-enders, with identical ends and the side wheels amidships. The Algonquin was given machinery designed by Edward N. Dickerson which was such a failure that the machinery was rejected and the ship never went into commission. The machinery of the others, designed by Benjamin F. Isherwood, produced 1,272 IHP with forced draft and was designed for 14.5 knots. Several ships, including the Ascutney, Chicopee, Eutaw, Massasoit, Mattabesett, and Tallapoosa were criticised as poorly built. The Osceola and Shamrock were fitted with rams in 1864. Satisfactory for inshore service, these ships tended to be poor sea boats which steered badly. The Mackinaw was in commission from 19 Aug 63 to 23 Aug 63 for a transit from New York to Baltimore. The Iosco was converted into a coal hulk in 1868 and her subsequent fate is uncertain. The Tallapoosa became a despatch vessel in 1869, a training ship in 1872, and a transport in 1873. She was completely rebuilt in 1874 by C. W. Booz at Baltimore with the same basic dimensions but as a single-ender. She resumed service in 1876 as a despatch vessel and was sunk in 1884 off Newport, R.I. in a collision. Salvaged and refitted, she then served as a cruising vessel.

WATEREE

Displacement: 1173 tons
Dimensions: 240'(wl.) x 35' x 9'6"
Armament: 2-100#R 4-9"; 2-100#R 4-9" 2-20#R (1865);
Rig: Schooner

Machinery: 1 inclined, direct-acting engine, 58" x 8'9", side wheels
Speed: 13 kts.
Complement: 200

	Hull	Machinery	Laid down	Launched	Commiss'd	Disposition
WATEREE	Reaney	Reaney	1863	12 Aug 63	20 Jan 64	Grounded Arica, Peru, 13 Aug 68.

Notes: Ordered 9 Sep 62, she was identical to the Sassacus class except that her hull was built of iron instead of wood. She was washed one-quarter mile inland in a tidal wave and was sold in place on 21 Nov 68.

1863

MOHONGO class

Displacement: 1370 tons
Dimensions: 255'(wl.) x 35'(e) x 9'6"(Mohongo, max), 9'4"
  Muscoota, max), 9'(others, max)
Armament: Ashuelot--4-8" 2-60#R 2-20#R (1866);
  Mohongo--2-100#R 4-9" (1868);
  Monocacy--4-8" 2-60#R 2-20#R (1869); 4-8" 2-60#BLR (1889);
  4-1# (1900);
  others--2-100#R 4-9" 2-20#R

Rig: Schooner
Machinery: 850 IHP; 1 inclined,
  direct-acting engine, 58" x 8'9",
  side wheels
Speed: 13.5 kts.
Complement: 190

	Hull	Machinery	Laid down	Launched	Commiss'd	Disposition
ASHUELOT	McKay	McKay	1864	12 Jul 65	4 Apr 66	Wrecked on Lamock Rocks, China, 18 Feb 83
MOHONGO	Zeno, Secor	Fulton Fdry	1863	9 Jul 64	23 May 65	Sold 17 Nov 70
MONOCACY	Denmead	Denmead	1863	14 Dec 64	11 May 66	Sold 1 Oct 1903
MUSCOOTA	Cont'l, B'klyn	Morgan	1863	1864	5 Jan 65	Sold 8 May 69
SHAMOKIN	Reaney	Reaney	1863	1864	17 Oct 65	Sold 21 Oct 69
SUWANEE	Reaney	Reaney	1863	13 Mar 64	23 Jan 65	Wrecked in Shadwell Passage, B.C., 9 Jul 68
WINNIPEC	Loring	Loring	1863	20 Aug 64	1865	Sold 17 Jun 69.

Notes: Ordered between 24 Jun 63 and 22 Aug 63. This class was an improved version of the Sassacus class in which iron hulls provided strength sufficient for sea service as well as for inland waters. The engines were built to the same Isherwood plans as those of the Sassacus class and the designed speed was 15 knots. The iron ships demonstrated considerably better performance in open ocean navigation than their predecessors and two saw long service on the China station. The Ashuelot was converted to a single-ender during construction.

Steamers (Lake)

1841

MICHIGAN

Displacement: 685 tons
Dimensions: 163'3"(b.p.) x 27'1", 45'10"(o.g.) x 7'10"(mean)
Armament: 2-8" 4-32#; 1-8" (1845); 1-30#R 5-20#R (1864);
  4-30#BLR (1884); 6-6# (1897); 6-3# (1913)
Rig: Bark

Machinery: 110 NHP, 365 AHP; 2
  inclined, direct-acting, condensing
  engines, 36" x 8', side wheels
Speed: 10.5 kts.
Complement: 85

	Hull	Machinery	Laid down	Launched	Commiss'd	Disposition
MICHIGAN	Stackhouse & Tomlinson		1842	5 Dec 43	29 Sep 44	To City of Erie, Pa., 19 Jul 1927.

Notes: Authorized 9 Sep 41. 4th rate. The first iron hulled vessel in the Navy, she was exceptionally well built. Her machinery suffered its first major accident in 1923. Samuel Hartt designed her hull and Charles W. Copeland her engines. Assembled at Pittsburgh, she was taken apart and then reassembled at Erie. She was rigged as a barkentine and as a schooner at various times in her career. She spent her entire service on the Great Lakes as either a patrol or training vessel. A replacement (PG-16) was authorized in fiscal year 1899 but was suspended in 1899 pending a study of treaty limits on Great Lakes naval ships.
Renaming: To Wolverine 17 Jun 05.
Reclassification: She was designated "unclassified" (IX-31) on 17 Jul 20.

Spar Torpedo Boats

1862

ALLIGATOR

Displacement: Unknown
Dimensions: 47' x 4'6" x 6'
Armament: 2-Spar Torpedoes

Machinery: Hand crank paddles
Speed: 2.5 kts.
Complement: 17

	Builder	Laid down	Launched	Commiss'd	Disposition
ALLIGATOR	Neafie & Levy	1862	30 Apr 62	by Jun 62	Foundered off Virginia Capes 2 Apr 63.

Notes: A hand-propelled submarine with special air purification equipment, she was designed by the French engineer Brutus de Villeroi. Martin Thomas was the contractor. She was built for use against the Virginia (ex-Merrimack) and commissioned for an attack on the Virginia II, but this idea was abandoned in August 1862 after the crew proved unable to move the boat and practically ran out of air. She was lost while being towed to Port Royal.

1864

SPUYTEN DUYVIL

Displacement: 207 tons
Dimensions: 84'2"(oa.) x 20'8"(e) x 9'1"(max)
Armament: 1-Spar Torpedo
Armor: 5" sides, 3" deck, 5" pilot house
Rig: None

Machinery: High-pressure engine, 1 screw
Speed: 5 kts.
Complement: 23

	Hull	Machinery	Laid down	Launched	Commiss'd	Disposition
SPUYTEN DUYVIL	Pook	Mystic	1864	1864	Oct 64	Stricken 1880.

Notes: Ordered 1 Jun 64. Designed by Chief Engineer William W. W. Wood, she used sinking tanks to reduce her exposed area when going into action. Although substantially built, she was slow and unwieldy and could not use her torpedo with headway on because of the danger of overrunning the explosion.
Renaming: Ex Stromboli 19 Nov 64.

1874

INTREPID

Displacement: 1150 tons
Dimensions: 170'(b.p.) x 35'4 (e) x 11'9'
Armament: 5-Spar torpedoes; none (1882)
Armor: 5" sides, 2" deck
Rig: Brig

Machinery: 643 IHP; 2 compound engines, 2 screws
Speed: 10.6 kts.
Complement: Unknown

	Hull	Machinery	Laid down	Launched	Commiss'd	Disposition
INTREPID	Boston	Morgan	1873	5 Mar 74	31 Jul 74	Sold 9 May 92.

Notes: Engines ordered 23 Dec 71. Built of iron to a design of Isaiah Hanscom, she was intended for experimental work for the Bureau of Ordnance. The Morgan Iron Works designed her engines. She had a large underwater ram, a complete armor belt, one spar torpedo forward and two on each broadside. New York Navy Yard started to convert her into a light-draft gunboat for Chinese waters mounting 2-8"R in 1882 but work ceased on 22 Sep 83 before completion.

ALARM

Displacement: 730 tons
Dimensions: 173'(oa.), 158'6"(b.p.) x 28'(e) x 11'1"
Armament: 1-15" 3-Spar Torpedoes; none (1893)
Armor: 4" bow

Rig: 3 masts
Machinery: 600 IHP; 2 compound engines, 1 Fowler wheel
Speed: 7 kts.
Complement: 25

	Hull	Machinery	Laid down	Launched	Commiss'd	Disposition
ALARM	New York	Morgan	1873	13 Nov 73	2 Nov 74	Sold 23 Feb 98.

Notes: Engines ordered 23 Dec 71. Another design by Isaiah Hanscom for the Bureau of Ordnance, she followed a general plan devised by Admiral David D. Porter. The Morgan Iron Works designed the engines. She had a double iron hull, a 32-foot underwater ram containing a submerged spar torpedo, a

The double-ended gunboat *Conemaugh*. (NH 49989)

The torpedo ram *Alarm* in drydock at the New York Navy Yard ca. 1874. (NH 57291)

spar torpedo on each beam, and sinking tanks. Only her bow was armored, the rest of the hull being unprotected. She used her Fowler horizontal feathering paddle wheel for both propulsion and steering. In 1881 this device was replaced with a Mallory steering propeller, which increased her draft to 14'. With it she developed 685 IHP and 11.42 kts. An armament of 1-6"BLR and 3 spar torpedoes was planned for her in 1890 as a gunnery ship in a training squadron with the <u>Lancaster</u> but was probably not fitted.

1876

LIGHTNING

<u>Tonnage</u>: 3.45 tons
<u>Dimensions</u>: 58'(oa.) x 6'3" x 1'10"
<u>Armament</u>: 2-Spar Torpedoes
<u>Rig</u>: None

<u>Machinery</u>: 60 HP; direct-acting
    engine, 1 screw
<u>Speed</u>: 17.5 kts.
<u>Complement</u>: Unknown

	Hull	Machinery	Laid down	Launched	Commiss'd	Disposition
LIGHTNING	Herreshoff		1876	1876	1876	Unknown.

<u>Notes</u>: She was a high-speed wooden steam launch designed by Nathaniel G. Herreshoff and was also known as <u>Steam Launch No. 6</u>. She reached 20 mph on trials on 24 May 76 and was delivered on 1 Jun 76. Steam launches 1-5, also in existence in 1876, were sometimes used for torpedo experiments although not designed as torpedo boats. Similarly, six picket boats (45' x 9'6") were built during the Civil War, and <u>Picket Boat No. 1</u> was fitted with a spar torpedo and used by Cushing to sink the Confederate ram <u>Albemarle</u> in 1864.

Armed Merchantmen (Steam)

1. Steamers (2nd and 3rd Rates)

1849

MASSACHUSETTS (ex-Massachusetts). Screw Steamer. 750 tons. 161'(d) x 32'2"(e) x 15'6". Armament: 2-9#;
8-32# (1854); 6-32# (1863); 6-32# 2-20#R (1865). Machinery: 170 HP, inclined, direct-acting engine, 1
Ericsson screw. Speed: 8 kts. Built by Hall, Boston, 1845. Transferred from War Dept. 1 Aug 49 and
commissioned same date. Converted to storeship (4th rate) and engine removed 1862. Renamed Farralones
Jan 63. Sold San Francisco 16 May 67.

1861

ALABAMA (ex-Alabama). Side-wheel Steamer, 3rd rate. 1261 tons. 214'4" x 35'2"(hull) x 14'6". Armament:
8-32# 1-20#R; 1-9" 6-32# 2-30#R (1862). Schooner rig. Machinery: Side-lever engine, side wheels.
Speed: 13 kts. Complement: 180. Built by Webb, launched 19 Jan 50. Engine by Novelty. Purchased New
York 1 Aug 61. Commissioned 30 Sep 61. Sold Philadelphia 10 Aug 65. Sister to the Florida.

AUGUSTA (ex-Augusta). Side-wheel Steamer, 3rd rate. 1310 tons. 220'8"(d) x 35'4"(hull) x 14'3".
Armament: 8-32#; 8-32# 1-20#R (1862); 1-100#R 6-8" 2-30#R (1863). Schooner rig. Machinery: Oscillating
engine, side wheels. Speed: 11 kts. Complement: 157. Built by Webb 1852. Engine by Novelty. Purchased
New York 1 Aug 61. Commissioned 28 Sep 61. Sold New York 2 Dec 68.

BIENVILLE (ex-Bienville). Side-wheel Steamer, 2nd rate. 1558 tons. 253' x 38'(hull) x 16'2". Armament:
8-32# 1-30#R; 8-32# (1861); 1-100#R 8-32# 1-30#R (1863). Brig rig. Machinery: 400 HP, vertical beam
engine, side wheels. Speed: 11 kts. Complement: 185. Built by Lawrence & Foulkes 1860. Engine by
Morgan. Purchased New York 14 Aug 61. Commissioned 23 Oct 61. Sold Boston 5 Oct 67. Sister to the
DeSoto.

CAMBRIDGE (ex-Cambridge). Screw Steamer, 3rd rate. 858 tons. 200' x 32' x 13'6". Armament: 2-8"; 4-8"
1-30#R (1861); 4-8" 4-30#R (1863). Brigantine rig. Machinery: Vertical, direct-acting engine, 1 screw.
Speed: 10.5 kts. Complement: 96. Built by Curtis, Medford, launched 18 Nov 59. Purchased Boston 30 Jul
61. Converted by Boston. Commissioned 29 Aug 61. Sold Philadelphia 20 Jun 65.

CONNECTICUT (ex-Mississippi). Side-wheel Steamer, 2nd rate. 1725 tons. 251'6" x 38'2"(hull) x 14'.
Brig rig. Armament: 4-32#; 2-8" 1-30#R (1861); 1-50#R 10-32# 1-30#R (1862); 1-100#R 8-8" 2-30#R
(1863). Machinery: Vertical beam engine, side wheels. Speed: 10 kts. Built by Webb, launched 15 Jan
61. Engine by Morgan. Purchased New York 18 Jul 61. Commissioned 23 Aug 61. Used as a storeship 1861-
62 and cruiser thereafter. Sold Philadelphia 21 Sep 65.

DE SOTO (ex-DeSoto). Side-wheel Steamer, 2nd rate. 1675 tons. Hull and machinery duplicate the
Bienville. Armament: 6-32# 1-30#R; 1-9" 6-32# 1-30#R (1863). Built by Lawrence & Foulkes, launched 25
Jun 59. Engine by Morgan. Purchased New York 21 Aug 61. Converted by New York. Commissioned 1861. Sold
New York 30 Sep 68.

FLAG (ex-Phineas Sprague). Screw Steamer, 3rd rate. 938 tons. 195'(b.p.) x 30'10" x 15'. Armament: 6-
8"; 1-10" 4-8" 2-30#R (1863). Machinery: 400 HP, vertical, direct-acting engine, 1 screw. Speed: 12
kts. Complement: 116. Built by Birely & Lynn 1857. Engine by Merrick & Sons. Purchased Philadelphia 26
Apr 61. Converted by Washington. Commissioned 28 May 61. Sold New York 12 Jul 65.

FLAMBEAU (ex-Flambeau). Screw Steamer, 3rd rate. 900 tons. 185'(d) x 30' x 11'. Armament: 1-30#R 1-
20#R; 2-30#R 1-20#R (1862); 2-8" 1-30#R (1865). Brigantine rig. Machinery: Vertical beam engine, 1
screw. Speed: 12 kts. Complement: 92. Built by Lawrence & Foulkes 1861. Engine by Esler. Purchased 14
Nov 61. Commissioned 27 Nov 61. Sold New York 12 Jul 65.

FLORIDA (ex-Florida). Side-wheel Steamer, 3rd rate. 1261 tons. Hull and machinery duplicate the
Alabama. Armament: 8-32# 1-20#R; 1-100#R 4-9" 1-50#R (1863). Built by Webb 1850. Engine by Novelty.
Purchased 12 Aug 61. Commissioned 5 Oct 61. Sold Philadelphia 5 Dec 68. Haitian gunboat Republique
1869-75.

HATTERAS (ex-St. Mary's). Side-wheel Steamer, 3rd rate. 1126 tons. 210'(b.p.) x 34'(hull) x 18'(h).
Armament: 4-32#; 4-32# 1-20#R (1861). 3-masted schooner rig. Machinery: 500 HP beam engine, side
wheels. Complement: 110. Iron hull. Built by Harlan & Hollingsworth 1861. Purchased Wilmington, Del.,
25 Sep 61. Commissioned Oct 61. Sunk by CSS Alabama off Galveston, Tex., 11 Jan 63.

HUNTSVILLE (ex-Huntsville). Screw Steamer, 3rd rate. 840 tons. 196'4" x 29'8"(e) x 14'4". Armament: 1-8" 3-32#; 1-8"R 2-32# 1-30#R (1862); 1-10" 2-32# 1-30#R (1862). 3-masted schooner rig. Machinery: Vertical, inverted, direct-acting engine, 1 screw. Speed: 11 kts. Complement: 143. Built by Westervelt 1858. Engine by Morgan. Chartered 24 Apr 61. Commissioned 9 May 61. Purchased New York 24 Aug 61. Sold New York 30 Nov 65. Sister to the Montgomery.

JAMES ADGER (ex-James Adger). Side-wheel Steamer, 3rd rate. 1152 tons. 215'(d) x 33'6"(hull) x 12'6". Armament: 8-32#; 8-32# 1-20#R (1861); 1-9" 6-32# 1-20#R (1863). 3-masted schooner rig. Machinery: 240 NHP, side-lever engine, side wheels. Speed: 12.5 kts. Complement: 120. Built by Webb 1852. Engine by Allaire. Purchased New York 26 Jul 61. Converted by New York. Commissioned 20 Sep 61. Sold New York 9 Oct 66.

KEYSTONE STATE (ex-Keystone State). Side-wheel Steamer, 3rd rate. 1364 tons. 219' x 35'6"(hull) x 14'6". Armament: 5-8" 2-32# 1-?#R; 6-8" 1-50#R 2-32# 2-30#R (1863); 3-8" 1-50#R 2-32# 2-30#R (1863); 2-8" 1-50#R 2-32# 1-30#R (1864); 2-8" 2-30#R (1864). Bark rig. Machinery: 300 HP, side-lever engine, side wheels. Speed: 9.5 kts. Complement: 163. Built by Vaughn & Lynn 1853. Engine by Merrick & Sons. Chartered 19 Apr 61. Purchased Philadelphia 10 Jun 61. Converted by Philadelphia. Commissioned 19 Jul 61. Sold Washington 15 Sep 65.

MERCEDITA (ex-Mercedita). Screw Steamer, 3rd rate. 776 tons. 183'6" x 30'3" x 12'3". Armament: 8-32#; 8-32# 1-20#R (1861); 1-100#R 4-32# 1-20#R (1863). Barkentine rig. Machinery: 300 HP, inverted, direct-acting engine, 1 screw. Speed: 14 kts. Complement: 121. Built by Lupton, launched 20 Apr 61. Engine by Murphy. Purchased New York 31 Jul 61. Commissioned 5 Dec 61. Sold New York 25 Oct 65.

MONTGOMERY (ex-Montgomery). Screw Steamer, 3rd rate. 787 tons. Hull and machinery duplicate the Huntsville. Armament: 1-10" 2-32#; 1-10" 4-32# (1861); 1-10" 4-32# 1-30#R (1862); 1-100#R 4-32# 2-30#R (1862); 1-100#R 2-9" 3-30#R (1864). Built by Westervelt, launched 9 Jan 58. Engine by Morgan. Chartered 2 May 61. Commissioned 27 May 61. Purchased New York 24 Aug 61. Sold Philadelphia 10 Aug 65.

QUAKER CITY (ex-Quaker City). Side-wheel Steamer, 2nd rate. 1600 tons. 244'8" x 36'(hull) x 13'8". Armament 2-32#; 8-32# 1-20#R (1861); 1-100#R 6-8" 1-30#R 1-20#R (1863); 1-100#R 4-8" 1-30#R 1-20#R (1864). Schooner rig. Machinery: Side-lever engine, side wheels. Speed: 13 kts. Complement: 142. Built by Vaughn & Lynn, launched 2 May 54. Engine by Merrick & Sons. Chartered 25 Apr 61. Purchased 12 Aug 61. Commissioned 14 Dec 61. Sold Philadelphia 20 Jun 65. Haitian gunboat Mont Organise 1869-71.

R. R. CUYLER (ex-R. R. Cuyler). Screw Steamer, 3rd rate. 1202 tons. 237' x 33'3" x 16'. Armament: 8-32#; 8-32# 1-30#R (1862); 10-32# 1-30#R (1863); 10-32# 2-30#R (1864). Hermaphrodite brig. Machinery: Vertical, direct-acting engine, 1 screw. Speed: 14 kts. Complement: 116. Built by Sneeden, launched 20 Aug 59. Engine by Allaire. Chartered 29 Apr 61. Converted by Westervelt. Commissioned May 61. Purchased 24 Aug 61. Sold New York 15 Aug 65. Colombian warship El Rayo 1866-67.

RHODE ISLAND (ex-Eagle, ex-John P. King). Side-wheel Steamer, 2nd rate. 1517 tons. 236'7" x 36'9"(hull) x 15' Armament: 4-32#; 2-8" 4-32# 1-30#R (1861); 1-9" 8-8" 1-30#R (1862); 2-8" 4-32# (1863); 1-9" 8-32# 2-30#R (1863); 1-9" 8-32# (1864). Brig rig. Machinery: Vertical beam engine, side wheels. Speed: 13 kts. Complement: 257. Built by Westervelt, launched 6 Sep 60. Engine by Allaire. Purchased New York 8 Jul 61. Commissioned 29 Jul 61. Used as a supply vessel 1861-62. Sold New York 1 Oct 67.

SANTIAGO DE CUBA (ex-Santiago de Cuba). Side-wheel Steamer, 2nd rate. 1567 tons. 238'(d) x 38'(hull) x 16'2". Armament: 8-32# 2-20#R; 8-32# 1-30#R 2-20#R (1864); 5-32# 1-30#R 2-20#R (1864); 4-32# 2-30#R 2-20#R (1865). Brigantine rig. Machinery: Vertical beam engine, side wheels. Speed: 14 kts. Complement: 179. Built by Simonson, launched 2 Apr 61. Engine by Neptune Works. Purchased New York 6 Sep 61. Commissioned 5 Nov 61. Sold Philadelphia 21 Sep 65.

SOUTH CAROLINA (ex-South Carolina). Screw Steamer, 3rd rate. 1165 tons. 217'11" x 33'6" x 14'6". Armament: 4-8" 1-32#; 4-8" 2-32# 1-30#R (1862). Machinery: Vertical, inverted, direct-acting engine, 1 screw. Speed: 10.5 kts. Complement: 115. Iron hull. Built by Atlantic 1860. Engine by builder. Purchased Boston 3 May 61. Converted by Boston. Commissioned 22 May 61. Sold New York 5 Oct 66.

STATE OF GEORGIA (ex-State of Georgia). Side-wheel Steamer, 3rd rate. 1204 tons. 210'(d) x 33'(hull) x 14'. Armament: 6-8" 2-32# 1-30#R; 1-100#R 6-9" 1-30#R (1863). Barkentine rig. Machinery: 400 HP, side-lever engine, side wheels. Complement: 113. Built by Vaughn & Lynn, launched 12 Feb 52. Engine by Merrick & Sons. Purchased Philadelphia 25 Sep 61. Commissioned 20 Nov 61. Sold New York 25 Oct 65.

VARUNA (ex-Varuna). Screw Steamer. 1300 tons. 218' x 34'8" x 13'8"(h). Armament: 8-8" 2-30#R.
Machinery: 1 screw. Complement: 157. Built by Mallory 1861. Purchased New York 31 Dec 61. Commissioned
Feb 62. Sunk by CSS Governor Moore below New Orleans 24 Apr 62.

1862

LODONA (ex-Lodona). Screw Steamer, 3rd rate. 861 tons. 210' x 27'6" x 11'6". Armament: 1-9" 1-100#R 1-
30#R. Bark rig. Machinery: Vertical, direct-acting engine, 1 screw. Speed: 7 kts. Complement: 97. Iron
hull. Built by Samuelson, Hull, 1862. Captured by Unadilla in Ossabaw Sound, S.C., 4 Aug 62 while
running blockade. Purchased from Philadelphia Prize Court 20 Sep 62. Commissioned 5 Jan 63. Sold
Philadelphia 20 Jun 65. Redesignated 4th rate 1865.

MEMPHIS (ex-Memphis). Screw Steamer, 3rd rate. 791 tons. 227' x 30'1" x 15'6". Armament: 1-30#R 4-24#;
1-30#R 4-24# 4-20#R (1864). Machinery: Inverted, direct-acting engine, 1 screw. Speed: 14 kts.
Complement: 100. Iron hull. Built by Denny, launched 3 Apr 62. Captured by Magnolia off the Carolinas
31 Jul 62 while running blockade. Purchased from New York Prize Court 4 Sep 62. Commissioned 4 Oct 62.
Converted to storeship (4th rate) 1865. Sold New York 8 Jun 69.

TENNESSEE (ex-Tennessee). Side-wheel Steamer, 3rd rate. 1275 tons. 210' x 33'11" x 12'. Armament: 2-
32# 1-30#R. Machinery: Vertical beam engine, side wheels. Complement: 217. Built by Robb, Baltimore,
launched 31 Aug 53. Engine by Reeder. Captured at New Orleans 25 Apr 62. Commissioned 8 May 62.
Renamed Mobile 1 Sep 64. Sold New York 30 Mar 65.

VANDERBILT (ex-Vanderbilt). Side-wheel Steamer, 2nd rate. 3360 tons. 340'(oa.) x 47'6"(hull) x 21'6".
Armament: 2-100#R 12-9"; 12-9" (1863); 2-100#R 12-9" 2-30#R (1864); 1-100#R 12-9" 2-30#R (1865).
Brigantine rig. Machinery: 2800 IHP, two vertical beam engines, side wheels. Speed: 14 kts,
Complement: 209. Built by Simonson, launched 17 Dec 55. Engine by Allaire. Donated to Army 17 Mar 62.
Transferred from War Dept. 2 Sep 62. Fitted out by New York. Redesignated 1st rate 1865. Sold Mare I.
1 Apr 73.

1863

ARIES (ex-Aries). Screw Steamer, 3rd rate. 820 tons. 201'(d) x 27'10" x 16'. Armament: 4-8" 1-30#R; 4-
8" 2-30#R (1863). 3-masted schooner rig. Machinery: Vertical, inverted, direct-acting engine, 1 screw.
Speed: 12 kts. Complement: 90. Iron hull. Built by Laing, Sunderland, launched 12 Feb 62. Captured by
Stettin in Bulls Bay, S. C., 28 Mar 63 while running blockade. Purchased from Boston Prize Court 20
May 63. Commissioned 25 Jul 63. Sold Boston 1 Aug 65.

ARIZONA (ex-Caroline, ex-Arizona). Side-wheel Steamer, 3rd rate. 950 tons. 201'6" x 34' x 8'.
Armament: 4-32# 1-30#R. 2-masted schooner rig. Machinery: Vertical beam engine, side wheels.
Complement: 91. Iron hull. Built by Harlan & Hollingsworth 1859. Engine by Morgan. Captured by
Montgomery off Pensacola 29 Oct 62 while running blockade. Purchased from Philadelphia Prize Court 23
Jan 63. Commissioned 9 Mar 63. Destroyed by fire below New Orleans 27 Feb 65.

ARKANSAS (ex-Tonawanda). Screw Steamer, 3rd rate. 752 tons. 191' x 30' x 14'. Armament: 4-32#; 4-32#
1-20#R (1863). Barkentine rig. Machinery: Vertical, direct-acting engine, 1 screw. Speed: 15 kts.
Complement: 88. Built by Cramp 1863. Purchased Philadelphia 27 Jun 63. Commissioned 5 Sep 63. Sold
Portsmouth 20 Jul 65. Also used as transport and tug.

AUGUSTA DINSMORE (ex-Augusta Dinsmore). Screw schooner, 3rd rate. 850 tons. 169' x 32'6" x 12'6".
Armament: 2-24# 1-20#R. 2-masted schooner rig. Machinery: Ericsson monitor type engine, 1 screw.
Speed: 11 kts. Complement: 70. Built by Mallory 1863. Purchased New York 17 Jul 63. Commissioned 1863.
Sold New York 5 Sep 65.

FORT JACKSON (ex-Union). Side-wheel Steamer, 2nd rate. 1850 tons. 250' x 38'6"(e) x 18'. Armament: 1-
100#R 8-9" 2-30#R. Brigantine rig. Machinery: Vertical, beam engine, side wheels. Speed: 14 kts.
Complement: 194. Built by Simonson 1862. Engine by Allaire. Purchased New York 22 Jul 63. Commissioned
18 Aug 63. Sold New York 27 Sep 65.

GALATEA (ex-Galatea). Screw Steamer, 3rd rate. 1244 tons. 209' x 35'6" x 14'. Armament: 1-100#R 8-32#
2-30#R; 8-32# (1864); 1-100#R 6-32# 2-30#R (1865). Schooner rig. Machinery: Inverted, direct-acting
engine, 1 screw. Speed: 11 kts. Complement: 164. Built by Van Deusen 1863. Engine by Esler. Purchased
New York 17 Sep 63. Commissioned 29 Jan 64. Sold to Haiti 27 Sep 65 as gunboat Alexandre Petion.
Sister to Glaucus, Neptune, Nereus, and Proteus.

GLAUCUS (ex-Glaucus). Screw Steamer, 3rd rate. 1244 tons. Hull and machinery duplicate the Galatea.
Armament: 1-100#R 8-8" 2-30#R. Built by Van Deusen 1863. Engine by Esler. Purchased New York 17 Jul

63. Commissioned 18 Feb 64. Sold New York 12 Jul 65. Sister to the Galatea, Neptune, Nereus, and Proteus.

GOVERNOR BUCKINGHAM (ex-Governor Buckingham). Screw Steamer, 3rd rate. 886 tons. 177'6" x 32'2" x 13'6". Armament: 1-100#R 4-30#R 1-20#R. Brigantine rig. Machinery: Vertical, direct-acting engine, 1 screw. Speed: 8 kts. Complement: 112. Built by Mallory 1863. Purchased Stonington, Conn., 29 Jul 63. Converted by Webb. Commissioned 13 Nov 63. Sold New York 12 Jul 65.

GRAND GULF (ex-Onward). Screw Steamer, 3rd rate. 1200 tons. 216' x 34'6" x 24'(h). Armament: 1-100#R 8-8" 2-30#R. Machinery: Vertical, direct-acting engine, 1 screw. Speed: 11 kts. Complement: 201. Built by Poillon 1863. Purchased New York 14 Sep 63. Commissioned 28 Sep 63. Sold New York 30 Nov 65.

NEPTUNE (ex-Neptune). Screw Steamer, 3rd rate. 1244 tons. Hull and machinery duplicate the Galatea. Armament: 1-100#R 8-32# 2-30#R; 1-100#R 6-32# 2-30#R (1864); 1-60#R 2-32# 2-30#R (1865). Built by Van Deusen 1863. Engine by Esler. Purchased New York 17 Jul 63. Commissioned 19 Dec 63. Sold New York 12 Jul 65. Sister to the Galatea, Glaucus, Nereus, and Proteus.

NEREUS (ex-Nereus). Screw Steamer, 3rd rate. 1244 tons. Hull and machinery duplicate the Galatea. Armament: 1-100#R 1-60#R 6-32# 2-30#R; 1-100#R 6-32# 2-30#R (1864); 6-32# 2-30#R (1865). Built by Van Deusen 1863. Engine by Esler. Purchased New York 5 Oct 63. Commissioned 19 Apr 64. Sold New York 12 Jul 65. Sister to the Galatea, Glaucus, Neptune, and Proteus.

PETERHOFF (ex-Peterhoff). Screw Steamer. 800 tons. 220' x 29' x 17'. Machinery: 1 screw. Iron hull. Built by Oswald, Sunderland, launched 25 Jul 61. Captured by Vanderbilt off St. Thomas 25 Feb 63 while running blockade. Purchased from New York Prize Court Feb 63. Commissioned Feb 64. Sunk in collision with Monticello off North Carolina 6 Mar 64.

PRINCESS ROYAL (ex-Princess Royal). Screw Steamer, 3rd rate. 828 tons. 196'9" x 27'3" x 11'. Armament: 1-9" 2-30#R. Machinery: Horizontal geared engine, 1 screw. Speed: 11 kts. Complement: 90. Built by Tod & McGregor, Glasgow, launched 20 Jun 61. Captured by Unadilla off Charleston 29 Jan 63 while running blockade. Purchased from Philadelphia Prize Court 18 Mar 63. Commissioned 29 May 63. Sold Philadelphia 17 Aug 65.

PROTEUS (ex-Proteus). Screw Steamer, 3rd rate. 1244 tons. Hull and machinery duplicate the Galatea. Armament: 1-100#R 6-32# 2-30#R; 1-60#R 6-32# 2-30#R (1864); 1-60#R 6-32# 2-20#R (1865). Built by Van Deusen 1863. Purchased New York 5 Oct 63. Commissioned 10 Mar 64. Sold New York 12 Jul 65. Sister to the Galatea, Glaucus, Neptune, and Nereus.

VICKSBURG (ex-Vicksburg). Screw Steamer, 3rd rate. 886 tons. 185'(oa.) x 33' x 13'8". Armament: 1-100#R 2-30#R 3-20#R. Brigantine rig. Machinery: 200 IHP, vertical, direct-acting engine, 1 screw. Speed: 9 kts. Complement: 122. Built by Maxon, Fish 1863. Purchased New York 20 Oct 63. Converted by New York. Commissioned 2 Dec 63. Sold New York 12 Jul 65.

1864

FORT DONELSON (ex-Robert E. Lee, ex Giraffe). Side-wheel Steamer, 3rd rate. 900 tons. 283' x 26' x 10'. Armament: 2-30#R. Schooner rig. Machinery: 290 NHP, oscillating engine, side wheels. Speed: 11 kts. Complement: 137. Iron hull. Built by Thomson, launched 16 May 60. Captured by Iron Age and James Adger off Wilmington 9 Nov 63 while running blockade. Purchased from Boston Prize Court Jan 64. Commissioned 29 Jun 64. Sold New York 25 Oct 65. Chilean naval steamer Concepcion 1865-68.

IUKA (ex-Commodore). Screw Steamer, 3rd rate. 944 tons. 200' x 31'6" x 20'(h). Armament: 1-100#R 2-8" 2-30#R; 1-100#R 2-8" 1-30#R (1865). Machinery: Horizontal, direct-acting engine, 1 screw. Speed: 10 kts. Complement: 116. Built by Pook 1863. Engine by Delamater. Purchased New York 8 Mar 64. Commissioned 23 May 64. Sold Boston 1 Aug 65.

2. Steamers (Large 4th Rates)

1855

DESPATCH (ex-City of Boston). Screw Steamer (Tender). 558 tons. 169'6" x 30'6" x 12'. Machinery: 1 screw. Complement: 95. Built at Medford, Mass., 1852. Engine by Fulton IrWks. Purchased Boston 20 Mar 55. Commissioned 17 Jan 56. Decommissioned 2 Jan 59 at Norfolk and rebuilt as the sloop Pocahontas.

1858

CRUSADER (ex-Southern Star). Screw Steamer, 4th rate. 545 tons. 169' x 28' x 12'6". Bark rig.
Armament: 8-24#; 2-9" (1859); 1-32# (1861); 4-32# (1861); 4-32# 2-20#R (1862). Machinery: Inclined,
direct-acting engine, 1 screw. Speed: 8 kts. Complement: 92. Built in Murfreesboro, N. C., 1858.
Chartered Oct 58. Commissioned 27 Oct 58. Purchased 1859. Sold Washington 20 Jul 65.

MOHAWK (ex-Caledonia). Screw Steamer, 4th rate. 459 tons. 162'4" x 24'4" x 14'. Armament: 4-32#; 2-9"
(1859); 6-32# (1861); 6-32# 1-30#R (1862). Machinery: Vertical, direct-acting engine, 1 screw. Speed:
8 kts. Complement: 90. Built by Teas & Birely, launched 11 Jun 53. Engine by Sutton. Chartered 13 Sep
58. Purchased 26 May 59. Renamed 14 Jun 59. Commissioned 19 Sep 59. Sold Philadelphia 12 Jul 64.

MYSTIC (ex-Memphis, ex-Mount Savage). Screw Steamer, 4th rate. 452 tons. 157' x 24'7" x 13'6".
Armament: 4-32#; 2-9" (1859); 6-32# 1-20#R (1862). Machinery: Vertical, direct-acting engine, 1 screw.
Speed: 6 kts. Bark rig. Complement: 90. Built by Cramp, launched 2 Apr 53. Engine by Reanie & Neafie.
Chartered 13 Sep 58. Commissioned 3 Dec 58. Purchased 26 May 59. Renamed Mystic 14 Jun 59. Sold
Washington 24 Jun 65.

PULASKI (ex-Metacomet). Side-wheel Steamer, 4th rate. 395 tons. 169'11' x 26' x 9'(h). Armament: 3
small. Machinery: Crosshead engine, side wheels. Built by Sneeden 1854. Chartered and commissioned
1858, purchased 1859. Sold at Montevideo 22 Jan 63.

SUMTER (ex-Atalanta, ex-Parker Vein). Screw Steamer, 4th rate. 460 tons. 163' x 24'4" x 11'9".
Armament: 4-32#; 2-9" (1859); 4-32# 1-20#R (1863). Machinery: Vertical, back-acting engine, 1 screw.
Complement: 90. Built by Hillman & Streaker, launched 19 Mar 53. Engine by Reanie & Neafie. Chartered
13 Sep 58. Purchased 26 May 59. Renamed Sumter (sometimes spelled Sumpter) 14 Jun 59. Sunk in
collision with USAT General Meigs off Smith I., N. C., 24 Jun 63.

WYANDOTTE (ex-Western Port). Screw Steamer, 4th rate. 453 tons. 162'4"x 24'3" x 13'6". Armament: 4-
32#; 2-9" (1859); 4-32# 1-20#R (1862). Machinery: Vertical, direct-acting engine, 1 screw. Speed: 7
kts. Complement: 90. Built by Birely & Lynn, launched 26 Mar 53. Engine by Reanie & Neafie. Chartered
13 Sep 58. Commissioned 27 Oct 58. Purchased 26 May 59. Renamed 14 Jun 59. Sold New York 12 Jul 65.

1861

ALBATROSS (ex-Albatross). Screw Steamer, 4th rate. 378 tons. 158' x 30' x 13'. Armament: 1-8" 2-32#;
4-32# (1861); 1-8" (1862); 4-32# 1-30#R (1863). 3-masted schooner rig. Machinery: Vertical, direct-
acting engine, 1 screw. Speed: 11 kts. Complement: 95. Built by Greenman, launched 31 Oct 58. Engine
by Corliss. Purchased Brooklyn 23 May 61. Commissioned 25 Jun 61. Sold Boston 8 Sep 65.

DAWN (ex-Dawn). Screw Steamer, 4th rate. 399 tons. 154' x 28'10" x 12'. Armament: 2-32#; 4-32# 1-20#R
(1861); 1-100#R 2-32# 1-30#R (1863); 1-100#R 1-20#R (1863). 3-masted schooner rig. Machinery: Rotary
engine, 1 screw. Speed: 11 kts. Complement: 60. Built by Sneeden 1857. Engine by Delamater. Chartered
26 Apr 61. Converted by Boston. Commissioned 9 May 61. Purchased 12 Oct 61. Sold Boston 1 Nov 65.

DAYLIGHT (ex-Daylight). Screw Steamer, 4th rate. 682 tons. 170' x 30'6" x 13'. Armament: 4-32#; 4-32#
1-30#R (1862). Barkentine rig. Machinery: Half-trunk (rotary) engine, 1 screw. Speed: 5 kts.
Complement: 57. Built by Sneeden 1859. Engine by Delamater. Chartered 10 May 61. Converted by New
York. Commissioned 7 Jun 61. Purchased New York 12 Oct 61. Sold New York 25 Oct 65.

DELAWARE (ex-Delaware, ex-Virginia Dare). Side-wheel Steamer, 4th rate. 357 tons. 161' x 27' x 6'(h).
Armament: 4-32#; 1-9" 1-32# (1862). Schooner rig. Machinery: Beam engine, side wheels. Speed: 13 kts.
Complement: 65. Iron hull. Built by Harlan & Hollingsworth 1861. Purchased Wilmington, Del., 14 Oct
61. Commissioned 1861. Transferred to Revenue Cutter Service 30 Aug 65.

ISAAC SMITH (ex-Isaac Smith). Screw Steamer, 4th rate. 453 tons. 171'6" x 31'4" x 7'. Armament: 6-8"
2-32# 1-30#R; 8-8" 1-30#R (1861); 1-30#R (1862). Machinery: Beam engine, 1 screw. Complement: 119.
Built by Lawrence & Foulkes 1861. Purchased New York 9 Sep 61. Commissioned 16 Oct 61. Captured by
Confederate batteries in Stono R., S. C., 30 Jan 63.

MONTICELLO (ex-Monticello). Screw Steamer, 4th rate. 655 tons. 180' x 29' x 12'10". Armament: 1-10" 2-
32#; 1-10" 4-32# (1861); 1-10" 4-32# 2-30#R (1862); 1-100#R 4-32# 2-30#R (1862); 1-100#R 2-9" 3-30#R
(1864). Schooner rig. Machinery: 220 NHP, vertical, direct-acting engine, 1 screw. Speed: 11.5 kts.
Complement: 137. Built by Williams 1859. Chartered 23 Apr 61. Converted by New York. Commissioned by 2
May 61. Renamed Star 3 May 61; name changed back 25 May 61. Purchased New York 12 Sep 61. Sold Boston
1 Nov 65.

MOUNT VERNON (ex-Mount Vernon). Screw Steamer, 4th rate. 625 tons. 173'6" x 28'8" x 14'. Armament: 3-32#; 8-32# 1-?#R (1861); 1-100#R 4-32# (1863); 1-100#R 2-9" 2-20#R (1863). Schooner rig. Machinery: 220 NHP, vertical, direct-acting engine, 1 screw. Speed: 11.5 kts. Complement: 50. Built by Sneeden, launched 10 Jul 59. Chartered 23 Apr 61. Commissioned May 61. Purchased New York 12 Sep 61. Sold New York 12 Jul 65.

MOUNT WASHINGTON (ex-USS Mount Vernon, ex-Mount Vernon). Side-wheel Steamer, 4th rate. 500 tons. 200' x 24' x 6'6". Armament: 1-32#. Machinery: Vertical beam engine, side wheels. Speed: 12 kts. Complement: 40. Built by Birely, launched 11 Apr 46. Engine by Reaney & Neafie. Transferred from War Department 21 Apr 61. Commissioned May 61. Renamed 4 Nov 61. Sold Baltimore 21 Jun 65.

NORWICH (ex-Norwich). Screw Steamer, 4th rate. 431 tons. 132'5" x 24'6" x 10'. Armament: 4-8" 1-30#R. 3-masted schooner rig. Machinery: Vertical, direct-acting engine, 1 screw. Speed: 6 kts. Complement: 80. Built in Norwich, Conn., 1861. Purchased New York 26 Sep 61. Commissioned 28 Dec 61. Sold Philadelphia 10 Aug 65.

PENGUIN (ex-Penguin). Screw Steamer, 4th rate. 389 tons. 155' x 30'5" x 12'. Armament: 1-8" 2-32#; 4-32# (1861); 4-32# 1-20#R (1863). 3-masted schooner rig. Machinery: Vibrating-lever engine, 1 screw. Speed: 10 kts. Complement: 69. Built by Mallory, launched 26 Nov 59. Engine by Delamater. Purchased New York 23 May 61. Commissioned 25 Jun 61. Sold 18 Sep 65.

STARS AND STRIPES (ex-Stars and Stripes). Screw Steamer, 4th rate. 407 tons. 150'6"(d) x 34'6"(m) x 9'. Armament: 4-32#; 4-8" (1861); 4-8" 1-20#R (1862). Schooner rig. Machinery: Vertical, direct-acting engine, 1 screw. Speed: 10.5 kts. Complement: 94. Built by Mallory 1861. Engine by Delamater. Purchased New York 27 Jul 61. Commissioned 19 Sep 61. Sold Philadelphia 10 Aug 65.

UNDERWRITER (ex-Underwriter). Side-wheel Steamer, 4th rate. 341 tons. 185' x 23'7" x 8'1". Armament: 1-100#R 1-8"; 2-8" (1863). Machinery: Oscillating engine, side wheels. Complement: 69. Built at Brooklyn 1852. Purchased New York 23 Aug 61. Commissioned 23 Aug 61. Captured and destroyed by Confederates 2 Feb 64 on Neuse River, N.C.

UNION (ex-Union). Chartered Philadelphia 24 Apr 61. Commissioned 16 May 61. Decommissioned 10 Dec 61 and transferred to War Dept. A "long, low steamer" with a maximum draft of 10'. The Union acquired in 1862 and used as a transport was a different ship.

WESTERN WORLD (ex-Western World). Screw Steamer, 4th rate. 441 tons. 178' x 34'3" x 8'6". Armament: 2-32# 1-30#R; 4-32# 1-30#R (1863). Machinery: Vertical, direct-acting engine, 1 screw. Speed: 7 kts. Complement: 86. Built by William Collyer, Brooklyn 1857. Engine by Allaire. Purchased New York 21 Sep 61. Commissioned 3 Jan 62. Sold Washington 24 Jun 65.

YOUNG ROVER (ex-Young Rover). Screw Steamer, 4th rate. 418 tons. 141' x 28'2" x 11'. Armament: 4-32#. Bark rig. Machinery: 75 HP, 1 screw. Speed: 7 kts. Complement: 48. Built by Curtis, Medford, 1860. Purchased Boston 27 Jul 61. Converted by Boston. Commissioned 10 Sep 61. Sold Boston 22 Jun 65.

1862

CALHOUN (ex-Cuba). Side-wheel Steamer, 4th rate. 508 tons. Armament: 2-32# 3-30#R. Machinery: Side wheels. Built by Sneeden 1851. Confederate privateer captured by Samuel Rotan off Southwest Pass, La., 23 Jan 62. Commissioned 19 Mar 62. Purchased from Philadelphia Prize Court 28 Nov 62. Transferred to War Dept. 4 Jun 64 as General Sedgwick.

COLUMBIA (ex-Columbia). Screw Steamer, 4th rate. 503 tons. 168' x 25' x 14'(h). Armament: 6-24# 1-30#R. Machinery: Inverted engine, 1 screw. Complement: 100. Iron hull. Built by A. Denny, Dumbarton, launched 19 Jul 62. Captured by Santiago de Cuba off Florida 3 Aug 62 while running blockade. Purchased from Key West Prize Court 4 Nov 62. Commissioned Dec 62. Wrecked off Masonboro Inlet, N.C., 14 Jan 63 and wreck burned 17 Jan 63.

ESTRELLA (ex-Estrella). Side-wheel Steamer, 4th rate. 438 tons. 178' x 26' x 6'. Armament: 2-32# 1-30#R; 1-30#R (1865). Machinery: Oscillating engine, side wheels. Complement: 57. Iron hull. Built in London 1853. Captured Jun 62 while running blockade. Transferred from Army 1862. Commissioned 1862. Sold New York 9 Oct 67.

HENDRICK HUDSON (ex-Florida). Screw Steamer, 4th rate. 460 tons. 171'(d) x 29'11" x 9'6"(h). Armament: 4-8" 2-20#R. 2-masted schooner rig. Machinery: 100 HP, Vertical direct-acting engine, 1 screw. Speed: 11 kts. Complement: 88. Built by Whitlock, launched 30 Jun 59. Captured by Pursuit N of St.

Andrewstown, Fla., 6 Apr 62 while running blockade. Purchased from Philadelphia Prize Court 20 Sep 62. Commissioned 30 Dec 62. Sold Philadelphia 12 Sep 65.

MAGNOLIA (ex-Magnolia). Side-wheel Steamer, 4th rate. 843 tons. 242'5" x 33'11" x 5'. Armament: 2-24# 1-20#R; 4-24# 1-20#R (1864). Schooner rig. Machinery: Vertical beam engine, side wheels. Speed: 12 kts. Complement: 95. Built by Simonson, launched 22 Aug 54. Engine by Allaire. Captured by Brooklyn and South Carolina off Pass a l'Outre, Louisiana, 19 Feb 62 while running blockade. Purchased from Key West Prize Court 9 Apr 62. Commissioned 22 Jul 62. Sold New York 12 Jul 65.

STETTIN (ex-Stettin). Screw Steamer, 4th rate. 600 tons. 171' x 28' x 12'. Armament: 1-30#R. Brig rig. Machinery: Inverted engine, 1 screw. Speed: 6 kts. Complement: 72. Iron hull. Built by Pile, Sunderland, launched 19 Sep 61. Captured by Bienville off Charleston 24 May 62 while running blockade. Purchased from New York Prize Court 4 Sep 62. Commissioned 12 Nov 62. Sold Boston 22 Jun 65.

1863

ADELA (ex-Adela). Side-wheel Steamer, 4th rate. 585 tons. 211' x 23'6" x 9'3". Armament: 4-24# 2-20#R. Brig rig. Machinery: Oscillating engine, side wheels. Speed: 12 kts. Complement: 70. Iron hull. Built in Britain. Captured by Quaker City and Huntsville in the Bahamas 7 Jul 62 while running blockade. Purchased from Key West Prize Court 23 May 63. Commissioned Jun 63. Sold New York 30 Nov 65.

ANTONA (ex-Antona). Screw Steamer, 4th rate. 549 tons. 166'9" x 23'1" x 13'. Armament: 2-32# 2-24# 1-20#R; 2-32# 2-24# (1864). Machinery: Vertical engine, 1 screw. Speed: 8 kts. Complement: 56. Iron hull. Built by Neilson, Glasgow, 1859. Captured by Pocahontas off Mobile 6 Jan 63 while running blockade. Commissioned 19 Mar 63. Purchased from New York Prize Court 28 Mar 64. Sold New York 30 Nov 65.

BRITANNIA (ex-Britannia). Side-wheel Steamer, 4th rate. 495 tons. 189' x 26' x 9'. Armament: 1-30#R. Machinery: Vertical steeple engine, side wheels. Speed: 12.5 kts. Complement: 75. Iron hull. Built by Barclay Curle, Glasgow, 1862. Captured by Santiago de Cuba in the Bahamas 25 Jun 63 while running blockade. Commissioned 16 Sep 63. Purchased from Boston Prize Court 29 Sep 63. Sold Philadelphia 10 Aug 65.

CALYPSO (ex-Calypso). Screw Steamer, 4th rate. 630 tons. 190'3" x 26'6" x 12'. Armament: 4-24# 2-30#R; 4-24# 3-30#R (1863); 4-24# 1-30#R (1865). 3-masted schooner rig. Machinery: 140 HP, geared steeple engine, 1 screw. Speed: 12 kts. Complement: 70. Iron hull. Built by A. Denny, Dumbarton, launched 15 Apr 55. Captured by Florida off Wilmington 11 Jun 63 while running blockade. Commissioned 24 Sep 63. Purchased from Philadelphia Prize Court 12 Oct 63. Sold New York 30 Nov 65.

CLYDE (ex-Neptune). Side-wheel Steamer, 4th rate. 294 tons. 200'6" x 18'6" x 8"(h). Armament: 2 small. Machinery: Inclined engine, side wheels. Speed: 9 kts. Complement: 67. Iron hull. Built by Napier, Glasgow, 1861. Captured by Lackawanna 14 Jun 63 while running blockade. Purchased from New York Prize Court 25 Jul 63. Commissioned 29 Jul 63. Renamed 11 Aug 63. Sold New York 25 Oct 65.

CORNUBIA (ex-Lady Davis, ex-Cornubia). Side-wheel Steamer, 4th rate. 589 tons. 210' x 24'6" x 10'. Armament: 2-24# 1-20#R; 2-24# 1-30#R (1864). Machinery: 230 HP, oscillating engine, side wheels. Speed: 13 kts. Complement: 76. Iron hull. Built by Harvey, Hayle, launched 27 Feb 58. Captured by Niphon and James Adger off New Inlet, N.C., 8 Nov 63 while running blockade. Purchased from Boston Prize Court Nov 63. Commissioned 17 Mar 64. Sold New York 25 Oct 65.

DAI CHING (ex-Dai Ching). Screw Steamer, 4th rate. 520 tons. 175'2" x 29'4" x 9'6". Armament: 1-100#R 4-24# 2-20#R. Machinery: Low pressure, direct-acting engine, 1 screw. Speed: 6 kts. Complement: 83. Built by Jewett, Brooklyn, 1862, for Ward's Chinese navy. Engine by McLeod. Purchased New York 21 Apr 63. Commissioned 11 Jun 63. Grounded in Combahee River, S.C. and burned 26 Jan 65.

EMMA (ex-Emma). Screw Steamer, 4th rate. 350 tons. 156' x 21' x 9'4". Armament: 1-20#R. Schooner rig. Machinery: Oscillating engine, 1 screw. Speed: 12 kts. Complement: 68. Iron hull. Built by Barclay Curle, Glasgow, launched 24 Nov 62. Captured by USAT Arago 24 Jul 63 while running blockade. Purchased from New York Prize Court 30 Sep 63. Commissioned 4 Nov 63. Sold Boston 1 Nov 65. Sister to the Gertrude.

GERTRUDE (ex-Gertrude). Screw Steamer, 4th rate. 350 tons. Hull and machinery duplicate the Emma. Armament: 8 small. Built by Barclay Curle, Glasgow, launched 28 Nov 62. Captured by Vanderbilt off Eleuthera 16 Apr 63 while running blockade. Purchased from New York Prize Court 4 Jun 63. Commissioned 22 Jul 63. Sold New York 30 Nov 65.

GETTYSBURG (ex-Margaret & Jessie, ex-Douglas). Side-wheel Steamer, 4th rate. 726 tons. 211' x 26'3" x 10'. Armament: 1-30#R; 2-32# 1-30#R (1864). Brigantine rig. Machinery: Oscillating engine, side wheels. Speed: 15 kts. Complement: 96. Iron hull. Built by Napier, Glasgow, launched 28 May 58. Captured by Nansemond, Keystone State, and Howquah off Wilmington 5 Nov 63 while running blockade. Purchased from New York Prize Court 20 Nov 63. Commissioned 2 May 64. Sold at Genoa 8 May 79.

GRANITE CITY (ex-Granite City). Side-wheel Steamer, 4th rate. 315 tons. 160' x 23' x 5'6". Armament: 1-20#R. Machinery: Inclined engine, side wheels. Complement: 69. Iron hull. Built by A. Denny, Dumbarton, launched 11 Nov 62. Captured by Tioga in the Bahamas 22 Mar 63 while running blockade. Purchased from New York Prize Court Apr 63. Commissioned 16 Apr 63. Captured by Confederate batteries at Calcasieu Pass, La., 28 Apr 64.

HARVEST MOON (ex-Harvest Moon). Side-wheel Steamer, 4th rate. 546 tons. 193' x 29' x 8'. Armament: 1-20#R. Machinery: Vertical beam engine, side wheels. Speed: 15 mph. Complement: 72. Built by Dyer, 1862. Purchased Boston 16 Nov 63. Commissioned 12 Feb 64. Sunk by mine 1 May 65 in Winyah Bay, S.C.

IRON AGE (ex-Iron Age). Screw Steamer, 4th rate. 424 tons. 144' x 25' x 12'6"(h). Armament: 6-8" 3-30#R. Machinery: 1 screw. Complement: 107. Built by Thompson 1862. Purchased Boston 28 Apr 63. Converted by Boston. Commissioned 25 Jun 63. Grounded in Lockwood's Folly Inlet, N. C., 11 Jan 64 and destroyed.

MALVERN (ex-Ella and Annie) Side-wheel Steamer, 4th rate. 627 tons. 240' x 23'2" x 8'5". Armament: 4-20#R. Machinery: Beam engine, side wheels. Complement: 68. Iron hull. Captured by Niphon off New Inlet, N.C., 9 Nov 63 while running blockade. Purchased from Boston Prize Court 1863. Commissioned 9 Feb 64. Sold New York 25 Oct 65. The Ella and Annie has been identified as the former William G. Hewes, launched by Harlan & Hollingsworth 15 Oct 60 with a reported tonnage of 1477 tons (which would have made her a 3rd rate), dimensions of 239'4" x 33' x 9', and 500 HP machinery by Morgan.

NANSEMOND (ex-James F. Freeborn). Side-wheel Steamer, 4th rate. 335 tons. 155'(d) x 26' x 8'3". Armament: 1-30#R 2-24#. Machinery: Vertical beam engine, side wheels. Speed: 15 kts. Complement: 63. Built by Lawrence & Foulkes 1862. Engine by Fletcher. Purchased New York 18 Aug 63. Commissioned 19 Aug 63. Sold to Revenue Cutter Service 22 Aug 65.

NIPHON (ex-Niphon). Screw Steamer, 4th rate. 475 tons. 153'2" x 24'7" x 13'3". Armament: 4-32# 1-20#R; 6-32# 1-20#R (1864). Fore and aft rig on fore and mizzen masts, square sails on main. Machinery: Vertical, inverted, direct-acting engine, 1 screw. Speed: 10 kts. Complement: 100. Composite hull. Built by S. Smith 1863. Engine by Atlantic. Purchased Boston 9 May 63. Converted by Boston. Commissioned 24 Apr 63. Sold Boston 17 Apr 65.

TRITONIA (ex-Sarah S. B. Cary). Side-wheel Steamer, 4th rate. 202 tons. 178' x 22'4" x 7'6"(h). Armament: 1-30#R. Machinery: Side wheels. Complement: 26. Built at East Haddam, Ct., 1863. Purchased Hartford, Ct., 1 Dec 63. Commissioned 23 Apr 64. Sold New York 5 Oct 66.

VIRGINIA (ex-Virginia, ex-Noe-Daquy, ex-Pet). Screw Steamer, 4th rate. 581 tons. 175'6" x 26' x 8'. Armament: 1-30#R. Bark rig. Machinery: Vertical, direct-acting engine, 1 screw. Speed: 9 kts. Complement: 61. Iron hull. Built at Dumbarton, Scotland, 1861. Captured by Wachusett and Sonoma off Mujeres Is., Mexico, 18 Jan 63 while running blockade. Commissioned 12 Jun 63. Purchased from New York Prize Court 1 Sep 63. Sold New York 30 Nov 65.

1864

ADVANCE (ex-A. D. Vance, ex-Lord Clyde). Side-wheel Steamer, 4th rate. 808 tons. 243' x 26' x 11'8". Armament: 1-20#R. Schooner rig. Machinery: Side-lever engine, side wheels. Speed: 12 kts. Complement: 107. Iron hull. Built by Caird, Greenock, launched 3 Jul 62. Captured by Santiago de Cuba 10 Sep 64 while running blockade. Purchased from New York Prize Court Sep 64. Commissioned 28 Oct 64. Renamed Frolic 2 Jun 65. Sold 1 Oct 83.

BANSHEE (ex-Banshee). Side-wheel Steamer, 4th rate. 533 tons. 220' x 20'4" x 10'. Armament: 1-30#R. 2-masted schooner rig. Machinery: Oscillating engine, side wheels. Speed: 12 kts. Complement: 89. Steel hull. Built by Jones Quiggin, Liverpool, launched 22 Nov 62. Captured by Grand Gulf and USAT Fulton off Wilmington 21 Nov 63 while running blockade. Purchased from New York Prize Court 12 Mar 64. Commissioned Jun 64. Sold New York 30 Nov 65.

BAT (ex-Bat). Side-wheel Steamer, 4th rate. 530 tons. 230' x 26' x 8'. Armament: 1-30#R. Schooner rig. Machinery: 180 NHP, oscillating engine, side wheels. Speed: 16 kts. Complement: 82. Iron hull. Built by Jones Quiggin, Liverpool, launched 21 Jun 64. Captured by Montgomery off Wilmington 10 Oct 64 while running blockade. Purchased from Boston Prize Court Nov 64. Commissioned 13 Dec 64. Sold New York 25 Oct 65.

CHEROKEE (ex-Thistle). Screw Steamer, 4th rate. 606 tons. 194'6" x 25'2" x 11'6". Armament: 4-24# 2-20#R. Schooner rig. Machinery: Geared beam engine, 1 screw. Speed: 13 kts. Complement: 92. Iron hull. Built by Hall, Renfrew, launched 2 Jul 59. Captured by Canandaigua off Charleston 8 May 63 while running blockade. Purchased Boston 13 Jan 64. Commissioned 21 Apr 64. Sold Boston 1 Aug 65. Chilean naval steamer Ancud 1865-78.

DON (ex-Don). Screw Steamer, 4th rate. 390 tons. 162' x 23' x 6'. Armament: 6-24# 2-20#R. Machinery: 600 IHP, horizontal engines, 2 screws. Speed: 14 kts. Complement: 94. Iron hull. Built by Dudgeon, Millwall, 1863. Captured by Pequot off Beaufort, N.C., 4 Mar 64 while running blockade. Purchased from Boston Prize Court 21 Apr 64. Commissioned May 64. Sold 29 Aug 68.

DUMBARTON (ex-Thistle). Side-wheel Steamer, 4th rate. 636 tons. 204' x 29' x 10'. Armament: 2-32#; 2-32# 1-20#R (1865). Schooner rig. Machinery: Oscillating engine, side wheels. Speed: 10 kts. Complement: 96. Iron hull. Built by Hall, Renfrew, 1863. Captured by Fort Jackson off North Carolina 4 Jun 64 while running blockade. Purchased from Boston Prize Court 20 Jul 64. Commissioned 13 Aug 64. Sold New York 15 Oct 67.

HIBISCUS (ex-Hibiscus). Screw Steamer, 4th rate. 406 tons. 175' x 30' x 7'. Armament: 2-30#R. Machinery: Wright's segmental engines, 2 screws. Speed: 9 kts. Complement: 86. Built by Pook, Fairhaven, 1864. Purchased 16 Nov 64. Commissioned 29 Dec 64. Sold New York 5 Oct 66. Sister to the Spirea.

ISONOMIA (ex-Shamrock). Side-wheel Steamer, 4th rate. 593 tons. 215'3" x 29'6" x 7'. Armament: 1-30#R. Machinery: Vertical beam engine, side wheels. Speed: 12 kts. Complement: 63. Built by Stack 1864. Engine by Murphy. Purchased New York 16 Jul 64. Commissioned 16 Aug 64. Sold New York 12 Jul 65.

LADY STERLING (ex-Lady Sterling). Side-wheel Steamer, 4th rate. 835 tons. 242' x 26'6" x 13'3"(h). Armament: 8 guns. Machinery: Oscillating engine, side wheels. Speed: 13 kts. Iron hull. Built by Ash, Millwall, launched 18 Jun 64. Captured by Eolus and Calypso off Wilmington 28 Oct 64 while running blockade. Purchased from New York Prize Court Nov 64. Commissioned 24 Apr 65. Renamed Hornet 17 Jun 65. Sold 26 Jun 69.

LILIAN (ex-Lilian). Side-wheel Steamer, 4th rate. 630 tons. 225'6" x 26'5" x 8'2". Armament: 1-30#R 1-20#R. Schooner rig. Machinery: Oscillating engine, side wheels, 3 funnels. Speed: 14 kts. Complement: 63. Steel hull. Built by Thomson 1864. Captured by Keystone State and Gettysburg off Cape Fear 24 Aug 64 while running blockade. Purchased from Philadelphia Prize Court 6 Sep 64. Commissioned 6 Oct 64. Sold New York 30 Nov 65. Spanish navy corvette Victoria de los Tunas 1870, wrecked Nov 70.

MERRIMAC (ex-Merrimac). Side-wheel Steamer, 4th rate. 684 tons. 230' x 30' x 8'6". Armament: 4-24# 2-30#R; 4-24# 1-30#R (1864). Machinery: Oscillating engine, side wheels. Speed: 11.5 kts. Complement: 116. Iron hull. Built in Britain. Captured by Iroquois off Cape Fear, N.C., 24 Jul 63 while running blockade. Purchased from New York Prize Court 10 Mar 64. Commissioned 1 May 64. Foundered in a gale off Florida 15 Feb 65.

PRESTON (ex-Annie). Screw Steamer, 4th rate. 428 tons. 179' x 23'1" x 10'. Armament: 2-24# 1-30#R. 2-masted schooner rig. Machinery: Direct-acting engines, 2 screws. Speed: 14 kts. Iron hull. Built by Dudgeon, Millwall, 1863. Captured by Wilderness and Niphon off New Inlet, N.C., 1864 while running blockade. Purchased from New York Prize Court 31 Oct 64. Commissioned 6 Feb 65. Sold New York 30 Nov 65.

SELMA (ex-CSS Selma, ex-Florida). Side-wheel Steamer, 4th rate. 590 tons. 252' x 30' x 6'. Armament: 2-9"R 1-8"R 1-6"R. Machinery: Inclined, direct-acting engine, side wheels. Speed: 9 kts. Complement: 99. Built at Mobile, Ala., 1856. Captured by Metacomet in Mobile Bay 5 Aug 64. Commissioned 5 Aug 64. Sold New Orleans 15 Jul 65.

SPIREA (ex-Spirea). Screw Steamer, 4th rate. 406 tons. Hull and machinery duplicate the Hibiscus. Armament: 2-30#R. Built by Pook, Fairhaven, 1864. Purchased 30 Dec 64. Commissioned 9 Jan 65. Sold New York 5 Oct 66. Sister to the Hibiscus.

TRISTAM SHANDY (ex-Tristam Shandy). Side-wheel Steamer, 4th rate. 444 tons. 222' x 23'6" x 6'4". Armament: 1-20#R. Schooner rig. Machinery: Inclined, direct-acting engine, side wheels. Speed: 12 kts. Complement: 80. Iron hull. Built by Aitken & Mansel, Greenock, launched 13 Jan 64. Captured by Kansas off Wilmington 15 May 64 while running blockade. Purchased from Boston Prize Court May 64.

Commissioned 12 Aug 64. Renamed Boxer 21 Jun 65. Sold Philadelphia 1 Sep 68.

WANDO (ex-Wando, ex Let Her Rip). Side-wheel Steamer, 4th rate. 645 tons. 230' x 26' x 7'. Armament: 1-30#R. Machinery: Oscillating engine, side wheels. Complement: 86. Iron hull. Built by Kirkpatrick, Glasgow, launched 25 Mar 64. Captured by Fort Jackson off Cape Romain, S.C., 21 Oct 64 while running blockade. Purchased from Boston Prize Court 5 Nov 64. Commissioned 22 Dec 64. Sold New York 30 Nov 65.

1865

EMMA HENRY (ex-Emma Henry). Side-wheel Steamer, 4th rate. 521 tons. 212' x 25'2" x 6'. Armament: 1-30#R. Machinery: Oscillating engine, side wheels. Iron hull. Built by Thomson 1864. Captured by Cherokee 8 Dec 64 while running blockade. Purchased from New York Prize Court 13 Jan 65. Commissioned 11 May 65. Renamed Wasp 13 Jun 65. Sold at Montevideo 5 Jan 76.

3. Ferryboats

1861

CLIFTON (ex-Clifton). Side-wheel Ferry, 4th rate. 892 tons. 210' x 40' x 13'4"(h). Armamant: 2-9" 4-32#; 3-9" 4-32# 1-30#R (1862); 2-9" 4-32# 1-30#R (1863); 2-9" 4-32# 2-30#R (1863). Machinery: Vertical beam engine, side wheels. Complement: 121. Built by Simonson 1861. Engine by Allaire. Purchased New York 2 Dec 61. Converted by Westervelt. Commissioned 1862. Captured by Confederate squadron in Sabine Pass, Tex., 8 Sep 63.

COMMODORE BARNEY (ex-Ethan Allen). Side-wheel Ferry, 4th rate. 512 tons. 143'(b.p.) x 33' x 9'. Armament: 3-9"; 1-100#R 3-9" 1-32# (1863); 1-100#R 5-9" (1863). Machinery: 500 IHP, vertical beam engine, side wheels. Speed: 11 kts. Complement: 96. Built by Stack & Joyce 1859. Engine by Novelty. Purchased New York 2 Oct 61. Commissioned 1861. Sold Washington 20 Jul 65. Sister to the Commodore Perry and Morse.

COMMODORE PERRY (ex-Commodore Perry). Side-wheel Ferry, 4th rate. 512 tons. Hull and machinery duplicate the Commodore Barney. Armament: 2-9" 2-32#; 1-100#R 4-9" (1864). Built by Stack & Joyce 1859. Engine by Novelty. Purchased New York 2 Oct 61. Commissioned Oct 61. Sold New York 12 Jul 65. Sister to the Commodore Barney and Morse.

ELLEN (ex-Ellen). Side-wheel Ferry, 4th rate. 341 tons. 125'(k) x 28' x 8'. Armament: 2-32# 2-30#R. Machinery: Inclined engine, side wheels. Speed: 12 kts. Complement: 50. Built by Eckford Webb, launched 1 Feb 53. Engine by Novelty. Purchased Brooklyn 10 Oct 61. Converted by Copeland and New York. Commissioned 16 Oct 61. Sold Bay Point, S. C., 2 Sep 65.

HUNCHBACK (ex-Hunchback). Side-wheel Ferry, 4th rate. 517 tons. 179' x 29' x 9'. Armament: 1-100#R 3-9"; 1-100#R 4-9" (1863); 1-100#R 5-9" (1865). Machinery: Vertical beam engine, side wheels. Speed: 12 kts. Complement: 99. Built by Simonson 1852. Purchased New York 16 Dec 61. Converted by Webb. Commissioned 3 Jan 62. Sold New York 12 Jul 65.

JOHN P. JACKSON (ex-John P. Jackson). Side-wheel Ferry, 4th rate. 787 tons. 210'(d) x 36'6" x 5'6". Armament: 1-10" 1-6"R 4-32#; 1-100#R 1-9" 4-32# (1862); 1-10" 4-32# (1864); 1-100#R 1-10" 4-32# (1865). Machinery: Vertical beam engine, side wheels. Speed: 8 kts. Complement: 99. Built by Burtis, launched 2 Aug 60. Engine by Fulton IrWks. Purchased Jersey City 6 Nov 61. Commissioned 4 Feb 62. Sold New Orleans 27 Sep 65.

MORSE (ex-Marion) Side-wheel Ferry, 4th rate. 512 tons. Hull and machinery duplicate the Commodore Barney. Armament: 2-9"; 2-100#R 2-9" (1863). Built by Roosevelt 1859. Engine by Novelty. Purchased New York 7 Nov 61. Commissioned 9 Nov 61. Sold Washington 20 Jul 65. Sister to the Commodore Barney and Commodore Perry.

SOUTHFIELD (ex-Southfield). Side-wheel Ferry, 4th rate. 751 tons. 200' x 34' x 6'6". Armament: 1-100#R 1-9"; 1-100#R 3-9" (1862); 1-100#R 5-9" (1863). Machinery: Vertical beam engine, side wheels. Speed: 12 kts. Complement: 61. Built by Englis 1857. Engine by Murphy. Purchased New York 16 Dec 61. Converted by Webb. Commissioned Dec 61. Rammed and sunk by CSS Albemarle in Roanoke R., Va., 19 Apr 64.

WESTFIELD (ex-Westfield). Side-wheel Ferry. 891 tons. 215' x 35' x 13'6"(h). Armament: 1-100#R 1-9" 4-8". Machinery: Vertical beam engine, side wheels. Complement: 116. Built by Simonson 1861. Engine by Morgan. Purchased New York 22 Nov 61. Converted by Westervelt. Commissioned Jan 62. Blown up to avoid capture off Galveston, Tex., 1 Jan 63.

WHITEHALL (ex-Whitehall). Side-wheel Ferry, 4th rate. 326 tons. 126'(k) x 28'2" x 8'. Armament: 2-32# 2-30#R. Machinery: Inclined engine, side wheels. Built by Burtis 1850. Purchased Brooklyn 10 Oct 61. Converted by Copeland. Commissioned Oct 61. Burned at Old Point Comfort, Va., 10 Mar 62.

1862

COMMODORE HULL (ex-Nuestra Senora de Regla). Side-wheel Ferry, 4th rate. 376 tons. 141' x 28'4" x 9'. Armament: 4-24# 2-30#R; 4-24# 1-32#R 1-30#R. Machinery: Inclined engine, side wheels. Speed: 10 kts. Complement: 68. Built at Brooklyn 1861. Seized at Port Royal, S.C. Purchased at New York 1 Sep 62. Commissioned 27 Nov 62. Sold New York 27 Sep 65.

COMMODORE McDONOUGH. Side-wheel Ferry, 4th rate. 532 tons. 154' x 32'6" x 8'6". Armament: 1-9" 1-20#R; 1-100#R 1-11" 2-50#R (1863). Machinery: Inclined engine, side wheels. Speed: 8 kts. Complement: 75. Probably built in New York 1862. Purchased New York 5 Aug 62. Converted by New York. Commissioned 24 Nov 62. Foundered under tow enroute to New York from Port Royal 23 Aug 65.

COMMODORE MORRIS (ex-Clinton). Side-wheel Ferry, 4th rate. 532 tons. Hull and machinery duplicate the Commodore McDonough. Armament: 1-100#R 1-9"; 1-100#R 1-9" 2-30#R (1864). Built in New York 1862. Purchased New York 5 Aug 62. Converted by New York. Commissioned 19 Nov 62. Sold New York 12 Jul 65.

FORT HENRY. Side-wheel Ferry, 4th rate. 519 tons. 150'6" x 32' x 11'9"(h). Armament: 2-9" 4-32#. Machinery: Side wheels. Complement: 120. Probably built in New York 1862. Purchased New York 25 Mar 62. Commissioned 3 Apr 62. Sold New York 15 Aug 65.

SOMERSET (ex-Somerset). Side-wheel Ferry, 4th rate. 521 tons. 151' x 32'4" x 11'3"(h). Armament: 2-9" 4-32#. Machinery: Side wheels. Complement: 110. Built in Brooklyn 1862. Purchased Washington 4 Mar 62. Commissioned 3 Apr 62. Sold New York 12 Jul 65.

1863

COMMODORE JONES (ex-Commodore Jones). Side-wheel Ferry, 4th rate. 542 tons. 154' x 32'6" x 11'8". Armament: 4-9" 1-50#R; 1-9" 1-50#R (1863); 1-9" 1-50#R 2-30#R (1863). Machinery: Side wheels. Speed: 12 kts. Complement: 103. Probably built in New York 1863. Purchased New York 12 May 63. Commissioned 21 May 63. Mined, Deep Bottom, James R., Va., 6 May 64.

COMMODORE READ (ex-Atlantic). Side-wheel Ferry, 4th rate. 650 tons. 179' x 33'6" x 6'3". Armament: 2-100#R; 2-100#R 4-9" (1864). Machinery: Vertical beam engine, side wheels. Complement: 84. Built by Brutus 1857. Purchased New York 19 Aug 63. Converted by New York. Commissioned 8 Sep 63. Sold Washington 20 Jun 65.

SHOKOKON (ex-Clifton). Side-wheel Ferry, 4th rate. 709 tons. 181' x 32' x 8'6". Armament: 2-30#R; 2-9" 2-30#R (1865). Machinery: 570 IHP, vertical beam engine, side wheels. Speed: 10 kts. Complement: 120. Built in Greenpoint, N. Y., 1862. Engine by Allaire. Purchased New York 3 Apr 63. Converted by Simonson. Commissioned 18 May 63. Sold New York 25 Oct 65.

4. River Steamers

1861

CONESTOGA (ex-Conestoga). River Steamer ("timberclad"), 4th rate. 572 tons. Armament: 4-32#; 3-32# 3-30#R (1864). Machinery: High pressure engine, side wheels. Speed: 12 kts. Built in Brownsville, Pa., 1859. Purchased 3 Jun 61 by Army. Commissioned 1861. Transferred from War Dept. 30 Sep 62. Sunk in collision with General Price off Bondurant Pt., La., 8 Mar 64.

LEXINGTON (ex-Lexington). River Steamer ("timberclad"), 4th rate. 448 tons. 177'7" x 36'10" x 6'. Armament: 4-8" 2-32#; 4-8" 1-32# 2-30#R (1862); 6-8" 1-32# 2-30#R (1864). Machinery: High pressure engines, side wheels. Speed: 7 kts. (upstream). Built by L. M. Speer, Belle Vernon, Pa., 1860. Purchased 5 Jun 61 by Army. Fitted out at New Albany. Commissioned by 12 Aug 61. Transferred from the War Dept. 30 Sep 62. Sold Mound City 17 Aug 65.

TYLER (ex-A. O. Tyler). River Steamer ("timberclad"), 4th rate. 575 tons. 180' x 45'4" x 6'. Armament: 6-8" 3-30#R; 4-8" 2-30#R (1865). Machinery: High pressure engine, side wheels. Speed: 8 kts. (upstream). Complement: 67. Built in Cincinnati 1857. Purchased 5 Jun 61 by Army. Transferred from War Dept. 30 Sep 62. Sold Mound City 17 Aug 65. Sometimes called Taylor.

1862

BLACK HAWK (ex-New Uncle Sam). River Steamer, 3rd rate. 902 tons. 260' x 45'6" x 6'. Armament: 4-32# 2-30#R; 2-30#R (1864). Machinery: Side wheels. Complement: 141. Built in New Albany, Ind., 1848. Purchased Cairo, Ill., 24 Nov 62. Commissioned 6 Dec 62. Renamed Black Hawk 13 Dec 62. Burned and sank off Cairo 22 Apr 65. A large "tinclad" without an identifying number.

GENERAL BRAGG (ex-CSS General Bragg, ex-Mexico). River Steamer, 4th rate. 840 tons. 208' x 32'8" x 12'. Armament: 1-32# 1-30#R. Machinery: Low pressure beam engine, side wheels. Speed: 10 kts. Built by Westervelt 1850. Engine by Morgan. Confederate "cottonclad" captured after Battle of Memphis 6 Jun 62. Commissioned 9 Jul 62. Transferred from Army to Navy 30 Sep 62. Sold Mound City 1 Sep 65.

GENERAL PRICE (ex-CSS General Sterling Price, ex-Laurent Millaudon). River Ram, 4th rate. 633 tons. 182' x 30' x 9'3"(h). Armament: 4-9"; 2-9" (1863). Machinery: Side wheels. Speed: 12 mph. Complement: 77. Built in Cincinnati 1856. Sunk in Battle of Memphis 6 Jun 62 but raised and repaired by the Army. Transferred from the War Dept. 30 Sep 62. Commissioned 11 Mar 63. Sold Mound City, Ill., 3 Oct 65.

SUMTER (ex-CSS General Sumter, ex-Junius Beebe). River Steamer. 524 tons. 182' x 28'4". Machinery: Low pressure engine, side wheels. Built at Algiers, La., 1853. Confederate "cottonclad" captured after Battle of Memphis 6 Jun 62. Commissioned 1862. Grounded and abandoned Aug 62 off Bayou Sara, La.

1863

HASTINGS (ex-Emma Duncan). River Steamer, 4th rate. 293 tons. 173' x 34'2" x 5'4"(h). Armament: 2-32# 2-30#R. Machinery: Side wheels. Built in Monongahela, Pa., 1860. Purchased Cairo, Ill., 24 Mar 63. Renamed 7 Apr 63. Commissioned Apr 63. Sold Mound City 17 Aug 65. The largest of 73 numbered "tinclads" which served in the river campaigns, she was number 15.

OUACHITA (ex-Louisville). River Steamer, 4th rate. 720 tons. 227'6" x 38' x 7'. Armament: 5-30#R. Machinery: Side wheels. Speed: 8 mph. (upstream). Built in New Albany, Ind., 1861. Confederate army cargo ship captured in Little Red River by Manitou (ex-Fort Hindman) and Rattler 13 Jul 63. Purchased Cairo, Ill., 29 Sep 63. Commissioned 18 Jan 64. Sold Mount City 25 Sep 65. A large "tinclad" without an identifying number.

1864

AVENGER (ex-Balize). River Ram, 4th rate. 750 tons. 210' x 41'5" x 6'. Armament: 1-100#R 4-24#; 1-100#R 5-24# (1864); 1-100#R 11-24# (1865). Machinery: Side wheels. Speed: 11 mph. Built at New Albany, Ind., 1863 for the Army. Transferred to the Navy on completion and commissioned 29 Feb 64. Sold Mound City 29 Nov 65. Originally listed as 3rd rate.

VINDICATOR (ex-Vindicator). River Ram, 4th rate. 750 tons. 210' x 41'5" x 9'5". Armament: 1-100#R 2-24# howitzers; 1-100#R 1-30#R 10-24# howitzers (1864); 1-100#R 1-30#R 8-24# howitzers (1864). Machinery: Side wheels. Speed: 12 mph. Built at New Albany, Ind., 1863 for the Army. Transferred to the Navy upon completion and commissioned 24 May 64. Sold Mound City 29 Nov 65. Originally listed as 3rd rate.

3

The New Navy, 1883–1990

Monitors (BM)

1874

PURITAN

Displacement: 6060 tons
Dimensions: 296'3"(oa.) x 60'2"(e) x 18'6"(max)
Armament: 4-12"/35 6-4"/40 *
Armor (Steel): 14" belt, 8" turrets (Harvey), 2" deck, 10"
  conning tower

Machinery: 3700 IHP; 2 compound
  engines, 2 screws
Speed: 12.4 kts.
Complement: 208

No.		Hull	Machinery	Laid down	Launched	Commiss'd	Disposition
1	PURITAN	Roach	Morgan	May 76	6 Dec 82	10 Dec 96	Stk. 18 Feb 13, sold 26 Jan 22.

Notes: Officially considered to be the old monitor Puritan rebuilt, she was completed under fiscal year 1887. Designed in 1874 as an iron hulled copy of the Civil War ship, she was suspended from 1877 to 1882 when Congress authorized her launching. She was transferred to the New York Navy Yard after launch and was redesigned in 1886 with 4-10" breechloaders as in the Miantonomoh. She was completed to a third set of plans drafted in 1889. She served as a training ship 1899-1901, 1904-10 and a target (Target B) 1910-17. Two 4" guns were put ashore during her 1901-03 commission.

AMPHITRITE class

Displacement: 3990 tons
Dimensions: 262'9"(Amphitrite, oa.), 262'3"(Monadnock, oa.),
  263'1"(others, oa.) x 55'10"(e) x 15'0"(Miantonomoh, max),
  15'4"(Terror, max), 14'8" (others, max)
Armament: 2-10"/30 2-10"/34 (Miantonomoh); 4-10"/30 (Terror);
  4-10"/30 2-4"/40 (others); 4-10"/30 4-4"/40 (Terror, 1904)
Armor (Steel): 9" (Amphitrite and Monadnock), 7" (others)
  belt; 7 1/2" (Amphitrite and Monadnock), 11 1/2" (others)
  turrets; 1 3/4" deck; 10" conning tower

Machinery: 3000 IHP, 2 horizontal
  triple-expansion engines, 2 screws
  (Monadnock); 1426 IHP, 2 inclined
  compound engines, 2 screws
  (Miantonomoh); 1600 IHP, 2 inclined
  compound engines, 2 screws (others)
Speed: 12 kts. (Monadnock); 10.5 kts.
  (others)
Complement: 149 (Miantonomoh), 171
  (others)

No.		Hull	Machinery	Laid down	Launched	Commiss'd	Disposition
2	AMPHITRITE	Harlan&Hollingsworth		1874	7 Jun 83	23 Apr 95	Stk. 24 Jul 19, sold 3 Jan 20
3	MONADNOCK	Continen-tal,Vallejo	Mare I.	15 Jan 75	19 Sep 83	20 Feb 96	Stk. 2 Feb 23, sold 24 Aug 23
4	TERROR	Cramp	Cramp	1874	24 Mar 83	15 Apr 96	Stk. 31 Dec 15, sold 10 Mar 21
5	MIANTONOMOH	Roach	Morgan	1874	5 Dec 76	27 Oct 91	Stk. 31 Dec 15, sold 26 Jan 22.

Notes: Officially considered to be the old monitors of the same names rebuilt, they were completed under fiscal years 1887 (Nos. 2-4) and 1888 (5). They were initially designed in 1874 as iron hulled copies of the Civil War ships of the same names. The Continental Iron Works fabricated the hull of the Monadnock at their Brooklyn works and shipped the pieces to California for assembly at Vallejo by Phineas Burgess. The ships were suspended from 1877 to 1882, when Congress authorized their launchings and transfers to navy yards for completion. The Monadnock was completed by Mare Island, Amphitrite by Norfolk Navy Yard, and Miantonomoh and Terror by New York Navy Yard. (The incomplete Miantonomoh was commissioned on 6 Oct 82, steamed to New York, and decommissioned on 13 Mar 83.) The ships were redesigned around 1886 with 4-10" breechloaders. The Miantonomoh was completed to this design, while the others were again modified in 1889 to the extent that their state of advancement permitted. The Miantonomoh had compound instead of steel armor on her turrets. Poor sea boats because of their low freeboard, they were also difficult to steer. They failed to make their designed speeds, which were 14.5 knots (Monadnock) and 12 knots (Terror and Amphitrite). The Amphitrite served as a training vessel 1898-1904 and 1910-17 as did the Terror in 1902-06 and the Miantonomoh in 1905-15. The Monadnock served as a submarine tender 1912-18. She was put on the sale list on 1 Jul 21 but removed on 11 Aug 21. The Miantonomoh and Terror served as Targets C and D before their disposal, Terror being so designated on 1 Jun 16.
Reclassification: Monadnock to "unclassified" (IX-17) 1 Jul 21.

* Hereafter, unless otherwise stated, all guns may be assumed to be breech-loading rifles and all armor is Krupp Nickel-Cemented (KNC).

The ''rebuilt'' double-turret monitor *Miantonomoh* (BM-5) ca. 1907. (NH 60649)

The battleship *Kentucky* (BB-6). (NH 61959)

1887

MONTEREY

Displacement: 4084 tons
Dimensions: 260'11"(oa.) x 59'(e) x 15'4"(max)
Armament: 2-12"/35 2-10"/30
Armor (Steel): 13" belt, 8" fore turret, 7 1/2" aft turret, 2
    1/2" deck, 10" conning tower

Machinery: 5400 IHP; 2 vertical,
    triple-expansion engines, 2 screws
Speed: 13.6 kts.
Complement: 191

No.		Hull	Machinery	Laid down	Launched	Commiss'd	Disposition
6	MONTEREY	Union	Union	20 Dec 89	28 Apr 91	13 Feb 93	To sale list 1 Jul 21, sold 25 Feb 22.

Notes: Fiscal year 1888. She was built for West Coast defense. The initial design called for an
armament of 1-16" 1-12" and 1-15" pneumatic dynamite gun. She had sinking tanks to allow her to
reduce her freeboard while in action. She failed to make her design speed of 16 kts and was
considered a slow vessel which steered poorly and was a bad sea boat.

1889

Unnamed

Displacement: 3130 tons
Dimensions: 235'(wl.) x 55'(e) x 14'6"(mean)
Armament: 2-10" 1-6" 1-15" pneumatic dynamite gun
Armor: 4 1/2" deck, 10" turrets

Machinery: 7500 IHP; 2 vertical,
    triple-expansion engines, 2 screws
Speed: 17 kts.
Complement: Unknown

Notes: Fiscal year 1890. Congressman B. R. Thomas of the House Naval Committee caused Congress to
authorize this "armored cruising monitor" of his own design. The hull armor consisted of a curved
protective deck. The Navy's Board of Construction reported that she would have to be lengthened 30
feet to carry her weights, and Congress cancelled her on 2 Mar 91 after the design exceeded the limits
of the appropriated funds.

1898

ARKANSAS class

Displacement: 3225 tons
Dimensions: 255'1"(oa.) x 50'(e) x 12'11"(max)
Armament: 2-12"/40 4-4"/50; 2-12" 4-4" 1-3"/50AA (1918);
    2-12" 4-4" 2-3"AA (Cheyenne, ex-Wyoming, 1924); 4-4" 2-3"AA
    (Cheyenne, 1931)
Armor (Harvey): 11" belt, 10" turret, 1 1/2" deck, 8" conning
    tower

Machinery: 2400 IHP; 2 vertical,
    triple-expansion engines, 2 screws
Speed: 12.5 kts.
Complement: 171

No.		Hull	Machinery	Laid down	Launched	Commiss'd	Disposition
7	ARKANSAS	-Newport	News-	14 Nov 99	10 Nov 00	28 Oct 02	To sale list 1 Jul 21, sold 26 Jan 22
8	NEVADA	Bath	Bath	17 Apr 99	24 Nov 00	5 Mar 03	To sale list 1 Jul 21, sold 26 Jan 22
9	FLORIDA	Nixon	Nixon	23 Jan 99	30 Nov 01	18 Jun 03	To sale list 16 Jan 22, sold 25 Jul 22
10	WYOMING	Union	Union	11 Apr 99	8 Sep 00	8 Dec 02	Stk. 25 Jan 37, sold 20 Apr 39.

Notes: Fiscal year 1899. They were built to a Navy Department design which was lengthened 27' after
the contracts had been let. All served as trials ships and training vessels from 1906 and as
submarine tenders after 1912-14.
Renamings: BM-7 to Ozark 2 Mar 09; BM-8 ex Connecticut Jan 01, to Tonopah 2 Mar 09; BM-9 to
Tallahassee 20 Jun 08; and BM-10 to Cheyenne 1 Jan 09.
Reclassifications: BM-9 to "unclassified" (no number) and BM-10 to "unclassified" (IX-4) 1 Jul 21.

Battleships (BB)

1886

TEXAS

Displacement: 6315 tons
Dimensions: 308'10"(oa.) x 64'1"(e) x 24'6"(max)
Armament: 2-12"/35 2-6"/35 4-6"/30 4-18"T; 2-12" 2-6" 4-6"
  2-18"T (1898); 2-12" 6-6"/35 (1904)
Armor (Harvey): 12" belt, 12" turrets, 3" deck, 9" conning
  tower

Machinery: 8000 IHP; 2 vertical,
  triple-expansion engines, 2 screws
Speed: 17 kts.
Complement: 392

	Hull	Machinery	Laid down	Launched	Commiss'd	Disposition
TEXAS	Norfolk	Richmond	1 Jun 89	28 Jun 92	15 Aug 95	Sunk as target 22 Mar 11 in Chesapeake Bay, stk. 11 Oct 11

Notes: Fiscal year 1887. Her plans, drawn by Sir William John, were purchased from the Naval Construction and Armaments Co., Ltd., Barrow-in-Furness, England. She was not a total success because of weak armor protection and heavy coal consumption. She was used as a receiving ship 1908-11 and was sunk as a target off Tangier I., Md., by the battleship New Hampshire.
Renaming: To San Marcos 16 Feb 11.
Reclassification: Launched as a battleship, she was referred to as a 2d class battleship after 1894.

MAINE

Displacement: 6682 tons
Dimensions: 324'4"(oa.) x 57'(e) x 22'6"(max)
Armament: 4-10"/30 6-6"/30 4-18"T; 4-10" 6-6" 2-18"T (1897)
Armor (Harvey): 12" belt, 8" turrets, 3" deck, 10" conning
  tower

Machinery: 9000 IHP; 2 vertical,
  triple-expansion engines, 2 screws
Speed: 17 kts.
Complement: 374

	Hull	Machinery	Laid down	Launched	Commiss'd	Disposition
MAINE	New York	Quintard	17 Oct 88	18 Nov 90	17 Sep 95	Blew up at Havana, Cuba, 15 Feb 98.

Notes: Fiscal year 1887. Designed by the Navy Department, she generally followed contemporary foreign central citadel designs, notably that of the Brazilian Riachuelo. When first commissioned she carried small (3d class) torpedo boats. Recent research indicates that the cause of her loss was probably a fire in a coal bunker which detonated an adjacent 6" magazine. Her wreck was raised on 13 Feb 1912 and sunk in the Strait of Florida on 16 Mar 12.
Reclassification: Launched as Armored Cruiser No. 1, the Maine was referred to as a 2d class battleship after 1894.

1890

INDIANA class

Displacement: 10,288 tons
Dimensions: 351'2"(Oregon, oa.), 350'11"(others, oa) x
  69'3"(e) x 27'2"(max)
Armament: 4-13"/35 8-8"/35 4-6"/30 4-18"T (Indiana); 4-13"
  8-8" 4-6" 3-18"T (others); 4-13" 8-8" 3-18"T (Indiana,
  1908); 4-13" 8-8" 12-3"/50 (1910-11); 4-13" 8-8" 4-3"
  (1917-18); none (Oregon, 1921)

Armor (Steel): 18" belt, 15" turrets,
  3" deck, 10" conning tower
Machinery: 9000 IHP; 2 vertical,
  inverted, triple-expansion engines,
  2 screws
Speed: 15 kts.
Complement: 473

No.		Builder	Laid down	Launched	Commiss'd	Disposition
1	INDIANA	Cramp	7 May 91	28 Feb 93	20 Nov 95	Sunk as target in Chesapeake Bay 1 Nov 20
2	MASSACHUSETTS	Cramp	25 Jun 91	10 Jun 93	10 Jun 96	Stk. 22 Nov 20, sunk as target off Pensacola, Fla., Jan 21
3	OREGON	Union	19 Nov 91	26 Oct 93	15 Jul 96	To State of Oregon 25 Jun 25.

Notes: Fiscal year 1891. Built to a Navy Department design modified by Cramp with the builders supplying both the hulls and the machinery. The ships made between 15.5 and 16.8 kts. on trials. The class sacrificed space and coal supply for protection because of the limitations written into the authorization act by Congress. They were designed for 6 torpedo tubes but the number actually carried fluctuated between 1 and 3 between 1897 and 1910. Cage mainmasts were fitted in 1910-11. The Indiana was sunk as a target off Tangier I., Md., in 1920 and her hulk was sold on 19 Mar 24. The Massachusetts was transferred to the War Department and sunk as a target by Army coastal batteries off Pensacola, Fla. The Oregon was demilitarized on 4 Jan 24 and loaned as a relic at Portland, Oregon.

She was stricken on 2 Nov 42 and sold for scrap on 7 Dec 42. The Navy reacquired the stripped hulk in September 1943 for use as an ammunition barge. The hulk was sold 15 Mar 56 and scrapped in Japan later that year.
Renamings: BB-1 and BB-2 to Coast Battleship No. 1 and Coast Battleship No. 2 29 Mar 19.
Reclassification: BB-1 to "unclassified" 17 Jul 20, BB-3 to "unclassified" (IX-22) 1 Jul 21.

1892

IOWA

Displacement: 11,410 tons
Dimensions: 362'5"(oa.) x 72'3"(e) x 26'10"(max)
Armament: 4-12"/35 8-8"/35 6-4"/40 4-14"T; 4-12" 8-8" 6-4" 2-14"T (1905); 4-12" 8-8" 4-4" (1906); 4-12" 8-8" 10-4" (1910); 4-12" 8-8" 4-4" (1917); none (1921)
Armor (Harvey): 14" belt, 17" turrets, 3" deck, 10" conning tower

Machinery: 11,000 IHP; 2 vertical, triple-expansion engines, 2 screws
Speed: 16 kts.
Complement: 486

No.		Builder	Laid down	Launched	Commiss'd	Disposition
4	IOWA	Cramp	5 Aug 93	28 Mar 96	16 Jun 97	Sunk as target 23 Mar 23 in Panama Bay, stk. 27 Mar 23.

Notes: Fiscal year 1893. Cramp built both the hull and the machinery. She followed a Navy Department design which introduced a long, high forecastle for better seakeeping, increased coal capacity, medium-caliber quick-firing guns, and Harveyized armor which was lighter but stronger than the steel armor in the Indiana class. She reached 17.09 kts. on trials. A cage mainmast was fitted in 1911. She was converted to a radio controlled target in 1920 and was sunk by the battleship Mississippi in 1923.
Renaming: To Coast Battleship No. 4 30 Apr 19.
Reclassification: To "unclassified" (IX-6) 10 Feb 20.

1895

KEARSARGE class

Displacement: 11,525 tons
Dimensions: 375'4"(oa.) x 72'3"(e) x 25'10"(max)
Armament: 4-13"/35 4-8"/35 14-5"/40 4-18"T; 4-13" 4-8" 14-5" 1-18"T (1905-6); 4-13" 4-8" 14-5" (1908); 4-13" 4-8" 18-5" (1912); 4-13" 4-8" 8-5" (1917); 4-13" 4-8" 8-5" 2-3"/50AA (1918-19); none (Kearsarge, 1920)

Armor (Harvey): 16 1/2" belt, 17" turrets, 5" (aft) deck, 10" conning tower
Machinery: 10,000 IHP; 2 vertical, triple-expansion engines, 2 screws
Speed: 16 kts.
Complement: 553

No.		Builder	Laid down	Launched	Commiss'd	Disposition
5	KEARSARGE	Newport News	30 Jun 96	24 Mar 98	20 Feb 00	Stk. 22 Jun 55, sold 9 Aug 55
6	KENTUCKY	Newport News	30 Jun 96	24 Mar 98	15 May 00	To sale list 27 May 22, sold 24 Mar 23.

Notes: Fiscal year 1896. Newport News built both the hulls and the machinery. They were built to a Navy design which returned to the 13" guns of the Indiana class for smashing effect and introduced a large quick-firing 5" secondary battery for torpedo boat defense. The use of superposed 8" and 13" turrets forced the designers to accept low freeboard, which made the ships very wet in high seas. Coal capacity and trial speed (16.82 and 16.90 kts.) were somewhat less than in the Iowa. Cage mainmasts were fitted in 1911. The Kearsarge was converted into a crane ship in 1920 and was given the additional designation Crane Ship No. 1 on 5 Aug 20.
Renaming: Kearsarge to Crane Ship No. 1 6 Nov 41.
Reclassifications: BB-5 to "unclassified" (IX-16) 17 Jul 20 and to AB-1 15 Apr 39.

1896

ILLINOIS class

Displacement: 11,565 tons
Dimensions: 375'4" (Illinois, oa.), 374'(Alabama, oa.), 373'10" (Wisconsin, oa.) x 72'3"(e) x 25'10"(Illinois, max), 25'0" (Alabama, max), 25'7" (Wisconsin, max)
Armament: 4-13"/35 14-6"/40 4-18"T; 4-13" 14-6" 1-18"T (1906-8); 4-13" 14-6" 4-3"/50 (1912); 4-13" 8-6" (1917); none (Illinois, 1922); 2-4/50" (Illinois, 1938); none (Prairie State, ex Illinois, 1945)

Armor (Harvey): 16 1/2" belt, 14" turrets, 4" (aft) deck, 10" conning tower
Machinery: 10,000 IHP; 2 vertical, inverted, triple-expansion engines, 2 screws
Speed: 16 kts.
Complement: 536

No.		Builder	Laid down	Launched	Commiss'd	Disposition
7	ILLINOIS	Newport News	10 Feb 97	4 Oct 98	16 Sep 01	Stk. 26 Mar 56, sold 18 May 56
8	ALABAMA	Cramp	1 Dec 96	18 May 98	16 Oct 00	Sunk as target 27 Sep 21 in Chesapeake Bay
9	WISCONSIN	Union	9 Feb 97	26 Nov 98	4 Feb 01	To sale list 1 Jul 21, sold 26 Jan 22.

Notes: Fiscal year 1897. Designed by the Navy after a thorough review of earlier designs. The intermediate 8" armament was deleted, partly because of the availability of the new 6" quick-fire gun. Seakeeping qualities were emphasized in the design, which caused the long forecastle of the Iowa to be restored. The builders supplied both the hull and the machinery. The ships made between 17.1 and 17.45 kts. on trials. The Wisconsin received a cage foremast in 1909 and all had two cage masts by 1911. The Illinois was delivered to the New York State Naval Militia on 25 Oct 21 and served as a housed-over training hulk until 1955. The Alabama was transferred to the War Department on 15 Sep 21 and sunk as a target by the Air Corps; her hulk was sold 19 Mar 24.
Renaming: BB-7 to Prairie State 23 Jan 41.
Reclassification: BB-7 to "unclassified" (IX-15) 26 Jun 22.

1898

MAINE class

Displacement: 12,500 tons
Dimensions: 393'10"(Ohio, oa.), 393'11"(others, oa.) x
    72'3"(e) x 26'8"(max)
Armament: 4-12"/40 16-6"/50 6-3"/50 2-18"T; 4-12" 10-6" 6-3"
    2-18"T (1917); 4-12" 8-6" 2-18"T (Ohio, 1918); 4-12" 8-6"
    2-3"/50AA 2-18"T (Missouri, 1918); 4-12" 8-6" 6-3" 2-3"AA
    2-18"T (Maine, 1919); 4-12" 4-6" 2-18"T (Ohio, 1919); 4-12"
    4-6" (Ohio, 1921)

Armor: 11" belt, 12" turrets, 4"
    (aft) deck, 10" conning tower
Machinery: 16,000 IHP; 2 vertical,
    inverted, triple-expansion engines,
    2 screws
Speed: 18 kts.
Complement: 561

No.		Builder	Laid down	Launched	Commiss'd	Disposition
10	MAINE	Cramp	15 Feb 99	27 Jul 01	29 Dec 02	To sale list 1 Jul 21, sold 26 Jan 22
11	MISSOURI	Newport News	7 Feb 00	28 Dec 01	1 Dec 03	To sale list 1 Jul 21, sold 26 Jan 22
12	OHIO	Union	22 Apr 99	18 May 01	4 Oct 04	Stk. 14 Aug 22, sold 24 Mar 23.

Notes: Fiscal year 1899. Originally to have been repeats of the Illinois class, they were built to a new design with water-tube boilers because of dissatisfaction with the 16-knot designed speed of the earlier class. The new design also took advantage of the new smokeless gunpowder which, with its higher velocities, allowed a return to the 12" gun. It also introduced Krupp nickel-cemented armor, lighter and stronger than the earlier Harvey armor. (Krupp armor was used in all subsequent U.S. armored ships.) Finally, it was the first U.S. battleship design to use underwater torpedo tubes. The builders constructed both the hulls and the machinery. The Maine, with 24 Niclausse boilers of a type preferred by her builder, was a notorious coal eater. The ships were mediocre sea boats with comparatively shallow draft. The Missouri and Ohio received cage foremasts in 1909 and all had two cage masts by 1911.

1899

VIRGINIA class

Displacement: 14,948 tons
Dimensions: 441'3"(oa.) x 76'3"(e) x 26'(max)
Armament: 4-12"/40 8-8"/40 12-6"/50 12-3"/50 4-21"T; 4-12"
    8-8"/45 12-6" 12-3" 4-21"T (1908-10); 4-12" 8-8" 12-6" 6-3"
    4-21"T (1917); 4-12" 8-8" 6-3" 2-3"/50AA 4-21"T (all but
    Nebraska, 1918); 4-12" 8-8" 4-3" 4-3"AA 4-21"T (Nebraska,
    1919); 4-12" 8-8" 4-21"T (New Jersey, 1920)
Armor: 11" belt, 12" turrets, 3" deck, 9" conning tower

Machinery: 19,000 IHP; 2 vertical,
    inverted, triple-expansion engines,
    2 screws
Speed: 19 kts.
Complement: 812

No.		Builder	Laid down	Launched	Commiss'd	Disposition
13	VIRGINIA	Newport News	21 May 02	5 Apr 04	7 May 06	Stk. 12 Jul 22, sunk as target off Cape Hatteras 5 Sep 23
14	NEBRASKA	Moran	4 Jul 02	7 Oct 04	1 Jul 07	Stk. 12 Jul 22, sold 30 Nov 23
15	GEORGIA	Bath	31 Aug 01	11 Oct 04	24 Sep 06	Stk. 12 Jul 22, sold 1 Nov 23
16	NEW JERSEY	Fore River	2 Apr 02	10 Nov 04	12 May 06	Stk. 12 Jul 22, sunk as target off Cape Hatteras 5 Sep 23
17	RHODE ISLAND	Fore River	1 May 02	17 May 04	19 Feb 06	Stk. 12 Jul 22, sold 1 Nov 23.

The battleship *Georgia* (BB-15) in 1907. (NH 73911)

The battleship *Florida* (BB-30) ca. 1918. (NH 54174)

Notes: Fiscal years 1900 (BB 13-15) and 1901 (16-17). The design was the first to incorporate the lessons learned in the Spanish-American War, which showed the need for a true ocean-going battle fleet with great endurance and seakeeping qualities. The 8" gun was reintroduced after its success at the Battle of Santiago. The construction of the first two ships was delayed because of Congressional limitations on the price which could be paid for armor plate and because of lengthy debates within the navy on the arrangement of the guns. As with the other battleships powered with reciprocating engines, the machinery was provided by the shipbuilder. All considerably exceeded the designed HP on trials. The Nebraska, Georgia, and New Jersey were completed without torpedo tubes, which were added in 1907-11. In 1908-10, after an accident in the armored cruiser Colorado, all 8"/40 Mark 5 guns in the fleet were replaced by the 8"/45 Mark 6. The Virginia, Nebraska, and Rhode Island received cage foremasts in 1909 and all had two cage masts by 1911. The armaments of individual ships varied in 1917-18 as most of the 3" guns, then all of the 6" guns, were progressively removed. The Virginia and New Jersey were transferred to the War Department on 6 Aug 23 and sunk as targets by the Army Air Service. All were stricken again on 1 Nov 23 to show compliance with the Washington Naval Treaty.
Renaming: BB-13 ex New Jersey, BB-14 ex Pennsylvania, and BB-16 ex Virginia 7 Mar 01.

1902

CONNECTICUT class

Displacement: 16,000 tons
Dimensions: 455'10"(Vermont. oa.), 456'4"(others, oa.) x 76'10"(e) x 26'9"(max)
Armament: 4-12"/45 8-8"/45 12-7"/45 20-3"/50 4-21"T; 4-12" 8-8" 12-7" 18-3" 4-21"T (1914-16); 4-12" 8-8" 12-7" 4-3" (1917); 4-12" 8-8" 6-3" 2-3"/50AA 4-21"T (1918); 4-12" 8-8" 12-3" 2-3"AA 4-21"TT (1919-20, except 6-3" in Louisiana)

Armor: 11"(Louisiana, Connecticut), 9"(others) belt, 12" turrets, 3" deck, 9" conning tower
Machinery: 16,500 HP; 2 vertical, triple-expansion engines, 2 screws
Speed: 18 kts.
Complement: 881

No.		Builder	Laid down	Launched	Commiss'd	Disposition
18	CONNECTICUT	New York	10 Mar 03	29 Sep 04	29 Sep 06	Sold 1 Nov 23, stk. 10 Nov 23
19	LOUISIANA	Newport News	7 Feb 03	27 Aug 04	2 Jun 06	Sold 1 Nov 23, stk. 10 Nov 23
20	VERMONT	Fore River	21 May 04	31 Aug 05	4 Mar 07	Stk. 10 Nov 23, sold 30 Nov 23
21	KANSAS	New York SB	10 Feb 04	12 Aug 05	18 Apr 07	Stk. 10 Nov 23, scrapped 1924
22	MINNESOTA	Newport News	27 Oct 03	8 Apr 05	9 Mar 07	Stk. 10 Nov 23, scrapped 1924
25	NEW HAMPSHIRE	New York SB	1 May 05	30 Jun 06	19 Mar 08	Sold 1 Nov 23, stk. 10 Nov 23.

Notes: Fiscal years 1903 (BB 18-19), 1904 (20-22) and 1905 (25). Each of these three groups had a slightly different armor distribution scheme. The arrangement of the 8" guns and the adoption of the 7" gun represented the final outcome of the debate that had begun over the armament of the Virginia class. All but the New Hampshire were completed without torpedo tubes, which were added in 1909-10. The Minnesota received a cage foremast in 1909 and all had two cage masts by 1911. The armaments of individual ships varied in 1917-18 as most of the 3" guns, then all of the 7" guns, were progressively removed. The torpedo tubes of the Louisiana, Kansas and New Hampshire were removed after the war.

1903

MISSISSIPPI class

Displacement: 13,000 tons
Dimensions: 382'(oa.) x 77'(e) x 27'(max)
Armament: 4-12"/45 8-8"/45 8-7"/45 12-3"/50 2-21"T
Armor: 9" belt, 12" turrets, 3" deck, 9" conning tower

Machinery: 10,000 IHP; 2 vertical, triple-expansion engines, 2 screws
Speed: 17 kts.
Complement: 744

No.		Builder	Laid down	Launched	Commiss'd	Disposition
23	MISSISSIPPI	Cramp	12 May 04	30 Sep 05	1 Feb 08	Stk. 21 Jul 14, to Greece 21 Jul 14 as Kilkis
24	IDAHO	Cramp	12 May 04	9 Dec 05	1 Apr 08	Stk. 30 Jul 14, to Greece 30 Jul 14 as Lemnos.

Notes: Fiscal year 1904. This class resulted from Congress espousing a theory put forth by some naval officers (including Admirals Mahan and Dewey) that a battle fleet needed numerous as well as strong ships and that the tendency towards increased size and cost of ships should be resisted. The design was essentially a scaled-down Connecticut with speed decreased by a knot. In service these ships were substantially slower than the Connecticuts, had less endurance, and were much worse sea boats. Both ships received cage mainmasts in 1908 and cage foremasts in 1910-12. Sold to Greece in 1914, they were sunk by German aircraft at Salamis on 10 Apr 41. Cramp supplied the hulls and the machinery.

1905

SOUTH CAROLINA class

Displacement: 16,000 tons
Dimensions: 452'9"(oa.) x 80'3"(e) x 27'1"(max)
Armament: 8-12"/45 22-3"/50 2-21"T; 8-12" 14-3" 2-3"/50AA
  2-21"T (1917)
Armor: 11" belt, 12" turrets, 3" (aft) deck, 12" conning
  tower

Machinery: 16,500 IHP; 2 vertical,
  triple-expansion engines, 2 screws
Speed: 18.5 kts.
Complement: 869

No.	Builder	Laid down	Launched	Commiss'd	Disposition
26 SOUTH CAROLINA	Cramp	18 Dec 06	11 Jul 08	1 Mar 10	Stk. 10 Nov 23, scrapped 1924
27 MICHIGAN	New York SB	17 Dec 06	26 May 08	4 Jan 10	Stk. 10 Nov 23, scrapped 1924.

Notes: Fiscal year 1906. The first American "all big gun" battleships. Progress in guns and torpedoes led U.S. Navy officers to begin considering this type in 1901, and serious design work began in September 1904, a year before the Dreadnought was laid down. The design was essentially complete in June 1905 and the plans were approved by the Secretary of the Navy in December. Superfiring 12" turrets were adopted in part as a means of remaining within the 16,000 ton limit set by Congress. They were also consistent with the new theory that, with the advent of long-range gunnery, broadside fire had become a key objective of battleship design. The ships were the first to be completed with cage masts, which were designed to get gunnery spotters as high as possible while being largely invulnerable to shot because individual parts were too light to detonate shells. The ships were good sea boats but bad rollers.

1906

DELAWARE class

Displacement: 20,000 tons
Dimensions: 518'9"(oa.) x 85'3"(e) x 28'10"(max)
Armament: 10-12"/45 14-5"/50 2-21"T; 10-12" 14-5" 2-3"/50AA
  2-21"T (1917); 10-12" 14-5" 8-3"AA 2-21"T (1921); none
  (North Dakota, 1924)
Armor: 11" belt, 12" turrets, 3" (aft) deck, 11 1/2" conning
  tower

Machinery: Delaware--25,000 IHP; 2
  vertical, triple-expansion engines,
  2 screws;
  North Dakota--25,000 SHP; direct
  drive turbines, 2 screws
Speed: 21 kts.
Complement: 933

No.	Builder	Laid down	Launched	Commiss'd	Disposition
28 DELAWARE	Newport News	11 Nov 07	6 Feb 09	4 Apr 10	Stk. 27 Nov 23, sold 5 Feb 24
29 NORTH DAKOTA	Fore River	16 Dec 07	10 Nov 08	11 Apr 10	Stk. 7 Jan 31, sold 16 Mar 31.

Notes: Fiscal years 1907 (BB-28) and 1908 (29). With this class, Congress ceased imposing displacement limits in its authorizing acts and instead required the Navy to produce the most powerful ship possible with the funds specified. As a result, the Delawares were the largest battleships in the world when authorized. Their design caused great controversy as the armor belt was largely submerged when the vessels were normally loaded. The builders supplied both the hulls and the machinery. The North Dakota was given experimental Curtis turbines for comparison with the reciprocating engines in Delaware. She was re-engined in 1915 with 31,300 SHP geared turbines. She was designated on 24 Aug 23 as a mobile target under the provisions of the Washington Naval Treaty and was demilitarized on 29 May 24. Her new turbines were subsequently transferred to the battleship Nevada.
Reclassification: BB-29 to "unclassified" 31 May 24.

1908

FLORIDA class

Displacement: 21,825 tons
Dimensions: 521'6"(oa.) x 88'3"(e) x 30'1"(max)
Armament: 10-12"/45 16-5"/51 2-21"T; 10-12" 12-5" 2-3"/50AA
  2-21"T (1917); 10-12" 16-5" 8-3"AA 2-21"T (1922); 10-12"
  12-5" 8-3"AA (1926); none (Utah, 1931); 4-5"/25AA (Utah,
  1939); 4-5"/38AA 4-5"/25AA (Utah, 1941)
Armor: 11" belt, 12" turrets, 3" (aft) deck, 11 1/2" conning
  tower

Machinery: 28,000 SHP; direct-drive
  turbines, 4 screws
Speed: 20.75 kts.
Complement: 1001

No.	Builder	Laid down	Launched	Commiss'd	Disposition
30 FLORIDA	New York	9 Mar 09	12 May 10	15 Sep 11	Stk. 6 Apr 31, scrapped 1931
31 UTAH	New York SB	15 Mar 09	23 Dec 09	31 Aug 11	Sunk by Japanese aircraft, Pearl Harbor, 7 Dec 41.

Notes: Fiscal year 1909. These ships were generally repeats of the Delaware class, although they introduced the 5"/51 secondary gun and had their machinery spaces rearranged and beam increased to accomodate Parsons turbines. The building yards provided the machinery. They were reconstructed in 1925-27 at the Boston Navy Yard, receiving oil-fired boilers from cancelled battleships and having the uptakes trunked into a single funnel, the after cage mast removed, and the secondary batteries rearranged. They also received enhanced underwater protection and horizontal armor, including an additional protective deck with a maximum thickness of 4 3/4" (4 1/4" in Utah) above the old protective deck. Hull blisters increased their beam to 106'(e) and their displacement to 23,700 tons (normal). The Utah was converted to a target vessel in 1931 as the replacement for the North Dakota. After 1935 she also served as anti-aircraft gunnery training ship.
Reclassification: BB-31 to AG-16 1 Jul 31.

1909

WYOMING class

Displacement: 26,000 tons
Dimensions: 562'(oa.) x 93'3"(e) x 29'7"(max)
Armament: 12-12"/50 21-5"/51 2-21"T; 12-12" 16-5" 2-3"/50AA 2-21"T (1918); 12-12" 16-5" 8-3"AA 2-21"T (1921); 12-12" 16-5" 8-3"AA (1926); 6-12" 16-5" 8-3"AA (Wyoming, 1931); 12-12" 14-5" 8-3"AA (Arkansas, 1941); 6-12" 10-5"/51 4-5"/38AA 4-3"AA (Wyoming, 1941); 12-12" 6-5"/51 8-3"AA (Arkansas, 1942); 6-12" 8-5"/38AA 4-3"AA (Wyoming, 1942); 14-5"/38AA 4-3"AA (Wyoming, 1944); 12-12" 6-5"/51 10-3"AA (Arkansas, 1944)

Armor: 11" belt, 12" turrets, 3" (aft) deck, 11.5" conning tower
Machinery: 28,000 SHP; direct-drive turbines, 4 screws
Speed: 20.5 kts.
Complement: 1063

No.		Builder	Laid down	Launched	Commiss'd	Disposition
32	WYOMING	Cramp	9 Feb 10	25 May 11	25 Sep 12	Stk. 16 Sep 47, sold 30 Oct 47
33	ARKANSAS	New York SB	25 Jan 10	14 Jan 11	17 Sep 12	Sunk as target 25 Jul 46 at Bikini Atoll, stk. 15 Aug 46.

Notes: Fiscal year 1910. The first battleships designed in the light of experience from the world cruise of the Great White Fleet in 1907-9. The cruise showed that armor belts needed to be deeper to protect hulls below the waterline in a seaway, that protection needed to be better for bows and steering gear, and that the main and anti-torpedo boat armaments needed to be higher to be fully usable in a seaway at high battle speeds. A large increase in size made these improvements possible. The Navy had already decided to arm future battleships with 10-14" but used 12"/50 guns for this class because the 14" were not yet ready. The two ships were reconstructed in 1925-27 at the Philadelphia Navy Yard along the same lines as the Florida class--their beams were increased to 106' and displacement to 27,900 tons (normal) and they received an extra protective deck of 4 3/4". The Wyoming was converted to a gunnery training vessel in 1931. The Arkansas had her one remaining cage mast replaced by a tripod in early 1942 and the Wyoming had hers replaced by a pole in 1944. The Arkansas was sunk in the Bikini atomic bomb tests.
Reclassification: BB-32 to AG-17 1 Jul 31.

1910

NEW YORK class

Displacement: 27,000 tons
Dimensions: 573'(oa.) x 95'3"(e) x 29'7"(max)
Armament: 10-14"/45 21-5"/51 4-21"T; 10-14" 21-5" 2-3"/50AA 4-21"T (Texas, 1916); 10-14" 16-5" 2-3"AA 4-21"T (1917); 10-14" 16-5" 8-3"AA 4-21"T (1922); 10-14" 16-5" 8-3"AA (1926); 10-14" 14-5" 10-3" (1941); 10-14" 6-5" 8-3"AA (1942); 10-14" 6-5" 10-3"AA (1944)

Armor: 12" belt, 14" turrets, 3" (aft) deck, 12" conning tower
Machinery: 28,100 IHP; 2 vertical, triple-expansion engines, 2 screws
Speed: 21 kts.
Complement: 1052

No.		Builder	Laid down	Launched	Commiss'd	Disposition
34	NEW YORK	New York	11 Sep 11	30 Oct 12	15 Apr 14	Sunk as target 8 Jul 48 off Hawaii, stk. 13 Jul 48
35	TEXAS	Newport News	17 Apr 11	18 May 12	12 Mar 14	Memorial near Houston, Texas, 21 Apr 48, stk. 30 Apr 48.

Notes: Fiscal year 1911. The successful trials of the new 14"/45 gun permitted its use in this class, which otherwise was very similar to the Arkansas class. The ships were built with reciprocating engines because the turbine builders refused to comply with Navy standards. The Texas was the first U.S. battleship with anti-aircraft guns and was also the first U.S. dreadnought fitted with aircraft, for which she received platforms on two turrets in early 1918. The two ships were reconstructed in 1925-27 at the New York (New York) and Norfolk Navy Yards along the same lines as the Florida class--their beams were increased to 106'1" and displacement to 28,700 tons (normal) and they received an extra protective deck of 3 1/2". They also received completely new fire controls like those in later battleships and had their forward cage masts replaced with tripods. The reconstruction made them poor sea boats in rough weather and dropped their maximum speed to 19.5 kts. The New York was sunk as a target after use in the Bikini atomic bomb tests.

1911

NEVADA class

Displacement: 27,500 tons
Dimensions: 583'(oa.) x 95'3"(e) x 29'7"(max)
Armament: 10-14"/45 21-5"/51 2-21"T; 10-14" 12-5" 2-3"/50AA 2-21"T (1917); 10-14" 12-5" 8-3"AA 2-21"T (1921); 10-14" 12-5" 8-5"/25AA (1929); 10-14" 10-5" 8-5"AA (Nevada, 1941); 10-14" 10-5" 8-5"AA 4-3"/50AA (Oklahoma, 1941); 10-14" 16-5"/38AA (Nevada, 1942)
Armor: 13 1/2" belt, 18" triple turrets, 16" twin turrets, 3" second (armor) deck + 2 1/2" third (splinter) deck, 16" conning tower

Machinery: Nevada--26,500 SHP; geared turbines, 2 screws; Oklahoma--24,800 IHP; 2 vertical, triple-expansion engines, 2 screws
Speed: 20.5 kts.
Complement: 864

No.		Builder	Laid down	Launched	Commiss'd	Disposition
36	NEVADA	Fore River	4 Nov 12	11 Jul 14	11 Mar 16	Sunk as target 31 Jul 48 off Hawaii, stk. 12 Aug 48
37	OKLAHOMA	New York SB	26 Oct 12	23 Mar 14	2 May 16	Sunk by Japanese aircraft, Pearl Harbor, 7 Dec 41.

Notes: Fiscal year 1912. Epoch-making vessels, they were the first Dreadnoughts to incorporate the "all or nothing" concept of armor. They were designed for action at very long ranges with heavy armor-piercing shells and had thick side armor, two strong protective decks, and practically no thinner armor. The need to limit the length of the ships caused the designers to adopt oil fuel and triple-gun main-battery turrets, both firsts in U.S. battleships. Both ships were engined by their builders but the Nevada had her engines replaced in 1924 with the 31,300 SHP geared turbines from the North Dakota. The two ships were reconstructed in 1927-29 at the Norfolk (Nevada) and Philadelphia Navy Yards with boilers from cancelled battleships, new fire controls on two large tripods, and aircraft catapults on turret tops. The elevation of their main guns was increased, their secondary batteries were raised one deck and rearranged, and 5"/25AA guns were added. The armor deck of each ship received an additional 2" layer (increasing it to 5") and underwater protection was enhanced. Hull blisters increased the beam to 107'11" and the displacement to 29,000 tons (standard). The Nevada was again rebuilt in 1942 at Puget Sound following her damage at Pearl Harbor. She was sunk as a target by the battleship Iowa and three cruisers after use in the Bikini atomic bomb tests. The Oklahoma's hulk was raised on 28 Dec 43 and sold at Pearl Harbor on 5 Dec 46, but it sank on 17 May 47 while being towed to California for scrapping.

1912

PENNSYLVANIA class

Displacement: 31,400 tons
Dimensions: 608'(oa.) x 97'1"(e) x 29'10"(max)
Armament: 12-14"/45 22-5"/51 2-21"T; 12-14" 14-5" 4-3"/50AA 2-21"T (1917); 12-14" 14-5" 8-3"AA 2-21"T (1921); 12-14" 12-5" 8-5"/25AA (1931); 12-14" 10-5" 8-5"AA (Arizona, 1941); 12-14" 10-5" 8-5"AA 4-3"/50AA (Pennsylvania, 1941); 12-14" 16-5"/38AA (Pennsylvania, 1942)
Armor: 13 1/2" belt, 18" turrets, 3" + 2" decks, 16" conning tower
Machinery: 31,500 SHP (Pennsylvania), 34,000 SHP (Arizona); geared turbines, 4 screws
Speed: 21 kts.
Complement: 915

No.		Builder	Laid down	Launched	Commiss'd	Disposition
38	PENNSYLVANIA	Newport News	27 Oct 13	16 Mar 15	12 Jun 16	Scuttled off Kwajalein 10 Feb 48, stk. 19 Feb 48
39	ARIZONA	New York	16 Mar 14	19 Jun 15	17 Oct 16	Sunk by Japanese aircraft, Pearl Harbor, 7 Dec 41.

Notes: Fiscal years 1913 (BB-38) and 1914 (39). They were improved Nevadas with an extra 2-14" guns and 1/2 knot of speed. They were successful vessels which were comfortable and steady in most seas. They were engined by their builders. They were reconstructed in 1929-31 at the Philadelphia (Pennsylvania) and Norfolk Navy Yards along the same lines as the Nevada class--their beams were increased to 106'3" and standard displacement to 33,100 tons (Pennsylvania) and 32,600 tons (Arizona). They also received an extra 1 3/4" layer on their armor deck and their turbines (except for the low pressure turbines in Arizona) were replaced with turbines from the cancelled battleship Washington. The Pennsylvania was again rebuilt in 1942-43 at Mare Island. She was scuttled after use in the Bikini atomic bomb tests.

The battleship *Arizona* (BB-39) during gunnery practice ca. 1917. Her forward 5″ guns have not yet been removed. (NH 95244)

The battleship *Wisconsin* (BB-64) alongside the hulk of the *Oklahoma* (BB-37) at Pearl Harbor on 11 November 1944. (NH 78940)

1914

NEW MEXICO class

Displacement: 32,000 tons
Dimensions: 624'(oa.) x 97'5"(e) x 31'1"(max)
Armament: 12-14"/50 22-5"/51 2-21"T; 12-14" 14-5" 4-3"/50AA
  2-21"T (1918); 12-14" 12-5" 8-3"AA 2-21"T (1921); 12-14"
  12-5" 8-5"/25AA (1932); 12-14" 10-5" 8-5"AA 4-3"/50AA
  (1941); 12-14" 6-5" 8-5"AA (New Mexico, Mississippi, 1942);
  12-14" 8-5"/25AA (Idaho, 1942); 12-14" 10-5"/38AA (Idaho,
  1945); 12-14" 16-5"/25AA (Mississippi, 1945); 3-14"
  2-6"/47AA 2-5"/54AA 6-5"/38AA 4-3"/50AA (Mississippi,
  1949); 2-6" 2-5" 6-5" 4-3" 4-Terrier SAM (Mississippi,
  1952)

Armor: 13 1/2" belt, 18" turrets, 3
  1/2"+ 2" decks, 16" conning tower
Machinery: New Mexico--27,500 SHP; G.
  E. turbines with electric drive, 4
  screws;
  others--32,000 SHP; geared
  turbines, 4 screws
Speed: 21 kts.
Complement: 1084

No.	Hull	Laid down	Launched	Commiss'd	Disposition
40 NEW MEXICO	New York	14 Oct 15	23 Apr 17	20 May 18	Stk. 25 Feb 47, sold 9 Nov 47
41 MISSISSIPPI	Newport News	5 Apr 15	25 Jan 17	18 Dec 17	Stk. 30 Jul 56, sold 28 Nov 56
42 IDAHO	New York SB	20 Jan 15	30 Jun 17	24 Mar 19	Stk. 16 Sep 47, sold 24 Nov 47.

Notes: Fiscal year 1915. The Navy's General Board wanted to develop a new, larger design with 10-16"
guns for these ships, but in January 1914 the Secretary of the Navy ordered that they essentially
duplicate the Pennsylvania. Some important changes were worked into the design, including a new
14"/50 gun, a new turret design that permitted individual elevation of the guns, a new hull form with
a clipper bow and bulbous forefoot, and a new distribution of the secondary battery. The New Mexico
was fitted with turbo-electric machinery as an experimental alternative to reduction gearing. The
Idaho was built with the proceeds from the sale of the old Idaho and Mississippi. The three ships
were reconstructed in 1931-34 at the Philadelphia (New Mexico) and Norfolk Navy Yards along the same
lines as the Nevada class--their beams were increased to 106'3" and standard displacement to 33,000
(Mississippi) and 33,400 (others) tons. Each also received an extra 2" layer on its armor deck, new
40,000 SHP Westinghouse geared turbines, and a tower bridge. The Mississippi became a trials ship and
gunnery training vessel after World War II.
Renaming: BB-40 ex California 22 Mar 16.
Reclassification: BB-41 to AG-128 15 Feb 46.

1915

TENNESSEE class

Displacement: 32,300 tons
Dimensions: 624'(oa.) x 97'4"(e) x 31'0"(max)
Armament: 12-14"/50 14-5"/51 4-3"/50AA 2-21"T; 12-14" 12-5"
  8-3"AA 2-21"T (1922); 12-14" 12-5" 8-5"/25AA 2-21"T (1929);
  12-14" 12-5" 8-5"AA (1935); 12-14" 10-5" 8-5"AA 4-3"/50AA
  (1941); 12-14" 16-5"/38AA (1943)

Armor: 13.5" belt, 18" turrets, 3
  1/2" + 1 1/2" decks, 16" conning
  tower
Machinery: 26,800 SHP (Tennessee),
  28,500 SHP (California); turbines
  with electric drive, 4 screws
Speed: 21 kts.
Complement: 1083

No.	Hull	Machinery	Laid down	Launched	Commiss'd	Disposition
43 TENNESSEE	New York	Westing-house	14 May 17	30 Apr 19	3 Jun 20	Stk. 1 Mar 59, sold 16 Jul 59
44 CALIFORNIA	Mare I.	G. E.	25 Oct 16	20 Nov 19	10 Aug 21	Stk. 1 Mar 59, sold 1 Jul 59.

Notes: Fiscal year 1916. The Secretary of the Navy ordered in July 1914 that these ships essentially
duplicate the New Mexico class. Improvements worked into the design included enhanced underwater
protection, increased elevation of the main guns, larger bridges, and more robust cage masts with
larger fire controls. Both ships were completely rebuilt at Puget Sound in 1942-44, emerging as
modern battleships except for their speed. Their many improvements included bulges which increased
the beam to 114', an extra 2" layer on their armor deck, and modern fire control systems.

1916

COLORADO class

Displacement: 32,600 tons
Dimensions: 624'(oa.) x 97'4"(e) x 31'4"(max)
Armament: 8-16"/45 14-5"/51 4-3"/50AA 2-21"T; 8-16" 12-5"
  8-3"AA 2-21"T (1922); 8-16" 12-5" 8-5"/25AA 2-21"T (1929);

Armor: 13 1/2" belt, 18" turrets,
  3 1/2" + 1 1/2" decks, 16" conning
  tower

8-16" 12-5" 8-5"AA (1938); 8-16" 10-5" 8-5"AA 4-3"/50AA
(Colorado, Maryland, 1941); 8-16" 9-5" 7-5"AA 4-3"AA (West
Virginia, 1941); 8-16" 8-5" 8-5"AA (Colorado, Maryland,
1943); 8-16" 16-5"/38AA (West Virginia, 1944; Maryland,
1945)

Machinery: 28,900 SHP; turbines with
electric drive, 4 screws
Speed: 21 kts.
Complement: 1080

No.		Hull	Machinery	Laid down	Launched	Commiss'd	Disposition
45	COLORADO	New York SB	Westing-house	29 May 19	22 Mar 21	30 Aug 23	Stk. 1 Mar 59, sold 6 Jul 59
46	MARYLAND	Newport News	G. E.	24 Apr 17	20 Mar 20	21 Jul 21	Stk. 1 Mar 59, sold 15 Jul 59
47	WASHINGTON	New York	Westing-house	30 Jun 19	1 Sep 21	No	Stk. 10 Nov 23, sunk as target off Virginia Capes 25 Nov 24
48	WEST VIRGINIA	Newport News	G. E.	12 Apr 20	19 Nov 21	1 Dec 23	Stk. 1 Mar 59, sold 24 Aug 59.

Notes: Fiscal year 1917. In June 1916 the Secretary of the Navy ordered that these ships duplicate
the Tennessee class except that 16" guns could be substituted. The construction of the Washington was
stopped on 8 Feb 22 when 75.9 percent complete because of the Washington Naval Treaty and she was sunk
as a target by the battleship Texas after tests of her protective systems. The Colorado received
bulges at Puget Sound in 1941-2, increasing her beam to 108'1", and the Maryland was similarly altered
there immediately after the Pearl Harbor attack. The West Virginia received the same complete
reconstruction as the Tennessee class at Puget Sound in 1942-44. The Maryland received 5"/38AA guns
in 1945 after a Kamikaze attack.

1917

SOUTH DAKOTA class

Displacement: 43,200 tons
Dimensions: 684'(oa.) x 106'(e) x 33'4"(max)
Armament: 12-16"/50 16-6"/53 6-3"/50AA 2-21"T
Armor: 13 1/2" belt, 18" turrets, 3 1/2" + 1 1/4" decks, 16"
  conning tower

Machinery: 60,000 SHP; G. E. (BB 53-
  54), Westinghouse (others) turbines
  with electric drive, 4 screws
Speed: 23 kts.
Complement: 1351

No.		Hull	Laid down	Launched	Commiss'd	Disposition
49	SOUTH DAKOTA	New York	15 Mar 20	No	No	Sold 25 Oct 23, stk. 10 Nov 23
50	INDIANA	New York	1 Nov 20	No	No	Sold 25 Oct 23, stk. 10 Nov 23
51	MONTANA	Mare I.	1 Sep 20	No	No	Sold 25 Oct 23, stk. 10 Nov 23
52	NORTH CAROLINA	Norfolk	12 Jan 20	No	No	Sold 25 Oct 23, stk. 10 Nov 23
53	IOWA	Newport News	17 May 20	No	No	Sold 8 Nov 23, stk. 10 Nov 23
54	MASSACHUSETTS	Quincy	4 Apr 21	No	No	Sold 8 Nov 23, stk. 10 Nov 23.

Notes: Fiscal years 1918 (BB 49-51) and 1919 (52-54). The cap on battleship size imposed by the
Secretary of the Navy was lifted for these ships. They were essentially enlarged Colorados with
triple rather than twin 16" turrets, new 16"/50 guns, a 6" secondary battery, and increased speed.
They were to have been laid down in late 1917 or early 1918, but the U-boat war caused all
shipbuilding resources to be shifted to destroyers, ASW vessels, and merchant ships. Construction on
all stopped on 8 Feb 22 when they were between 27.6 and 38.5 percent complete (11 percent for the
Massachusetts) and the hulls were scrapped under the Washington Naval Treaty. Some of their armor and
boilers were used in the battleship reconstructions of the 1920s and 1930s.

1934

NORTH CAROLINA class

Displacement: 35,000 tons standard
Dimensions: North Carolina--728'9"(oa.) x 108'4"(e) x 35'6'
  (max); Washington--729'(oa.) x 108'4"(e) x 34'9"(max)
Armament: 9-16"/45 20-5"/38AA
Armor: 12" belt, 16" turrets, 1 1/2" main deck + 5 1/2"
  second (armor) deck + 3/4" third deck, 16" conning tower

Machinery: 115,000 SHP; G. E. geared
  turbines, 4 screws
Speed: 27 kts.
Complement: 1880

No.		Hull	Laid down	Launched	Commiss'd	Disposition
55	NORTH CAROLINA	New York	27 Oct 37	13 Jun 40	9 Apr 41	Stk. 1 Jun 60, memorial at Wilmington, N.C., 6 Sep 61
56	WASHINGTON	Philadelphia	14 Jun 38	1 Jun 40	15 May 41	Stk. 1 Jun 60, sold 6 Jun 61.

Notes: Fiscal year 1937. Their design was restricted by the provisions of the Washington and London
Naval Treaties. It included a main armament of 12-14"/50 guns in three quadruple turrets but also
provided for the substitution of 16" guns if treaty conditions permitted. The change in armament was
approved in November 1937, but the protection scheme remained as designed against 14" shells.

1938

SOUTH DAKOTA class

Displacement: 35,000 tons standard
Dimensions: 680"4", 680'0", 680'10" and 679'5" (respectively,
    oa.) x 108'2"(e) x 36'2"(max)
Armament: 9-16"/45 16-5"/38AA (South Dakota), 9-16" 20-5"AA
    (others)
Armor: 12 1/4" belt, 18" turrets, 1 1/2" + 6" + 1/3" decks,
    15" conning tower

Machinery: 130,000 SHP; G. E. (BB-57,
    59), Westinghouse (BB 58, 60)
    geared turbines, 4 screws
Speed: 27 kts.
Complement: 1793

No.		Hull	Laid down	Launched	Commiss'd	Disposition
57	SOUTH DAKOTA	New York SB	5 Jul 39	7 Jun 41	20 Mar 42	Stk. 1 Jun 62, sold Nov 62
58	INDIANA	Newport News	20 Nov 39	21 Nov 41	30 Apr 42	Stk. 1 Jun 62, sold 23 Oct 63
59	MASSACHUSETTS	Quincy	20 Jul 39	23 Sep 41	12 May 42	Stk. 1 Jun 62, memorial at Fall R., Mass., 8 Jun 65
60	ALABAMA	Norfolk	1 Feb 40	16 Feb 42	16 Aug 42	Stk. 1 Jun 62, memorial at Mobile, Ala., 11 Jun 64.

Notes: Fiscal year 1939. They were built to a new compact design which incorporated balanced
protection against contemporary 16" shells while remaining within treaty limits. Their 5" battery was
set a deck higher than in the North Carolinas, and in the South Dakota the center 5" mount on each
side was eliminated in order to provide an extra level in the conning tower for a fleet (force)
commander and his staff. General Electric designed the turbines.

1939

IOWA class

Displacement: 45,000 tons standard
Dimensions: 887'7"(New Jersey, oa.), 887'3"(others, oa.) x
    108'1"(New Jersey, e), 108'2"(others, e) x 38'(New Jersey,
    max), 37'9"(others, max)
Armament: 9-16"/50 20-5"/38AA; 9-16" 12-5" 32-Tomahawk-SSM
    16-Harpoon-SSM (1983)

Armor: 12 1/8" belt, 17" turrets,
    1 1/2" + 6" + 5/8" (splinter) +
    5/8" decks, 17 1/4" conning tower
Machinery: 212,000 SHP; G. E. (BB 61,
    63, 66), Westinghouse (others)
    geared turbines, 4 screws
Speed: 33 kts.
Complement: 1921

No.		Hull	Laid down	Launched	Commiss'd	Disposition
61	IOWA	New York	27 Jun 40	27 Aug 42	22 Feb 43	USN
62	NEW JERSEY	Philadelphia	16 Sep 40	7 Dec 42	23 May 43	USN
63	MISSOURI	New York	6 Jan 41	29 Jan 44	11 Jun 44	USN
64	WISCONSIN	Philadelphia	25 Jan 41	7 Dec 43	16 Apr 44	USN
65	ILLINOIS	Philadelphia	15 Jan 45	No	No	Cancelled 12 Aug 45, scrapped Sep 58
66	KENTUCKY	Norfolk	6 Dec 44	20 Jan 50	No	Stk. 9 Jun 58, sold Nov 58.

Notes: Fiscal years 1940 (BB 61-62) and 1941 (63-66). Built to the first modern U.S. battleship
design not hampered by the 35,000-ton limit of the Washington and London Naval Treaties, these were
fast and successful vessels. The Navy felt it needed some fast battleships to protect forces of
carriers and cruisers against similar Japanese forces which might also contain fast Kongo class
battlecruisers. The new class was therefore designed as 33-knot South Dakotas with new 16"/50 guns.
Such a design was made possible by the increase in 1938 of the treaty limit on battleship displacement
to 45,000 tons. The conning tower of the Iowa had an extra level for a fleet (force) commander. The
Kentucky was initially laid down on 7 Mar 42 but her bottom section was launched on 10 Jun 42 to make
way for LST construction. Hull construction was resumed in December 1944, suspended in August 1946
and resumed in August 1948 to permit launching. She was 73 percent complete when laid up in 1950.
Plans were begun in 1956 for her conversion in Fiscal Year 1958 to a guided missile battleship (BBG)
with Regulus II missiles, but the project was dropped later in 1956. Her bow was used to repair the
Wisconsin in 1956 and her machinery was used in the replenishment ships Sacramento and Camden in the
1960s. The Illinois was 22 percent complete when cancelled in 1945. The New Jersey was
recommissioned for service in the Vietnam War on 6 Apr 68 and decommissioned on 17 Dec 69. All four
ships were refitted and recommissioned beginning in 1982 as follows: New Jersey (Long Beach Naval
Shipyard, 28 Dec 82), Iowa (Avondale Shipyard and Ingalls Shipbuilding, 28 Apr 84), Missouri (Long
Beach, 10 May 86) and Wisconsin (Avondale and Ingalls, 22 Oct 88). The Iowa suffered a major
explosion in number two turret on 19 Apr 89.

1940

MONTANA class

Displacement: 63,221 tons standard
Dimensions: 925'0"(oa.) x 121'2"(e) x 36'2"(max)
Armament: 12-16/50" 20-5"/54AA
Armor: 16 1/8" belt, 22 1/2" turrets, 2 1/4" + 7 1/3" + 3/4"
  decks, 18" conning tower

Machinery: 172,000 SHP; geared
  turbines, 4 screws
Speed: 28 kts. (designed)
Complement: 2247 (Maine), 2149
  (others)

No.	Hull	Laid down	Launched	Commiss'd	Disposition
67 MONTANA	Philadelphia	No	No	No	Cancelled 21 Jul 43
68 OHIO	Philadelphia	No	No	No	Cancelled 21 Jul 43
69 MAINE	New York	No	No	No	Cancelled 21 Jul 43
70 NEW HAMPSHIRE	New York	No	No	No	Cancelled 21 Jul 43
71 LOUISIANA	Norfolk	No	No	No	Cancelled 21 Jul 43.

Notes: Fiscal year 1941. With this class the Navy returned to slower battleships for the main battle line. The design, which received its final refinements in June 1942, was unconstrained by treaty limits or by the width of the Panama Canal (which was to have been increased while the ships were under construction). Improvements included heavier armor effective against a new heavy 16" projectile (which was introduced after the Iowas were designed) and greatly improved underwater protection including hull blisters, a separate, internal underwater belt up to 8 1/2" thick, elaborate subdivision, and a triple bottom. The Maine was to be a fleet (force) flagship and the others were to be division flagships. When ordered on 19 May 40 the scheduled completion dates of the ships ranged from July to November 1945. With the war, however, escort vessels, landing craft, and carriers received higher precedence, and construction of the class was suspended on 20 May 42.

Battle Cruisers (CC)

1916

LEXINGTON class

Displacement: 43,500 tons
Dimensions: 874'(oa.) x 105'5"(e) x 31'(mean)
Armament: 8-16"/50 16-6"/53 4-3"/50AA 8-21"T
Armor: 7" belt, 11" turrets, 1 3/4" + 1 1/2" + 1 1/2" + 2"
  decks, 12" conning tower

Machinery: 180,000 SHP; Westinghouse
  (CC 2, 4), G. E. (others) turbines
  with electric drive, 4 screws
Speed: 33.25 kts.
Complement: 1297

No.	Hull	Laid down	Launched	Commiss'd	Disposition
1 LEXINGTON	Quincy	8 Jan 21	Completed as CV		To CV-2 1 Jul 22
2 CONSTELLATION	Newport News	18 Aug 20	No	No	Sold 8 Nov 23, stk. 10 Nov 23
3 SARATOGA	New York SB	25 Sep 20	Completed as CV		To CV-3 1 Jul 22
4 RANGER	Newport News	23 Jun 21	No	No	Sold 8 Nov 23, stk. 10 Nov 23
5 CONSTITUTION	Philadelphia	25 Sep 20	No	No	Sold 25 Oct 23, stk. 10 Nov 23
6 UNITED STATES	Philadelphia	25 Sep 20	No	No	Sold 25 Oct 23, stk. 10 Nov 23.

Notes: Fiscal years 1917 (CC 1-4), 1918 (5), and 1919 (6). The original design, completed in June 1916, called for seven-funneled, 34,300 ton vessels, 874'(oa.) x 90'11", mounting 10-14"/50 18-5"/51 4-3/"50 8-21"T. Their speed was 35 knots and their protection was 5" belt, 6" turrets, 1" + 1 1/2" + 1 1/2" + 1 1/8" decks, and 5" conning tower. The number of funnels was reduced to five in May 1917 and the main battery was changed to 8-16" in October 1918. The class was suspended in March 1919 for redesign in the light of war experience, and the final design (described above) was completed in June 1919. It featured two large funnels, a substantial increase in deck protection, and side armor inclined as in the British battlecruiser Hood. Construction of the four vessels slated for scrapping under the Washington Naval Treaty stopped on 8 Feb 22 when between 4 and 22.7 percent complete.
Renamings (all 10 Dec 17): Lexington ex Constitution, Ranger ex Lexington, and Constitution ex Ranger.

Aircraft Carriers (CV)

1919

LANGLEY

Displacement: 11,050 tons
Dimensions: 542'(oa.) x 65'5" x 24'(max)
Armament: 4-5"/51 36 planes; 4-5" (1937)

Machinery: 7152 SHP; G. E. turbines
  with electric drive, 2 screws
Speed: 15 kts.
Complement: 411

No.		Converted	Conv. begun	Commiss'd	Disposition
1	LANGLEY	Norfolk	24 Mar 20	20 Mar 22	Sunk by Japanese aircraft E. of Bali 27 Feb 42.

Notes: Built at Mare Island in 1911-13 as the collier Jupiter, she was reclassified CV-1 on 11 Jul 19 and renamed Langley on 21 Apr 20. She was selected for conversion because she had large holds and hatches for storing aircraft and had hoisting gear already in place. An experimental conversion, she was never regarded as a combatant. Her flight deck measured 534' x 64' and she had two catapults (removed in 1928) and one elevator. In 1937 the forward part of her flight deck was removed and she was converted to a seaplane tender to free up tonnage under U. S. legislation for the construction of the Wasp (CV-7).
Reclassification: From Fuel Ship No. 3 21 Apr 20; to AV-3 21 Apr 37.

1922

LEXINGTON class

Displacement: 33,000 tons standard
Dimensions: 888'(oa.) x 105'6"(hull, e), 130'(f.d.) x
  32'(max)
Armament: 8-8"/55 12-5"/25AA 90 planes; 12-5"AA 93 planes
  (CV-3 1941, CV-2 1942); 16-5"/38AA 83 planes (CV-3 (1942);
  12-5"AA 75 planes (1945)

Armor: 7" belt, 2" deck
Machinery: 180,000 SHP; G. E.
  turbines with electric drive, 4
  screws
Speed: 34 kts.
Complement: 2122

No.		Hull	Laid down	Launched	Commiss'd	Disposition
2	LEXINGTON	Quincy	8 Jan 21	3 Oct 25	14 Dec 27	Sunk by Japanese aircraft in the Coral Sea 8 May 42
3	SARATOGA	New York SB	25 Sep 20	7 Apr 25	16 Nov 27	Sunk 25 Jul 46, stk. 15 Aug 46.

Notes: The large Lexington class battle cruisers, then on the ways, were prime candidates for cancellation under proposed arms limitation treaties, and in November 1921 the Navy began studies for their conversion to aircraft carriers. The Washington Naval Treaty permitted the conversion of two of them, which were reclassified CV on 1 Jul 22. They retained their battle cruiser machinery and some protection. Their strength deck was the flight deck, not the hangar deck, and the hangar was a fully enclosed integral part of the hull. The 866' x 106' flight deck was fitted with a catapult (removed in 1934) and two elevators. Distinctive looking ships with their massive funnels and knuckled bows, they were difficult to maneuver and had a large tactical radius. Their 8" guns were removed in 1941-42 because successive modifications had made the ships overweight. The Saratoga was sunk in the Baker atomic bomb test at Bikini Atoll.
Reclassifications: From CC-1 and CC-3 respectively 1 Jul 22.

1929

RANGER

Displacement: 14,500 tons standard
Dimensions: 769'(oa.) x 80'1"(hull), 109'6"(f.d.) x 24'(max)
Armament: 8-5"/25AA 86 planes
Armor: None

Machinery: 53,500 SHP; geared
  turbines, 2 screws
Speed: 29.5 kts.
Complement: 1788

No.		Hull	Machinery	Laid down	Launched	Commiss'd	Disposition
4	RANGER	Newport News		26 Sep 31	25 Feb 33	4 Jun 34	Stk. 29 Oct 46, sold 31 Jan 47.

Notes: Fiscal year 1930. The first American carrier built as such from the keel up, her displacement was fixed as one fifth of the total still available to the U. S. under the Washington Naval Treaty. Speed was sacrificed to stay within this limit--her designers felt that 29.5 knots would allow her to operate with the battle line and, under most conditions, with the scouting force. Her relatively low speed and lack of underwater protection, however, prevented her use in the Pacific during the war. She introduced the configuration that became standard in other prewar carrier designs: her strength

The aircraft carrier *Lexington* (CV-2) on 31 May 1934. (NARA 80-G-415861)

The ASW support aircraft carrier *Tarawa* (CVS-40) on 13 August 1958, in a configuration typical of unmodified *Essex*-class carriers. (NARA 80-G-1046503)

deck was the hangar deck, her hangar was largely open, and her flight deck was surrounded with galleries containing her armament and other equipment. She was designed without an island, but one was added in the late stages of construction. She had two elevators but no catapults.

1933

YORKTOWN class

Displacement: 19,800 tons standard
Dimensions: 809'6"(oa.) x 83'1"(hull), 114'(f.d.) x 28'6"(max)
Armament: 8-5"/38AA 90 planes
Armor: 4" belt, 1 1/2" deck, 4" conning tower (3/4" in CV-8)

Machinery: 120,000 SHP; geared turbines, 4 screws
Speed: 32.5 kts.
Complement: 1889 (later 2919)

No.		Hull	Machinery	Laid down	Launched	Commiss'd	Disposition
5	YORKTOWN	Newport News		21 May 34	4 Apr 36	30 Sep 37	Sunk by HIJMS I-168 off Midway I. 7 Jun 42
6	ENTERPRISE	Newport News		16 Jul 34	3 Oct 36	12 May 38	Stk. 2 Oct 56, sold 2 Jul 58
8	HORNET	Newport News		25 Sep 39	14 Dec 40	20 Oct 41	Sunk by Japanese aircraft and destroyers off Sta. Cruz Is. 26 Oct 42.

Notes: Fiscal years 1934 (CV 5-6) and 1939 (8). After the Ranger was begun, the Navy decided to use its remaining treaty tonnage to build only one more small carrier of her size and two larger ones of around 20,000 tons. The main purpose of increasing carrier size was to add some protection against gunfire and torpedoes. Exercises with earlier carriers also showed the tactical importance of speed and the ability to operate in rough weather. The design included three catapults (two on the flight deck and one on the hangar deck) and three elevators. Although obsolescent by 1939, it was reused for the Hornet because the navy's ship designers were then fully occupied with the design of the Iowa class battleships. In 1942 the Enterprise and Hornet lost their hangar deck catapults, and in 1943 the Enterprise received bulges, increasing her hull beam to 95"8".
Reclassifications: CV-6 to CVA-6 1 Oct 52 and to CVS-6 8 Aug 53.

1934

WASP

Displacement: 14,700 tons standard
Dimensions: 741'4"(oa.) x 80'8"(hull), 109'(f.d.) x 22'2"(max)
Armament: 8-5"/38AA 72 planes
Armor: 3/4" belt, 1 1/4" deck, 1 1/2" conning tower

Machinery: 75,000 SHP; geared turbines, 2 screws
Speed: 29.5 kts.
Complement: 1889

No.	Hull	Machinery	Laid down	Launched	Commiss'd	Disposition
7 WASP	Quincy	Quincy	1 Apr 36	4 Apr 39	25 Apr 40	Sunk by HIJMS I-19 off Guadalcanal 15 Sep 42.

Notes: Fiscal year 1936. The initial characteristics for this ship were developed at the same time as those of the Yorktown class, of which she was in many ways a smaller edition. Unlike the larger ships, she had practically no side armor, no torpedo bulkheads, and reverted to the lower speed of the Ranger. The last transversely framed combat vessel built for the Navy, she was fitted with four catapults (two on the flight deck and a transverse pair on the hangar deck) and three elevators (including the first deck edge installation). She proved to be too slow and too weak for satisfactory fleet service and was the last American effort to build a small fleet carrier until the emergency Independence class of 1942.

1940

ESSEX class

Displacement: 27,100 tons standard
Dimensions: 872'(oa.) x 93'(hull), 147'6"(f.d.) x 28'7"(max)
Armament: 12-5"/38AA 82 planes; 8-5"AA 28-3"/50AA 83 planes (SCB-27 conversions); 7 to 8-5"AA, 8 to 16-3"AA, 83 planes (SCB-125 conversions); 7 to 8-5"AA, 83 planes (both conversions, 1959); 4-5"AA 29 planes 18 helicopters (same, as CVS in 1960s)

Armor: 4" belt, 2 1/2" hangar deck, 1 1/2" deck, 1 1/2" conning tower
Machinery: 150,000 SHP; Westinghouse geared turbines, 4 screws
Speed: 33 kts.
Complement: 3448

No.		Hull	Laid down	Launched	Commiss'd	Disposition
9	ESSEX	Newport News	28 Apr 41	31 Jul 42	31 Dec 42	Stk. 1 Jun 73, sold 14 May 75
10	YORKTOWN	Newport News	1 Dec 41	21 Jan 43	15 Apr 43	Stk. 1 Jun 73, memorial at Charleston, S.C., 9 Jun 75
11	INTREPID	Newport News	1 Dec 41	26 Apr 43	16 Aug 43	Stk. 23 Feb 82, memorial at New York City 23 Feb 82
12	HORNET	Newport News	3 Aug 42	30 Aug 43	29 Nov 43	Stk. 25 Jul 89
13	FRANKLIN	Newport News	7 Dec 42	14 Oct 43	31 Jan 44	Stk. 1 Oct 64, sold 27 Jul 66
16	LEXINGTON	Quincy	15 Jul 41	26 Sep 42	17 Feb 43	USN
17	BUNKER HILL	Quincy	15 Sep 41	7 Dec 42	25 May 43	Stk. 1 Nov 66, sold 19 Jun 73
18	WASP	Quincy	18 Mar 42	17 Aug 43	24 Nov 43	Stk. 1 Jul 72, sold 21 May 73
20	BENNINGTON	New York	15 Dec 42	26 Feb 44	6 Aug 44	Stk. 20 Sep 89
31	BON HOMME RICHARD	New York	1 Feb 43	29 Apr 44	26 Nov 44	Stk. 20 Sep 89.

Notes: Fiscal years (Essex, Ticonderoga, and Oriskany classes): 1941 (CV 9-19), 1942 (20-21), 1943 (31-40), 1944 (45-47), 1945 (50-55). These ships were a development of the Hornet design produced after treaty tonnage restrictions had been lifted. The main purpose of the new design was to allow operation of a larger air group. Important new features were the unit machinery arrangement with alternating boiler and engine rooms, deck protection strengthened against bombs as well as gunfire, more speed, and a larger gun battery. The ships were fitted with two centerline and one deck edge elevators and a pair of catapults. (Six ships, CV 10, 12, 13, 14, 17, and 18, were completed with a third catapult on the hangar deck, which was soon removed.) The early ships of the Essex class (this group) were completed with the short bow of the original design with a single antiaircraft gun position and were referred to as the "short hulled" group. The order for CV-12 was transferred on 9 Sep 40 from the Norfolk Navy Yard.

The Bunker Hill and Franklin were not modified after the war, and the former was used as a floating electronics laboratory after being stricken. The others underwent a series of conversions to allow them to operate jet fighters and the largest attack aircraft that could be accomodated without major structural changes. During 1949-55 the Essex, Yorktown, Hornet, Wasp, and Bennington got SCB-27A rebuildings which included hydraulic catapults, and the Intrepid, Lexington, and Bon Homme Richard underwent SCB-27C modernizations which featured more powerful steam catapults. Following the success of the Forrestal (CVA-59), all of these also received the SCB-125 modernization which gave them angled decks and enclosed bows. Their new specifications were: 30,800 tons; 899'(oa.) x 129'(hull), 147'(f.d.) x 30'6"(max). The start and completion dates for major modifications to individual ships were as follows:

Essex: SCB-27A, 15 Feb 49-1 Feb 51, Puget Sd.; SCB-125, 1 Aug 55-9 Mar 56, Puget Sd;
Yorktown: SCB-27A, 19 Mar 51-2 Jan 53, Puget Sd.; SCB-125, 9 Mar 55-15 Aug 55, Puget Sd;
Intrepid: SCB-27C, 12 Apr 52-18 Jun 54, Newport News; SCB-125, 30 Sep 56-2 May 57, New York;
Hornet: SCB-27A, 16 Jul 51-1 Oct 53, New York; SCB-125, 15 Jan 56-15 Aug 56, Puget Sd;
Lexington: SCB-27C and SCB-125 together, 1 Sep 53-1 Sep 55, Puget Sd;
Wasp: SCB-27A, 1 May 49-28 Sep 51, New York; SCB-125, 1 May 55-1 Dec 55, San Francisco;
Bennington: SCB-27A, 1 Dec 50-30 Nov 52, New York; SCB-125, 9 Sep 54-15 Apr 55, New York;
Bon Homme Richard: SCB-27C and SCB-125 together, 1 May 53-1 Nov 55, San Francisco.
Renamings: CV-10 ex Bon Homme Richard 26 Sep 42; CV-12 ex Kearsarge 25 Jan 43; CV-16 ex Cabot 18 Jun 42; and CV-18 ex Oriskany 13 Nov 42.
Reclassifications:
Essex (CV-9) to CVA-9 1 Oct 52; CVS-9 8 Mar 60;
Yorktown (CV-10) to CVA-10 1 Oct 52; CVS-10 1 Sep 57;
Intrepid (CV-11) to CVA-11 1 Oct 52; CVS-11 31 Mar 62;
Hornet (CV-12) to CVA-12 1 Oct 52; CVS-12 27 Jun 58;
Franklin (CV-13) to CVA-13 1 Oct 52; CVS-13 8 Aug 53; AVT-8 15 May 59;
Lexington (CV-16) to CVA-16 1 Oct 52; CVS-16 1 Oct 62; CVT-16 1 Jan 69;
    AVT-16 1 Jul 78;
Bunker Hill (CV-17) to CVA-17 1 Oct 52; CVS-17 8 Aug 53; AVT-9 15 May 59;
Wasp (CV-18) to CVA-18 1 Oct 52; CVS-18 1 Nov 56;
Bennington (CV-20) to CVA-20 1 Oct 52; CVS-20 30 Jun 59;
Bon Homme Richard (CV-31) to CVA-31 1 Oct 52 (still CVA 1989).

TICONDEROGA class

Displacement: 27,100 tons standard
Dimensions: 888'(oa.) x 93'(hull), 147'6"(f.d.) x 28'7"(max)
Armament: 12-5"/38AA 82 planes; 10-5"AA 60 planes (Antietam, 1954); 8-5"AA 28-3"/50AA 85 planes (SCB-27 conversions); 7 to 8-5"AA, 8 to 16-3"AA, 85 planes (SCB-125 conversions); 7 to 8-5"AA, 85 planes (both conversions, 1959); 4-5"AA 29 planes 18 helicopters (same, as CVS in 1960s); 6-5"AA 40 helicopters (LPH 5 and 8)

Armor: 4" belt, 2 1/2" hangar deck, 1 1/2" deck, 1 1/2" conning tower
Machinery: 150,000 SHP; Westinghouse geared turbines, 4 screws
Speed: 33 kts.
Complement: 3448

No.		Hull	Laid down	Launched	Commiss'd	Disposition
14	TICONDEROGA	Newport News	1 Feb 43	7 Feb 44	8 May 44	Stk. 16 Nov 73, sold 16 Sep 74
15	RANDOLPH	Newport News	10 May 43	28 Jun 44	9 Oct 44	Stk. 1 Jun 73, sold 14 May 75
19	HANCOCK	Quincy	26 Jan 43	24 Jan 44	15 Apr 44	Stk. 31 Jan 76, sold 23 Aug 76
21	BOXER	Newport News	13 Sep 43	14 Dec 44	16 Apr 45	Stk. 1 Dec 69, sold Feb 71
32	LEYTE	Newport News	21 Feb 44	23 Aug 45	11 Apr 46	Stk. 1 Jun 69, sold Sep 70
33	KEARSARGE	New York	1 Mar 44	5 May 45	2 Mar 46	Stk. 1 May 73, sold 6 Feb 74
35	REPRISAL	New York	1 Jul 44	1945	No	Cancelled 12 Aug 45, test hulk, sold 2 Aug 49
36	ANTIETAM	Philadelphia	15 Mar 43	20 Aug 44	28 Jan 45	Stk. 1 May 73, sold 18 Jan 74
37	PRINCETON	Philadelphia	14 Sep 43	8 Jul 45	18 Nov 45	Stk. 30 Jan 70, sold 20 May 71
38	SHANGRI LA	Norfolk	15 Jan 43	24 Feb 44	15 Sep 44	Stk. 15 Jul 82, sold Aug 88
39	LAKE CHAMPLAIN	Norfolk	15 Mar 43	2 Nov 44	3 Jun 45	Stk. 1 Dec 69, sold 5 Jul 72
40	TARAWA	Norfolk	1 Mar 44	12 May 45	8 Dec 45	Stk. 1 Jun 67, sold 3 Oct 68
45	VALLEY FORGE	Philadelphia	7 Sep 44	18 Nov 45	3 Nov 46	Stk. 15 Jan 70, sold 29 Oct 71
46	IWO JIMA	Newport News	29 Jan 45	No	No	Cancelled 12 Aug 45
47	PHILIPPINE SEA	Quincy	19 Aug 44	5 Sep 45	11 May 46	Stk. 1 Dec 69, sold 23 Mar 71
50	Unnamed	Quincy	No	No	No	Cancelled 27 Mar 45
51	Unnamed	New York	No	No	No	Cancelled 27 Mar 45
52	Unnamed	New York	No	No	No	Cancelled 27 Mar 45
53	Unnamed	Philadelphia	No	No	No	Cancelled 27 Mar 45
54	Unnamed	Norfolk	No	No	No	Cancelled 27 Mar 45
55	Unnamed	Norfolk	No	No	No	Cancelled 27 Mar 45.

Notes: This group, referred to as the "long hulled" Essex class carriers, was identical with the earlier Essex group except that they were completed with a longer bow extending beyond the flight deck and containing two quadruple 40mm mounts and a stern sponson for another quadruple 40mm mount. These alterations, which doubled the 40mm batteries at the ends of the ships, were approved in March 1943 for ships still in the early stages of construction. The order for CV-32 was transferred from the New York Navy Yard on 23 Mar 43.

The hull of the Reprisal was used in underwater explosive tests in Chesapeake Bay in 1948. The Antietam received the prototype American angled deck but was not otherwise modified. During 1950-55 the Randolph, Kearsarge, and Lake Champlain received SCB-27A (hydraulic catapult) alterations and the Ticonderoga, Hancock, and Shangri La were given SCB-27C (steam catapult) modernizations. All of the SCB-27 ships except the Lake Champlain soon also received the SCB-125 modernization with enclosed bows and angled decks. Their new specifications were 30,800 tons; 899'(oa.) x 129'(hull), 147'(f.d.) x 30'6"(max). The Randolph and Shangri La were also fitted to carry Regulus missiles in 1956. The start and completion dates for major modifications to individual ships were as follows:
Ticonderoga: SCB-27C, 15 Apr 52-1 Oct 54, New York; SCB-125, 17 Aug 56-1 Apr 57, Norfolk;
Randolph: SCB-27A, 4 Jun 51-1 Jul 53, Newport News; SCB-125, 11 Jul 55-12 Feb 56, Norfolk;
Hancock: SCB-27C, 15 Dec 51-1 Mar 54, Puget Sd.; SCB-125, 15 Apr 56-15 Nov 56, San Francisco;
Kearsarge: SCB-27A, 24 Feb 50-1 Mar 52, Puget Sd.; SCB-125, 6 Jul 56-31 Jan 57, Puget Sd.;
Shangri La: SCB-27C and SCB-125 together, 15 Oct 52-1 Feb 55, Puget Sd;
Lake Champlain: SCB-27A, 22 Aug 50-19 Sep 52, Norfolk.
Renamings: CV-14 ex Hancock and CV-19 ex Ticonderoga 1 May 43; CV-37 ex Valley Forge 20 Nov 44; CV-47 ex Wright 12 Feb 45; and CV-32 ex Crown Point 8 May 45.
Reclassifications:
Ticonderoga (CV-14) to CVA-14 1 Oct 52; CVS-14 21 Oct 69;
Randolph (CV-15) to CVA-15 1 Oct 52; CVS-15 31 Mar 59;
Hancock (CV-19) to CVA-19 1 Oct 52; CV-19 30 Jun 75;
Boxer (CV-21) to CVA-21 1 Oct 52; CVS-21 1 Feb 56; LPH-4 30 Jan 59;
Leyte (CV-32) to CVA-32 1 Oct 52; CVS-32 8 Aug 53; AVT-10 15 May 59;
Kearsarge (CV-33) to CVA-33 1 Oct 52; CVS-33 1 Oct 58;
Antietam (CV-36) to CVA-36 1 Oct 52; CVS-36 8 Aug 53;
Princeton (CV-37) to CVA-37 1 Oct 52; CVS-37 1 Jan 54; LPH-5 2 Mar 59;
Shangri La (CV-38) to CVA-38 1 Oct 52; CVS-38 30 Jun 69;
Lake Champlain (CV-39) to CVA-39 1 Oct 52; CVS-39 1 Aug 57;
Tarawa (CV-40) to CVA-40 1 Oct 52; CVS-40 10 Jan 55; AVT-12 1 May 61;
Valley Forge (CV-45) to CVA-45 1 Oct 52; CVS-45 1 Jan 54; LPH-8 1 Jul 61;
Philippine Sea (CV-47) to CVA-47 1 Oct 52; CVS-47 15 Nov 55; AVT-11 15 May 59.

ORISKANY

Displacement: 30,800 tons light
Dimensions: 904'(oa.) x 129'(hull), 147'6"(f.d.) x 30'6"(max)
Armament: 8-5"/38AA 28-3"/50AA 100 planes; 8-5"AA 16-3"AA 100 planes (1954); 7-5"AA 85 planes (1959); 4-5"AA 85 planes (1967); 2-5" (1977)
Armor: 4" belt, 2 1/2" + 1 1/2" decks

Machinery: 150,000 SHP; Westinghouse geared turbines, 4 screws
Speed: 33 kts.
Complement: 3460

No.		Hull	Laid down	Launched	Commiss'd	Disposition
34	ORISKANY	Philadelphia	1 May 44	13 Oct 45	25 Sep 50	Stk. 25 Jul 89.

Notes: The last Ticonderoga class carrier, she was completed to a modified design as the prototype SCB-27A. She sported two center line and one deck edge elevators and a pair of hydraulic catapults. Between 2 Jan 57 and 29 May 59 she was given an enclosed bow, angled deck, and steam catapults (SCB-125A design) at San Francisco Naval Shipyard.
Reclassification: To CVA-34 1 Oct 52 and to CV-34 30 Jun 75.

1942

INDEPENDENCE class

Displacement: 11,000 tons standard
Dimensions: 622'6"(oa.) x 71'6"(hull), 109'2"(f.d.) x 26'(max)
Armament: 2-5"/38 45 planes (CV-22, 1943); 45 planes (all, 1943)
Armor: 5" belt (none in CV 22-23), 2" deck

Machinery: 100,000 SHP; G. E. geared turbines, 4 screws
Speed: 31.5 kts.
Complement: 1569

No.		Hull	Laid down	Launched	Commiss'd	Disposition
22	INDEPENDENCE	New York SB	1 May 41	22 Aug 42	14 Jan 43	Sunk as target 26 Jan 51 off California, stk. 27 Feb 51
23	PRINCETON	New York SB	2 Jun 41	18 Oct 42	25 Feb 43	Sunk by Japanese aircraft E of Luzon 25 Oct 44
24	BELLEAU WOOD	New York SB	11 Aug 41	6 Dec 42	31 Mar 43	To France 5 Sep 53 as Bois Belleau, stk. 1 Oct 60
25	COWPENS	New York SB	17 Nov 41	17 Jan 43	28 May 43	Stk. 1 Nov 59, sold 9 May 60
26	MONTEREY	New York SB	29 Dec 41	28 Feb 43	17 Jun 43	Stk. 1 Jun 70, sold 20 May 71
27	LANGLEY	New York SB	11 Apr 42	22 May 43	31 Aug 43	To France 8 Jan 51 as Lafayette, stk. 22 Jan 51
28	CABOT	New York SB	16 Mar 42	4 Apr 43	24 Jul 43	To Spain 28 May 67 as Dedalo, stk. 1 Aug 72
29	BATAAN	New York SB	31 Aug 42	1 Aug 43	17 Nov 43	Stk. 1 Sep 59, sold 1 May 61
30	SAN JACINTO	New York SB	26 Oct 42	26 Sep 43	15 Dec 43	Stk. 1 Jun 70, sold 15 Dec 71.

Notes: Fiscal year 1941. President Roosevelt noted in August 1941 that no carriers were scheduled to be delivered between the Hornet in 1941 and the Essex in 1944. He pressured the Navy to convert some Cleveland class light cruisers as an emergency measure. The first proposals for the conversions were rejected because they were too elaborate and would take too long to complete, and ultimately the same level of austerity was adopted for these as for the escort carrier conversions. Unlike the CVEs, however, the cruiser conversions were designed for fleet use, with a bit less than half the air group of regular fleet carriers. The first conversion was ordered in January 1942 and a CVE island was added to the plans in February. The ships were fitted with a pair of center line elevators and two catapults. The Independence was used in the 1946 Bikini atomic bomb tests and was later sunk as a target. The Belleau Wood was returned by France 12 Sep 60 and sold 14 Dec 60; the Langley was returned on 20 Mar 63 and sold in March 1964.
Renamings: CV-27 ex Crown Point 13 Nov 42; CV-30 ex Reprisal 6 Jan 43.
Reclassifications: The entire class was reclassified CVL from CV on 15 Jul 43. CVL 25, 26, 28, 29, and 30 became AVT 1-5 respectively on 15 May 59. The former cruiser names, numbers, and dates of reclassification to CV were:

Independence ex-Amsterdam (CL-59) 10 Jan 42;
Princeton ex-Tallahassee (CL-61) 16 Feb 42;
Belleau Wood ex-New Haven (CL-76) 16 Feb 42;
Cowpens ex-Huntington (CL-77) 27 Mar 42;
Monterey ex-Dayton (CL-78) 27 Mar 42;

Crown Point ex-Fargo (CL-85) 27 Mar 42;
Cabot ex-Wilmington (CL-79) 2 Jun 42;
Bataan ex-Buffalo (CL-99) 2 Jun 42;
Reprisal ex-Newark (CL-100) 2 Jun 42.

Small Aircraft Carriers (CVL)

1943

SAIPAN class

Displacement: 14,500 tons standard
Dimensions: 683'7"(oa.) x 76'8"(hull), 108'(f.d.) x 28'(max)
Armament: 42 planes; 6 helicopters (as CC); 8-3"/50AA (as AGMR)
Armor: 4" belt, 2 1/2" deck

Machinery: 120,000 SHP; G. E. geared turbines, 4 screws
Speed: 33 kts.
Complement: 1721 (Saipan), 1787 (Wright)

No.		Hull	Laid down	Launched	Commiss'd	Disposition
48	SAIPAN	New York SB	10 Jul 44	8 Jul 45	14 Jul 46	Stk. 15 Aug 75, sold 3 Jun 76
49	WRIGHT	New York SB	21 Aug 44	1 Sep 45	9 Feb 47	Stk. 1 Dec 77, sold Jul 80.

Notes: Fiscal year 1944. These two ships were ordered to offset expected attrition of Independence class CVLs. By 1944, the mission of CVLs was to provide fighter cover while larger Essex class ships launched strike aircraft--one CVL was to accompany every two CVs. To augment the capabilities of the new ships, their design was based on the Baltimore instead of the Cleveland class hull. Unlike their predecessors, the new ships were designed and built from the keel up as CVLs. They had a pair of center line elevators and two catapults. The Wright was converted to a command ship (CC) at Puget Sound Naval Shipyard. A similar conversion for the Saipan was cancelled and she was converted into a communications relay ship (AGMR) instead.

Renaming: Saipan to Arlington 8 Apr 65 as AGMR-2.

Reclassifications: To AVT-6 and 7 respectively 15 May 59. Wright to CC-2 1 Sep 62. Saipan to CC-3 1 Jan 64 and to AGMR-2 1 Sep 64.

Large Aircraft Carriers (CVB)

1942

MIDWAY class

Displacement: 45,000 tons standard
Dimensions: 968'(oa.) x 113'(hull), 136'(f.d.) x 35'(max)
Armament: Midway--18-5"/54AA 137 planes; 14-5"AA 40-3"/50AA 137 planes (1950); 10-5"AA 22-3"AA 137 planes (1957); 10-5"AA 137 planes (1960); 4-5"AA 75 planes (1963); 3-5"AA 75 planes (1970)
Franklin D. Roosevelt--18-5"/54AA 137 planes; 14-5"AA 36-3"/50AA 137 planes (1951); 10-5"AA 22-3"AA 137 planes (1956); 10-5"AA 137 planes (1959); 4-5"AA 75 planes (1963); 2-5"AA 75 planes (1977)
Coral Sea--14-5"/54AA 137 planes; 14-5"AA 36-3"/50AA 137 planes (1949); 6-5"AA 137 planes (1960); 3-5"AA 75 planes (1962)

Armor: 7.6" belt, 3 1/2" flight deck, 2" hangar deck, 2" deck, 6 1/2" conning tower (2" in CV-43)
Machinery: 212,000 SHP; geared turbines, 4 screws
Speed: 33 kts.
Complement: 4104

No.		Hull	Machinery	Laid down	Launched	Commiss'd	Disposition
41	MIDWAY	Newport News	Westinghouse	27 Oct 43	20 Mar 45	10 Sep 45	USN
42	FRANKLIN D. ROOSEVELT	New York	G. E.	1 Dec 43	29 Apr 45	27 Oct 45	Stk. 1 Oct 77, sold 11 Apr 78
43	CORAL SEA	Newport News	Westinghouse	10 Jul 44	2 Apr 46	1 Oct 47	Stk. 30 Apr 90
44	Unnamed	Newport News	Unknown	No	No	No	Cancelled 11 Jan 43
56	Unnamed	Newport News	Unknown	No	No	No	Cancelled 27 Mar 45
57	Unnamed	Newport News	Unknown	No	No	No	Cancelled 27 Mar 45.

Notes: Fiscal years 1943 (41-44) and 1945 (56-57). In August 1940 the Navy began to study the possibility of developing a new large carrier with an armored flight deck and a heavy gun battery. The first of these requirements resulted from British experience against dive bombers earlier in 1940; the second resulted from fears that cruisers might not always be available to escort carriers in the Pacific. In March 1942 the Navy decided on a 45,000-ton design with deck armor and a large 5"/54AA battery, and in May it included four of the ships in a program of 690 combatants to be laid down in calendar years 1943 and 1944. CV 41-44 were all ordered from Newport News on 7 Aug 42. President Roosevelt approved the rest of the program but withheld his approval for the four large carriers. He felt that these large ships could not be completed soon enough and suspected that the Navy was "gold plating" its building program. He clearly preferred a larger number of 11,000-ton carriers. The Navy finally persuaded him to approve two ships on 29 Dec 1942, and it cancelled its orders for the other two, CV 43-44, on 11 Jan 43. To spread the work around, it also cancelled CV-42 at Newport News on 11 Jan 43 and reordered her at the New York Navy Yard on 21 Jan 43. Roosevelt approved a third ship on 26 May 1943 as a part of a program to use remaining authorized combatant tonnage, and CV-43 was reinstated at Newport News on 14 Jun 43 under her original contract. In March 1945 an 84-ship combatant program for fiscal year 1945 which included CVB 56-57 was disapproved. This type introduced

The large aircraft carrier *Midway* (CVB-41) near Norfolk on 4 April 1947. (NH 49826)

The nuclear powered aircraft carrier *Dwight D. Eisenhower* (CVN-69) during sea trials on 23 August 1977. (USN 1170824)

the armored flight deck into the American Navy, had water-tight integrity and damage control equal to a battleship, and had protection against 8" gunfire. The ships originally had two center line and one deck edge elevators along with a pair of catapults. Their machinery duplicated that of the Iowa class battleships. Because of their armored flight deck, their freeboard was relatively low (no greater than the Essex class) and they were wet in service.

The three completed ships were rebuilt at Puget Sound Naval Shipyard to the SCB-110 design between 1954 and 1960 with angled decks, three steam catapults, and other equipment to handle heavier planes. Their new dimensions were 974'(oa.) x 209'(f.d.). The Coral Sea was rebuilt to modified plans with three deck edge elevators (SCB-110A), and this configuration was extended to the others during additional modernizations in 1966-70. All remaining 5" guns had been removed by 1980. The start and completion dates for major modifications to individual ships were as follows:

   Midway: SCB-110, 1 Sep 55-25 Nov 57, Puget Sd.; SCB-101.66, 15 Feb 66-15 Jun 70, San Francisco;
   Franklin D. Roosevelt: SCB-110, 1 May 54-1 Jun 56, Puget Sd.;
   Coral Sea: SCB-110A, 16 Apr 57-15 Mar 60, Puget Sd.
Renaming: CVB-42 ex Coral Sea 8 May 45.
Reclassifications: CV 41-43 to CVB 41-43 15 Jul 43; CVA 41-43 1 Oct 52; and CV 41-43 again 30 Jun 75.

Attack Aircraft Carriers (CVA)

1948

UNITED STATES

Displacement: 65,000 tons standard
Dimensions: 1090'(oa.) x 190'(f.d.) x unknown
Armament: 8-5"/54 16-3"/70 98 planes
Armor: 1 1/2" belt, 2" flight deck, 1 1/2" hangar deck, 1 1/2" deck

Machinery: 280,000 SHP; geared turbines, 4 screws
Speed: 33 kts. (designed)
Complement: 4127

No.	Hull	Laid down	Launched	Commiss'd	Disposition
58 UNITED STATES	Newport News	18 Apr 49	No	No	Cancelled 23 Apr 49.

Notes: Fiscal year 1949. SCB-6A design. This ship was designed to launch strategic bombing strikes by relatively small numbers of large bombers. The design reverted to an entirely flush-decked configuration to permit the operation of oversized aircraft--plans called for a 100,000 pound bomber with a 2000 mile combat radius. The ship was to have an armored axial flight deck with large sponsons on each side, four elevators, and four catapults. She was cancelled by Secretary of Defense Johnson in favor of the Air Force's B-36 bomber program.

1951

FORRESTAL class

Displacement: 56,000 (CVA 59-60), 56,300 (CVA 61-62) tons light
Dimensions: 1039'(CVA 59-61, oa.), 1046'6"(CVA-62, oa.) x 129'1" (hull), 252'(f.d.) x 37'(max)
Armament: 8-5"/54AA 100 planes; 4-5"AA 100 planes (1961-66); 85 planes (CV-59, 1967; CV 60-62, 1973-77)
Armor: Unknown

Machinery: 260,000 (CVA-59), 280,000 (others) SHP; geared turbines, 4 screws
Speed: 33 (CVA-59), 34 (others) kts.
Complement: 3800-4280

No.	Hull	Machinery	Laid down	Launched	Commiss'd	Disposition
59 FORRESTAL	Newport News	Westinghouse	14 Jul 52	11 Dec 54	1 Oct 55	USN
60 SARATOGA	New York	G. E.	16 Dec 52	8 Oct 55	14 Apr 56	USN
61 RANGER	Newport News	G. E.	2 Aug 54	29 Sep 56	10 Aug 57	USN
62 INDEPENDENCE	New York	G. E.	1 Jul 55	6 Jun 58	10 Jan 59	USN.

Notes: Fiscal years 1952, 1953, 1954 and 1955 respectively. The original design for these ships was a scaled-down version of the United States with a flush deck and a retracting island. The smaller design was made possible by the reduction in size of the proposed heavy bomber from 100,000 to 70,000 pounds (it materialized as the Douglas A3D Skywarrior). The new ship also had a modified mission: launching tactical air strikes by large groups of smaller aircraft (including the nuclear-capable Douglas A4D Skyhawk). The ships were redesigned after a directive of 4 May 53 specified that the entire class was to be fitted with an angled deck; an island was also adopted at this time. Although the four ships have individual differences, all were built to the SCB-80 design. They have four deck

edge elevators and four steam catapults. To expedite construction, the Forrestal was built with a 600-psi, 850-degree steam plant; the others received the new 1200-psi, 950-degree plant. The gun armaments of these ships were eventually replaced by Sea Sparrow point defense missiles. Three ships were refurbished under the Service Life Extension Program (SLEP): Saratoga in 1980-83, Forrestal in 1983-85, and Independence in 1985-88.
Reclassifications: CVA-59 ex CVB-59 1 Oct 52. All were redesignated CV (multi-role carrier) in the early 1970s, CV-60 on 30 Jun 72, CV-62 on 28 Feb 73, and the others on 30 Jun 75.

1955

KITTY HAWK class

Displacement: 60,100 (CVA 63-64), 60,300 (CVA-66), 61,000 (CVA-67) tons light
Dimensions: 1047'(CVA-63, oa.), 1051'3" (CVA-67), 1047'6" (others, oa.) x 129'4" (hull), 251'8"(f.d.) x 37'(max)
Armament: 4-Terrier-SAM, 100 planes (except CVA-67); 85 planes (CVA-67 as built, others in 1978-83)

Armor: Unknown
Machinery: 280,000 SHP: G. E. geared turbines, 4 screws
Speed: 34 kts.
Complement: 4154-4580

No.		Hull	Laid down	Launched	Commiss'd	Disposition
63	KITTY HAWK	New York SB	27 Dec 56	21 May 60	29 Apr 61	USN
64	CONSTELLATION	New York	14 Sep 57	8 Oct 60	27 Oct 61	USN
66	AMERICA	Newport News	9 Jan 61	1 Feb 64	23 Jan 65	USN
67	JOHN F. KENNEDY	Newport News	22 Oct 64	27 May 67	7 Sep 68	USN.

Notes: Fiscal years 1956, 1957, 1961, and 1963 respectively. Based on the Forrestal class, the design of this class (SCB-127) has a flight deck layout modified to increase the flexibility and speed of air operations. The individual vessels differ considerably but all have four deck edge elevators and four steam catapults. Terrier SAMs were substituted for guns during construction--the Constellation had the first fully integrated Terrier installation. The Terrier systems were later replaced by Sea Sparrow point defense missiles. The design of the America (SCB-127B) added an SQS-23 sonar. In the John F. Kennedy (SCB-127C), the main machinery was rearranged and the side protection system modified. Her original design included two Tartar SAM launchers, which were not fitted. The Kitty Hawk began a SLEP refurbishment in 1988 and the Constellation began one in 1990.
Reclassifications: All were redesignated CV in the early 1970s, CV-63 on 29 Apr 73, CV-67 on 1 Dec 74, and the others on 30 Jun 75.

Nuclear Powered Attack Aircraft Carriers (CVAN)

1957

ENTERPRISE

Displacement: 75,700 tons light
Dimensions: 1101'2"(oa.) x 133'(hull), 255'(f.d.) x 37'1"(max)
Armament: 100 planes
Armor: Unknown

Machinery: 280,000 SHP; 8 Westinghouse (A2W) reactors driving geared turbines, 4 screws
Speed: 30+ kts.
Complement: 5382

No.		Hull	Laid down	Launched	Commiss'd	Disposition
65	ENTERPRISE	Newport News	4 Feb 58	24 Sep 60	25 Nov 61	USN.

Notes: Fiscal year 1958. Early efforts to design a nuclear carrier failed for lack of a suitable reactor, but in 1954 successful efforts were begun to develop both the reactor and the design (SCB-160) used for this ship. The flight deck layout and missile armament fitted in the Kitty Hawk class were also features of the SCB-160 design, although the planned 4-Terrier SAM were never mounted. Sea Sparrow point defense missiles were installed in their place in 1967. The ship has four steam catapults and four deck edge elevators. Instead of a funnel, the island featured fixed (phased-array) radars and futuristic ECM equipment. These were removed during a long refit between 1979 and 1982. She began another refit and a refueling under fiscal year 1990.
Reclassification: To CVN-65 30 Jun 75.

1966

NIMITZ class

Displacement: 72,805 tons light, 91,300 tons full load
Dimensions: 1088'(oa.) x 134'(hull), 257'6"(f.d.) x 37'8"
  (max)
Armament: 90 planes (designed)
Armor: Unknown

Machinery: 260,000 SHP; 2 Westinghouse (A4W) reactors driving geared
  turbines, 4 screws
Speed: 30+ kts.
Complement: 5617

No.		Hull		Laid down	Launched	Commiss'd	Disposition
68	NIMITZ	Newport News		22 Jun 68	13 May 72	3 May 75	USN
69	DWIGHT D. EISENHOWER	Newport News		15 Aug 70	11 Oct 75	18 Oct 77	USN
70	CARL VINSON	Newport News		11 Oct 75	15 Mar 80	13 Mar 82	USN
71	THEODORE ROOSEVELT	Newport News		31 Oct 81	27 Oct 84	25 Oct 86	USN
72	ABRAHAM LINCOLN	Newport News		3 Nov 84	13 Feb 88	11 Nov 89	USN
73	GEORGE WASHINGTON	Newport News		25 Aug 86	21 Jul 90		USN
74	JOHN C. STENNIS	Newport News					USN
75	UNITED STATES	Newport News					USN.

Notes: Fiscal years 1967 (CVAN-68), 1970 (69), 1974 (CVN-70), 1980 (71), 1983 (72-73), 1988 (74-75).
The main improvement in this class over the Enterprise was the introduction of a reactor so powerful
that only two, instead of eight, were required. The flight deck layout was also adjusted to even out
the airflow aft of the ship. The ships carry four catapults and four elevators. Their shipboard
armament is limited to point defenses (Sea Sparrow missiles and CIWS gatling guns).
Reclassifications: CVAN 68-69 to CVN on 30 Jun 75.

Aircraft Escort Vessels (AVG)

1940

LONG ISLAND class

Displacement: 7886 (Long Island), 8000 (others) tons
Dimensions: 492'(oa.) x 69'6"(hull), 102'(Long Island, f.d.),
  111'2"(others, f.d.) x 25'6"(Long Island, max),
  26'3"(others, max)
Armament: 1-5"/38AA 2-3"/50AA 21 planes

Machinery: 8500 BHP; diesel engine, 1
  screw
Speed: 16 kts.
Complement: 970

No.		MC-#	Hull	Launched	Acquired	Commiss'd	Disposition
1	LONG ISLAND	47	Sun	11 Jan 40	6 Mar 41	2 Jun 41	Stk. 12 Apr 46, sold 24 Apr 47 by War Shipping Admin.
*1	(ARCHER)	46	Sun	14 Dec 39	6 May 41	No	To Britain 17 Nov 41 as Archer, stk. 26 Feb 46
*2	(AVENGER)	59	Sun	27 Nov 40	2 Aug 41	No	To Britain 2 Mar 42 as Avenger, lost 15 Nov 42
*3	(BITER)	60	Sun	18 Dec 40	15 Sep 41	No	To Britain 1 May 42 as Biter, to France 9 Apr 45 as Dixmude, stk. 24 Jan 51
*4	CHARGER	61	Sun	1 Mar 41	4 Oct 41	3 Mar 42	Stk. 28 Mar 46, sold 15 Apr 47
*5	(DASHER)	62	Sun	12 Apr 41	22 Nov 41	No	To Britain 5 Jul 42 as Dasher, lost 27 Mar 43.

* BAVG number.
Notes: Fiscal year 1941 (AVG-1). The others were funded under the Lend Lease program. In October
1940 President Roosevelt proposed a merchant ship conversion to protect convoys against submarines.
In January 1941 the type also acquired the mission of supporting expeditionary forces. The President
rejected all conversion plans which would take more than three months to complete, forcing the Navy to
adopt the most austere configuration possible. The first six ships were converted from early diesel-
engined Maritime Commission C3 merchant ships built by Sun Shipbuilding. The first two were designed
as C3 Cargo ships and served as merchant ships for about a year before acquisition by the navy; the
other four were designed as C3 Passenger and Cargo ships and were acquired while fitting out. They

were converted by Newport News (AVG-1, BAVG-1, 4); Bethlehem, Staten Island (BAVG-2); Atlantic Basin
Iron Works, Brooklyn (BAVG-3); and Tietjen and Lang Drydock Co., Brooklyn (BAVG-5). They had one
elevator, one catapult, and a partial hangar limited to the after portion of the ship. The Charger
was intended for the Royal Navy but was taken over for American use on 2 Mar 42 as a training ship,
although retaining her British name. The Archer was returned 9 Jan 46 and sold 30 Sep 47; the Biter
was re-transferred to France 9 Apr 45; and the Avenger and Dasher were war losses.
Previous mercantile names: Ex Mormacmail, Mormacland, Rio Hudson, Rio Parana, Rio de la Plata, and Rio
de Janeiro respectively.
Reclassifications: BAVG-4 to AVG-30 24 Jan 42. She and AVG-1 were redesignated auxiliary aircraft
carriers (ACV) 20 Aug 42 and escort aircraft carriers (CVE) 15 Jun 43. The others became British
auxiliary aircraft carriers (BACV) around 20 Aug 42 and reverted to BAVG around 15 Jun 43.

AVG 2-5

In January 1941 the Navy began to consider the possibility of converting large ocean liners to
aircraft transports for the delivery of aircraft to overseas theaters. Such a ship would be able to
carry about fifty aircraft for delivery by flying off or up to a hundred if its deck was completely
filled. Designations were proposed for four ships during further planning in 1941: AVG 2-4 would have
been converted from the transports Wakefield (AP-21), Mount Vernon (AP-22), and West Point (AP-23)
while AVG-5 was to have been the ex-Swedish Kungsholm. These ships were also in great demand as
troopships, however, and the AVG 2-5 conversions were cancelled by the CNO on 31 Dec 41.

Auxiliary Aircraft Carriers (ACV)

1941

SANGAMON class

Displacement: 11,400 tons standard
Dimensions: 553'(oa.) x 75'(hull), 105'2"(f.d.) x 32'(max)
Armament: 2-5"/38AA 34 planes

Machinery: 13,500 SHP; geared
    turbines, 2 screws
Speed: 18 kts.
Complement: 830

No.		Hull	Machinery	Built	Decommiss'd	Recommiss'd	Disposition
26	SANGAMON	Kearny	G. E.	1939	25 Feb 42	25 Aug 42	Stk. 1 Nov 45, sold 11 Feb 48
27	SUWANNEE	Kearny	G. E.	1940	21 Feb 42	24 Sep 42	Stk. 1 Mar 59, sold May 61
28	CHENANGO	Sun	Westing-house	1939	16 Mar 42	19 Sep 42	Stk. 1 Mar 59, sold May 61
29	SANTEE	Sun	Westing-house	1940	20 Mar 42	24 Aug 42	Stk. 1 Mar 59, sold 5 Dec 59.

Notes: Fiscal year 1941. Austere escort carrier conversions were also performed on four Navy oilers,
even though these were also in high demand as tankers. The results were generally regarded as far
more successful than the freighter conversions. The ex-tankers, although a bit slower, had much
larger flight decks, had flush hangar decks (without the camber and sheer of the freighter decks), and
retained many of their tanker capabilities, including the ability to refuel escorts. Converted from
the oilers of the same names, they were fitted with two elevators and a catapult. Newport News
converted the Sangamon and Suwannee; Bethlehem, Staten Island, the Chenango; and Norfolk Navy Yard the
Santee. The Chemung (AO-30) was selected on 1 Feb 42 for conversion to AVG-29; the Santee was
substituted on 11 Feb 42. The Suwannee's name was commonly misspelled Suwanee.
Previous mercantile names: Esso Trenton, Markay, Esso New Orleans, and Seakay respectively.
Reclassifications: Ex AO 28, 33, 31, and 29 on 14 Feb 42; to ACV from AVG 20 Aug 42 and to CVE 15 Jul
43. CVE 27-29 to CVHE 27-29 12 Jun 55.

BOGUE class

Displacement: 7800 (AVG 6-25, BAVG-6), 8333 (others) tons
Dimensions: 495'8"(oa.) x 69'6"(hull), 111'6"(f.d.) x
    26'(max)
Armament: 2-5"/38AA 28 planes; none (AKV conversions)

Machinery: 8500 SHP; Allis-Chalmers
    geared turbines, 1 screw
Speed: 17.5 kts.
Complement: 890

The escort aircraft carrier *Altamaha* (CVE-18) off San Francisco on 16 July 1943 with a deck load of P-51 fighters. (NARA 80-G-74453)

The escort aircraft carrier *Badoeng Strait* (CVE-116). (NH 67541)

No.		MC-#	Hull	Laid down	Launched	Commiss'd	Disposition
*6	TRACKER	233	Sea-Tac, Tacoma	3 Nov 41	7 Mar 42	No	To Britain 31 Jan 43 as Tracker, stk. 21 Jan 46
6	ALTAMAHA	160	Ingalls	15 Apr 41	4 Apr 42	No	To Britain 31 Oct 42 as Battler, stk. 28 Mar 46
7	BARNES	171	Western Pipe	7 Apr 41	27 Sep 41	30 Sep 42	To Britain 30 Sep 42 as Attacker, stk. 26 Feb 46
8	BLOCK ISLAND	161	Ingalls	12 May 41	22 May 42	No	To Britain 9 Jan 43 as Trailer, later Hunter, stk. 26 Feb 46
9	BOGUE	170	Sea-Tac, Tacoma	1 Oct 41	15 Jan 42	26 Sep 42	Stk. 1 Mar 59, sold 22 Jun 60
10	BRETON	162	Ingalls	28 Jun 41	19 Jun 42	9 Apr 43	To Britain 9 Apr 43 as Chaser, stk. 3 Jul 46
11	CARD	178	Sea-Tac, Tacoma	27 Oct 41	21 Feb 42	8 Nov 42	Stk. 15 Sep 70, sold 14 May 71
12	COPAHEE	169	Sea-Tac, Tacoma	18 Jun 41	21 Oct 41	15 Jun 42	Stk. 1 Mar 59, sold 1 Feb 61
13	CORE	179	Sea-Tac, Tacoma	2 Jan 42	15 May 42	10 Dec 42	Stk. 15 Sep 70, sold 28 Apr 71
14	CROATAN	197	Western Pipe	5 Sep 41	4 Apr 42	No	To Britain 27 Feb 43 as Fencer, stk. 28 Jan 47
15	HAMLIN	174	Western Pipe	6 Oct 41	5 Mar 42	21 Dec 42	To Britain 21 Dec 42 as Stalker, stk. 20 Mar 46
16	NASSAU	234	Sea-Tac, Tacoma	27 Nov 41	4 Apr 42	20 Aug 42	Stk. 1 Mar 59, sold 28 Feb 61
17	ST. GEORGE	163	Ingalls	31 Jul 41	18 Jul 42	No	To Britain 14 Jun 43 as Pursuer, stk. 28 Mar 46
18	ALTAMAHA	235	Sea-Tac, Tacoma	19 Dec 41	22 May 42	15 Sep 42	Stk. 1 Mar 59, sold 25 Apr 61
19	(STRIKER)	198	Western Pipe	15 Dec 41	7 May 42	No	To Britain 28 Apr 43 as Striker, stk. 28 Mar 46
20	BARNES	236	Sea-Tac, Tacoma	19 Jan 42	22 May 42	20 Feb 43	Stk. 1 Mar 59, sold 1 Oct 59
21	BLOCK ISLAND	237	Sea-Tac, Tacoma	19 Jan 42	6 Jun 42	8 Mar 43	Sunk by U-549 in N. Atlantic 29 May 44
22	(SEARCHER)	238	Sea-Tac, Tacoma	2 Feb 42	20 Jun 42	No	To Britain 7 Apr 43 as Searcher, stk. 7 Feb 46
23	BRETON	239	Sea-Tac, Tacoma	25 Feb 42	27 Jun 42	12 Apr 43	Stk. 6 Aug 71, sold 29 Feb 72
24	(RAVAGER)	240	Sea-Tac, Tacoma	11 Apr 42	16 Jul 42	No	To Britain 25 Apr 43 as Ravager (ex Charger), stk. 12 Apr 46
25	CROATAN	241	Sea-Tac, Tacoma	15 Apr 42	1 Aug 42	28 Apr 43	Stk. 15 Sep 70, sold 5 Feb 71
31	PRINCE WILLIAM	242	Sea-Tac, Tacoma	18 May 42	23 Aug 42	9 Apr 43	Stk. 1 Mar 59, sold 21 Sep 60
32	CHATHAM	243	Sea-Tac, Tacoma	25 May 42	19 Sep 42	No	To Britain 11 Aug 43 as Slinger, stk. 12 Apr 46
33	GLACIER	244	Sea-Tac, Tacoma	9 Jun 42	7 Sep 42	3 Jul 43	To Britain 31 Jul 43 as Atheling, stk. 7 Feb 47
34	PYBUS	245	Sea-Tac, Tacoma	23 Jun 42	7 Oct 42	31 May 43	To Britain 6 Aug 43 as Emperor, stk. 28 Mar 46
35	BAFFINS	246	Sea-Tac, Tacoma	18 Jul 42	18 Oct 42	28 Jun 43	To Britain 19 Jul 43 as Ameer, stk. 20 Mar 46
36	BOLINAS	247	Sea-Tac, Tacoma	3 Aug 42	11 Nov 42	22 Jul 43	To Britain 2 Aug 43 as Begum, stk. 19 Jun 46
37	BASTIAN	248	Sea-Tac, Tacoma	25 Aug 42	15 Dec 42	No	To Britain 4 Aug 43 as Trumpeter (ex Lucifer), stk. 21 May 46
38	CARNEGIE	249	Sea-Tac, Tacoma	9 Sep 42	31 Dec 42	9 Aug 43	To Britain 12 Aug 43 as Empress, stk. 28 Mar 46
39	CORDOVA	250	Sea-Tac, Tacoma	22 Sep 42	30 Jan 43	No	To Britain 25 Aug 43 as Khedive (ex Slinger), stk. 19 Jul 46
40	DELGADA	251	Sea-Tac, Tacoma	9 Oct 42	20 Feb 43	No	To Britain 20 Nov 43 as Speaker, stk. 25 Sep 46
41	EDISTO	252	Sea-Tac, Tacoma	20 Oct 42	9 Mar 43	No	To Britain 7 Sep 43 as Nabob, damaged, returned 16 Mar 45
42	ESTERO	253	Sea-Tac, Tacoma	31 Oct 42	22 Mar 43	No	To Britain 3 Nov 43 as Premier (ex Speaker), stk. 21 May 46
43	JAMAICA	254	Sea-Tac, Tacoma	13 Nov 42	21 Apr 43	No	To Britain 27 Sep 43 as Shah, stk. 7 Feb 46
44	KEWEENAW	255	Sea-Tac, Tacoma	27 Nov 42	6 May 43	No	To Britain 22 Oct 43 as Patroller, stk. 7 Feb 47
45	PRINCE	256	Sea-Tac, Tacoma	17 Dec 42	18 May 43	No	To Britain 17 Jan 44 as Rajah, stk. 7 Feb 47
46	NIANTIC	257	Sea-Tac, Tacoma	5 Jan 43	2 Jun 43	No	To Britain 8 Nov 43 as Ranee, stk. 22 Jan 47

No.		MC-#	Hull		Laid down	Launched	Commiss'd	Disposition
47	PERDIDO	258	Sea-Tac, Tacoma		1 Feb 43	16 Jun 43	28 Jan 44	To Britain 31 Jan 44 as Trouncer, stk. 12 Apr 46
48	SUNSET	259	Sea-Tac, Tacoma		23 Feb 43	15 Jul 43	No	To Britain 19 Nov 43 as Thane, damaged, stk. 16 Nov 45
49	ST. ANDREWS	260	Sea-Tac, Tacoma		12 Mar 43	2 Aug 43	No	To Britain 7 Dec 43 as Queen (ex Trouncer), stk. 22 Jan 47
50	ST. JOSEPH	261	Sea-Tac, Tacoma		25 Mar 43	21 Aug 43	No	To Britain 22 Dec 43 as Ruler (ex Trouncer), stk. 20 Mar 46
51	ST. SIMON	262	Sea-Tac, Tacoma		26 Apr 43	9 Sep 43	No	To Britain 31 Dec 43 as Arbiter, stk. 12 Apr 46
52	VERMILLION	–	Sea-Tac, Tacoma		10 May 43	27 Sep 43	No	To Britain 20 Jan 44 as Smiter, stk. 21 May 46
53	WILLAPA	–	Sea-Tac, Tacoma		21 May 43	8 Nov 43	No	To Britain 5 Feb 44 as Puncher, stk. 12 Mar 46
54	WINJAH	–	Sea-Tac, Tacoma		5 Jun 43	22 Nov 43	No	To Britain 18 Feb 44 as Reaper (ex Smiter), stk. 3 Jul 46.

* BAVG number.

Notes: Fiscal year 1942 except BAVG-6 (Lend Lease). These ships received a slightly more complete conversion than the Long Island group. Their merchant ship superstructure was removed and the hangar deck was extended to cover most of the length of the ship instead of just the after half. They also had heavier aircraft, more fuel, and much improved underwater protection. As in the other escort carriers, an island superstructure was added to the design in February 1942. Converted from Maritime Commission C3-S-A1 type hulls while building, they carried either one (ACV 12, 16, 18, 20, 21, 23, 25) or two (others) catapults and two center line elevators. ACV 6, 12, 16, 18, 31, 33, and BAVG-6 were completed by Puget Sound Navy Yard; ACV 24, 32, 40, and 45 by Willamette Iron & Steel Corp.; and ACV 22, 37, 42, and 47 by Commercial Iron Works. The dates of return and disposal for the Lend-Lease vessels were:

BAVG-6 returned 29 Nov 45; sold 14 May 47
CVE-6 returned 12 Feb 46; sold 12 Jun 46
CVE-7 returned 5 Jan 46; sold 28 Oct 46
CVE-8 returned 29 Dec 45; sold 17 Jan 46
CVE-10 returned 12 May 46; sold 20 Dec 46
CVE-14 returned 11 Dec 46; sold 30 Dec 47
CVE-15 returned 29 Dec 45; sold 18 Dec 46
CVE-17 returned 12 Feb 46; sold 14 May 46
CVE-19 returned 12 Feb 46; sold 5 Jun 46
CVE-22 returned 29 Nov 45; sold 30 Sep 47
CVE-24 returned 27 Feb 46; sold 14 Jan 47
CVE-32 returned 27 Feb 46; sold 7 Nov 46
CVE-33 returned 13 Dec 46; sold 26 Nov 47
CVE-34 returned 12 Feb 46; sold 14 May 46
CVE-35 returned 17 Jan 46; sold 17 Sep 46
CVE-36 returned 4 Jan 46; sold 16 Apr 47
CVE-37 returned 6 Apr 46; sold 2 May 47

CVE-38 returned 4 Feb 46; sold 21 Jun 46
CVE-39 returned 26 Jan 46; sold 23 Jan 47
CVE-40 returned 27 Jul 46; sold 22 Apr 47
CVE-41 returned 16 Mar 45; sold 26 Oct 46
CVE-42 returned 12 Apr 46; sold 14 Feb 47
CVE-43 returned 6 Dec 45; sold 20 Jun 47
CVE-44 returned 13 Dec 46; sold 26 Aug 47
CVE-45 returned 13 Dec 46; sold 7 Jul 47
CVE-46 returned 21 Nov 46; sold 1 Jul 47
CVE-47 returned 3 Mar 46; sold 6 Mar 47
CVE-48 returned 5 Dec 45; sold 26 Oct 46
CVE-49 returned 31 Oct 46; sold 29 Jul 47
CVE-50 returned 29 Jan 46; sold 13 May 46
CVE-51 returned 3 Mar 46; sold 30 Jan 47
CVE-52 returned 6 Apr 46; sold 28 Jan 47
CVE-53 returned 17 Jan 46; sold 4 Feb 47
CVE-54 returned 20 May 46; sold 12 Feb 47.

Previous mercantile names: BAVG-6 ex Mormacmail; ACV-7 ex Steel Artisan; ACV-8 ex Mormacpenn; ACV-12 ex Steel Architect; and ACV-17 ex Mormacland.

Renamings: A proposal in April 1942 to name AVG-19 Block Island was disapproved because the ship had already been designated for transfer to Britain. ACV-45 ex McClure 13 Nov 42 and ACV-36 ex Balinas 16 Feb 43 (to correct a misspelling).

Reclassifications: All except BAVG-6 originally AVG, to ACV 20 Aug 42 and CVE 15 Jul 43. All ten survivors to CVHE 12 Jun 55. CVE 11, 13, 23, and 25 to CVU 11, 13, 23, and 25 on 1 Jul 58 and to AKV-40, 41, 42 and 43 on 7 May 59.

1943

CASABLANCA class

Displacement: 7800 tons standard
Dimensions: 512'3"(oa.) x 65'2"(hull), 108'1"(f.d.) x 22'4"(max)
Armament: 1-5"/38AA 28 planes; 20 helicopters (CVHA conversion)

Complement: 860
Machinery: 9000 IHP; 2 Skinner Uniflow engines built by Nordberg, 2 screws
Speed: 19 kts.

No.		Hull	Laid down	Launched	Commiss'd	Disposition
55	CASABLANCA	Vancouver	3 Nov 42	5 Apr 43	8 Jul 43	Stk. 3 Jul 46, sold 23 Apr 47
56	LISCOME BAY	Vancouver	9 Dec 42	19 Apr 43	7 Aug 43	Sunk by HIJMS I-175 off Tarawa 24 Nov 43
57	CORAL SEA	Vancouver	12 Dec 42	1 May 43	27 Aug 43	Stk. 1 Mar 59, sold 24 Nov 59
58	CORREGIDOR	Vancouver	17 Dec 42	12 May 43	31 Aug 43	Stk. 1 Oct 58, sold 28 Apr 59
59	MISSION BAY	Vancouver	28 Dec 42	26 May 43	13 Sep 43	Stk. 1 Sep 58, sold 30 Apr 59
60	GUADALCANAL	Vancouver	5 Jan 43	5 Jun 43	25 Sep 43	Stk. 27 May 58, sold 30 Apr 59
61	MANILA BAY	Vancouver	15 Jan 43	10 Jul 43	5 Oct 43	Stk. 27 May 58, sold 30 Jul 59
62	NATOMA BAY	Vancouver	17 Jan 43	20 Jul 43	14 Oct 43	Stk. 1 Sep 58, sold 30 Jul 59
63	MIDWAY	Vancouver	23 Jan 43	17 Aug 43	23 Oct 43	Sunk by Japanese aircraft off Samar 25 Oct 44
64	TRIPOLI	Vancouver	1 Feb 43	2 Sep 43	31 Oct 43	Stk. 1 Feb 59, sold 1960
65	WAKE ISLAND	Vancouver	6 Feb 43	15 Sep 43	7 Nov 43	Stk. 17 Apr 46, sold 19 Apr 47
66	WHITE PLAINS	Vancouver	11 Feb 43	27 Sep 43	15 Nov 43	Stk. 27 Jun 58, sold 29 Jul 58
67	SOLOMONS	Vancouver	19 Apr 43	6 Oct 43	21 Nov 43	Stk. 5 Jun 46, sold 22 Dec 46
68	KALININ BAY	Vancouver	26 Apr 43	15 Oct 43	27 Nov 43	Stk. 5 Jun 46, sold 8 Dec 46
69	KASAAN BAY	Vancouver	11 May 43	24 Oct 43	4 Dec 43	Stk. 1 Mar 59, sold 24 Nov 59
70	FANSHAW BAY	Vancouver	18 May 43	1 Nov 43	9 Dec 43	Stk. 1 Mar 59, sold 29 Aug 59
71	KITKUN BAY	Vancouver	31 May 43	8 Nov 43	15 Dec 43	Stk. 8 May 46, sold 18 Nov 46
72	TULAGI	Vancouver	7 Jun 43	15 Nov 43	21 Dec 43	Stk. 8 May 46, sold 30 Dec 46
73	GAMBIER BAY	Vancouver	10 Jul 43	22 Nov 43	28 Dec 43	Sunk by Japanese squadron off Samar 25 Oct 44
74	NEHENTA BAY	Vancouver	20 Jul 43	28 Nov 43	3 Jan 44	Stk. 1 Aug 59, sold 29 Jan 60
75	HOGGATT BAY	Vancouver	17 Aug 43	4 Dec 43	11 Jan 44	Stk. 1 Aug 59, sold 8 Apr 60
76	KADASHAN BAY	Vancouver	2 Sep 43	11 Dec 43	18 Jan 44	Stk. 1 Aug 59, sold 3 Feb 60
77	MARCUS ISLAND	Vancouver	15 Sep 43	16 Dec 43	26 Jan 44	Stk. 1 Sep 59, sold 29 Feb 60
78	SAVO ISLAND	Vancouver	27 Sep 43	22 Dec 43	3 Feb 44	Stk. 1 Sep 59, sold 29 Feb 60
79	OMMANEY BAY	Vancouver	6 Oct 43	29 Dec 43	11 Feb 44	Sunk by Japanese aircraft off Mindoro 4 Jan 45
80	PETROF BAY	Vancouver	15 Oct 43	5 Jan 44	18 Feb 44	Stk. 27 Jun 58, sold 30 Jul 59
81	RUDYERD BAY	Vancouver	24 Oct 43	12 Jan 44	25 Feb 44	Stk. 1 Aug 59, sold 4 Feb 60
82	SAGINAW BAY	Vancouver	1 Nov 43	19 Jan 44	2 Mar 44	Stk. 1 Mar 59, sold 27 Nov 59
83	SARGENT BAY	Vancouver	8 Nov 43	31 Jan 44	9 Mar 44	Stk. 27 Jun 58, sold 30 Jul 59
84	SHAMROCK BAY	Vancouver	15 Nov 43	4 Feb 44	15 Mar 44	Stk. 27 Jun 58, sold 23 Nov 59
85	SHIPLEY BAY	Vancouver	22 Nov 43	12 Feb 44	21 Mar 44	Stk. 1 Mar 59, sold 2 Oct 59
86	SITKOH BAY	Vancouver	28 Nov 43	19 Feb 44	28 Mar 44	Stk. 1 Apr 60, sold 30 Aug 60
87	STEAMER BAY	Vancouver	4 Dec 43	26 Feb 44	4 Apr 44	Stk. 1 Mar 59, sold 29 Aug 59
88	CAPE ESPERANCE	Vancouver	11 Dec 43	3 Mar 44	9 Apr 44	Stk. 1 Mar 59, sold 14 May 59
89	TAKANIS BAY	Vancouver	16 Dec 43	10 Mar 44	15 Apr 44	Stk. 1 Aug 59, sold 29 Jun 60
90	THETIS BAY	Vancouver	22 Dec 43	16 Mar 44	21 Apr 44	Stk. 1 Mar 64, sold Dec 66
91	MAKASSAR STRAIT	Vancouver	29 Dec 43	22 Mar 44	27 Apr 44	Stk. 1 Sep 58, sunk as target off S. California
92	WINDHAM BAY	Vancouver	5 Jan 44	29 Mar 44	3 May 44	Stk. 1 Feb 59, sold 1960
93	MAKIN ISLAND	Vancouver	12 Jan 44	5 Apr 44	9 May 44	Stk. 5 Jun 46, sold 5 Jan 47
94	LUNGA POINT	Vancouver	19 Jan 44	11 Apr 44	14 May 44	Stk. 1 Apr 60, sold 3 Aug 60
95	BISMARCK SEA	Vancouver	31 Jan 44	17 Apr 44	20 May 44	Sunk by Japanese aircraft off Iwo Jima 21 Feb 45
96	SALAMAUA	Vancouver	4 Feb 44	22 Apr 44	26 May 44	Stk. 21 May 46, sold 28 Dec 46
97	HOLLANDIA	Vancouver	12 Feb 44	28 Apr 44	1 Jun 44	Stk. 1 Apr 60, sold 9 Aug 60
98	KWAJALEIN	Vancouver	19 Feb 44	4 May 44	7 Jun 44	Stk. 1 Apr 60, sold 16 Aug 60
99	ADMIRALTY ISLANDS	Vancouver	26 Feb 44	10 May 44	13 Jun 44	Stk. 8 May 46, sold 2 Jan 47
100	BOUGAINVILLE	Vancouver	3 Mar 44	16 May 44	18 Jun 44	Stk. 1 Apr 60, sold 9 Sep 60
101	MATANIKAU	Vancouver	10 Mar 44	22 May 44	24 Jun 44	Stk. 1 Apr 60, sold 5 Aug 60
102	ATTU	Vancouver	16 Mar 44	27 May 44	30 Jun 44	Stk. 3 Jul 46, sold 3 Jan 47
103	ROI	Vancouver	22 Mar 44	2 Jun 44	6 Jul 44	Stk. 21 May 46, sold 31 Dec 46
104	MUNDA	Vancouver	29 Mar 44	8 Jun 44	8 Jul 44	Stk. 1 Sep 58, sold 28 Jun 60.

Notes: Fiscal year 1944. In June 1942, President Roosevelt stated that he felt that more escort carriers besides the conversions already ordered were needed to cope with the ASW situation. He was impressed with a design by Gibbs and Cox which Henry J. Kaiser had shown him. Kaiser offered to build up to 100 of the ships; 50 were ordered. To speed production, the whole program was turned over to the Maritime Commission, Navy participation being limited to reviewing the plans. The ships, the first to be built from the keel up as escort carriers, were built to MC design S4-S2-BB3 with MC hull numbers 1092-1141 respectively. They had two elevators and one catapult as well as level hangar decks, staggered engine and boiler rooms and two screws. They reverted to reciprocating steam machinery, in the form of a 5-cylinder Uniflow engine. There was no room in their hulls for underwater protection, and their magazines were considered vulnerable. The Thetis Bay was converted to an assault helicopter aircraft carrier in 1955. The Makassar Strait was used as a target by the Pacific Missile Range at Pt. Mugu, California and still existed as a hulk aground on San Nicholas Is. in April 1961.

Renamings: These 50 ships received a total of 95 names. 16 of these were British names, assigned before the Allies decided on 21 Jun 43 to reallocate all Casablanca class carriers to the U.S. and all of the CVE 32-54 group to the U.K. The British names were Ameer (CVE-55, transferred to CVE-56 on 20 Jan 43), Atheling (58, soon transferred to 59), Begum (62), Emperor (67), Empress (71), Khedive (74), Nabob (79), Premier (83), Shah (86), Queen (90), Rajah (94), Ranee (99), Ruler (103), and Thane (104). The use of "bay" names for the class was approved on 22 Jan 43, and between then and 23 Sep 43 CVE 55-118 all received bay names. Beginning on 3 Apr 43, names of World War II battles were substituted for many ships. The changes for individual ships were as follows:

CVE 55, 58, 60-61, 64-66 ex Alazon Bay (55), Anguilla Bay (58), Astrolabe Bay (60), Bucareli Bay (61), Didrickson Bay (64), Dolomi Bay (65), and Elbour Bay (66) 3 Apr 43;
CVE-57 ex Alikula Bay 3 Apr 43, renamed Anzio 15 Sep 44;
CVE-63 ex Chapin Bay 3 Apr 43, renamed St. Lo 15 Sep 44;
CVE 67, 72, 77, 78, 88, 91, 94, 96, 102, and 104 ex Nassuk Bay (67), Fortazela Bay (72), Kanalku Bay (77), Kaita Bay (78), Tananek Bay (88), Ulitka Bay (91), Alazon Bay (94), Anguilla Bay (96), Elbour Bay (102), and Tonowek Bay (104) 6 Nov 43;
CVE-93 ex Woodcliff Bay 17 Dec 43;
CVE-95 ex Alikula Bay 16 May 44;
CVE-97 ex Astrolabe Bay 30 May 44;
CVE-98, 99, 100, 101, and 103 ex Bucareli Bay (98), Chapin Bay (99), Didrickson Bay (100), Dolomi Bay (101), and Alava Bay (103) 26 Apr 44.

In addition, corrected spellings for the names of 5 ships were proposed on 22 Oct 43 but not used in later documents: Nossuk Bay (67), Fortaleza Bay (72), Alazan Bay (94), Elbow Bay (102), and Moser Bay (114, Commencement Bay class).

Reclassifications: All originally AVG, to ACV 20 Aug 42 and CVE 15 Jun 43. CVE-90 became CVHA-1 on 25 Feb 55 and LPH-6 on 28 May 59. CVE 57, 69, 70, 75, 77, 78, 82, 85, 87, and 101 became escort helicopter aircraft carriers (CVHE) on 12 Jun 55. All the other survivors became utility aircraft carriers (CVU) at the same time. CVE 74, 75, 76, 77, 78, 81, 86, 89, 94, 97, 98, 100, and 101 were reclassified aircraft transports, AKV 24-36 respectively, on 7 May 59.

Escort Aircraft Carriers (CVE)

1943

COMMENCEMENT BAY class

Displacement: 11,373 tons standard
Dimensions: 557'7"(oa.) x 75'(hull), 105'2"(f.d.) x 30'8"(max)
Armament: 2-5"/38AA 34 planes; 1-5"AA 34 planes (1951)

Machinery: 16,000 SHP; Allis-Chalmers geared turbines, 2 screws
Speed: 19 kts.
Complement: 1066

No.		Hull	Laid down	Launched	Commiss'd	Disposition
105	COMMENCEMENT BAY	Todd, Tacoma	23 Sep 43	9 May 44	27 Nov 44	Stk. 1 Apr 71, sold 25 Aug 72
106	BLOCK ISLAND	Todd, Tacoma	25 Oct 43	10 Jun 44	30 Dec 44	Stk. 1 Jul 59, sold 23 Feb 60
107	GILBERT ISLANDS	Todd, Tacoma	29 Nov 43	20 Jul 44	5 Feb 45	Stk. 15 Oct 76, sold Dec 79
108	KULA GULF	Todd, Tacoma	16 Dec 43	15 Aug 44	12 May 45	Stk. 15 Sep 70, sold 12 Mar 71
109	CAPE GLOUCESTER	Todd, Tacoma	10 Jan 44	12 Sep 44	5 Mar 45	Stk. 1 Apr 71, sold 20 Nov 72
110	SALERNO BAY	Todd, Tacoma	7 Feb 44	26 Sep 44	19 May 45	Stk. 1 Jun 61, sold 13 Nov 61
111	VELLA GULF	Todd, Tacoma	7 Mar 44	19 Oct 44	9 Apr 45	Stk. 1 Dec 70, sold 22 Oct 71
112	SIBONEY	Todd, Tacoma	1 Apr 44	9 Nov 44	14 May 45	Stk. 1 Jun 70, sold 18 May 71
113	PUGET SOUND	Todd, Tacoma	12 May 44	30 Nov 44	18 Jun 45	Stk. 1 Jun 60, sold 4 Apr 62
114	RENDOVA	Todd, Tacoma	15 Jun 44	28 Dec 44	22 Oct 45	Stk. 1 Apr 71, sold 20 Nov 72
115	BAIROKO	Todd, Tacoma	25 Jul 44	25 Jan 45	16 Jul 45	Stk. 1 Apr 60, sold 17 Aug 60
116	BADOENG STRAIT	Todd, Tacoma	18 Aug 44	15 Feb 45	14 Nov 45	Stk. 1 Dec 70, sold 8 May 72
117	SAIDOR	Todd, Tacoma	29 Sep 44	17 Mar 45	4 Sep 45	Stk. 1 Dec 70, sold 22 Oct 71
118	SICILY	Todd, Tacoma	23 Oct 44	14 Apr 45	27 Feb 46	Stk. 1 Jul 60, sold 15 Nov 60
119	POINT CRUZ	Todd, Tacoma	4 Dec 44	18 May 45	16 Oct 45	Stk. 15 Sep 70, sold 12 Mar 71

No.		Hull		Laid down	Launched	Commiss'd	Disposition
120	MINDORO	Todd, Tacoma		2 Jan 45	27 Jun 45	4 Dec 45	Stk. 1 Dec 59, sold 31 May 60
121	RABAUL	Todd, Tacoma		29 Jan 45	14 Jul 45	No	Stk. 1 Sep 71, sold 25 Aug 72
122	PALAU	Todd, Tacoma		19 Feb 45	6 Aug 45	15 Jan 46	Stk. 1 Apr 60, sold 26 Jul 60
123	TINIAN	Todd, Tacoma		20 Mar 45	5 Sep 45	No	Stk. 1 Jun 70, sold 15 Dec 71
124	BASTOGNE	Todd, Tacoma		2 Apr 45	No	No	Cancelled 12 Aug 45
125	ENIWETOK	Todd, Tacoma		20 Apr 45	No	No	Cancelled 12 Aug 45
126	LINGAYEN	Todd, Tacoma		1 May 45	No	No	Cancelled 12 Aug 45
127	OKINAWA	Todd, Tacoma		22 May 45	No	No	Cancelled 12 Aug 45
128	Unnamed	Todd, Tacoma		17 Jul 45	No	No	Cancelled 12 Aug 45
129	Unnamed	Todd, Tacoma		9 Aug 45	No	No	Cancelled 12 Aug 45
130 -131	Unnamed	Todd, Tacoma		No	No	No	Cancelled 12 Aug 45
132 -139	Unnamed	Vancouver		No	No	No	Cancelled 12 Aug 45.

Notes: Fiscal years 1943 (CVE 105-19), 1944 (CVE 120-27), and 1945. These ships were ordered to continue production of CVEs at the two main yards participating in the program through 1944 and 1945 (Todd had taken over the Seattle-Tacoma yards). With the requirement for austerity somewhat reduced, the Navy was able to choose the design it preferred, that of the Sangamon class, and incorporate some improvements from the Casablanca class and elsewhere. The main improvement over the Sangamon was the separation of the two engine rooms to improve survivability. The ships had two elevators and a pair of catapults. CVE-108, 114, and 118 were completed by Willamette Iron and Steel Co.; CVE-110, 116, and 121 by Commercial Iron Works. The Rabaul and Tinian were completed on 27 May 46 and 30 Jul 46 respectively but were never commissioned. The Gilbert Islands was converted to a communications ship in 1963 by the New York Naval Shipyard and recommissioned 7 Mar 64 as the Annapolis. The projected conversion of the Vella Gulf to AGMR-2 was dropped as was that of Block Island to LPH-1.

Renamings: CVE 105-10 originally received names previously carried by CVE 48-50 and 52-54 with the word "bay" added when appropriate. These and the "bay" names of CVE 111-19 were assigned on 23 Sep 43, but most were later replaced by names of World War II actions:

  CVE-105 ex St. Joseph Bay 10 Jul 44;
  CVE-106 ex Sunset (named after an island) 5 Jul 44;
  CVE 107, 109, 111, and 112 ex St. Andrews Bay (107), Willapa Bay (109), Totem Bay (111), and Frosty Bay (112) 26 Apr 44;
  CVE 108, 110, 114, and 116 ex Vermillion Bay (108), Winjah Bay (110), Mosser Bay (114), and San Alberto Bay (116) 6 Nov 43;
  CVE 113, 115, 117, 118, and 119 ex Hobart Bay (113), Portage Bay (115), Saltery Bay (117), Sandy Bay (118), and Trocadero Bay (119) 5 Jun 44.
  AGMR-1 to Annapolis 22 Jun 63.

Reclassifications: CVE 105-19 originally ACV, to CVE 15 Jul 43. CVE-105, 109, 111, 113, 117, 121, and 122 were reclassified CVHE on 12 Jun 55. CVE-106 was reclassified LPH-1 on 22 Dec 57 and reverted to CVE-106 on 17 Feb 59. The entire class was reclassified to AKV on 7 May 59, CVE/CVHE 108-123, 105-107 becoming AKV 8-23 and 37-39 respectively. AKV-39 (ex CVE-107) became AGMR-1 on 1 Jun 63.

Armored Cruisers (CA)

1888

NEW YORK

Displacement: 8150 tons
Dimensions: 384'(oa.) x 64'10"(e) x 26'8"(max)
Armament: 6-8"/35 12-4"/40 3-18"T; 6-8" 12-4" 2-18"T (1897);
  4-8"/45 10-5"/50 8-3"/50 (1909); 4-8" 10-5" (1917); 4-8"
  8-5" (1919); 4-8" 8-5" 2-3"/50AA (1925)
Armor (steel): 4" belt, 5 1/2" turrets, 6" deck, 7" conning
  tower

Machinery: 16,000 IHP; 2 vertical
  inverted, triple-expansion engines,
  2 screws
Speed: 20 kts.
Complement: 566

No.		Hull	Machinery	Laid down	Launched	Commiss'd	Disposition
2	NEW YORK	Cramp	Cramp	30 Sep 90	2 Dec 91	1 Aug 93	Stk. 28 Oct 38, sunk 24 Dec 41.

Notes: Fiscal year 1889. She was authorized in 1888 as a second "armored cruiser" or small battleship
to follow the Maine but was redesigned in 1890 as a different type of ship, a long-range fast cruiser
with limited protection whose primary mission was to destroy commerce raiders. Built to Navy
Department plans, she was an exceptionally good sea boat and an efficient steamer. She made 21.09
knots on trials. She was rebuilt in 1905-9 with modern guns, the 8" being in new turrets with 6 1/2"
Krupp armor. Her fore funnel and its boilers were removed in 1927, reducing her horsepower to 7700.
She was decommissioned at Olongapo Naval Station on 29 Apr 33 and remained there as a hulk until
scuttled in Subic Bay to keep her out of Japanese hands.
Renamings: To Saratoga 16 Feb 11 and to Rochester 1 Dec 17.

1892

BROOKLYN

Displacement: 9215 tons
Dimensions: 402'7"(oa.) x 64'8"(e) x 26'2"(max)
Armament: 8-8"/35 12-5"/40 5-18"T; 8-8" 12-5" 4-18"T (1897);
  8-8" 12-5" (1903); 8-8" 8-5" 2-3"/50AA (1917)
Armor (Harvey): 3" belt, 5 1/2" turrets, 6" deck, 7 1/2"
  conning tower

Machinery: 16,000 IHP; 2 vertical,
  triple-expansion engines, 2 screws
Speed: 20 kts.
Complement: 561

No.		Hull	Machinery	Laid down	Launched	Commiss'd	Disposition
3	BROOKLYN	Cramp	Cramp	2 Aug 93	2 Oct 95	1 Dec 96	Ordered sold 21 Apr 21, sold 20 Dec 21.

Notes: Fiscal year 1893. Officially described as an improved New York, she had an extra 1000 tons
displacement which allowed adding a forecastle for better seakeeping and two more 8" guns amidships.
She steamed well and reached 21.9 knots on trials but not in service. She was a Navy Department
design.

1899

PENNSYLVANIA class

Displacement: 13,680 tons
Dimensions: 504'(Cramp vessels, oa.), 503'11"(others, oa.) x
  69'7"(e) x 26'6"(max)
Armament: 4-8"/40 14-6"/50 18-3"/50 2-18"T; 4-8"/45 14-6"/50
  18-3"/50 2-18"T (1909); 4-8" 10-6" 10-3" 2-3"/50AA 2-18"T
  (Pittsburgh, 1918); 4"8" 4-6" 10-3" 2-3"AA 2-18"T (others,
  1918)
Armor: 6" belt, 6 1/2" turrets, 4" deck, 9" conning tower

Machinery: 23,000 IHP; 2 vertical,
  inverted, triple-expansion engines,
  2 screws
Speed: 22 kts.
Complement: 828

No.		Builder	Laid down	Launched	Commiss'd	Disposition
4	PENNSYLVANIA	Cramp	7 Aug 01	22 Aug 03	9 Mar 05	Stk. 28 Oct 31, sold 21 Dec 31
5	WEST VIRGINIA	Newport News	16 Sep 01	18 Apr 03	23 Feb 05	Stk. 12 Mar 30, scrapped 1930
6	CALIFORNIA	Union	7 May 02	28 Apr 04	1 Aug 07	Mined off Fire I., N.Y., 19 Jul 18
7	COLORADO	Cramp	25 Apr 01	25 Apr 03	19 Jan 05	Stk. 21 Feb 30, scrapped 1931
8	MARYLAND	Newport News	29 Oct 01	12 Sep 03	18 Apr 05	Stk. 13 Nov 29, sold 11 Feb 30
9	SOUTH DAKOTA	Union	30 Sep 02	21 Jul 04	27 Jan 08	Stk. 15 Nov 29, sold 11 Feb 30.

Notes: Fiscal years 1900 (CA 4-6) and 1901 (7-9). This new type of armored cruiser was designed to
operate in a high-speed squadron in the van of a battle fleet. The builders supplied both the hulls

The armored cruiser *Brooklyn* (CA-3) in 1898 just after the Spanish American War. (NH 61501)

The large cruiser *Guam* (CB-2) near Trinidad in January 1945. (NARA 80-G-290578)

and the machinery. The refusal of manufacturers to sell armor within the price limits set by Congress delayed the ships' construction. In 1908-10, following an accident in the Colorado, all 8"/40 Mark 5 guns in the fleet were replaced with 8"/45 Mark 6 guns. The entire class received cage foremasts around 1911. The Huntington (ex-West Virginia) carried an experimental aircraft catapult in 1917. The Pueblo (ex-Colorado) served as a receiving ship 1921-27. The Pittsburgh (ex-Pennsylvania) had her forward funnel and boilers removed in 1926 when she was refitted as flagship of the Asiatic Fleet.
Renamings: CA-4 ex Nebraska 7 Mar 01, to Pittsburgh 27 Aug 12; CA-5 to Huntington 11 Nov 16; CA-6 to San Diego 1 Sep 14; CA-7 to Pueblo and CA-8 to Frederick 9 Nov 16; CA-9 to Huron 7 Jun 20.

1902

TENNESSEE class

Displacement: 14,500 tons
Dimensions: 504'5"(oa.) x 72'11"(e) x 27'2"(max)
Armament: 4-10"/40 16-6"/50 22-3"/50 4-21"T; 4-10" 4-6" 12-3"
  2-3"/50AA 4-21"T (1918); 4-10" 4-6" 4-21"T (Seattle, ex-
  Washington, 1922); 4-10" 4-6" (Seattle, 1938)
Armor: 5" belt, 9" turrets, 4" deck 9" conning tower

Machinery: 23,000 IHP; 2 vertical,
  inverted, triple-expansion engines,
  2 screws
Speed: 22 kts.
Complement: 829

No.		Builder	Laid down	Launched	Commiss'd	Disposition
10	TENNESSEE	Cramp	20 Jun 03	3 Dec 04	17 Jul 06	Wrecked Santo Domingo, 29 Aug 16
11	WASHINGTON	New York SB	23 Sep 03	18 Mar 05	7 Aug 06	Stk. 19 Jul 46, sold 3 Dec 46
12	NORTH CAROLINA	Newport News	21 Mar 05	6 Oct 06	7 May 08	Stk. 15 Jul 30, sold 29 Sep 30
13	MONTANA	Newport News	29 Apr 05	15 Dec 06	21 Jul 08	Stk. 15 Jul 30, sold 29 Sep 30.

Notes: Fiscal years 1903 (CA 10-11) and 1905 (12-13). These two groups had slightly different armor distribution schemes. The entire class received cage foremasts around 1911. The North Carolina carried an experimental aircraft catapult in 1915-17 and the Seattle (ex-Washington) carried one in 1917. (One was also planned for the Montana, but it was not installed.) The Seattle was fitted as administrative flagship of the United States Fleet in 1922-23 and served as a receiving ship from 1927 to 1946. The hulk of the Memphis (ex-Tennessee) was sold on 17 Jan 22.
Renamings: CA-10 to Memphis 25 May 15; CA-11 to Seattle 9 Nov 16; CA-12 to Charlotte and CA-13 to Missoula 7 Jun 20.
Reclassification: CA-11 to "unclassified" (IX-39) 11 Jul 31.

Large Cruisers (CB)

1940

ALASKA class

Displacement: 27,000 tons standard
Dimensions: 808'6"(oa.) x 90'9"(e) x 31'9"(max)
Armament: 9-12"/50 12-5"/38AA
Armor: 9" belt, 12 4/5" turrets, 1 2/5" + 4" + 5/8" decks,
  10 3/5" conning tower

Machinery: 150,000 SHP; G. E. geared
  turbines, 4 screws
Speed: 33 kts.
Complement: 1517

No.		Hull	Laid down	Launched	Commiss'd	Disposition
1	ALASKA	New York SB	17 Dec 41	15 Aug 43	17 Jun 44	Stk. 1 Jun 60, sold 30 Jun 61
2	GUAM	New York SB	2 Feb 42	12 Nov 43	17 Sep 44	Stk. 1 Jun 60, sold 20 Jun 61
3	HAWAII	New York SB	20 Dec 43	3 Nov 45	No	Stk. 9 Jun 58, sold 23 Apr 59
4	PHILIPPINES	New York SB	No	No	No	Cancelled 24 Jun 43
5	PUERTO RICO	New York SB	No	No	No	Cancelled 24 Jun 43
6	SAMOA	New York SB	No	No	No	Cancelled 24 Jun 43.

Notes: Fiscal year 1941. A new type, designed to hunt down 8" gun cruisers and protect carrier groups against enemy cruiser groups. Although they looked like capital ships and were popularly called battlecruisers, they were in reality exactly what their official classification indicated, large cruisers. Their armor, underwater protection, and 5"AA armament all followed cruiser practice. Their belts, however, extended a deck higher than in other cruisers and their hulls and machinery were similar to those of Essex class carriers. CB 3-6 were suspended on 20 May 42 along with the Montana class battleships. CB-3 was reinstated on 24 Jun 43 and was 85 percent complete when construction was suspended on 17 Feb 47. Funds were included in the Fiscal Year 1952 budget for her conversion to a Large Tactical Command Ship (CBC) but work was not begun and the project was dropped in 1954.
Reclassifications: CB-3 to CBC-1 26 Feb 52; reverted to CB-3 9 Sep 54.

Heavy Cruisers (CA)

1925

PENSACOLA class

Displacement: 9100 tons standard
Dimensions: 585'6"(oa.) x 65'3"(e) x 22'(max)
Armament: 10-8"/55 4-5"/25AA 6-21"T; 10-8" 4-5"AA (1934);
  10-8" 8-5"AA (1941)
Armor: 4" belt, 2 1/2" turrets, 1" deck, 1 1/4" conning tower

Machinery: 107,000 SHP; geared
  turbines, 4 screws
Speed: 32.7 kts.
Complement: 653

No.		Hull	Machinery	Laid down	Launched	Commiss'd	Disposition
24	PENSACOLA	New York Navy Yd.	New York SB	27 Oct 26	25 Apr 29	6 Feb 30	Sunk as target 10 Nov 48 off Bremerton, WA, stk. 26 Nov 48
25	SALT LAKE CITY	New York SB	New York SB	9 Jun 27	23 Jan 29	11 Dec 29	Sunk as target 25 May 48 off California, stk. 18 Jun 48.

Notes: Fiscal year 1926. The first post-Washington Treaty American cruisers, their design emphasized armament and speed at the expense of protection. They suffered from a low freeboard and a tendency to roll at low speeds. The contract for the Salt Lake City was originally let to Cramp but when that yard closed it was transferred to New York Ship on 16 Apr 27. Both ships were used in the Bikini atomic bomb tests and later expended as targets.
Reclassification: Designated light cruisers (CL) until 1 Jul 31. At this time the symbol CA was redefined from "cruisers" (the old armored cruisers) to "heavy cruisers" (the new treaty type with 8" guns or larger).

1926

NORTHAMPTON class

Displacement: 9300 (Chicago), 9200 (Chester), 9050 (others)
  tons standard
Dimensions: 600'3"(oa.) x 66'1"(e) x 23'(max)
Armament: 9-8"/45 4-5"/25AA 6-21"T; 9-8" 4-5"AA (1934); 9-8"
  8-5"AA (1941)
Armor: 3 3/4" belt, 2 1/2" turrets, 1" deck, 1 1/4" conning
  tower

Machinery: 107,000 SHP; geared
  turbines, 4 screws
Speed: 32.7 kts.
Complement: 621

No.		Hull	Machinery	Laid down	Launched	Commiss'd	Disposition
26	NORTHAMPTON	Quincy		12 Apr 28	5 Sep 29	17 May 30	Sunk by HIJMS Oyashio off Guadalcanal 30 Nov 42
27	CHESTER	New York SB		6 Mar 28	3 Jul 29	24 Jun 30	Stk. 1 Mar 59, sold 11 Aug 59
28	LOUISVILLE	Puget Sd.		4 Jul 28	1 Sep 30	15 Jan 31	Stk. 1 Mar 59, sold 30 Sep 59
29	CHICAGO	Mare I.	G. E.	10 Sep 28	10 Apr 30	9 Mar 31	Sunk by Japanese aircraft off Rennell I. 30 Jan 43
30	HOUSTON	Newport News		1 May 28	7 Sep 29	17 Jun 30	Sunk by HIJMS Mikuma and Mogami in Bantam Bay, Java, 28 Feb 42
31	AUGUSTA	Newport News		2 Jul 28	1 Feb 30	30 Jan 31	Stk. 1 Mar 59, sold 12 Nov 59.

Notes: Fiscal year 1927. This class introduced what became the standard main battery arrangement for U.S. heavy cruisers, three triple turrets, as part of an effort to overcome the shortcomings of the Pensacola class. The Augusta, Chicago, and Houston were fitted as fleet flagships with additional accommodations in an extended forecastle. Some of these ships carried 4-3"/50AA as a temporary measure in 1941-2 until quadruple 1.1"AA gun mounts became available to replace them.
Reclassification: Designated light cruisers (CL) until 1 Jul 31.

1929

PORTLAND class

Displacement: 9950 (Indianapolis), 9800 (Portland) tons
  standard
Dimensions: 610'3"(oa.) x 66'1"(e) x 24'(max)
Armament: 9-8"/55 8-5"/25AA
Armor: 5" belt, 2 1/2" turrets, 2 1/2" deck, 1 1/4" conning
  tower

Machinery: 107,000 SHP; geared
  turbines, 4 screws
Speed: 32.7 kts.
Complement: 952

The heavy cruiser *Louisville* (CA-28) in the early 1930s. (NH 51903)

The heavy cruiser *Rochester* (CA-124) off the east coast of Korea on 16 March 1954. (NARA 80-G-644206)

No.		Builder	Laid down	Launched	Commiss'd	Disposition
33	PORTLAND	Quincy	17 Feb 30	21 May 32	23 Feb 33	Stk. 1 Mar 59, sold 8 Oct 59
35	INDIANAPOLIS	New York SB	31 Mar 30	7 Nov 31	15 Nov 32	Sunk by HIJMS I-58 off the Philippines 29 Jul 45.

Notes: Fiscal year 1930. These ships were improved Northamptons, with the Indianapolis fitted as a fleet flagship. Their deck protection (originally 1") and side protection forward were augmented while under construction. The builders supplied both hull and machinery. Both rolled badly until fitted with bilge keels.
Reclassification: Designated light cruisers (CL) until 1 Jul 31.

NEW ORLEANS class

Displacement: 9975 (Tuscaloosa), 9400 (Vincennes), 9375 (Quincy), 9950 (others) tons standard
Dimensions: 588'0"(oa.) x 61'10"(Quincy, Vincennes, e), 61'9" (others, e) x 22'6"(Quincy, Vincennes, max), 23'6"(others, max)
Armament: 9-8"/55 8-5"/25AA
Armor: 5" belt, 8" turrets, 2 1/4" deck, 5" conning tower

Machinery: 107,000 SHP; geared turbines, 4 screws
Speed: 32.0 kts. (Quincy and Vincennes), 32.7 kts. (others)
Complement: 751

No.		Hull	Machinery	Laid down	Launched	Commiss'd	Disposition
32	NEW ORLEANS	New York	Westinghouse	14 Mar 31	12 Apr 33	15 Feb 34	Stk. 1 Mar 59, sold 1 Oct 59
34	ASTORIA	Puget Sd.	Westinghouse	1 Sep 30	16 Dec 33	28 Apr 34	Sunk by Japanese squadron off Savo I. 9 Aug 42
36	MINNEAPOLIS	Philadelphia	Westinghouse	27 Jun 31	6 Sep 33	19 May 34	Stk. 1 Mar 59, sold 29 Sep 59
37	TUSCALOOSA	New York SB		3 Sep 31	15 Nov 33	17 Aug 34	Stk. 1 Mar 59, sold Jul 59
38	SAN FRANCISCO	Mare I.	Westinghouse	9 Sep 31	9 Mar 33	10 Feb 34	Stk. 1 Mar 59, sold 29 Sep 59
39	QUINCY	Quincy	Quincy	15 Nov 33	19 Jun 35	9 Jun 36	Sunk by Japanese squadron off Savo I. 9 Aug 42
44	VINCENNES	Quincy	Quincy	2 Jan 34	21 May 36	24 Feb 37	Sunk by Japanese squadron off Savo I. 9 Aug 42.

Notes: Fiscal years 1930 (CA 32, 34, 36), 1931 (37-38), 1933 (39), and 1934 (44). When the first U.S. treaty cruisers were completed, they were found to be up to 1000 tons lighter than expected. An entirely new design was therefore developed in 1929 for the Fiscal Year 1931 ships which used this tonnage to remedy the earlier ships' severe deficiencies in protection. The three Fiscal Year 1930 ships that had been ordered from navy yards were also shifted to the new design. With its increased subdivision and concentrated armor, this class represented a turning point in American heavy cruiser design. The final design became very tight, however, and in the Quincy and Vincennes, the forward turret was moved aft eight feet and other changes in details were made to conserve weight.
Reclassification: Designated light cruisers (CL) until 1 Jul 31.

1934

WICHITA

Displacement: 10,000 tons standard
Dimensions: 608'4"(oa.) x 61'9"(e) x 25'(max)
Armament: 9-8"/55 8-5"/38AA
Armor: 6" belt, 8" turrets, 2 1/4" deck, 6" conning tower

Machinery: 100,000 SHP; geared turbines, 4 screws
Speed: 33.5 kts.
Complement: 863

No.		Hull	Machinery	Laid down	Launched	Commiss'd	Disposition
45	WICHITA	Philadelphia	New York SB	28 Oct 35	16 Nov 37	16 Feb 39	Stk. 1 Mar 59, sold 29 Sep 59.

Notes: Fiscal year 1935. This, the last new heavy cruiser allowed to the U.S. under the London Naval Treaty, was built using the hull design of the Brooklyn class modified for three 8" turrets. She introduced a new type of 8" turret and was the first U.S. cruiser to place part of her anti-aircraft battery in enclosed gun mounts.
Reclassification: Authorized in 1929 and designated a light cruiser (CL) until 1 Jul 31.

1940

BALTIMORE class

Displacement: 13,600 tons standard
Dimensions: 673'5"(CA 68-71, oa.). 674'11"(others, oa.) x 70'10"(e) x 26'10"(max)

Armor: 6" belt, 8" turrets, 2 1/2" deck, 6 1/2" conning tower (not in CA 68-73)

Armament: 9-8"/55 12-5"/38AA; 9-8" 12-5"AA 20-3"/50AA (CA 72-75, 130, 132, 133, 135; 1951); 9-8" 12-5"AA 18-3"AA 3-Regulus-I-SSM (CA 75, 132, 133, 135; 1955-58); 9-8" 12-5"AA 14-3"AA (CA 68, 1956; CA 75, 132, 133, 135; 1959-62); 9-8" 10-5"AA 14-3"AA (CA-73, 1963); 9-8" 10-5"AA 12-3"AA (CA-73, 1965)

Machinery: 120,000 SHP; G. E. geared turbines, 4 screws
Speed: 33 kts.
Complement: 1142

No.	Hull	Laid down	Launched	Commiss'd	Disposition
68 BALTIMORE	Quincy	26 May 41	28 Jul 42	15 Apr 43	Stk. 15 Feb 71, sold 10 May 72
69 BOSTON	Quincy	30 Jun 41	26 Aug 42	30 Jun 43	To CAG-1 4 Jan 52
70 CANBERRA	Quincy	3 Sep 41	19 Apr 43	14 Oct 43	To CAG-2 4 Jan 52
71 QUINCY	Quincy	9 Oct 41	23 Jun 43	15 Dec 43	Stk. 1 Oct 73, sold 20 Aug 74
72 PITTSBURGH	Quincy	3 Feb 43	22 Feb 44	10 Oct 44	Stk. 1 Jul 73, sold 22 Jul 74
73 ST. PAUL	Quincy	3 Feb 43	16 Sep 44	17 Feb 45	Stk. 31 Jul 78, sold Jan 80
74 COLUMBUS	Quincy	28 Jun 43	30 Nov 44	8 Jun 45	To CG-12 30 Sep 59
75 HELENA	Quincy	9 Sep 43	28 Apr 45	4 Sep 45	Stk. 1 Jan 74, sold 13 Nov 74
130 BREMERTON	New York SB	1 Feb 43	2 Jul 44	29 Apr 45	Stk. 1 Oct 73, sold 22 Jul 74
131 FALL RIVER	New York SB	12 Apr 43	13 Aug 44	1 Jul 45	Stk. 19 Feb 71, sold 28 Aug 72
132 MACON	New York SB	14 Jun 43	15 Oct 44	26 Aug 45	Stk. 1 Nov 69, sold 5 Jul 73
133 TOLEDO	New York SB	13 Sep 43	6 May 45	27 Oct 46	Stk. 1 Jan 74, sold 13 Nov 74
135 LOS ANGELES	Philadelphia	28 Jul 43	20 Aug 44	22 Jul 45	Stk. 1 Jan 74, sold 16 May 75
136 CHICAGO	Philadelphia	28 Jul 43	20 Aug 44	10 Jan 45	To CG-11 1 Nov 58.

Notes: Fiscal years 1941 (CA 68-75) and 1943 (130-36). They were the first U.S. heavy cruisers not subject to the limitations of the Washington and London Naval Treaties. They were designed as 12,000-ton improved Wichitas, their increased size permitting improvements in protection and seakeeping capabilities and expansion of the 5"/38AA battery. They were also large enough to absorb wartime modifications without becoming overweight. Bethlehem prepared the detailed plans and G. E. designed the power plants. Most of the ships received 3"/50AA guns in place of their 40mm guns during the early 1950s. The Baltimore received hers during her final inactivation overhaul in 1956. During the mid-1950s, the Helena, Macon, Toledo, and Los Angeles were equipped to carry Regulus surface-to-surface missiles on the fantail. Around 1960 the St. Paul, Helena, and Los Angeles underwent limited flagship conversions with enlarged foremasts, and the St. Paul received additional flagship modifications after 1962. The Boston and Canberra were converted to CAG 1-2 in 1952-56 and the Chicago and Columbus were converted to CG 11-12 in 1959-64 (see Guided Missile Heavy Cruisers and Guided Missile Cruisers, below). The Fall River was to have become CG-12 on 1 Nov 58 but her conversion was cancelled on 9 Oct 58 before the renumbering took effect.
Renamings: CA-70 ex Pittsburgh 12 Oct 42; CA-71 ex St. Paul 16 Oct 42; CA-72 ex Albany 26 Nov 42; CA-73 ex Rochester 26 Nov 42; and CA-75 ex Des Moines 6 Nov 44. CA-135 dropped her name 5 May 71.
Reclassifications: Two ships to CAG and two to CG as listed above. CAG 1-2 reverted to CA 69-70 1 May 68.

1942

OREGON CITY class

Displacement: 13,700 tons standard
Dimensions: 674'11"(oa.) x 70'10"(e) x 26'4"(max)
Armament: 9-8"/55 12-5"/38AA; 9-8" 12-5"AA 20-3"/50AA (CA 123-124, 1954)
Armor: 6" belt, 8" turrets, 2 1/2" deck, 6" conning tower

Machinery: 120,000 SHP; G. E. geared turbines, 4 screws
Speed: 33 kts.
Complement: 1142

No.	Hull	Laid down	Launched	Commiss'd	Disposition
122 OREGON CITY	Quincy	8 Apr 44	9 Jun 45	16 Feb 46	Stk. 1 Nov 70, sold 17 Aug 73
123 ALBANY	Quincy	6 Mar 44	30 Jun 45	15 Jun 46	To CG-10 1 Nov 58
124 ROCHESTER	Quincy	29 May 44	28 Aug 45	20 Dec 46	Stk. 1 Oct 73, sold 20 Aug 74
125 NORTHAMPTON	Quincy	31 Aug 44	Completed as CLC		Cancelled 12 Aug 45, to CLC-1 1 Nov 47
126 CAMBRIDGE	Quincy	16 Dec 44	No	No	Cancelled 12 Aug 45
127 BRIDGEPORT	Quincy	13 Jan 45	No	No	Cancelled 12 Aug 45
128 KANSAS CITY	Quincy	9 Jul 45	No	No	Cancelled 12 Aug 45
129 TULSA	Quincy	No	No	No	Cancelled 12 Aug 45
137 NORFOLK	Philadelphia	27 Dec 44	No	No	Cancelled 12 Aug 45
138 SCRANTON	Philadelphia	27 Dec 44	No	No	Cancelled 12 Aug 45.

Notes: Fiscal year 1943. The Baltimore, Cleveland, and Atlanta class cruiser designs were all modified in mid-1942 to reduce topweight and improve resistance to underwater damage. In the new designs (the Oregon City, Fargo, and Juneau classes), superstructures and some smaller guns were

lowered, superstructures were made more compact to clear firing arcs for the relocated antiaircraft guns, and hull subdivision was enhanced. The Oregon City and Fargo classes were given a single large funnel. The Northampton was reclassified as a task force command ship (CLC-1) on 1 Nov 47 and reordered to her new design on 1 Jul 48 (see Tactical Command Ships, below). The Albany was converted to CG-10 in 1959-62 (see Guided Missile Cruisers, below).
Renaming: The original name of CA-127, Chicago, was reassigned to CA-136 on 15 Jun 43 and the name Bridgeport was assigned to CA-127 on 28 Jun 44.
Reclassifications: One ship to CLC and one to CG as listed above.

DES MOINES class

Displacement: 17,000 tons
Dimensions: 716'6"(oa.) x 76'4"(e) x 26'(max)
Armament: 9-8"/55 12-5"/38AA 24-3"/50AA; 9-8" 12-5"AA 22-3"AA (1955); 9-8" 12-5"AA 20-3"AA (CA-134, 1960); 9-8" 12-5"AA 16-3"AA (CA-148, 1962); 9-8" 12-5"AA 8-3"AA (CA-148, 1966); 6-8" 12-5"AA 4-3"AA (CA-148, 1973)
Armor: 6" belt, 8" turrets, 1" + 3 1/2" decks, 6 1/2" conning tower

Machinery: 120,000 SHP; G. E. geared turbines, 4 screws
Speed: 33 kts.
Complement: 1799

No.		Hull	Laid down	Launched	Commiss'd	Disposition
134	DES MOINES	Quincy	28 May 45	27 Sep 46	16 Nov 48	USN
139	SALEM	Quincy	4 Jul 45	25 Mar 47	14 May 49	USN
140	DALLAS	Quincy	15 Oct 45	No	No	Cancelled 6 Jun 46
141	Unnamed	Quincy	No	No	No	Cancelled 7 Jan 46
142	Unnamed	Quincy	No	No	No	Cancelled 12 Aug 45
143	Unnamed	Quincy	No	No	No	Cancelled 12 Aug 45
148	NEWPORT NEWS	Newport News	1 Oct 45	6 Mar 47	29 Jan 49	Stk. 31 Jul 78
149	Unnamed	Newport News	No	No	No	Cancelled 12 Aug 45
150	DALLAS	New York SB	No	No	No	Cancelled 28 Mar 45
151	Unnamed	New York SB	No	No	No	Cancelled 28 Mar 45.
-153						

Notes: Fiscal years 1943 (CA-134), 1944 (139-43, 148-49), and 1945 (150-53). In May 1943 the Bureau of Ordnance proposed a new 8-inch gun derived from the 6" gun in the Worcester class that used cased ammunition and was nearly automatic. The need for such a weapon was shown in the night surface actions in the Solomons in 1942 in which 6" guns fired rapidly enough but lacked range while 8" guns using bag ammunition had the necessary range but fired too slowly to hit fast moving targets. The first ships of the new type were CA 139-42, ordered as Oregon City class ships on 14 Jun 43 and shifted to the new design in August. The Des Moines was originally ordered from New York Shipbuilding Corp. as a Baltimore class ship but was cancelled there on 18 Sep 43 and reordered to the new design at Quincy on 25 Sep 43. CA-143 was originally ordered from New York Ship on 15 Jun 43 and CA 148-149 were initially ordered from Cramp on 14 Jun 43, all as Worcester class CLs. These orders were cancelled and the new contracts awarded on 8 Apr 44. The Newport News was refitted as a flagship in 1962. She lost the center gun in No. 2 turret in an explosion on 1 Oct 72 and the turret was not restored to service.

1945

PRINZ EUGEN

Displacement: 14,800 tons
Dimensions: 654'6"(oa.) x 71' x 15'
Armament: 8-8" 12-4.1"AA 12-21"T
Armor: 3" belt, 5 1/2" turrets, 1" + 1" decks

Machinery: 80,000 SHP, geared turbines, 3 screws
Speed: 32 kts.
Complement: 830

	Builder	Launched	Acquired	In Serv.	Disposition
PRINZ EUGEN	Germania, Kiel	22 Aug 38	14 Dec 45	5 Jan 46	Foundered off Kwajalein 22 Dec 46, stk. 10 Jun 47.

Notes: Formerly the German cruiser Prinz Eugen, surrendered to the British at Copenhagen on 8 May 45, allocated to the United States in August 1945, and placed in service in January 1946 with her German name and the U.S. hull number IX-300. She was used as a target in the Bikini atomic bomb tests in July 1946 and eventually flooded and capsized because of test damage. Except for two destroyers (DD-935 and DD-939), she was the only German combatant acquired after either World War to receive a U.S. Navy hull number. After World War I several German ships, including the battleship Ostfriesland, the cruiser Frankfurt, and some destroyers and submarines, were brought to the United States but were not given U.S. designations.

Protected and Unprotected Cruisers

1883

ATLANTA class

Displacement: 3189 tons
Dimensions: 283'(oa.) x 42'(e) x 21'1"(max)
Armament: 2-8"/30 6-6"/30; none (Boston, 1917)
Armor: 2" shields, 1 1/2" deck, 2" conning tower

Machinery: 4030 IHP; horizontal,
  compound engine, 1 screw
Speed: 15.6 kts. (trials)
Complement: 284

	Hull	Machinery	Laid down	Launched	Commiss'd	Disposition
ATLANTA	Roach	Morgan	8 Nov 83	9 Oct 84	19 Jul 86	Stk. 24 Apr 12, sold 10 Jun 12
BOSTON	Roach	Morgan	15 Nov 83	4 Dec 84	2 May 87	Sunk as target 8 Apr 46 off San Francisco, stk. 17 Apr 46.

Notes: The first ships of the new navy were authorized by Congress on 3 Mar 83 (fiscal year 1884): the cruisers Atlanta, Boston, and Chicago and the dispatch vessel Dolphin. The first two, the smaller of the ABC cruisers, were initially regarded as successors to the Hartford and Omaha types of the old navy. They were underpowered vessels (designed for only 13 kts.) with protective decks covering only the engines and boilers. Their main battery was mounted en echelon to permit use on either broadside, ahead, or astern. They were rigged to carry 10,400 sq.ft. of canvas. Both vessels were completed by New York Navy Yard. The Atlanta was partially rebuilt in 1897-99, receiving new 3500 IHP triple-expansion engines and having her 6" guns converted to rapid firing. She served as a training vessel in 1905 and a barracks ship thereafter. The Boston was partially reconstructed in 1900-01, at which time her 6" guns were converted to rapid firing. She was stricken on 12 Jul 10 but was reinstated and served as a training vessel 1911-17. She was stricken on 3 May 1917 and loaned to the Shipping Board. On 18 Jun 18 she reappeared on the navy list and acted as a receiving ship (1918-40) and a training vessel (1940-46).
Renaming: Boston to Despatch 9 Aug 40.
Reclassification: Boston to "unclassified" (IX-2) 17 Jul 20.

CHICAGO

Displacement: 4500 tons
Dimensions: 342'2"(oa.) x 48'2"(e) x 22'7"(max)
Armament: 4-8"/30 8-6"/30 2-5"/30; 4-8"/35 14-5"/40 (1898);
  12-4"/40 (1915); 4-5"/51 (1918); none (1920)
Armor: 4" shields, 1 1/2" deck, 3" conning tower

Machinery: 5084 IHP; 2 compound,
  overhead-beam engines, 2 screws
Speed: 15.3 kts. (trials)
Complement: 409

	Hull	Machinery	Laid down	Launched	Commiss'd	Disposition
CHICAGO	Roach	Morgan	29 Dec 83	5 Dec 85	17 Apr 89	Stk. 16 Aug 35, sold 15 May 36.

Notes: Fiscal year 1884. The largest of the ABC cruisers, she was initially regarded as a successor to the Wabash, Tennessee, and Trenton types of the old navy. Her hull was designed by F. L. Fernald and her machinery by Miers Coryell. As built her protective deck was 136' long and covered only the machinery. She was rigged to carry 14,880 sq. ft. of sails and was designed for 15 knots. The original engines were inadequate and in 1895-99 New York Navy Yard fitted her with new 9000 IHP triple-expansion ones designed for 18 knots. In 1902 an additional reconstruction increased her displacement to 5000 tons and extended the armored deck. She served as a training ship 1907-17, as a submarine force flagship 1917-23, and as a barracks ship at Pearl Harbor 1923-35. She was scuttled by her purchaser on 8 Jul 36.
Renaming: To Alton 16 Jul 28.
Reclassifications: To CA-14 17 Jul 20. She was to have been reclassified CL-14 8 Aug 21 but was instead designated "unclassified" (IX-5) 1 Jul 21.

1885

NEWARK

Displacement: 4083 tons
Dimensions: 328'(oa.) x 49'2"(e) x 22'8"(max)
Armament: 12-6"/30; 12-6" 6-3"/50 (1902); 12-6" (1908); none
  (1913);
Armor: 2" shields, 3" deck, 3" conning tower

Machinery: 8500 IHP; 2 horizontal
  triple-expansion engines, 2 screws
Speed: 18 kts.
Complement: 384

No.		Builder	Laid down	Launched	Commiss'd	Disposition
1	NEWARK	Cramp	12 Jun 88	19 Mar 90	2 Feb 91	Stk. 26 Jun 13, sold 7 Sep 26.

Notes: Fiscal year 1886. The hull was designed by the Navy Department and the engines by Cramp. The builder supplied both hull and machinery. The design included 6-14"T which were never mounted. Her

The protected cruiser *Atlanta* ca. 1886. (NH 57444)

The ''semi-armored'' cruiser *Charleston* (No. 22) alongside the receiving ship *Philadelphia* (formerly protected cruiser No. 4) at Puget Sound before World War I. (NH 92172)

guns were converted to rapid firing in 1898 and she was rebuilt at the Boston Navy Yard in 1901. She served as a training vessel 1905-1908. She was stricken in 1913 and was turned over to the Public Health Service as a quarantine vessel. The Navy took her back on 18 Jun 18 as a floating annex to hospitals ashore and returned her to the Public Health Service on 31 May 19. She reverted to the Navy on 7 Jul 26 and was sold.

CHARLESTON

Displacement: 3730 tons
Dimensions: 320'(oa.) x 46'(e) x 21'9"(max)
Armament: 10-6"/30; 2-8"/35 6-6"/30 (1891)
Armor: 3" shields, 3" deck, 2" conning tower

Machinery: 7500 IHP; 2 horizontal, compound engines, 2 screws
Speed: 18 kts.
Complement: 300

No.		Builder	Laid down	Launched	Commiss'd	Disposition
2	CHARLESTON	Union	20 Jan 87	19 Jul 88	26 Dec 89	Wrecked on Camiguin I., Philippines, 2 Nov 99.

Notes: Fiscal year 1886. The plans, purchased from Sir William Armstrong & Co., Ltd., Newcastle-on-Tyne, had to be completely reworked by Union before the start of construction. The design called for 4-14"T which were never mounted. Union built both the hull and the machinery.

1886

BALTIMORE

Displacement: 4413 tons
Dimensions: 335'(oa.) x 48'6"(e) x 23'11"(max)
Armament: 4-8"/35 6-6"/30; 12-6"/40 6-3"/50 (1903); 4-6" 180 mines (1915); 4-5"/51 2-3"/50AA 180 mines (1918)
Armor: 4 1/2" shields, 4" deck, 3" conning tower

Machinery: 10,500 IHP; 2 horizontal, triple-expansion engines, 2 screws
Speed: 19 kts.
Complement: 386

No.		Builder	Laid down	Launched	Commiss'd	Disposition
3	BALTIMORE	Cramp	5 May 87	6 Oct 88	7 Jan 90	Stk. 14 Oct 37, sold 16 Feb 42.

Notes: Fiscal year 1887. The design was purchased from Humphreys, Tennant & Co., Ltd. and proved to be very successful. It included 4-14"T which were never mounted. Cramp built both the hull and the machinery. The ship had excellent sea keeping qualities and good speed. She was rebuilt in 1902, served as a receiving ship 1911-12, and was converted to a minelayer at the Charleston Navy Yard in 1913-14. After being stricken from the Navy List in 1937 she became a storage hulk at Pearl Harbor and remained there until scuttled at sea on 22 Sep 44.
Reclassification: To mine planter ca. 1912 (numbered CM-1 17 Jul 20).

1887

PHILADELPHIA

Displacement: 4324 tons
Dimensions: 335'(oa.) x 48'6"(e) x 23'5"(max)
Armament: 12-6"/30; none (1904)
Armor: 3" shields, 4" deck, 3" conning tower

Machinery: 10,500 IHP; 2 horizontal, triple-expansion engines, 2 screws
Speed: 19 kts.
Complement: 384

No.		Builder	Laid down	Launched	Commiss'd	Disposition
4	PHILADELPHIA	Cramp	22 Mar 88	7 Sep 89	28 Jul 90	Stk. 24 Nov 26, sold 1 Jun 27.

Notes: Fiscal year 1888. She was built to the same hull plans as the Baltimore but with the armament modified and rearranged. Cramp built the machinery as well as the hull. The design included 4-14"T which were never mounted. Her 6" guns were converted to rapid firing in 1898. She was housed over in 1904 and served as a receiving ship 1904-12 and 1916-26 and as a prison ship 1912-16.
Reclassification: To "unclassified" (IX-24) 17 Jul 20.

SAN FRANCISCO

Displacement: 4083 tons
Dimensions: 324'6" (oa.) x 49'2"(e) x 22'4"(max)
Armament: 12-6"/30; 12-6" 4-18"T (1894); 12-6" (1902); 8-5"/40 300 mines (1911); 4-5"/51 2-3"/50AA 300 mines (1918); 3-5" 2-3" 300 mines (1925)
Armor: 2" shields, 3" deck, 3" conning tower

Machinery: 10,500 IHP; 2 horizontal triple-expansion engines, 2 screws
Speed: 19 kts.
Complement: 383

No.		Builder	Laid down	Launched	Commiss'd	Disposition
5	SAN FRANCISCO	Union	14 Aug 88	26 Oct 89	15 Nov 90	Stk. 8 Jun 37, sold 20 Apr 39.

Notes: Fiscal year 1888. She was built to the same hull plans as the Newark but with the guns rearranged. She was the last U.S. cruiser to carry a full rig of sails. The builders supplied both

hull and machinery. The guns of the San Francisco were converted to rapid firing in 1902, and the ship was ordered refitted as a mine planter on 12 Jun 08.
Renaming: To Yosemite 1 Jan 31. (The name Tahoe was initially selected but was not used.)
Reclassification: To mine planter 19 Dec 12 (numbered CM-2 17 Jul 20).

1888

OLYMPIA

Displacement: 5870 tons
Dimensions: 344'1"(oa.) x 53'1"(m) x 24'10"(max)
Armament: 4-8"/35 10-5"/40 6-18"T; 4-8" 10-5" (1902); 12-4"/40 (1916); 10-5"/51 (1918)
Armor: 3 1/2" turrets, 4 3/4" deck, 5" conning tower

Machinery: 13,500 IHP; 2 vertical, triple-expansion engines, 2 screws
Speed: 20 kts.
Complement: 412

No.		Builder	Laid down	Launched	Commiss'd	Disposition
6	OLYMPIA	Union	17 Jun 91	5 Nov 92	5 Feb 95	Stk. 2 Jan 57, memorial at Philadelphia 11 Sep 57.

Notes: Fiscal year 1889. This ship was initially described as a very fast commerce raider with great endurance. She was a successful vessel whose hull and machinery were both provided by Union. On trials she produced 17,313 IHP for 21.69 knots. She was partially rebuilt in 1901-03. Plans to replace her 4-8" with 2-7" in 1909 were not carried out.
Reclassifications: To CA-15 17 Jul 20, CL-15 8 Aug 21, and "unclassified" (IX-40) 30 Jun 31.

CINCINNATI class

Displacement: 3213 tons
Dimensions: 305'10"(Raleigh, oa). 305'9"(Cincinnati, oa.) x 42'(e) x 20'2"(max)
Armament: 1-6"/40 10-5"/40 4-18"T; 1-6" 10-5" 2-18"T (1897); 11-5"/40 (Cincinnati 1901, Raleigh 1903); 9-5" (1918)

Armor: 2 1/2" deck, 2" conning tower
Machinery: 10,000 IHP; 2 vertical, triple-expansion engines, 2 screws
Speed: 19 kts.
Complement: 312

No.		Builder	Laid down	Launched	Commiss'd	Disposition
7	CINCINNATI	New York	29 Jan 90	10 Nov 92	16 Jun 94	Ordered sold 16 Mar 20, sold 5 Aug 21
8	RALEIGH	Norfolk	19 Dec 89	31 Mar 92	17 Apr 94	Ordered sold 10 Apr 20, sold 5 Aug 21.

Notes: Fiscal year 1889. They were an attempt to produce a small high-speed cruiser for use on foreign stations. The original machinery provided by the builders had a high coal consumption and could not maintain the designed speed. The ships received new 8500 IHP triple-expansion engines in 1901-03 which drove them at 18 knots. Plans to rearm them in 1919 with 7-5"/51 were not carried out.
Reclassification: The hull numbers PG 25-26 were probably reserved for them, but they were ordered sold before the new hull numbers became effective on 17 Jul 20.

MONTGOMERY class

Displacement: 2089 tons
Dimensions: 269'6"(oa.) x 37'(e) x 16'8"(max)
Armament: Montgomery--8-5"/40 3-18"T; 9-5" 3-18"T (1895); 10-5" 2-18"T (1897); 10-5" (1901); 1"21"T 3-18"T 2-14"T (1905); 2-21"T 2-18"T (1912); 4-4" 2-21"T 2-18"T (1914);
Detroit--2-6"/35 8-5"/40 3-18"T; 8-5" 3-18"T (1894); 10-5" 2-18"T (1897); 10-5" (1902);
Marblehead--8-5"/40 3-18"T; 9-5" 3-18"T (1896); 10-5" 2-18"T (1897); 10-5" (1901); 8-4"/40 (1915)

Armor: 7/16" deck, 2" conning tower
Machinery: 5400 IHP; 2 vertical, triple-expansion engines, 2 screws
Speed: 18 kts.
Complement: 274

No.		Hull	Machinery	Laid down	Launched	Commiss'd	Disposition
9	MONTGOMERY	Columbian	Columbian	Feb 90	5 Dec 91	21 Jun 94	Stk. 25 Aug 19, sold 14 Nov 19
10	DETROIT	Columbian	Columbian	Feb 90	28 Oct 91	20 Jul 93	Stk. 12 Jul 10, sold 22 Dec 10
11	MARBLEHEAD	City Pt.	Quintard	Oct 90	11 Aug 92	2 Apr 94	Ordered sold 21 Oct 20, sold 5 Aug 21.

Notes: Fiscal year 1889. Authorized as 2000-ton "gunboats or cruisers," they were classified cruisers because of their designed speed of 18 knots. Trial speeds ranged from 18.44 to 19.05 knots. The Montgomery was converted to a torpedo practice and experimental vessel in 1905 and served as a training ship until 1918. The Marblehead also served as a training vessel between 1910 and 1917.
Renaming: Montgomery to Anniston 14 Mar 18.
Reclassification: Marblehead to PG-27 17 Jul 20.

1890

COLUMBIA class

Displacement: 7375 tons
Dimensions: 413'1"(oa.) x 58'2"(e) x 25'7"(max)
Armament: 1-8"/40 2-6"/40 8-4"/40 4-18"T; 1-8" 2-6" 8-4"
  (1904); 3-6"/45 8-4"/40 (Columbia, 1915); 3-6" 6-4" (both,
  1917); 3-6" 4-4" (1918)
Armor: 4" shields, 4" deck, 5" conning tower

Machinery: 21,000 IHP; 3 vertical,
  inverted, triple-expansion engines,
  3 screws
Speed: 21 kts.
Complement: 477

No.		Builder	Laid down	Launched	Commiss'd	Disposition
12	COLUMBIA	Cramp	30 Dec 90	26 Jul 92	23 Apr 94	To sale list 22 Jun 21, sold 26 Jan 22
13	MINNEAPOLIS	Cramp	16 Dec 91	12 Aug 93	13 Dec 94	Ordered sold 16 Jun 21, sold 5 Aug 21.

Notes: Fiscal years 1891 (No. 12) and 1892 (13). Designed by the Navy Department as specialized commerce raiders to hunt down fast North Atlantic liners, they were a great technical success. They made 22.8 (Columbia) and 23.07 knots (Minneapolis) on trials and could sustain nearly 20 knots at sea. They were, however, very expensive to operate. The original design called for 400-foot vessels.
Renaming: Columbia to Old Columbia 17 Nov 21.
Reclassifications: To CA 16-17 respectively 17 Jul 20

1898

NEW ORLEANS class

Displacement: 3769 tons
Dimensions: 354'4"(Albany, oa.). 354'5"(New Orleans, oa.) x
  43'9"(e) x 19'1"(max)
Armament: 6-6"/50 4-4.7"/50 3-18"T; 6-6" 4-4.7" (1900-2);
  5-6" 1-5"/50 4-4.7" (Albany, 1903); 10-5"/50 (1907-9); 8-5"
  (1917-18); 8-5" 1-3"/50AA (Albany, 1921)

Armor: 4" shields, 3 1/2" deck, 4"
  conning tower
Machinery: 7500 IHP; 2 vertical,
  inverted, triple-expansion engines,
  2 screws
Speed: 20 kts.
Complement: 365

	Hull	Machinery	Laid down	Launched	Commiss'd	Disposition
NEW ORLEANS	Elswick	Humphreys &Tennant	1895	4 Dec 96	18 Mar 98	Stk. 13 Nov 29, sold 11 Feb 30
ALBANY	Elswick	Hawthorne Leslie	1897	14 Jan 99	29 May 00	Stk. 13 Nov 29, sold 11 Feb 30.

Notes: Designed by their builder, they proved to be unsatisfactory as built. They were over-gunned and had poor accommodations by American standards. They were purchased from Brazil 16 Mar 98 in a last minute effort to strengthen the Navy before the outbreak of the Spanish-American War. They were formerly the Amazonas and Almirante Abreu respectively.
Reclassifications: To PG-34 and PG-36 respectively 17 Jul 20 and to CL 22-23 8 Aug 21.

REINA MERCEDES

Displacement: 2835 tons
Dimensions: 292'(b.p.) x 43'3" x 21'11"
Armament: 2-6.3" (1898); none (1899)

Machinery: 3700 IHP, compound engine,
  1 screw
Speed: 17.05 kts.
Complement: 375

	Builder	Launched	Acquired	Commiss'd	Disposition
REINA MERCEDES	Cartagena Dockyard	9 Sep 87	17 Jul 98	May 05	Stk. 6 Sep 57, sold 1957.

Notes: Formerly the Spanish unprotected cruiser Reina Mercedes, she was scuttled in the entrance to the harbor of Santiago de Cuba on 4 Jul 98. The wreck was captured with the port on 17 Jul 98 and raised on 1 Mar 99. Plans to convert her to a seagoing training ship were cancelled and she was converted in 1902-5 to a non-self-propelled receiving ship. She served at the Naval Academy at Annapolis from 1912 to 1957. She was laid down in 1881 and was originally armed with 6-6.3" guns. Another ex-Spanish cruiser, the Infanta Maria Teresa, was salvaged near Santiago de Cuba on 24 Sep 98 but was wrecked on 1 Nov 98 while being towed to the United States.
Reclassifications: To "unclassified" (IX-25) 17 Jul 20.

1899

DENVER class

Displacement: 3200 tons
Dimensions: 309'10"(Des Moines, oa.), 308'11" (Chattanooga, oa.), 308'10"(Cleveland, Galveston, oa.), 308'9"(Denver, oa.), 308'6"(Tacoma, oa.) x 44'(e) x 17'3"(max)
Armament: 10-5"/50; 8-5" (1918); 8-5" 1-3"/50AA (1920)
Armor: 1 3/4" shields, 2 1/2" deck

Machinery: 4700 IHP; 2 vertical, inverted, triple-expansion engines, 2 screws
Speed: 16.5 kts.
Complement: 327

No.		Builder	Laid down	Launched	Commiss'd	Disposition
14	DENVER	Neafie & Levy	28 Jun 00	21 Jun 02	17 May 04	Stk. 12 Mar 31, sold 13 Sep 33
15	DES MOINES	Fore River	28 Aug 00	20 Sep 02	5 Mar 04	Stk. 13 Dec 29, sold 11 Mar 30
16	CHATTANOOGA	Crescent	29 Mar 00	7 Mar 03	11 Oct 04	Stk. 13 Dec 29, sold 11 Mar 30
17	GALVESTON	Trigg	19 Jan 01	23 Jul 03	15 Feb 05	Stk. 1 Nov 30, sold 13 Sep 33
18	TACOMA	Union	27 Sep 00	2 Jun 03	30 Jan 04	Wrecked off Vera Cruz, Mexico, 16 Jan 24
19	CLEVELAND	Bath	1 Jun 00	28 Sep 01	2 Nov 03	Stk. 13 Dec 29, sold 11 Mar 30.

Notes: Fiscal year 1900. Sometimes called "peace cruisers," they were in effect large gunboats for patrolling the new U.S. sphere of influence in the Caribbean. They were thus successors to the Montgomery class. They could berth 480 men in an emergency. Construction of the Chattanooga stopped 18 Jun 03 on the closing of the Crescent yard. Her contract was declared forfeited on 15 Aug 03 and the hull taken to New York Navy Yard for completion. Work on the Galveston halted 24 Dec 02 when Trigg closed. The contract was declared forfeited on 14 May 03 and she went to Norfolk Navy Yard for completion.
Reclassifications: To PG 28-33 respectively 17 Jul 20 and to CL 16-21 8 Aug 21.

1900

ST. LOUIS class

Displacement: 9700 tons
Dimensions: 426'6"(oa.) x 66'(e) x 25'6"(max)
Armament: 14-6"/50 18-3"/50; 12-6" 4-3" 2-3"/50AA (1918)
Armor: 4" belt, 4" shields, 3" deck, 5" conning tower

Machinery: 21,000 IHP; 2 vertical, triple-expansion engines, 2 screws
Speed: 22 kts.
Complement: 670

No.		Builder	Laid down	Launched	Commiss'd	Disposition
20	ST. LOUIS	Neafie & Levy	31 Jul 02	6 May 05	18 Aug 06	Stk. 20 Mar 30, scrapped 1930
21	MILWAUKEE	Union	30 Jul 02	10 Sep 04	10 Dec 06	Wrecked near Eureka, Calif., 13 Jan 17
22	CHARLESTON	Newport News	30 Jan 02	23 Jan 04	17 Oct 05	Stk. 25 Nov 29, sold 11 Feb 30.

Notes: Fiscal year 1901. Originally conceived of as 6000-ton "improved Olympia" type protected cruisers, their design grew because of a desire to provide sufficient endurance and speed plus protection against modern shells. Because of their patch of side armor amidships, they were officially described as "semi-armored." The builders provided both the hulls and the machinery. The Milwaukee stranded while attempting to salvage the submarine H-3. Her hulk was sold on 5 Aug 19.
Reclassifications: St. Louis and Charleston to CA 18-19 respectively 17 Jul 20.

Dynamite Cruisers

1886

VESUVIUS

Displacement: 930 tons
Dimensions: 252'4"(oa.) x 26'5"(e) x 11'3"(max)
Armament: 3-15" pneumatic dynamite guns; 2-21"T 3-18"T (1905); 1-21"T 3-18"T (1912); 1-3" (1918); none (1920)

Machinery: 3200 IHP; 2 vertical, triple-expansion engines, 2 screws
Speed: 20 kts.
Complement: 70

	Builder	Laid down	Launched	Commiss'd	Disposition
VESUVIUS	Cramp	Sep 87	28 Apr 88	7 Jun 90	To sale list 13 Oct 21, sold 19 Apr 22.

Notes: Fiscal year 1887. Both the hull and the machinery were built by Cramp under a contract from the Pneumatic Dynamite Gun Co. She was an experimental vessel which hurled dynamite filled shells by means of compressed air. She developed 4216 IHP and 21.65 knots on trials. The dynamite guns were

judged a failure, however, and in 1905 the ship became a torpedo practice vessel.
Reclassification: To "unclassified" 17 Jul 20.

1890

Unnamed

A second dynamite gun cruiser, to have had 2-15" dynamite guns and a speed of 21 kts., was authorized in fiscal year 1890 but was deferred pending trials of the Vesuvius. She was never designed or built, and Congress transferred her appropriation to three torpedo boats (the Foote class) on 26 Jul 94.

Torpedo Cruisers

1890

Unnamed

Displacement: 800 tons
Dimensions: 259'(wl.) x 27'6"(e) x 9'
Armament: 6" guns and 5 torpedo tubes
Armor: 3/4" deck

Machinery: 6000 IHP; 2 vertical,
    triple-expansion engines, 2 screws
Speed: 23 kts.
Complement: Unknown

Notes: Fiscal year 1891. This ship was intended to accompany seagoing battleships while the smaller torpedo boats concentrated on coast defense. Bids were to be opened on 11 Feb 91 but none was received, probably because the engines alone would have used up all of the funds appropriated for the ship. The Navy requested supplemental funding in 1891-93 and redesigned the ship in 1893 to reduce costs, but Congress did not respond and the project was dropped.

Scout Cruisers

1904

CHESTER class

Displacement: 3750 tons
Dimensions: 423'1"(oa.) x 47'1"(e) x 19'3"(max)
Armament: 2-5"/50 6-3"/50 2-21"T; 4-5"/51 2-3" 1-3"/50AA 2-
    21"T (1917)
Armor: 2" belt
Complement: 356

Machinery: Chester--23,000 SHP;
    direct drive turbines, 4 screws;
    Birmingham--15,670 IHP; 2 vertical,
    triple-expansion engines, 2 screws;
    Salem--22,242 SHP; direct drive
    turbines, 2 screws
Speed (trials): 26.52 (Chester),
    25.95 (Salem), 24.33 (Birmingham)
    kts.

No.		Builder	Laid down	Launched	Commiss'd	Disposition
1	CHESTER	Bath	25 Sep 05	26 Jun 07	25 Apr 08	Stk. 21 Jan 30, sold 13 May 30
2	BIRMINGHAM	Fore River	14 Aug 05	29 May 07	11 Apr 08	Stk. 21 Jan 30, sold 13 May 30
3	SALEM	Fore River	28 Aug 05	27 Jul 07	1 Aug 08	Stk. 13 Nov 29, sold 11 Feb 30.

Notes: Fiscal year 1905. The design called for the equivalent of 16,000 IHP and a speed of 24 knots with different machinery in each ship. The Chester had turbines of Parsons type and reached 26.52 knots on trials, which broke the existing speed record for vessels over 1500 tons. The Salem's Curtis type turbines were replaced in 1916-17 by new 20,000 SHP ones built by G. E. The armored deck covered only the steering gear. The Birmingham served as a destroyer tender in 1914.
Renaming: CL-1 to York 10 Jul 28.
Reclassifications: All were reclassified light cruisers (CL) from scout cruisers 17 Jul 20.

Light Cruisers (CL)

1916

OMAHA class

Displacement: 7050 tons
Dimensions: 555'6"(oa.) x 55'4"(e) x 20'(max)
Armament: 12-6"/53 4-3"/50AA 10-21"T;
 12-6" 4-3"AA 6-21"T (1925);
 11-6" 4-3"AA 6-21"T (Marblehead 1930);
 10-6" 4-3"AA 6-21"T (Cincinnati, Raleigh, Detroit, Richmond
 1931; Marblehead 1938);
 12-6" 6 to 9-3"AA 6-21"T (Concord 1938; Omaha, Milwaukee,
 Trenton, Memphis 1940);
 10-6" 6 to 9-3"AA 6-21"T (Cincinnati, Raleigh, Richmond, Concord, Marblehead 1940; Milwaukee,
 Detroit, Trenton, Memphis 1941; Omaha 1943);
 10-6" 6 to 9-3"AA (Omaha, Cincinnati, Raleigh, Detroit, Marblehead 1945)

Armor: 3" belt, 1 1/2" deck, 1 1/4"
 conning tower
Machinery: 90,000 SHP; geared
 turbines, 4 screws
Speed: 35 kts.
Complement: 458

No.		Hull	Machinery	Laid down	Launched	Commiss'd	Disposition
4	OMAHA	Todd, Tacoma	Westing-house	6 Dec 18	14 Dec 20	24 Feb 23	Stk. 28 Nov 45, scrapped 1946
5	MILWAUKEE	Todd, Tacoma	Westing-house	13 Dec 18	24 Mar 21	20 Jun 23	Stk. 27 Oct 49, sold 22 Nov 49
6	CINCINNATI	Todd, Tacoma	Westing-house	15 May 20	23 May 21	1 Jan 24	Stk. 28 Nov 45, scrapped 1946
7	RALEIGH	Quincy	Quincy	16 Aug 20	25 Oct 22	6 Feb 24	Stk. 28 Nov 45, scrapped 1946
8	DETROIT	Quincy	Quincy	10 Nov 20	29 Jun 22	31 Jul 23	Stk. 21 Jan 46, sold 27 Dec 46
9	RICHMOND	Cramp	Cramp	16 Feb 20	29 Sep 21	2 Jul 23	Stk. 21 Jan 46, sold 14 Jan 47
10	CONCORD	Cramp	Cramp	29 Mar 20	15 Dec 21	3 Nov 23	Stk. 8 Jan 46, sold 21 Jan 47
11	TRENTON	Cramp	Cramp	18 Aug 20	16 Apr 23	19 Apr 24	Stk. 21 Jan 46, sold 29 Dec 46
12	MARBLEHEAD	Cramp	Cramp	4 Aug 20	9 Oct 23	8 Sep 24	Stk. 28 Nov 45, scrapped 1946
13	MEMPHIS	Cramp	Cramp	14 Oct 20	17 Apr 24	4 Feb 25	Stk. 8 Jan 46, sold 10 Jan 47.

Notes: Fiscal years 1917 (Nos. 4-7), 1918 (8-10), and 1919 (11-13). All were authorized and designed
as scout cruisers. The original design called for 8-6" but was altered to include light turrets on
the forecastle and quarterdeck. The ships were built with geared turbines because space limitations
prevented the installation of electric drive. Normally they carried two seaplanes. The contracts for
Scout Cruisers 4-6 were originally placed with Seattle Construction & Dry Dock Co. The Milwaukee was
loaned to the Soviet Union under the name Murmansk 20 Apr 44 - 16 Mar 49.
Reclassifications: All were reclassified from scout cruisers to light cruisers 17 Jul 20.

1933

BROOKLYN class

Displacement: 9700 (Brooklyn, Philadelphia, Boise), 9650
 (Honolulu), 9575 (Phoenix), 9475 (Savannah, Nashville) tons
 standard
Dimensions: 608'4"(oa.) x 61'8"(Nashville, Savannah, Phoenix,
 Boise, e), 61'9" (others, e) x 24'(max)
Armament: 15-6"/47 8-5"/25AA; 15-6" 8-5"/38AA (Savannah,
 Honolulu, 1945)
Armor: 5" belt, 6 1/2" turrets, 2" deck, 5" conning tower

Machinery: 100,000 SHP; geared
 turbines, 4 screws
Speed: 32.5 kts.
Complement: 868

No.		Builder	Laid down	Launched	Commiss'd	Disposition
40	BROOKLYN	New York	12 Mar 35	30 Nov 36	30 Sep 37	To Chile 9 Jan 51 as O'Higgins, stk. 22 Jan 51
41	PHILADELPHIA	Philadelphia	28 May 35	17 Nov 36	23 Sep 37	To Brazil 9 Jan 51 as Barroso, stk. 22 Jan 51
42	SAVANNAH	New York SB	31 May 34	8 May 37	10 Mar 38	Stk. 1 Mar 59, sold 6 Jan 60
43	NASHVILLE	New York SB	24 Jan 35	2 Oct 37	6 Jun 38	To Chile 9 Jan 51 as Capitan Prat, stk. 22 Jan 51
46	PHOENIX	New York SB	15 Apr 35	12 Mar 38	3 Oct 38	To Argentina 11 Jan 51 as 17 de Octubre, stk. 25 Jan 51
47	BOISE	Newport News	1 Apr 35	3 Dec 36	12 Aug 38	To Argentina 11 Jan 51 as 9 de Julio, stk. 25 Jan 51
48	HONOLULU	New York	10 Sep 35	26 Aug 37	15 Jun 38	Stk. 1 Mar 59, sold 17 Dec 59.

The light cruiser *St. Louis* (CL-49) on trials off Rockland, Maine, on 28 April 1939. Her 5″/38 gun mounts have not yet been installed. (NH 48998)

The nuclear powered guided missile cruiser *Long Beach* (CGN-9) on sea trials on 7 July 1961. (USN 1056853)

Notes: Fiscal years 1934 (CL 40-43) and 1935 (46-48). This class was a result of the 1930 London Naval Treaty, which limited U.S. heavy cruiser construction to 18 ships. The hull protection was on the same scale as the New Orleans class heavy cruisers. The armament was increased from 12 to 15-6" in response to the Japanese Mogamis. The large hanger in the stern allowed them to carry six seaplanes. Some temporarily carried 2-3"/50AA in 1941-2 while awaiting the delivery of quadruple 1.1"AA mounts. The Brooklyn, Philadelphia, Savannah, and Honolulu had their beam increased to 69'6" when fitted with bulges in 1944-45. During that refit the Savannah and Honolulu had their single 5"AA replaced with twin 5"/38 mounts. The Phoenix, renamed General Belgrano in 1956, was sunk on 2 May 82 in the Falklands War. The builders provided the machinery.

1935

ST. LOUIS class

Displacement: 10,000 tons standard				Machinery: 100,000 SHP; geared		
Dimensions: 608'4"(oa.) x 61'8"(e) x 25'10"(max)				turbines, 4 screws		
Armament: 15-6"/47 8-5"/38AA				Speed: 32.5 kts.		
Armor: 5" belt, 6 1/2" turrets, 2" deck, 5" conning tower				Complement: 888		

No.		Builder	Laid down	Launched	Commiss'd	Disposition
49	ST. LOUIS	Newport News	10 Dec 36	15 Apr 38	19 May 39	To Brazil 9 Jan 51 as Tamandare, stk. 22 Jan 51
50	HELENA	New York	9 Dec 36	27 Aug 38	18 Sep 39	Sunk by Japanese destroyers in Kula Gulf, Solomons, 6 Jul 43.

Notes: Fiscal year 1936. These were the last light cruisers ordered before the 1936 London Naval Treaty limited new cruisers to 8000 tons. They were modified Brooklyns with their 5"AA in twin turrets to provide protection to the secondary battery. The builders supplied the machinery.

1938

ATLANTA class

Displacement: 6000 tons standard				Machinery: 75,000 SHP; Westinghouse		
Dimensions: 541'6"(San Diego, San Juan, oa.), 541'0" (others, oa.) x 53'2"(e) x 26'6"(max)				geared turbines, 2 screws		
Armament: CL 51-54--16-5"AA 8-21"T;				Speed: 32.5 kts.		
CL 95-98--12-5"AA 8-21"T; 12-5"AA (Oakland, 1945);				Complement: 673		
Armor: 3 3/4" belt, 1 1/4" turrets, 1 1/4" deck, 2 1/2"conning tower						

No.		Hull	Laid down	Launched	Commiss'd	Disposition
51	ATLANTA	Kearny	22 Apr 40	6 Sep 41	24 Dec 41	Sunk by Japanese squadron off Guadalcanal 13 Nov 42
52	JUNEAU	Kearny	27 May 40	25 Oct 41	14 Feb 42	Sunk by HIJMS I-26 off Guadalcanal 13 Nov 42
53	SAN DIEGO	Quincy	27 Mar 40	26 Jul 41	10 Jan 42	Stk. 1 Mar 59, sold 3 Feb 60
54	SAN JUAN	Quincy	15 May 40	6 Sep 41	28 Feb 42	Stk. 1 Mar 59, sold 9 Nov 61
95	OAKLAND	Beth-SF	15 Jul 41	23 Oct 42	17 Jul 43	Stk. 1 Mar 59, sold 1 Dec 59
96	RENO	Beth-SF	1 Aug 41	23 Dec 42	28 Dec 43	Stk. 1 Mar 59, sold 26 Mar 62
97	FLINT	Beth-SF	23 Oct 42	25 Jan 44	31 Aug 44	Stk. 1 Sep 65, sold 6 Oct 66
98	TUCSON	Beth-SF	23 Dec 42	3 Sep 44	3 Feb 45	Stk. 1 Jun 66, sold 24 Feb 71.

Notes: Fiscal years 1939 (CL 51-54) and 1941 (95-98). Initially intended to work with destroyers in support of a battle fleet, they were later used to give anti-aircraft protection to carriers. Designed for 32.5 knots, the Atlanta made 33.67 knots on trials.
Renaming: CL-96 ex Tucson and CL-98 ex Reno 15 Mar 41. CL-97 ex Spokane 26 Nov 42.
Reclassifications: All to anti-aircraft light cruisers (CLAA) 18 Mar 49.

1939

CLEVELAND class

Displacement: 10,000 tons standard		Machinery: 100,000 SHP; G. E. geared
Dimensions: 610'1"(oa.) x 66'6"(CL 101-105, e), 66'4"(others, e) x 25'(max)		turbines, 4 screws
Armament: 12-6"/47 12-5"/38AA; 12-6" 12-5"AA 16-3"/50AA (Manchester, 1952)		Speed: 32.5 kts.
Armor: 5" belt, 6" turrets, 2" deck, 5" conning tower		Complement: 1255

No.		Hull	Laid down	Launched	Commiss'd	Disposition
55	CLEVELAND	New York SB	1 Jul 40	1 Nov 41	15 Jun 42	Stk. 1 Mar 59, sold 8 Feb 60
56	COLUMBIA	New York SB	19 Aug 40	17 Dec 41	29 Jul 42	Stk. 1 Mar 59, sold 28 Dec 59
57	MONTPELIER	New York SB	2 Dec 40	12 Feb 42	9 Sep 42	Stk. 1 Mar 59, sold 28 Jan 60
58	DENVER	New York SB	26 Dec 40	4 Apr 42	15 Oct 42	Stk. 1 Mar 59, sold 4 Feb 60
59	AMSTERDAM	New York SB	1 May 41	Completed as CV		To CV-22 10 Jan 42
60	SANTA FE	New York SB	7 Jun 41	10 Jun 42	24 Nov 42	Stk. 1 Mar 59, sold 9 Nov 59
61	TALLAHASSEE	New York SB	2 Jun 41	Completed as CV		To CV-23 16 Feb 42
62	BIRMINGHAM	Newport News	17 Feb 41	20 Mar 42	29 Jan 43	Stk. 1 Mar 59, sold 12 Nov 59
63	MOBILE	Newport News	14 Apr 41	15 May 42	24 Mar 43	Stk. 1 Mar 59, sold 21 Dec 59
64	VINCENNES	Quincy	7 Mar 42	17 Jul 43	21 Jan 44	Stk. 1 Apr 66, sunk as target off S. California 28 Oct 69
65	PASADENA	Quincy	6 Feb 43	28 Dec 43	8 Jun 44	Stk. 1 Dec 70, sold 5 Jul 72
66	SPRINGFIELD	Quincy	13 Feb 43	9 Mar 44	9 Sep 44	To CLG-7 23 May 57
67	TOPEKA	Quincy	21 Apr 43	19 Aug 44	23 Dec 44	To CLG-8 23 May 57
76	NEW HAVEN	New York SB	11 Aug 41	Completed as CV		To CV-24 16 Feb 42
77	HUNTINGTON	New York SB	17 Nov 41	Completed as CV		To CV-25 27 Mar 42
78	DAYTON	New York SB	29 Dec 41	Completed as CV		To CV-26 27 Mar 42
79	WILMINGTON	New York SB	16 Mar 42	Completed as CV		To CV-28 2 Jun 42
80	BILOXI	Newport News	9 Jul 41	23 Feb 43	31 Aug 43	Stk. 1 Sep 61, sold 5 Mar 62
81	HOUSTON	Newport News	4 Aug 41	19 Jun 43	20 Dec 43	Stk. 1 Mar 59, sold 1 Jun 61
82	PROVIDENCE	Quincy	27 Jul 43	28 Dec 44	15 May 45	To CLG-6 23 May 57
83	MANCHESTER	Quincy	25 Sep 44	5 Mar 46	29 Oct 46	Stk. 1 Apr 60, sold 16 Nov 60
84	BUFFALO	Kearny	No	No	No	Cancelled 16 Dec 40
85	FARGO	New York SB	Built as CV			To CV-27 27 Mar 42
86	VICKSBURG	Newport News	26 Oct 42	14 Dec 43	12 Jun 44	Stk. 1 Oct 62, sold 25 Aug 64
87	DULUTH	Newport News	9 Nov 42	13 Jan 44	18 Sep 44	Stk. 1 Jan 60, sold 26 Sep 60
88	NEWARK	Kearny	No	No	No	Cancelled 16 Dec 40
89	MIAMI	Cramp	2 Aug 41	8 Dec 42	28 Dec 43	Stk. 1 Sep 61, sold 31 Jul 62
90	ASTORIA	Cramp	6 Sep 41	6 Mar 43	17 May 44	Stk. 1 Nov 69, sold 12 Jan 71
91	OKLAHOMA CITY	Cramp	8 Dec 42	20 Feb 44	22 Dec 44	To CLG-5 23 May 57
92	LITTLE ROCK	Cramp	6 Mar 43	27 Aug 44	17 Jun 45	To CLG-4 23 May 57
93	GALVESTON	Cramp	20 Feb 44	22 Apr 45	No	To CLG-93 4 Feb 56
94	YOUNGSTOWN	Cramp	4 Sep 44	No	No	Cancelled 12 Aug 45
99	BUFFALO	New York SB	Built as CV			To CV-29 2 Jun 42
100	NEWARK	New York SB	Built as CV			To CV-30 2 Jun 42
101	AMSTERDAM	Newport News	3 Mar 43	25 Apr 44	8 Jan 45	Stk. 2 Jan 71, sold 11 Feb 72
102	PORTSMOUTH	Newport News	28 Jun 43	20 Sep 44	25 Jun 45	Stk. 1 Dec 70, sold 21 Mar 74
103	WILKES BARRE	New York SB	14 Dec 42	24 Dec 43	1 Jul 44	Stk. 15 Jan 71, sunk as target off Key West 12 May 72
104	ATLANTA	New York SB	25 Jan 43	6 Feb 44	3 Dec 44	Stk. 1 Apr 70, sunk as target off S. California 1 Oct 70
105	DAYTON	New York SB	8 Mar 43	19 Mar 44	7 Jan 45	Stk. 1 Sep 61, sold 6 Apr 62.

Notes: Fiscal years 1940 (CL 55-56), 1941 (57-67, 76-94, 99-100), 1942 (101-02), and 1943 (103-05). The design of these ships was begun in October 1939 as a modified Helena with two additional 5" mounts on the centerline in place of one 6" turret. The beam was also increased to augment stability. The design left little space or weight for additional small-caliber AA guns, and wartime modifications quickly overloaded the ships. The design was, however, retained for the sake of production efficiency, and the class became the largest single class of cruisers ever laid down for any navy. New York Ship prepared the detailed plans and G. E. designed the engines. CL-84 and CL-88 were cancelled on 16 Dec 40 to allow Kearny to concentrate on building destroyers; they were replaced in the program by CL 99-100. The Fargo (85), Vicksburg (86), and Duluth (87) were originally ordered from Kearny but the contracts were transferred on 4 Feb 42 (CL 86-87) and 5 Feb 42. The Galveston (CL-93) was completed 24 May 46 but not commissioned before her conversion to CLG.
Renamings: CL-64 ex Flint and CL-90 ex Wilkes Barre 16 Oct 42; CL-81 ex Vicksburg 12 Oct 42; CL-86 ex Cheyenne 26 Nov 42.
Reclassifications: Nine ships to CV and six ships to CLG as listed above. The Atlanta was stricken on 1 Oct 62 but reinstated on the list as IX-304 on 15 May 64 for use as a target.

1942

FARGO class

Displacement: 10,000 tons standard
Dimensions: 611'2"(oa.) x 66'6"(e) x 25'1"(max)
Armament: 12-6"/47 12-5"/38AA
Armor: 5" belt, 6" turrets, 2" deck, 5" conning tower

Machinery: 100,000 SHP; G. E. geared turbines, 4 screws
Speed: 32.5 kts.
Complement: 992

No.	Hull	Laid down	Launched	Commiss'd	Disposition
106 FARGO	New York SB	23 Aug 43	25 Feb 45	9 Dec 45	Stk. 1 Mar 70, sold 18 Aug 71
107 HUNTINGTON	New York SB	4 Oct 43	8 Apr 45	23 Feb 46	Stk. 1 Sep 61, sold 17 Apr 62
108 NEWARK	New York SB	17 Jan 44	14 Dec 45	No	Cancelled 12 Aug 45, test hulk, sold 2 Apr 49
109 NEW HAVEN	New York SB	28 Feb 44	No	No	Cancelled 12 Aug 45
110 BUFFALO	New York SB	3 Apr 44	No	No	Cancelled 12 Aug 45
111 WILMINGTON	Cramp	5 Mar 45	No	No	Cancelled 12 Aug 45
112 VALLEJO	New York SB	No	No	No	Cancelled 5 Oct 44
113 HELENA	New York SB	No	No	No	Cancelled 5 Oct 44
114 ROANOKE	New York SB	No	No	No	Cancelled 5 Oct 44
115 Unnamed	New York SB	No	No	No	Cancelled 5 Oct 44
116 TALLAHASSEE	Newport News	31 Jan 44	No	No	Cancelled 12 Aug 45
117 CHEYENNE	Newport News	29 May 44	No	No	Cancelled 12 Aug 45
118 CHATTANOOGA	Newport News	9 Oct 44	No	No	Cancelled 12 Aug 45.

Notes: Fiscal year 1943. The Cleveland class cruiser design was modified in mid-1942 to reduce topweight and improve resistance to underwater damage. The new design had a single funnel and compact superstructure which permitted more effective use of the anti-aircraft defenses. CL 111-115 were cancelled at New York SB on 2 Sep 44 due to a lack of labor at that yard; priority was given instead to carriers and the Alaska and Worcester class cruisers. The Wilmington was reordered from Cramp on 4 Sep 44 but the other four remained cancelled because Cramp also had a backlog. The Newark's unfinished hull was used in underwater explosive tests in Chesapeake Bay in 1948.
Renaming: CL-118 ex Norfolk 18 Aug 44.

JUNEAU class

Displacement: 6000 tons standard
Dimensions: 541'0" (oa.) x 53'2"(e) x 26'6"(max)
Armament: 12-5"/38AA; 12-5"/38 14-3"/50 (Juneau, 1952); none (Spokane as AG)
Armor: 3 3/4" belt, 1 1/4" turrets, 1 1/4" deck, 2 1/2"conning tower

Machinery: 75,000 SHP; Westinghouse geared turbines, 2 screws
Speed: 32.7 kts.
Complement: 673

No.	Hull	Laid down	Launched	Commiss'd	Disposition
119 JUNEAU	Kearny	15 Sep 44	15 Jul 45	15 Feb 46	Stk. 1 Nov 59, sold 29 Apr 60
120 SPOKANE	Kearny	15 Nov 44	22 Sep 45	17 May 46	Stk. 15 Apr 72, sold 17 May 73
121 FRESNO	Kearny	12 Feb 45	5 Mar 46	27 Nov 46	Stk. 1 Apr 65, sold 17 Jun 66.

Notes: Fiscal year 1943. The Atlanta class cruiser design was modified in mid-1942 to reduce topweight and improve resistance to underwater damage. Four of the six 5" gun mounts were lowered one deck and the superstructure was redesigned to improve firing arcs for AA guns. The contracts for these ships were transferred from Bethlehem, San Francisco on 27 Sep 43. Spokane was designated for conversion to test conformal arrary sonar in 1966 but the project was not begun.
Reclassifications: All to anti-aircraft light cruisers (CLAA) 18 Mar 49. CLAA-120 to AG-191 1 Apr 66.

WORCESTER class

Displacement: 14,700 tons standard
Dimensions: 679'6"(oa.) x 70'8"(e) x 25'(max)
Armament: 12-6"/47AA 24-3"/50AA; 12-6"AA 22-3"AA (1955)
Armor: 5" belt, 6 1/2" turrets, 1" + 3 1/2" decks, 5" conning tower

Machinery: 120,000 SHP; G. E. geared turbines, 4 screws
Speed: 33 kts.
Complement: 1401

No.	Hull	Laid down	Launched	Commiss'd	Disposition
144 WORCESTER	New York SB	29 Jan 45	4 Feb 47	26 Jun 48	Stk. 1 Dec 70, sold 5 Jul 72
145 ROANOKE	New York SB	15 May 45	16 Jun 47	4 Apr 49	Stk. 1 Dec 70, sold 22 Feb 72
146 VALLEJO	New York SB	16 Jul 45	No	No	Cancelled 12 Aug 45
147 GARY	New York SB	No	No	No	Cancelled 12 Aug 45.

Notes: Fiscal year 1944. This class was designed to carry a twin dual-purpose automatic 6" turret which the Bureau of Ordnance had begun to develop before the war. The design was developed in response to a 1941 demand for a ship to defend the fleet from high level bombing (possibly inspired by the Crete campaign) and a 1943 requirement to counter large guided missiles (such as those encountered at Salerno).

1945

CL-154 Class

Displacement: 7,370 tons
Dimensions: 591'6"(oa.) x 55'6"(wl.) x 19'0"(mean)
Armament: 12-5"/54
Armor: 3 3/4" belt, 1 1/4" deck

Machinery: 100,000 SHP
Speed: 34.8 kts.
Complement: 692

No.	Hull	Laid down	Launched	Commiss'd	Disposition
154 Unnamed -159	Not assigned	No	No	No	Cancelled 26 Mar 45.

Notes: Fiscal year 1945. These ships were designed around a twin 5"/54 mount initially developed for the Montana class battleships. The new class was first proposed in May 1944 as a follow-on to the Juneau (CL-119) class, which was overweight and ill adapted to further improvement. The design was not quite complete and builders had not been selected when the 1945 building program was cancelled on 26 Mar 45.

Tactical Command Ships (CLC)

1948

NORTHAMPTON

Displacement: 12,320 tons (light)
Dimensions: 677'2"(oa.) x 70'3"(wl.) x 19'2"(mean)
Armament: 4-5"/54AA 8-3"/50AA; 4-5" 8-3"/70AA (1956); 4-5" (1962); 1-5" (1970)
Armor: none

Machinery: 120,000 SHP; G. E. geared turbines, 4 screws
Speed: 33 kts.
Complement: 1675

No.	Hull	Laid down	Launched	Commiss'd	Disposition
1 NORTHAMPTON	Quincy	31 Aug 44	27 Jan 51	7 Mar 53	Stk. 1 Dec 77, sold Mar 80.

Notes: Fiscal year 1949. Originally a heavy cruiser of the Oregon City class, she was cancelled on 12 Aug 45 when 56.2 percent complete. She was reinstated on the list on 24 Jul 46 and construction resumed to a new design as a tactical command ship on 1 Jul 48. Capable of acting as either a fleet flagship or an amphibious force flagship, she had an extra deck added to her hull for command and control spaces. She was converted into a National Emergency Command Post Afloat (NECPA) in 1961 with the designation CC (Command Ship).
Reclassifications: From CA-125 1 Nov 47; to CC-1 15 Sep 61.

Guided Missile Heavy Cruisers (CAG)

1952

BOSTON class

Displacement: 13,300 tons light
Dimensions: 674'(oa) x 71'(e) x 29'(max)
Armament: 6-8" 10-5"AA 12-3"AA 4-Terrier-SAM (CAG-1, 1955); 6-8" 10-5"AA 8-3"AA 4-Terrier-SAM (CAG-2, 1956; CAG-1, 1957); 6-8" 10-5"AA 8-3"AA (CA-70, ca. 1971)
Armor: 6" belt, 8" turrets, 2 1/2" deck

Machinery: 120,000 SHP; G. E. geared turbines, 4 screws
Speed: 33 kts.
Complement: 1730

No.	Conv. yard	Conv. began	Recommissioned	Disposition
1 BOSTON	New York SB	11 Apr 52	1 Nov 55	Stk. 4 Jan 74, sold 28 Mar 75
2 CANBERRA	New York SB	30 Jun 52	15 Jun 56	Stk. 31 Jul 78, sold 31 Jul 80

Notes: Fiscal year 1952. In 1952-56, the Boston and Canberra were converted to the Navy's first anti-aircraft guided missile ships. The reworking, to the SCB-48 design, replaced the after 8-inch turret with missile launchers. Because of the limitations of their early model Terrier systems both ships reverted to CAs in 1968, and the Canberra later had her missile equipment removed. One additional CAG conversion was authorized in fiscal year 1956 but was dropped to save funds.
Reclassifications: From CA 69-70 4 Jan 52, back to CA 69-70 1 May 68.

Guided Missile Light Cruisers (CLG)

1955

GALVESTON class

Displacement: 10,670 tons light
Dimensions: 610'(oa) x 66'4"(e) x 26'(max)
Armament: 6-6"/47 6-5"/38AA 2-Talos-SAM (Galveston); 3-6"
  2-5"AA 2-Talos-SAM (others)
Armor: 5" belt, 6" turrets, 2" deck

Machinery: 100,000 SHP; G. E. geared
  turbines, 4 screws
Speed: 32 kts.
Complement: 1200

No.		Conv. yard	Conv. began	Recommissioned	Disposition
3	GALVESTON	Philadelphia	15 Aug 56	28 May 58	Stk. 21 Dec 73, sold 16 May 75
4	LITTLE ROCK	New York SB	30 Jan 57	3 Jun 60	Stk. 22 Nov 76, memorial at Buffalo, N.Y. 21 Jun 77
5	OKLAHOMA CITY	Beth-SF	21 May 57	7 Sep 60	Stk. 15 Dec 79.

Notes: Fiscal years 1956 (CLG-3) and 1957 (4-5). They were converted from Cleveland class light cruisers according to the SCB-140 (Galveston) and 140A designs. They differ from the Providence conversions only in the missiles mounted. CLG 4-5 were converted as fleet flagships without their second 6" turret.
Renaming: CLG-5 dropped her name as of 2 May 85.
Reclassifications: Galveston ex CLG-93 23 May 57, from CL-93 4 Feb 56; others from CL-92 and 91 respectively 23 May 57.

1956

PROVIDENCE class

Displacement: 10,670 tons light
Dimensions: 610'(oa.) x 66'4"(e) x 25'(max)
Armament: 6-6"/47 6-5"/38AA 2-Terrier-SAM (Topeka); 3-6"
  2-5"AA 2-Terrier-SAM (others)
Armor: 5" belt, 6" turrets, 2" deck

Machinery: 100,000 SHP; G. E. geared
  turbines, 4 screws
Speed: 32 kts.
Complement: 1200

No.		Conv. yard	Conv. began	Recommissioned	Disposition
6	PROVIDENCE	New York	1 Jun 57	17 Sep 59	Stk. 31 Jul 78, sold 31 Jul 80
7	SPRINGFIELD	Quincy	1 Aug 57	2 Jul 60	Stk. 31 Jul 78, sold 11 Mar 80
8	TOPEKA	Boston	19 Aug 57	26 Mar 60	Stk. 1 Dec 73, sold 28 Mar 75.

Notes: Fiscal year 1957. These SCB-146 (Topeka) and 146A conversions differ from the Galveston class only in their missiles. The conversion of the Springfield was completed by Boston Naval Shipyard when Quincy was closed by a strike. The Pasadena (CL-65) was initially slated for conversion at Boston to CLG-6.
Reclassifications: From CL-82, 66, and 67 respectively 23 May 57.

Nuclear Powered Guided Missile Cruisers (CGN)

1955

LONG BEACH

Displacement: 14,200 tons light
Dimensions: 721'3"(oa.) x 73'3"(e) x 31'(max)
Armament: 4-Terrier-SAM 2-Talos-SAM 1-ASROC; 2-5"/38AA 4-
  Terrier 2-Talos 1-ASROC (1961); 2-5"AA 4-Terrier 2-Talos 1-
  ASROC 6-12.75"T (1963); 2-5"AA 4-Terrier 1-ASROC 6-12.75"T
  (1978); 2-5"AA 4-Terrier 8-Harpoon-SSM 1-ASROC 6-12.75"T
  (1982); Same plus 8-Tomahawk-SSM (1985)
Armor: Unknown

Machinery: 80,000 SHP; 2 Westinghouse
  reactors (C1W) with G. E. geared
  turbines, 2 screws
Speed: 30.5 kts.
Complement: 1060

No.		Hull	Laid down	Launched	Commiss'd	Disposition
9	LONG BEACH	Quincy	2 Dec 57	14 Jul 59	9 Sep 61	USN.

Notes: Fiscal year 1957. The world's first nuclear surface combat vessel, she was the SCB-169 design. The original concept was for an enlarged Terrier missile frigate to escort the nuclear carrier Enterprise, but it quickly grew to include Talos missiles and a capability to operate

independently. A plan to install 8 Polaris SSM was dropped. She was completed with the Navy Tactical Data System (NTDS). Plans to modernize her with the Aegis radar/fire control system were cancelled in December 1976. Her Talos missiles were removed around 1979 and she received an austere modernization in 1982.
Reclassification: Ex CGN-160 1 Jul 57, ex CLGN-160 6 Dec 56.

Guided Missile Cruisers (CG)

1957

ALBANY class

Displacement: 13,700 tons light	Machinery: 120,000 SHP; G. E. geared
Dimensions: 674'(oa.) x 71'(e) x 30'(max)	turbines, 4 screws
Armament: 2-5"/38AA 4-Talos-SAM 4-Tartar-SAM 1-ASROC; 2-5"AA	Speed: 31.5 kts.
4-Talos-SAM 4-Tartar-SAM 1-ASROC 6-12.75"T (1968)	Complement: 1155
Armor: 6" belt, 2 1/2" deck	

No.		Conv. yard	Conv. began	Recommissioned	Disposition
10	ALBANY	Boston	2 Jan 59	3 Nov 62	Stk. 30 Jun 85, sold Aug 90
11	CHICAGO	Puget Sd.	1 Jul 59	2 May 64	Stk. 31 Jan 84
12	COLUMBUS	Puget Sd.	1 Jun 59	1 Dec 62	Stk. 9 Aug 76, sold 3 Oct 77.

Notes: Fiscal years 1958 (CG-10) and 1959 (11-12). "Double-ended" conversions of Baltimore and Oregon City class heavy cruisers, they were originally CA-123, 136, and 74 respectively. The Oregon City (CA-122) was originally slated for conversion to CG-10 but was replaced by the Albany early in the planning process. CG 11-12 were originally included with CG-10 in Fiscal year 1958 but were dropped in June 1958 because of fund shortages. They would have been the Chicago, assigned to the San Francisco Naval Shipyard and cancelled there 9 Jun 58, and the Fall River (CA-131), assigned to Puget Sound. The Albany and Chicago were reclassified CG 10-11 on 1 Nov 58 and the Fall River was to have been reclassified CG-12 on the same date, but the Columbus was substituted on 9 Oct 58 and was reclassified CG-12 on 30 Sep 59. SCB-173 design. Plans to include Regulus SSM in their armament were abandoned. One more conversion (SCB-173A, with Polaris instead of Regulus SSM) was authorized for fiscal year 1960 but was cancelled to provide additional funds for Polaris submarines; candidate ships were the Rochester and Bremerton. The Chicago was completed with an early version of NTDS, and the Albany received this system as part of an AAW modernization in 1967-9.
Reclassifications: CG 10-11 from CA-123 and 136 respectively 1 Nov 58; CG-12 from CA-74 30 Sep 59.

Gunboats (Seagoing) (PG)

1885

YORKTOWN class

Displacement: 1700 tons	Machinery: 3400 IHP; 2 horizontal,
Dimensions: 230' x 36'(e) x 16'7"(max)	triple-expansion engines, 2 screws
Armament: 6-6"/30; 6-5"/40 (Yorktown, 1913)	Speed: 16 kts.
Armor: 2" conning tower	Complement: 197

No.		Hull	Machinery	Laid down	Launched	Commiss'd	Disposition
1	YORKTOWN	Cramp	Cramp	14 May 87	28 Apr 88	23 Apr 89	For sale 1919, sold 30 Sep 21
3	CONCORD	DelawareR	Quintard	May 88	8 Mar 90	14 Feb 91	Stk. 31 Dec 15, sold 28 Jun 29
4	BENNINGTON	DelawareR	Quintard	Jun 88	3 Jun 90	20 Jun 91	Stk. 10 Sep 10, sold 14 Nov 10.

Notes: Fiscal years 1886 (PG-1) and 1888 (3-4). This class represented an attempt to produce the smallest possible cruising ship with good seakeeping qualities and a heavy battery. They were sometimes unofficially called 3rd class cruisers. They were also referred to at times as torpedo gunboats or torpedo cruisers, and their design included six torpedo tubes which were never fitted. The Bureau of Construction & Repair produced the hull plans and Cramp those for the machinery. All exceeded their designed speed of 16 knots on trials, the Bennington reaching 17.5 knots. The contracts for the Concord and Bennington were let to N. F. Palmer & Co., proprietors of Quintard, who sub-let the hulls to Delaware River. The Concord was stricken on 12 Jul 10 but was reinstated and served as a training ship 1910-14. She was on loan to the Coast Guard as a quarantine vessel from 22 Apr 15 to 19 Mar 29. The Bennington was sunk by a boiler explosion on 21 Jul 05. She served the Matson line as a water barge at Honolulu from 1912 until 1924 and was subsequently scuttled off Oahu.

The gunboat *Bennington* (PG-4) ca. 1891. (NH 63248)

The gunboat *Erie* (PG-50) photographed by the New York Navy Yard on 19 October 1936. (NH 54262)

PETREL

Displacement: 890 tons
Dimensions: 188'(oa.) x 31'(e) x 13'1"(max)
Armament: 4-6"/30; 4-4"/40 (1911)
Armor: 1" shields

Machinery: 1350 IHP; 2 horizontal,
  compound engines, 2 screws
Speed: 11.5 kts.
Complement: 132

No.		Hull	Machinery	Laid down	Launched	Commiss'd	Disposition
2	PETREL	Columbian		27 Aug 87	13 Oct 88	10 Dec 89	Stk. 16 Apr 20, sold 1 Nov 20.

Notes: Fiscal year 1886. This gunboat was a small, slow cruising ship armed with cruiser weapons. A Navy Department design, she proved to be a satisfactory vessel although handicapped by a moderate coal capacity and a low speed. She failed to reach her designed speed of 13 knots.

1888

BANCROFT

Displacement: 839 tons
Dimensions: 189'6"(oa.) x 32'(e) x 12'11"(max)
Armament: 4-4"/40 2-18"T; 4-4" 1-18"T (1898); 4-4" (1901)

Machinery: 1300 IHP; 2 vertical,
  triple-expansion engines, 2 screws
Speed: 13 kts.
Complement: 130

	Hull	Machinery	Laid down	Launched	Commiss'd	Disposition
BANCROFT	Moore		Feb 91	30 Apr 92	3 Mar 93	Stk. 30 Jun 06, to Treasury Dept. same date.

Notes: Fiscal year 1889. She was built as a practice vessel for the U.S. Naval Academy which could also be used for other purposes in case of emergencies. She made 14.37 knots on trials. She later served as the Coast Guard's training ship Itasca.

1889

MACHIAS class

Displacement: 1177 tons
Dimensions: 212'4"(oa.) x 32'(e) x 14'0"(max)
Armament: Machias--8-4"/40; 4-4" (1915);
  Castine--8-4"/40; 2-6# 1-18"T (1908); 2-4" (1913)

Machinery: 2000 IHP; 2 vertical,
  expansion engines, 2 screws
Speed: 15.5 kts.
Complement: 154

No.		Builder	Laid down	Launched	Commiss'd	Disposition
5	MACHIAS	Bath	Feb 91	8 Dec 91	20 Jul 93	For sale 1919, sold 29 Oct 20
6	CASTINE	Bath	Feb 91	11 May 92	22 Oct 94	Ordered sold 19 May 20, sold 5 Aug 21.

Notes: Fiscal year 1890. These ships were authorized by Congress as "cruisers or gun-boats" of 800 to 1200 tons. They were larger and faster than the Petrel but had only a gunboat armament of 4" guns. They were unstable when first put into service and so were lengthened 14'amidships at the New York Navy Yard. (The dimensions above are for the lengthened vessels.) The light armor on their gun sponsons was also removed. They were designed to carry 1-18"T but the Machias never carried hers. Bath built both the hulls and the machinery. The Castine served as a training vessel 1907-09 and as a submarine tender thereafter. After being sold, the Machias served in the Mexican navy to around 1935 as the Agua Prieta and the Castine served as a merchant ship.

1893

NASHVILLE

Displacement: 1371 tons
Dimensions: 233'8"(oa.) x 38'2" x 12'7"(max)
Armament: 8-4"/40
Armor: 2 1/4" shields

Machinery: 1790 IHP; 2 vertical
  quadruple-expansion engines, 2
  screws
Speed: 16 kts.
Complement: 169

No.		Builder	Laid down	Launched	Commiss'd	Disposition
7	NASHVILLE	Newport News	9 Aug 94	19 Oct 95	19 Aug 97	Ordered sold 20 Apr 21, sold 20 Oct 21.

Notes: Fiscal year 1894. A shallow-draft, lightly-armored ship built for service in the Far East, she was a departmental design whose hull and machinery were both provided by Newport News. The design called for a bow torpedo tube but it was never mounted. She operated as a training vessel 1909-13.
Renaming: It was originally intended to name her Albatross but Nashville was substituted before launching.

WILMINGTON class

Displacement: 1392 tons
Dimensions: 251'10"(oa.) x 40'2"(e) x 9'10"(max)
Armament: 8-4"/40; 2-4"/50 (Wilmington, 1941); 1-5"/38 1-
  4"/50 1-3"/50 (Dover ex Wilmington, 1945)
Armor: 1" belt, 2 1/2" shields

Machinery: 1600 IHP; 2 vertical
  triple-expansion engines, 2 screws
Speed: 15.5 kts.
Complement: 170

No.		Builder	Laid down	Launched	Commiss'd	Disposition
8	WILMINGTON	Newport News	8 Oct 94	19 Oct 95	13 May 97	Stk. 8 Jan 46, sold 30 Dec 46
9	HELENA	Newport News	11 Oct 94	30 Jan 96	8 Jul 97	Stk. 27 May 32, sold 7 Jul 32.

Notes: Fiscal year 1894. They were a Navy Department design intended for use on the lower part of the Yangtse River in China. Thus they combined light draft with powerful engines and a large berthing capacity to permit the carrying of either refugees or a landing party. Newport News provided the machinery as well as the hulls. The design called for a torpedo tube which was never fitted. The Wilmington served as a training vessel after 1922.
Renamings: Intended to be named Penguin and Porpoise respectively but their names were changed before launching. Wilmington became Dover on 27 Jan 41.
Reclassification: Wilmington to "unclassified" (IX-30) 26 Jun 22

1895

ANNAPOLIS class

Displacement: 1010 tons
Dimensions: 203'6"(Annapolis, oa.), 204'5"(others, oa.) x
  36'(e) x 13'1"(max)
Armament: Annapolis--6-4"/40; 4-6# (1907); 6-4" (1912);
  1-4"(1920); none (1929);
  Vicksburg--6-4"/40; none (1920);
  Newport--6-4"/40; none (1911); 1-4" 2-3"/50 (1918);
  2-3"(1924); none (1929);
  Princeton--6-4"/40; 4-6# (1915); none (1918)

Machinery: 800 IHP; vertical triple-
  expansion engine, 1 screw
Speed: 12 kts.
Complement: 135

No.		Builder	Laid down	Launched	Commiss'd	Disposition
10	ANNAPOLIS	Nixon	Apr 96	23 Dec 96	20 Jul 97	To Maritime Commission 11 Apr 40, stk. 30 Jun 40
11	VICKSBURG	Bath	Mar 96	5 Dec 96	23 Oct 97	To Coast Guard 2 May 21
12	NEWPORT	Bath	Mar 96	5 Dec 96	5 Oct 97	Stk. 12 Oct 31, to city of Aberdeen, Wash., 24 Oct 35
13	PRINCETON	Dialogue	May 96	3 Jun 97	27 May 98	Stk. 22 Jul 19, sold 13 Nov 19.

Notes: Fiscal year 1896. They were low-powered cruising gunboats which had a full barkentine rig, single screws, uncoupling engines, and composite hulls. The Annapolis reached 13.17 knots on trials. She served as a training vessel 1899-1901 and 1919-39 (Pennsylvania Marine School Ship). After transfer to the Maritime Commission she continued to serve as the school ship Keystone State until 1950. The Vicksburg was a training vessel in 1899 and 1913-17 and became the Coast Guard's Alexander Hamilton in 1921. She was decommissioned in 1930 and became the station ship Beta in 1939. She was returned to the Navy on 12 Mar 45 and was sold by the Maritime Commission for the Navy on 28 Mar 46. The Newport was a training ship in 1899-1901 and 1905-31 and was given to the city of Aberdeen, Wash. as a naval reserve training ship by an Act of Congress of 14 May 34. The Princeton was stricken on 3 May 1917 and loaned to the Shipping Board. She was returned and recommissioned on 17 Jan 18.
Reclassifications: Annapolis and Newport to "unclassified" (IX-1 and IX-19 respectively) 1 Jul 21, Vicksburg to "unclassified" (no number) same date.

WHEELING class

Displacement: 990 tons
Dimensions: 189'7"(oa.) x 34' x 12'11"(max)
Armament: Marietta--6-4"/40; 4-4" (1918); none (1919);
  Wheeling--6-4"/40; 4-4" (1918); 2-3# (1920); none (1921);
  4-4" (1929); 1-4"/50 (1938); 7-4" (1943); none (1945)

Machinery: 1100 IHP; 2 vertical
  triple-expansion engines, 2 screws
Speed: 12 kts.
Complement: 144

No.		Builder	Laid down	Launched	Commiss'd	Disposition
14	WHEELING	Union	11 Apr 96	18 Mar 97	10 Aug 97	Stk. 28 Mar 46, sold 5 Oct 46
15	MARIETTA	Union	13 Apr 96	18 Mar 97	1 Sep 97	Ordered sold 12 Jan 20, sold 25 Mar 20.

Notes: Fiscal year 1896. This was a companion design to the Annapolis class in which steam was emphasized instead of sail--it had two screws and only steadying sails. The hulls were designed by the Navy Department and the machinery by Union, who built it. The ships had composite hulls. The Marietta reached 13.03 knots on trials. The Wheeling served as a training vessel after 1920
Reclassification: Wheeling to "unclassified" (IX-28) 1 Jul 21.

1898

TOPEKA

Displacement: 2755 tons
Dimensions: 259'4"(oa.) x 35'(e) x 19'5"(max)
Armament: 6-4"; none (1899)

Machinery: 2000 IHP; 2 horizontal compound engines, 2 screws
Speed: 16 kts.
Complement: 152

	Hull	Machinery	Laid down	Launched	Commiss'd	Disposition
TOPEKA	Howaldt	Howaldt ?	1881	1883	2 Apr 98	Stk. 2 Jan 30, sold 13 May 30.

Notes: She was built for Peru as the Callao (ex Diogenes) but was never taken over. She later passed into the hands of the Thames Iron Works under the name Diogenes and was sold by them to the United States 2 Apr 98. She was reengined in 1916-17 with 2000 SHP DeLaval geared turbines. After 1901 she served as a training, receiving, or prison ship except for one cruise in 1919. She was ordered sold on 22 Mar 22, withdrawn from the sale list on 29 Sep 22 for lack of a buyer, and put back in service on 2 Jul 23 as a naval reserve training ship. She was a sister to the Peruvian Lima (ex-Socrates).
Reclassifications: To PG-35 17 Jul 20, to "unclassified" (no number) 1 Jul 21.

1899

DON JUAN DE AUSTRIA

Displacement: 1130 tons
Dimensions: 215'6"(oa.) x 32'(m) x 15'8"(max)
Armament: 4-4.7" 3-14"T (1898); 4-5" (1900); 6-3" (1906); 2-4"/40 (1911); 6-3# (1916); 4-4"/40 (1918)

Machinery: 941 IHP, horizontal compound engine, 1 screw
Speed: 12.2 kts.
Complement: 153

	Builder	Launched	Acquired	Commiss'd	Disposition
DON JUAN DE AUSTRIA	Cartagena	23 Jan 87	1 May 98	11 Apr 00	Stk. 23 Jul 19, sold 16 Oct 19.

Notes: Formerly a small Spanish cruiser of the same name, she was sunk at the battle of Manila Bay on 1 May 98. She was raised and reconditioned by the Hongkong and Whampoa Dock Co. under a Navy contract approved on 31 Oct 98. She served as a training vessel after 1907. She became the merchant ship Dewey in 1921 and was scrapped in 1932.

ISLA DE LUZON class

Displacement: 1030 tons
Dimensions: 196'9"(oa.) x 30'1"(e) x 12'8"(max)
Armament: 4-4.7" 3-14"T (1898); 4-4"/40 3-14"T (1900); 4-4" (both, 1904); 6-3" (Cuba, 1906); 2-4"/40 (Cuba, 1911); 4-3# (Luzon, 1918)
Armor: 2 1/2" deck

Machinery: 516 IHP (Luzon), 844 IHP (Cuba), horizontal triple-expansion engines, 2 screws
Speed: 11.23 kts. (Luzon), 13.08 kts. (Cuba)
Complement: 145

	Builder	Launched	Acquired	Commiss'd	Disposition
ISLA DE LUZON	Elswick	13 Nov 86	1 May 98	31 Jan 00	Stk. 23 Jul 19, sold 10 Mar 20
ISLA DE CUBA	Elswick	11 Dec 86	1 May 98	11 Apr 00	Stk. 17 May 12, to Venezuela 1912 as Mariscal Sucre.

Notes: Formerly small Spanish cruisers of the same names, they were sunk at the battle of Manila Bay on 1 May 98. They were raised on 2 Dec 98 and reconditioned by the Hongkong and Whampoa Dock Co. under a Navy contract approved on 31 Oct 98. They were used as training vessels after 1903 and 1907 respectively. The Isla de Luzon became the merchant salvage ship Reviver and was scrapped in 1940; the Isla de Cuba was scrapped in 1940.

ELCANO

Displacement: 620 tons
Dimensions: 165'6"(oa.) x 26' x 11'9"(max)
Armament: 3-4.7" 1-14"T (1898); 4-4"/40 (1902)

Machinery: 435 IHP, vertical compound engines, 2 screws
Speed: 11 kts.
Complement: 103

	Builder	Launched	Acquired	Commiss'd	Disposition
ELCANO	Carraca	28 Jan 84	9 Nov 99	20 Nov 02	Stk. 4 Oct 28, sunk as target.

Notes: As the Spanish gunboat Elcano, this ship spent the entire Spanish-American War at Ilo Ilo in the Philippines. She and 11 small gunboats were sold to the U.S. Army by the departing Spanish authorities on 15 Mar 99 and were resold by the Army to the Navy on 9 Nov 99. The President authorized her use as a target on 29 Dec 27.
Reclassification: To PG-38 17 Jul 20. The hull numbers PG-37 and PG 39-42 were assigned to ex-Spanish small gunboats.

1902

DUBUQUE class

Displacement: 1085 tons
Dimensions: 200'5"(oa.) x 35'(e) x 13'4"(max)
Armament: Dubuque--6-4"/40; 4-6# (1916); 2-4" (1918); 4-4"
  1-3"AA (1920); none (1921); 4-4"/50 1-3"/23 (1941);
  1-5"/38AA 2-4"/50 1-3"/50AA (1943);
  Paducah--6-4"/40; 4-4" (1916); none (1919); 4-4" 1-3"AA
  (1920); none (1922); 4-4"/50 1-3"/23 (1941); 1-5"/38AA
  2-4"/50 1-3"/50AA (1943)

Machinery: 1220 IHP; 2 vertical, triple-expansion engines, 2 screws
Speed: 13 kts.
Complement: 156

No.		Hull	Machinery	Laid down	Launched	Commiss'd	Disposition
17	DUBUQUE	Gas Engine		22 Sep 03	15 Aug 04	3 Jun 05	Stk. 17 Sep 45, sold 23 Nov 46
18	PADUCAH	Gas Engine		22 Sep 03	11 Oct 04	2 Sep 05	Stk. 17 Sep 45, sold 19 Dec 46 by War Shipping Admin.

Notes: Fiscal year 1903. Designed for police and surveying duties in the Caribbean, they were composite hulled vessels which served in many capacities during their long lives. The Dubuque served as a training vessel 1911-15 and as a surveying vessel 1920-21. She was placed on the sale list 25 Nov 21 but was removed 28 Mar 22 and served as a training vessel 1922-45. The Paducah was a surveying vessel 1920-21 and a training vessel 1922-45. Both later became merchant ships.
Reclassifications: To miscellaneous auxiliaries (AG 6-7 respectively) 17 Jul 20; to "unclassified" (IX 9 and 23) 24 Apr 22; and back to gunboats (PG 17-18) 4 Nov 40.

1911

SACRAMENTO

Displacement: 1425 tons
Dimensions: 226'2"(oa.) x 40'10"(e) x 12'7"(max)
Armament: 3-4"/50; 2-4" (1940); 1-4" 1-3"/50AA (1945)

Machinery: 836 IHP; vertical, triple-expansion engine, 1 screw
Speed: 12.5 kts.
Complement: 164

No.		Hull	Machinery	Laid down	Launched	Commiss'd	Disposition
19	SACRAMENTO	Cramp		30 Apr 13	21 Feb 14	26 Apr 14	Stk. 12 Mar 46, sold 23 Aug 47 by War Shipping Admin.

Notes: Fiscal year 1912. The "peace cruisers" of the Denver class were effective in patrolling the Caribbean but were large and expensive to operate. This type was developed as a less expensive oceangoing gunboat in which size, cost, and complement were halved by eliminating the requirement to carry troops and by reducing the ship's armament. The ship had good seakeeping qualities and ample coal capacity. She later became a merchant ship.
Reclassification: To "unclassified" 17 Feb 40, to PG-19 4 Nov 40.

1915

ASHEVILLE class

Displacement: 1575 tons
Dimensions: 241'2"(oa.) x 41'3"(e) x 12'9"(max)
Armament: 3-4"/50; 5-3"/50AA (1945)

Machinery: 800 SHP; geared turbines, 1 screw
Speed: 12 kts.
Complement: 185

No.		Hull	Machinery	Laid down	Launched	Commiss'd	Disposition
21	ASHEVILLE	Charleston		9 Jun 17	4 Jul 18	6 Jul 20	Sunk by Japanese squadron south of Java 3 Mar 42
22	TULSA	Charleston		9 Dec 19	25 Aug 22	3 Dec 23	Stk. 17 Apr 46, sold 12 Oct 46.

Notes: Fiscal years 1916 (PG-21) and 1918. Gunboats were in great demand in Mexican and Central American waters, and these ships were built to a slightly modified Sacramento design with additional length for an extra boiler. This boiler facilitated boiler maintenance underway and provided additional endurance. The Asheville, initially a coal burner, was converted to oil fuel in 1922.
Renaming: Tulsa to Tacloban 27 Nov 44.

1917

SCHURZ

Displacement: 1590 tons
Dimensions: 249'4" x 33'10" x 15'(max)
Armament: 8-3.9" 2-14"T (1917); 4-5"/51 (1917)

Machinery: 2930 IHP, triple-expansion
  engines, 1 screw
Speed: 16 kts.
Complement: 217

	Builder	Launched	Acquired	Commiss'd	Disposition
SCHURZ	Wilhelmshaven	18 Oct 94	7 Apr 17	15 Sep 17	Sunk in collision 21 Jun 18 off North Carolina.

Notes: Formerly the small German cruiser Geier, she was interned at Honolulu on 7 Nov 14 after a commerce raiding cruise. Her German crew sabotaged her machinery in February 1917 and decommissioned her on 16 Mar 17. She was seized in April after the U.S. entered World War I. She was sunk in a collision with the merchant ship Florida.
Renaming: Ex Geier 9 Jun 17.

1933

ERIE class

Displacement: 2000 tons standard
Dimensions: 328'6"(oa.) x 41'3"(e) x 14'10"(max)
Armament: 4-6"/47
Armor: 3 1/2" belt, 1" shields, 1 1/4" deck, 4" conning tower

Machinery: 6200 SHP; geared turbines,
  2 screws
Speed: 20 kts.
Complement: 243

No.		Hull	Machinery	Laid down	Launched	Commiss'd	Disposition
50	ERIE	New York		17 Dec 34	29 Jan 36	1 Jul 36	Torpedoed by German U-163 off Curacao 12 Nov 42
51	CHARLESTON	Charleston		27 Oct 34	25 Feb 36	8 Jul 36	Stk. 12 Mar 48, to Maritime Commission 25 Mar 48.

Notes: Fiscal year 1934. The London Naval Treaty of 1930 placed no restrictions on surface ships under 2000 tons with guns of up to 6.1" and speeds up to 20 knots. This class represented an effort to obtain some peacetime cruising and wartime trade protection and fleet support capabilities without using treaty-limited cruiser tonnage. The burned-out hulk of the Erie was beached at Willemstad, Curacao, and remained there until 1952. The Charleston was turned over by the Maritime Commission to the Massachusetts Maritime Academy on 25 Mar 48 as a training ship but was soon replaced by a merchant ship.

Dispatch Vessels

1883

DOLPHIN

Displacement: 1485 tons
Dimensions: 256'6"(oa.) x 32'(e) x 17'2"(max)
Armament: 1-6"/30; 2-4"/40 (1891); 3-4" (1898); 2-4" (1899);
  6-6# (1913); 2-3"/50 (1918); 1-4"/50 (1919)

Machinery: 2240 IHP; vertical
  compound engine, 1 screw
Speed: 15.5 kts.
Complement: 115

	Hull	Machinery	Laid down	Launched	Commiss'd	Disposition
DOLPHIN	Roach	Morgan	11 Oct 83	12 Apr 84	8 Dec 85	To sale list 26 Oct 21, sold 25 Feb 22.

Notes: Fiscal year 1884. Ordered with the ABC cruisers. Her hull was designed by F. L. Fernald. She was deficient as a combatant ship in that her engines were exposed above the waterline. When built she was the second fastest sea-going steamer of her size in the United States. After being sold, she served in the Mexican navy to around 1927 as the Plan de Guadalupe.
Reclassification: To PG-24 1 Jul 21.

Armored Rams

1889

KATAHDIN

Displacement: 2155 tons
Dimensions: 251'(oa.) x 43'5"(e) x 16'(max)
Armament: 4-6#
Armor: 6" sides and deck

Machinery: 4800 IHP; 2 horizontal triple-expansion engines, 2 screws
Speed: 16 kts.
Complement: 97

	Hull	Machinery	Laid down	Launched	Commiss'd	Disposition
KATAHDIN	Bath	Bath	Jul 91	4 Feb 93	8 Jun 96	Stk. 9 Jul 09, sunk as target, Rappahannock Spit, Va., 1916.

Notes: Fiscal year 1890. She was designed by Rear Admiral Daniel Ammen for use as a harbor defense vessel and so had a very limited range. The original plans called for a 2050 ton vessel, 243'(oa.) x 43'5"(e) x 15'(max), with 4800 IHP vertical, triple-expansion engines. She was designed for 17 knots but made only 16.11 on trials. When stricken, she was transferred to the Bureau of Ordnance for use as a target (Target A). Her wreck was raised in 1950.

Torpedo Boats

1886

CUSHING

Displacement: 116 tons
Dimensions: 138'9"(oa.) x 15'1"(e) x 5'3"(max)
Armament: 3-6#; 3-6# 3-18"T (1892)

Machinery: 1720 IHP; 2 vertical quadruple-expansion engines, 2 screws
Speed: 22.5 kts. (trials)
Complement: 22

No.		Hull	Machinery	Laid down	Launched	Commiss'd	Disposition
1	CUSHING	Herreshoff		Apr 88	23 Jan 90	22 Apr 90	Stk. 8 Apr 12, sunk as target 24 Sep 20.

Notes: Fiscal year 1887. Designed by Nathaniel Herreshoff, she was built of galvanized steel and carried Howell torpedoes. Although highly maneuverable, she was effective only in smooth waters. Her trial speed fell above her contract speed of 22 knots but below her designed speed of 23 knots.

1890

ERICSSON

Displacement: 120 tons
Dimensions: 149'7"(oa.) x 15'7"(e) x 4'9"(mean)
Armament: 4-1# 3-18"T

Machinery: 1800 IHP; 2 vertical quadruple-expansion engines, 2 screws
Speed: 24 kts.
Complement: 22

No.		Hull	Machinery	Laid down	Launched	Commiss'd	Disposition
2	ERICSSON	Iowa	Iowa	21 Jul 92	12 May 94	18 Feb 97	Stk. 8 Apr 12, sunk as target.

Notes: Fiscal year 1891. A modified Cushing built to Navy plans.

1894

FOOTE class

Displacement: 142 tons
Dimensions: 161'7"(oa.) x 16'1"(e) x 5'(mean)
Armament: 4-1# 3-18"T; 3-1# 3-18"T (1909); 3-1# (1915)

Machinery: 2000 IHP; 2 vertical quadruple-expansion engines, 2 screws
Speed: 24.5 kts.
Complement: 20

The torpedo boat *Cushing* (No. 1). (NH 69186)

The destroyer *Stewart* (DD-13) with the *Preble* (DD-12) at Guaymas, Mexico, on 26 December 1915. (NH 92183)

No.		Hull	Machinery	Laid down	Launched	Commiss'd	Disposition
3	FOOTE	Columbian		1 May 96	1 Oct 96	7 Aug 97	Stk. 28 Oct 19, sold 19 Jul 20
4	RODGERS	Columbian		6 May 96	10 Nov 96	2 Apr 98	Stk. 28 Oct 19, sold 19 Jul 20
5	WINSLOW	Columbian		8 May 96	6 Jan 97	29 Dec 97	Stk. 12 Jul 10, sold 3 Jan 11.

Notes: Fiscal year 1895. Designed as somewhat enlarged versions of the Ericsson, they were built to Navy plans. The Rodgers's commissioning was delayed by the breaking of a crank shaft during trials. Trial speeds were 24.53, 24.49, and 24.82 knots respectively. The Rodgers and Foote served as training vessels 1910-17 and 1911-17 respectively.
Renamings: TB 3-4 to Coast Torpedo Boat No. 1 and 2 respectively 1 Aug 18.

1895

PORTER class

Displacement: 165 tons
Dimensions: 175'6"(oa.) x 17'9"(e) x 6'9"(max)
Armament: 4-1# 3-18"T; 3-1# 3-18"T (1909); 3-1# (1915)

Machinery: 3400 IHP; 2 vertical quadruple-expansion engines, 2 screws
Speed: 27.5 kts.
Complement: 24

No.		Hull	Machinery	Laid down	Launched	Commiss'd	Disposition
6	PORTER	Herreshoff		Feb 96	9 Sep 96	20 Feb 97	Stk. 6 Nov 12, sold
7	DUPONT	Herreshoff		Feb 96	30 Mar 97	23 Sep 97	Stk. 28 Oct 19, sold 19 Jul 20.

Notes: Fiscal year 1896. Designed by Nathaniel Herreshoff, they reached trial speeds of 28.63 and 28.58 knots respectively and were considered reliable and fast in service. The Dupont served as a training vessel 1914-17
Renaming: TB-7 to Coast Torpedo Boat No. 3 1 Aug 18.

ROWAN

Displacement: 182 tons
Dimensions: 175'6"(oa.) x 17'(e) x 7'6"(max)
Armament: 4-1# 3-18"T

Machinery: 3200 IHP; 2 vertical quadruple-expansion engines, 2 screws
Speed: 26 kts.
Complement: 24

No.		Hull	Machinery	Laid down	Launched	Commiss'd	Disposition
8	ROWAN	Moran	Moran	22 Jun 96	8 Apr 98	1 Apr 99	Stk. 29 Oct 12, sold 3 Jun 18.

Notes: Fiscal year 1896. A Navy-designed counterpart to the previous class, she reached 27.07 knots on trials. She was used as a target before disposal.

1896

DAHLGREN class

Displacement: 146 tons
Dimensions: 151'7"(oa.) x 16'5"(e) x 8'9"(max)
Armament: 4-1# 2-18"T; 2-1# (Dahlgren, 1918)

Machinery: 4200 IHP; 2 vertical triple-expansion engines, 2 screws
Speed: 30.5 kts.
Complement: 29

No.		Hull	Machinery	Laid down	Launched	Commiss'd	Disposition
9	DAHLGREN	Bath	Bath	11 Dec 97	29 May 99	16 Jun 00	Stk. 28 Oct 19, sold 19 Jul 20
10	T.A.M. CRAVEN	Bath	Bath	6 Dec 97	25 Sep 99	9 Jun 00	Stk. 15 Nov 13, sunk as target.

Notes: Fiscal year 1897. The 1897 budget included three torpedo boats with a speed of not less than 30 knots. Bath chose to use without modification the plans of the successful French 30-knot oceangoing torpedo boat Forban, which it purchased from the French designer, Normand. Following French practice, these boats had bow and stern rudders. They reached around 30 knots on trials.
Renamings: After 1910 the T.A.M. Craven appeared in Navy lists as simply Craven. TB-9 to Coast Torpedo Boat No. 4 1 Aug 18.

FARRAGUT

Displacement: 279 tons
Dimensions: 214'(oa.) x 20'8"(e) x 6'(max)
Armament: 6-6# 2-18"T; 4-6# 2-18"T (1907); 4-3# (1915)

Machinery: 5600 IHP; 2 vertical triple-expansion engines, 2 screws
Speed: 30 kts.
Complement: 66

No.		Hull	Machinery	Laid down	Launched	Commiss'd	Disposition
11	FARRAGUT	Union	Union	23 Jul 97	16 Jul 98	22 Mar 99	Stk May 19, sold 9 Sep 19.

TORPEDO BOATS   165

Notes: Fiscal year 1897. An oceangoing boat designed by her builder, she reached 30.13 knots on trials. Her large size reflected a belief that oceangoing capabilities in torpedo boats would compensate for lack of numbers and enable the torpedo boat force to cover more of the coastline. She was the only American torpedo boat with a ram bow. The Farragut served as a training vessel 1915-17.
Renaming: To Coast Torpedo Boat No. 5 1 Aug 18.

DAVIS class

Displacement: 154 tons
Dimensions: 148'(oa.) x 15'4"(e) x 5'10"(mean)
Armament: 3-1# 3-18"T; 3-1# (Fox 1916)

Machinery: 1750 IHP; 2 vertical triple-expansion engines, 2 screws
Speed: 22.5 kts.
Complement: 24

No.		Hull	Machinery	Laid down	Launched	Commiss'd	Disposition
12	DAVIS	Wolf & Zwicker		2 Mar 97	4 Jun 98	10 May 99	Stk. 12 Nov 13, sold 21 Apr 20
13	FOX	Wolf & Zwicker		4 Mar 97	4 Jul 98	8 Jul 99	Stk. 31 Aug 16, sold 27 Oct 16.

Notes: Fiscal year 1897. In addition to the three oceangoing boats (TB 9-11), the 1897 budget included "not more than ten" smaller and slower torpedo boats for use in and near harbors, the actual number being limited by their cost. The boats actually built were three of intermediate size, designed for 22.5 knots (TB 12-14) and four small ones designed for 20 knots (TB 15-18). TB 12-13 were designed by their builder and reached 23.41 and 23.13 knots on trials respectively.

MORRIS

Displacement: 105 tons
Dimensions: 147'(oa.) x 15'6"(e) x 4'1"(mean)
Armament: 3-1# 3-18"T; 3-1# (1915)

Machinery: 1750 IHP; 2 vertical triple-expansion engines, 2 screws
Speed: 22.5 kts.
Complement: 22

No.		Hull	Machinery	Laid down	Launched	Commiss'd	Disposition
14	MORRIS	Herreshoff		17 Nov 97	13 Apr 98	11 May 98	Stk. 24 Jan 24, sold 10 Oct 24.

Notes: Fiscal year 1897. Designed by her builder, she made around 24 knots on trials.
Renaming: To Coast Torpedo Boat No. 6 1 Aug 18.
Reclassification: To "unclassified" 17 Jul 20, to unclassified district craft 1 Jul 21.

TALBOT class

Displacement: 46 tons
Dimensions: 100'(oa.) x 12'6"(e) x 4'6"(max)
Armament: 1-1# 2-18"T

Machinery: 850 IHP; vertical triple-expansion engine, 1 screw
Speed: 20 kts.
Complement: 12

No.		Hull	Machinery	Laid down	Launched	Commiss'd	Disposition
15	TALBOT	Herreshoff		8 Apr 97	14 Nov 97	4 Apr 98	Stk. 18 Jul 44, scrapped 1944
16	GWIN	Herreshoff		14 Apr 97	15 Nov 97	4 Apr 98	Stk. 30 Apr 25, sold 24 Sep 25.

Notes: Fiscal year 1897. Designed by their builder, they reached 21.15 and 20.88 knots on trials. They served as training vessels 1900-07. The Talbot was stricken on 1 May 12 and the Gwin was stricken on 20 Apr 14, but both were reinstated in 1915 when they were converted to ferry boats.
Renamings: To Berceau and Cyane respectively on 11 Apr 18.
Reclassifications: To YFB 3-4 respectively 17 Jul 20.

MACKENZIE class

Displacement: 65 tons
Dimensions: 101'6"(oa.) x 12'9"(e) x 6'(max)
Armament: 1-1# 2-18"T; 1-1# (1916)

Machinery: 850 IHP; vertical triple-expansion engine, 1 screw
Speed: 20 kts.
Complement: 12

No.		Hull	Machinery	Laid down	Launched	Commiss'd	Disposition
17	MACKENZIE	Hillman		15 Apr 97	19 Feb 98	1 May 99	Stk. 10 Mar 16, sunk as target
18	McKEE	Columbian		11 Sep 97	5 Mar 98	16 May 98	Stk. 8 Apr 12, scuttled near Craney I., Va. 24 Sep 20.

Notes: Fiscal year 1897. Designed by the Columbian Iron Works, they made 20.11 and 19.82 knots respectively on trials. The Mackenzie served as a training vessel 1912-16 and the McKee was used as a target after 1912.

1897

STRINGHAM

Displacement: 340 tons
Dimensions: 232'4"(oa.) x 22'(e) x 8'(max)
Armament: 7-6# 2-18"T; 4-6# 2-18"T (1902)

Machinery: 7200 IHP; 2 vertical
  triple-expansion engines, 2 screws
Speed: 30 kts.
Complement: 59

No.	Hull	Machinery	Laid down	Launched	Commiss'd	Disposition
19 STRINGHAM	Harlan&Hollingsworth		21 Mar 98	10 Jun 99	7 Nov 05	Stk. 26 Nov 13, sold 18 Mar 23.

Notes: Fiscal year 1898. Designed by her builder as a 30-knot oceangoing torpedo boat, she was larger than many contemporary British destroyers. She was completed in 1899 but failed to pass her acceptance trials. She was re-engined and finally accepted in 1904 with a trial speed of only 25.33 knots. She served as a training vessel 1906-13 and then as a target.

GOLDSBOROUGH

Displacement: 255 tons
Dimensions: 198'(wl.) x 20'7"(e) x 6'10"(mean)
Armament: 4-6# 2-18"T; 4-6# (1915)

Machinery: 6000 IHP; 2 vertical
  triple-expansion engines, 2 screws
Speed: 30 kts.
Complement: 59

No.	Hull	Machinery	Laid down	Launched	Commiss'd	Disposition
20 GOLDSBOROUGH	Wolf & Zwicker		14 Jul 98	29 Jul 99	9 Apr 08	Stk. May 19, sold 8 Sep 19.

Notes: Fiscal year 1898. Designed by her builder as a 30-knot oceangoing torpedo boat and completed in 1899, she failed her acceptance trials. Puget Sound Navy Yard re-engined her in 1901 following the bankruptcy of the builders. In the ensuing trials the new port engine was destroyed, further delaying her acceptance until 1908. She ultimately achieved a trial speed of 27.40 knots. She served as a training vessel 1914-17.
Renaming: To Coast Torpedo Boat No. 7 1 Aug 18.

BAILEY

Displacement: 235 tons
Dimensions: 205'(oa.) x 19'3"(e) x 6'10"(max)
Armament: 4-6# 2-18"T

Machinery: 5600 IHP; 2 vertical
  triple-expansion engines, 2 screws
Speed: 30 kts.
Complement: 56

No.	Hull	Machinery	Laid down	Launched	Commiss'd	Disposition
21 BAILEY	Gas Engine		30 Apr 98	5 Dec 99	10 Jun 01	Stk. 28 Oct 19, sold 10 Mar 20.

Notes: Fiscal year 1898. This, the third 30-knot oceangoing torpedo boat in the 1898 budget, was a relative success, reaching 30.20 knots on trials. She was the Navy's first four stack torpedo boat and the first naval vessel to use Seabury water-tube boilers. She served as a training vessel 1911-17.
Renaming: To Coast Torpedo Boat No. 8 1 Aug 18.

1898

SOMERS

Displacement: 150 tons
Dimensions: 156'(oa.) x 17'6"(e) x 5'10"(mean)
Armament: none; 4-1# (1900); 1-1# 3-18"T (1900); none (1914);
  3-1# (1915)

Machinery: 1900 IHP; vertical
  quadruple-expansión engine, 1 screw
Speed: 23 kts.
Complement: 22

No.	Hull	Machinery	Laid down	Launched	Commiss'd	Disposition
22 SOMERS	Schichau	Schichau	ca. 1891	ca. 1892	28 Mar 98	Stk. 7 Oct 19, sold 19 Jul 20.

Notes: She was built by Schichau as an experimental vessel (their hull 450) and was purchased from them on 25 Mar 98 as part of a crash effort at the beginning of the Spanish American War to buy warships overseas. She was a training vessel between 1909 and 1920. The Navy estimated her speed at 17.5 knots but did not record a trial speed.
Renaming: To Coast Torpedo Boat No. 9 1 Aug 18.

MANLEY

Displacement: 30 tons
Dimensions: 60'8"(wl.) x 9'5"(e) x 2'11"(mean)
Armament: 2-18"T; none (1901)

Machinery: 250 IHP; vertical triple-
  expansion engine, 1 screw
Speed: 17.5 kts.
Complement: 5

No.		Hull	Machinery	Laid down	Launched	Commiss'd	Disposition
23	MANLEY	Yarrow	Yarrow	ca. 1894	ca. 1894	No	Sold 21 Apr 20.

Notes: Built on speculation and purchased from Charles R. Flint on 13 Apr 98 during the Spanish-American War, she was delivered after the war and served as a training ship at Annapolis without ever being commissioned. She was stricken on 2 Apr 14 but was reinstated as a ferry.

Renaming: Name sometimes spelled Manly. To Levant 11 Apr 18.

BAGLEY class

Displacement: 175 tons
Dimensions: 157'4"(oa.) x 17'8"(e) x 9'5"(max)
Armament: 3-3# 3-18"T; 3-1# 3-18"T (1902); 2-1# (TB-24, 1918); 3-1# (others, 1918)

Machinery: 4200 IHP; 2 vertical triple-expansion engines, 2 screws
Speed: 28 kts.
Complement: 29

No.		Hull	Machinery	Laid down	Launched	Commiss'd	Disposition
24	BAGLEY	Bath	Bath	4 Jan 00	25 Sep 00	18 Oct 01	Stk. 31 Mar 19, sold 9 Apr 19
25	BARNEY	Bath	Bath	3 Jan 00	28 Jul 00	21 Oct 01	Stk. 28 Oct 19, sold 19 Jul 20
26	BIDDLE	Bath	Bath	21 Feb 00	18 May 01	26 Oct 01	Stk. 28 Oct 19, sold 19 Jul 20.

Notes: Fiscal year 1899. For this class, Bath modified the plans of the French Forban for which it held the American rights, lengthening and widening them slightly. The machinery, although rearranged, closely followed the Normand design and achieved trial speeds of 29.15, 29.04, and 28.57 knots in the three boats respectively. Although lightly built, these were considered strong vessels. The Bagley served as a training vessel 1907-13 and the others 1912-17.

Renamings: To Coast Torpedo Boat No. 10, 11, and 12 respectively 1 Aug 18.

BLAKELY class

Displacement: 200 (TB 31-33), 196 (TB 27-28), 175 (TB-35), 165 (TB-34) tons
Dimensions: 175'1"(TB 27-28, oa.), 175'(others, oa.) x 17'9" (TB 27-28, e), 17'8"(TB-35, e), 17'6"(others, e) x 7'6"(max)
Armament: 3-1# 3-18"T; 3-3# (TB-27, 1918); 2-1# (TB-28, 31, 34, 1918); none (TB-33, 1918)

Machinery: 3000 IHP; 2 vertical, inverted triple-expansion engines, 2 screws
Speed: 26.5 kts. (Wilkes), 26 kts. (others)
Complement: 29

No.		Hull	Machinery	Laid down	Launched	Commiss'd	Disposition
27	BLAKELY	Lawley		12 Jan 99	22 Nov 00	27 Dec 04	Stk. May 19, sold 10 Mar 20
28	DE LONG	Lawley		24 Jan 99	23 Nov 00	27 Oct 02	Stk. 7 Oct 19, sold 19 Jul 20
31	SHUBRICK	Trigg		11 Mar 99	31 Oct 99	Nov 01	Stk. 28 Oct 19, sold 10 Mar 20
32	STOCKTON	Trigg		18 Mar 99	27 Dec 99	Nov 01	Stk. 15 Nov 13, sunk as target Sep 16
33	THORNTON	Trigg		16 Mar 99	15 May 00	9 Jun 02	Stk. 12 May 19, sold 28 Aug 20
34	TINGEY	Columbian		29 Mar 99	25 Mar 01	7 Jan 04	Stk. 28 Oct 19, sold 10 Mar 20
35	WILKES	Gas Engine		3 Jun 99	28 Sep 01	18 Sep 02	Stk. 15 Nov 13, sunk as target.

Notes: Fiscal year 1899. The design by the Bureau of Construction and Repair was based on the Winslow (TB-5) and called for an armament of 3# guns. They were, however, built with 1# guns, as were all but the largest U.S. torpedo boats. The acceptance speed of these boats was reduced from 28 to 26 knots (26.5 knots for the Wilkes) because of problems in the Navy design, but only one boat succeeded in reaching the reduced speeds—trial results were 25.88, 25.52, 26.07, 25.79, 24.88, 24.94, and 25.99 knots respectively.

Renamings: The Blakely, De Long, Shubrick, Thornton, and Tingey were renamed Coast Torpedo Boats No. 13 thru 17 respectively 1 Aug 18.

NICHOLSON class

Displacement: 218 (Nicholson), 220 (O'Brien) tons
Dimensions: 175'(oa.) x 17'(e) x 6'6"(O'Brien, mean), 6'5" (Nicholson, mean)
Armament: 3-1# 3-18"T

Machinery: 3000 IHP; 2 vertical triple-expansion engines, 2 screws
Speed: 26 kts.
Complement: 28

No.		Hull	Machinery	Laid down	Launched	Commiss'd	Disposition
29	NICHOLSON	Crescent	Box	6 Dec 98	23 Sep 01	10 Jan 05	Stk. 3 Mar 09, sunk as target near Norfolk
30	O'BRIEN	Crescent	Box	29 Dec 98	24 Sep 00	15 Jul 05	Stk. 3 Mar 09, scrapped.

Notes: Fiscal year 1899. Work on both vessels stopped 18 Jun 03 when the Crescent Yard closed. The contract was declared forfeit on 15 Aug 03 and the vessels completed by New York Navy Yard. They made 25.74 and 25.0 knots respectively on trials. In 1909 they became Battle Towing Targets #6 and #5 respectively.

Destroyers (DD)

1898

BAINBRIDGE class

Displacement: 420 tons
Dimensions: 250'6"(DD-13, oa.), 250'2"(DD 10-12, oa.), 250'
  (others, oa.) x 23'8"(DD-13, e), 23'6"(DD 10-12, e), 23'7"
  (others, e) x 9'2"(DD 4-5, 10-12, max), 9'3"(DD-13, max),
  9'4" (others, max)
Armament: 2-3"/50 5-6# 2-18"T

Machinery: 7000 IHP (DD 10-12), 8000
  IHP (others); 2 vertical, inverted
  triple-expansion engines, 2 screws
Speed: 28 kts. (DD 4-5); 29 kts.
  (others)
Complement: 75

No.		Hull	Machinery	Laid down	Launched	Commiss'd	Disposition
1	BAINBRIDGE	Neafie & Levy		15 Aug 99	27 Aug 01	24 Nov 02	Stk. 15 Sep 19, sold 3 Jan 20
2	BARRY	Neafie & Levy		2 Sep 99	22 Mar 02	24 Nov 02	Stk. 15 Sep 19, sold 3 Jan 20
3	CHAUNCEY	Neafie & Levy		2 Dec 99	26 Oct 01	20 Nov 02	Sunk in collision off Gibraltar 19 Nov 17
4	DALE	Trigg		12 Jul 99	24 Jul 00	24 Oct 02	Stk. 15 Sep 19, sold 3 Jan 20
5	DECATUR	Trigg		26 Jul 99	26 Sep 00	19 May 02	Stk. 15 Sep 19, sold 3 Jan 20
10	PAUL JONES	Union		20 Apr 99	14 Jun 02	19 Jul 02	Stk. 15 Sep 19, sold 3 Jan 20
11	PERRY	Union		19 Apr 99	27 Oct 00	4 Sep 02	Stk. 15 Sep 19, sold 3 Jan 20
12	PREBLE	Union		21 Apr 99	2 Mar 01	21 Jun 02	Stk. 15 Sep 19, sold 3 Jan 20
13	STEWART	Gas Engine		24 Jan 00	10 May 02	17 Dec 02	Stk. 15 Sep 19, sold 3 Jan 20.

Notes: Fiscal year 1899. This, the Navy Department's first destroyer design, emphasized seakeeping over speed and guns over torpedo armament, although speed and torpedo capabilities remained important design objectives. It featured a high forecastle for seakeeping and strength and introduced the 3" gun into the torpedo force. The ships were considered to be excellent sea boats. Trial speeds ranged between 28.0 and 28.91 knots except for Stewart which reached 29.69 knots.

HOPKINS class

Displacement: 408 tons
Dimensions: 248'8"(oa.) x 24'6"(e) x 10'6"(Hopkins, max),
  10'3" (Hull, max)
Armament: 2-3"/50 5-6# 2-18"T; 2-3" 4-18"T (1918)

Machinery: 7200 IHP; 2 vertical,
  inverted triple-expansion engines,
  2 screws
Speed: 29 kts.
Complement: 73

No.		Hull	Machinery	Laid down	Launched	Commiss'd	Disposition
6	HOPKINS	Harlan&Hollingsworth		2 Feb 99	24 Apr 02	23 Sep 03	Stk. 2 Oct 19, sold 7 Sep 20
7	HULL	Harlan&Hollingsworth		22 Feb 99	21 Jun 02	20 May 03	Stk. 15 Sep 19, sold 3 Jan 20.

Notes: Fiscal year 1899. Private bidders in the destroyer program were given the option of providing their own designs, and some chose to focus on trial speed in smooth water instead of seakeeping capabilities. In this class, the builder essentially followed the Department's design except for reverting to a low turtleback forecastle typical of torpedo boats. Trial results were 29.02 and 28.04 knots respectively.

LAWRENCE class

Displacement: 400 tons
Dimensions: 246'3"(oa.) x 22'3"(e) x 9'5"(max)
Armament: 2-3"/50 5-6# 2-18"T; 7-6# 2-18"T (1906)

Machinery: 8400 IHP; 2 vertical,
  inverted triple-expansion engines,
  2 screws
Speed: 30 kts.
Complement: 72

No.		Hull	Machinery	Laid down	Launched	Commiss'd	Disposition
8	LAWRENCE	Fore River		10 Apr 99	7 Nov 00	14 Apr 03	Stk. 15 Sep 19, sold 3 Jan 20
9	MACDONOUGH	Fore River		21 Apr 99	24 Dec 00	5 Sep 03	Stk. 7 Nov 19, sold 10 Mar 20.

Notes: Fiscal year 1899. Designed by their builders, they were considered the least successful of the 1898 vessels. They were unable to carry their 3" guns, and 6-pounders were eventually substituted. Trial speeds were 28.41 and 28.03 knots respectively.

TRUXTUN class

Displacement: 433 tons
Dimensions: 259'6"(oa.) x 23'3"(e) x 9'10"(max)
Armament: 2-3"/50 6-6# 2-18"T; 2-3" 4-18"T (DD-14, 16, 1918)

Machinery: 8300 IHP; 2 vertical,
  inverted triple-expansion engines,
  2 screws
Speed: 30 kts.
Complement: 72

No.		Hull	Machinery	Laid down	Launched	Commiss'd	Disposition
14	TRUXTUN	Maryland Steel		13 Nov 99	15 Aug 01	11 Sep 02	Stk. 15 Sep 19, sold 3 Jan 20
15	WHIPPLE	Maryland Steel		13 Nov 99	15 Aug 01	21 Oct 02	Stk. 15 Sep 19, sold 3 Jan 20
16	WORDEN	Maryland Steel		13 Nov 99	15 Aug 01	31 Dec 02	Stk. 15 Sep 19, sold 3 Jan 20.

Notes: Fiscal year 1899. Designed by the builder, they were regarded as very successful. In general they followed the Navy design except for reverting to a turtleback forecastle. They carried one more 6-pounder than the other boats in their group. All three were sold into merchant service as banana carriers, and Whipple was not scrapped until 1956.

1906

SMITH class

Displacement: 700 tons
Dimensions: 293'10"(oa.) x 26'5"(DD 17-18, e), 26'11"(others, e) x 10'7"(DD 17-18, max), 10'11"(DD-19, max), 10'(DD 20-21, max)
Armament: 5-3"/50 3-18"T; 4-3" 6-18"T (1916)

Machinery: 10,000 SHP; direct drive turbines, 3 screws
Speed: 28 kts.
Complement: 89

No.		Hull	Machinery	Laid down	Launched	Commiss'd	Disposition
17	SMITH	Cramp		18 Mar 08	20 Apr 09	26 Nov 09	Ordered sold 1 Sep 21, sold 20 Dec 21
18	LAMSON	Cramp		18 Mar 08	16 Jun 09	10 Feb 10	Stk. 15 Sep 19, sold 21 Nov 19
19	PRESTON	New York SB		28 Apr 08	14 Jul 09	24 Dec 09	Stk. 15 Sep 19, sold 21 Nov 19
20	FLUSSER	Bath		3 Aug 08	20 Jul 09	28 Oct 09	Stk. 15 Sep 19, sold 21 Nov 19
21	REID	Bath		3 Aug 08	17 Aug 09	3 Dec 09	Stk. 15 Sep 19, sold 21 Nov 19.

Notes: Fiscal years 1907 (DD 17-19) and 1908. This class was built to a Navy design derived from the 420-ton type. Its primary function was to protect the battle line against torpedo craft, and the design emphasized guns over torpedoes and seakeeping and endurance over speed. It and the next class came to be known as "flivvers" or lightweights compared to their larger thousand-ton successors. In this and subsequent classes through DD-74, individual builders were given considerable leeway in implementing the Navy designs, resulting in differences in funnel spacing and in other details within classes. These were the first American destroyers to have turbines and the last to be coal-fired. A single high-pressure turbine was on the center propeller shaft and two low-pressure turbines drove the wing shafts. All served as training vessels in 1916-17. The Smith was originally ordered sold on 28 Feb 20 but was instead converted to a target vessel.
Reclassification: DD-17 to "unclassified" as a target 11 Jun 20.

1908

PAULDING class

Displacement: 742 tons
Dimensions: 293'10"(oa.) x 26'11"(DD 24-32, e), 27'(others, e) x 9'6"(DD 22-23, max), 10'1"(DD 26-27, max), 10'11"(DD 24-25, max), 9'5"(others, max)
Armament: Sterett, Burrows--5-3"/50 6-18"T; 4-3" 6-18"T (1920);
5-3" 6-18"T (1921);
Perkins, Mayrant--5-3" 6-18"T;
Paulding, Drayton, Roe, Terry--5-3" 6-18"T; 4-3" 6-18"T (1918); 5-3" 6-18"T (1921);
Warrington--5-3" 6-18"T; 4-3" 6-18"T (1920);
Monaghan--5-3" 6-18"T; 4-3" 6-18"T (1918); none (1931);
Others--5-3" 6-18"T; 4-3" 6-18"T (1918)

Machinery: 12,000 SHP; direct drive turbines, 2 screws (DD 26-27, 30-31, 34), 3 screws (others)
Speed: 30 kts. (DD 30-31), 29.5 kts. (others)
Complement: 86

No.		Hull	Machinery	Laid down	Launched	Commiss'd	Disposition
22	PAULDING	Bath		24 Jul 09	12 Apr 10	29 Sep 10	Stk. 28 Jun 34, scrapped 1934
23	DRAYTON	Bath		19 Aug 09	22 Aug 10	29 Oct 10	Stk. 8 Mar 35, sold 28 Jun 35
24	ROE	Newport News		18 Jan 09	24 Jul 09	17 Sep 10	Stk. 28 Jun 34, scrapped 1934
25	TERRY	Newport News		8 Feb 09	21 Aug 09	18 Oct 10	Stk. 28 Jun 34, scrapped 1934
26	PERKINS	Fore River		22 Mar 09	9 Apr 10	18 Nov 10	Stk. 8 Mar 35, sold 28 Jun 35
27	STERETT	Fore River		22 Mar 09	12 May 10	15 Dec 10	Stk. 8 Mar 35, sold 28 Jun 35
28	McCALL	New York SB		8 Jun 09	4 Jun 10	23 Jan 11	Stk. 28 Jun 34, scrapped 1934
29	BURROWS	New York SB		19 Jun 09	23 Jun 10	21 Feb 11	Stk. 5 Jul 34, scrapped 1934
30	WARRINGTON	Cramp		21 Jun 09	18 Jun 10	20 Mar 11	Stk. 8 Mar 35, sold 28 Jun 35
31	MAYRANT	Cramp		22 Apr 09	23 Apr 10	12 Jul 11	Stk. 8 Mar 35, sold 28 Jun 35

No.		Hull	Machinery	Laid down	Launched	Commiss'd	Disposition
32	MONAGHAN	Newport News		1 Jun 10	18 Feb 11	21 Jun 11	Stk. 5 Jul 34, scrapped 1934
33	TRIPPE	Bath		12 Apr 10	20 Dec 10	23 Mar 11	Stk. 5 Jul 34, scrapped 1934
34	WALKE	Fore River		5 Mar 10	3 Nov 10	22 Jul 11	Stk. 8 Mar 35, scrapped 1935
35	AMMEN	New York SB		29 Mar 10	20 Sep 10	23 May 11	Stk. 5 Jul 34, scrapped 1934
36	PATTERSON	Cramp		27 Apr 10	29 Apr 11	11 Oct 11	Stk. 28 Jun 34, scrapped 1934
37	FANNING	Newport News		29 Apr 11	11 Jan 12	21 Jun 12	Stk. 28 Jun 34, scrapped 1934
38	JARVIS	New York SB		1 Jul 11	3 Apr 12	22 Oct 12	Stk. 8 Mar 35, scrapped 1935
39	HENLEY	Fore River		17 Jul 11	3 Apr 12	6 Dec 12	Stk. 5 Jul 34, scrapped 1934
40	BEALE	Cramp		8 May 11	30 Apr 12	30 Aug 12	Stk. 28 Jun 34, scrapped 1934
41	JOUETT	Bath		7 Mar 11	15 Apr 12	25 May 12	Stk. 5 Jul 34, scrapped 1934
42	JENKINS	Bath		24 Mar 11	29 Apr 12	15 Jun 12	Stk. 8 Mar 35, scrapped 1935.

Notes: Fiscal years 1909 (DD 22-31), 1910 (32-36), and 1911. A refinement of the previous class, these ships introduced oil fuel and twin torpedo tubes and had increased horsepower. The Cramp, Newport News, and Fore River ships (except the Fanning, Henley, and Beale) had three funnels. The Henley had reciprocating engines for cruising in addition to her main turbines, and she and the Mayrant were re-engined in 1915 with 13,000 SHP Westinghouse geared turbines. The following were loaned to the Coast Guard: Paulding (CG-17), Patterson (CG-16), and Beale (CG-9), 28 Apr 24-18 Oct 30; Burrows (CG-10), 28 Apr 24-2 May 31; Roe (CG-18), Terry (CG-19), and McCall (CG-14), 7 Jun 24-18 Oct 30; Monaghan (CG-15), 7 Jun 24-8 May 31; Trippe (CG-20), 7 Jun 24-2 May 31; Ammen (CG-8) and Jouett (CG-13), 28 Apr 24-22 May 31; Fanning (CG-11), 7 Jun 24-24 Nov 30; and Henley (CG-12), 16 May 24-8 May 31.
Renamings: The Drayton, Monaghan, Walke, Ammen, and Patterson lost their names on 1 Jul 33 and the Perkins hers on 1 Nov 33.

CASSIN class

Displacement: 1072 (DD-45), 1020 (DD 43-44), 1014 (DD-46) tons
Dimensions: 305'3"(oa.) x 31'2"(e) x 10'6"(max)
Armament: 4-4"/50 8-18"T; 4-4" 1-3"/23AA 8-18"T (DD-46, 1929)

Machinery: 16,000 SHP; direct drive turbines with triple-expansion cruising engines, 2 screws
Speed: 29.5 kts.
Complement: 97

No.		Hull	Machinery	Laid down	Launched	Commiss'd	Disposition
43	CASSIN	Bath		1 May 12	20 May 13	9 Aug 13	Stk. 5 Jul 34, scrapped 1934
44	CUMMINGS	Bath		21 May 12	6 Aug 13	19 Sep 13	Stk. 5 Jul 34, scrapped 1934
45	DOWNES	New York SB		27 Jun 12	8 Nov 13	11 Feb 15	Stk. 5 Jul 34, scrapped 1934
46	DUNCAN	Fore River		17 Jun 12	5 Apr 13	30 Aug 13	Stk. 8 Mar 35, scrapped 1935.

Notes: Fiscal year 1912. This class was built to a new Navy design with increased steaming radius, larger guns, and more torpedo tubes. Together with DD 47-68 they were known as the "thousand tonners." The thousand tonners had several different types of machinery installations for cruising at moderate speeds, needed to offset the low endurance of the direct drive main turbines. Within the Cassin class, DD 43-44 had a single reciprocating cruising engine which could be clutched to one of their two shafts, while DD 45-46 had two such engines, one per shaft. They used the reciprocating engines at speeds under 15 knots only and were economical vessels. The Cassin (CG-1) was loaned to the Coast Guard 7 Jun 24-30 Jun 33; the Cummings (CG-3) 7 Jun 24-23 May 32; and the Downes (CG-4) 28 Apr 24-2 May 31.
Renamings: The Cassin lost her name on 1 Nov 33 and the Cummings and Downes dropped theirs on 1 Jul 33.

1911

AYLWIN class

Displacement: 1036 tons
Dimensions: 305'3"(oa.) x 31'2"(e) x 10'6"(max)
Armament: 4-4"/50 8-18"T; 4-4" 1-3"/23AA 8-18"T (1929, except DD-48)

Machinery: 16,000 SHP; direct drive turbines with triple-expansion cruising engines, 2 screws
Speed: 29.5 kts.
Complement: 99

No.		Hull	Machinery	Laid down	Launched	Commiss'd	Disposition
47	AYLWIN	Cramp		7 Mar 12	23 Nov 12	17 Jan 14	Stk. 8 Mar 35, scrapped 1935
48	PARKER	Cramp		11 Mar 12	8 Feb 13	30 Dec 13	Stk. 8 Mar 35, scrapped 1935
49	BENHAM	Cramp		14 Mar 12	22 Mar 13	20 Jan 14	Stk. 8 Mar 35, scrapped 1935
50	BALCH	Cramp		7 May 12	21 Dec 12	26 Mar 14	Stk. 8 Mar 35, scrapped 1935.

Notes: Fiscal year 1912. These ships closely resembled the Cassin class and had two reciprocating cruising engines. They were very economical steamers. The Benham was experimentally fitted with twin 4" mounts in 1917 but they were removed before she sailed for war service in Europe.
Renamings: The Balch dropped her name on 1 Nov 33 and the Aylwin hers on 1 Jul 33.

1912

O'BRIEN class

Displacement: 1090 (DD-56), 1020 (DD-54), 1050 (others) tons
Dimensions: 305'3"(oa.) x 31'1"(e) x 10'7"(max)
Armament: 4-4"/50 8-21"T; 4-4" 1-3"/23AA 8-21"T (DD 51-53,
  55, 1929)
Complement: 101

Machinery: 17,000 SHP; direct drive
  turbines with triple-expansion
  cruising engines (DD 51-54, 56) or
  with geared cruising turbines (DD-
  55); 2 screws
Speed: 29 kts.

No.		Hull	Machinery	Laid down	Launched	Commiss'd	Disposition
51	O'BRIEN	Cramp		8 Sep 13	20 Jul 14	22 May 15	Stk. 8 Mar 35, scrapped 1935
52	NICHOLSON	Cramp		8 Sep 13	19 Aug 14	30 Apr 15	Stk. 7 Jan 36, sold 30 Jun 36
53	WINSLOW	Cramp		1 Oct 13	11 Feb 15	7 Aug 15	Stk. 7 Jan 36, sold 30 Jun 36
54	McDOUGAL	Bath		29 Jul 13	22 Apr 14	16 Jun 14	Stk. 5 Jul 34, scrapped 1934
55	CUSHING	Fore River		23 Sep 13	16 Jan 15	21 Aug 15	Stk. 7 Jan 36, sold 30 Jun 36
56	ERICSSON	New York SB		10 Nov 13	22 Aug 14	14 Aug 15	Stk. 5 Jul 34, scrapped 1934.

Notes: Fiscal year 1913. This class featured an increase from 18" to 21" torpedo tubes. It also featured three types of cruising machinery installations--DD 51-53 had two reciprocating cruising engines; DD-54 and 56 had one such engine; and DD-55 had two geared cruising turbines, one per shaft. The McDougal (CG-6) was loaned to the Coast Guard 7 Jun 24-30 Jun 33; the Ericsson (CG-5) 7 Jun 24-23 May 32.
Renamings: The Winslow and Cushing lost their names 1 Jul 33 and the McDougal hers on 1 Nov 33.

1913

TUCKER class

Displacement: 1150 (DD-61, 62), 1060 (DD-60), 1090 (others)
  tons
Dimensions: 315'3"(oa.) x 29'11"(DD-57, 60, 62, e),
  30'7"(others, e) x 10'5"(max)
Armament: 4-4"/50 8-21"T; 4-4" 1-3"/23AA 8-21"T (DD-60,
  1929); 3-4"(in Coast Guard service)

Machinery: 17,500 (DD-60), 18,000 (DD
  58-59), 17,000 (others) SHP; geared
  turbines (DD-60), direct drive
  turbines with geared cruising
  turbines (others); 2 screws
Speed: 29.5 kts.
Complement: 99

No.		Hull	Machinery	Laid down	Launched	Commiss'd	Disposition
57	TUCKER	Fore River		9 Nov 14	4 May 15	11 Apr 16	Stk. 24 Oct 36, sold 10 Dec 36
58	CONYNGHAM	Cramp		27 Jul 14	8 Jul 15	21 Jan 16	Stk. 5 Jul 34, scrapped 1934
59	PORTER	Cramp		24 Aug 14	26 Aug 15	17 Apr 16	Stk. 5 Jul 34, scrapped 1934
60	WADSWORTH	Bath		23 Feb 14	29 Apr 15	23 Jul 15	Stk. 7 Jan 36, sold 30 Jun 36
61	JACOB JONES	New York SB		3 Aug 14	29 May 15	10 Feb 16	Sunk by U-53 off Scilly Is. 6 Dec 17
62	WAINWRIGHT	New York SB		1 Sep 14	12 Jun 15	12 May 16	Stk. 5 Jul 34, scrapped 1934.

Notes: Fiscal year 1914. Five of these ships had a single geared cruising turbine on one of their two shafts while the sixth, DD-60, was a testbed for reduction gearing on the main turbines and had no cruising engines. The Tucker (CG-23) was on loan to the Coast Guard 25 Mar 26-30 Jun 33; the Conyngham (CG-2) and Porter (CG-7) from 7 Jun 24 to 30 Jun 33; and the Wainwright (CG-24), 2 Apr 26-27 Apr 34.
Renamings: The Tucker and Conyngham dropped their names on 1 Nov 33 while the Porter shed hers 1 Jul 33.

1914

SAMPSON class

Displacement: 1111 (DD 63-64), 1110 (DD 67-68), 1071 (DD 65-
  66) tons
Dimensions: 315'3"(oa.) x 30'7"(e) x 9'9"(DD 65-66), 10'8"
  (others)
Armament: 4-4"/50 12-21"T; 4-4" 1-3"/23AA 12-21"T (1919);
  4-4" 2-3"AA 12-21"T (DD-66, 1939); 3-4" 3-3"/50 6-21"T (DD-
  66, 1940)

Machinery: 17,500 SHP; direct drive
  turbines with geared cruising
  turbines, 2 screws
Speed: 29.5 kts.
Complement: 99

No.		Hull	Machinery	Laid down	Launched	Commiss'd	Disposition
63	SAMPSON	Fore River		21 Apr 15	4 Mar 16	27 Jun 16	Stk. 7 Jan 36, sold 8 Sep 36
64	ROWAN	Fore River		10 May 15	23 Mar 16	22 Aug 16	Stk. 7 Jan 36, sold 20 Apr 39

No.		Hull	Machinery	Laid down	Launched	Commiss'd	Disposition
65	DAVIS	Bath		7 May 15	15 Aug 16	5 Oct 16	Stk. 5 Jul 34, scrapped 1934
66	ALLEN	Bath		10 May 15	5 Dec 16	24 Jan 17	Stk. 1 Nov 45, sold 26 Sep 46
67	WILKES	Cramp		11 Mar 15	18 May 16	10 Nov 16	Stk. 5 Jul 34, scrapped 1934
68	SHAW	Mare I.		7 Feb 16	9 Dec 16	9 Apr 17	Stk. 5 Jul 34, scrapped 1934.

Notes: Fiscal year 1915. These ships were repeats of the Tucker class except that they introduced triple torpedo tubes. The first three had two cruising turbines and the last three had single cruising turbines. The Davis (CG-21), Wilkes (CG-25), and Shaw (CG-22) were loaned to the Coast Guard on 25 Mar 26. The Davis and Shaw were returned 30 Jun 33 and the Wilkes on 27 Apr 34. The Rowan was reduced to a hulk on 4 Dec 36.
Renaming: The Shaw dropped her name on 1 Nov 33.

1915

CALDWELL class

Displacement: 1020 (standard), 1125 (normal) tons
Dimensions: 315'6"(oa.) x 31'2"(DD 69-70, e), 31'4"(DD-71, e), 31'3"(others, e) x 11'6"(max)
Armament: 4-4"/50 12-21"T; 5-4" 2-3"/23AA 12-21"T (DD-73, 1919 only); 4-4" 2-3" 12-21"T (others, 1919); 4-4" 1-3"/50AA (APD-1, 1940); 3-3"/50 (DD 70, 72-73, 1940); 3-4"(APD-1, 1943)

Machinery: 20,000 (DD-70), 21,000 (DD-69), 18,500 (others) SHP; direct drive turbines with geared cruising turbines, 3 screws (DD 72-73); geared turbines, 2 screws (others)
Speed: 30 kts.
Complement: 100

No.		Hull	Machinery	Laid down	Launched	Commiss'd	Disposition
69	CALDWELL	Mare I.	G. E.	9 Dec 16	10 Jul 17	1 Dec 17	Stk. 7 Jan 36, sold 30 Jun 36
70	CRAVEN	Norfolk		20 Nov 17	29 Jun 18	19 Oct 18	To Britain 23 Oct 40 as Lewes, stk. 8 Jan 41
71	GWIN	Seattle		21 Jun 17	22 Dec 17	18 Mar 20	Stk. 25 Jan 37, sold 16 Mar 39
72	CONNER	Cramp		16 Oct 16	21 Aug 17	12 Jan 18	To Britain 23 Oct 40 as Leeds, stk. 8 Jan 41
73	STOCKTON	Cramp		16 Oct 16	17 Jul 17	26 Nov 17	To Britain 23 Oct 40 as Ludlow, stk. 8 Jan 41
74	MANLEY	Bath		22 Aug 16	23 Aug 17	15 Oct 17	Stk. 5 Dec 45, sold 26 Nov 46.

Notes: Fiscal year 1916. In these ships the Navy introduced a new flush deck hull configuration which was expected to reduce rolling and pitching and increase hull strength. Otherwise the new design was very similar to the previous class. The Cramp ships followed the Navy plans; the other builders introduced various modifications. The Cramp ships had direct drive turbines on two wing shafts and a geared cruising turbine on a central shaft; the others had the machinery installation that became standard in the war-built ships: geared main turbines, no cruising turbine, and two shafts. The Cramp and Seattle ships had three funnels. The Gwin was reduced to a hulk on 28 Dec 36. The Manley was converted to the prototype high-speed transport (reclassified AG-28 in 1938 and APD-1 in 1940 after a second, more extensive conversion).
Renamings: The Craven lost her name 31 May 35 and became the Conway on 20 Nov 39.
Reclassifications: Manley (DD-74) to AG-28 28 Nov 38; APD-1 2 Aug 40; DD-74 25 Jun 45.

1916

WICKES class

Displacement: 1090 (standard), 1154 (normal) tons
Dimensions: 314'5"(oa.) x 31'8"(e) x 9'6"(DD-133, max), 9'8" (DD 75-78, 93-94, 131-132, 135-138, 140-141, max), 9'10" (others, max)
Armament: 4-4"/50 2-3"/23AA 12-21"T; 4-4" 1-3"AA 12-21"T (1921); 3-4" 1-3"AA 12-21"T (DD-113, 1924); 6-3"/50AA 6-21"T (DD-118, 142, 144, 145, 147, 152-156, 1941); 4-4" 6-21"T (others, 1943); 3-4" 6-21"T (DD-113, 1943); 2-3"AA (DMS conversions); 3-3"AA (APD conversions)

Machinery: 24,200 (DD 75-78, 93-94), 26,000 (others) SHP; geared turbines, 2 screws
Speed: 35 kts.
Complement: 103

No.		Hull	Machinery	Laid down	Launched	Commiss'd	Disposition
75	WICKES	Bath		26 Jun 17	25 Jun 18	31 Jul 18	To Britain 23 Oct 40 as Montgomery, stk. 8 Jan 41
76	PHILIP	Bath		1 Sep 17	25 Jul 18	24 Aug 18	To Britain 23 Oct 40 as Lancaster, stk. 8 Jan 41
77	WOOLSEY	Bath		1 Nov 17	17 Sep 18	30 Sep 18	Sunk in collision off Balboa, C.Z., 26 Feb 21

The destroyer *Preston* (DD-19) soon after completion. (NH 44198)

A World War I destroyer, probably *Gilmer* (DD-233) or *Kane* (DD-235), on sea trials. She has 5"/51 instead of the usual 4"/50 guns. (NH 43771)

No.		Hull	Machinery	Laid down	Launched	Commiss'd	Disposition
78	EVANS	Bath		28 Dec 17	30 Oct 18	11 Nov 18	To Britain 23 Oct 40 as Mansfield, stk. 8 Jan 41
93	FAIRFAX	Mare I.		10 Jul 17	15 Dec 17	6 Apr 18	To Britain 26 Nov 40 as Richmond, stk. 8 Jan 41
94	TAYLOR	Mare I.		15 Oct 17	14 Feb 18	1 Jun 18	Stk. 6 Dec 38, sold 8 Aug 45
113	RATHBURNE	Cramp		12 Jul 17	27 Dec 17	24 Jun 18	Stk. 28 Nov 45, sold 21 Nov 46
114	TALBOT	Cramp		12 Jul 17	20 Feb 18	20 Jul 18	Stk. 24 Oct 45, sold 30 Jan 46
115	WATERS	Cramp		26 Jul 17	3 Mar 18	8 Aug 18	Stk. 24 Oct 45, sold 21 Nov 46
116	DENT	Cramp		30 Aug 17	23 Mar 18	9 Sep 18	Stk. 3 Jan 46, sold 13 Jun 46
117	DORSEY	Cramp		18 Sep 17	9 Apr 18	16 Sep 18	Wrecked Okinawa 9 Oct 45, destroyed 11 Jan 46
118	LEA	Cramp		18 Sep 17	29 Apr 18	2 Oct 18	Stk. 13 Aug 45, sold 30 Nov 45
131	BUCHANAN	Bath		29 Jun 18	2 Jan 19	20 Jan 19	To Britain 9 Sep 40 as Campbeltown, stk. 8 Jan 41
132	AARON WARD	Bath		1 Aug 18	10 Apr 19	21 Apr 19	To Britain 9 Sep 40 as Castleton, stk. 8 Jan 41
133	HALE	Bath		7 Oct 18	29 May 19	12 Jun 19	To Britain 9 Sep 40 as Caldwell, stk. 8 Jan 41
134	CROWNINSHIELD	Bath		5 Nov 18	24 Jul 19	6 Aug 19	To Britain 9 Sep 40 as Chelsea, stk. 8 Jan 41
135	TILLMAN	Charleston		29 Jul 18	7 Jul 19	30 Apr 21	To Britain 26 Nov 40 as Wells, stk. 8 Jan 41
136	BOGGS	Mare I.		15 Nov 17	25 Apr 18	23 Sep 18	Stk. 12 Apr 46, sold 27 Nov 46
137	KILTY	Mare I.		15 Dec 17	25 Apr 18	17 Dec 18	Stk. 16 Nov 45, sold 26 Aug 46
138	KENNISON	Mare I.		14 Feb 18	8 Jun 18	2 Apr 19	Stk. 5 Dec 45, sold 18 Nov 46
139	WARD	Mare I.		15 May 18	1 Jun 18	24 Jul 18	Sunk by Japanese suicide planes off Leyte 7 Dec 44
140	CLAXTON	Mare I.		25 Apr 18	15 Jan 19	15 Sep 19	To Britain 26 Nov 40 as Salisbury, stk. 8 Jan 41
141	HAMILTON	Mare I.		8 Jun 18	15 Jan 19	7 Nov 19	Stk. 1 Nov 45, sold 21 Nov 46
142	TARBELL	Cramp		31 Dec 17	28 May 18	27 Nov 18	Stk. 13 Aug 45, sold 30 Nov 45
143	YARNALL	Cramp		12 Feb 18	19 Jun 18	29 Nov 18	To Britain 23 Oct 40 as Lincoln, stk. 8 Jan 41
144	UPSHUR	Cramp		19 Feb 18	4 Jul 18	23 Dec 18	Stk. 16 Nov 45, sold 26 Sep 47
145	GREER	Cramp		24 Feb 18	1 Aug 18	31 Dec 18	Stk. 13 Aug 45, sold 30 Nov 45
146	ELLIOT	Cramp		23 Feb 18	4 Jul 18	25 Jan 19	Stk. 24 Oct 45, scrapped 1946
147	ROPER	Cramp		19 Mar 18	17 Aug 18	15 Feb 19	Stk. 11 Oct 45, sold 31 Mar 46
148	BRECKINRIDGE	Cramp		11 Mar 18	17 Aug 18	27 Feb 19	Stk. 19 Dec 45, sold 31 Oct 46
149	BARNEY	Cramp		26 Mar 18	5 Sep 18	14 Mar 19	Stk. 19 Dec 45, sold 31 Oct 46
150	BLAKELEY	Cramp		26 Mar 18	19 Sep 18	8 May 19	Stk. 13 Aug 45, sold 30 Nov 45
151	BIDDLE	Cramp		22 Apr 18	3 Oct 18	22 Apr 19	Stk. 24 Oct 45, sold 3 Dec 46
152	DU PONT	Cramp		2 May 18	22 Oct 18	30 Apr 19	Stk. 5 Jun 46, sold 12 Mar 47
153	BERNADOU	Cramp		4 Jun 18	7 Nov 18	19 May 19	Stk. 13 Aug 45, sold 30 Nov 45
154	ELLIS	Cramp		8 Jul 18	30 Nov 18	7 Jun 19	Stk. 16 Nov 45, sold 17 Jul 47
155	COLE	Cramp		25 Jun 18	11 Jan 19	19 Jun 19	Stk. 16 Nov 45, sold 6 Oct 47
156	J. FRED TALBOTT	Cramp		8 Jul 18	14 Dec 18	30 Jun 19	Stk. 19 Jun 46, sold 22 Dec 46.

Notes: Fiscal years 1917 (DD 75-78, 93-94) and 1918. DD 75-94 were repeats of the previous (DD 69-74) type except that the designed speed was increased from 30 to 35 knots to allow the ships to operate with the new Lexington class battlecruisers and Omaha class cruisers. The increased speed was obtained by adding about 100 tons of machinery, using reduction gearing on the main turbines, introducing a new more powerful type of boiler, and modifying the hull lines. Two builders prepared detail designs for this type, Bath Iron Works (this class) and Bethlehem Steel (the Little class). The type was then put into mass production for World War I, resulting in orders for DD 95-185). All builders except Bethlehem used the Bath plans, including Newport News in the Lamberton and New York SB in the Tattnall classes. Ships of the Bath group (especially those built by Bath and Cramp) were generally more successful than the Bethlehem ships in reaching or exceeding the steaming radius in their contracts (3600 nm at 15 knots), an important consideration for transatlantic convoy operations.

The Boggs (DD-136) and Kilty (DD-137) were designated Light Targets No. 2 and No. 3 (IX 36-37, later AG 19-20) in 1931, but the Kilty reverted to destroyer status in 1932. The Dorsey (DD-117) and Elliot (DD-146) served as control ships for radio controlled targets during the 1930s. The Taylor (DD-94) became Damage Control Hulk No. 40 on 11 Jul 40, and her bow was used to repair the Blakeley (DD-150) in 1942.

Renamings: DD-139 ex Cowell 20 May 18.

Reclassifications:
   Rathburne (DD-113) to APD-25 20 May 44; DD-113
20 Jul 45;
   Talbot (DD-114) to APD-7 15 Mar 43; DD-114 16
Jul 45;
   Waters (DD-115) to APD-8 3 Feb 43; DD-115 2
Aug 45;
   Dent (DD-116) to APD-9 7 Mar 43;
   Dorsey (DD-117) to DMS-1 19 Nov 40;
   Boggs (DD-136) to IX-36 11 Aug 31;
AG-19 5 Sep 31; DMS-3 19 Nov 40;
AG-19 5 Jun 45;
   Kilty (DD-137) to IX-37 11 Aug 31; AG-20 5
Sep 31; DD-137 16 Apr 32; APD-15 1 Mar 43;
DD-137 20 Jul 45;

   Kennison (DD-138) to AG-83 1 Oct 44;
   Ward (DD-139) to APD-16 6 Feb 43;
   Hamilton (DD-141) to DMS-18 11 Oct 41; AG-111
5 Jun 45;
   Upshur (DD-144), Breckinridge (DD-148), Barney
(DD-149), Biddle (DD-151), Ellis (DD-154), and
Cole (DD-155) to AG-103 and 112-116 30 Jun 45;
   Elliot (DD-146) to DMS-4 19 Nov 40; AG-104 5
Jun 45;
   Roper (DD-147) to APD-20 20 Oct 43;
   Du Pont (DD-152) and J. Fred Talbott (DD-156)
to AG 80-81 25 Sep 44.

LITTLE class

Displacement: 1060 (standard), 1191 (normal) tons
Dimensions: 315'5"(DD 79-92, oa.), 314'5"(others, oa.) x
   31'8" (DD 79-84, 87-92, 161-180, e), 31'9"(DD-85, 95-112,
   e), 32' (DD-86, e) x 9'10"(max)
Armament: 4-4"/50 2-3"/23AA 12-21"T; 4-4" 1-3"AA 12-21"T
   (1929); 4-4" 1-3"AA 80m (DM conversions, 1930); 3-3"/50AA
   (APD conversions, 1940); 2-3"AA (DMS conversions, 1940);
   6-3"AA 6-21"T (DD, 1941); 3-3"AA 80m (DM conversions, 1943)

Machinery: 27,000 SHP; geared
   turbines, 2 screws
Speed: 35 kts.
Complement: 103

No.		Hull	Machinery	Laid down	Launched	Commiss'd	Disposition
79	LITTLE	Fore River		18 Jun 17	11 Nov 17	6 Apr 18	Sunk by Japanese destroyers off Guadalcanal 5 Sep 42
80	KIMBERLY	Fore River		21 Jun 17	4 Dec 17	26 Apr 18	Stk. 25 Jan 37, sold 20 Apr 39
81	SIGOURNEY	Fore River		25 Aug 17	16 Dec 17	15 May 18	To Britain 26 Nov 40 as Newport, stk. 8 Jan 41
82	GREGORY	Fore River		25 Aug 17	27 Jan 18	1 Jun 18	Sunk by Japanese destroyers off Guadalcanal 5 Sep 42
83	STRINGHAM	Fore River		19 Sep 17	30 Mar 18	2 Jul 18	Stk. 5 Dec 45, scrapped 1946
84	DYER	Fore River		26 Sep 17	13 Apr 18	1 Jul 18	Stk. 7 Jan 36, sold 8 Sep 36
85	COLHOUN	Fore River		19 Sep 17	21 Feb 18	13 Jun 18	Sunk by Japanese aircraft off Guadalcanal 30 Aug 42
86	STEVENS	Fore River		20 Sep 17	13 Jan 18	24 May 18	Stk. 7 Jan 36, sold 8 Sep 36
87	McKEE	Union	G. E.	29 Oct 17	23 Mar 18	7 Sep 18	Stk. 7 Jan 36, sold 8 Sep 36
88	ROBINSON	Union	G. E.	31 Oct 17	28 Mar 18	19 Oct 18	To Britain 26 Nov 40 as Newmarket, stk. 8 Jan 41
89	RINGGOLD	Union	G. E.	20 Oct 17	14 Apr 18	14 Nov 18	To Britain 26 Nov 40 as Newark, stk. 8 Jan 41
90	McKEAN	Union	G. E.	12 Feb 18	4 Jul 18	25 Feb 19	Sunk by Japanese aircraft off Bougainville 17 Nov 43
91	HARDING	Union	G. E.	12 Feb 18	4 Jul 18	24 Jan 19	Stk. 7 Jan 36, sold 29 Sep 36
92	GRIDLEY	Union	G. E.	1 Apr 18	4 Jul 18	8 Mar 19	Stk. 25 Jan 37, sold 18 Apr 39
95	BELL	Fore River		16 Nov 17	20 Apr 18	31 Jul 18	Stk. 25 Jan 37, sold 18 Apr 39
96	STRIBLING	Fore River		14 Dec 17	29 May 18	16 Aug 18	Stk. 1 Dec 36, sunk as target off Pearl Harbor 28 Jul 37
97	MURRAY	Fore River		22 Dec 17	8 Jun 18	21 Aug 18	Stk. 7 Jan 36, sold 29 Sep 36
98	ISRAEL	Fore River		26 Jan 18	22 Jun 18	13 Sep 18	Stk. 25 Jan 37, sold 18 Apr 39
99	LUCE	Fore River		9 Feb 18	29 Jun 18	11 Sep 18	Stk. 7 Jan 36, sold 29 Sep 36
100	MAURY	Fore River		26 Feb 18	4 Jul 18	23 Sep 18	Stk. 22 Oct 30, sold 17 Jan 31
101	LANSDALE	Fore River		20 Apr 18	21 Jul 18	26 Oct 18	Stk. 25 Jan 37, sold 16 Mar 39
102	MAHAN	Fore River		4 May 18	4 Aug 18	24 Oct 18	Stk. 22 Oct 30, sold 17 Jan 31
103	SCHLEY	Union		29 Oct 17	28 Mar 18	20 Sep 18	Stk. 5 Dec 45, scrapped 1946
104	CHAMPLIN	Union		31 Oct 17	7 Apr 18	11 Nov 18	Stk. 19 May 36, sunk in tests off San Diego 12 Aug 36
105	MUGFORD	Union		20 Oct 17	14 Apr 18	25 Nov 18	Stk. 19 May 36, sold 29 Sep 36
106	CHEW	Union		2 Jan 18	26 May 18	12 Dec 18	Stk. 1 Nov 45, sold 4 Oct 46
107	HAZELWOOD	Union		24 Dec 17	22 Jun 18	20 Feb 19	Stk. 5 Jun 35, sold 3 Aug 35
108	WILLIAMS	Union		25 Mar 18	4 Jul 18	1 Mar 19	To Britain 24 Sep 40 as St. Clair, stk. 8 Jan 41
109	CRANE	Union		7 Jan 18	4 Jul 18	18 Apr 19	Stk. 19 Dec 45, sold 1 Nov 46

No.		Hull	Machinery	Laid down	Launched	Commiss'd	Disposition
110	HART	Union		8 Jan 18	4 Jul 18	26 May 19	Stk. 11 Nov 31, sold 25 Feb 32
111	INGRAHAM	Union		12 Jan 18	4 Jul 18	15 May 19	Stk. 1 Dec 36, sunk as target off Pearl Harbor 23 Jul 37
112	LUDLOW	Union		7 Jan 18	9 Jun 18	23 Dec 18	Stk. 18 Nov 30, scrapped 1931
161	PALMER	Fore River		29 May 18	18 Aug 18	22 Nov 18	Sunk by Japanese aircraft in Lingayen Gulf, 7 Jan 45
162	THATCHER	Fore River		8 Jun 18	31 Aug 18	14 Jan 19	To Britain 24 Sep 40 as Niagara, stk. 8 Jan 41
163	WALKER	Fore River		19 Jun 18	14 Sep 18	31 Jan 19	Scuttled off Hawaii 28 Dec 41
164	CROSBY	Fore River		23 Jun 18	28 Sep 18	24 Jan 19	Stk. 24 Oct 45, sold 23 May 46
165	MEREDITH	Fore River		26 Jun 18	22 Sep 18	29 Jan 19	Stk. 7 Jan 36, sold 29 Sep 36
166	BUSH	Fore River		4 Jul 18	27 Oct 18	19 Feb 19	Stk. 7 Jan 36, sold 8 Sep 36
167	COWELL	Fore River		15 Jul 18	23 Nov 18	17 Mar 19	To Britain 23 Sep 40 as Brighton, stk. 8 Jan 41
168	MADDOX	Fore River		20 Jul 18	27 Oct 18	10 Mar 19	To Britain 23 Sep 40 as Georgetown, stk. 8 Jan 41
169	FOOTE	Fore River		7 Aug 18	14 Dec 18	21 Mar 19	To Britain 23 Sep 40 as Roxborough, stk. 8 Jan 41
170	KALK	Fore River		17 Aug 18	21 Dec 18	29 Mar 19	To Britain 23 Sep 40 as Hamilton, stk. 8 Jan 41
171	BURNS	Union		15 Apr 18	4 Jul 18	7 Aug 19	Stk. 18 Nov 30, scrapped 1932
172	ANTHONY	Union		18 Apr 18	10 Aug 18	19 Jun 19	Stk. 1 Dec 36, sunk as target off California 22 Jul 37
173	SPROSTON	Union		20 Apr 18	10 Aug 18	12 Jul 19	Stk. 1 Dec 36, sunk as target off California 20 Jul 37
174	RIZAL	Union		26 Jun 18	21 Sep 18	28 May 19	Stk. 11 Nov 31, scrapped 1932
175	MACKENZIE	Union		4 Jul 18	29 Sep 18	25 Jul 19	To Britain 24 Sep 40 as Annapolis, stk. 8 Jan 41
176	RENSHAW	Union		8 May 18	21 Sep 18	31 Jul 19	Stk. 19 May 36, sold 29 Sep 36
177	O'BANNON	Union		12 Nov 18	28 Feb 19	27 Aug 19	Stk. 19 May 36, sold 29 Sep 36
178	HOGAN	Union		25 Nov 18	12 Apr 19	1 Oct 19	Stk. 1 Nov 45, sunk as target off San Diego 8 Nov 45
179	HOWARD	Union		9 Dec 18	26 Apr 19	29 Jan 20	Stk. 19 Dec 45, sold 13 Jun 46
180	STANSBURY	Union		9 Dec 18	16 May 19	8 Jan 20	Stk. 3 Jan 46, sold 26 Oct 46.

Notes: Fiscal years 1917 (DD 79-92) and 1918. This class was built to the same specifications as the Wickes class using detail plans prepared by Bethlehem Steel for use in its shipyards at Quincy, Mass. (Fore River) and San Francisco (Union). The ships were not quite as successful as those built to the Bath plans, particularly in steaming endurance. In addition, Bethlehem used a type of Yarrow boiler in all of its flush-deckers which deteriorated rapidly in service. The Navy still had 58 destroyers and destroyer minelayers with Yarrow boilers on active duty in late 1929 and decided, instead of repairing them, to replace them with ships from the reserve fleet and scrap them. (These ships were DD 107, 276-78, 280-295, 298-308, and 313-335 plus DM 5, 7, and 10-11.)

The Rizal (DD-174) was built at the expense of the Philippine government for service with a Filipino crew. The Hazelwood (DD-107) was designated Light Target No. 2 (IX-36) in 1930 but reverted to destroyer status in 1931 because of boiler defects. (She was initially renamed with her Light Target designation but recovered her destroyer name on 24 Apr 31.) The Kimberly (DD-80), ex-Gridley (DD-92), Bell (DD-95), Israel (DD-98), and Lansdale (DD-101) were reduced to hulks 28 Dec 36. The Walker (DD-163) was stricken on 23 Mar 38, retained as an unpowered water barge (YW-57), and converted in 1941 to the damage control training hulk DCH-1 (IX-44) for use at Pearl Harbor. She was scuttled while under tow to Pearl Harbor after the Japanese attack rendered her services unnecessary.

Renamings: DD-99 ex unnamed 4 Dec 17, ex Schley 24 Sep 17; DD-170 ex Rodgers 23 Dec 18. The Gridley (DD-92) and Mugford (DD-105) dropped their names 31 May 35.

Reclassifications:

Little (DD-79), Gregory (DD-82), Colhoun (DD-85), and McKean (DD-90) to APD-4, 3, 2, and 5 2 Aug 40;

Stringham (DD-83) to APD-6 2 Aug 40; DD-83 25 Jun 45;

Stribling (DD-96), Murray (DD-97), Israel (DD-98), Luce (DD-99), Maury (DD-100), Lansdale (DD-101), Mahan (DD-102), Hart (DD-110), Ingraham (DD-111), Ludlow (DD-112), Burns (DD-171), Anthony (DD-172), Sproston (DD-173), and Rizal (DD-174) to DM 1-14 17 Jul 20;

Schley (DD-103) to APD-14 6 Feb 43; DD-103 5 Jul 45;

Hazelwood (DD-107) to IX-36 5 Nov 30; DD-107 11 Aug 31;

Palmer (DD-161) to DMS-5 19 Nov 40;

Walker (DD-163) to YW-57 1 Apr 39; IX-44 6 Jan 41;

Crosby (DD-164) to APD-17 22 Feb 43;

Hogan (DD-178), Howard (DD-179), and Stansbury (DD-180) to DMS 6-8 19 Nov 40; AG 105-107 5 Jun 45.

1917

LAMBERTON class

Displacement: 1090 (standard), 1213 (normal) tons
Dimensions: 314'5"(oa.) x 31'8"(e) x 10'3"(DD-120, 122, 124, 184, 185, max), 9'6"(DD-123, max), 9'10"(others, max)
Armament: 4-4"/50 2-3"AA/23 12-21"T; 4-4" 1-3"AA 12-21"T (1921); 4-4" 1-3"AA 80m (DM conversions, 1930); 4-3"/50AA (DMS conversions, 1940); 6-3"AA 6-21"T (DD, 1941); 4-4" 80m (DM conversions except DD-124/DM-16, 1943); 4-3"AA 80m (DD-124/DM-16, 1943)

Machinery: 24,900 (DD 120-124), 24,100 (others) SHP; direct drive turbines with geared cruising turbines, 2 screws
Speed: 35 kts.
Complement: 101

No.	Hull	Machinery	Laid down	Launched	Commiss'd	Disposition
119 LAMBERTON	Newport News		1 Oct 17	30 Mar 18	22 Aug 18	Stk. 28 Jan 47, sold 9 May 47
120 RADFORD	Newport News		2 Oct 17	5 Apr 18	30 Sep 18	Stk. 19 May 36, sunk as target off San Diego 5 Aug 36
121 MONTGOMERY	Newport News		2 Oct 17	23 Mar 18	26 Jul 18	Stk. 28 Apr 45, sold 11 Mar 46
122 BREESE	Newport News		10 Nov 17	11 May 18	23 Oct 18	Stk. 7 Feb 46, sold 16 May 46
123 GAMBLE	Newport News		12 Nov 17	11 May 18	29 Nov 18	Stk. 22 Jun 45, scuttled off Guam 16 Jul 45
124 RAMSAY	Newport News		21 Dec 17	8 Jun 18	15 Feb 19	Stk. 13 Nov 45, sold 21 Nov 46
181 HOPEWELL	Newport News		19 Jan 18	8 Jun 18	22 Mar 19	To Britain 23 Sep 40 as Bath, stk. 8 Jan 41
182 THOMAS	Newport News		23 Mar 18	4 Jul 18	25 Apr 19	To Britain 23 Sep 40 as St. Albans, stk. 8 Jan 41
183 HARADEN	Newport News		30 Mar 18	4 Jul 18	7 Jun 19	To Britain 24 Sep 40 as Columbia, stk. 8 Jan 41
184 ABBOT	Newport News		5 Apr 18	4 Jul 18	19 Jul 19	To Britain 23 Sep 40 as Charlestown, stk. 8 Jan 41
185 BAGLEY	Newport News		11 May 18	19 Oct 18	27 Aug 19	To Britain 23 Sep 40 as St. Marys, stk. 8 Jan 41.

Notes: Fiscal year 1918. War emergency legislation gave priority to naval over civilian shipbuilding contracts and allowed two large yards, Newport News and New York SB, to join the expanded destroyer program in May and June 1917. These firms closely followed the Bath plans for the Wickes class, although the normal displacement of their ships was slightly heavier. The Newport News ships had an older type of machinery installation with two direct-drive main turbines and two geared cruising turbines, all driving two shafts. Despite this, their steaming radius was better than some of the less-well built ships with geared main turbines.
The Lamberton (DD-119) was designated Light Target No. 1 (AG-21) in 1932. At the same time the Radford (DD-120) was reclassified AG-22 for conversion to Light Target No. 3, but the conversion was not undertaken due to budget limitations and she reverted to destroyer status. The Montgomery was irreparably damaged by a mine at Ngulu Lagoon, Carolines, on 17 Oct 44 and the Gamble was damaged by Japanese aircraft off Iwo Jima on 17 Feb 45.
Renamings: The Bagley dropped her name 31 May 35 and became the Doran 22 Dec 39.
Reclassifications:
Lamberton (DD-119) to AG-21 16 Apr 32; DMS-2 19 Nov 40; AG-21 5 May 45;
Radford (DD-120) to AG-22 16 Apr 32; DD-120 27 Jun 32;
Montgomery (DD-121) and Breese (DD-122) to DM 17-18 5 Jan 31
Gamble (DD-123) to DM-15 13 Jun 30;
Ramsey (DD-124) to DM-16 13 Jun 30; AG-98 5 Jun 45.

TATTNALL class

Displacement: 1090 (standard). 1211 (normal) tons
Dimensions: 314'5"(oa.) x 31'8"(e) x 10'1"(DD-126, 128-129, max), 9'10"(others, max)
Armament: 4-4"/50 2-3"/23AA 12-21"T; 4-4" 1-3"AA 12-21"T (all except DD-130, 1921); 4-4" 6-21"T (DD-125, 1941); 6-3"AA 6-21"T (DD-126, 128, 130, 157, 159, 1941); 3-3"AA (APD conversions, 1943)

Machinery: 24,900 (DD 125-130) 26,300 (others) SHP; geared turbines, 2 screws
Speed: 35 kts.
Complement: 101

No.	Hull	Machinery	Laid down	Launched	Commiss'd	Disposition
125 TATTNALL	New York SB		1 Dec 17	5 Sep 18	26 Jun 19	Stk. 8 Jan 46, sold 13 Nov 46
126 BADGER	New York SB		9 Jan 18	24 Aug 18	29 May 19	Stk. 13 Aug 45, sold 30 Nov 45
127 TWIGGS	New York SB		23 Jan 18	28 Sep 18	28 Jul 19	To Britain 23 Oct 40 as Leamington, stk. 8 Jan 41
128 BABBITT	New York SB		19 Feb 18	30 Sep 18	24 Oct 19	Stk. 25 Feb 46, sold 5 Jun 46
129 DE LONG	New York SB		21 Feb 18	29 Oct 18	20 Sep 19	Wrecked Half Moon Bay, Calif., 1 Dec 21
130 JACOB JONES	New York SB		21 Feb 18	20 Nov 18	20 Oct 19	Sunk by U-578 off Cape May, N.J., 28 Feb 42
157 DICKERSON	New York SB		25 May 18	12 Mar 19	3 Sep 19	Scuttled at Kerama Retto 4 Apr 45, stk. 28 Apr 45
158 LEARY	New York SB		6 Mar 18	18 Dec 18	5 Dec 19	Sunk by U-275 N off the Azores 24 Dec 43
159 SCHENCK	New York SB		26 Mar 18	23 Apr 19	30 Oct 19	Stk. 5 Jun 46, sold 25 Nov 46
160 HERBERT	New York SB		9 Apr 18	8 May 19	21 Nov 19	Stk. 24 Oct 45, sold 23 May 46.

Notes: Fiscal year 1918. New York SB joined the wartime destroyer program in June 1917 and closely followed the Bath plans for the Wickes class, although the normal displacement of its ships was slightly greater. The steaming radius of these ships was not as good as that of their Bath- and Cramp-built sisters. The wreck of the De Long was sold 25 Sep 22. The Dickerson was damaged by suicide planes off Okinawa on 2 Apr 45.

Reclassifications:

Tattnall (DD-125) to APD-19 24 Jul 43;   Schenck (DD-159) to AG-82 25 Sep 44;
Babbitt (DD-128) to AG-102 10 Jun 45;   Herbert (DD-160) to APD-22 1 Dec 43.
Dickerson (DD-157) to APD-21 21 Aug 43;

1917

CLEMSON class

Displacement: 1190 (standard), 1215 (normal) tons
Dimensions: 314'5"(oa.) x 31'8"(DD-231, 335-347, e), 31'9" (others, e) x 9'10"(max)
Armament: 5-4"/50 1-3"/23AA 12-21"T (DD-189); 8-4" 12-21"T (DD 208-209); 4-5"/51 1-3"AA 12-21"T (DD 231-235); 4-4" 1-3"AA 12-21"T (others); 4-4" 6-21"T (DD-187, 211, 213, 215-218, 222, 228, 230-231, 234, 242, 247-248, 250, 336, 343, 1943); 6-3"/50AA 6-21"T (DD-199, 210, 220-221, 223, 229-239, 246, 341, 1941); 2-3"AA (DD-237, 1945); 3-3"AA (APD conversions); 2-3"AA (DMS conversions); 3-3"AA 80m (DM conversions)

Machinery: 26,500 (DD 186-205), 25,200 (DD 206-230), 27,700 (DD 231-235), 27,600 (DD 251-260), 27,000 (DD 236-250), 26,000 (DD 261-344), 24,800 (DD 345-347); geared turbines, 2 screws
Speed: 35 kts.
Complement: 101

No.	Hull	Machinery	Laid down	Launched	Commiss'd	Disposition
186 CLEMSON	Newpt.News	W'house	11 May 18	5 Sep 18	29 Dec 19	Stk. 24 Oct 45, sold 21 Nov 46
187 DAHLGREN	Newpt.News	W'house	8 Jun 18	20 Nov 18	6 Jan 20	Stk. 8 Jan 46, sold 17 Jun 46
188 GOLDSBOROUGH	Newpt.News	W'house	8 Jun 18	20 Nov 18	26 Jan 20	Stk. 24 Oct 45, sold 21 Nov 46
189 SEMMES	Newpt.News	W'house	10 Jul 18	21 Dec 18	21 Feb 20	Stk. 3 Jul 46, sold 25 Nov 46
190 SATTERLEE	Newpt.News	W'house	10 Jul 18	21 Dec 18	23 Dec 19	To Britain 9 Oct 40 as Belmont, stk. 8 Jan 41
191 MASON	Newpt.News	W'house	10 Jul 18	8 Mar 19	28 Feb 20	To Britain 9 Oct 40 as Broadwater, stk. 8 Jan 41
192 GRAHAM	Newpt.News	W'house	7 Sep 18	22 Mar 19	13 Mar 20	Stk. 4 May 22, sold 19 Sep 22
193 ABEL P. UPSHUR	Newpt.News	W'house	20 Aug 18	14 Feb 20	23 Nov 20	To Britain 9 Sep 40 as Clare, stk. 8 Jan 41
194 HUNT	Newpt.News	W'house	20 Aug 18	14 Feb 20	30 Sep 20	To Britain 9 Oct 40 as Broadway, stk. 8 Jan 41
195 WELBORN C. WOOD	Newpt.News	W'house	24 Sep 18	6 Mar 20	14 Jan 21	To Britain 9 Sep 40 as Chesterfield, stk. 8 Jan 41
196 GEORGE E. BADGER	Newpt.News	W'house	24 Sep 18	6 Mar 20	28 Jul 20	Stk. 24 Oct 45, scrapped 1946
197 BRANCH	Newpt.News	W'house	25 Oct 18	19 Apr 19	26 Jul 20	To Britain 9 Oct 40 as Beverly, stk. 8 Jan 41
198 HERNDON	Newpt.News	W'house	25 Nov 18	31 May 19	14 Sep 20	To Britain 9 Oct 40 as Churchill, stk. 8 Jan 41
199 DALLAS	Newpt.News	W'house	25 Nov 18	31 May 19	29 Oct 20	Stk. 13 Aug 45, sold 30 Nov 45
200 Unnamed -205	Newpt.News	W'house	No	No	No	Cancelled 3 Feb 19

No.		Hull	Machinery	Laid down	Launched	Commiss'd	Disposition
206	CHANDLER	Cramp		19 Aug 18	19 Mar 19	5 Sep 19	Stk. 5 Dec 45, sold 18 Nov 46
207	SOUTHARD	Cramp		18 Aug 18	31 Mar 19	24 Sep 19	Grounded on Tsugen Jima 9 Oct 45, destroyed 14 Jan 46
208	HOVEY	Cramp		7 Sep 18	26 Apr 19	2 Oct 19	Sunk by Japanese aircraft in Lingayen Gulf, Luzon, 6 Jan 45
209	LONG	Cramp		23 Sep 18	26 Apr 19	20 Oct 19	Sunk by Japanese suicide planes in Lingayen Gulf, 6 Jan 45
210	BROOME	Cramp		8 Oct 18	14 May 19	31 Oct 19	Stk. 19 Jun 46, sold 20 Nov 46
211	ALDEN	Cramp		24 Oct 18	7 Jun 19	24 Nov 19	Stk. 13 Aug 45, sold 30 Nov 45
212	SMITH THOMPSON	Cramp		24 Mar 19	14 Jul 19	10 Dec 19	Stk. 19 May 36, scuttled off Subic Bay 25 Jul 36
213	BARKER	Cramp		30 Apr 19	11 Sep 19	27 Dec 19	Stk. 13 Aug 45, sold 30 Nov 45
214	TRACY	Cramp		3 Apr 19	12 Aug 19	9 Mar 20	Stk. 7 Feb 46, sold 16 May 46
215	BORIE	Cramp		30 Apr 19	4 Oct 19	24 Mar 20	Sunk as result of ramming U-405 in N. Atlantic 2 Nov 43
216	JOHN D. EDWARDS	Cramp		21 May 19	18 Oct 19	6 Apr 20	Stk. 13 Aug 45, sold 30 Nov 45
217	WHIPPLE	Cramp		12 Jun 19	6 Nov 19	23 Apr 20	Stk. 5 Dec 45, scrapped 1946
218	PARROTT	Cramp		23 Jul 19	25 Nov 19	11 May 20	Stk. 18 Jul 44, sold 5 Apr 47
219	EDSALL	Cramp		15 Sep 19	29 Jul 20	26 Nov 20	Sunk by Japanese squadron S of Java 1 Mar 42
220	MACLEISH	Cramp		19 Aug 19	18 Dec 19	2 Aug 20	Stk. 13 Nov 46, sold 3 Dec 46
221	SIMPSON	Cramp		9 Oct 19	28 Apr 20	3 Nov 20	Stk. 19 Jun 46, sold 21 Nov 46
222	BULMER	Cramp		11 Aug 19	22 Jan 20	16 Aug 20	Stk. 25 Sep 46, sold 28 Feb 47
223	McCORMICK	Cramp		11 Aug 19	14 Feb 20	30 Aug 20	Stk. 24 Oct 45, sold 15 Dec 46
224	STEWART	Cramp		9 Sep 19	4 Mar 20	15 Sep 20	Stk. 17 Apr 46, sunk as target off San Francisco 24 May 46
225	POPE	Cramp		9 Sep 19	23 Mar 20	27 Oct 20	Sunk by Japanese aircraft in Bali Strait 1 Mar 42
226	PEARY	Cramp		9 Sep 19	6 Apr 20	22 Oct 20	Sunk by Japanese aircraft at Darwin, Australia, 19 Feb 42
227	PILLSBURY	Cramp		23 Oct 19	3 Aug 20	15 Dec 20	Sunk by Japanese squadron in Bali Strait 1 Mar 42
228	FORD	Cramp		11 Nov 19	2 Sep 20	30 Dec 20	Stk. 16 Nov 45, sold 30 Sep 47
229	TRUXTUN	Cramp		3 Dec 19	28 Sep 20	16 Feb 21	Wrecked in Placenta Bay, Newfoundland, 18 Feb 42
230	PAUL JONES	Cramp		23 Dec 19	30 Sep 20	19 Apr 21	Stk. 28 Nov 45, sold 5 Oct 47
231	HATFIELD	N.York SB	W'house	10 Jun 18	17 Mar 19	16 Apr 20	Stk. 28 Jan 47, sold 9 May 47
232	BROOKS	N.York SB	W'house	11 Jun 18	24 Apr 19	18 Jun 20	Stk. 17 Sep 45, sold 30 Jan 46
233	GILMER	N.York SB	W'house	25 Jun 18	24 May 19	30 Apr 20	Stk. 25 Feb 46, sold 3 Dec 46
234	FOX	N.York SB	W'house	25 Jun 18	12 Jun 19	17 May 20	Stk. 19 Dec 45, sold 12 Nov 46
235	KANE	N.York SB	W'house	3 Jul 18	12 Aug 19	11 Jun 20	Stk. 25 Feb 46, sold 21 Jun 46
236	HUMPHREYS	N.York SB	W'house	31 Jul 18	28 Jul 19	21 Jul 20	Stk. 13 Nov 45, sold 26 Aug 46
237	McFARLAND	N.York SB	W'house	31 Jul 18	30 Mar 20	30 Sep 20	Stk. 19 Dec 45, sold 29 Oct 46
238	JAMES K. PAULDING	N.York SB	W'house	31 Jul 18	20 Apr 20	29 Nov 20	Stk. 25 Jan 37, sold 16 Mar 39
239	OVERTON	N.York SB	W'house	30 Oct 18	10 Jul 19	30 Jun 20	Stk. 13 Aug 45, sold 30 Nov 45
240	STURTEVANT	N.York SB	W'house	23 Nov 18	29 Jul 20	21 Sep 20	Mined off Key West, Fla., 26 Apr 42
241	CHILDS	N.York SB	W'house	19 Mar 19	15 Sep 20	22 Oct 20	Stk. 3 Jan 46, sold 23 May 46
242	KING	N.York SB	W'house	28 Apr 19	14 Oct 20	16 Dec 20	Stk. 16 Nov 45, sold 29 Sep 46
243	SANDS	N.York SB	W'house	22 Mar 19	28 Oct 19	10 Nov 20	Stk. 1 Nov 45, sold 23 May 46
244	WILLIAMSON	N.York SB	W'house	27 Mar 19	16 Oct 19	29 Oct 20	Stk. 19 Dec 45, sold 30 Oct 46
245	REUBEN JAMES	N.York SB	W'house	2 Apr 19	4 Oct 19	24 Sep 20	Sunk by U-562 S of Iceland 31 Oct 41
246	BAINBRIDGE	N.York SB	W'house	27 May 19	12 Jun 20	9 Feb 21	Stk. 13 Aug 45, sold 30 Nov 45
247	GOFF	N.York SB	W'house	16 Jun 19	2 Jun 20	19 Jan 21	Stk. 13 Aug 45, sold 30 Nov 45
248	BARRY	N.York SB	W'house	26 Jul 19	28 Oct 20	28 Dec 20	Sunk by Japanese suicide planes off Okinawa 21 Jun 45
249	HOPKINS	N.York SB	W'house	30 Jul 19	26 Jun 20	21 Mar 21	Stk. 8 Jan 46, sold 8 Nov 46
250	LAWRENCE	N.York SB	W'house	14 Aug 19	10 Jul 20	18 Apr 21	Stk. 13 Nov 45, sold 1 Oct 46
251	BELKNAP	Quincy		31 Jul 18	14 Jan 19	28 Apr 19	Stk. 13 Aug 45, sold 30 Nov 45
252	McCOOK	Quincy		11 Sep 18	31 Jan 19	30 Apr 19	To Britain 24 Sep 40 as St. Croix, stk. 8 Jan 41
253	McCALLA	Quincy		25 Sep 18	28 Mar 19	19 May 19	To Britain 23 Oct 40 as Stanley, stk. 8 Jan 41

No.		Hull	Machinery	Laid down	Launched	Commiss'd	Disposition
254	RODGERS	Quincy		25 Sep 18	26 Apr 19	22 Jul 19	To Britain 23 Oct 40 as Sherwood, stk. 8 Jan 41
255	INGRAM	Quincy		15 Oct 18	28 Feb 19	28 Jun 19	Stk. 21 Jan 46, sold 17 Jun 46
256	BANCROFT	Quincy		4 Nov 18	21 Mar 19	30 Jun 19	To Britain 24 Sep 40 as St. Francis, stk. 8 Jan 41
257	WELLES	Quincy		13 Nov 18	8 May 19	2 Sep 19	To Britain 9 Sep 40 as Cameron, stk. 8 Jan 41
258	AULICK	Quincy		3 Dec 18	11 Apr 19	26 Jul 19	To Britain 9 Oct 40 as Burnham, stk. 8 Jan 41
259	TURNER	Quincy		19 Dec 18	17 May 19	24 Sep 19	Stk. 17 Apr 46, sold 20 Feb 47 by Maritime Commission
260	GILLIS	Quincy		27 Dec 18	29 May 19	3 Sep 19	Stk. 1 Nov 45, sold 29 Jan 46
261	DELPHY	Squantum	Buffalo	20 Apr 18	18 Jul 18	30 Nov 18	Wrecked on Honda Pt., Calif., 8 Sep 23
262	McDERMUT	Squantum	Buffalo	20 Apr 18	6 Aug 18	27 Mar 19	Stk. 11 Nov 31, scrapped 1932
263	LAUB	Squantum	Buffalo	20 Apr 18	25 Aug 18	17 Mar 19	To Britain 9 Oct 40 as Burwell, stk. 8 Jan 41
264	McLANAHAN	Squantum	Buffalo	20 Apr 18	22 Sep 18	5 Apr 19	To Britain 9 Oct 40 as Bradford, stk. 8 Jan 41
265	EDWARDS	Squantum	Buffalo	20 Apr 18	10 Oct 18	24 Apr 19	To Britain 9 Oct 40 as Buxton, stk. 8 Jan 41
266	GREENE	Squantum	Buffalo	3 Jun 18	2 Nov 18	9 May 19	Grounded Okinawa 9 Oct 45, destroyed 11 Feb 46
267	BALLARD	Squantum	Buffalo & G. E.	3 Jun 18	7 Dec 18	5 Jun 19	Stk. 3 Jan 46, sold 23 May 46
268	SHUBRICK	Squantum	Buffalo	3 Jun 18	31 Dec 18	3 Jul 19	To Britain 26 Nov 40 as Ripley, stk. 8 Jan 41
269	BAILEY	Squantum	Buffalo	3 Jun 18	5 Feb 19	27 Jun 19	To Britain 26 Nov 40 as Reading, stk. 8 Jan 41
270	THORNTON	Squantum	Buffalo & G. E.	3 Jun 18	22 Mar 19	15 Jul 19	Beached and abandoned 2 May 45, Kerama Retto, stk. 13 Aug 45
271	MORRIS	Squantum	Buffalo	20 Jul 18	12 Apr 19	21 Jul 19	Stk. 19 May 36, sold 29 Sep 36
272	TINGEY	Squantum	Buffalo	8 Aug 18	24 Apr 19	25 Jul 19	Stk. 19 May 36, sold 29 Sep 36
273	SWASEY	Squantum	Buffalo	27 Aug 18	7 May 19	8 Aug 19	To Britain 26 Nov 40 as Rockingham, stk. 8 Jan 41
274	MEADE	Squantum	Buffalo	23 Sep 18	24 May 19	8 Sep 19	To Britain 26 Nov 40 as Ramsey, stk. 8 Jan 41
275	SINCLAIR	Squantum	Buffalo	15 Oct 18	2 Jun 19	8 Oct 19	Stk. 5 Jun 35, sold 30 Aug 35
276	McCAWLEY	Squantum	Buffalo	5 Nov 18	14 Jun 19	22 Sep 19	Stk. 13 Aug 30, scrapped 1931
277	MOODY	Squantum	Buffalo	9 Dec 18	28 Jun 19	10 Dec 19	Stk. 3 Nov 30, scrapped 1931
278	HENSHAW	Squantum	Buffalo	3 Jan 19	28 Jun 19	10 Dec 19	Stk. 22 Jul 30, scrapped 1930
279	MEYER	Squantum	Buffalo	6 Feb 19	18 Jul 19	17 Dec 19	Stk. 25 Nov 30, scrapped 1932
280	DOYEN	Squantum	Buffalo	24 Mar 19	26 Jul 19	17 Dec 19	Stk. 12 Jul 30, scrapped 1930
281	SHARKEY	Squantum	Buffalo	14 Apr 19	12 Aug 19	28 Nov 19	Stk. 22 Oct 30, sold 17 Jan 31
282	TOUCEY	Squantum	Buffalo	26 Apr 19	5 Sep 19	9 Dec 19	Stk. 22 Oct 30, sold 17 Jan 31
283	BRECK	Squantum	Buffalo	8 May 19	5 Sep 19	1 Dec 19	Stk. 22 Oct 30, sold 17 Jan 31
284	ISHERWOOD	Squantum	Buffalo	24 May 19	10 Sep 19	4 Dec 19	Stk. 22 Oct 30, sold 17 Jan 31
285	CASE	Squantum	Buffalo	3 Jun 19	21 Sep 19	8 Dec 19	Stk. 22 Oct 30, sold 17 Jan 31
286	LARDNER	Squantum	Buffalo	16 Jun 19	29 Sep 19	10 Dec 19	Stk. 22 Oct 30, sold 17 Jan 31
287	PUTNAM	Squantum	Buffalo	30 Jun 19	30 Sep 19	18 Dec 19	Stk. 22 Oct 30, sold 17 Jan 31
288	WORDEN	Squantum	Buffalo	30 Jun 19	24 Oct 19	24 Feb 20	Stk. 22 Oct 30, sold 17 Jan 31
289	FLUSSER	Squantum	Buffalo	21 Jul 19	7 Nov 19	25 Feb 20	Stk. 22 Oct 30, sold 17 Jan 31
290	DALE	Squantum	Buffalo	28 Jul 19	19 Nov 19	16 Feb 20	Stk. 22 Oct 30, sold 17 Jan 31
291	CONVERSE	Squantum	Buffalo	13 Aug 19	28 Nov 19	28 Apr 20	Stk. 22 Oct 30, sold 17 Jan 31
292	REID	Squantum	Buffalo	9 Sep 19	15 Oct 19	3 Dec 19	Stk. 22 Oct 30, sold 17 Jan 31
293	BILLINGSLEY	Squantum	Buffalo	8 Sep 19	10 Dec 19	1 Mar 20	Stk. 22 Oct 30, sold 17 Jan 31
294	CHARLES AUSBURN	Squantum	Buffalo	11 Sep 19	18 Dec 19	23 Mar 20	Stk. 22 Oct 30, sold 17 Jan 31
295	OSBORNE	Squantum	Buffalo	23 Sep 19	29 Dec 19	17 May 20	Stk. 22 Oct 30, sold 17 Jan 31
296	CHAUNCEY	Beth-SF	G. E.	17 Jun 18	29 Sep 18	25 Jun 19	Wrecked on Honda Pt., Calif., 8 Sep 23
297	FULLER	Beth-SF	G. E.	4 Jul 18	5 Dec 18	28 Feb 20	Wrecked on Honda Pt., Calif., 8 Sep 23
298	PERCIVAL	Beth-SF	G. E.	4 Jul 18	5 Dec 18	31 Mar 20	Stk. 18 Nov 30, scrapped 1931

No.		Hull	Machinery	Laid down	Launched	Commiss'd	Disposition
299	JOHN FRANCIS BURNS	Beth-SF	G. E.	4 Jul 18	10 Nov 18	1 May 20	Stk. 22 Jul 30, scrapped 1931
300	FARRAGUT	Beth-SF	G. E.	4 Jul 18	21 Nov 18	4 Jun 20	Stk. 22 Jul 30, scrapped 1930
301	SOMERS	Beth-SF	G. E.	4 Jul 18	28 Dec 18	23 Jun 20	Stk. 18 Nov 30, scrapped 1931
302	STODDERT	Beth-SF	G. E.	4 Jul 18	8 Jan 19	30 Jun 20	Stk. 5 Jun 35, sold 30 Aug 35
303	RENO	Beth-SF	G. E.	4 Jul 18	22 Jan 19	23 Jul 20	Stk. 8 Jul 30, scrapped 1931
304	FARQUHAR	Beth-SF	G. E.	13 Aug 18	18 Jan 19	5 Aug 20	Stk. 18 Nov 30, scrapped 1932
305	THOMPSON	Beth-SF	G. E.	14 Aug 18	19 Jan 19	16 Aug 20	Stk. 22 Jul 30, scrapped 1931
306	KENNEDY	Beth-SF	G. E.	25 Sep 18	15 Feb 19	28 Aug 20	Stk. 18 Nov 30, scrapped 1931
307	PAUL HAMILTON	Beth-SF	G. E.	25 Sep 18	21 Feb 19	24 Sep 20	Stk. 8 Jul 30, scrapped 1931
308	WILLIAM JONES	Beth-SF	G. E.	2 Oct 18	9 Apr 19	30 Sep 20	Stk. 13 Aug 30, scrapped 1931
309	WOODBURY	Beth-SF	G. E.	3 Oct 18	6 Feb 19	20 Oct 20	Wrecked on Honda Pt., Calif., 8 Sep 23
310	S. P. LEE	Beth-SF	G. E.	31 Dec 18	22 Apr 19	30 Oct 20	Wrecked on Honda Pt., Calif., 8 Sep 23
311	NICHOLAS	Beth-SF	G. E.	11 Jan 19	1 May 19	23 Nov 20	Wrecked on Honda Pt., Calif., 8 Sep 23
312	YOUNG	Beth-SF	G. E.	28 Jan 19	8 May 19	29 Nov 20	Wrecked on Honda Pt., Calif., 8 Sep 23
313	ZEILIN	Beth-SF	G. E.	20 Feb 19	28 May 19	10 Dec 20	Stk. 8 Jul 30, scrapped 1930
314	YARBOROUGH	Beth-SF	G. E.	27 Feb 19	20 Jun 19	31 Dec 20	Stk. 3 Nov 30, scrapped 1931
315	LA VALLETTE	Beth-SF	G. E.	14 Apr 19	15 Jul 19	24 Dec 20	Stk. 22 Jul 30, scrapped 1931
316	SLOAT	Beth-SF	G. E.	18 Jan 19	14 May 19	30 Dec 20	Stk. 28 Jan 35, sunk as target off San Diego 26 Jun 35
317	WOOD	Beth-SF	G. E.	23 Jan 19	28 May 19	28 Jan 21	Stk. 22 Jul 30, scrapped 1930
318	SHIRK	Beth-SF	G. E.	13 Feb 19	20 Jun 19	5 Feb 21	Stk. 22 Jul 30, scrapped 1931
319	KIDDER	Beth-SF	G. E.	5 Mar 19	10 Jul 19	7 Feb 21	Stk. 22 Jul 30, scrapped 1930
320	SELFRIDGE	Beth-SF	G. E.	28 Apr 19	25 Jul 19	17 Feb 21	Stk. 3 Nov 30, scrapped 1931
321	MARCUS	Beth-SF	G. E.	20 May 19	22 Aug 19	23 Feb 21	Stk. 28 Jan 35, sunk as target off San Diego 25 Jun 35
322	MERVINE	Beth-SF	G. E.	28 Apr 19	11 Aug 19	1 Mar 21	Stk. 3 Nov 30, scrapped 1931
323	CHASE	Beth-SF	G. E.	5 May 19	2 Sep 19	10 Mar 21	Stk. 13 Aug 30, scrapped 1931
324	ROBERT SMITH	Beth-SF	G. E.	13 May 19	19 Sep 19	17 Mar 21	Stk. 12 Jul 30, scrapped 1931
325	MULLANY	Beth-SF	G. E.	3 Jun 19	9 Jul 20	29 Mar 21	Stk. 18 Nov 30, scrapped 1931
326	COGHLAN	Beth-SF	G. E.	25 Jun 19	16 Jun 20	31 Mar 21	Stk. 22 Oct 30, sold 17 Jan 31
327	PRESTON	Beth-SF	G. E.	19 Jul 19	7 Aug 20	13 Apr 21	Stk. 6 Nov 31, scrapped 1932
328	LAMSON	Beth-SF	G. E.	13 Aug 19	1 Sep 20	19 Apr 21	Stk. 22 Oct 30, sold 17 Jan 31
329	BRUCE	Beth-SF	G. E.	30 Jul 19	20 May 20	29 Sep 20	Stk. 6 Nov 31, scrapped 1932
330	HULL	Beth-SF	G. E.	13 Sep 20	18 Feb 21	26 Apr 21	Stk. 22 Jul 30, scrapped 1931
331	MACDONOUGH	Beth-SF	G. E.	24 May 20	15 Dec 20	30 Apr 21	Stk. 8 Jul 30, scrapped 1930
332	FARENHOLT	Beth-SF	G. E.	13 Sep 20	9 Mar 21	10 May 21	Stk. 12 Jul 30, scrapped 1930
333	SUMNER	Beth-SF	G. E.	27 Aug 19	24 Nov 20	27 May 21	Stk. 18 Nov 30, scrapped 1934
334	CORRY	Beth-SF	G. E.	15 Sep 20	28 Mar 21	25 May 21	Stk. 22 Jul 30, scrapped 1930
335	MELVIN	Beth-SF	G. E.	15 Sep 20	11 Apr 21	31 May 21	Stk. 3 Nov 30, scrapped 1931
336	LITCHFIELD	Mare I.		15 Jan 19	12 Aug 19	12 May 20	Stk. 28 Nov 45, scrapped 1946
337	ZANE	Mare I.		15 Jan 19	12 Aug 19	15 Feb 21	Stk. 8 Jan 46, sold 22 Oct 46
338	WASMUTH	Mare I.		12 Aug 19	15 Sep 20	16 Dec 21	Foundered in Aleutians 29 Dec 42
339	TREVER	Mare I.		12 Aug 19	15 Sep 20	3 Aug 22	Stk. 5 Dec 45, sold 12 Nov 46
340	PERRY	Mare I.		15 Sep 20	29 Oct 21	7 Aug 22	Mined off Palau 13 Sep 44
341	DECATUR	Mare I.		15 Sep 20	29 Oct 21	9 Aug 22	Stk. 13 Aug 45, sold 30 Nov 45
342	HULBERT	Norfolk		18 Nov 18	28 Jun 19	27 Oct 20	Stk. 28 Nov 45, sold 31 Oct 46
343	NOA	Norfolk		18 Nov 18	28 Jun 19	15 Feb 21	Sunk in collision off Palau 12 Sep 44
344	WILLIAM B. PRESTON	Norfolk		18 Nov 18	9 Aug 19	23 Aug 20	Stk. 3 Jan 46, sold 26 Nov 46
345	PREBLE	Bath		12 Apr 19	8 Mar 20	19 Mar 20	Stk. 3 Jan 46, sold 26 Oct 46
346	SICARD	Bath		18 Jun 19	20 Apr 20	9 Jun 20	Stk. 19 Dec 45, sold 22 Jun 46
347	PRUITT	Bath		25 Jun 19	2 Aug 20	2 Sep 20	Stk. 5 Dec 45, scrapped 1946.

Notes: Fiscal years 1918 (DD 186-344) and 1919 (345-47). DD 348-59 were also authorized for fiscal year 1919 but were not ordered because no building ways were open for them before the end of the war. This class was essentially a repeat of the earlier mass production type (DD 75-185) except that fuel capacity was increased by 35 percent to ensure an adequate steaming radius (designed to be 4900 nm at 15 knots). The extra fuel was put in wing bunkers in the boiler rooms. Other enhancements included modifications to the rudder and hull lines to reduce the turning radius and a short mainmast that could be dismounted to clear antiaircraft gun firing arcs and allow the use of kite balloons. The design also provided for 5" guns to compete with foreign destroyers and with submarines carrying large deck guns, but 4" guns were mounted in all but five ships (DD 231-35) because of supply problems. Director fire control, additional depth charges, and better weather protection for the crew were added as a result of U.S. and allied war experience. The Semmes was the testbed for a twin 4" mount which was later mounted in the Hovey and Long. For this large program, existing shipbuilding facilities were expanded as much as possible and entirely new yards were created at San Francisco and at Squantum, Mass. by Bethlehem Steel.

The Charles Ausburn (DD-294) and Noa (DD-343) were experimentally fitted with seaplanes in 1923 and 1939-40 respectively. The Stoddert (DD-302) and Sinclair (DD-275) were designated Light Targets No. 1 (IX-35, later AG-18) and No. 3 (IX-37) in 1930. Because of boiler defects they reverted to destroyer status in 1932 and 1931 respectively. (They were initially renamed with their Light Target designations but recovered their destroyer names on 24 Apr 31.) The Dahlgren (DD-187) was re-engined in 1937 with high pressure (1300 psi, 925 degree) forced circulation boilers aft and new G.E. geared turbines. The following vessels were loaned to the Coast Guard during the periods shown for use on the rum runner patrol in replacement of thousand tonners: Abel P. Upshur (DD-193/CG-15) 5 Nov 30-21 May 34; George E. Badger (DD-196/CG-16) 1 Oct 30-21 May 34; Herndon (DD-198/CG-17) and Hunt (DD-194/CG-18) 13 Sep 30-28 May 34; Welborn C. Wood (DD-195/CG-19) 1 Oct 30-21 May 34; and Semmes (DD-189/CG-20) 25 Apr 32-20 Apr 34.

The Graham (DD-192) was damaged in a collision on 16 Dec 21, the Smith Thompson was damaged on 14 Apr 36 in a collision with the Whipple (DD-217), the Parrott (DD-218) was damaged in a collision at Norfolk on 2 May 44, the Brooks (DD-232) was damaged by a suicide plane on 6 Jan 45, and the Thornton (DD-270) was damaged in a collision in the Ryukyus on 5 Apr 45. The wrecks of the Delphy (DD-261), Chauncey (DD-296), Fuller (DD-297), Woodbury (DD-309), S. P. Lee (DD-310), Nicholas (DD-311), and Young (DD-312) were sold on 19 Oct 25. The Putnam (DD-287), Worden (DD-288), Dale (DD-290), and Osborne (DD-295) were sold into mercantile service and became banana carriers, DD-287 surviving to 1955. Some of the ships "scrapped" in navy yards in the early 1930s were sold as gutted hulks, and one, the Thompson (DD-305), still existed as a wreck into the 1970s. The Farquhar (DD-304) and Sumner (DD-333) were used as barracks hulks after being stricken on 18 Nov 30. The Preston (DD-327) and Bruce (DD-329) were used for strength tests at Norfolk Navy Yard in 1931 and the Marcus (DD-321) and Sloat (DD-316) were used in 1935 to test the effect on destroyers of aircraft bombs and strafing. The Turner (DD-259) was stricken on 5 Aug 36 and retained as an unpowered water barge (YW-56). She was stricken again on 24 Jul 42 but was then reactivated as an electronics training vessel by the San Diego Destroyer Base and on 10 Feb 43 was reclassified IX-98 and renamed Moosehead. The James K. Paulding (DD-238) was reduced to a hulk 28 Dec 36. The Barry (DD-248) was irreparably damaged by a suicide plane on 25 May 45 and was in use as a decoy hulk when sunk in June. The Stewart (DD-224) was scuttled at Suribaya, N. E. I., on 2 Mar 42 and was stricken on 25 Mar 42. She was raised by the Japanese and used by them in 1942-45 as the Patrol Boat No. 102. She was recovered at Kure 28 Oct 45 and again hoisted the American flag the following day as USS DD-224.

Renamings: DD-216 ex Stewart 11 Nov 19; DD-199 to Alexander Dallas 31 Mar 45; DD-228 to John D. Ford 17 Nov 21; DD-254 ex Kalk 23 Dec 18; DD-255 to Osmond Ingram 11 Nov 19; DD-266 ex Anthony 1 Aug 18; DD-291 ex Stewart 20 Oct 19; DD-292 ex Stewart 7 Oct 19; DD-294 ex Ausburn 20 Feb 20; and DD-299 ex unnamed 18 Oct 18 ex Swasey 1 Oct 18. DD-307 was originally named Hamilton. An error in the General Order that assigned the name Branch to DD-197 also associated that name with DD-310.

Reclassifications:

Clemson (DD-186) to AVP-17 15 Nov 39; AVD-4 2 Aug 40; DD-186 1 Dec 43; APD-31 7 Mar 44; DD-186 16 Jul 45;

Dahlgren (DD-187) to AG-91 1 Mar 45;

Goldsborough (DD-188) to AVP-18 15 Nov 39; AVD-5 2 Aug 40; DD-188 1 Dec 43; APD-32 7 Mar 44; DD-188 10 Jul 45;

Semmes (DD-189) to AG-24 1 Jul 35;

George E. Badger (DD-196) to AVP-16 1 Oct 39; AVD-3 2 Aug 40; DD-196 1 Dec 43; APD-33 10 Apr 44; DD-196 20 Jul 45;

Chandler (DD-206), Zane (DD-337), and Trever (DD-339) to DMS-9, 14, 16 19 Nov 40; AG 108-110 5 Jun 45;

Southard (DD-207), Hovey (DD-208), Long (DD-209), Hopkins (DD-249), Wasmuth (DD-338), and Perry (DD-340) to DMS 10-13, 15, 17, 19 Nov 40;

Broome (DD-210) and Simpson (DD-221) to AG 96-97 23 May 45;

Tracy (DD-214) to DM-19 30 Jun 37;

Whipple (DD-217), McCormick (DD-223), John D. Ford (DD-228), and Paul Jones (DD-230) to AG 117-120 30 Jun 45;

MacLeish (DD-220) to AG-87 5 Jan 45;

Bulmer (DD-222) to AG-86 30 Nov 44;

Hatfield (DD-231) and Fox (DD-234) to AG 84-85 1 Oct 44;

Brooks (DD-232) to APD-10 5 Jan 43;

Gilmer (DD-233) to APD-11 22 Jan 43;

Kane (DD-235) to APD-18 25 Mar 43;

Humphreys (DD-236) to APD-12 18 Dec 42; DD-236 20 Jul 45;

McFarland (DD-237) to AVD-14 2 Aug 40; DD-237 1 Dec 43; projected conversion to APD-26 cancelled 10 Jun 44;

Overton (DD-239) to APD-23 21 Aug 43;

Childs (DD-241) to AVP-14 1 Jul 38; AVD-1 2 Aug 40;

Sands (DD-243) to APD-13 17 Dec 42;

Williamson (DD-244) to AVP-15 1 Jul 38; AVD-2 2 Aug 40; DD-244 1 Dec 43; projected conversion to APD-27 cancelled 10 Jun 44;
Reuben James (DD-245) to AVP-16 1 Aug 39 but change cancelled 1 Oct 39;
Barry (DD-248) to APD-29 15 Jan 44;
Belknap (DD-251), Osmond Ingram (DD-255) to AVD 8-9 2 Aug 40; DD 251, 255 1 Dec 43; APD 34-35 22 Jun 44;
Turner (DD-259) to YW-56 23 Oct 36; IX-98 13 Feb 43;
Gillis (DD-260), Ballard (DD-267), and Thornton (DD-270) to AVD-12, 10, 11 2 Aug 40;
Greene (DD-266) to AVD-13 2 Aug 40; DD-266 1 Dec 43; APD-36 1 Feb 44;

Sinclair (DD-275) to IX-37 24 Nov 30; DD-275 11 Aug 31;
Stoddert (DD-302) to IX-35 5 Nov 30; AG-18 30 Jun 31; DD-302 16 Apr 32;
Litchfield (DD-336) to AG-95 31 Mar 45;
Decatur (DD-341) projected conversion to APD-30 cancelled 17 Jan 44;
Hulbert (DD-342) to AVP-19 15 Nov 39; AVD-6 2 Aug 40; DD-342 1 Dec 43; projected conversion to APD-28 cancelled 10 Jun 44;
Noa (DD-343) to APD-24 10 Aug 43;
William B. Preston (DD-344) to AVP-20 15 Nov 39; AVD-7 2 Aug 40;
Preble (DD-345), Sicard (DD-346), and Pruitt (DD-347) to DM 20-22 30 Jun 37; AG 99-101 5 Jun 45.

1933

FARRAGUT class

Displacement: 1410 (DD-352), 1375 (DD-355), 1365 (DD-348), 1345 (DD-349), 1395 (others) tons standard
Dimensions: 341'3"(oa.) x 34'3"(e) x 16'4"(max)
Armament: 5-5"/38AA 8-21"T; 4-5"AA 8-21"T (1942)
Machinery: 42,800 SHP; geared turbines, 2 screws
Speed: 36.5 kts.
Complement: 160

No.	Hull	Machinery	Laid down	Launched	Commiss'd	Disposition
348 FARRAGUT	Quincy		20 Sep 32	15 Mar 34	18 Jun 34	Stk. 28 Jan 47, sold 14 Aug 47
349 DEWEY	Bath	Quincy	16 Dec 32	28 Jul 34	4 Oct 34	Stk. 1 Nov 45, sold 20 Dec 46
350 HULL	New York		7 Mar 33	31 Jan 34	11 Jan 35	Foundered E of Luzon 17 Dec 44
351 MACDONOUGH	Boston		15 May 33	22 Aug 34	15 Mar 35	Stk. 1 Nov 45, sold 20 Dec 46
352 WORDEN	Puget Sd.		29 Dec 32	27 Oct 34	15 Jan 35	Grounded off Amchitka, Aleutians, 12 Jan 43
353 DALE	New York		10 Feb 34	23 Jan 35	17 Jun 35	Stk. 1 Nov 45, sold 20 Dec 46
354 MONAGHAN	Boston		21 Nov 33	9 Jan 35	19 Apr 35	Foundered E of Luzon 17 Dec 44
355 AYLWIN	Philadelphia		23 Sep 33	10 Jul 34	1 Mar 35	Stk. 1 Nov 45, sold 20 Dec 46.

Notes: Fiscal years 1932 (DD 348-52) and 1933. The design for these, our first post-war destroyers, reflected a belief that, with the advent of torpedo aircraft, the gun had become the primary weapon of destroyers. It also emphasized seakeeping qualities, for which it reverted to a raised forecastle. The class introduced the longitudinal system of hull framing; the 5"/38 dual purpose main battery; and quadruple torpedo tubes. The detailed plans were prepared by Bethlehem Steel, who chose a propulsion plant consisting of two Parsons turbines, single reduction gears, and boilers operating at 400 psi and 648 degrees with integral superheaters. Designed with a standard displacement of 1500 tons and a normal displacement of 1726 tons, the ships were found to be somewhat lighter when completed.
Renamings: The Farragut and the Dewey were renamed Smith and Phelps respectively 15 Jul 33 only to regain their original names 13 Aug 33.

PORTER class

Displacement: 1825 (DD 362-363), 1805 (DD 360-361), 1850 (others) tons standard
Dimensions: 381'1"(oa.) x 36'11"(e) x 17'9"(max)
Armament: 8-5"/38 8-21"T; 6-5"/38 8-21"T (DD 358, 360-63, 1943); 5-5"/38AA 8-21"T (DD 357, 358, 360, 1944); 5-5"/38AA (DD-357, 359, 360, 1945); 4-5"/38AA (AG 126-27, 1945)
Machinery: 50,000 SHP; geared turbines, 2 screws
Speed: 36.5 kts.
Complement: 194

No.	Hull	Machinery	Laid down	Launched	Commiss'd	Disposition
356 PORTER	New York SB		18 Dec 33	12 Dec 35	27 Aug 36	Sunk by HIJMS I-12 off Santa Cruz Is. 26 Oct 42
357 SELFRIDGE	New York SB		18 Dec 33	18 Apr 36	25 Nov 36	Stk. 1 Nov 45, sold 20 Dec 46
358 McDOUGAL	New York SB		18 Dec 33	17 Jul 36	23 Dec 36	Stk. 15 Aug 49, sold 22 Sep 49
359 WINSLOW	New York SB		18 Dec 33	21 Sep 36	17 Feb 37	Stk. 5 Dec 57, sold 23 Feb 59
360 PHELPS	Quincy		2 Jan 34	18 Jul 35	26 Feb 36	Stk. 28 Jan 47, sold 10 Aug 47
361 CLARK	Quincy		2 Jan 34	15 Oct 35	20 May 36	Stk. 16 Nov 45, scrapped 1946
362 MOFFETT	Quincy		2 Jan 34	11 Dec 35	28 Aug 36	Stk. 28 Jan 47, sold 16 May 47
363 BALCH	Quincy		16 May 34	24 Mar 36	20 Oct 36	Stk. 1 Nov 45, scrapped 1946.

Notes: Fiscal year 1934. These ships were intended to serve as leaders for destroyer squadrons. They were larger than regular destroyers, being designed to displace 1850 tons standard and 2131 tons normal. Their extra size was used to increase offensive power instead of command facilities, however, and they were classified DD as heavy destroyers rather than DL as leaders. They carried a very heavy gun armament for surface actions--their 5"/38 guns were a single-purpose model without anti-aircraft capabilities. The detailed plans were prepared by New York SB and used boilers operating at 400 psi and 648 degrees. The McDougal and Winslow were reclassified miscellaneous auxiliaries (AG) in 1945 and reconfigured to resemble the Gearing class radar picket destroyers. They were intended for use in developing defensive measures against suicide aircraft. The McDougal later served as a training vessel and the Winslow became an ordnance experimental vessel.
Reclassifications: DD 358-359 to AG 126-127 respectively 17 Sep 45.

MAHAN class

Displacement: 1480 (DD 366-369, 378-379), 1465 (DD-365, 376-377), 1450 (DD-364), 1500 (others) tons standard
Dimensions: 341'4"(oa.) x 34'8"(e) x 17'2"(max)
Armament: 5-5"/38AA 12-21"T; 4-5"AA, 12-21"T (1942); 4-5"AA 8-21"T (DD 372, 375, 1943); 4-5"AA (DD-367, 1945); 3-5"AA (DD-373, 1945)

Machinery: 48,000 SHP; G. E. geared turbines, 2 screws
Speed: 36.5 kts.
Complement: 158

No.	Hull	Laid down	Launched	Commiss'd	Disposition
364 MAHAN	United	12 Jun 34	15 Oct 35	18 Sep 36	Sunk by Japanese suicide plane, Ormoc Bay, Leyte, 7 Dec 44
365 CUMMINGS	United	26 Jun 34	11 Dec 35	25 Nov 36	Stk. 28 Jan 47, sold 17 Jul 47
366 DRAYTON	Bath	20 Mar 34	26 Mar 36	1 Sep 36	Stk. 24 Oct 45, sold 20 Dec 46
367 LAMSON	Bath	20 Mar 34	17 Jun 36	21 Oct 36	Sunk in atomic test, Bikini, 2 Jul 46, stk. 15 Aug 46
368 FLUSSER	Kearny	4 Jun 34	28 Sep 35	1 Oct 36	Stk. 4 Apr 47, sold 6 Jan 48
369 REID	Kearny	25 Jun 34	11 Jan 36	2 Nov 36	Sunk by Japanese suicide plane, Ormoc Bay, Leyte, 11 Dec 44
370 CASE	Boston	19 Sep 34	14 Sep 35	15 Sep 36	Stk. 28 Jan 47, sold 31 Dec 47
371 CONYNGHAM	Boston	19 Sep 34	14 Sep 35	4 Nov 36	Sunk as a target off California 2 Jul 48, stk. 13 Jun 48
372 CASSIN	Philadelphia	1 Oct 34	28 Oct 35	21 Aug 36	Stk. 28 Jan 47, sold 25 Nov 47
373 SHAW	Philadelphia	1 Oct 34	28 Oct 35	18 Sep 36	Stk. 24 Oct 45, scrapped 1946
374 TUCKER	Norfolk	15 Aug 34	26 Feb 36	23 Jul 36	Mined off Espiritu Santo 4 Aug 42
375 DOWNES	Norfolk	15 Aug 34	22 Apr 36	15 Jan 37	Stk. 28 Jan 47, sold 18 Nov 47
376 CUSHING	Puget Sd.	15 Aug 34	31 Dec 35	28 Aug 36	Sunk by Japanese squadron off Guadalcanal 13 Nov 42
377 PERKINS	Puget Sd.	15 Nov 34	31 Dec 35	18 Sep 36	Sunk in collision off Cape Vogel, New Guinea, 29 Nov 43
378 SMITH	Mare I.	27 Oct 34	20 Feb 36	19 Sep 36	Stk. 25 Feb 47, sold 20 Aug 47
379 PRESTON	Mare I.	27 Oct 34	22 Apr 36	27 Oct 36	Sunk by HIJMS Nagara off Guadalcanal 15 Nov 42.

Notes: Fiscal year 1934. This new 1500-ton design resulted from a desire for more torpedo tubes (still considered the primary destroyer weapon by many in the fleet). The hull design, which remained in use through the Benham (DD-397) class, was made one foot wider than the Farragut and given fuller lines aft, in part to use the full 1500 tons allowed by the naval treaties. The class also introduced a new type of propulsion plant favored by the naval architect W. F. Gibbs with boilers operating at 400 psi and 700 degrees, two compact high speed Curtis main turbines, a third turbine for cruising, and double reduction gears. This class was also the earliest group of destroyers to have largely welded hulls. Gibbs and Cox prepared the detailed plans as design agent for the lead yard for the class, Federal Shipbuilding, Kearny, and General Electric designed the power plants. The Cassin and Downes were completely rebuilt with new hulls at Mare Island Navy Yard in 1942-43 following extensive damage at Pearl Harbor.

1934

DUNLAP class

Displacement: 1490 tons standard
Dimensions: 341'2"(oa.) x 35'5"(e) x 17'2"(max)
Armament: 5-5"/38AA 12-21"T; 4-5"AA 12-21"T (1941)

Machinery: 48,000 SHP; G. E. geared turbines, 2 screws
Speed: 36 kts.
Complement: 158

The destroyer *Cassin* (DD-372) on 2 February 1937. (NARA 19-N-17931)

The destroyer *Anderson* (DD-411) at high speed, probably on sea trials. Her fifth 5″/38 gun has not yet been removed and her Mk. 37 gun director has not yet been fitted. (NH 96119)

No.	Hull	Laid down	Launched	Commiss'd	Disposition
384 DUNLAP	United	10 Apr 35	18 Apr 36	12 Jun 37	Stk. 28 Jan 47, sold 31 Dec 47
385 FANNING	United	10 Apr 35	18 Sep 36	8 Oct 37	Stk. 28 Jan 47, sold 6 Jan 48.

Notes: Fiscal year 1935. These were built as repeat Mahan class ships to save costs at the yard, which already had two Mahans under construction. They had the same hull and machinery as the Mahan class but had lighter superstructure and rig and completely enclosed 5" gun mounts forward.

GRIDLEY class

Displacement: 1500 tons standard
Dimensions: 341'5"(DD-380, 382, oa.), 341'8"(others, oa.) x
    35'6" x 17'1"(max)
Armament: 4-5"/38AA 16-21"T; 4-5"AA 8-21"T (1944)

Machinery: 50,000 SHP; geared
    turbines, 2 screws
Speed: 35.5 kts.
Complement: 158

No.	Hull	Machinery	Laid down	Launched	Commiss'd	Disposition
380 GRIDLEY	Quincy		3 Jun 35	1 Dec 36	24 Jun 37	Stk. 25 Feb 47, sold 20 Aug 47
382 CRAVEN	Quincy		3 Jun 35	25 Feb 37	2 Sep 37	Stk. 25 Feb 47, sold 2 Oct 47
400 McCALL	Beth-SF		17 Mar 36	20 Nov 37	22 Jun 38	Stk. 28 Jan 47, sold 17 Nov 47
401 MAURY	Beth-SF		24 Mar 36	14 Feb 38	5 Aug 38	Stk. 1 Nov 45, sold 13 Jun 46.

Notes: Fiscal years 1935 (DD 380, 382) and 1936. This class introduced another increase in the torpedo armament--its sixteen tubes were the most ever fitted in an American destroyer. In compensation, it gave up one 5" gun. Bethlehem Steel made the initial proposal for such a ship and was allowed to use its design for the four ships built in its shipyards while the Bagley and Benham classes were being built elsewhere. In its design, Bethlehem used high-pressure boilers (operating at 565 psi and 700 degrees with integral superheaters) but reverted to a Parsons-type turbine installation similar to that in the Farragut class, for which it had a strong preference. During World War II, the Navy discovered that the four Bethlehem ships had inadequate stability, which made them the only modern destroyers not to receive 40mm guns during the war and forced the removal of eight torpedo tubes in 1944-45.

BAGLEY class

Displacement: 1500 tons standard
Dimensions: 341'4"(oa.) x 35'5"(DD 386-391, e), 35'6"(others,
    e) x 17'1"(max)
Armament: 4-5"/38AA 16-21"T

Machinery: 48,000 SHP; geared
    turbines, 2 screws
Speed: 35.5 kts.
Complement: 158

No.	Hull	Machinery	Laid down	Launched	Commiss'd	Disposition
386 BAGLEY	Norfolk	G. E.	31 Jul 35	3 Sep 36	12 Jun 37	Stk. 25 Feb 47, sold 3 Oct 47
387 BLUE	Norfolk	G. E.	25 Sep 35	27 May 37	14 Aug 37	Sunk by HIJMS Kawakaze off Guadalcanal 22 Aug 42
388 HELM	Norfolk	G. E.	25 Sep 35	27 May 37	16 Oct 37	Stk. 25 Feb 47, sold 2 Oct 47
389 MUGFORD	Boston	G. E.	28 Oct 35	31 Oct 36	16 Aug 37	Scuttled off Kwajalein 22 Mar 48, stk. 5 Apr 48
390 RALPH TALBOT	Boston	G. E.	28 Oct 35	31 Oct 36	14 Oct 37	Scuttled off Kwajalein 8 Mar 48, stk. 5 Apr 48
391 HENLEY	Mare I.	G. E.	28 Oct 35	12 Jan 37	14 Aug 37	Sunk by HIJMS RO-108 off Finschhaffen, New Guinea, 3 Oct 43
392 PATTERSON	Puget Sd.	G. E.	23 Jul 35	6 May 37	22 Sep 37	Stk. 25 Feb 47, sold 18 Aug 47
393 JARVIS	Puget Sd.	G. E.	21 Aug 35	6 May 37	27 Oct 37	Sunk by Japanese aircraft E of Guadalcanal 9 Aug 42.

Notes: Fiscal year 1935. The Navy prepared its own plans for these ships, following the layout of Bethlehem's Gridley class but using the hull and machinery designs of the Mahan and Dunlap classes.

SOMERS class

Displacement: 1850 tons standard
Dimensions: 381'(DD-383, oa.), 381'2"(DD-381, oa.), 380'11"
    (others, oa.) x 36'7"(DD 381-383, e), 36'11"(others, e) x
    18'(max)
Armament: 8-5"/38 12-21"T; 8-5"/38 8-21"T (1943-44); 6-5"/38,
    8-21"T (1943-44); 5-5"/38AA 8-21"T (DD 395-96, 1944-45);
    5-5"/38AA (DD 395-96, 1945)

Machinery: 52,000 SHP; G. E. geared
    turbines, 2 screws
Speed: 37.5 kts.
Complement: 235

No.		Hull	Laid down	Launched	Commiss'd	Disposition
381	SOMERS	Kearny	27 Jun 35	13 Mar 37	1 Dec 37	Stk. 28 Jan 47, sold 16 May 47
383	WARRINGTON	Kearny	10 Oct 35	15 May 37	9 Feb 38	Foundered N of Bahamas 13 Sep 44
394	SAMPSON	Bath	8 Apr 36	16 Apr 38	19 Aug 38	Stk. 28 Nov 45, scrapped 1946
395	DAVIS	Bath	28 Jul 36	30 Jul 38	9 Nov 38	Stk. 1 Nov 45, sold 24 Nov 47
396	JOUETT	Bath	26 Mar 36	24 Sep 38	25 Jan 39	Stk. 28 Nov 45, scrapped 1946.

Notes: Fiscal years 1935 (DD-381, 383) and 1936. These ships were originally to have been duplicates of the Porter class destroyer leaders, but during the detailed design phase Federal, Kearny, and their design agent, Gibbs and Cox, produced a very different ship with the heaviest torpedo broadside—12 tubes—in any American destroyer. (Contemporary 1500-ton destroyers had more tubes but fewer per broadside.) The new design also included all of the machinery innovations of the Mahan class plus separately-fired superheaters in the boilers, which operated at 565 psi and 730 degrees. (They were designed to operate at temperatures up to 850 degrees.) This type engineering plant became a standard in American destroyers until the introduction of 1200 psi steam after World War II.

1935

BENHAM class

Displacement: 1500 tons standard
Dimensions: 340'6"(DD-405, oa.), 340'9"(DD-406, oa.), 341' (DD-403, 407, oa.), 341'1"(DD-399, 402, oa.), 341'2"(DD-397, oa.), 341'3"(DD-398, oa.), 341'4"(DD-404, 408, oa.) x 35'5"(DD 402-403, e), 35'6"(others, e) x 17'3"(max)
Armament: 4-5"/38AA 16-21"T; 4-5"AA 8-21"T (1941 except DD-397, 402); 4-5"AA (DD-399, 407, 1945)

Machinery: 50,000 SHP; Westinghouse geared turbines, 2 screws
Speed: 36.5 kts.
Complement: 184

No.		Hull	Laid down	Launched	Commiss'd	Disposition
397	BENHAM	Kearny	1 Sep 36	16 Apr 38	2 Feb 39	Sunk by Japanese squadron off Guadalcanal 15 Nov 42
398	ELLET	Kearny	3 Dec 36	11 Jun 38	17 Feb 39	Stk. 13 Nov 45, sold 1 Aug 47
399	LANG	Kearny	5 Apr 37	28 Aug 38	30 Mar 39	Stk. 1 Nov 45, sold 20 Dec 46
402	MAYRANT	Boston	15 Apr 37	14 May 38	19 Sep 39	Scuttled off Kwajalein 4 Apr 48, stk. 30 Apr 48
403	TRIPPE	Boston	15 Apr 37	14 May 38	1 Nov 39	Scuttled off Kwajalein 3 Feb 48, stk. 19 Feb 48
404	RHIND	Philadelphia	22 Sep 37	28 Jul 38	10 Nov 39	Scuttled off Kwajalein 22 Mar 48, stk. 5 Apr 48
405	ROWAN	Norfolk	25 Jun 37	5 May 38	23 Sep 39	Sunk by German MTBs off Salerno, It., 11 Sep 43
406	STACK	Norfolk	25 Jun 37	5 May 38	20 Nov 39	Sunk as target off Kwajalein 24 Apr 48, stk. 28 May 48
407	STERETT	Charleston	2 Dec 36	27 Oct 38	15 Aug 39	Stk. 25 Feb 47, sold 10 Aug 47
408	WILSON	Puget Sd.	22 Mar 37	12 Apr 39	5 Jul 39	Scuttled off Kwajalein 8 Mar 48, stk. 5 Apr 48.

Notes: Fiscal year 1936. They were improved versions of the Bagley class with machinery as in the Somers class. To reduce machinery weight, they had three boilers instead of the four slightly smaller ones in the Bagleys. The boilers operated at 565 psi and 700 degrees. The class also had base-ring instead of pedestal mounts for the after 5" guns (which remained open). Federal was the lead yard and Gibbs and Cox prepared the plans. The Benham and others bettered 40 kts. on trials.

1936

SIMS class

Displacement: 1570 tons standard
Dimensions: 347'7"(DD-417, oa.), 347'8"(DD-419, oa.), 347'10" (DD-415, oa.), 347'11"(DD-411, oa.), 348'(DD-412, 418, oa.), 348'2"(DD-409, 410, oa.), 348'3"(DD-420, oa.), 348'4"(DD-413, 414, oa.) x 36'1"(e) x 17'4"(max)
Armament: 5-5"/38AA 12-21"T (DD 409-13); 5-5"AA 8-21"T (all, 1939-40); 4-5"AA 8-21"T (1941); 4-5"AA (DD-413, 414, 417, 1945)

Machinery: 50,000 SHP; Westinghouse geared turbines, 2 screws
Speed: 37 kts.
Complement: 192

No.		Hull	Laid down	Launched	Commiss'd	Disposition
409	SIMS	Bath	15 Jul 37	8 Apr 39	1 Aug 39	Sunk by Japanese aircraft in Coral Sea 7 May 1942
410	HUGHES	Bath	15 Sep 37	17 Jun 39	21 Sep 39	Sunk as target 16 Oct 48, stk. 26 Nov 48
411	ANDERSON	Kearny	15 Nov 37	4 Feb 39	19 May 39	Sunk in atomic test, Bikini, 1 Jul 46, stk. 25 Sep 46
412	HAMMANN	Kearny	17 Jan 38	4 Feb 39	11 Aug 39	Sunk by HIJMS I-168 in Battle of Midway, 6 Jun 42
413	MUSTIN	Newport News	20 Dec 37	8 Dec 38	15 Sep 39	Scuttled off Kwajalein 18 Apr 48, stk. 30 Apr 48
414	RUSSELL	Newport News	20 Dec 37	8 Dec 38	3 Nov 39	Stk. 28 Nov 45, sold 28 Sep 47
415	O'BRIEN	Boston	31 May 38	20 Oct 39	2 Mar 40	Foundered off Samoa 19 Oct 42
416	WALKE	Boston	31 May 38	20 Oct 39	27 Apr 40	Sunk by Japanese squadron off Guadalcanal 15 Nov 42
417	MORRIS	Norfolk	7 Jun 38	1 Jun 39	5 Mar 40	Stk. 28 Nov 45, sold 2 Aug 47
418	ROE	Charleston	23 Apr 38	21 Jun 39	5 Jan 40	Stk. 16 Nov 45, sold 1 Aug 47
419	WAINWRIGHT	Norfolk	7 Jun 38	1 Jun 39	15 Apr 40	Sunk as target in Pacific 5 Jul 48, stk. 13 Jul 48
420	BUCK	Philadelphia	6 Apr 38	22 May 39	15 May 40	Sunk by U-616 off Salerno, It., 9 Oct 43.

Notes: Fiscal year 1937. This was the first new destroyer design which was not required to remain under the 1500-ton limit in the 1930 London Naval Treaty. It was developed in response to concern that destroyers had become excessively flimsy in an effort to maximize speed. A 70-ton increase was adopted to allow strengthening the hull structure, providing light armor on the bridge, and introducing the Mk-37 gun fire control system. A reevaluation of operational requirements also led to the restoration of a fifth 5"AA at the expense of four torpedo tubes. The machinery was nearly identical to that in the Benham class, although the boiler operating temperature was raised to 715 degrees. The detailed plans were produced by Gibbs and Cox. The first ships completed were found to be overweight and unstable, and in compensation another four torpedo tubes and the bridge armor were removed. The fifth 5"AA was soon also removed to make room for additional small AA guns. The O'Brien foundered as a result of damage incurred when torpedoed by the I-15 south of the Solomons 15 Sep 42. The Wainwright had four of her eight torpedo tubes removed temporarily for Mediterranean service in 1944.

1937

BENSON class

Displacement: 1620 tons standard
Dimensions: 347'4"(DD 421-422), 347'9"(DD-492), 347'10" (DD-422, 459-460), 347'11"(DD 425-426), 348'(DD-427), 348'3"(DD-428, 491), 348'4"(others) (all oa.) x 36' (DD 616-617, e), 36'1"(others, e) x 17'6"(max)
Armament: 5-5"/38AA 10-21"T (DD 421, 425-428); 5-5"AA 5-21"T (DD-421, 425-428, 1941); 4-5"AA 5-21"T (DD-459-460, 491-492, 598-617); 4-5"AA 10-21"T (DD 421-422, 425, 427-428, 1945); 4-5"AA (DD 600-601, 603-604, 608, 612-617, 1945)

Machinery: 47,000 (DD 421-422, 425-428), 50,000 (others) SHP; Bethlehem geared turbines, 2 screws
Speed: 36.5 kts.
Complement: 191

No.		Hull	Laid down	Launched	Commiss'd	Disposition
421	BENSON	Quincy	16 May 38	15 Nov 39	25 Jul 40	To Taiwan 26 Feb 54 as Lo Yang, stk. 1 Nov 74
422	MAYO	Quincy	16 May 38	26 Mar 40	18 Sep 40	Stk. 1 Dec 70, sold 8 May 72
425	MADISON	Boston	19 Dec 38	20 Oct 39	6 Aug 40	Stk. 1 Jun 68, sunk as target off SE Florida 14 Oct 69
426	LANSDALE	Boston	19 Dec 38	20 Oct 39	17 Sep 40	Sunk by German aircraft NW of Anzio, It., 20 Apr 44
427	HILARY P. JONES	Charleston	16 Nov 38	14 Dec 39	7 Sep 40	To Taiwan 26 Feb 54 as Han Yang, stk. 1 Nov 74
428	CHARLES F. HUGHES	Puget Sd.	3 Jan 39	16 May 40	5 Sep 40	Stk. 1 Jun 68, sunk as target off Virginia 26 Mar 69
459	LAFFEY	Beth-SF	13 Jan 41	30 Oct 41	31 Mar 42	Sunk by HIJMS Hiei & Teratsuki off Guadalcanal 13 Nov 42
460	WOODWORTH	Beth-SF	13 Jan 41	29 Nov 41	30 Apr 42	To Italy 15 Jan 51 as Artigliere, stk. 22 Jan 51
491	FARENHOLT	Staten I.	11 Dec 40	19 Nov 41	2 Apr 42	Stk. 1 Jun 71, sold 22 Nov 72
492	BAILEY	Staten I.	29 Jan 41	19 Dec 41	11 May 42	Stk. 1 Jun 68, sunk as target off NE Florida 4 Nov 69

No.		Hull	Laid down	Launched	Commiss'd	Disposition
598	BANCROFT	Quincy	1 May 41	31 Dec 41	30 Apr 42	Stk. 1 Jun 71, sold 16 Mar 73
599	BARTON	Quincy	20 May 41	31 Jan 42	29 May 42	Sunk by HIJMS Amatsukaze off Guadalcanal 13 Nov 42
600	BOYLE	Quincy	31 Dec 41	15 Jun 42	15 Aug 42	Stk. 1 Jun 71, sunk as target off NE Florida 3 May 73
601	CHAMPLIN	Quincy	31 Jan 42	25 Jul 42	12 Sep 42	Stk. 2 Jan 71, sold 8 May 72
602	MEADE	Staten I.	25 Mar 41	15 Feb 42	22 Jun 42	Stk. 1 Jun 71, sunk as target off NE Florida 18 Feb 73
603	MURPHY	Staten I.	19 May 41	29 Apr 42	27 Jul 42	Stk. 1 Nov 70, sold 6 Oct 72
604	PARKER	Staten I.	9 Jun 41	12 May 42	31 Aug 42	Stk. 1 Jul 71, sold 25 May 73
605	CALDWELL	Beth-SF	24 Mar 41	15 Jan 42	10 Jun 42	Stk. 1 May 65, sold 4 Nov 66
606	COGHLAN	Beth-SF	28 Mar 41	12 Feb 42	10 Jul 42	Stk. 1 Jul 71, sold 12 Jun 74
607	FRAZIER	Beth-SF	5 Jul 41	17 Mar 42	30 Jul 42	Stk. 1 Jul 71, sold 6 Oct 72
608	GANSEVOORT	Beth-SF	16 Jun 41	11 Apr 42	25 Aug 42	Stk. 1 Jul 71, sunk as target off NE Florida 23 Mar 72
609	GILLESPIE	Beth-SF	16 Jun 41	8 May 42	18 Sep 42	Stk. 1 Jul 71, sunk as target off Puerto Rico 16 Jul 73
610	HOBBY	Beth-SF	30 Jun 41	4 Jun 42	18 Nov 42	Stk. 1 Jul 71, sunk as target off South Carolina 28 Jun 72
611	KALK	Beth-SF	30 Jun 41	18 Jul 42	17 Oct 42	Stk. 1 Jun 68, sunk as target off NE Florida 20 Mar 69
612	KENDRICK	San Pedro	1 May 41	2 Apr 42	12 Sep 42	Stk. 1 May 66, sunk as target off Key West 2 Mar 68
613	LAUB	San Pedro	1 May 41	28 Apr 42	24 Oct 42	Stk. 1 Jul 71, sold 14 Jan 75
614	MACKENZIE	San Pedro	29 May 41	27 Jun 42	21 Nov 42	Stk. 1 Jul 71, sunk as target off NE Florida 6 May 74
615	McLANAHAN	San Pedro	29 May 41	7 Sep 42	19 Dec 42	Stk. 1 Jul 71, sold 12 Jun 74
616	NIELDS	Quincy	15 Jun 42	1 Oct 42	15 Jan 43	Stk. 15 Sep 70, sold 8 May 72
617	ORDRONAUX	Quincy	25 Jul 42	9 Nov 42	13 Feb 43	Stk. 1 Jul 71, sold 16 Mar 73.

Notes: Fiscal years for Benson and Gleaves classes: 1938 (DD 421-28), 1939 (429-36), 1940 (437-44), 1941 (453/497), 1942 (598/648). This class was an improvement on the Sims design on the same basic hull dimensions. It introduced the unit machinery arrangement with alternating boiler and engine rooms which increased survivability (and also caused a reversion to four boilers and two funnels). Additional features of the ships as built included additional hull strengthening, light protection for the bridge and director, and quintuple torpedo tubes. Bethlehem Steel won the contract to prepare the detailed plans for the fiscal year 1938 ships, and the Navy reluctantly allowed them to use the machinery arrangement that they preferred (two high-speed turbines, single reduction gears, and boilers operating at 575 psi and 700 degrees with integral superheaters). Bethlehem continued to use these plans for later ships of this type built in its yards. DD 616-617 were transferred from San Pedro to Quincy 7 Oct 41. DD 421-22 and 425-28 had five of their ten torpedo tubes removed temporarily for Mediterranean service in 1944.

GLEAVES class

Displacement: 1620 (DD 423-424, 429-436, 492), 1630 (others) tons standard
Dimensions: 347'5"(DD-424), 347'7"(DD-437), 347'8"(DD-429, 442), 347'9"(DD-430, 434, 441, 444, 638-639), 347'10"(DD-433, 453-454, 459-462), 347'11"(DD-455, 456), 348'(DD-440, 443), 348'1"(DD-431, 432, 439, 463-464, 634-635), 348'2"(DD-423, 436, 457-458, 636-637), 348'3"(DD 483-490), 348'4"(DD-435, 438, 493-497, 618-628, 632-633, 645-648) (all oa.) x 36'(DD-434, 638-641), 36'2" (DD-442), 36'3"(DD 636-637), 36'1"(others) (all e) x 17'6"(max)

Armament: 5-5"/38AA 10-21"T (DD 423-24, 429-44) 5-5"AA 5-21"T (DD 423-24, 431, 1941); 4-5"AA 10-21"T (DD 429-30, 432-44, 1941; 423-24, 431, 1943); 4-5"AA 5-21"T (others, as built); 4-5"AA (DD 423-24, 429-32, 435, 437-40, 443, 497, 623-24, 628, 1945); 3-5"AA (DMS conversions)
Machinery: 50,000 SHP; geared turbines, 2 screws
Speed: 37 kts.
Complement: 208

No.		Hull	Machinery	Laid down	Launched	Commiss'd	Disposition
423	GLEAVES	Bath	W'house	16 May 38	9 Dec 39	14 Jun 40	Stk. 1 Nov 69, sold 29 Jun 72
424	NIBLACK	Bath	W'house	8 Aug 38	18 May 40	1 Aug 40	Stk. 31 Jul 68, sold 16 Aug 73
429	LIVERMORE	Bath	G. E.	6 Mar 39	3 Aug 40	7 Oct 40	Stk. 19 Jul 56, sold 3 Mar 61
430	EBERLE	Bath	G. E.	12 Apr 39	14 Sep 40	4 Dec 40	To Greece 22 Jan 51 as Niki, stk. 24 Jan 51
431	PLUNKET	Kearny	G. E.	1 Mar 39	9 Mar 40	17 Jul 40	To Taiwan 16 Feb 59 as Nan Yang, stk. 1 Nov 74
432	KEARNY	Kearny	G. E.	1 Mar 39	9 Mar 40	13 Sep 40	Stk. 1 Jun 71, sold 6 Oct 72

No.		Hull	Machinery	Laid down	Launched	Commiss'd	Disposition
433	GWIN	Boston	Boston	1 Jun 40	25 May 40	15 Jan 41	Sunk by Japanese squadron off Kolombangara 13 Jul 43
434	MEREDITH	Boston	Boston	1 Jun 40	24 Apr 40	1 Mar 41	Sunk by Japanese aircraft off San Cristobal, Solomon Is., 15 Oct 42
435	GRAYSON	Charleston	G. E.	17 Jul 39	7 Aug 40	14 Feb 41	Stk. 1 Jun 71, sold 22 Nov 72
436	MONSSEN	Puget Sd.	G. E.	12 Jul 39	16 May 40	14 Mar 41	Sunk by Japanese squadron off Guadalcanal 13 Nov 42
437	WOOLSEY	Bath	W'house	9 Oct 39	12 Feb 41	7 May 41	Stk. 1 Jul 71, sold 12 Jun 74
438	LUDLOW	Bath	Westing-house	18 Dec 39	11 Nov 40	5 Mar 41	To Greece 22 Jan 51 as Doxa, stk. 24 Jan 51
439	EDISON	Kearny	W'house	18 Mar 40	23 Nov 40	31 Jan 41	Stk. 1 Apr 66, sold 29 Dec 66
440	ERICSSON	Kearny	W'house	18 Mar 40	23 Nov 40	13 Mar 41	Stk. 1 Jun 70, sunk as target 17 Nov 70
441	WILKES	Boston	G. E.	1 Nov 39	31 May 40	22 Apr 41	Stk. 1 Mar 71, sold 29 Jun 72
442	NICHOLSON	Boston	G. E.	1 Nov 39	31 May 40	3 Jun 41	To Italy 15 Jan 51 as Aviere, stk. 22 Jan 51
443	SWANSON	Charleston	G. E.	15 Nov 39	2 Nov 40	29 May 41	Stk. 1 Mar 71, sold 29 Jun 72
444	INGRAHAM	Charleston	G. E.	15 Nov 39	15 Feb 41	17 Jul 41	Sunk in collision N of Azores 22 Aug 42
453	BRISTOL	Kearny	G. E.	2 Dec 40	25 Jul 41	22 Oct 41	Sunk by U-371 off Algeria 13 Oct 43
454	ELLYSON	Kearny	G. E.	2 Dec 40	25 Jul 41	28 Nov 41	To Japan 19 Oct 54 as Asakaze, stk. 1 Feb 70
455	HAMBLETON	Kearny	G. E.	16 Dec 40	26 Sep 41	22 Dec 41	Stk. 1 Jun 71, sold 22 Nov 72
456	RODMAN	Kearny	G. E.	16 Dec 40	26 Sep 41	27 Jan 42	To Taiwan 28 Jul 55 as Hsuen Yang, stk. 1 Nov 72
457	EMMONS	Bath	Westing-house	14 Nov 40	23 Aug 41	5 Dec 41	Sunk by Japanese suicide plane off Okinawa 6 Apr 45
458	MACOMB	Bath	Westing-house	3 Sep 40	23 Sep 41	26 Jan 42	To Japan 19 Oct 54 as Hatakaze, stk 1 Feb 70, to Taiwan 6 Aug 70 as Hsuen Yang
461	FORREST	Boston	Boston	6 Jan 41	14 Jun 41	13 Jan 42	Stk. 19 Dec 45, sold 20 Nov 46
462	FITCH	Boston	Boston	6 Jan 41	14 Jun 41	3 Feb 42	Stk. 1 Jul 71, sunk as target off NE Florida 15 Nov 73
463	CORRY	Charleston	G. E.	4 Sep 40	28 Jul 41	18 Dec 41	Mined off Carentan R., France, 6 Jun 44
464	HOBSON	Charleston	G. E.	14 Nov 40	8 Sep 41	22 Jan 42	Sunk in collision with USS Wasp in N Atlantic 26 Apr 52
483	AARON WARD	Kearny	Westing-house	11 Feb 41	22 Nov 41	4 Mar 42	Sunk by Japanese aircraft off Guadalcanal 7 Apr 43
484	BUCHANAN	Kearny	Westing-house	11 Feb 41	22 Nov 41	21 Mar 42	To Turkey 28 Apr 49 as Gelibolu, stk. 7 Jun 49
485	DUNCAN	Kearny	Westing-house	31 Jul 41	20 Feb 42	16 Apr 42	Sunk by Japanese squadron off Guadalcanal 12 Oct 42
486	LANSDOWNE	Kearny	Westing-house	31 Jul 41	20 Feb 42	29 Apr 42	To Turkey 10 Jun 49 as Gaziantep, stk. 15 Aug 49
487	LARDNER	Kearny	Westing-house	15 Sep 41	20 Mar 42	13 May 42	To Turkey 10 Jun 49 as Gemlik, stk. 15 Aug 49
488	McCALLA	Kearny	Westing-house	15 Sep 41	20 Mar 42	27 May 42	To Turkey 28 Apr 49 as Giresun, stk. 7 Jun 49
489	MERVINE	Kearny	W'house	3 Nov 41	3 May 42	17 Jun 42	Stk. 31 Jul 68, sold 27 Oct 69
490	QUICK	Kearny	W'house	3 Nov 41	3 May 42	3 Jul 42	Stk. 15 Jan 72, sold 27 Aug 73
493	CARMICK	Sea-Tac, Seattle	G. E.	29 May 41	8 Mar 42	28 Dec 42	Stk. 1 Jul 71, sold 7 Aug 72
494	DOYLE	Sea-Tac, Seattle	A. C.	26 May 41	17 Mar 42	27 Jan 43	Stk. 1 Dec 70, sold 6 Oct 72
495	ENDICOTT	Sea-Tac, Seattle	A. C.	1 May 41	5 Apr 42	25 Feb 43	Stk. 1 Nov 69, sold 6 Oct 70
496	McCOOK	Sea-Tac, Seattle	G. E.	1 May 41	30 Apr 42	15 Mar 43	Stk. 15 Jan 72, sold 27 Aug 73
497	FRANKFORD	Sea-Tac, Seattle	A. C.	5 Jun 41	17 May 42	31 Mar 43	Stk. 1 Jun 71, sunk as target off Puerto Rico 4 Dec 73

No.		Hull	Machinery	Laid down	Launched	Commiss'd	Disposition
618	DAVIDSON	Kearny	W'house	26 Feb 42	19 Jul 42	11 Sep 42	Stk. 15 Jan 72, sold 27 Aug 73
619	EDWARDS	Kearny	W'house	26 Feb 42	19 Jul 42	18 Sep 42	Stk. 1 Jul 71, sold 25 May 73
620	GLENNON	Kearny	Westinghouse	25 Mar 42	26 Aug 42	8 Oct 42	Mined off Quineville, Fr., 8 Jun 44
621	JEFFERS	Kearny	W'house	25 Mar 42	26 Aug 42	5 Nov 42	Stk. 1 Jul 71, sold 25 May 73
622	MADDOX	Kearny	Westinghouse	7 May 42	15 Sep 42	31 Oct 42	Sunk by German aircraft off Gela, Sicily, 10 Jul 43
623	NELSON	Kearny	W'house	7 May 42	15 Sep 42	26 Nov 42	Stk. 1 Mar 68, sold 18 Jul 69
624	BALDWIN	Sea-Tac, Seattle	Westinghouse	19 Jul 41	14 Jun 42	30 Apr 43	Grounded under tow on Montauk Pt., N.Y., 16 Apr 61, stk. 1 Jun 61, scuttled 5 Jun 61
625	HARDING	Sea-Tac, Seattle	Westinghouse	22 Jul 41	28 Jun 42	25 May 43	Stk. 16 Nov 45, sold 16 Apr 47
626	SATTERLEE	Sea-Tac, Seattle	Westinghouse	10 Sep 41	17 Jul 42	1 Jul 43	Stk. 1 Dec 70, sold 8 May 72
627	THOMPSON	Sea-Tac, Seattle	Westinghouse	22 Sep 41	15 Jul 42	10 Jul 43	Stk. 1 Jul 71, sold 7 Aug 72
628	WELLES	Sea-Tac, Seattle	Westinghouse	27 Sep 41	7 Sep 42	16 Aug 43	Stk. 1 Mar 68, sold 18 Jul 69
632	COWIE	Boston	G. E.	18 Mar 41	27 Sep 41	1 Jun 42	Stk. 1 Dec 70, sold 22 Feb 72
633	KNIGHT	Boston	G. E.	18 Mar 41	27 Sep 41	23 Jun 42	Stk. 1 Dec 66, sunk as target off S. California 27 Oct 67
634	DORAN	Boston	G. E.	14 Jun 41	10 Dec 41	4 Aug 42	Stk. 15 Jan 72, sold 27 Aug 73
635	EARLE	Boston	G. E.	14 Jun 41	10 Dec 41	1 Sep 42	Stk. 1 Dec 69, sold Oct 70
636	BUTLER	Philadelphia	G. E.	16 Sep 41	12 Feb 42	15 Aug 42	Stk. 28 Nov 45, sold 10 Jan 48
637	GHERARDI	Philadelphia	G. E.	16 Sep 41	12 Feb 42	15 Sep 42	Stk. 1 Jun 71, sunk as target off Puerto Rico 3 Jun 73
638	HERNDON	Norfolk	G. E.	26 Aug 41	5 Feb 42	20 Dec 42	Stk. 1 Jul 71, sunk as target off NE Florida 24 May 73
639	SHUBRICK	Norfolk	G. E.	17 Feb 42	18 Apr 42	7 Feb 43	Stk. 28 Nov 45, sold 28 Sep 47
640	BEATTY	Charleston	G. E.	1 May 41	20 Dec 41	7 May 42	Sunk by German aircraft off Cape Bougaroun, Algeria, 6 Nov 43
641	TILLMAN	Charleston	G. E.	1 May 41	20 Dec 41	4 Jun 42	Stk. 1 Jun 70, sold 8 May 72
645	STEVENSON	Kearny	A. C.	23 Jul 42	11 Nov 42	15 Dec 42	Stk. 1 Jun 68, sold 2 Jun 70
646	STOCKTON	Kearny	W'house	24 Jul 42	11 Nov 42	11 Jan 43	Stk. 1 Jul 71, sold 25 May 73
647	THORN	Kearny	Westinghouse	15 Nov 42	28 Feb 43	1 Apr 43	Stk. 1 Jul 71, sunk as target off NE Florida 26 Aug 74
648	TURNER	Kearny	Westinghouse	15 Nov 42	28 Feb 43	16 Apr 43	Sunk by explosion off New York 3 Jan 44.

Notes: Fiscal years: see Benson class, above. For the fiscal year 1939 ships (the Livermore group), the Navy planned to repeat the Benson design but to specify the use of 850 degree steam. In May 1938 the Navy extended this specification to the two fiscal year 1938 ships to be built by Bath (the Gleaves and Niblack). Bath and Kearny subsequently won the fiscal year 1939 contracts, and their design agent, Gibbs and Cox, produced the detailed plans for the new class. These included the machinery arrangement preferred by the Navy (three high-speed turbines including a cruising turbine, double reduction gears, and boilers operating at 580 psi and 825 degrees with separately-fired superheaters). Beginning with the Bristol (DD-453), the designed gun armament was reduced to 4-5". Later war-built ships of this class (DD 493-97, 618-28, and 645-48) had a modified, square-faced bridge with a lowered gun director. DD 423-24, 429-32, and 437-40 had five of their ten torpedo tubes removed temporarily for Mediterranean service in 1944. The Livermore (DD-429) was used as a test hulk before her sale.
Renamings: DD-429 ex Grayson and DD-435 ex Livermore 23 Dec 38. DD-496 ex Farley 10 Jun 41. The Wilkes (DD-441) dropped her name 16 July 1968.
Reclassifications:
   Ellyson (DD-454), and Macomb (DD-458) to DMS 19, 23 15 Nov 44; DD 454, 458 4 May 54;
   Hambleton (DD-455), Rodman (DD-456), and Jeffers (DD-621) to DMS 20, 21, 27 15 Nov 44; DD 455, 456, 621 15 Jan 55;
   Emmons (DD-457), Forrest (DD-461), Hobson (DD-464), Harding (DD-625), and Butler (DD-636) to DMS 22, 24, 26, 28, 29 15 Nov 44;
   Fitch (DD-462), and Gherardi (DD-637) to DMS 25, 30 15 Nov 44; DD 462, 637 15 Jul 55;

   Mervine (DD-489), Endicott (DD-495), McCook (DD-496), Thompson (DD-627), Cowie (DD-632), and Doran (DD-634) to DMS-31, 35-36, 38-39, 41 30 May 45; DD-489, 495-496, 627, 632, 634 15 Jul 55;
   Quick (DD-490), Carmick (DD-493), Davidson (DD-618), Knight (DD-633), and Earle (DD-635) to DMS 32-33, 37, 40, 42 23 Jun 45; DD-490, 493, 618, 633, 635 15 Jul 55;
   Doyle (DD-494) to DMS-34, 23 Jun 45; DD-494 15 Jan 55

1940

FLETCHER class

Displacement: 2050 tons standard
Dimensions: 375'10"(DD-683). 375'11"(DD 526-527, 535-536, 569, 572), 376'(DD 533-534, 570-571, 579-580), 376'1"(DD-528, 537, 539, 577-578, 684), 376'2"(DD-530, 538, 573-576), 376'3"(DD 445-446, 448, 529, 531), 376'4"(DD-447, 449-450, 594-597), 376'5"(DD 480-481, 532, 574-575, 594, 596), 376'7"(DD-472, 479), 376'6"(others) (all oa.) x 39'4"(DD-451, 518-519, 540-541), 39'5"(DD-447), 39'6"(DD-684), 39'7"(DD 502-508, 512-517, 526-533, 629-631, 642-644, 650-653), 39'9"(DD 477-478, 481), 40' (DD 509-511, 688-691), 39'8"(others) (all e) x 17'9"(max)
Complement: 273-334

Armament: 5-5"/38AA 10-21"T; 5-5"AA 5-21"T (53 ships, 1945); 2-5"AA 4-3"AA 4-21"T (DDE conversions, 1948); 4-5"AA 6-3"/50AA 5-21"T (39 ships, 1952); 2-5"AA 6-12.75"T DASH (DDE 446-447, 449, 1960); 2-5"AA 4-3"AA 6-12.75"T (DD-445, 450, 466, 468, 498-499, 507-508, 510, 517, 1965)
Machinery: 60,000 SHP; geared turbines, 2 screws
Speed: 38 kts.

No.	Hull	Machinery	Laid down	Launched	Commiss'd	Disposition
445 FLETCHER	Kearny	G. E.	2 Oct 41	3 May 42	30 Jun 42	Stk. 1 Aug 69, sold 22 Feb 72
446 RADFORD	Kearny	G. E.	2 Oct 41	3 May 42	22 Jul 42	Stk. 10 Nov 69, sold Oct 70
447 JENKINS	Kearny	G. E.	27 Nov 41	21 Jun 42	31 Jul 42	Stk. 2 Jul 69, sold 17 Feb 71
448 LA VALLETTE	Kearny	G. E.	27 Nov 41	21 Jun 42	12 Aug 42	Stk. 1 Feb 74, sold 26 Jul 74 to Peru for spare parts
449 NICHOLAS	Bath	W'house	3 Mar 41	19 Feb 42	4 Jun 42	Stk. 30 Jan 70, sold Oct 70
450 O'BANNON	Bath	W'house	3 Mar 41	14 Mar 42	26 Jun 42	Stk. 30 Jan 70, sold 6 Jun 72
451 CHEVALIER	Bath	G. E.	30 Apr 41	11 Apr 42	20 Jul 42	Sunk by La Vallette 7 Oct 43 after torpedoing by HIJMS Yugumo off Vella Lavella, Solomons
465 SAUFLEY	Kearny	G. E.	27 Jan 42	19 Jul 42	29 Aug 42	Stk. 1 Sep 66, sunk as target off Key West 20 Feb 68
466 WALLER	Kearny	G. E.	12 Feb 42	15 Aug 42	1 Oct 42	Stk. 15 Jul 69, sunk as target off Rhode Island 17 Jun 70
467 STRONG	Bath	G. E.	30 Apr 41	17 May 42	7 Aug 42	Sunk by Japanese destroyers off Bairoko Harbor, New Georgia, 5 Jul 43
468 TAYLOR	Bath	Westing-house	28 Aug 41	7 Jun 42	28 Aug 42	To Italy 2 Jul 69 as Lanciere, stk. 2 Jul 69
469 DE HAVEN	Bath	G. E.	27 Sep 41	28 Jun 42	21 Sep 42	Sunk by Japanese aircraft off Guadalcanal 1 Feb 43
470 BACHE	Staten I.	G. E.	19 Nov 41	7 Jul 42	14 Nov 42	Wrecked on Isle of Rhodes 6 Feb 68, scrapped there
471 BEALE	Staten I.	G. E.	19 Dec 41	24 Aug 42	23 Dec 42	Stk. 1 Oct 68, sunk as target off Virginia 24 Jun 69
472 GUEST	Boston	A. C.	27 Sep 41	20 Feb 42	15 Dec 42	To Brazil 5 Jun 59 as Para, stk. 1 Aug 73
473 BENNETT	Boston	A. C.	10 Dec 41	16 Apr 42	9 Feb 43	To Brazil 15 Dec 59 as Paraiba, stk. 1 Aug 73
474 FULLAM	Boston	A. C.	10 Dec 41	16 Apr 42	2 Mar 43	Stk. 1 Jun 62, sunk as target off Virginia 7 Jul 62
475 HUDSON	Boston	A. C.	20 Feb 42	3 Jun 42	13 Apr 43	Stk. 1 Dec 72, sold 27 Nov 73
476 HUTCHINS	Boston	A. C.	27 Sep 41	20 Feb 42	17 Nov 42	Stk. 19 Dec 45, sold 10 Jan 48
477 PRINGLE	Charleston	G. E.	31 Jul 41	2 May 42	15 Sep 42	Sunk by Japanese suicide plane off Okinawa 16 Apr 45
478 STANLY	Charleston	W'house	15 Sep 41	2 May 42	15 Oct 42	Stk. 1 Dec 70, sold 16 Dec 71
479 STEVENS	Charleston	A. C.	30 Dec 41	24 Jun 42	1 Feb 43	Stk. 1 Dec 72, sold 27 Nov 73
480 HALFORD	Puget Sd.	G. E.	3 Jun 41	29 Oct 42	10 Apr 43	Stk. 1 May 68, sold 2 Apr 70
481 LEUTZE	Puget Sd.	A. C.	3 Jun 41	29 Oct 42	4 Mar 44	Stk. 3 Jan 46, sold 11 Feb 47
498 PHILIP	Kearny	G. E.	7 May 42	13 Oct 42	21 Nov 42	Stk. 1 Oct 68, sold 15 Dec 71
499 RENSHAW	Kearny	G. E.	7 May 42	13 Oct 42	5 Dec 42	Stk. 14 Feb 70, sold Oct 70
500 RINGGOLD	Kearny	G. E.	25 Jun 42	11 Nov 42	24 Dec 42	To W. Germany 14 Jul 59 as Z-2, stk. 1 Oct 74
501 SCHROEDER	Kearny	G. E.	25 Jun 42	11 Nov 42	1 Jan 43	Stk. 1 Oct 72, sold 2 Jan 74
502 SIGSBEE	Kearny	G. E.	22 Jul 42	7 Dec 42	23 Jan 43	Stk. 1 Dec 74, sold 31 Jul 75
507 CONWAY	Bath	Westing-house	5 Nov 41	16 Aug 42	9 Oct 42	Stk. 15 Nov 69, sunk as target 26 Jun 70

No.		Hull	Machinery	Laid down	Launched	Commiss'd	Disposition
508	CONY	Bath	A. C.	24 Dec 41	16 Aug 42	30 Oct 42	Stk. 2 Jul 69, sunk as target off Puerto Rico 20 Mar 70
509	CONVERSE	Bath	A. C.	23 Feb 42	30 Aug 42	20 Nov 42	To Spain 1 Jul 59 as Almirante Valdes, stk. 1 Oct 72
510	EATON	Bath	G. E.	17 Mar 42	20 Sep 42	4 Dec 42	Stk. 2 Jul 69, sunk as target off NE Florida 27 Mar 70
511	FOOTE	Bath	G. E.	14 Apr 42	11 Oct 42	22 Dec 42	Stk. 1 Oct 72, sold 2 Jan 74
512	SPENCE	Bath	G. E.	18 May 42	27 Oct 42	8 Jan 43	Foundered E of Samar 18 Dec 44
513	TERRY	Bath	G. E.	8 Jun 42	22 Nov 42	26 Jan 43	Stk. 1 Apr 74, sold 26 Jul 74 to Peru for spare parts
514	THATCHER	Bath	G. E.	29 Jun 42	6 Dec 42	10 Feb 43	Stk. 5 Dec 45, sold 23 Jan 48
515	ANTHONY	Bath	G. E.	17 Aug 42	20 Dec 42	26 Feb 43	To W. Germany 17 Jan 58 as Z-1, stk. 15 Apr 72
516	WADSWORTH	Bath	G. E.	18 Aug 42	10 Jan 43	16 Mar 43	To W. Germany 6 Oct 59 as Z-3, stk. 1 Oct 74
517	WALKER	Bath	G. E.	31 Aug 42	31 Jan 43	3 Apr 43	To Italy 2 Jul 69 as Fante, stk. 2 Jul 69
518	BROWNSON	Staten I.	G. E.	15 Feb 42	24 Sep 42	3 Feb 43	Sunk by Japanese aircraft off Cape Gloucester, New Guinea, 26 Dec 43
519	DALY	Staten I.	G. E.	29 Apr 42	24 Oct 42	10 Mar 43	Stk. 1 Dec 74, sold 22 Apr 76
520	ISHERWOOD	Staten I.	G. E.	12 May 42	24 Nov 42	12 Apr 43	To Peru 8 Oct 61 as Almirante Guise, stk. 15 Jan 74
521	KIMBERLY	Staten I.	G. E.	27 Jul 42	4 Feb 43	22 May 43	To Taiwan 1 Jun 67 as An Yang, stk. 25 Jan 74
522	LUCE	Staten I.	G. E.	24 Aug 42	6 Mar 43	21 Jun 43	Sunk by Japanese suicide plane E of Okinawa 4 May 45
523 -525	Unnamed	Staten I.	Unknown	No	No	No	Cancelled 16 Dec 40
526	ABNER READ	Beth-SF	Westinghouse	30 Oct 41	18 Aug 42	5 Feb 43	Sunk by Japanese suicide plane off Samar 1 Nov 44
527	AMMEN	Beth-SF	W'house	29 Nov 41	17 Sep 42	12 Mar 43	Stk. 1 Oct 60, sold 21 Mar 61
528	MULLANY	Beth-SF	Westinghouse	15 Jan 42	12 Oct 42	23 Apr 43	To Taiwan 6 Oct 71 as Chiang Yang, stk. 6 Oct 71
529	BUSH	Beth-SF	Westinghouse	12 Feb 42	27 Oct 42	10 May 43	Sunk by Japanese suicide planes N of Okinawa 6 Apr 45
530	TRATHEN	Beth-SF	Westinghouse	17 Mar 42	22 Oct 42	28 May 43	Stk. 1 Nov 72, target hulk Nov 73
531	HAZELWOOD	Beth-SF	W'house	11 Apr 42	20 Nov 42	18 Jun 43	Stk. 1 Dec 74, sold 14 Apr 76
532	HEERMAN	Beth-SF	A. C.	8 May 42	5 Dec 42	6 Jul 43	To Argentina 14 Aug 61 as Alm. Brown, stk. 1 Sep 75
533	HOEL	Beth-SF	Westinghouse	4 Jun 42	19 Dec 42	29 Jul 43	Sunk by Japanese squadron E of Samar 25 Oct 44
534	McCORD	Beth-SF	W'house	17 Mar 42	10 Jan 43	19 Aug 43	Stk. 1 Oct 72, sold 2 Jan 74
535	MILLER	Beth-SF	W'house	18 Aug 42	7 Mar 43	31 Aug 43	Stk. 1 Dec 74, sold 31 Jul 75
536	OWEN	Beth-SF	W'house	17 Sep 42	21 Mar 43	20 Sep 43	Stk. 15 Apr 73, sold 27 Nov 73
537	THE SULLIVANS	Beth-SF	Westinghouse	10 Oct 42	4 Apr 43	30 Sep 43	Stk. 1 Dec 74, memorial at Buffalo, N.Y., 21 Jun 77
538	STEPHEN POTTER	Beth-SF	Westinghouse	27 Oct 42	28 Apr 43	21 Oct 43	Stk. 1 Dec 72, sold 27 Nov 73
539	TINGEY	Beth-SF	Westinghouse	22 Oct 42	28 May 43	25 Nov 43	Stk. 1 Nov 65, sunk as target off San Francisco May 66
540	TWINING	Beth-SF	Westinghouse	20 Nov 42	11 Jul 43	1 Dec 43	Stk. 1 Jul 71, to Taiwan as Kwei Yang 16 Aug 71
541	YARNALL	Beth-SF	A. C.	5 Dec 42	25 Jul 43	30 Dec 43	To Taiwan 10 Jun 68 as Kun Yang, stk. 25 Jan 74
542	Unnamed	Beth-SF	Unknown	No	No	No	Cancelled 16 Dec 40
543	Unnamed	Beth-SF	Unknown	No	No	No	Cancelled 16 Dec 40
544	BOYD	San Pedro	G. E.	2 Apr 42	29 Oct 42	8 May 43	To Turkey 1 Oct 69 as Iskenderun, stk. 1 Oct 69
545	BRADFORD	San Pedro	G. E.	28 Apr 42	12 Dec 42	12 Jun 43	To Greece 27 Sep 62 as Thyella, stk. 1 Sep 75
546	BROWN	San Pedro	A. C.	27 Jun 42	21 Feb 43	10 Jul 43	To Greece 27 Sep 62 as Navarinon, stk. 1 Sep 75

No.		Hull	Machinery	Laid down	Launched	Commiss'd	Disposition
547	COWELL	San Pedro	A. C.	7 Sep 42	18 Mar 43	23 Aug 43	To Argentina 17 Aug 71 as Alm. Storni, stk. 17 Aug 71
548	Unnamed	San Pedro	Unknown	No	No	No	Cancelled 16 Dec 40
549	Unnamed	San Pedro	Unknown	No	No	No	Cancelled 16 Dec 40
550	CAPPS	Gulf	A. C.	12 Jun 41	31 May 42	23 Jun 43	To Spain 15 May 57 as Lepanto, stk. 1 Oct 72
551	DAVID W. TAYLOR	Gulf	A. C.	12 Jun 41	4 Jul 42	18 Sep 43	To Spain 15 May 57 as Almirante Ferrandiz, stk. 1 Oct 72
552	EVANS	Gulf	W'house	21 Jul 41	4 Oct 42	11 Dec 43	Stk. 28 Nov 45, sold 11 Feb 47
553	JOHN D. HENLEY	Gulf	Westing-house	21 Jul 41	15 Nov 42	2 Feb 44	Stk. 1 May 68, sold May 70
554	FRANKS	Sea-Tac, Seattle	G. E.	8 Mar 42	7 Dec 42	30 Jul 43	Stk. 1 Dec 72, sold 27 Aug 73
555	HAGGARD	Sea-Tac, Seattle	G. E.	27 Mar 42	9 Feb 43	31 Aug 43	Stk. 16 Nov 45, scrapped 1946
556	HAILEY	Sea-Tac, Seattle	G. E.	11 Apr 42	9 Mar 43	30 Sep 43	To Brazil 20 Jul 61 as Pernambuco, stk. 1 Aug 73
557	JOHNSTON	Sea-Tac, Seattle	Westing-house	6 May 42	25 Mar 43	27 Oct 43	Sunk by Japanese squadron E of Samar 25 Oct 44
558	LAWS	Sea-Tac, Seattle	G. E.	19 May 42	22 Apr 43	18 Nov 43	Stk. 15 Apr 73, sold 3 Dec 73
559	LONGSHAW	Sea-Tac, Seattle	G. E.	16 Jun 42	4 Jun 43	4 Dec 43	Sunk by Japanese batteries after grounding off Okinawa 14 May 45
560	MORRISON	Sea-Tac, Seattle	Westing-house	30 Jun 42	4 Jul 43	18 Dec 43	Sunk by Japanese suicide plane N of Okinawa 4 May 45
561	PRITCHETT	Sea-Tac, Seattle	G. E.	20 Jul 42	31 Jul 43	15 Jan 44	Stk. 10 Jan 70, to Italy as Geniere 17 Jan 70
562	ROBINSON	Sea-Tac, Seattle	G. E.	12 Aug 42	28 Aug 43	31 Jan 44	Stk. 1 Dec 74, sunk as target off Puerto Rico 13 Apr 82
563	ROSS	Sea-Tac, Seattle	Westing-house	7 Sep 42	18 Sep 43	21 Feb 44	Stk. 1 Dec 74, sunk as target off Puerto Rico 26 Jan 78
564	ROWE	Sea-Tac, Seattle	G. E.	7 Dec 42	30 Sep 43	13 Mar 44	Stk. 1 Dec 74, sunk as target off Puerto Rico 23 Feb 78
565	SMALLEY	Sea-Tac, Seattle	G. E.	9 Feb 43	27 Oct 43	31 Mar 44	Stk. 1 Apr 65, sold 4 Jan 66
566	STODDARD	Sea-Tac, Seattle	G. E.	10 Mar 43	19 Nov 43	15 Apr 44	Stk. 1 Jun 75, target hulk Oct 80
567	WATTS	Sea-Tac, Seattle	G. E.	26 Mar 43	31 Dec 43	29 Apr 44	Stk. 1 Feb 74, sold 16 Aug 74
568	WREN	Sea-Tac, Seattle	G. E.	24 Apr 43	29 Jan 44	20 May 44	Stk. 1 Dec 74, sold 22 Oct 75
569	AULICK	Orange	G. E.	14 May 41	2 Mar 42	27 Oct 42	To Greece 21 Aug 59 as Sfendoni, stk. 1 Sep 75
570	CHARLES AUSBURNE	Orange	G. E.	14 May 41	16 Mar 42	24 Nov 42	To W. Germany 12 Apr 60 as Z-6, stk. 1 Dec 67
571	CLAXTON	Orange	G. E.	25 Jun 41	1 Apr 42	8 Dec 42	To W. Germany 16 Dec 59 as Z-4, stk. 1 Oct 74
572	DYSON	Orange	G. E.	25 Jun 41	15 Apr 42	30 Dec 42	To W. Germany 23 Feb 60 as Z-5, stk. 1 Oct 74
573	HARRISON	Orange	G. E.	25 Jul 41	4 May 42	25 Jan 43	Stk. 1 May 68, to Mexico as Cuauhtemoc 19 Aug 70
574	JOHN RODGERS	Orange	G. E.	25 Jul 41	7 May 42	9 Feb 43	Stk. 1 May 68, to Mexico as Cuitlahuac 19 Aug 70
575	McKEE	Orange	G. E.	2 Mar 42	2 Aug 42	31 Mar 43	Stk. 1 Oct 72, sold 2 Jan 74
576	MURRAY	Orange	G. E.	16 Mar 42	16 Aug 42	20 Apr 43	Stk. 1 Jun 65, sold 16 Aug 66
577	SPROSTON	Orange	G. E.	1 Apr 42	31 Aug 42	19 May 43	Stk. 1 Oct 68, sold 15 Dec 71
578	WICKES	Orange	G. E.	15 Apr 42	13 Sep 42	16 Jun 43	Stk. 1 Nov 72, sunk as target 8 Apr 74
579	WILLIAM D. PORTER	Orange	G. E.	7 May 42	27 Sep 42	6 Jul 43	Sunk by Japanese suicide planes NW of Okinawa 10 Jun 45
580	YOUNG	Orange	G. E.	7 May 42	15 Oct 42	31 Jul 43	Stk. 1 May 68, sunk as target off Virginia 16 Apr 70

No.		Hull	Machinery	Laid down	Launched	Commiss'd	Disposition
581	CHARETTE	Boston	A. C.	20 Feb 42	3 Jun 42	18 May 43	To Greece 16 Jun 59 as Velos, stk. 1 Sep 75
582	CONNER	Boston	A. C.	16 Apr 42	18 Jul 42	8 Jun 43	To Greece 15 Sep 59 as Aspis, stk. 1 Sep 75
583	HALL	Boston	G. E.	16 Apr 42	18 Jul 42	6 Jul 43	To Greece 9 Feb 60 as Lonchi, stk. 1 Sep 75
584	HALLIGAN	Boston	G. E.	9 Nov 42	19 Mar 43	19 Aug 43	Mined off Naha, Okinawa, 26 Mar 45
585	HARADEN	Boston	G. E.	9 Nov 42	19 Mar 43	16 Sep 43	Stk. 1 Nov 72, target hulk Nov 73
586	NEWCOMB	Boston	A. C.	19 Mar 43	4 Jul 43	10 Nov 43	Stk. 28 Mar 46, scrapped 1947
587	BELL	Charleston	A. C.	30 Dec 41	24 Jun 42	4 Mar 43	Stk. 1 Nov 72, sunk as target 11 May 75
588	BURNS	Charleston	A. C.	9 May 42	8 Aug 42	3 Apr 43	Stk. 1 Nov 72, sunk as target 20 Jun 74
589	IZARD	Charleston	A. C.	9 May 42	8 Aug 42	15 May 43	Stk. 1 May 68, sold 2 Apr 70
590	PAUL HAMILTON	Charleston	A. C.	20 Jan 43	7 Apr 43	25 Oct 43	Stk. 1 May 68, sold 2 Apr 70
591	TWIGGS	Charleston	A. C.	20 Jan 43	7 Apr 43	4 Nov 43	Sunk by Japanese aircraft S of Okinawa 16 Jun 45
592	HOWORTH	Puget Sd.	A. C.	26 Nov 41	10 Jan 43	3 Apr 44	Stk. 1 Jun 61, sunk as target off San Diego 8 Mar 62
593	KILLEN	Puget Sd.	A. C.	26 Nov 41	10 Jan 43	4 May 44	Stk. 1 Jan 63, target hulk, sold 15 Apr 75
594	HART	Puget Sd.	W'house	10 Aug 43	25 Sep 44	4 Nov 44	Stk. 15 Apr 73, sold 3 Dec 73
595	METCALF	Puget Sd.	W'house	10 Aug 43	25 Sep 44	18 Nov 44	Stk. 2 Jan 71, sold 6 Jun 72
596	SHIELDS	Puget Sd.	Westinghouse	10 Aug 43	25 Sep 44	8 Feb 45	To Brazil 1 Jul 72 as Maranhao, stk. 1 Jul 72
597	WILEY	Puget Sd.	A. C.	10 Aug 43	25 Sep 44	22 Feb 45	Stk. 1 May 68, sold 2 Apr 70
629	ABBOT	Bath	G. E.	21 Sep 42	17 Feb 43	23 Apr 43	Stk. 1 Dec 74, sold 31 Jul 75
630	BRAINE	Bath	G. E.	12 Oct 42	7 Mar 43	11 May 43	To Argentina 17 Aug 71 as Almirante Domecq Garcia, stk. 17 Aug 71
631	ERBEN	Bath	G. E.	28 Oct 42	21 Mar 43	28 May 43	To S. Korea 16 May 63 as Chung Mu, stk. 2 Jun 75
642	HALE	Bath	G. E.	23 Nov 42	4 Apr 43	15 Jun 43	To Colombia 5 Dec 60 as Antioquia, stk. 2 Jun 75
643	SIGOURNEY	Bath	G. E.	7 Dec 42	24 Apr 43	29 Jun 43	Stk. 1 Dec 74, sold 31 Jul 75
644	STEMBEL	Bath	G. E.	21 Dec 42	8 May 43	16 Jul 43	To Argentina 7 Aug 61 as Rosales, stk. 1 Sep 75
649	ALBERT W. GRANT	Charleston	A. C.	30 Dec 42	29 May 43	24 Nov 43	Stk. 14 Apr 71, sold 30 May 72
650	CAPERTON	Bath	G. E.	11 Jan 43	22 May 43	30 Jul 43	Stk. 1 Dec 74
651	COGSWELL	Bath	G. E.	1 Feb 43	5 Jun 43	17 Aug 43	To Turkey 1 Oct 69 as Izmit, stk. 1 Oct 69
652	INGERSOLL	Bath	G. E.	18 Feb 43	28 Jun 43	31 Aug 43	Stk. 20 Jan 70, sunk as target 19 May 74
653	KNAPP	Bath	G. E.	8 Mar 43	10 Jul 43	16 Sep 43	Stk. 6 Mar 72, sold 27 Aug 73
654	BEARSS	Gulf	A. C.	14 Jul 42	25 Jul 43	12 Apr 44	Stk. 1 Dec 74, sold 14 Apr 76
655	JOHN HOOD	Gulf	A. C.	12 Oct 42	25 Oct 43	7 Jun 44	Stk. 1 Dec 74, sold 12 Apr 76
656	VAN VALKENBURGH	Gulf	A. C.	15 Nov 42	19 Dec 43	2 Aug 44	To Turkey 28 Feb 67 as Izmir, stk. 1 Feb 73
657	CHARLES J. BADGER	Staten I.	G. E.	24 Sep 42	3 Apr 43	23 Jul 43	Stk. 1 Feb 74, sold 10 May 74 to Chile for spare parts
658	COLAHAN	Staten I.	G. E.	24 Oct 42	3 May 43	23 Aug 43	Stk. 1 Aug 66, sunk as target off S. California 18 Dec 66
659	DASHIELL	Kearny	G. E.	1 Oct 42	6 Feb 43	20 Mar 43	Stk. 1 Dec 74, sold 21 Sep 75
660	BULLARD	Kearny	G. E.	16 Oct 42	28 Feb 43	9 Apr 43	Stk. 1 Dec 72, sold 3 Dec 73
661	KIDD	Kearny	G. E.	16 Oct 42	28 Feb 43	23 Apr 43	Stk. 1 Dec 74, memorial at Baton Rouge, La.
662	BENNION	Boston	A. C.	19 Mar 43	4 Jul 43	14 Dec 43	Stk. 15 Apr 71, sold 30 May 72
663	HEYWOOD L. EDWARDS	Boston	A. C.	4 Jul 43	6 Oct 43	26 Jan 44	To Japan 10 Mar 59 as Ariake, stk. 18 Mar 74
664	RICHARD P. LEARY	Boston	A. C.	4 Jul 43	6 Oct 43	23 Feb 44	To Japan 10 Mar 59 as Yugure, stk. 18 Mar 74

No.		Hull	Machinery	Laid down	Launched	Commiss'd	Disposition
665	BRYANT	Charleston	A. C.	30 Dec 42	29 May 43	4 Dec 43	Stk. 30 Jun 68, sunk as target off S. California 24 Aug 69
666	BLACK	Kearny	G. E.	14 Nov 42	28 Mar 43	21 May 43	Stk. 26 Sep 69, sold 17 Feb 71
667	CHAUNCEY	Kearny	G. E.	14 Nov 42	28 Mar 43	31 May 43	Stk. 1 Oct 72, sold 2 Jan 74
668	CLARENCE K. BRONSON	Kearny	G. E.	9 Dec 42	18 Apr 43	11 Jun 43	To Turkey 14 Jan 67 as Istanbul, stk. 1 Feb 73
669	COTTEN	Kearny	G. E.	8 Feb 43	12 Jun 43	24 Jul 43	Stk. 1 Dec 74, sold 31 Jul 75
670	DORTCH	Kearny	G. E.	2 Mar 43	20 Jun 43	7 Aug 43	To Argentina 14 Aug 61 as Espora, stk. 1 Sep 75
671	GATLING	Kearny	G. E.	3 Mar 43	20 Jun 43	19 Aug 43	Stk. 1 Dec 74, sold 22 Feb 77
672	HEALY	Kearny	G. E.	4 Mar 43	4 Jul 43	3 Sep 43	Stk. 1 Dec 74, sold 12 Apr 76
673	HICKOX	Kearny	G. E.	12 Mar 43	4 Jul 43	10 Sep 43	To S. Korea 15 Nov 68 as Pusan, stk. 2 Jun 75
674	HUNT	Kearny	G. E.	31 Mar 43	1 Aug 43	22 Sep 43	Stk. 1 Dec 74, sold 14 Aug 75
675	LEWIS HANCOCK	Kearny	G. E.	31 Mar 43	1 Aug 43	29 Sep 43	To Brazil 2 Aug 67 as Piaui, stk. 15 Mar 73
676	MARSHALL	Kearny	G. E.	19 Apr 43	29 Aug 43	16 Oct 43	Stk. 19 Jul 69, sold Jul 70
677	McDERMUT	Kearny	G. E.	14 Jun 43	17 Oct 43	19 Nov 43	Stk. 1 Apr 65, sold 4 Jan 66
678	McGOWAN	Kearny	G. E.	30 Jun 43	14 Nov 43	20 Dec 43	To Spain 30 Nov 60 as Jorge Juan, stk. 1 Oct 72
679	McNAIR	Kearny	G. E.	30 Jun 43	14 Nov 43	30 Dec 43	Stk. 1 Dec 74, sold 10 Jun 76
680	MELVIN	Kearny	G. E.	6 Jul 43	17 Oct 43	24 Nov 43	Stk. 1 Dec 74, sold 14 Aug 75
681	HOPEWELL	San Pedro	Westing-house	29 Oct 42	2 May 43	30 Sep 43	Stk. 2 Jan 70, sunk as target off S. California 11 Feb 72
682	PORTERFIELD	San Pedro	W'house	12 Dec 42	13 Jun 43	30 Oct 43	Stk. 1 Mar 75, target hulk 1976
683	STOCKHAM	Beth-SF	Westing-house	19 Dec 42	25 Jun 43	11 Feb 44	Stk. 1 Mar 75, sunk as target off Puerto Rico 17 Feb 77
684	WEDDERBURN	Beth-SF	W'house	10 Jan 43	1 Aug 43	9 Mar 44	Stk. 1 Oct 69, sold 16 Dec 71
685	PICKING	Staten I.	G. E.	24 Nov 42	1 Jun 43	21 Sep 43	Stk. 1 Mar 75, target hulk Jun 76
686	HALSEY POWELL	Staten I.	G. E.	4 Feb 43	30 Jun 43	25 Oct 43	To S. Korea 27 Apr 68 as Seoul, stk. 2 Jun 75
687	UHLMANN	Staten I.	G. E.	6 Mar 43	30 Jul 43	22 Nov 43	Stk. 15 Jul 72, sold 21 Mar 74
688	REMEY	Bath	W'house	22 Mar 43	25 Jul 43	30 Sep 43	Stk. 1 Dec 74, sold 10 Jun 76
689	WADLEIGH	Bath	Westing-house	5 Apr 43	7 Aug 43	19 Oct 43	To Chile 26 Jul 62 as Blanco Encalada, stk. 1 Sep 75
690	NORMAN SCOTT	Bath	G. E.	26 Apr 43	28 Aug 43	5 Nov 43	Stk. 15 Apr 73, sold 3 Dec 73
691	MERTZ	Bath	G. E.	10 May 43	11 Sep 43	19 Nov 43	Stk. 1 Oct 70, sold 16 Dec 71
792	CALLAGHAN	San Pedro	Westing-house	21 Feb 43	1 Aug 43	27 Nov 43	Sunk by Japanese aircraft E of Okinawa 28 Jul 45
793	CASSIN YOUNG	San Pedro	Westing-house	18 Mar 43	12 Sep 43	31 Dec 43	Stk. 1 Dec 74, memorial at Boston, Mass., 1981
794	IRWIN	San Pedro	G. E.	2 May 43	31 Oct 43	14 Feb 44	To Brazil 10 May 68 as Santa Catarina, stk. 15 Mar 73
795	PRESTON	San Pedro	Westing-house	13 Jun 43	12 Dec 43	20 Mar 44	To Turkey 15 Nov 69 as Icel, stk. 15 Nov 69
796	BENHAM	Staten I.	G. E.	3 Apr 43	30 Aug 43	20 Dec 43	To Peru 15 Dec 60 as Villar, stk. 15 Jan 74
797	CUSHING	Staten I.	G. E.	3 May 43	30 Sep 43	17 Jan 44	To Brazil 20 Jul 61 as Parana, stk. 1 Aug 73
798	MONSSEN	Staten I.	G. E.	1 Jun 43	30 Oct 43	14 Feb 44	Stk. 1 Feb 63, sold 21 Oct 63
799	JARVIS	Sea-Tac, Seattle	G. E.	7 Jun 43	14 Feb 44	3 Jun 44	To Spain 3 Nov 60 as Alcala Galiano, stk. 1 Oct 72
800	PORTER	Sea-Tac, Seattle	G. E.	6 Jul 43	13 Mar 44	24 Jun 44	Stk. 1 Oct 72, sold 21 Mar 74
801	COLHOUN	Sea-Tac, Seattle	G. E.	3 Aug 43	10 Apr 44	8 Jul 44	Sunk by Japanese aircraft N of Okinawa 6 Apr 45
802	GREGORY	Sea-Tac, Seattle	G. E.	31 Aug 43	8 May 44	29 Jul 44	Stk. 1 May 66, grounded as target, San Clemente Is., Cal., 4 Mar 71
803	LITTLE	Sea-Tac, Seattle	G. E.	13 Sep 43	22 May 44	19 Aug 44	Sunk by Japanese suicide plane NE of Okinawa 3 May 45
804	ROOKS	Sea-Tac, Seattle	G. E.	27 Oct 43	6 Jun 44	2 Sep 44	To Chile 26 Jul 62 as Cochrane, stk. 1 Sep 75.

The *Fletcher*-class destroyer *Anthony* (DD-515) on 8 December 1944. (NARA 80-G-77161)

The *Gearing*-class destroyer *Rich* (DD-820) photographed by the New York Navy Yard on 17 September 1947. She is in her original configuration except that Mount 52 has been removed to make room for a training hedgehog. (NH 86114)

Notes: Fiscal years 1941 (DD 445/644) and 1942 (649-691, 792-804). The design for this class resulted from a complete reappraisal of destroyer design requirements following the elimination of treaty restrictions on destroyer tonnage. Compared to earlier classes, it added splinter protection against bomb attack for the machinery spaces, an expanded anti-aircraft battery, and a higher designed speed (38 knots) to allow it to escort Iowa class battleships and Yorktown class carriers. The flush-deck hull was adopted to improve stability, increase freeboard amidships, and augment hull strength. The boilers operated at 565 psi and 850 degrees. The detailed plans were prepared by Gibbs and Cox. Later war-built ships of this class (DD 518-22, 526-41, 544-47, 554-68, 581-91, 594-97, 629-44, 649-91, and 792-804) had a modified, square-faced bridge with a lowered gun director. DD 523-524 were originally ordered from Bethlehem, San Francisco, and DD-525 from Bethlehem, San Pedro. They along with DD 542-3 and 548-49 were replaced in the building program in 1940 by seven Benson class ships in the DD 602-17 group to expedite production.

    DD 476-481 were scheduled to be built with a catapult in place of 1-5" and 5-21"T. Only DD 477, 479, and 480 actually operated with aircraft and DD-481 never received her catapult. The removal of the catapult was ordered on 15 Oct 43 and the ships resumed a conventional configuration. In 1945, 53 ships had one bank of torpedo tubes removed and additional small anti-aircraft guns added to enhance defenses against suicide aircraft. Ships reactivated for the Korean War were similarly fitted. Under the fiscal year 1952 program, 39 ships were fitted with 3"/50 AA guns, losing one 5"AA. These ships were DD 519-20, 527-528, 530, 532, 535, 537, 544, 547, 556, 561, 563-64, 566, 629-30, 642, 644, 650-652, 655, 659, 666, 669-70, 674, 677-79, 681, 685, 687, 689, 795-96, 799, and 804. (DD-538 and 541 were also scheduled but not refitted; others were later modified for foreign owners.) Eighteen ships were converted to escort destroyers (DDE) in 1948-52 in an effort to produce ASW ships that could keep up with fast modern submarines. Three of these (DDE 446, 447, 449) received Fram II modernizations in 1960-61; planned modernizations of the other 15 were dropped in December 1961. The Hazelwood (DD-531) was converted into a DASH helicopter trials ship with 2-5"AA and a flight deck in 1958. The Gregory (DD-802) served as the training hulk Indoctrinator at San Diego from 20 May 66 to 8 Jan 71.
Renamings: DD-451 ex unnamed 8 Aug 40 ex Pringle 13 Jul 40; DD-528 ex Beatty 10 Jun 41; DD-535 to James Miller 5 Aug 71; DD-537 ex Putnam 10 Feb 43; DD-594 ex Mansfield 21 Mar 44; DD-655 ex Hood 16 Apr 43; and DD-686 ex Powell 16 Oct 42.
Reclassifications: DD 445-446, 449-450, 465-466, 498-499, 507-508, 517, and 577 to DDE 26 Mar 49; reverted to DD on 30 Jun 62. DD-447, 468, 470-471, 510, and 576 to DDE on 2 Jan 51, also reverted to DD 30 Jun 62.

PERCIVAL and WATSON

Displacement: 2050 tons standard   Speed: 35 kts. (designed)
Dimensions: 376'5"(oa.) x 39'7"(e) x 17'9"(max)   Complement: 329
Armament: 5-5"/38AA 10-21"T
Machinery: 60,000 SHP; G. E. geared turbines, 2 screws
    (Percival); 60,000 BHP; 24 General Motors diesel engines
    with electric drive, 2 screws (Watson)

No.	Hull	Machinery	Laid down	Launched	Commiss'd	Disposition
452 PERCIVAL	Kearny	G. E.	No	No	No	Cancelled 7 Jan 46
482 WATSON	Kearny	G. M.	No	No	No	Cancelled 7 Jan 46.

Notes: Fiscal year 1941. Fletcher class hulls with experimental power plants, they were never built because of the outbreak of World War II. The construction of a testbed for ultra-high pressure boilers was approved in March 1940 and construction of an experimental ship with lightweight diesels and diesel-electric propulsion was approved in June 1940. Machinery for the former, the successor to the Dahlgren (DD-187), was nearly ready by the end of the war and was being tested ashore at Philadelphia; it was later put in the Timmerman (DD-828). Very little work was done on the diesel plant.

STEVENSON and THORN classes

Displacement: 1175 tons standard   Machinery: 12,000 SHP
Dimensions: 300' (wl) x 34'6" x 9'9"   Speed: 24.5 kts.
Armament: 4-5"/38AA   Complement: Unknown

No.	Hull	Machinery	Laid down	Launched	Commiss'd	Disposition
503 STEVENSON	Kearny	Unknown	No	No	No	Cancelled 10 Feb 41
504 STOCKTON	Kearny	Unknown	No	No	No	Cancelled 10 Feb 41
505 THORN	Kearny	Unknown	No	No	No	Cancelled 10 Feb 41
506 TURNER	Kearny	Unknown	No	No	No	Cancelled 10 Feb 41.

Notes: Fiscal year 1941. This group originated in an interest inside and outside the Navy in a small, mass-produceable destroyer. In August 1940 Gibbs and Cox presented two designs for fast, lightweight destroyers to President Roosevelt, and on 9 Sep 40 the Navy ordered two ships to each design. DD 503-4 were to be 750-ton ships with dimensions of 264'(wl) x 28' x 9'3", 25,000 SHP producing 35 knots, and an armament of 2-3"/50 or 4"/50 and 6-21"T. DD 505-6 were to be 1050-ton ships with dimensions of 292'(wl) x 31' x 10'4", 35,000 SHP producing 35 knots, and an armament of 2-5"/38AA and 8-21"T. In November 1940 all four ships were changed to a very different 1175-ton Navy design (details above). The new design was for an escort ship rather than a light destroyer and emphasized seakeeping rather than speed. The contract was modified for the new design in December 1940, but the project was dropped soon afterwards because the design did not offer large enough savings in cost or industrial resources over Gleaves class destroyers. When the contract was cancelled in February 1941, it was replaced in the building program with a contract for four Gleaves class ships, DD 645-48. Development of the design continued, however, and eventually led to the destroyer escort (DE) type.

1942

ALLEN M. SUMNER class

Displacement: 2200 tons standard
Dimensions: 376'5"(DD 747-762), 376'(DD 725-728, 730-734), 376'6"(others) (all oa.) x 40'10"(DD 692-709, 735-740, 744, e), 41'(DD 749-751, 757-762, e), 41'2"(DD 742-743, e), 41'1"(others, e) x 19'(max)
Armament: 6-5"/38AA 10-21"T; 6-5"AA 5-21"T (1945); 6-5"AA 100m (DM conversions); 6-5"AA 6-3"/50AA 5-21"T (1952); 6-5"AA 2-21"T 6-12.75"T (FRAM-II conversions, 1959)

Machinery: 60,000 SHP; geared turbines, 2 screws
Speed: 34 kts.
Complement: 345

No.		Hull	Machinery	Laid down	Launched	Commiss'd	Disposition
692	ALLEN M. SUMNER	Kearny	G. E.	7 Jul 43	15 Dec 43	26 Jan 44	Stk. 15 Aug 73, sold 13 Nov 74
693	MOALE	Kearny	G. E.	5 Aug 43	16 Jan 44	28 Feb 44	Stk. 1 Jul 73, sold 13 Nov 74
694	INGRAHAM	Kearny	G. E.	4 Aug 43	16 Jan 44	10 Mar 44	To Greece 16 Jul 71 as Miaoulis, stk. 16 Jul 71
695	COOPER	Kearny	G. E.	30 Aug 43	9 Feb 44	27 Mar 44	Sunk by HIJMS Take in Ormoc Bay, Leyte, 3 Dec 44
696	ENGLISH	Kearny	G. E.	19 Oct 43	27 Feb 44	4 May 44	Stk. 15 May 70, to Taiwan as Huei Yang 11 Aug 70
697	CHARLES S. SPERRY	Kearny	G. E.	19 Oct 43	13 Mar 44	17 May 44	Stk. 15 Dec 73, to Chile as Ministro Zenteno 8 Jan 74
698	AULT	Kearny	G. E.	15 Nov 43	26 Mar 44	31 May 44	Stk. 1 Sep 73, sold 30 Apr 74
699	WALDRON	Kearny	G. E.	16 Nov 43	26 Mar 44	8 Jun 44	To Colombia 30 Oct 73 as Santander, stk. 31 Oct 73
700	HAYNSWORTH	Kearny	G. E.	16 Dec 43	15 Apr 44	22 Jun 44	Stk. 30 Jan 70, to Taiwan as Yuen Yang 12 May 70
701	JOHN W. WEEKS	Kearny	G. E.	17 Jan 44	21 May 44	21 Jul 44	Stk. 12 Aug 70, sunk as target off Virginia 19 Nov 70
702	HANK	Kearny	G. E.	17 Jan 44	21 May 44	28 Aug 44	To Argentina 1 Jul 72 as Segui, stk. 1 Jul 72
703	WALLACE L. LIND	Kearny	G. E.	14 Feb 44	14 Jun 44	8 Sep 44	To S. Korea 4 Dec 73 as Daegu, stk. 4 Dec 73
704	BORIE	Kearny	G. E.	29 Feb 44	4 Jul 44	21 Sep 44	To Argentina 1 Jul 72 as Hipolito Bouchard, stk. 1 Jul 72
705	COMPTON	Kearny	G. E.	28 Mar 44	17 Sep 44	4 Nov 44	To Brazil 27 Sep 72 as Matto Grosso, stk. 27 Sep 72
706	GAINARD	Kearny	G. E.	29 Mar 44	17 Sep 44	23 Nov 44	Stk. 26 Feb 71, sold 26 Mar 74
707	SOLEY	Kearny	G. E.	18 Apr 44	8 Sep 44	8 Dec 44	Stk. 13 Feb 70, sunk as target 18 Sep 70
708	HARLAN R. DICKSON	Kearny	G. E.	23 May 44	17 Dec 44	17 Feb 45	Stk. 1 Jul 72, sold 18 May 73
709	HUGH PURVIS	Kearny	G. E.	23 May 44	17 Dec 44	1 Mar 45	To Turkey 1 Jul 72 as Zafer, stk. 1 Feb 73
722	BARTON	Bath	G. E.	24 May 43	10 Oct 43	30 Dec 43	Stk. 1 Oct 68, sunk as target off Virginia 8 Oct 69
723	WALKE	Bath	G. E.	7 Jun 43	27 Oct 43	21 Jan 44	Stk. 1 Feb 74, sold 19 Mar 75
724	LAFFEY	Bath	G. E.	28 Jun 43	21 Nov 43	8 Feb 44	Stk. 1 Mar 75, memorial at Charleston, S. C.
725	O'BRIEN	Bath	G. E.	12 Jul 43	8 Dec 43	25 Feb 44	Stk. 18 Feb 72, sunk as target off S. California 13 Jul 72
726	MEREDITH	Bath	G. E.	26 Jul 43	21 Dec 43	14 Mar 44	Sunk 9 Jun 44 after being mined off Quineville, Fr.

No.		Hull	Machinery	Laid down	Launched	Commiss'd	Disposition
727	DE HAVEN	Bath	G. E.	9 Aug 43	9 Jan 44	31 Mar 44	Stk. 3 Dec 73, to S. Korea as Inchon 5 Dec 73
728	MANSFIELD	Bath	G. E.	28 Aug 43	29 Jan 44	14 Apr 44	Stk. 1 Feb 74, sold 4 Jun 74 to Argentina for spare parts
729	LYMAN K. SWENSON	Bath	G. E.	11 Sep 43	12 Feb 44	2 May 44	Stk. 1 Feb 74, sold 6 May 74 to Taiwan for spare parts
730	COLLETT	Bath	G. E.	11 Oct 43	5 Mar 44	16 May 44	Stk. 1 Feb 74, to Argentina as Piedra Buena 4 Jun 74
731	MADDOX	Bath	G. E.	28 Oct 43	19 Mar 44	2 Jun 44	To Taiwan 6 Jul 72 as Po Yang, stk. 6 Jul 72
732	HYMAN	Bath	G. E.	22 Nov 43	8 Apr 44	16 Jun 44	Stk. 14 Nov 69, sold 13 Oct 70
733	MANNERT L. ABELE	Bath	G. E.	9 Dec 43	23 Apr 44	4 Jul 44	Sunk by Japanese suicide planes NE of Okinawa 12 Apr 45
734	PURDY	Bath	G. E.	22 Dec 43	7 May 44	18 Jul 44	Stk. 1 Jul 73, sold 11 Jun 74
735	ROBERT H. SMITH	Bath	G. E.	10 Jan 44	25 May 44	4 Aug 44	Stk. 26 Feb 71, sold 3 Dec 73
736	THOMAS E. FRASER	Bath	G. E.	31 Jan 44	10 Jun 44	22 Aug 44	Stk. 1 Nov 70, sold 12 Jun 74
737	SHANNON	Bath	G. E.	14 Feb 44	24 Jun 44	8 Sep 44	Stk. 1 Nov 70, sold 18 May 73
738	HARRY F. BAUER	Bath	G. E.	6 Mar 44	9 Jul 44	22 Sep 44	Stk. 15 Aug 71, sold 12 Jun 74
739	ADAMS	Bath	G. E.	20 Mar 44	23 Jul 44	10 Oct 44	Stk. 1 Dec 70, sold 16 Dec 71
740	TOLMAN	Bath	G. E.	10 Apr 44	13 Aug 44	27 Oct 44	Stk. 1 Dec 70, test hulk 1973
741	DREXLER	Bath	G. E.	24 Apr 44	3 Sep 44	14 Nov 44	Sunk by Japanese suicide planes SW of Okinawa 28 May 45
744	BLUE	Staten I.	G. E.	30 Jun 43	28 Nov 43	20 Mar 44	Stk. 1 Feb 74, sunk as target off S. California 28 Apr 77
745	BRUSH	Staten I.	G. E.	30 Jul 43	28 Dec 43	17 Apr 44	Stk. 27 Oct 69, to Taiwan as Hsiang Yang 9 Dec 69
746	TAUSSIG	Staten I.	G. E.	30 Aug 43	25 Jan 44	20 May 44	Stk. 1 Feb 74, to Taiwan as Lo Yang 6 May 74
747	SAMUEL N. MOORE	Staten I.	G. E.	30 Sep 43	23 Feb 44	24 Jun 44	Stk. 24 Oct 69, to Taiwan as Heng Yang 9 Dec 69
748	HARRY E. HUBBARD	Staten I.	Westing-house	30 Oct 43	24 Mar 44	22 Jul 44	Stk. 17 Oct 69, sold Jul 70
749	HENRY A. WILEY	Staten I.	A. C.	28 Nov 43	21 Apr 44	31 Aug 44	Stk. 15 Oct 70, sold 30 May 72
750	SHEA	Staten I.	G. E.	28 Dec 43	20 May 44	30 Sep 44	Stk. 1 Sep 73, sold 16 Aug 74
751	J. WILLIAM DITTER	Staten I.	G. E.	25 Jan 44	4 Jul 44	28 Oct 44	Stk. 11 Oct 45, scrapped 1946
752	ALFRED A. CUNNINGHAM	Staten I.	Westing-house	23 Feb 44	3 Aug 44	23 Nov 44	Stk. 1 Feb 74, sunk as target off S. California 12 Oct 79
753	JOHN R. PIERCE	Staten I.	Westing-house	24 Mar 44	1 Sep 44	30 Dec 44	Stk. 1 Jul 73, sold 6 Nov 74
754	FRANK E. EVANS	Staten I.	Westing-house	21 Apr 44	3 Oct 44	3 Feb 45	Stk. 1 Jul 69, sunk as target off Subic Bay 10 Oct 69
755	JOHN A. BOLE	Staten I.	G. E.	20 May 44	1 Nov 44	3 Mar 45	Stk. 1 Feb 74, sold 6 May 74 to Taiwan for spare parts
756	BEATTY	Staten I.	G. E.	4 Jul 44	30 Nov 44	31 Mar 45	To Venezuela 14 Jul 72 as Carabobo, stk. 14 Jul 72
757	PUTNAM	Beth-SF	G. E.	11 Jul 43	26 Mar 44	12 Oct 44	Stk. 6 Aug 73, sold 24 Jun 74
758	STRONG	Beth-SF	G. E.	25 Jul 43	23 Apr 44	8 Mar 45	To Brazil 31 Oct 73 as Rio Grande do Norte, stk. 31 Oct 73
759	LOFBERG	Beth-SF	Westing-house	4 Nov 43	12 Aug 44	26 Apr 45	Stk. 1 Feb 74, sold 6 May 74 to Taiwan for spare parts
760	JOHN W. THOMASON	Beth-SF	G. E.	21 Nov 43	30 Sep 44	11 Oct 45	Stk. 1 Feb 74, to Taiwan as Nan Yang 6 May 74
761	BUCK	Beth-SF	G. E.	1 Feb 44	11 Mar 45	28 Jun 46	Stk. 15 Jul 73, to Brazil as Alagoas 16 Jul 73
762	HENLEY	Beth-SF	G. E.	8 Feb 44	8 Apr 45	8 Oct 46	Stk. 1 Jul 73, sold 24 Jun 74
770	LOWRY	San Pedro	G. E.	1 Aug 43	6 Feb 44	23 Jul 44	To Brazil 29 Oct 73 as Espirito Santo, stk. 31 Oct 73

No.		Hull	Machinery	Laid down	Launched	Commiss'd	Disposition
771	LINDSEY	San Pedro	G. E.	12 Sep 43	5 Mar 44	20 Aug 44	Stk. 1 Oct 70, sunk as target off Virginia 9 May 72
772	GWIN	San Pedro	G. E.	31 Oct 43	9 Apr 44	30 Sep 44	Stk. 15 Aug 71, to Turkey as Muavenet 22 Oct 71
773	AARON WARD	San Pedro	G. E.	12 Dec 43	5 May 44	28 Oct 44	Stk. 11 Oct 45, scrapped 1946
774	HUGH W. HADLEY	San Pedro	G. E.	6 Feb 44	16 Jul 44	25 Nov 44	Stk. 8 Jan 46, sold 2 Sep 47
775	WILLARD KEITH	˜an Pedro	G. E.	5 Mar 44	29 Aug 44	27 Dec 44	To Colombia 1 Jul 72 as Caldas, stk. 1 Jul 72
776	JAMES C. OWENS	San Pedro	G. E.	9 Apr 44	1 Oct 44	17 Feb 45	Stk. 15 Jul 73, to Brazil as Sergipe 16 Jul 73
777	ZELLARS	Todd, Seattle	A. C.	24 Dec 43	19 Jul 44	25 Oct 44	To Iran 19 Mar 71 as Babr, stk. 19 Mar 71
778	MASSEY	Todd, Seattle	A. C.	14 Jan 44	19 Aug 44	24 Nov 44	Stk. 17 Sep 73, sold 13 Nov 74
779	DOUGLAS H. FOX	Todd, Seattle	A. C.	31 Jan 44	30 Sep 44	26 Dec 44	Stk. 15 Dec 73, to Chile as Ministro Portales 8 Jan 74
780	STORMES	Todd, Seattle	A. C.	15 Feb 44	4 Nov 44	27 Jan 45	To Iran 16 Feb 72 as Palang, stk. 16 Feb 72
781	ROBERT K. HUNTINGTON	Todd, Seattle	A. C.	29 Feb 44	5 Dec 44	3 Mar 45	To Venezuela 31 Oct 73 as Falcon, stk. 31 Oct 73
857	BRISTOL	San Pedro	G. E.	5 May 44	29 Oct 44	17 Mar 45	Stk. 21 Nov 69, to Taiwan as Hua Yang 9 Dec 69.

Notes: Fiscal years for Allen M. Sumner and Gearing classes: 1942 (DD 805-808), 1943 (692-791), 1944 (809-890), 1945 (891-926). The Allen M. Sumner class was the result of an effort to increase antiaircraft firepower. Its design introduced the twin 5"/38-gun dual purpose turret and the quad 40mm mount in destroyers. The beam and tonnage were increased, but the power plant of the Fletcher class was retained and a reduction in speed was therefore accepted. In service the ships were wet forward, and the forward 5" mounts had to be strengthened against heavy seas.

The ships reclassified as light minelayers (DM) were converted while building. Many ships exchanged five of their ten torpedo tubes for additional small antiaircraft guns in 1945 to increase defenses against suicide aircraft. 40 of the 53 surviving DDs received 3"/50AA guns in the early 1950s, the exceptions being DD 699-701, 730, 734, 747, 756, 759-61, 778, 781, and 857. 33 ships received FRAM II conversions in 1959-63: DD 692-694, 697-699, 703-704, 709, 723-725, 727-730, 744, 746, 752, 754-755, 757-761, 770, 776-781. Conversion of 17 other ships was dropped in December 1961. The Frank E. Evans (DD-754) was cut in half in a collision with HMAS Melbourne off Luzon on 3 Jun 69. Her stern stayed afloat but was not worth repairing and was used as a target.
Renamings: DD-709 ex Purvis 6 Jul 44; DD-734 ex Gainard 18 Mar 44; and DD-751 ex William Ditter 3 Jul 44 ex Ditter 14 Mar 44.
Reclassifications: DD 735-740, 749-751, and 771-773 to DM 23-34 19 Jul 44; DM 23-30, 32-33 to MMD (retaining their DM numbers) 1 Jan 69.

GEARING class

Displacement: 2425 tons standard
Dimensions: 389'8"(DD-888), 390'2"(DD-765), 390'9"(DD 763-764), 391'(DD-890), 390'6"(others) (all oa.) x 40'10"(DD 766-769), 40'11"(DD-765, 782-791), 41'(DD 763-764, 888, 890), 41'2"(DD 742-743), 41'1"(others) (all e) x 18'6"(max)
Armament: 6-5"/38AA 10-21"T; 6-5"AA 5-21"T (1945); 6-5"AA (DDR conversions, 1945); 4-5"AA 5-21"T (DD-837, 847, 848, 871, 1947); 4-5"AA 4-3"/50AA (DDE-824, 1949); 4-5"AA (DDE-719, 764-765, 818-820, 824, 847-848, 858-861, 871 1949); 4-3"/50AA (DDK-825, 827, 1949); 6-5"AA 6-3"AA 5-21"T (1950); 6-5"AA 6-3"AA (DDR conversions, 1950); 6-5"AA 1-3"AA 5-21"T (DD-838, 868, 1951); 4-5"AA 2-3"AA (DD-849 as AG, 1952); 4-5"AA 6-3"AA (DDE-719, 1954); 4-5"AA 2-Terrier-SAM (DD-712 as DDG, 1956); 4-3"/70AA (DDK-825, 827, 1957); 4-3"/50AA 5-21"T (DDE 764-765, 858-861, 1958); 6-5"AA 6-3"AA 2-21"T (DDR conversions, 1958); 4-5"AA 6-12.75"T DASH ASROC (FRAM I conversions); 4-5"AA 2-21"T 6-12.75"T DASH (FRAM II conversions); 6-5"AA 6-12.75"T DASH (DDR FRAM conversions, 1960); 2-5"AA 6-12.75"T DASH (DD-825, 827, 1964)

Machinery: 100,000 (DD-828), 60,000 (others) SHP; geared turbines, 2 screws
Speed: 40 (DD-828), 35 (others) kts.
Complement: 355

No.		Hull	Machinery	Laid down	Launched	Commiss'd	Disposition
710	GEARING	Port Newark	Westing-house	10 Aug 44	18 Feb 45	3 May 45	Stk. 1 Jul 73, sold 6 Nov 74
711	EUGENE A. GREENE	Port Newark	Westing-house	17 Aug 44	18 Mar 45	8 Jun 45	To Spain 31 Aug 72 as Churruca, stk. 2 Jun 75
712	GYATT	Port Newark	Westing-house	7 Sep 44	15 Apr 45	2 Jul 45	Stk. 22 Oct 69, sunk as target off Virginia 11 Jun 70
713	KENNETH D. BAILEY	Port Newark	G. E.	21 Sep 44	17 Jun 45	31 Jul 45	Stk. 1 Feb 74, sold 13 Jan 75 to Iran for spare parts
714	WILLIAM R. RUSH	Port Newark	Westing-house	19 Oct 44	8 Jul 45	21 Sep 45	To S. Korea 1 Jul 78 as Kang Won, stk. 1 Jul 78
715	WILLIAM M. WOOD	Port Newark	Westing-house	2 Nov 44	29 Jul 45	24 Nov 45	Stk. 1 Dec 76, sunk as target Mar 83
716	WILTSIE	Port Newark	G. E.	13 Mar 45	31 Aug 45	12 Jan 46	Stk. 30 Jan 76, to Pakistan as Tariq 29 Apr 77
717	THEODORE E. CHANDLER	Port Newark	Westing-house	23 Apr 45	20 Oct 45	22 Mar 46	Stk. 1 Apr 75, sold 1 Dec 75
718	HAMNER	Port Newark	Westing-house	25 Apr 45	24 Nov 45	12 Jul 46	Stk. 1 Oct 79, to Taiwan as Chao Yang 17 Dec 80
719	EPPERSON	Port Newark	G. E.	20 Jun 45	22 Dec 45	19 Mar 49	Stk. 30 Jan 76, to Pakistan as Taimur 29 Apr 77
720	CASTLE	Port Newark	G. E.	11 Jul 45	No	No	Stk. 2 Nov 54, sold on ways 29 Aug 55
721	WOODROW R. THOMPSON	Port Newark	G. E.	1 Aug 45	No	No	Stk. 2 Nov 54, sold on ways 29 Aug 55
742	FRANK KNOX	Bath	Westing-house	8 May 44	17 Sep 44	11 Dec 44	To Greece 23 Jan 71 as Themistocles, stk. 30 Jan 71
743	SOUTHERLAND	Bath	Westing-house	27 May 44	5 Oct 44	22 Dec 44	Stk. 23 Feb 81, target hulk 1983
763	WILLIAM C. LAWE	Beth-SF	G. E.	12 Mar 44	21 May 45	18 Dec 46	Stk. 1 Oct 83
764	LLOYD THOMAS	Beth-SF	A. C.	26 Mar 44	5 Oct 45	21 Mar 47	To Taiwan 12 Oct 72 as Dang Yang, stk. 12 Oct 72
765	KEPPLER	Beth-SF	A. C.	23 Apr 44	24 Jun 46	23 May 47	To Turkey 1 Jul 72 as Tinaztepe, stk. 1 Jul 72
766	LANSDALE	Beth-SF	G. E.	2 Apr 44	20 Dec 46	No	Stk. 9 Jun 58, sold 23 Mar 59
767	SEYMOUR D. OWENS	Beth-SF	G. E.	3 Apr 44	24 Feb 47	No	Stk. 9 Jun 58, sold 23 Mar 59
768	HOEL	Beth-SF	G. E.	21 Apr 44	No	No	Cancelled. 13 Sep 46, scrapped Jan 47, stk. 2 Nov 54
769	ABNER READ	Beth-SF	G. E.	21 May 44	No	No	Cancelled. 13 Sep 46, scrapped Jan 47, stk. 2 Nov 54
782	ROWAN	Todd, Seattle	G. E.	25 Mar 44	29 Dec 44	31 Mar 45	Stk. 30 Jan 76, to Taiwan as Chao Yang 10 Jun 77
783	GURKE	Todd, Seattle	G. E.	1 Jul 44	15 Feb 45	12 May 45	Stk. 30 Jan 76, to Greece as Tombazis 17 Mar 77
784	McKEAN	Todd, Seattle	G. E.	15 Sep 44	31 Mar 45	9 Jun 45	Stk. 1 Oct 81, sold 2 Nov 82 to Turkey for spare parts
785	HENDERSON	Todd, Seattle	G. E.	27 Oct 44	28 May 45	4 Aug 45	To Pakistan 30 Sep 80 as Tughril, stk. 1 Oct 80
786	RICHARD B. ANDERSON	Todd, Seattle	G. E.	1 Dec 44	7 Jul 45	26 Oct 45	Stk. 30 Jan 76, to Taiwan as Kai Yang 10 Jun 77
787	JAMES B. KYES	Todd, Seattle	G. E.	27 Dec 44	4 Aug 45	8 Feb 46	Stk. 31 Mar 73, to Taiwan as Chien Yang 18 Apr 73
788	HOLLISTER	Todd, Seattle	G. E.	18 Jan 45	9 Oct 45	29 Mar 46	Stk. 31 Aug 79, to Taiwan as Chen Yang 3 Mar 83
789	EVERSOLE	Todd, Seattle	A. C.	28 Feb 45	8 Jan 46	10 May 46	To Turkey 21 Sep 73 as Gayret, stk. 21 Sep 73
790	SHELTON	Todd, Seattle	G. E.	31 May 45	8 Mar 46	21 Jun 46	Stk. 31 Mar 73, to Taiwan as Lao Yang 18 Apr 73
791	SEAMAN	Todd, Seattle	G. E.	10 Jul 45	29 May 46	No	Stk. 1 Mar 61, sold 12 Sep 61
805	CHEVALIER	Bath	G. E.	12 Jun 44	29 Oct 44	9 Jan 45	To Taiwan 5 Jul 72 as Chung Bok, stk. 2 Jun 75
806	HIGBEE	Bath	G. E.	26 Jun 44	12 Nov 44	27 Jan 45	Stk. 15 Jul 79, sunk as target in Pacific Jun 83

No.		Hull	Machinery	Laid down	Launched	Commiss'd	Disposition
807	BENNER	Bath	G. E.	10 Jul 44	30 Nov 44	13 Feb 45	Stk. 1 Feb 74, sold 19 Mar 75
808	DENNIS J. BUCKLEY	Bath	G. E.	24 Jul 44	20 Dec 44	2 Mar 45	Stk. 1 Jul 73, sold 29 Apr 74
809 -812	Unnamed	Bath	G. E.	No	No	No	Cancelled 12 Aug 45
813 -814	Unnamed	Staten I.	Westing-house	No	No	No	Cancelled 12 Aug 45
815	CHARLES H. ROAN	Orange	Westing-house	No	No	No	Cancelled 12 Aug 45
816	TIMMERMAN	Orange	A. C.	No	No	No	Cancelled 12 Aug 45
817	CORRY	Orange	G. E.	5 Apr 45	28 Jul 45	27 Feb 46	Stk. 27 Feb 81, to Greece as Kriezis 8 Jul 81
818	NEW	Orange	G. E.	14 Apr 45	18 Aug 45	5 Apr 46	Stk. 1 Jul 76, to S. Korea as Taejon 23 Feb 77
819	HOLDER	Orange	G. E.	23 Apr 45	25 Aug 45	18 May 46	Stk. 1 Oct 76, to Ecuador as Presidente Eloy Alfaro 1 Sep 78
820	RICH	Orange	G. E.	16 May 45	5 Oct 45	3 Jul 46	Stk. 15 Dec 77, sold Dec 79
821	JOHNSTON	Orange	G. E.	5 Jun 45	19 Oct 45	23 Aug 46	To Taiwan 27 Feb 81 as Yung Yang, stk. 27 Feb 81
822	ROBERT H. McCARD	Orange	Westing-house	20 Jun 45	9 Nov 45	26 Oct 46	To Turkey 5 Jun 80 as Kilic Ali Pasa, stk. 6 Aug 87
823	SAMUEL B. ROBERTS	Orange	Westing-house	27 Jun 45	30 Nov 45	20 Dec 46	Stk. 2 Nov 70, sunk as target off Puerto Rico 11 Nov 71
824	BASILONE	Orange	G. E.	7 Jul 45	21 Dec 45	26 Jul 49	Stk. 1 Nov 77, sunk as target off NE Florida 9 Apr 82
825	CARPENTER	Orange	G. E.	30 Jul 45	28 Dec 45	15 Dec 49	To Turkey 20 Feb 81 as Anittepe, stk. 6 Aug 87
826	AGERHOLM	Bath	G. E.	10 Sep 45	30 Mar 46	20 Jun 46	Stk. 1 Dec 78, sunk as target off S. California 18 Jul 82
827	ROBERT A. OWENS	Bath	G. E.	29 Oct 45	15 Jul 46	5 Nov 49	To Turkey 22 Feb 82 as Alcitepe, stk. 6 Aug 87
828	TIMMERMAN	Bath	G. E. & W'house	1 Oct 45	19 May 51	26 Sep 52	Stk. 4 Apr 58, sold 21 Apr 59
829	MYLES C. FOX	Bath	G. E.	14 Aug 44	13 Jan 45	20 Mar 45	Stk. 1 Oct 79, sold 2 Aug 80 to Greece for spare parts
830	EVERETT F. LARSON	Bath	G. E.	4 Sep 44	28 Jan 45	6 Apr 45	To S. Korea 30 Oct 72 as Jeong Buk, stk. 2 Jun 75
831	GOODRICH	Bath	G. E.	18 Sep 44	25 Feb 45	24 Apr 45	Stk. 1 Feb 74, sold 12 Sep 77
832	HANSON	Bath	G. E.	7 Oct 44	11 Mar 45	11 May 45	Stk. 31 Mar 73, to Taiwan as Liao Yang 18 Apr 73
833	HERBERT J. THOMAS	Bath	G. E.	30 Oct 44	25 Mar 45	29 May 45	Stk. 1 Feb 74, to Taiwan as Han Yang 6 May 74
834	TURNER	Bath	G. E.	13 Nov 44	8 Apr 45	12 Jun 45	Stk. 26 Sep 69, sold 13 Oct 70
835	CHARLES P. CECIL	Bath	G. E.	2 Dec 44	22 Apr 45	29 Jun 45	Stk. 1 Oct 79, to Greece as Apostolis 2 Aug 80
836	GEORGE K. MACKENZIE	Bath	G. E.	21 Dec 44	13 May 45	13 Jul 45	Stk. 1 Oct 76, sunk as target off S. California 15 Oct 76
837	SARSFIELD	Bath	G. E.	15 Jan 45	27 May 45	31 Jul 45	To Taiwan 1 Oct 77 as Te Yang, stk. 1 Oct 77
838	ERNEST G. SMALL	Bath	G. E.	30 Jan 45	14 Jun 45	21 Aug 45	Stk. 13 Nov 70, to Taiwan as Fu Yang 13 Apr 71
839	POWER	Bath	G. E.	26 Feb 45	30 Jun 45	13 Sep 45	To Taiwan 1 Oct 77 as Shen Yang, stk. 1 Oct 77
840	GLENNON	Bath	G. E.	12 Mar 45	14 Jul 45	4 Oct 45	Stk. 1 Oct 76, sunk as target off Puerto Rico 26 Feb 81
841	NOA	Bath	G. E.	26 Mar 45	30 Jul 45	2 Nov 45	To Spain 31 Oct 73 as Blas de Lezo, stk. 2 Jun 75
842	FISKE	Bath	G. E.	9 Apr 45	8 Sep 45	28 Nov 45	To Turkey 5 Jun 80 as Piyale Pasa, stk. 6 Aug 87
843	WARRINGTON	Bath	G. E.	23 Apr 45	27 Sep 45	20 Dec 45	Stk. 1 Oct 72, sold 24 Apr 73 to Taiwan for spare parts
844	PERRY	Bath	G. E.	14 May 45	25 Oct 45	17 Jan 46	Stk. 1 Jul 73, sold 24 Jun 74
845	BAUSELL	Bath	G. E.	28 May 45	19 Nov 45	7 Feb 46	Stk. 30 May 78
846	OZBOURN	Bath	G. E.	16 Jun 45	22 Dec 45	5 Mar 46	Stk. 1 Jun 75, sold 1 Dec 75

No.		Hull	Machinery	Laid down	Launched	Commiss'd	Disposition
847	ROBERT L. WILSON	Bath	G. E.	2 Jul 45	5 Jan 46	28 Mar 46	Stk. 30 Sep 74, sunk as target off Puerto Rico 25 Jan 80
848	WITEK	Bath	Westing-house	16 Jul 45	2 Feb 46	25 Apr 46	Stk. 17 Sep 68, sunk as target off Virginia 4 Jun 69
849	RICHARD E. KRAUS	Bath	G. E.	31 Jul 45	2 Mar 46	23 May 46	Stk. 1 Jul 76, to S. Korea as Kwang Ju 23 Feb 77
850	JOSEPH P. KENNEDY, JR.	Quincy	Westing-house	2 Apr 45	26 Jul 45	15 Dec 45	Stk. 1 Jul 73, memorial at Fall River, Mass., Dec 73
851	RUPERTUS	Quincy	Westing-house	2 May 45	21 Sep 45	8 Mar 46	To Greece 10 Jul 73 as Kountouriotis, stk. 10 Jul 73
852	LEONARD F. MASON	Quincy	Westing-house	6 Aug 45	4 Jan 46	28 Jun 46	Stk. 2 Nov 76, to Taiwan as Lai Yang 10 Mar 78
853	CHARLES H. ROAN	Quincy	Westing-house	27 Sep 45	15 Mar 46	12 Sep 46	To Turkey 21 Sep 73 as Maresal Fevzi Cakmak, stk. 21 Sep 73
854	ROBERT A. OWENS	Staten I.	G. E.	7 Jul 45	No	No	Cancelled 12 Aug 45
855	Unnamed	Staten I.	G. E.	6 Aug 45	No	No	Cancelled 12 Aug 45
856	Unnamed	Staten I.	G. E.	No	No	No	Cancelled 12 Aug 45
858	FRED T. BERRY	SanPedro	G. E.	16 Jul 44	28 Jan 45	12 May 45	Stk. 15 Sep 70, scuttled after tests off Key West 14 May 72
859	NORRIS	San Pedro	Westing-house	29 Aug 44	25 Feb 45	9 Jun 45	Stk. 1 Feb 74, to Turkey as Kocatepe 7 Jul 74
860	McCAFFERY	San Pedro	G. E.	1 Oct 44	12 Apr 45	26 Jul 45	Stk. 30 Sep 73, sold 11 Jun 74
861	HARWOOD	San Pedro	G. E.	29 Oct 44	22 May 45	28 Sep 45	To Turkey 17 Dec 71 as Kocatepe, stk. 1 Feb 73
862	VOGELGESANG	Staten I.	G. E.	3 Aug 44	15 Jan 45	28 Apr 45	To Mexico 24 Feb 82 as Quetzalcoatl, stk. 24 Feb 82
863	STEINAKER	Staten I.	G. E.	1 Sep 44	13 Feb 45	26 May 45	To Mexico 24 Feb 82 as Netzahualcoyotl, stk. 24 Feb 82
864	HAROLD J. ELLISON	Staten I.	G. E.	3 Oct 44	14 Mar 45	23 Jun 45	To Pakistan 1 Oct 83 as Shah Jahan, stk. 1 Oct 83
865	CHARLES R. WARE	Staten I.	G. E.	1 Nov 44	12 Apr 45	21 Jul 45	Stk. 30 Nov 74, sunk as target in the Caribbean 15 Nov 81
866	CONE	Staten I.	G. E.	30 Nov 44	10 May 45	18 Aug 45	To Pakistan 1 Oct 82 as Alamgir, stk. 1 Oct 82
867	STRIBLING	Staten I.	G. E.	15 Jan 45	8 Jun 45	29 Sep 45	Stk. 1 Jul 76, sunk as target off Puerto Rico 27 Jul 80
868	BROWNSON	Staten I.	W'house	13 Feb 45	7 Jul 45	17 Nov 45	Stk. 30 Sep 76, sold 10 Jun 77
869	ARNOLD J. ISBELL	Staten I.	Westing-house	14 Mar 45	6 Aug 45	5 Jan 46	To Greece 4 Dec 73 as Sachtouris, stk. 1 Feb 74
870	FECHTELER	Staten I.	W'house	12 Apr 45	19 Sep 45	2 Mar 46	Stk. 11 Sep 70, sold 29 Jun 72
871	DAMATO	Staten I.	Westing-house	10 May 45	21 Nov 45	27 Apr 46	To Pakistan 30 Sep 80 as Tippu Sultan, stk. 1 Oct 80
872	FORREST ROYAL	Staten I.	G. E.	8 Jun 45	17 Jan 46	29 Jun 46	To Turkey 27 Mar 71 as Adatepe, stk. 1 Feb 73
873	HAWKINS	Orange	G. E.	14 May 44	7 Oct 44	10 Feb 45	Stk. 1 Oct 79, to Taiwan as Shao Yang 17 Mar 83
874	DUNCAN	Orange	G. E.	22 May 44	27 Oct 44	25 Feb 45	Stk. 1 Feb 74, sunk as target off S. California 31 Jul 80
875	HENRY W. TUCKER	Orange	G. E.	29 May 44	8 Nov 44	12 Mar 45	To Brazil 3 Dec 73 as Marcilio Dias, stk. 3 Dec 73
876	RODGERS	Orange	G. E.	3 Jun 44	20 Nov 44	26 Mar 45	Stk. 1 Oct 80, to S. Korea as Jeong Ju 25 Jul 81
877	PERKINS	Orange	G. E.	19 Jun 44	7 Dec 44	4 Apr 45	To Argentina 15 Jan 73 as Comodoro Py, stk. 15 Jan 73
878	VESOLE	Orange	G. E.	3 Jul 44	29 Dec 44	23 Apr 45	Stk. 1 Dec 76, sunk as target off Puerto Rico 14 Apr 83
879	LEARY	Orange	Westing-house	11 Aug 44	20 Jan 45	7 May 45	To Spain 31 Oct 73 as Langara, stk. 2 Jun 75
880	DYESS	Orange	Westing-house	17 Aug 44	26 Jan 45	21 May 45	Stk. 27 Feb 81, sold 8 Jul 81 to Greece for spare parts
881	BORDELON	Orange	G. E.	9 Sep 44	3 Mar 45	5 Jun 45	Stk. 1 Feb 77, sold Jul 77 to Iran for spare parts
882	FURSE	Orange	G. E.	23 Sep 44	9 Mar 45	10 Jul 45	To Spain 31 Aug 72 as Gravina, stk. 2 Jun 75

No.		Hull	Machinery	Laid down	Launched	Commiss'd	Disposition
883	NEWMAN K. PERRY	Orange	G. E.	10 Oct 44	17 Mar 45	26 Jul 45	To S. Korea 27 Feb 81 as Kyong Ki, stk. 27 Feb 81
884	FLOYD B. PARKS	Orange	G. E.	30 Oct 44	31 Mar 45	31 Jul 45	Stk. 2 Jul 83, sold 29 Apr 74
885	JOHN R. CRAIG	Orange	G. E.	17 Nov 44	14 Apr 45	20 Aug 45	Stk. 27 Jul 79, sunk as target off S. California 6 Jun 80
886	ORLECK	Orange	Westinghouse	28 Nov 44	12 May 45	15 Sep 45	To Turkey 1 Oct 82 as Yucetepe, stk. 6 Aug 87
887	BRINKLEY BASS	Orange	G. E.	20 Dec 44	26 May 45	1 Oct 45	To Brazil 3 Dec 73 as Mariz e Barros, stk. 3 Dec 73
888	STICKELL	Orange	G. E.	5 Jan 45	16 Jun 45	31 Oct 45	To Greece 1 Jul 72 as Kanaris, stk. 1 Jul 72
889	O'HARE	Orange	G. E.	27 Jan 45	22 Jun 45	29 Nov 45	To Spain 31 Oct 73 as Mendez Nunez, stk. 2 Jun 75
890	MEREDITH	Orange	G. E.	27 Jan 45	28 Jun 45	31 Dec 45	Stk. 29 Jun 79, to Turkey as Savastepe 7 Dec 79
891 -893	Unnamed	Kearny	Unknown	No	No	No	Cancelled 8 Mar 45
894 -895	Unnamed	Orange	Unknown	No	No	No	Cancelled 27 Mar 45
896	Unnamed	Kearny	Unknown	No	No	No	Cancelled 8 Mar 45
897 -904	Unnamed	Bath	Unknown	No	No	No	Cancelled 28 Mar 45
905 -908	Unnamed	Boston	Unknown	No	No	No	Cancelled 27 Mar 45
909 -916	Unnamed	Staten I.	Unknown	No	No	No	Cancelled 28 Mar 45
917 -924	Unnamed	Orange	Unknown	No	No	No	Cancelled 27 Mar 45
925 -926	Unnamed	Charleston	Unknown	No	No	No	Cancelled 27 Mar 45.

Notes: Fiscal years: see Allen M. Sumner class, above. In 1943 the Navy became aware that ships in task forces in the Pacific were falling short of their designed steaming endurance. In January 1944 it decided to lengthen the design of the Sumner class 14 feet amidships to add 168 tons of fuel and increase steaming radius by 30 percent. Ships ordered as Sumner-class ships on which little or no work had been done were built to the modified design and became the Gearing class. The detailed plans were prepared by Gibbs and Cox. The contracts for DD 850-56 were transferred from Bethlehem, San Francisco, on 1 Oct 43. DD 809-28 were also shifted as follows: DD 826 from Federal, Kearny and DD 827-28 from Federal, Newark on 10 Nov 44, DD 817-22 from Federal, Newark and DD 823-25 from Federal, Kearny, on 29 Nov 44, and DD 809-16 from Federal, Newark on 16 May 45. Among the fiscal year 1945 ships, DD 891-96 were cancelled at Federal, Kearny on 8 Mar 45. DD 894-95 were reordered from Consolidated, Orange, on 22 Mar 45. DD 891-93 were to have gone to Bath and DD-896 to the Charleston Navy Yard, but these contracts had not been awarded when the 1945 program was cancelled on 26 Mar 45.

This class, the last and most powerful built during World War II, underwent many modifications for wartime and postwar service. As a result of the Leyte campaign, 24 ships were converted during the war to radar picket destroyers (designated DDR in 1949): DD 742-43, 805-8, 829-35, and 873-83. A few initially retained one bank of torpedo tubes but soon traded these for additional small antiaircraft guns. Twelve more ships were converted to DDRs in 1952: DD 711, 713-15, 784, 817, 838, 842, 863, 870, and 888-89. In 1945, some ships exchanged five of their ten torpedo tubes for additional small antiaircraft guns to increase defenses against suicide aircraft. In 1948 four ships that were still incomplete were ordered finished as specialized ASW ships, two as Escort Destroyers (DDE) and two as Hunter Killer Destroyers (DDK). Of these, the two DDKs, Carpenter (825) and Robert A. Owens (827), were completed by Newport News and Bath and the DDEs, Epperson (719) and Basilone (824), were completed by Bath and Bethlehem, Quincy respectivley. The DDKs were merged into the DDE category in 1950 and two more groups totaling 11 ships were converted to DDEs: DD 764-65 and 858-61 (full conversions) and 818-20, 847, and 871 (austere conversions). Most Gearing class ships received 3"/50AA guns in the early 1950s. The exceptions were DD-710, 712, 782-83, 785, 787, 828, 836-37, 848-49, 851, 864, 869, 886, and DDE 764-65, 818-20, 847, and 871. Two of these, Sarsfield (DD-837) and Witek (DD-848), served as experimental ASW ships (EDD) with an armament of 4-5"AA. The Witek (DD-848) was later fitted with an experimental pump jet propulsion system. A third, Richard E Kraus (DD-849) served as an ordnance and missile trials ship in 1946-49 and as a miscellaneous trials ship (AG) in 1949-54. A fourth, the Timmerman (DD-828), was completed with experimental machinery as an engineering test ship. She had four boilers operating at 1050 degrees, one pair at 875 psi and one at 2000 psi, driving experimental machinery and theoretically producing 100,000 SHP and a speed of 43 knots. She was given increased freeboard forward to keep her dry at high speeds. She produced valuable data even though she appears never to have been run at over half power. In 1955 the Gyatt (DD-712) became the prototype guided missile destroyer (DDG).

The FRAM program produced a second round of modifications. A total of 79 Gearings were given FRAM I (SCB-206 design) conversions in 1959-65: DD 710-711, 714-719, 743, 763, 782-790, 806, 808, 817-827, 829, 832-833, 835-837, 839-847, 849-853, 862-873, 875-876, and 878-890. This conversion was intended to extend the active lives of the vessels eight years. During 1961-64 ten ships, DD 764-765, 805, 807, 830, 858-861, and 877, were given FRAM II modernizations intended to extend their useful lives by five years. In December 1961, 29 other Gearing class ships were shifted from the FRAM II to the FRAM I program. All DDEs and most DDRs reverted to DDs under the FRAM program, but six ships underwent FRAM II overhauls as DDRs in 1960-61: DDR-713, 742, 831, 834, 838, and 874.

Renamings: DD-783 ex John A. Bole 15 Jun 44; DD-850 ex Charles P. Cecil 13 Nov 44; DD-872 ex Forrest B. Royal 4 Aug 45; DD-873 ex Beatty 22 Jun 44; and DD-887 ex Harry B. Bass 27 Feb 45.

Reclassifications:

Eugene A. Greene (DD-711) to DDR 18 Jul 52; DD 15 Mar 63;

Gyatt (DD-712) to DDG-1 1 Dec 55; DDG-712 30 Dec 56; DDG-1 23 May 57; DD-712 1 Oct 62;

Kenneth D. Bailey (DD-713) to DDR 9 Apr 53; DD 1 Jan 69;

William R. Rush (DD-714) and Steinaker (DD-863) to DDR 18 Jul 52; DD 1 Jul 64;

William M. Wood (DD-715) to DDR 9 Apr 53; DD 1 Jul 64;

Epperson (DD-719) and Basilone (DD-824) to DDE 28 Jan 48; DD 30 Jun 62;

Frank Knox (DD-742), Goodrich (DD-831), Turner (DD-834), and Duncan (DD-874) to DDR 18 Mar 49; DD 1 Jan 69;

Southerland (DD-743), Dennis J. Buckley (DD-808), Myles C. Fox (DD-829), Hanson (DD-832), Hawkins (DD-873), Vesole (DD-878), and Dyess (DD-880) to DDR 18 Mar 49; DD 1 Apr 64;

Lloyd Thomas (DD-764), Keppler (DD-765), New (DD-818), Holder (DD-819), Rich (DD-820), Robert L. Wilson (DD-847), Fred T. Berry (DD-858), Norris (DD-859), McCaffrey (DD-860), Harwood (DD-861) and Damato (DD-871) to DDE 4 Mar 50; DD 30 Jun 62;

McKean (DD-784) and Fiske (DD-842) to DDR 18 Jul 52; DD 1 Apr 64;

Chevalier (DD-805) to DDR 18 Mar 49; DD 13 Jul 62;

Higbee (DD-806) to DDR 18 Mar 49; DD 1 Jun 63;

Benner (DD-807) to DDR 18 Mar 49; DD 15 Nov 62;

Corry (DD-817) to DDR 9 Apr 53; DD 1 Jan 64;

Carpenter (DD-825) and Robert A. Owens (DD-827) to DDK 28 Jan 48; DDE 4 Mar 50; DD 30 Jun 62;

Timmerman (DD-828) to AG-152 11 Jan 54;

Everett F. Larson (DD-830) to DDR 18 Mar 49; DD 30 Nov 62;

Herbert J. Thomas (DD-833), Leary (DD-879), and Newman K. Perry (DD-883) to DDR 18 Mar 49; DD 1 Jul 64;

Charles P. Cecil (DD-835) and Rodgers (DD-876) to DDR 18 Mar 49; DD 30 Jul 63;

Ernest G. Small (DD-838) to DDR 18 Jul 52; DD 1 Jan 69;

Richard E. Kraus (DD-849) to AG-151 24 Aug 49; DD-849 11 Jan 54;

Fechteler (DD-870) and O'Hare (DD-889) to DDR 9 Apr 53; DD 15 Mar 63;

Henry W. Tucker (DD-875), Bordelon (DD-881), and Furse (DD-882) to DDR 18 Mar 49; DD 15 Mar 63;

Perkins (DD-877) to DDR 18 Mar 49; DD 30 Sep 62;

Stickell (DD-888) to DDR 9 Apr 53; DD 1 Jun 63.

1945

DD-934

Displacement: 2701 tons
Dimensions: 440'4"(oa.) x 38'1"(e) x 23'2"
Armament: 8-3.9"/65AA 4-24"T; none (1947)

Machinery: 52,000 SHP, geared turbines, 2 screws
Speed: 33 kts.
Complement: 290

	Builder	Launched	Acquired	In Serv.	Disposition
(HANATSUKI)	Maizuru	10 Oct 44	28 Aug 47	Unknown	Sunk as target 3 Feb 48 E of Tsingtao, China.

Notes: One of a class of large Japanese destroyers with a main armament of anti-aircraft guns. Formerly the Japanese Hanatsuki, she was surrendered at Kure in August 1945 and, after repatriation duties, was transferred to the U.S. Navy on 28 Aug 47 without armament and designated DD-934. She was the only Japanese warship acquired after World War II to receive a U.S. Navy hull number.

DD-935

Displacement: 1200 tons
Dimensions: 313' x 31' x 9'
Armament: 4-4.1"/45AA 6-21"T

Machinery: 28,000 SHP, geared turbines, 2 screws
Speed: 34 kts.
Complement: 190

	Builder	Launched	Acquired	In Serv.	Disposition
(T-35)	Schichau, Elbing	1944	12 Jul 45	12 Jul 45	To France 1947 for spare parts.

Notes: Formerly the German torpedo boat T-35, she was taken over by the U.S. Navy and placed in service at Plymouth, England, with the designation DD-935. She was taken to the U.S. and used for engineering tests. Three similar torpedo boats, the T-4, T-14, and T-19, were taken over by the U.S. on 9 Jan 46 but did not receive U.S. Navy hull numbers.

DD-939

Displacement: 2660 tons
Dimensions: 403'6" x 38'4" x 9'6"
Armament: 4-5.9"/48 8-21"T

Machinery: 70,000 SHP, geared turbines, 2 screws
Speed: 36.5 kts.
Complement: 320

	Builder	Launched	Acquired	In Serv.	Disposition
(Z-39)	Germania, Kiel	2 Dec 41	12 Jul 45	12 Jul 45	To France 10 Nov 47 for spare parts.

Notes: Formerly the German destroyer Z-39, she was taken over by the U.S. Navy and placed in service at Plymouth, England, with the designation DD-939. She was taken to the U.S. and used in tests of her high-pressure steam propulsion plant and other equipment. The Germans removed her fifth 5.9" gun during the war.

1951

FORREST SHERMAN class

Displacement: 2780 (DD 931-933, 936-938), 2810 (others) tons
Dimensions: 418'5"(oa.) x 45'2"(DD 931-933, e), 45'1"(others, e) x 20'(max)
Armament: 3-5"/54AA 4-3"/50AA 0 to 4-21"T; 3-5"AA 4-3"AA 6-12.75"T (1965); 1-5"AA 1-Tartar-SAM ASROC 6-12.75"T (DDG conversions, 1965-67); 2-5"AA ASROC 6-12.75"T (ASW conversions, 1967-71); 3-5"AA 6-12.75"T (DD-931, 942, 944, 1978)

Machinery: 70,000 SHP; geared turbines, 2 screws
Speed: 33 kts.
Complement: 324

No.		Hull	Machinery	Laid down	Launched	Commiss'd	Disposition
931	FORREST SHERMAN	Bath	Westinghouse	27 Oct 53	5 Feb 55	9 Nov 55	Stk. 27 Jul 90
932	JOHN PAUL JONES	Bath	Westinghouse	18 Jan 54	7 May 55	5 Apr 56	Stk. Apr 86
933	BARRY	Bath	Westinghouse	15 Mar 54	1 Oct 55	31 Aug 56	Stk. 31 Jan 83, memorial at Washington, D.C. 15 Nov 83
936	DECATUR	Quincy	G. E.	13 Sep 54	15 Dec 55	7 Dec 56	Stk. 16 Mar 88
937	DAVIS	Quincy	G. E.	1 Feb 55	28 Mar 56	28 Feb 57	Stk. 27 Jul 90
938	JONAS INGRAM	Quincy	G. E.	15 Jun 55	7 Aug 56	19 Jul 57	Stk. 15 Jun 83, sunk as target Jul 88
940	MANLEY	Bath	G. E.	10 Feb 55	12 Apr 56	1 Feb 57	Stk. 1 Jun 90
941	DU PONT	Bath	G. E.	11 May 55	8 Sep 56	1 Jul 57	Stk. 1 Jun 90
942	BIGELOW	Bath	G. E.	6 Jul 55	2 Feb 57	8 Nov 57	Stk. 1 Jun 90
943	BLANDY	Quincy	G. E.	29 Dec 55	19 Dec 56	26 Nov 57	Stk. 27 Jul 90
944	MULLINIX	Quincy	G. E.	5 Apr 56	18 Mar 57	7 Mar 58	Stk. 26 Jul 90.

Notes: Fiscal years 1953 (DD 931-33), 1954 (936-38), and 1955 (940-44). SCB-85 design. Studies of a "large destroyer" conducted during World War II led to the Mitscher class ships, which were so large that they were reclassified destroyer leaders (q.v.) in 1951. They could not be reproduced in quantity, and in 1951 the Navy began development of a smaller mobilization destroyer that could be mass produced if necessary. The design began as an updated Fletcher and resulted in a general purpose destroyer with emphasis on ASW. Their rapid fire guns gave them firepower superior to any previous class. They had 1200-psi, 950-degree power plants and a new model of 5"/54 dual purpose gun. DD-933 received a bow sonar in 1959. The bows were 3' higher in DD-936 and later ships. DD-931 and 932 were completed with 2-21"T for long ASW torpedoes, which were soon abandoned. DD 931-33 got 4-21"T for Mk-37 torpedoes in the late 1950s. DD-932 and 936 were converted to DDGs (the SCB-240 design) by the Boston and Philadelphia Naval Shipyards in 1965-67 and DD 933, 937, 938, 940, 941, and 943 received an ASW modernization in 1967-71.
Renaming: The name of DDG-32 (ex DD-932) was cancelled 24 Mar 86.
Reclassifications: DD 936 to DDG-31 15 Sep 66; DD-932 to DDG-32 15 Mar 67.

1955

HULL class

Displacement: 2850 tons
Dimensions: 418'(oa.) x 45'(e) x 20'(max)
Armament: 3-5"/54AA 4-3"/50AA; 3-5"AA 4-3"AA 6-12.75"T
  (1965); 1-5"AA 1-Tartar-SAM ASROC 6-12.75"T (DDG
  conversions, 1965-68); 2-5"AA ASROC 6-12.75"T (ASW
  conversions, 1969-71); 1-8"/55 2-5" 6-12.75"T (DD-945,
  1974); 3-5"AA 6-12.75"T (DD-946, 951, 1978; DD-945, 1979)

Machinery: 70,000 SHP; G. E. geared
  turbines, 2 screws
Speed: 33 kts.
Complement: 324

No.	Hull	Laid down	Launched	Commiss'd	Disposition
945 HULL	Bath	12 Sep 56	10 Aug 57	3 Jul 58	Stk. 15 Nov 83, target hulk
946 EDSON	Bath	3 Dec 56	4 Jan 58	7 Nov 58	Stk. 31 Jan 89, memorial at New York City 30 Jun 89
947 SOMERS	Bath	4 Mar 57	30 May 58	3 Apr 59	Stk. Apr 88
948 MORTON	Ingalls	4 Mar 57	23 May 58	26 May 59	Stk. 7 Feb 90
949 PARSONS	Ingalls	17 Jun 57	19 Aug 58	29 Oct 59	Stk. 15 May 84
950 RICHARD S. EDWARDS	Puget Sd. Br.	20 Dec 56	24 Sep 57	5 Feb 59	Stk. 7 Feb 90
951 TURNER JOY	Puget Sd. Br.	30 Sep 57	5 May 58	3 Aug 59	Stk. 13 Feb 90.

Notes: Fiscal year 1956. SCB-85A design. A modification of the Forrest Sherman class, they had higher freeboard forward for dryness and had the positions of their main and secondary gun directors reversed. DD 947 and 949 were converted to DDGs (the SCB-240 design) at San Francisco and Long Beach Naval Shipyards in 1965-68 and DD 948 and 950 received an ASW modernization in 1969-71. Between 1974 and 1978 DD-945 served as trials ship for a new lightweight 8"/55 gun, which took the place of her forward 5"/54.
Reclassifications: DD-947 to DDG-34 and DD-949 to DDG-33 15 Mar 67.
Renaming: DD-951 ex Joy 26 Jul 57.

1956

DD-960 class

Displacement: 2350 tons
Dimensions: 387'2"(oa.) x 39'4"(e) x 13'2"
Armament: 3-5"AA 4-3"AA 4-21"T

Machinery: 45,000 SHP; geared
  turbines, 2 screws
Speed: 32 kts.
Complement: 330

No.	Hull	Machinery	Laid down	Launched	Commiss'd	Disposition
960 (TERUZUKI)	Mitsubishi, Kobe	Westinghouse	15 Aug 58	24 Jun 59	No	To Japan Feb 60
961 (AKIZUKI)	Mitsubishi, Nagasaki		31 Jul 58	26 Jun 59	No	To Japan Feb 60.

Notes: Fiscal year 1957 (offshore procurement). They are a modification of the Fletcher design built in Japan as part of the Military Aid Program.

1957

DD-962

Displacement: 2020 tons
Dimensions: 362'9"(oa.) x 35'8"(e) x 16'(max)
Armament: 3-4.5"AA 4-21"T

Machinery: 40,000 SHP; geared
  turbines, 2 screws
Speed: 34 kts.
Complement: 186

No.	Hull	Machinery	Launched	Acquired	Commiss'd	Disposition
962 (SHAH JAHAN)	Thornycroft		30 Nov 44	16 Dec 58	No	To Pakistan 16 Dec 58.

Notes: Fiscal year 1958 (offshore procurement). The ex-HMS Charity, modernized in England under a U.S. contract of 16 Jun 58, purchased by the United States on 16 Dec 58, and simultaneously transferred to Pakistan under Military Assistance.

The destroyer *David R. Ray* (DD-971) off southern California ca. 1979. (NARA KN-27644)

The guided missile destroyer *Henry B. Wilson* (DDG-7) underway in October 1969. (USN 1142937)

1969

SPRUANCE class

Displacement: 5830 tons (light)   Machinery: 80,000 SHP, G. E. gas
Dimensions: 563'3"(oa.) x 55'(e) x 29'(max)   turbines, 2 screws
Armament: 2-5"/54 ASROC 6-12.75"T; 2-5" 8-Harpoon-SSM ASROC   Speed: 30 kts.
  6-12.75"T (1978-82); 2-5" 8-Tomahawk-SSM 8-Harpoon-SSM   Complement: 296
  ASROC 6-12.75"T (7 ships, 1984-86); 2-5" 1-Tomahawk-SSM/VLS
  6-12.75"T (others, 1987-)

No.		Hull	Laid down	Launched	Commiss'd	Disposition
963	SPRUANCE	Litton	27 Nov 72	10 Nov 73	20 Sep 75	USN
964	PAUL F. FOSTER	Litton	6 Feb 73	22 Feb 74	21 Feb 76	USN
965	KINKAID	Litton	19 Apr 73	25 May 74	10 Jul 76	USN
966	HEWITT	Litton	23 Jul 73	24 Aug 74	25 Sep 76	USN
967	ELLIOT	Litton	15 Oct 73	19 Dec 74	22 Jan 77	USN
968	ARTHUR W. RADFORD	Litton	31 Jan 74	21 Mar 75	16 Apr 77	USN
969	PETERSON	Litton	29 Apr 74	21 Jun 75	9 Jul 77	USN
970	CARON	Litton	1 Jul 74	23 Jun 75	1 Oct 77	USN
971	DAVID R. RAY	Litton	23 Sep 74	24 Aug 75	19 Nov 77	USN
972	OLDENDORF	Litton	27 Dec 74	21 Oct 75	4 Mar 78	USN
973	JOHN YOUNG	Litton	17 Feb 75	6 Jan 76	20 May 78	USN
974	COMTE DE GRASSE	Litton	4 Apr 75	26 Mar 76	5 Aug 78	USN
975	O'BRIEN	Litton	9 May 75	8 Jul 76	3 Dec 77	USN
976	MERRILL	Litton	16 Jun 75	1 Sep 76	11 Mar 78	USN
977	BRISCOE	Litton	21 Jul 75	28 Dec 76	3 Jun 78	USN
978	STUMP	Litton	22 Aug 75	21 Mar 77	19 Aug 78	USN
979	CONOLLY	Litton	29 Sep 75	3 Jun 77	14 Oct 78	USN
980	MOOSBRUGGER	Litton	3 Nov 75	23 Jul 77	16 Dec 78	USN
981	JOHN HANCOCK	Litton	16 Jan 76	28 Sep 77	10 Mar 79	USN
982	NICHOLSON	Litton	20 Feb 76	29 Nov 77	12 May 79	USN
983	JOHN RODGERS	Litton	12 Aug 76	25 Feb 78	14 Jul 79	USN
984	LEFTWICH	Litton	12 Nov 76	8 Apr 78	25 Aug 79	USN
985	CUSHING	Litton	2 Feb 77	17 Jun 78	21 Sep 79	USN
986	HARRY W. HILL	Litton	1 Apr 77	10 Aug 78	17 Nov 79	USN
987	O'BANNON	Litton	24 Jun 77	25 Sep 78	15 Dec 79	USN
988	THORN	Litton	29 Aug 77	22 Nov 78	16 Feb 80	USN
989	DEYO	Litton	14 Oct 77	20 Jan 79	22 Mar 80	USN
990	INGERSOLL	Litton	16 Dec 77	10 Mar 79	12 Apr 80	USN
991	FIFE	Litton	6 Mar 78	1 May 79	31 May 80	USN
992	FLETCHER	Litton	24 Apr 78	16 Jun 79	12 Jul 80	USN
997	HAYLER	Litton	20 Oct 80	2 Mar 82	5 Mar 83	USN.

Notes: Fiscal years 1970 (DD 963-65), 1971 (966-71), 1972 (972-78), 1974 (979-85), 1975 (986-92), and 1977 (997). In 1966 the Office of the Secretary of Defense proposed an economical way of coping with the bloc obsolescence of much of the Navy's general purpose force--large scale production in a single yard. The program was to include a guided missile destroyer or escort (DXG) and an ASW escort (DX). In 1967 OSD upgraded the DX from a DE type ship to a 30-knot ASW ship also capable of escorting carriers and providing gunfire support--characteristics which made it a destroyer. Litton won the contract for 30 ships in 1970. DD-997 was added to the 1977 building program by Congress as a DDH with enhanced helicopter facilities (for four LAMPS Mk III helicopters instead of two) but was finally built as a standard Spruance class ship. No DXGs were ordered for the U.S. Navy because of competition from the DLGN program, but Iran ordered four which later became the Kidd class DDGs. Under the fiscal year 1983-85 programs DD-974, 976, 979, 983-985, and 989 received Tomahawk missiles in armored box launchers. Beginning with DD-963 and 990 in fiscal year 1986, the remaining ships are to receive a vertical launch system (VLS) with Tomahawk missiles in place of the ASROC launcher. This system may also eventually be able to fire the ASROC and the Standard SM-2 SAM.

Guided Missile Destroyers (DDG)

1957

CHARLES F. ADAMS class

Displacement: 3370 tons (light)
Dimensions: 437'(oa.) x 47'(e) x 22'(max)
Armament: 2-5"/54AA 2-Tartar-SAM ASROC 6-12.75"T (DDG 2-14);
  2-5"AA 1-Tartar-SAM ASROC 6-12.75"T (others)

Machinery: 80,000 SHP; geared
  turbines, 2 screws
Speed: 32.5 kts.
Complement: 354

No.		Hull	Machinery	Laid down	Launched	Commiss'd	Disposition
2	CHARLES F. ADAMS	Bath	G. E.	16 Jun 58	8 Sep 59	10 Sep 60	USN
3	JOHN KING	Bath	G. E.	25 Aug 58	30 Jan 60	4 Feb 61	USN
4	LAWRENCE	New York SB	Westinghouse	27 Oct 58	27 Feb 60	6 Jan 62	Stk. 16 May 90
5	BIDDLE	New York SB	Westinghouse	18 May 59	4 Jun 60	5 May 62	Stk. 1 Jun 90
6	BARNEY	New York SB	Westinghouse	10 Aug 59	10 Dec 60	11 Aug 62	USN
7	HENRY B. WILSON	Defoe	G. E.	28 Feb 58	22 Apr 59	17 Dec 60	Stk. 26 Jan 90
8	LYNDE McCORMICK	Defoe	G. E.	4 Apr 58	28 Jul 59	3 Jun 61	USN
9	TOWERS	Todd, Seattle	Westinghouse	1 Apr 58	23 Apr 59	6 Jun 61	USN
10	SAMPSON	Bath	G. E.	2 Mar 59	21 May 60	24 Jun 61	USN
11	SELLERS	Bath	G. E.	3 Aug 59	9 Sep 60	28 Oct 61	USN
12	ROBISON	Defoe	G. E.	28 Apr 59	27 Apr 60	9 Dec 61	USN
13	HOEL	Defoe	G. E.	3 Aug 59	4 Aug 60	16 Jun 62	USN
14	BUCHANAN	Todd, Seattle	Westinghouse	23 Apr 59	11 May 60	7 Feb 62	USN
15	BERKELEY	New York SB	G. E.	29 Aug 60	29 Jul 61	15 Dec 62	USN
16	JOSEPH STRAUSS	New York SB	G. E.	27 Dec 60	9 Dec 61	20 Apr 63	USN
17	CONYNGHAM	New York SB	G. E.	1 May 61	19 May 62	13 Jul 63	USN
18	SEMMES	Avondale	G. E.	15 Aug 60	20 May 61	10 Dec 62	USN
19	TATTNALL	Avondale	G. E.	14 Nov 60	26 Aug 61	13 Apr 63	USN
20	GOLDSBOROUGH	Puget Sd. Br.	G. E.	3 Jan 61	15 Dec 61	9 Nov 63	USN
21	COCHRANE	Puget Sd. Br.	G. E.	31 Jul 61	18 Jul 62	21 Mar 63	USN
22	BENJAMIN STODDERT	Puget Sd. Br.	G. E.	11 Jun 62	8 Jan 63	12 Sep 64	USN
23	RICHARD E. BYRD	Todd, Seattle	Westinghouse	12 Apr 61	6 Feb 62	7 Mar 64	USN
24	WADDELL	Todd, Seattle	Westinghouse	6 Feb 62	26 Feb 63	28 Aug 64	USN
25	(PERTH)	Defoe	Unknown	21 Sep 62	26 Sep 63	No	To Australia 17 Jul 65
26	(HOBART)	Defoe	Unknown	26 Oct 62	9 Jan 64	No	To Australia 18 Dec 65
27	(BRISBANE)	Defoe	Unknown	15 Feb 65	5 May 66	No	To Australia 16 Dec 67
28	(LUTJENS)	Bath	Unknown	1 Mar 66	11 Aug 67	No	To W. Germany 12 Mar 69
29	(MOLDERS)	Bath	Unknown	12 Apr 66	13 Apr 68	No	To W. Germany 12 Sep 69
30	(ROMMEL)	Bath	Unknown	22 Aug 67	1 Feb 69	No	To W. Germany 24 Apr 70

Notes: Fiscal years 1957 (DDG 2-9), 1958 (10-14), 1959 (15-19), 1960 (20-22), 1961 (23-24), 1962 (25-26), 1964 (27), and 1965 (28-30). The first eight were initially assigned DD numbers but were reclassified DDG in 1957. They were planned as Tartar-armed versions of the Forrest Sherman class, but the final design (SCB-155) ended up a bit larger than the gun destroyers. Their high clipper bows made them relatively dry in heavy weather and they were considered good sea boats. DDG 2-15 had the twin-arm Mk.11 Tartar launcher; the rest had the faster single-arm Mk.13. Three ships (DDG 19, 20, and 22) were modernized in 1981-85 but modernization of the rest of the class was cancelled.
Renaming: Biddle (DDG-5) to Claude V. Ricketts on 28 Jul 64.
Reclassifications: DDG 2-9 ex DD 952-959 23 Apr 57.

1976

KIDD class

Displacement: 6950 tons (light)
Dimensions: 563'4"(oa.) x 55'(e) x 30'(max)
Armament: 2-5"/54 4-Standard-SAM 8-Harpoon-SSM 6-12.75"T

Machinery: 80,000 SHP; G. E. gas
turbines, 2 screws
Speed: 30 kts.
Complement: 338

No.	Hull	Laid down	Launched	Commiss'd	Disposition
993 KIDD	Litton	26 Jun 78	11 Aug 79	27 Jun 81	USN
994 CALLAGHAN	Litton	23 Oct 78	1 Dec 79	29 Aug 81	USN
995 SCOTT	Litton	12 Feb 79	1 Mar 80	24 Oct 81	USN
996 CHANDLER	Litton	7 May 79	24 May 80	13 Mar 82	USN.

Notes: Fiscal year 1977 (for Iran), 1979 (for USN). In August 1974 Iran ordered six variants of the Spruance class armed with Standard SAMs: Kouroosh, Daryush, Ardeshir, Nader, Shapour, and Anoushirvan, which were to have been designated DD 993-998 respectively. The Ardeshir and Shapour were cancelled in June 1976 because of cost escalation, and when the remaining four ships came under the U.S. Military Assistance Program with a contract on 23 Mar 78 they became DD 993-996 respectively. After the overthrow of the Shah, the Iranians cancelled DD 995-96 on 3 Feb 79 and the other two on 31 Mar 79. The ships were taken over under an Executive Order in July 1979 and given U.S. names and reclassified DDGs (with their original DD numbers) in August.
Reclassifications: Ex DD 993-996 8 Aug 79.

1984

ARLEIGH BURKE class

Displacement: 6624 tons (light)
Dimensions: 504'6"(oa.) x 67'(e) x 30'(max)
Armament: 1-5"/54 2-Standard-SAM/VLS 8-Harpoon-SSM 6-12.75"T

Machinery: 100,000 SHP, G. E. gas
turbines, 2 screws
Speed: 30+ kts.
Complement: 325

No.	Hull	Laid down	Launched	Commiss'd	Disposition
51 ARLEIGH BURKE	Bath	6 Dec 88	16 Sep 89		USN
52 BARRY	Litton	26 Feb 90			USN
53 JOHN PAUL JONES	Bath	8 Aug 90			USN
54 CURTIS WILBUR	Bath				USN
55 STOUT	Litton				USN
56 JOHN S. McCAIN	Bath				USN
57 MITSCHER	Litton				USN
58 LABOON	Litton				USN
59 RUSSELL	Litton				USN
60 PAUL HAMILTON	Bath				USN
61 RAMAGE	Litton				USN
62 FITZGERALD	Bath				USN
63 STETHEM	Litton				USN.

Notes: Fiscal years 1985 (DDG-51), 1987 (52-53), 1988 (54-58), 1990 (59-63). This class originated as an entirely new destroyer design smaller than the Ticonderoga (CG-47) class cruisers and with a less elaborate version of the AEGIS combat system. The Navy describes it as "by far the most powerful destroyer ever to go to sea" and plans to continue its procurement well into the 1990s. The Standard SAM vertical launch system (VLS) also fires Tomahawk SSM and ASROC.
Renaming: DDG-52 ex John Barry 8 Dec 89, ex Barry 9 May 89, ex John Barry 1 Feb 88.

Destroyer Leaders (DL)

1948

NORFOLK class

Displacement: 5600 tons
Dimensions: 540'2"(oa.) x 54'2"(e) x 26'(max)
Armament: 8-3"/50AA 4-21"T; 8-3"/70AA 4-21"T (1957); 8-3"AA
  4-21"T ASROC 6-12.75"T (1960)

Machinery: 80,000 SHP; G. E. geared
  turbines, 2 screws
Speed: 33 kts.
Complement: 480

No.		Hull	Laid down	Launched	Commiss'd	Disposition
1	NORFOLK	New York SB	1 Sep 49	29 Dec 51	4 Mar 53	Stk. 1 Nov 73, sold 22 Aug 74
-	NEW HAVEN	Philadelphia	No	No	No	Cancelled 9 Feb 51.

Notes: Fiscal year 1949 (Norfolk deferred from FY 1948). SCB-1 design. Designed as Cruiser-Hunter Killer Ships (CLK) with enough speed to chase down a 25-knot submarine in bad weather, substantial endurance and magazine capacity, and deep draft for sonar efficiency. These requirements led to a large ship, and the final design was based on the Atlanta (CL-51) class hull. Other cruiser features included a double bottom and some light protective side and deck plating. Their hulls incorporated the lessons learned in the Bikini atomic bomb experiments. The program was curtailed because the ships were too expensive for a type that might be needed in large numbers. The Norfolk spent her career as a test ship, evaluating new equipment including ASROC and large sonars.
Reclassifications: Norfolk from CLK-1 to destroyer leader (DL-1) 9 Feb 51 and to frigate (DL-1) 1 Jan 55. New Haven was CLK-2, designation cancelled 9 Feb 51.

MITSCHER class

Displacement: 3675 tons
Dimensions: 493'(oa.) x 50'(e) x 26'(max)
Armament: 2-5"/54AA 4-3"/50AA 4-21"T; 2-5"/54AA 4-3"/70AA
  4-21"T (1957); 2-5"AA 2-3"AA 4-21"T 6-12.75"T DASH (1960);
  2-5"AA 4-21"T 6-12.75"T DASH (DL 4-5, 1965); 2-5"AA
  1-Tartar-SAM ASROC 6-12.75"T (DDG conversions, 1967)

Machinery: 80,000 SHP; geared
  turbines, 2 screws
Speed: 35 kts.
Complement: 403

No.		Hull	Machinery	Laid down	Launched	Commiss'd	Disposition
2	MITSCHER	Bath	G. E.	3 Oct 49	26 Jan 52	15 May 53	Stk. 1 Jun 78, sold Jul 80
3	JOHN S. McCAIN	Bath	G. E.	24 Oct 49	12 Jul 52	12 Oct 53	Stk. 29 Apr 78, sold Jan 80
4	WILLIS A. LEE	Quincy	W'house	1 Nov 49	26 Jan 52	5 Oct 54	Stk. 15 May 72, sold 18 May 73
5	WILKINSON	Quincy	W'house	1 Feb 50	23 Apr 52	3 Aug 54	Stk. 1 May 74, sold 13 Jun 75.

Notes: Fiscal year 1949 (all deferred from FY 1948). SCB-5 design. This class was the result of "large destroyer" studies begun during World War II. It evolved into an AAW and ASW escort for fast carriers with residual surface warfare capabilities. It was also equipped to act as a radar picket. These were the first ships with the new 1200-psi, 950-degree steam plant. The ships were so large that they were reclassified destroyer leaders (DL) on 9 Feb 51 while building. Very good sea boats, they were intended as large general purpose destroyers but were used primarily as anti-submarine vessels. The 1200-psi machinery proved too light in fleet service and had to be strengthened. The Mitscher and John S. McCain were converted to DDGs at Philadelphia Naval Shipyard in 1966-70.
Reclassifications: Ex DD 927-930 respectively 9 Feb 51, to frigate (DL) 1 Jan 55. DL 2-3 to DDG 35-36 15 Mar 67.

Guided Missile Frigates (DLG)

1955

FARRAGUT class

Displacement: 4150 tons (standard)
Dimensions: 512'6"(oa.) x 52'6"(e) x 25'(max)
Armament: 1-5"/54AA 4-3"/50AA 2-Terrier-SAM ASROC 6-12.75"T;
  1-5"AA 2-Terrier-SAM ASROC 6-12.75"T (1977); 1-5"AA
  2-Terrier-SAM 8-Harpoon-SSM ASROC 6-12.75"T (1980)

Machinery: 85,000 SHP; geared
  turbines, 2 screws
Speed: 34 kts.
Complement: 375

No.		Hull	Machinery	Laid down	Launched	Commiss'd	Disposition
6	FARRAGUT	Quincy	DeLaval	3 Jun 57	18 Jul 58	10 Dec 60	USN
7	LUCE	Quincy	DeLaval	1 Oct 57	11 Dec 58	20 May 61	USN
8	MACDONOUGH	Quincy	DeLaval	15 Apr 58	9 Jul 59	4 Nov 61	USN
9	COONTZ	Puget Sd.	A. C.	1 Mar 57	6 Dec 58	15 Jul 60	Stk. 26 Jan 90
10	KING	Puget Sd.	A. C.	1 Mar 57	6 Dec 58	17 Nov 60	USN
11	MAHAN	San Francisco	A. C.	31 Jul 57	7 Oct 59	25 Aug 60	USN
12	DAHLGREN	Philadel- phia	A. C.	1 Mar 58	16 Mar 60	8 Apr 61	USN
13	WILLIAM V. PRATT	Philadel- phia	A. C.	1 Mar 58	16 Mar 60	4 Nov 61	USN
14	DEWEY	Bath	DeLaval	10 Aug 57	30 Nov 58	7 Dec 59	USN
15	PREBLE	Bath	DeLaval	16 Dec 57	23 May 59	9 May 60	USN.

Notes: Fiscal years 1956 (DLG 6-11) and 1957. SCB-142 design. Like the Mitscher class, these ships were designed as fast task force escorts with strong AAW and lesser ASW and surface warfare capabilities. Two designs were developed: an all-gun design (SCB-129) and a very similar design with a Terrier SAM system aft (SCB-143). The Navy initially decided to order three of each type in fiscal year 1956, but the three gun ships, DL 6-8, were reordered during 1956 to the design developed for the Coontz. ASROC and its SQS-23 sonar replaced a second 5"/54 gun forward during construction. All received AAW modernizations between 1968-75.
Renaming: DLG-7 ex Dewey 12 Feb 57.
Reclassifications: DLG 6-8 ex DL 6-8 and DLG 9-11 ex DLG 1-3 on 14 Nov 56; DLG 6-15 to DDG 37-46 respectively 30 Jun 75.

1958

LEAHY class

Displacement: 5670 tons (standard)
Dimensions: 533'(oa.) x 53'6"(e) x 25'3"(max)
Armament: 4-3"/50AA 4-Terrier-SAM ASROC 6-12.75"T; 4-Terrier-
    SAM 8-Harpoon-SSM ASROC 6-12.75"T (1978-80)

Machinery: 85,000 SHP; geared
    turbines, 2 screws
Speed: 34 kts.
Complement: 377

No.		Hull	Machinery	Laid down	Launched	Commiss'd	Disposition
16	LEAHY	Bath	G. E.	3 Dec 59	1 Jul 61	4 Aug 62	USN
17	HARRY E. YARNELL	Bath	G. E.	31 May 60	9 Dec 61	2 Feb 63	USN
18	WORDEN	Bath	G. E.	19 Sep 60	2 Jun 62	3 Aug 63	USN
19	DALE	New York SB	G. E.	6 Sep 60	28 Jul 62	23 Nov 63	USN
20	RICHMOND K. TURNER	New York SB	DeLaval	9 Jan 61	6 Apr 63	13 Jun 64	USN
21	GRIDLEY	Puget Sd. Br.	DeLaval	15 Jul 60	31 Jul 61	25 May 63	USN
22	ENGLAND	Todd, San Pedro	DeLaval	4 Oct 60	6 Mar 62	7 Dec 63	USN
23	HALSEY	San Francisco	A. C.	26 Aug 60	15 Jan 62	20 Jul 63	USN
24	REEVES	Puget Sd.	A. C.	1 Jul 60	12 May 62	15 May 64	USN.

Notes: Fiscal years 1958 (DLG 16-18) and 1959. SCB-172 design. The Navy decided to make a full commitment to missiles in its fiscal year 1958 fast task force escorts. The new design was a "double ender" with missiles at both ends and no guns for surface warfare. It had the Farragut's machinery and a Farragut type hull modified with a long forecastle and a knuckle for improved seakeeping. All received an AAW modernization in 1967-72 which included the addition of the Navy Tactical Data System (NTDS).
Reclassifications: All to CG (same numbers) 30 Jun 75.

1961

BELKNAP class

Displacement: 5340 tons (light)
Dimensions: 547'(oa.) x 54'10"(e) x 29'(max)
Armament: 1-5"/54AA 2-3"/50AA 2-Terrier-SAM 2-21"T 6-12.75"T
    DASH; 1-5"AA 2-3"AA 2-Terrier-SAM 6-12.75"T (1967); 1-5"AA
    2-Terrier-SAM 8-Harpoon-SSM 6-12.75"T (1976-80)

Machinery: 85,000 SHP; geared
    turbines, 2 screws
Speed: 34 kts.
Complement: 415

No.		Hull	Machinery	Laid down	Launched	Commiss'd	Disposition
26	BELKNAP	Bath	G. E.	5 Feb 62	20 Jul 63	7 Nov 64	USN
27	JOSEPHUS DANIELS	Bath	G. E.	23 Apr 62	2 Dec 63	8 May 65	USN
28	WAINWRIGHT	Bath	G. E.	2 Jul 62	25 Apr 64	8 Jan 66	USN
29	JOUETT	Puget Sd.	DeLaval	25 Sep 62	30 Jun 64	3 Dec 66	USN
30	HORNE	San Francisco	DeLaval	12 Dec 62	30 Oct 64	15 Apr 67	USN
31	STERETT	Puget Sd.	DeLaval	25 Sep 62	30 Jun 64	8 Apr 67	USN
32	WILLIAM H. STANDLEY	Bath	G. E.	29 Jul 63	19 Dec 64	9 Jul 66	USN
33	FOX	Todd, San Pedro	DeLaval	15 Jan 63	21 Nov 64	28 May 66	USN
34	BIDDLE	Bath	G. E.	9 Dec 63	2 Jul 65	21 Jan 67	USN.

Notes: Fiscal years 1961 (DLG 26-28) and 1962. This class was the final development in the series of fast task force escorts that began with the Mitscher class. The design (SCB-212) was the result of a merger of two designs, an improved Leahy (SCB-172A) and a more austere one (the original SCB-212) that began as a modified DDG. Features carried over from the improved Leahy included a lengthened hull, a new Terrier launcher that could also fire ASROC (permitting the deletion of the ASROC launcher), NTDS, the large SQS-26 sonar, and the DASH drone helicopter. Features retained from earlier SCB-212 designs were the reversion to a single-ended configuration (missiles at one end and a 5"/54 gun at the other) and the addition of two Mk-25 tubes for Mk-37 torpedoes beneath the helicopter deck. The Belknap was rebuilt in 1978-80 after being severely damaged in a collision with the carrier John F. Kennedy on 22 Nov 75.
Reclassifications: All to CG (same numbers) 30 Jun 75.

Nuclear Powered Guided Missile Frigates (DLGN)

1958

BAINBRIDGE

Displacement: 7800 tons (light)
Dimensions: 565'(oa.) x 57'8"(e) x 29'(max)
Armament: 4-3"/50AA 4-Terrier-SAM ASROC 6-12.75"T; 4-Terrier-SAM ASROC 6-12.75"T (1976); 4-Terrier-SAM 8-Harpoon-SSM ASROC 6-12.75"T (1979);

Machinery: 60,000 SHP; 2 G. E. (D2G) reactors driving geared turbines, 2 screws
Speed: 30 kts.
Complement: 497

No.		Hull	Laid down	Launched	Commiss'd	Disposition
25	BAINBRIDGE	Quincy	15 May 59	15 Apr 61	6 Oct 62	USN.

Notes: Fiscal year 1959. SCB-189 design. She was a nuclear version of the Leahy class which combined the weapons systems of the conventional ships with the newly-developed D2G nuclear reactor. The elimination of funnels allowed placing radar and radio antennae in more effective locations. She received an AAW modernization with NTDS in 1974-76.
Reclassification: To CGN-25 30 Jun 75.

1961

TRUXTUN

Displacement: 8200 tons (light)
Dimensions: 564'(oa.) x 58'(e) x 31'(max)
Armament: 1-5"/54AA 2-3"/50AA 2-Terrier-SAM 2-21"T 4-12.75"T DASH; 1-5"/54AA 2-3"/50AA 2-Terrier-SAM 4-12.75"T (1967); 1-5"/54AA 2-Terrier-SAM 8-Harpoon-SSM 4-12.75"T (1980)

Machinery: 60,000 SHP; 2 G. E. (D2G) reactors driving geared turbines, 2 screws
Speed: 30 kts.
Complement: 415

No.		Hull	Laid down	Launched	Commiss'd	Disposition
35	TRUXTUN	New York SB	17 Jun 63	19 Dec 64	27 May 67	USN.

Notes: Fiscal year 1962. SCB-222 design. The Navy requested only conventionally-powered DLGs in fiscal year 1962 but Congress substituted a nuclear powered DLGN for one of them. To take advantage of the nuclear-related design work done on the Bainbridge, the designers attempted to incorporate the Belknap-class improvements into the Bainbridge hull design. To accomodate the SQS-26 sonar forward, they had to put the Terrier missiles aft and the gun forward, the reverse of the arrangement in the Belknap class.
Reclassification: To CGN-35 30 Jun 75.

The guided missile frigate *Mahan* (DLG-11) preparing to refuel from the carrier *Kitty Hawk* on 14 November 1965. (USN 1115255)

The nuclear powered guided missile cruiser *Mississippi* (CGN-40) in Hampton Roads on 28 June 1978. (USN 1172840)

1966

CALIFORNIA class

Displacement: 9561 tons (light)
Dimensions: 596'(oa) x 61'(e) x 31'6"
Armament: 2-5"/54 2-Standard-SAM ASROC 4-12.75"T; 2-5"/54
  2-Standard-SAM 8-Harpoon-SSM ASROC 4-12.75"T (1980)

Machinery: 60,000 SHP; G. E. (D2G)
  reactors driving geared turbines, 2
  screws
Speed: 30 kts.
Complement: 540

No.		Hull	Laid down	Launched	Commiss'd	Disposition
36	CALIFORNIA	Newport News	23 Jan 70	22 Sep 71	16 Feb 74	USN
37	SOUTH CAROLINA	Newport News	1 Dec 70	1 Jul 72	25 Jan 75	USN.

Notes: Fiscal years 1967 (DLGN-36) and 1968. Congress purchased these ships in place of 8450-ton (full load) gas turbine DDGs proposed by the Navy and the Defense Department because it felt that any warship over 7000 tons should have nuclear propulsion. Long-lead items for a third ship were funded in fiscal year 1968 but she was dropped in favor of the DXGN type (the Virginia class). The combination of the Mk-13 launchers in these ships and the new Standard ER missile (also called Digital Tartar) had performance equal to earlier Terrier installations and a far higher launch rate.
Reclassifications: To CGN 36-37 30 Jun 75.

Nuclear Powered Guided Missile Cruisers (CGN, ex DLGN)

1970

VIRGINIA class

Displacement: 10,400 tons (light)
Dimensions: 585'(oa) x 63'(e) x 31'(max)
Armament: 2-5"/54 4-Standard-SAM 6-12.75"T; 2-5"/54 4-
  Standard-SAM 8-Harpoon-SSM 6-12.75"T (1980); 2-5"/54 4-
  Standard-SAM 8-Tomahawk-SSM 8-Harpoon-SSM 6-12.75"T (1985)

Machinery: 60,000 SHP; G. E. (D2G)
  reactors driving geared turbines, 2
  screws
Speed: 30 kts.
Complement: 473

No.		Hull	Laid down	Launched	Commiss'd	Disposition
38	VIRGINIA	Newport News	19 Aug 72	14 Dec 74	11 Sep 76	USN
39	TEXAS	Newport News	18 Aug 73	9 Aug 75	10 Sep 77	USN
40	MISSISSIPPI	Newport News	22 Feb 75	31 Jul 76	5 Aug 78	USN
41	ARKANSAS	Newport News	17 Jan 77	21 Oct 78	18 Oct 80	USN.

Notes: Fiscal years 1970, 1971, 1972, and 1975 respectively. The DX/DXG program of the 1960s which produced the Spruance class destroyers also included a nuclear version, the DXGN, of around 10,000 tons to escort nuclear carriers. This design used the weapon system developed for the DXG, including the Mk-26 missile launcher which could launch ASROC as well as the Standard (Tartar-D) SAM. Long lead items for DLGN-42 were funded in fiscal year 1975 but her procurement was stopped in 1976.
Reclassifications: Ex DLGN 38-41 30 Jun 75.

Guided Missile Cruisers (CG, ex DDG)

1977

TICONDEROGA class

Displacement: 7019 tons (light)
Dimensions: 565'10"(oa.) x 55'(e) x 31'6"(max)
Armament: 2-5"/54 4-Standard-SAM 8-Harpoon SSM 6-12.75"T (CG
  47-51); 2-5"/54 2-Standard-SAM/VLS 6-12.75"T (CG 52-73)

Machinery: 80,000 SHP, G. E. gas
  turbines, 2 screws
Speed: 30+ kts.
Complement: 364

No.		Hull	Laid down	Launched	Commiss'd	Disposition
47	TICONDEROGA	Litton	21 Jan 80	25 Apr 81	22 Jan 83	USN
48	YORKTOWN	Litton	19 Oct 81	17 Jan 83	4 Jul 84	USN
49	VINCENNES	Litton	20 Oct 82	14 Jan 84	6 Jul 85	USN
50	VALLEY FORGE	Litton	14 Apr 83	23 Jun 84	18 Jan 86	USN
51	THOMAS S. GATES	Bath	31 Aug 84	14 Dec 85	22 Aug 87	USN
52	BUNKER HILL	Litton	11 Jan 84	11 Mar 85	20 Sep 86	USN
53	MOBILE BAY	Litton	6 Jun 84	22 Aug 85	21 Feb 87	USN
54	ANTIETAM	Litton	15 Nov 84	14 Feb 86	6 Jun 87	USN
55	LEYTE GULF	Litton	18 Mar 85	20 Jun 86	26 Sep 87	USN
56	SAN JACINTO	Litton	24 Jul 85	14 Nov 86	23 Jan 88	USN
57	LAKE CHAMPLAIN	Litton	3 Mar 86	3 Apr 87	12 Aug 88	USN
58	PHILIPPINE SEA	Bath	8 May 86	12 Jul 87	18 Mar 89	USN
59	PRINCETON	Litton	15 Oct 86	2 Oct 87	11 Feb 89	USN
60	NORMANDY	Bath	7 Apr 87	19 Mar 88	9 Dec 89	USN
61	MONTEREY	Bath	19 Aug 87	23 Oct 88	16 Jun 90	USN
62	CHANCELLORS-VILLE	Litton	24 Jun 87	15 Jul 88	4 Nov 89	USN
63	COWPENS	Bath	23 Dec 87	11 Mar 89		USN
64	GETTYSBURG	Bath	17 Aug 88	22 Jul 89		USN
65	CHOSIN	Litton	22 Jul 88	1 Sep 89		USN
66	HUE CITY	Litton	20 Feb 89	1 Jun 90		USN
67	SHILOH	Bath	1 Aug 89	8 Sep 90		USN
68	ANZIO	Litton	21 Aug 89	2 Nov 90		USN
69	VICKSBURG	Litton	30 May 90			USN
70	LAKE ERIE	Bath	6 Mar 90			USN
71	CAPE ST. GEORGE	Litton	19 Nov 90			USN
72	VELLA GULF	Litton				USN
73	PORT ROYAL	Litton				USN.

Notes: Fiscal years 1978 (CG-47), 1980 (48), 1981 (49-50), 1982 (51-53), 1983 (54-56), 1984 (57-59), 1985 (60-62), 1986 (63-65), 1987 (66-68), and 1988 (69-73). This class was originally the low end of a program for AEGIS-equipped ships which included a large nuclear strike cruiser (CSGN, never built) and a conventionally-powered AEGIS destroyer based on the Spruance class hull. Because of its size and capabilities, the type was reclassified as a missile cruiser (CG) in 1980. The Standard SAM vertical launch system (VLS) in CG 52-73 also fires Tomahawk SSM and ASROC.
Renaming: CG-69 ex Port Royal 8 Dec 89.
Reclassification: CG 47-48 ex DDG 47-48 1 Jan 80 (remainder ordered as CG).

Escort Vessels (DE)

1941

EVARTS (GMT) class

Displacement: 1140 tons (standard)
Dimensions: 289'5"(oa.) x 35'2"(e) x 11'(max)
Armament: 3-3"/50AA

Machinery: 6000 BHP; 4 G. M. model
16-278A diesel engines with
electric drive, 2 screws
Speed: 21.5 kts.
Complement: 156

No.	Hull	Laid down	Launched	Commiss'd	Disposition
1 (BAYNTUN)	Boston	5 Apr 42	27 Jun 42	22 Aug 45	To Britain 20 Jan 43, stk. 1 Nov 45
2 (BAZELY)	Boston	5 Apr 42	27 Jun 42	20 Aug 45	To Britain 18 Feb 43, stk. 16 Nov 45
3 (BERRY)	Boston	22 Sep 42	23 Nov 42	No	To Britain 15 Mar 43, stk. 12 Mar 46
4 (BLACKWOOD)	Boston	22 Sep 42	23 Nov 42	No	To Britain 27 Mar 43, sunk 15 Jun 44
5 EVARTS	Boston	17 Oct 42	7 Dec 42	15 Apr 43	Stk. 24 Oct 45, sold 12 Jul 46
6 WYFFELS	Boston	17 Oct 42	7 Dec 42	21 Apr 43	To China 28 Aug 45 as Tai Kang, stk. 12 Mar 48
7 GRISWOLD	Boston	27 Nov 42	9 Jan 43	28 Apr 43	Stk. 5 Dec 45, sold 2 Dec 46
8 STEELE	Boston	27 Nov 42	9 Jan 43	4 May 43	Stk. 5 Dec 45, sold 2 Dec 46
9 CARLSON	Boston	27 Nov 42	9 Jan 43	10 May 43	Stk. 3 Jan 46, sold 25 Nov 46
10 BEBAS	Boston	27 Nov 42	9 Jan 43	15 May 43	Stk. 1 Nov 45, sold 8 Jan 47
11 CROUTER	Boston	8 Dec 42	26 Jan 43	25 May 43	Stk. 19 Dec 45, sold 25 Nov 46
12 (BURGES)	Boston	8 Dec 42	26 Jan 43	No	To Britain 2 Jun 43, stk. 28 Mar 46
13 BRENNAN	Mare I.	28 Feb 42	22 Aug 42	20 Jan 43	Stk. 24 Oct 45, scrapped 1946
14 DOHERTY	Mare I.	28 Feb 42	29 Aug 42	6 Feb 43	Stk. 8 Jan 46, sold 26 Dec 46
15 AUSTIN	Mare I.	14 Mar 42	25 Sep 42	13 Feb 43	Stk. 8 Jan 46, scrapped 1946
16 EDGAR G. CHASE	Mare I.	14 Mar 42	26 Sep 42	20 Mar 43	Stk. 1 Nov 45, sold 18 Mar 47
17 EDWARD C. DALY	Mare I.	1 Apr 42	21 Oct 42	3 Apr 43	Stk. 8 Jan 46, sold 8 Jan 47
18 GILMORE	Mare I.	1 Apr 42	22 Oct 42	17 Apr 43	Stk. 21 Jan 46, sold 1 Feb 47
19 BURDEN R. HASTINGS	Mare I.	15 Apr 42	20 Nov 42	1 May 43	Stk. 13 Nov 45, sold 1 Feb 47
20 LEHARDY	Mare I.	15 Apr 42	21 Nov 42	15 May 43	Stk. 13 Nov 45, sold 26 Dec 46
21 HAROLD C. THOMAS	Mare I	30 Apr 42	18 Dec 42	31 May 43	Stk. 28 Nov 45, sold 4 Jan 47
22 WILEMAN	Mare I.	30 Apr 42	19 Dec 42	11 Jun 43	Stk. 28 Nov 45, sold 8 Jan 47
23 CHARLES R. GREER	Mare I.	7 Sep 42	18 Jan 43	25 Jun 43	Stk. 16 Nov 45, sold 1 Feb 47
24 WHITMAN	Mare I.	7 Sep 42	19 Jan 43	3 Jul 43	Stk. 16 Nov 45, sold 31 Jan 47
25 WINTLE	Mare I.	1 Oct 42	18 Feb 43	10 Jul 43	Stk. 28 Nov 45, sold 25 Jul 47
26 DEMPSEY	Mare I.	1 Oct 42	19 Feb 43	24 Jul 43	Stk. 28 Nov 45, sold 18 Apr 47
27 DUFFY	Mare I.	29 Oct 42	16 Apr 43	5 Aug 43	Stk. 28 Nov 45, sold 27 Jul 47
28 EMERY	Mare I.	29 Oct 42	17 Apr 43	14 Aug 43	Stk. 28 Nov 45, sold 21 Jul 47
29 STADTFELD	Mare I.	26 Nov 42	17 May 43	26 Aug 43	Stk. 28 Nov 45, sold 22 Jul 47
30 MARTIN	Mare I.	26 Nov 42	18 May 43	4 Sep 43	Stk. 5 Dec 45, sold 3 Jun 47
31 SEDERSTROM	Mare I.	24 Dec 42	15 Jun 43	11 Sep 43	Stk. 28 Nov 45, sold 21 Jan 48
32 FLEMING	Mare I.	24 Dec 42	16 Jun 43	18 Sep 43	Stk. 28 Nov 45, sold 29 Jan 48
33 TISDALE	Mare I.	23 Jan 43	28 Jun 43	11 Oct 43	Stk. 28 Nov 45, sold 9 Feb 48
34 EISELE	Mare I.	23 Jan 43	29 Jun 43	18 Oct 43	Stk. 28 Nov 45, sold 29 Jan 48
35 FAIR	Mare I.	24 Feb 43	27 Jul 43	23 Oct 43	Stk. 28 Nov 45, to Army 20 May 47
36 MANLOVE	Mare I.	24 Feb 43	28 Jul 43	8 Nov 43	Stk. 28 Nov 45, sold 9 Feb 48
37 GREINER	Puget Sd.	7 Sep 42	20 May 43	18 Aug 43	Stk. 5 Dec 45, sold 11 Feb 47
38 WYMAN	Puget Sd.	7 Sep 42	3 Jun 43	1 Sep 43	Stk. 8 Jan 46, sold 16 May 47
39 LOVERING	Puget Sd.	7 Sep 42	18 Jun 43	17 Sep 43	Stk. 1 Nov 45, sold 31 Dec 46
40 SANDERS	Puget Sd.	7 Sep 42	18 Jun 43	1 Oct 43	Stk. 8 Jan 46, sold 8 May 47
41 BRACKETT	Puget Sd.	12 Jan 43	1 Aug 43	18 Oct 43	Stk. 5 Dec 45, sold 22 May 47
42 REYNOLDS	Puget Sd.	12 Jan 43	1 Aug 43	1 Nov 43	Stk. 19 Dec 45, sold 28 Apr 47
43 MITCHELL	Puget Sd.	12 Jan 43	1 Aug 43	17 Nov 43	Stk. 19 Dec 45, sold 11 Dec 46

No.		Hull	Laid down	Launched	Commiss'd	Disposition
44	DONALDSON	Puget Sd.	12 Jan 43	1 Aug 43	1 Dec 43	Stk. 19 Dec 45, sold 2 Jul 46
45	ANDRES	Philadelphia	12 Feb 42	24 Jul 42	15 Mar 43	Stk. 1 Nov 45, scrapped 1946
46	(DRURY)	Philadelphia	12 Feb 42	24 Jul 42	20 Aug 45	To Britain 12 Apr 43, stk. 16 Nov 45
47	DECKER	Philadelphia	1 Apr 42	24 Jul 42	3 May 43	To China 28 Aug 45 as Tai Ping, stk. 12 Mar 48
48	DOBLER	Philadelphia	1 Apr 42	24 Jul 42	17 May 43	Stk. 24 Oct 45, scrapped 1946
49	DONEFF	Philadelphia	1 Apr 42	24 Jul 42	10 Jun 43	Stk. 21 Jan 46, scrapped 1947
50	ENGSTROM	Philadelphia	1 Apr 42	24 Jul 42	21 Jun 43	Stk. 8 Jan 46, sold 26 Dec 46
256	SEID	Boston	10 Jan 43	22 Feb 43	11 Jun 43	Stk. 8 Jan 46, sold 8 Jan 47
257	SMARTT	Boston	10 Jan 43	22 Feb 43	18 Jun 43	Stk. 24 Oct 45, scrapped 1946
258	WALTER S. BROWN	Boston	10 Jan 43	22 Feb 43	25 Jun 43	Stk. 24 Oct 45, scrapped 1946
259	WILLIAM C. MILLER	Boston	10 Jan 43	22 Feb 43	2 Jul 43	Stk. 8 Jan 46, sold 18 Apr 47
260	CABANA	Boston	27 Jan 43	10 Mar 43	9 Jul 43	Stk. 21 Jan 46, sold 13 May 47
261	DIONNE	Boston	27 Jan 43	10 Mar 43	16 Jul 43	Stk. 7 Feb 46, sold 12 Jun 47
262	CANFIELD	Boston	23 Feb 43	6 Apr 43	22 Jul 43	Stk. 8 Jan 46, sold 12 Jun 47
263	DEEDE	Boston	23 Feb 43	6 Apr 43	29 Jul 43	Stk. 21 Jan 46, sold 12 Jun 47
264	ELDON	Boston	23 Feb 43	6 Apr 43	4 Aug 43	Stk. 7 Feb 46, sold 12 Jun 47
265	CLOUES	Boston	23 Feb 43	6 Apr 43	10 Aug 43	Stk. 5 Dec 45, sold 22 May 47
266	WINTLE	Boston	11 Mar 43	22 Apr 43	No	To Britain 16 Aug 43 as Capel, sunk 27 Dec 44
267	DEMPSEY	Boston	11 Mar 43	22 Apr 43	No	To Britain 23 Aug 43 as Cooke, stk. 8 May 46
268	DUFFY	Boston	7 Apr 43	19 May 43	No	To Britain 28 Aug 43 as Dacres, stk. 12 Apr 46
269	EISNER	Boston	7 Apr 43	19 May 43	No	To Britain 3 Sep 43 as Domett, stk. 8 May 46
270	GILLETTE	Boston	7 Apr 43	19 May 43	22 Aug 45	To Britain 8 Sep 43 as Foley, stk. 1 Nov 45
271	FLEMING	Boston	7 Apr 43	19 May 43	20 Aug 45	To Britain 13 Sep 43 as Garlies, stk. 1 Nov 45
272	LOVERING	Boston	23 Apr 43	4 Jun 43	No	To Britain 18 Sep 43 as Gould, sunk 1 Mar 44
273	SANDERS	Boston	23 Apr 43	4 Jun 43	20 Aug 45	To Britain 23 Sep 43 as Grindall, stk. 1 Nov 45
274	O'TOOLE	Boston	20 May 43	8 Jul 43	No	To Britain 28 Sep 43 as Gardiner, stk. 17 Apr 46
275	REYBOLD	Boston	20 May 43	8 Jul 43	No	To Britain 4 Oct 43 as Goodall, sunk 29 Apr 45
276	GEORGE	Boston	20 May 43	8 Jul 43	No	To Britain 9 Oct 43 as Goodson, stk. 22 May 47
277	HERZOG	Boston	20 May 43	8 Jul 43	No	To Britain 14 Oct 43 as Gore, stk. 31 Jul 46
278	TISDALE	Boston	5 Jun 43	17 Jul 43	No	To Britain 19 Oct 43 as Keats, stk. 20 Mar 46
279	TRUMPETER	Boston	5 Jun 43	17 Jul 43	20 Aug 45	To Britain 23 Oct 43 as Kempthorne, stk. 1 Nov 45
280	(KINGSMILL)	Boston	9 Jul 43	13 Aug 43	22 Aug 45	To Britain 29 Oct 43, stk. 16 Nov 45
301	LAKE	Mare I.	22 Apr 43	18 Aug 43	5 Feb 44	Stk. 19 Dec 45, sold 14 Dec 46
302	LYMAN	Mare I.	22 Apr 43	19 Aug 43	19 Feb 44	Stk. 19 Dec 45, sold 26 Dec 46
303	CROWLEY	Mare I.	24 May 43	22 Sep 43	25 Mar 44	Stk. 19 Dec 45, sold 21 Dec 46
304	RALL	Mare I.	24 May 43	23 Sep 43	8 Apr 44	Stk. 3 Jan 46, sold 18 Mar 47
305	HALLORAN	Mare I.	21 Jun 43	14 Jan 44	27 May 44	Stk. 28 Nov 45, sold 18 Mar 47
306	CONNOLLY	Mare I.	21 Jun 43	15 Jan 44	8 Jul 44	Stk. 19 Dec 45, scrapped 1946
307	FINNEGAN	Mare I.	5 Jul 43	22 Feb 44	19 Aug 44	Stk. 19 Dec 45, scrapped 1946
308	CREAMER	Mare I.	5 Jul 43	23 Feb 44	No	Cancelled 5 Sep 44
309	ELY	Mare I.	2 Aug 43	10 Apr 44	No	Cancelled 5 Sep 44
310	DELBERT W. HALSEY	Mare I.	2 Aug 43	11 Apr 44	No	Cancelled 5 Sep 44
311	KEPPLER	Mare I.	23 Aug 43	No	No	Cancelled 13 Mar 44
312	LLOYD THOMAS	Mare I.	23 Aug 43	No	No	Cancelled 13 Mar 44
313	WILLIAM C. LAWE	Mare I.	22 Jan 44	No	No	Cancelled 13 Mar 44

No.		Hull	Laid down	Launched	Commiss'd	Disposition
314	WILLARD KEITH	Mare I.	22 Jan 44	No	No	Cancelled 13 Mar 44
315	Unnamed	Mare I.	1 Mar 44	No	No	Cancelled 13 Mar 44
516	(LAWFORD)	Boston	9 Jul 43	13 Aug 43	No	To Britain 3 Nov 43, sunk 8 Jun 44
517	(LOUIS)	Boston	9 Jul 43	13 Aug 43	No	To Britain 9 Nov 43, stk. 17 Apr 46
518	(LAWSON)	Boston	9 Jul 43	13 Aug 43	No	To Britain 15 Nov 43, stk. 17 Apr 46
519	(PASLEY)	Boston	18 Jul 43	30 Aug 43	No	To Britain 20 Nov 43, stk. 16 Nov 45
520	(LORING)	Boston	18 Jul 43	30 Aug 43	No	To Britain 27 Nov 43, stk. 22 Jan 47
521	(HOSTE)	Boston	14 Aug 43	24 Sep 43	No	To Britain 3 Dec 43, stk. 16 Nov 45
522	(MOORSOM)	Boston	14 Aug 43	24 Sep 43	No	To Britain 10 Dec 43, stk. 5 Dec 45
523	(MANNERS)	Boston	14 Aug 43	24 Sep 43	No	To Britain 16 Dec 43, stk. 19 Dec 45
524	(MOUNSEY)	Boston	14 Aug 43	24 Sep 43	No	To Britain 23 Dec 43, stk. 28 Mar 46
525	(INGLIS)	Boston	25 Sep 43	2 Nov 43	No	To Britain 29 Dec 43, stk. 17 Apr 46
526	(INMAN)	Boston	25 Sep 43	2 Nov 43	No	To Britain 13 Jan 44, stk. 20 Mar 46
527	O'TOOLE	Boston	25 Sep 43	2 Nov 43	22 Jan 44	Stk. 1 Nov 45, scrapped 1946
528	JOHN J. POWERS	Boston	25 Sep 43	2 Nov 43	29 Feb 44	Stk. 1 Nov 45, scrapped 1946
529	MASON	Boston	14 Oct 43	17 Nov 43	20 Mar 44	Stk. 1 Nov 45, sold 18 Mar 47
530	JOHN M. BERMINGHAM	Boston	14 Oct 43	17 Nov 43	8 Apr 44	Stk. 1 Nov 45, scrapped 1946.

Notes: Fiscal years for wartime DEs: 1942 (DE 1-300), 1943 (DE 301-800), 1944 (DE 801-1005). In February 1941 the Navy began to formulate characteristics for an escort vessel to protect convoys against submarines in the western part of the North Atlantic. The plans of the 1175-ton light destroyer proposed in late 1940 as DD-503 were taken as a starting point. The U.S. Navy resisted the idea of building austerity escorts for itself, but in June 1941 the British asked the U.S. for 100 ships of the new type and in August President Roosevelt authorized construction of 50. These were ordered in November and were initially assigned BDE hull numbers indicative of their intended delivery to the Royal Navy under Lend-Lease. In November 1940 the British asked for 470 more, and in January 1942 another 250 were ordered. At the same time, all 300 were pooled for allocation between the U.S. Navy and Royal Navy as required.

The division of the World War II destroyer escorts into six different classes was brought about by bottlenecks in the production of propulsion machinery. Early designs called for the use of steam turbines, but there was a critical shortage of facilities to produce reduction gears for these. In late June 1941 the Navy decided to use submarine diesel engines in a composite arrangement: four operating through a diesel-electric drive and four operating through small, less critical reduction gears. These would give the same designed power and speed (12,000 HP, 24 knots) as the steam plant. Later, however, competition from the landing craft program made diesel engines a critical commodity, and in June 1942 half of the engines in each diesel DE were omitted. This reduced horsepower by half and designed speed by 4.5 knots.

The initial DE type, the Evarts class, had General Motors diesels with a diesel-electric drive in the short hull of the original design. It was called the General Motors Tandem motor drive (GMT) type. Gibbs and Cox prepared the detailed plans for this class. Most of the 50 ships built under the original British order never flew the White Ensign as they were taken over for American use and reclassified DE. Later ships were substituted under Lend Lease allocation procedures. The British ships returned to the U.S. in August 1945 were briefly commissioned in the U.S. Navy for their return voyage. Two ships were irreparably damaged in British service: DE-276 (25 Jun 44) and DE-523 (26 Jan 45).

Renamings: DE-28 ex Eisner 14 Jul 43; DE-31 ex Gillette 13 Jul 43; DE-308 ex Register 10 Sep 43. The following British names were assigned to vessels subsequently taken over by the U. S.: Bentinck (13), Berry (14), Blackwood (15), Burges (16), Byard (17), Calder (18), Duckworth (19), Duff (20), Essington (21), Foley (22), Capel (45), Cooke (47), Dacres (48), Domett (49), Drury (50), and Calder (307). The original British names of HMS Drury (46), Pasley (519), and Hoste (521) were Cockburn, Lindsay, and Mitchell respectively.

Reclassifications: BDE 5-11, 13-24, 45, 47-50 to DE on 25 Jan 43, BDE 25-44 to DE on 16 Jun 43.

1942

CANNON (DET) class

Displacement: 1240 tons (standard)
Dimensions: 306'(oa.) x 36'7"(e) x 11'8"(max)
Armament: 3-3/50" 3-21"T; 3-3" (1950)

Machinery: 6000 BHP; 4 G. M. model
16-278A diesel engines with
electric drive, 2 screws
Speed: 21 kts.
Complement: 186

No.		Hull	Laid down	Launched	Commiss'd	Disposition
99	CANNON	Dravo, Wilmington	14 Nov 42	25 May 43	26 Sep 43	To Brazil 19 Dec 44 as Baependi, stk. 20 Jul 53
100	CHRISTOPHER	Dravo, Wilmington	7 Dec 42	19 Jun 43	23 Oct 43	To Brazil 19 Dec 44 as Benevente, stk. 20 Jul 53
101	ALGER	Dravo, Wilmington	2 Jan 43	8 Jul 43	12 Nov 43	To Brazil 10 Mar 45 as Babitonga, stk. 20 Jul 53
102	THOMAS	Dravo, Wilmington	16 Jan 43	31 Jul 43	21 Nov 43	To China 29 Oct 48 as Tai Ho, stk. 22 Dec 48
103	BOSTWICK	Dravo, Wilmington	6 Feb 43	30 Aug 43	1 Dec 43	To China 14 Dec 48 as Tai Hu, stk. 10 Feb 49
104	BREEMAN	Dravo, Wilmington	20 Mar 43	4 Sep 43	12 Dec 43	To China 29 Oct 48 as Tai Chong, stk. 22 Dec 48
105	BURROWS	Dravo, Wilmington	24 Mar 43	2 Oct 43	19 Dec 43	To Netherlands 1 Jun 50 as Van Amstel, stk. 26 Sep 50
106	CORBESIER	Dravo, Wilmington	24 Apr 43	11 Nov 43	31 Dec 43	To France 2 Jan 44 as Senegalais, stk. 14 May 52
107	CRONIN	Dravo, Wilmington	13 May 43	27 Nov 43	22 Jan 44	To France 23 Jan 44 as Algerien, stk. 14 May 52
108	CROSLEY	Dravo, Wilmington	23 Jun 43	17 Dec 43	10 Feb 44	To France 11 Feb 44 as Tunisien, stk. 14 May 52
109	(MAROCAIN)	Dravo, Wilmington	7 Sep 43	1 Jan 44	No	To France 29 Feb 44, stk. 14 May 52
110	(HOVA)	Dravo, Wilmington	25 Sep 43	22 Jan 44	No	To France 18 Mar 44, stk. 14 May 52
111	(SOMALI)	Dravo, Wilmington	23 Oct 43	12 Feb 44	No	To France 9 Apr 44, stk. 14 May 52
112	CARTER	Dravo, Wilmington	19 Nov 43	29 Feb 44	3 May 44	To China 14 Dec 48 as Tai Chao, stk. 10 Feb 49
113	CLARENCE L. EVANS	Dravo, Wilmington	23 Dec 43	22 Mar 44	25 Jun 44	To France 29 Mar 52 as Berbere, stk. 18 Apr 52
114 -128	Unnamed	Dravo, Wilmington	No	No	No	Cancelled 2 Oct 43
162	LEVY	Port Newark	19 Oct 42	28 Mar 43	13 May 43	Stk. 1 Aug 73, sold 17 Jul 74
163	McCONNELL	Port Newark	19 Oct 42	28 Mar 43	28 May 43	Stk. 1 Oct 72, sold 21 Mar 74
164	OSTERHAUS	Port Newark	11 Nov 42	18 Apr 43	12 Jun 43	Stk. 1 Nov 72, sold 30 May 74
165	PARKS	Port Newark	11 Nov 42	18 Apr 43	23 Jun 43	Stk. 1 Jul 72, sold 15 Oct 73
166	BARON	Port Newark	30 Nov 42	9 May 43	5 Jul 43	To Uruguay 3 May 52 as Uruguay, stk. 14 May 52
167	ACREE	Port Newark	30 Nov 42	9 May 43	19 Jul 43	Stk. 1 Jul 72, sold 19 Jul 73
168	AMICK	Port Newark	7 Jan 43	27 May 43	26 Jul 43	To Japan 14 Jun 55 as Asahi, stk. 15 Jun 75, to Philippines 13 Sep 76 as Datu Siratuna
169	ATHERTON	Port Newark	14 Jan 43	27 May 43	29 Aug 43	To Japan 14 Jun 55 as Hatsuhi, stk. 15 Jun 75, to Philippines 13 Sep 76 as Rajah Humabon
170	BOOTH	Port Newark	30 Jan 43	21 Jun 43	19 Sep 43	To Philippines 15 Dec 67 as Datu Kalantiaw, stk. 15 Jul 78
171	CARROLL	Port Newark	30 Jan 43	21 Jun 43	24 Oct 43	Stk. 1 Aug 65, sold 29 Dec 66
172	COONER	Port Newark	22 Feb 43	23 Jul 43	21 Aug 43	Stk. 1 Jul 72, sold 1 Nov 73
173	ELDRIDGE	Port Newark	22 Feb 43	25 Jul 43	27 Aug 43	To Greece 15 Jan 51 as Leon, stk. 26 Mar 51
174	MARTS	Port Newark	26 Apr 43	8 Aug 43	3 Sep 43	To Brazil 20 Mar 45 as Bocaina, stk. 20 Jul 53

No.		Hull	Laid down	Launched	Commiss'd	Disposition
175	PENNEWELL	Port Newark	26 Apr 43	8 Aug 43	15 Sep 43	To Brazil 1 Aug 44 as Bertioga, stk. 20 Jul 53
176	MICKA	Port Newark	3 May 43	22 Aug 43	23 Sep 43	Stk. 1 Aug 65, sold 15 May 67
177	REYBOLD	Port Newark	3 May 43	22 Aug 43	29 Sep 43	To Brazil 15 Aug 44 as Bracui, stk. 20 Jul 53
178	HERZOG	Port Newark	17 May 43	5 Sep 43	6 Oct 43	To Brazil 1 Aug 44 as Beberibe, stk. 20 Jul 53
179	McANN	Port Newark	17 May 43	5 Sep 43	11 Oct 43	To Brazil 15 Aug 44 as Bauru, stk. 20 Jul 53
180	TRUMPETER	Port Newark	7 Jun 43	19 Sep 43	16 Oct 43	Stk. 1 Aug 73, sold 17 Jul 74
181	STRAUB	Port Newark	7 Jun 43	19 Sep 43	25 Oct 43	Stk. 1 Aug 73, sold 17 Jul 74
182	GUSTAFSON	Port Newark	5 Jul 43	3 Oct 43	1 Nov 43	To Netherlands 23 Oct 50 as Van Ewijck, stk. 20 Dec 50
183	SAMUEL S. MILES	Port Newark	5 Jul 43	3 Oct 43	4 Nov 43	To France 12 Aug 50 as Arabe, stk. 26 Sep 50
184	WESSON	Port Newark	29 Jul 43	17 Oct 43	11 Nov 43	To Italy 10 Jan 51 as Andromeda, stk. 26 Mar 51
185	RIDDLE	Port Newark	29 Jul 43	17 Oct 43	17 Nov 43	To France 12 Aug 50 as Kabyle, stk. 26 Sep 50
186	SWEARER	Port Newark	12 Aug 43	31 Oct 43	24 Nov 43	To France 16 Sep 50 as Bambara, stk. 20 Oct 50
187	STERN	Port Newark	12 Aug 43	31 Oct 43	1 Dec 43	To Netherlands 1 Mar 51 as Van Zijll, stk. 7 Mar 51
188	O'NEILL	Port Newark	26 Aug 43	14 Nov 43	6 Dec 43	To Netherlands 23 Oct 50 as Dubois, stk. 20 Dec 50
189	BRONSTEIN	Port Newark	26 Aug 43	14 Nov 43	13 Dec 43	To Uruguay 3 May 52 as Artigas, stk. 14 May 52
190	BAKER	Port Newark	9 Sep 43	28 Nov 43	23 Dec 43	To France 29 Mar 52 as Malgache, stk. 18 Apr 52
191	COFFMAN	Port Newark	9 Sep 43	28 Nov 43	27 Dec 43	Stk. 1 Jul 72, sold 17 Aug 73
192	EISNER	Port Newark	23 Sep 43	12 Dec 43	1 Jan 44	To Netherlands 1 Mar 51 as De Zeeuw, stk. 7 Mar 51
193	GARFIELD THOMAS	Port Newark	23 Sep 43	12 Dec 43	24 Jan 44	To Greece 15 Jan 51 as Panthir, stk. 26 Mar 51
194	WINGFIELD	Port Newark	7 Oct 43	30 Dec 43	28 Jan 44	To France 16 Sep 50 as Sakalave, stk. 20 Oct 50
195	THORNHILL	Port Newark	7 Oct 43	30 Dec 43	1 Feb 44	To Italy 10 Jan 51 as Aldebaran, stk. 26 Mar 51
196	RINEHART	Port Newark	21 Oct 43	9 Jan 44	12 Feb 44	To Netherlands 1 Jun 50 as De Bitter, stk. 26 Sep 50
197	ROCHE	Port Newark	21 Oct 43	9 Jan 44	21 Feb 44	Scuttled 11 Mar 46, stk. 5 Jun 46
739	BANGUST	Western Pipe	11 Feb 43	6 Jun 43	30 Oct 43	To Peru 21 Feb 52 as Castilla, stk. 18 Apr 52
740	WATERMAN	Western Pipe	24 Feb 43	20 Jun 43	30 Nov 43	To Peru 21 Feb 52 as Aguirre, stk. 18 Apr 52
741	WEAVER	Western Pipe	13 Mar 43	4 Jul 43	31 Dec 43	To Peru 21 Feb 52 as Rodriguez, stk. 18 Apr 52
742	HILBERT	Western Pipe	23 Mar 43	18 Jul 43	4 Feb 44	Stk. 1 Aug 72, sold 15 Oct 73
743	LAMONS	Western Pipe	10 Apr 43	1 Aug 43	29 Feb 44	Stk. 1 Aug 72, sold 15 Oct 73
744	KYNE	Western Pipe	16 Apr 43	15 Aug 43	4 Apr 44	Stk. 1 Aug 72, sold 1 Nov 73
745	SNYDER	Western Pipe	28 Apr 43	29 Aug 43	5 May 44	Stk. 1 Aug 72, sold 1 Nov 73
746	HEMMINGER	Western Pipe	8 May 43	12 Sep 43	30 May 44	To Thailand 22 Jul 59 as Pin Klao, stk. 3 Sep 74
747	BRIGHT	Western Pipe	9 Jun 43	26 Sep 43	30 Jun 44	To France 11 Nov 50 as Touareg, stk. 20 Dec 50
748	TILLS	Western Pipe	23 Jun 43	3 Oct 43	8 Aug 44	Stk. 23 Sep 68, sunk as target off Virginia 3 Apr 69
749	ROBERTS	Western Pipe	7 Jul 43	14 Nov 43	2 Sep 44	Stk. 23 Sep 68, sunk as target Nov 71
750	McCLELLAND	Western Pipe	21 Jul 43	28 Nov 43	19 Sep 44	Stk. 1 Aug 72, sold 1 Nov 73
751	GAYNIER	Western Pipe	4 Aug 43	30 Jan 44	No	Cancelled 1 Sep 44
752	CURTIS W. HOWARD	Western Pipe	18 Aug 43	26 Mar 44	No	Cancelled 1 Sep 44

No.	Hull	Laid down	Launched	Commiss'd	Disposition
753 JOHN J. VANBUREN	Western Pipe	31 Aug 43	16 Jan 44	No	Cancelled 1 Sep 44
754 WILLARD KEITH	Western Pipe	14 Sep 43	No	No	Cancelled 2 Oct 43
755 PAUL G. BAKER	Western Pipe	27 Sep 43	No	No	Cancelled 2 Oct 43
756 DAMON CUMMINGS	Western Pipe	No	No	No	Cancelled 2 Oct 43
757 Unnamed -762	Western Pipe	No	No	No	Cancelled 2 Oct 43
763 CATES	Tampa	1 Mar 43	10 Oct 43	15 Dec 43	To France 1 Nov 50 as Soudanais, stk. 20 Dec 50
764 GANDY	Tampa	1 Mar 43	12 Dec 43	7 Feb 44	To Italy 10 Jan 51 as Altair, stk. 26 Mar 51
765 EARL K. OLSEN	Tampa	9 Mar 43	13 Feb 44	10 Apr 44	Stk. 1 Aug 72, sold 15 Oct 73
766 SLATER	Tampa	9 Mar 43	13 Feb 44	1 May 44	To Greece 1 Mar 51 as Aetos, stk. 7 Mar 51
767 OSWALD	Tampa	1 Apr 43	25 Apr 44	12 Jun 44	Stk. 1 Aug 72, sold 1 Nov 73
768 EBERT	Tampa	1 Apr 43	11 May 44	12 Jul 44	To Greece 1 Mar 51 as Ierax, stk. 7 Mar 51
769 NEAL A. SCOTT	Tampa	1 Jun 43	4 Jun 44	31 Jul 44	Stk. 1 Jun 68, sold Jul 69
770 MUIR	Tampa	1 Jun 43	4 Jun 44	30 Aug 44	To S. Korea 2 Feb 56 as Kyong Ki, stk. 15 Nov 74
771 SUTTON	Tampa	23 Aug 43	6 Aug 44	22 Dec 44	To S. Korea 2 Feb 56 as Kang Won, stk. 15 Nov 74
772 MILTON LEWIS	Tampa	23 Aug 43	6 Aug 44	No	Cancelled 1 Sep 44
773 GEORGE M. CAMPBELL	Tampa	14 Oct 43	15 Oct 44	No	Cancelled 1 Sep 44
774 RUSSELL M. COX	Tampa	14 Oct 43	No	No	Cancelled 1 Sep 44
775 Unnamed -788	Tampa	No	No	No	Cancelled 2 Oct 43

Notes: This class had the same General Motors diesels and electric drive as the Evarts class but was built with the standard lengthened hull developed for the Buckley class, below. It was called the Diesel Electric Tandem motor drive (DET) type. It was the least successful of the long hulled types because of its low speed. The ships were seldom able to reach designed speed under service conditions. The Thomas (DE-102), Breeman (DE-104), Atherton (DE-169), Booth (DE-170), and Carroll (DE-171) were completed by Norfolk Navy Yard. The Roche (DE-197) was irreparably damaged on 22 Sep 45.
Renamings: DE-183 ex Miles 20 Jan 44; DE-190 ex Raby 3 Sep 43; DE-193 ex William G. Thomas 3 Nov 43; DE-765 ex Olsen 12 Jun 43; DE-772 ex Rogers 19 Jul 44.

EDSALL (FMR) class

Displacement: 1200 tons (standard)
Dimensions: 306'(oa.) x 36'7"(e) x 12'3"(max)
Armament: 3-3"/50AA 3-21"T; 2-5"/38AA (Camp, 1945); 3-3"AA
   (1950, except Camp)

Machinery: 6000 SHP; 4 F. M. model 38D81/8 geared diesel engines, 2 screws
Speed: 21 kts.
Complement: 186

No.	Hull	Laid down	Launched	Commiss'd	Disposition
129 EDSALL	Orange	2 Jul 42	1 Nov 42	10 Apr 43	Stk. 1 Jun 68, sold Jul 69
130 JACOB JONES	Orange	26 Jun 42	29 Nov 42	29 Apr 43	Stk. 2 Jan 71, sold 22 Aug 73
131 HAMMANN	Orange	10 Jul 42	13 Dec 42	17 May 43	Stk. 1 Oct 72, sold 18 Jan 74
132 ROBERT E. PEARY	Orange	30 Jun 42	3 Jan 43	31 May 43	Stk. 1 Jul 66, sold 6 Sep 67
133 PILLSBURY	Orange	18 Jul 42	10 Jan 43	7 Jun 43	Stk. 1 Jul 65, sold 1966
134 POPE	Orange	14 Jul 42	12 Jan 43	25 Jun 43	Stk. 2 Jan 71, sold 22 Aug 73
135 FLAHERTY	Orange	7 Nov 42	17 Jan 43	26 Jun 43	Stk. 1 Apr 65, sold 4 Nov 66
136 FREDERICK C. DAVIS	Orange	9 Nov 42	24 Jan 43	14 Jul 44	Sunk by U-546 in N Atlantic 24 Apr 45
137 HERBERT C. JONES	Orange	30 Nov 42	19 Jan 43	21 Jul 43	Stk. 1 Jul 72, sold 19 Jul 73
138 DOUGLAS L. HOWARD	Orange	8 Dec 42	24 Jan 43	29 Jul 43	Stk. 1 Oct 72, sold 14 May 74
139 FARQUHAR	Orange	14 Dec 42	13 Feb 43	5 Aug 43	Stk. 1 Oct 72, sold 21 Mar 74
140 J. R. Y. BLAKELY	Orange	16 Dec 42	7 Mar 43	16 Aug 43	Stk. 2 Jan 71, sold 22 Aug 73
141 HILL	Orange	21 Dec 42	28 Feb 43	16 Aug 43	Stk. 1 Oct 72, sold 18 Jan 74
142 FESSENDEN	Orange	4 Jan 43	9 Mar 43	25 Aug 43	Stk. 1 Sep 66, sunk as target off Pearl Harbor 20 Dec 67

No.		Hull	Laid down	Launched	Commiss'd	Disposition
143	FISKE	Orange	4 Jan 43	14 Mar 43	25 Aug 43	Sunk by U-804 in N Atlantic 2 Aug 44
144	FROST	Orange	13 Jan 43	21 Mar 43	30 Aug 43	Stk. 1 Apr 65, sold 29 Dec 66
145	HUSE	Orange	11 Jan 43	23 Mar 43	30 Aug 43	Stk. 1 Aug 73, sold 24 Jun 74
146	INCH	Orange	19 Jan 43	4 Apr 43	8 Sep 43	Stk. 1 Oct 72, sold 21 Mar 74
147	BLAIR	Orange	19 Jan 43	6 Apr 43	13 Sep 43	Stk. 1 Dec 72, sold 10 Sep 74
148	BROUGH	Orange	22 Jan 43	10 Apr 43	18 Sep 43	Stk. 1 Nov 65, sold 13 Oct 66
149	CHATELAIN	Orange	25 Jan 43	21 Apr 43	22 Sep 43	Stk. 1 Aug 73, sold 24 Jun 74
150	NEUNZER	Orange	29 Jan 43	27 Apr 43	27 Sep 43	Stk. 1 Jul 72, sold 1 Nov 73
151	POOLE	Orange	13 Feb 43	8 May 43	29 Sep 43	Stk. 2 Jan 71, sold 30 Jan 74
152	PETERSON	Orange	28 Feb 43	15 May 43	29 Sep 43	Stk. 1 Aug 73, sold 24 Jun 74
238	STEWART	Houston	15 Jul 42	22 Nov 42	31 May 43	Stk. 1 Oct 72, memorial at Galveston, Tex. 25 Jun 74
239	STURTEVANT	Houston	15 Jul 42	3 Dec 42	16 Jun 43	Stk. 1 Dec 72, sold 20 Sep 73
240	MOORE	Houston	20 Jul 42	21 Dec 42	1 Jul 43	Stk. 1 Aug 73, sunk as target off Virginia 13 Jun 75
241	KEITH	Houston	4 Aug 42	21 Dec 42	19 Jul 43	Stk. 1 Nov 72, sold 18 Jan 74
242	TOMICH	Houston	15 Sep 42	28 Dec 42	27 Jul 43	Stk. 1 Nov 72, sold 18 Jan 74
243	J. RICHARD WARD	Houston	30 Sep 42	6 Jan 43	5 Jul 43	Stk. 2 Jan 71, sold 10 Apr 72
244	OTTERSTETTER	Houston	9 Nov 42	19 Jan 43	6 Aug 43	Stk. 1 Aug 74, sunk as target off Puerto Rico 15 Feb 76
245	SLOAT	Houston	21 Nov 42	21 Jan 43	16 Aug 43	Stk. 2 Jan 71, sold 10 Apr 72
246	SNOWDEN	Houston	7 Dec 42	19 Feb 43	23 Aug 43	Stk. 23 Sep 68, sunk as target off Newport, R.I 27 Jun 69
247	STANTON	Houston	7 Dec 42	21 Feb 43	7 Aug 43	Stk. 1 Dec 70, sunk as target off Puerto Rico 16 Oct 72
248	SWASEY	Houston	30 Dec 42	18 Mar 43	31 Aug 43	Stk. 1 Nov 72, sold 21 Mar 74
249	MARCHAND	Houston	30 Dec 42	20 Mar 43	8 Sep 43	Stk. 2 Jan 71, sold 30 Jan 74
250	HURST	Houston	27 Jan 43	14 Apr 43	30 Aug 43	Stk. 1 Dec 72, to Mexico as Como. Manuel Azueta 1 Oct 73
251	CAMP	Houston	27 Jan 43	16 Apr 43	16 Sep 43	To S. Vietnam 13 Feb 71 as Tran Hung Dao, stk. 30 Dec 75, to Philippines 5 Apr 76 as Rajah Lakandula
252	HOWARD D. CROW	Houston	6 Feb 43	26 Apr 43	27 Sep 43	Stk. 23 Sep 68, sold Oct 70
253	PETTIT	Houston	6 Feb 43	28 Apr 43	23 Sep 43	Stk. 1 Aug 73, sunk as target off Puerto Rico 30 Sep 74
254	RICKETTS	Houston	16 Mar 43	10 May 43	5 Oct 43	Stk. 1 Nov 72, sold 18 Jan 74
255	SELLSTROM	Houston	16 Mar 43	12 May 43	12 Oct 43	Stk. 1 Nov 65, sold 1966
316	HARVESON	Orange	9 Mar 43	22 May 43	12 Oct 43	Stk. 1 Dec 66, sunk as target off S. California 10 Oct 67
317	JOYCE	Orange	8 Mar 43	26 May 43	30 Sep 43	Stk. 1 Dec 72, sold 11 Sep 73
318	KIRKPATRICK	Orange	15 Mar 43	5 Jun 43	23 Oct 43	Stk. 1 Aug 74, sold 12 Mar 75
319	LEOPOLD	Orange	24 Mar 43	12 Jun 43	18 Oct 43	Torpedoed by U-255 S of Iceland 9 Mar 44
320	MENGES	Orange	22 Mar 43	15 Jun 43	26 Oct 43	Stk. 2 Jan 71, sold 10 Apr 72
321	MOSLEY	Orange	6 Apr 43	26 Jun 43	30 Oct 43	Stk. 2 Jan 71, sold 22 Aug 73
322	NEWELL	Orange	5 Apr 43	29 Jun 43	30 Oct 43	Stk. 23 Sep 68, sold 15 Dec 71
323	PRIDE	Orange	12 Apr 43	3 Jul 43	13 Nov 43	Stk. 2 Jan 71, sold 30 Jan 74
324	FALGOUT	Orange	24 May 43	24 Jul 43	15 Nov 43	Stk. 1 Jun 75, sunk as target off S. California 12 Jan 77
325	LOWE	Orange	24 May 43	28 Jul 43	22 Nov 43	Stk. 23 Sep 68, sold 3 Sep 69
326	THOMAS J. GRAY	Orange	15 Jun 43	21 Aug 43	27 Nov 43	Stk. 30 Sep 73, to Tunisia as Pres. Bourguiba 22 Oct 73
327	BRISTER	Orange	14 Jun 43	24 Aug 43	30 Nov 43	Stk. 23 Sep 68, sold 15 Dec 71
328	FINCH	Orange	29 Jun 43	28 Aug 43	13 Dec 43	Stk. 1 Feb 74, sold 16 Aug 74
329	KRETCHMER	Orange	28 Jun 43	31 Aug 43	13 Dec 43	Stk. 30 Sep 73, sold 14 May 74
330	O'REILLY	Orange	29 Jul 43	2 Oct 43	28 Dec 43	Stk. 15 Jan 71, sold 10 Apr 72
331	KOINER	Orange	26 Jul 43	5 Oct 43	27 Dec 43	Stk. 23 Sep 68, sold 3 Sep 69
332	PRICE	Orange	24 Aug 43	30 Oct 43	12 Jan 44	Stk. 1 Aug 74, sold 12 Mar 75
333	STRICKLAND	Orange	23 Aug 43	2 Nov 43	10 Jan 44	Stk. 1 Dec 72, sold 10 Sep 74
334	FORSTER	Orange	31 Aug 43	13 Nov 43	25 Jan 44	To S. Vietnam 25 Sep 71 as Tran Khanh Du
335	DANIEL	Orange	30 Aug 43	16 Nov 43	24 Jan 44	Stk. 15 Jan 71, sold 30 Jan 74
336	ROY O. HALE	Orange	13 Sep 43	20 Nov 43	3 Feb 44	Stk. 1 Aug 74, sold 12 Mar 75

No.		Hull	Laid down	Launched	Commiss'd	Disposition
337	DALE W. PETERSON	Orange	25 Oct 43	22 Dec 43	17 Feb 44	Stk. 2 Jan 71, sold 10 Apr 72
338	MARTIN H. RAY	Orange	27 Oct 43	29 Dec 43	28 Feb 44	Stk. 1 May 66, sold 30 Mar 67
382	RAMSDEN	Houston	26 Mar 43	24 May 43	19 Oct 43	Stk. 1 Aug 74, sunk as target
383	MILLS	Houston	26 Mar 43	26 May 43	12 Oct 43	Stk. 1 Aug 74, sold 12 Mar 75
384	RHODES	Houston	19 Apr 43	29 Jun 43	25 Oct 43	Stk. 1 Aug 74, sold 12 Mar 75
385	RICHEY	Houston	19 Apr 43	30 Jun 43	30 Oct 43	Stk. 30 Jun 68, sunk as target off S. California Jul 69
386	SAVAGE	Houston	30 Apr 43	15 Jul 43	29 Oct 43	Stk. 1 Jun 75, sunk as target off S. California 25 Oct 82
387	VANCE	Houston	30 Apr 43	16 Jul 43	1 Nov 43	Stk. 1 Jun 75, disposed of ca. 1985
388	LANSING	Houston	15 May 43	2 Aug 43	10 Nov 43	Stk. 1 Feb 74, sold 16 Aug 74
389	DURANT	Houston	15 May 43	3 Aug 43	16 Nov 43	Stk. 1 Apr 74, sold 16 Aug 74
390	CALCATERRA	Houston	28 May 43	16 Aug 43	17 Nov 43	Stk. 2 Jul 73, sold 14 May 74
391	CHAMBERS	Houston	28 May 43	17 Aug 43	22 Nov 43	Stk. 1 Mar 75, sold 24 Sep 75
392	MERRILL	Houston	1 Jul 43	29 Aug 43	27 Nov 43	Stk. 2 Apr 71, sold 30 Sep 74
393	HAVERFIELD	Houston	1 Jul 43	30 Aug 43	29 Nov 43	Stk. 2 Jun 69, sold 15 Dec 71
394	SWENNING	Houston	17 Jul 43	13 Sep 43	1 Dec 43	Stk. 1 Jul 72, sold 17 Jan 74
395	WILLIS	Houston	17 Jul 43	14 Sep 43	10 Dec 43	Stk. 1 Jul 72, sold 17 Aug 73
396	JANSSEN	Houston	4 Aug 43	4 Oct 43	18 Dec 43	Stk. 1 Jul 72, sold 15 Oct 73
397	WILHOITE	Houston	4 Aug 43	5 Oct 43	16 Dec 43	Stk. 2 Jul 69, sold 19 Jul 72
398	COCKRILL	Houston	31 Aug 43	29 Oct 43	24 Dec 43	Stk. 1 Aug 73, sunk as target off NE Florida 19 Nov 74
399	STOCKDALE	Houston	31 Aug 43	30 Oct 43	31 Dec 43	Stk. 1 Jul 72, sunk as target off NE Florida 24 May 74
400	HISSEM	Houston	6 Oct 43	26 Nov 43	13 Jan 44	Stk. 1 Jun 75, sunk as target off S. California 24 Feb 82
401	HOLDER	Houston	6 Oct 43	27 Nov 43	18 Jan 44	Stk. 23 Sep 44, sold 20 Jun 47

Notes: The remaining diesel DEs were built with the other main type of submarine engine produced during the war, a Fairbanks Morse engine. Instead of electric drive, they used small single reduction gears to connect the diesels to the propellor shafts. All ships with this machinery were built with the standard lengthened DE hull developed for the Buckley class, below. They were called the Fairbanks Morse diesel Reversible gear drive (FMR) type.

The Holder (DE-401) was irreparably damaged by German aircraft off Algiers 11 Apr 44. Her stern was used to repair the Menges (DE-320). Plans were made during the war to refit the entire class with 2-5"/38 guns, but the only conversion carried out was Camp (DE-251) after an April 1945 collision. Because of their long endurance, ships of this type was selected after World War II for conversion to radar picket escorts (DER) to act as a seaward extension of the Continental Air Defense system. The first six retained their original high bridge, the later ones received a new, lower one. The Peterson (DE-152) received a major ASW upgrade (SCB-63A) in 1951. In 1951-52, fourteen DEs were loaned to the Coast Guard as weather ships: Newell (WDE-422) and Lowe (WDE-425) 20 Jul 51-1 Jun 54; Pride (WDE-423) 20 Jul 51-1 Jun 54; Falgout (WDE-424) 24 Aug 51-21 May 54; Finch (WDE-428) 24 Aug 51-23 Apr 54; Kretchmer (WDE-429) 20 Jun 51-12 Aug 54; Koiner (WDE-431) 20 Jun 51-14 May 54; Forster (WDE-434) 29 Jun 51-25 May 54; Ramsden (WDE-482) and Richey (WDE-485) 1 Apr 52-28 Jun 54; Vance (WDE-487) and Durant (WDE-489) 15 May 52-16 Jun 54; Lansing (WDE-488) 15 Jun 52-Jun 54; and Chambers (WDE-491) 11 Jun 52-30 Jul 54. The projected re-engining of the Mills (DE-383) in 1954-55 with a British built gas turbine was never accomplished.

Renamings: DE-131 ex Langley 1 Aug 42; DE-241 ex Scott 8 Dec 42; DE-243 ex James R. Ward 26 Jul 43; DE-326 ex Gary 1 Jan 45; DE-327 ex O'Toole 23 Jul 43.

Reclassifications:
Harveson (DE-316) and Joyce (DE-317) to DER 13 Sep 50;
Fessenden (DE-142), Otterstetter (DE-244), Kirkpatrick (DE-318), and Strickland (DE-333) to DER 1 Oct 51;
Pillsbury (DE-133), Savage (DE-386), Haverfield (DE-393), and Wilhoite (DE-397) to DER 2 Sep 54;
Falgout (DE-324), Lowe (DE-325), Koiner (DE-331), Rhodes (DE-384), Calcaterra (DE-390), and Chambers (DE-391) to DER 28 Oct 54;
Camp (DE-251) and Forster (DE-334) to DER 21 Oct 55; to FFR 30 Jun 75;
Sellstrom (DE-255), Brister (DE-327), Finch (DE-328), Kretchmer (DE-329), Price (DE-332), Roy O. Hale (DE-336), Vance (DE-387), Lansing (DE-388), Durant (DE-389), and Hissem (DE-400) to DER 21 Oct 55;
Blair (DE-147), Sturtevant (DE-239), Newell (DE-322), Thomas J. Gary (DE-326), Ramsden (DE-382), and Mills (DE-383) to DER 1 Nov 56.

BUCKLEY (TE) class

Displacement: 1400 tons (standard)
Dimensions: 306'(oa.) x 37'(e) x 13'6"(max)
Armament: 3-3"/50AA 3-21"T; 2-5"/38(DE 217-219, 678-680, 696-698, 700-701); 3-3"(3" types, 1950)

Machinery: 12,000 SHP; G. E. turbines with electric drive, 2 screws
Speed: 24 kts.
Complement: 186

No.		Hull	Laid down	Launched	Commiss'd	Disposition
51	BUCKLEY	Hingham	29 Jun 42	9 Jan 43	30 Apr 43	Stk. 1 Jun 68, sold Jul 69
52	BULL	Hingham	29 Jun 42	3 Feb 43	No	To Britain 19 May 43 as Bentinck, stk. 7 Feb 46
53	CHARLES LAWRENCE	Hingham	1 Aug 42	16 Feb 43	31 May 43	Stk. 1 Sep 64, sold 31 Jan 66
54	DANIEL T. GRIFFIN	Hingham	7 Sep 42	25 Feb 43	9 Jun 43	To Chile 15 Nov 66 as Uribe, stk. 1 Dec 66
55	DONALDSON	Hingham	15 Oct 42	6 Mar 43	No	To Britain 18 Jun 43 as Byard, stk. 7 Feb 46
56	DONNELL	Hingham	27 Nov 42	13 Mar 43	26 Jun 43	Stk. 16 Nov 45, sold 29 Apr 46
57	FOGG	Hingham	4 Dec 42	20 Mar 43	7 Jul 43	Stk. 1 Apr 65, sold 4 Jan 66
58	FORMOE	Hingham	11 Dec 42	27 Mar 43	No	To Britain 15 Jul 43 as Calder, stk. 5 Dec 45
59	FOSS	Hingham	31 Dec 42	10 Apr 43	23 Jul 43	Stk. 1 Nov 65, scrapped
60	GANTNER	Hingham	31 Dec 42	17 Apr 43	23 Jul 43	Stk. 15 Jan 66, to Taiwan as Wen Shan 22 Feb 66
61	THOMAS J. GARY	Hingham	16 Jan 43	1 May 43	No	To Britain 4 Aug 43 as Duckworth, stk. 21 Jan 46
62	GEORGE W. INGRAM	Hingham	6 Feb 43	8 May 43	11 Aug 43	Stk. 1 Jan 67, to Taiwan as Kang Shan Jul 67
63	IRA JEFFERY	Hingham	13 Feb 43	15 May 43	15 Aug 43	Stk. 1 Jun 60, sunk as target Jul 62
64	LAMONS	Hingham	22 Feb 43	22 May 43	No	To Britain 23 Aug 43 as Duff, stk. 17 Sep 45
65	LEE FOX	Hingham	1 Mar 43	29 May 43	30 Aug 43	Stk. 1 Sep 64, sold 31 Jan 66
66	AMESBURY	Hingham	8 Mar 43	5 Jun 43	31 Aug 43	Stk. 1 Jun 60, sunk as target, wreck sold 24 Oct 62
67	ESSINGTON	Hingham	15 Mar 43	19 Jun 43	No	To Britain 7 Sep 43 as Essington, stk. 5 Dec 45
68	BATES	Hingham	29 Mar 43	6 Jun 43	12 Sep 43	Sunk by Japanese suicide plane off Okinawa 25 May 45
69	BLESSMAN	Hingham	22 Mar 43	19 Jun 43	19 Sep 43	Stk. 1 Jun 67, to Taiwan as Chung Shan 3 Jul 67
70	JOSEPH E. CAMPBELL	Hingham	29 Mar 43	26 Jun 43	23 Sep 43	To Chile 15 Nov 66 as Riquelme, stk. 1 Dec 66
71	OSWALD	Hingham	5 Apr 43	30 Jun 43	No	To Britain 29 Sep 43 as Affleck, stk. 17 Sep 45
72	HARMON	Hingham	12 Apr 43	10 Jul 43	No	To Britain 30 Sep 43 as Aylmer, stk. 19 Dec 45
73	McANN	Hingham	19 Apr 43	10 Jul 43	No	To Britain 7 Oct 43 as Balfour, stk. 5 Dec 45
74	EBERT	Hingham	26 Apr 43	17 Jul 43	No	To Britain 13 Oct 43 as Bentley, stk. 19 Dec 45
75	EISELE	Hingham	3 May 43	26 Jul 43	No	To Britain 17 Oct 43 as Bickerton, sunk 22 Aug 44
76	LIDDLE	Hingham	10 May 43	31 Jul 43	No	To Britain 22 Oct 43 as Bligh, stk. 17 Apr 46
77	STRAUB	Hingham	10 May 43	31 Jul 43	No	To Britain 13 Nov 43 as Braithwaite, stk. 21 Jan 46
78	(BULLEN)	Hingham	17 May 43	7 Aug 43	No	To Britain 25 Oct 43, sunk 6 Dec 44
79	(BYRON)	Hingham	24 May 43	14 Aug 43	No	To Britain 30 Oct 43, stk. 3 Jan 46
80	(CONN)	Hingham	2 Jun 43	21 Aug 43	No	To Britain 31 Oct 43, stk. 3 Jan 46
81	(COTTON)	Hingham	2 Jun 43	21 Aug 43	No	To Britain 8 Nov 43, stk. 3 Jan 46
82	(CRANSTOUN)	Hingham	9 Jun 43	28 Aug 43	No	To Britain 13 Nov 43, stk. 7 Feb 46

No.		Hull	Laid down	Launched	Commiss'd	Disposition
83	(CUBITT)	Hingham	9 Jun 43	11 Sep 43	No	To Britain 17 Nov 43, stk. 12 Apr 46
84	(CURZON)	Hingham	23 Jun 43	18 Sep 43	No	To Britain 20 Nov 43, stk. 1 May 46
85	(DAKINS)	Hingham	23 Jun 43	18 Sep 43	No	To Britain 23 Nov 43, stk. 7 Feb 47
86	(DEANE)	Hingham	30 Jun 43	25 Sep 43	No	To Britain 26 Nov 43, stk. 12 Apr 46
87	(EKINS)	Hingham	5 Jul 43	2 Oct 43	No	To Britain 29 Nov 43, stk. 22 Jun 45
88	(FITZROY)	Hingham	24 Aug 43	1 Sep 43	No	To Britain 16 Oct 43, stk. 7 Feb 46
89	(REDMILL)	Hingham	14 Jul 43	2 Oct 43	No	To Britain 30 Nov 43, stk. 7 Feb 47
90	(RETALICK)	Hingham	21 Jul 43	9 Oct 43	No	To Britain 8 Dec 43, stk. 19 Dec 45
91	(REYNOLDS)	Hingham	28 Jul 43	14 Oct 43	No	To Britain 3 Nov 43, stk. 13 Nov 44
92	(RIOU)	Hingham	4 Aug 43	23 Oct 43	No	To Britain 14 Dec 43, stk. 28 Mar 46
93	(RUTHERFORD)	Hingham	4 Aug 43	23 Oct 43	No	To Britain 16 Dec 43, stk. 19 Dec 45
94	(COSBY)	Hingham	11 Aug 43	30 Oct 43	No	To Britain 20 Dec 43, stk. 13 Nov 46
95	(ROWLEY)	Hingham	18 Aug 43	30 Oct 43	No	To Britain 22 Dec 43, stk. 8 Jan 46
96	(RUPERT)	Hingham	25 Aug 43	31 Oct 43	No	To Britain 24 Dec 43, stk. 17 Apr 46
97	(STOCKHAM)	Hingham	25 Aug 43	31 Oct 43	No	To Britain 28 Dec 43, stk. 12 Mar 46
98	(SEYMOUR)	Hingham	1 Sep 43	1 Nov 43	No	To Britain 23 Dec 43, stk. 25 Feb 46
153	REUBEN JAMES	Norfolk	7 Sep 42	6 Feb 43	1 Apr 43	Stk. 30 Jun 68, sunk as target 1 Mar 71
154	SIMS	Norfolk	7 Sep 42	6 Feb 43	24 Apr 43	Stk. 1 Jun 60, sold 14 Apr 61
155	HOPPING	Norfolk	15 Dec 42	10 Mar 43	21 May 43	Stk. 1 Sep 64, sold 15 Aug 66
156	REEVES	Norfolk	7 Feb 43	22 Apr 43	9 Jun 43	Stk. 1 Jun 60, to Ecuador as power hulk Jul 61
157	FECHTELER	Norfolk	7 Feb 43	22 Apr 43	1 Jul 43	Sunk by U-967 N of Oran, Algeria, 5 May 44
158	CHASE	Norfolk	16 Mar 43	24 Apr 43	18 Jul 43	Stk. 7 Feb 46, sold 13 Nov 46
159	LANING	Norfolk	23 Apr 43	4 Jul 43	1 Aug 43	Stk. 1 Mar 75, sold 30 Sep 75
160	LOY	Norfolk	23 Apr 43	4 Jul 43	12 Sep 43	Stk. 1 Sep 64, sold 15 Aug 66
161	BARBER	Norfolk	27 Apr 43	20 May 43	10 Oct 43	Stk. 27 Nov 68, to Mexico as Coahuila Dec 69
198	LOVELACE	Norfolk	22 May 43	4 Jul 43	7 Nov 43	Stk. 1 Jul 67, sunk as target off S. California 25 Apr 68
199	MANNING	Charleston	15 Feb 43	1 Jun 43	1 Oct 43	Stk. 31 Jul 68, sold 27 Oct 69
200	NEUENDORF	Charleston	15 Feb 43	1 Jun 43	18 Oct 43	Stk. 1 Jul 67, sunk as target 30 Nov 67
201	JAMES E. CRAIG	Charleston	15 Apr 43	22 Jul 43	1 Nov 43	Stk. 30 Jun 68, sunk as target Feb 69
202	EICHENBERGER	Charleston	15 Apr 43	22 Jul 43	17 Nov 43	Stk. 1 Dec 72, sold 27 Nov 73
203	THOMASON	Charleston	5 Jun 43	23 Aug 43	10 Dec 43	Stk. 30 Jun 68, sold 30 Jun 69
204	JORDAN	Charleston	5 Jun 43	23 Aug 43	17 Dec 43	Stk. 8 Jan 46, scrapped 1947
205	NEWMAN	Charleston	8 Jun 43	9 Aug 43	26 Nov 43	Stk. 1 Sep 64, sold 15 Aug 66
206	LIDDLE	Charleston	8 Jun 43	9 Aug 43	6 Dec 43	Stk. 5 Apr 67, sold 25 Jan 68
207	KEPHART	Charleston	12 May 43	6 Sep 43	7 Jan 44	Stk. 1 May 67, to S. Korea as Kyong Puk 23 Jul 67
208	COFER	Charleston	12 May 43	6 Sep 43	19 Jan 44	Stk. 1 Apr 66, sold 5 Mar 68
209	LLOYD	Charleston	26 Jul 43	23 Oct 43	11 Feb 44	Stk. 1 Jun 66, sold 5 Mar 68
210	OTTER	Charleston	26 Jul 43	23 Oct 43	21 Feb 44	Stk. 1 Nov 69, sunk as target off Puerto Rico 10 Jul 70
211	HUBBARD	Charleston	11 Aug 43	11 Nov 43	6 Mar 44	Stk. 1 May 66, sold 1 Jul 68

The *Buckley*-class escort vessel *England* (DE-635) off San Francisco on 9 February 1944. (NARA 19-N-60938)

The *John C. Butler*-class escort vessel *Walter C. Wann* (DE-412) in 1944. (NH 90602)

No.		Hull	Laid down	Launched	Commiss'd	Disposition
212	HAYTER	Charleston	11 Aug 43	11 Nov 43	16 Mar 44	Stk. 1 Dec 66, to S. Korea as Jon Nam 23 Jul 67
213	WILLIAM T. POWELL	Charleston	26 Aug 43	27 Nov 43	28 Mar 44	Stk. 1 Nov 65, sold 3 Oct 66
214	SCOTT	Philadelphia	1 Jan 43	3 Apr 43	20 Jul 43	Stk. 1 Jul 65, sold 20 Jan 67
215	BURKE	Philadelphia	1 Jan 43	3 Apr 43	20 Aug 43	Stk. 1 Jun 68, to Colombia as Almirante Brion Jul 68
216	ENRIGHT	Philadelphia	22 Feb 43	29 May 43	21 Sep 43	To Ecuador 14 Jul 67 as 25 de Julio, stk. 31 Mar 78
217	COOLBAUGH	Philadelphia	22 Feb 43	29 May 43	15 Oct 43	Stk. 1 Jul 72, sold 17 Aug 73
218	DARBY	Philadelphia	22 Feb 43	29 May 43	15 Nov 43	Stk. 23 Sep 68, sunk as target 24 May 70
219	J. DOUGLAS BLACKWOOD	Philadelphia	22 Feb 43	29 May 43	15 Dec 43	Stk. 30 Jan 70, sunk as target 20 Jul 70
220	FRANCIS M. ROBINSON	Philadelphia	22 Feb 43	29 May 43	15 Jan 44	Stk. 1 Jul 72, sold 12 Jul 73
221	SOLAR	Philadelphia	22 Feb 43	29 May 43	15 Feb 44	Sunk by explosion off Earle, N. J., 30 Apr 46
222	FOWLER	Philadelphia	5 Apr 43	3 Jul 43	15 Mar 44	Stk. 1 Jul 65, sold 29 Dec 66
223	SPANGENBERG	Philadelphia	5 Apr 43	3 Jul 43	15 Apr 44	Stk. 1 Nov 65, sold 3 Oct 66
563	(SPRAGGE)	Hingham	15 Sep 43	16 Oct 43	No	To Britain 14 Jan 44, stk. 23 Dec 47
564	(STAYNER)	Hingham	22 Sep 43	6 Nov 43	No	To Britain 30 Dec 43, stk. 3 Jan 46
565	(THORNBOROUGH)	Hingham	22 Sep 43	13 Nov 43	No	To Britain 31 Dec 43, stk. 7 Feb 47
566	(TROLLOPE)	Hingham	29 Sep 43	20 Nov 43	No	To Britain 10 Jan 44, sold 9 Jan 47
567	(TYLER)	Hingham	6 Oct 43	20 Nov 43	No	To Britain 14 Jan 44, stk. 8 Jan 46
568	(TORRINGTON)	Hingham	22 Sep 43	27 Nov 43	No	To Britain 18 Jan 44, stk. 15 Oct 46
569	(NARBROUGH)	Hingham	6 Oct 43	27 Nov 43	No	To Britain 21 Jan 44, stk. 17 Apr 46
570	(WALDEGRAVE)	Hingham	16 Oct 43	4 Dec 43	No	To Britain 25 Jan 44, stk. 21 Jan 46
571	(WHITAKER)	Hingham	20 Oct 43	12 Dec 43	No	To Britain 28 Jan 44, sold 9 Jan 47
572	(HOLMES)	Hingham	27 Oct 43	18 Dec 43	No	To Britain 31 Jan 44, stk. 7 Feb 46
573	(HARGOOD)	Hingham	27 Oct 43	18 Dec 43	No	To Britain 7 Feb 44, stk. 12 Apr 46
574	(HOTHAM)	Hingham	5 Nov 43	21 Dec 43	No	To Britain 8 Feb 44, stk. 14 May 52
575	AHRENS	Hingham	5 Nov 43	21 Dec 43	12 Feb 44	Stk. 1 Apr 65, sold 20 Jan 67
576	BARR	Hingham	5 Nov 43	28 Dec 43	15 Feb 44	Stk. 1 Jun 60, sunk as target off Puerto Rico 26 Mar 63
577	ALEXANDER J. LUKE	Hingham	5 Nov 43	28 Dec 43	19 Feb 44	Stk. 1 May 70, sunk as target off Newport, R.I. 22 Oct 70
578	ROBERT I. PAINE	Hingham	5 Nov 43	30 Dec 43	26 Feb 44	Stk. 1 Jun 68, sold 18 Jul 69
633	FOREMAN	Beth-SF	9 Mar 43	1 Aug 43	22 Oct 43	Stk. 1 Apr 65, sold
634	WHITEHURST	Beth-SF	21 Mar 43	5 Sep 43	19 Nov 43	Stk. 12 Jul 69, sunk as target 28 Apr 71
635	ENGLAND	Beth-SF	4 Apr 43	26 Sep 43	10 Dec 43	Stk. 1 Nov 45, sold 26 Nov 46
636	WITTER	Beth-SF	28 Apr 43	17 Oct 43	29 Dec 43	Stk. 16 Nov 45, sold 2 Dec 46
637	BOWERS	Beth-SF	28 May 43	31 Oct 43	27 Jan 44	To Philippines 21 Apr 61 as Rajah Soliman, stk. 1 May 61
638	WILLMARTH	Beth-SF	25 Jun 43	21 Nov 43	13 Mar 44	Stk. 1 Dec 66, sold 1 Jul 68
639	GENDREAU	Beth-SF	1 Aug 43	12 Dec 43	17 Mar 44	Stk. 1 Dec 72, sold 11 Sep 73
640	FIEBERLING	Beth-SF	19 Mar 44	2 Apr 44	11 Apr 44	Stk. 1 Mar 72, sold 20 Nov 72
641	WILLIAM C. COLE	Beth-SF	5 Sep 43	29 Dec 43	12 May 44	Stk. 1 Mar 72, sold 20 Nov 72
642	PAUL G. BAKER	Beth-SF	26 Sep 43	12 Mar 44	25 May 44	Stk. 1 Dec 69, sold Oct 70
643	DAMON M. CUMMINGS	Beth-SF	17 Oct 43	18 Apr 44	29 Jun 44	Stk. 1 Mar 72, sold 18 May 73

No.		Hull	Laid down	Launched	Commiss'd	Disposition
644	VAMMEN	Beth-SF	1 Aug 43	21 May 44	27 Jul 44	Stk. 12 Jul 69, sunk as target 18 Feb 71
665	JENKS	Dravo, Pittsburgh	12 May 43	11 Sep 43	19 Jan 44	Stk. 1 Feb 66, sold 5 Mar 68
666	DURIK	Dravo, Pittsburgh	22 Jun 43	9 Oct 43	24 Mar 44	Stk. 1 Jun 65, sold 30 Jan 67
667	WISEMAN	Dravo, Pittsburgh	26 Jul 43	6 Nov 43	4 Apr 44	Stk. 15 Apr 73, sold 29 Apr 74
668	YOKES	Orange	22 Aug 43	27 Nov 43	18 Dec 44	Stk. 1 Apr 64, sold 23 Mar 65
669	PAVLIC	Orange	21 Sep 43	18 Dec 43	29 Dec 44	Stk. 1 Apr 67, sold 1 Jul 68
670	ODUM	Orange	15 Oct 43	19 Jan 44	12 Jan 45	To Chile 15 Nov 66 as Serrano, stk. 1 Dec 66
671	JACK C. ROBINSON	Orange	10 Nov 43	8 Jan 44	2 Feb 45	To Chile 15 Nov 66 as Orella, stk. 1 Dec 66
672	BASSETT	Orange	28 Nov 43	15 Jan 44	23 Feb 45	Stk. 1 May 67, to Colombia as Almirante Tono 6 Sep 68
673	JOHN P. GRAY	Orange	18 Dec 43	18 Mar 44	15 Mar 45	Stk. 1 Mar 67, sold 3 Sep 68
675	WEBER	Quincy	22 Feb 43	1 May 43	30 Jun 43	Stk. 1 Jun 60, sunk as target 15 Jul 62
676	SCHMITT	Quincy	22 Feb 43	29 May 43	24 Jul 43	Stk. 1 May 67, to Taiwan as Lung Shan 18 Feb 69
677	FRAMENT	Quincy	1 May 43	28 Jun 43	15 Aug 43	Stk. 1 Jun 60, to Ecuador as power hulk Jul 61
678	HARMON	Quincy	31 May 43	25 Jul 43	31 Aug 43	Stk. 1 Aug 65, sold 30 Jan 67
679	GREENWOOD	Quincy	29 Jun 43	21 Aug 43	25 Sep 43	Stk. 20 Feb 67, sold 6 Sep 67
680	LOESER	Quincy	27 Jul 43	11 Sep 43	10 Oct 43	Stk. 23 Sep 68, sunk as target
681	GILLETTE	Quincy	24 Aug 43	25 Sep 43	27 Oct 43	Stk. 1 Dec 72, sold 11 Sep 73
682	UNDERHILL	Quincy	16 Sep 43	15 Oct 43	15 Nov 43	Sunk by Japanese Kaiten torpedo off Luzon 24 Jul 45
683	HENRY R. KENYON	Quincy	29 Sep 43	30 Oct 43	30 Nov 43	Stk. 1 Dec 69, sold 22 Oct 70
693	BULL	Defoe	14 Dec 42	25 Mar 43	12 Aug 43	Stk. 15 Jun 66, to Taiwan as Lu Shan 12 Jul 66
694	BUNCH	Defoe	22 Feb 43	29 May 43	21 Aug 43	Stk. 1 Apr 64, scrapped 1965
695	RICH	Defoe	27 Mar 43	22 Jun 43	1 Oct 43	Mined off Quineville, Fr., 8 Jun 44
696	SPANGLER	Defoe	28 Apr 43	15 Jul 43	31 Oct 43	Stk. 1 Mar 72, sold 20 Nov 72
697	GEORGE	Defoe	22 May 43	14 Aug 43	20 Nov 43	Stk. 1 Nov 69, sold 12 Oct 70
698	RABY	Defoe	7 Jun 43	4 Sep 43	7 Dec 43	Stk. 1 Jun 68, sold 18 Jul 69
699	MARSH	Defoe	23 Jun 43	25 Sep 43	12 Jan 44	Stk. 15 Apr 73, sold 20 Feb 74
700	CURRIER	Defoe	21 Jul 43	14 Oct 43	1 Feb 44	Stk. 1 Dec 66, sunk as target off S. California 11 Jul 67
701	OSMUS	Defoe	17 Aug 43	4 Nov 43	23 Feb 44	Stk. 1 Dec 72, sold 27 Nov 73
702	EARL V. JOHNSON	Defoe	7 Sep 43	24 Nov 43	18 Mar 44	Stk. 1 May 67, sold 3 Sep 68
703	HOLTON	Defoe	28 Sep 43	15 Dec 43	1 May 44	Stk. 1 Nov 72, sold 30 May 74
704	CRONIN	Defoe	19 Oct 43	5 Jan 44	5 May 44	Stk. 1 Jun 70, sunk as target off NE Florida 16 Dec 71
705	FRYBARGER	Defoe	8 Nov 43	25 Jan 44	18 May 44	Stk. 1 Dec 72, sold 27 Nov 73
789	TATUM	Orange	22 Apr 43	7 Aug 43	22 Nov 43	Stk. 1 Jun 60, sold 8 May 61
790	BORUM	Orange	28 Apr 43	14 Aug 43	30 Nov 43	Stk. 1 Aug 65, sold 1966
791	MALOY	Orange	10 May 43	18 Aug 43	13 Dec 43	Stk. 1 Jun 65, sold 11 Mar 66
792	HAINES	Orange	17 May 43	26 Aug 43	27 Dec 43	Stk. 1 Jun 60, sold 3 May 61
793	RUNELS	Orange	7 Jun 43	4 Sep 43	3 Jan 44	Stk. 1 Jun 60, sold 10 Jul 61
794	HOLLIS	Orange	5 Jul 43	11 Sep 43	24 Jan 44	Stk. 15 Sep 74, sold 1 Jul 75
795	GUNASON	Orange	9 Aug 43	16 Oct 43	1 Feb 44	Stk. 1 Jul 73, sunk as target 28 Jul 74
796	MAJOR	Orange	16 Aug 43	23 Oct 43	12 Feb 44	Stk. 1 Dec 72, sold 27 Nov 73
797	WEEDEN	Orange	18 Aug 43	27 Oct 43	19 Feb 44	Stk. 30 Jun 68, sold 27 Oct 69
798	VARIAN	Orange	27 Aug 43	6 Nov 43	29 Feb 44	Stk. 1 Dec 72, sold 2 Jan 74
799	SCROGGINS	Orange	4 Sep 43	6 Nov 43	30 Mar 44	Stk. 1 Jul 65, sold 5 Apr 67
800	JACK W. WILKE	Orange	18 Oct 43	18 Dec 43	7 Mar 44	Stk. 1 Aug 72, sold 1 Feb 74

Notes: When the DE program was expanded from 50 to 300 ships in January 1942, the Navy realized that there would not be enough diesel engines for all the ships and turned to General Electric to develop a new turbo-electric steam plant. This plant was bulkier than the geared turbine plant in the original design and required a longer hull. To facilitate production, the lengthened 306-foot hull was adopted as the standard hull for all DEs, including the later diesel-propelled ones of the Cannon and Edsall classes, above. The new design, called the Turbo-Electric drive (TE) type, allowed a return to the 12,000 SHP and 24 knots of the original design. Bethlehem Shipbuilding at Quincy, Mass., prepared the detailed plans.

Contracts for some ships were reallocated before construction as follows: DE 51-98 from "Bethlehem Steel Co." 10 Feb 42; DE-198 and DE 214-23 from Newport News 3 Mar 42 and from its planned subsidiary, James River Shipbuilding, 8 Jun 42; DE 199-213 from Newport News 3 Mar 42, from James River Shipbuilding 8 Jun 42, and from the Norfolk Navy Yard 7 Aug 42; DE 665-67 from the Charleston Navy Yard 2 Nov 42; DE 668-73 from the Charleston Navy Yard 2 Nov 42 and from Dravo, Pittsburgh 13 Jun 44; DE 675-83 from the Charleston Navy Yard 29 Oct 42; DE 693-98 from the Norfolk Navy Yard 9 Oct 42; and DE 699-705 from the Philadelphia Navy Yard 9 Oct 42.

During the war, plans were developed to refit the entire class with 2-5"/38 guns, but only eleven ships (above) were converted. By mid-1943 it was clear that there would be more DEs than were necessary to meet ASW requirements, and alternative uses were sought for some of the ships. In May 1944 the Navy decided to convert 50 TE-type DEs to fast transports (APDs), including six (DE-668-673) still under construction. The ships were reclassified as they became available for conversion, and ultimately only 43 TEs were converted. The numbers APD 64, 67-68, and 82-83 were reserved for DE 214, 665-666, and 790-791 which were later selected for conversion to DERs instead; and the conversions of DE 635-636 to APD-41 and 58 were begun but not completed. By May 1945, twenty TE-type DEs were scheduled for conversion to radar picket ships, presumably to provide fighter cover for slow amphibious groups. Only seven were completed, and the projected conversions of DE 204, 210, 214, 220-222, 665-666, 790-791, and 798-800 were dropped on 4 Aug 45. The wartime conversions were reclassified DER in 1949 but they did not meet the requirements of the postwar DER type and reverted to DEs in 1954. The following were irreparably damaged in British service: DE-71 (26 Dec 44), DE-85 (25 Dec 44), DE-87 (16 Apr 45), DE-89 (27 Apr 45), DE-91 (10 Jun 44), DE-566 (6 Jul 44), and DE-571 (1 Nov 44). The hulk of Solar (DE-221) was scuttled 9 Jun 46 off New York.

This class was favored over other DE types for continued service after World War II, in part because commanders in the Pacific had preferred its open bridge to the covered bridges in the later TEV and WGT types. Four received major ASW upgrades in 1947: Coolbaugh (DE-217), Darby (DE-218), Greenwood (DE-679) and Currier (DE-700). Another, Vammen (DE-644), received a SCB-63A ASW refit in 1951. The Foss (DE-59), Whitehurst (DE-634), Wiseman (DE-667), and Marsh (DE-699) were fitted out in 1950 as electric power supply vessels to support amphibious operatons. Three other ships received additional communications gear and were reclassified Destroyer Escorts (Control), DEC, in 1949-50.
Renamings: DE-63 ex Jeffery 29 Jul 43; DE-70 ex Campbell 23 Jun 43; DE-219 ex James D. Blackwood 3 Apr 43. The original British name of DE-94 was Reeves.
Reclassifications:
    Buckley (DE-51) to DER 26 Apr 49; DE 29 Sep 54;
    Charles Lawrence (DE-53), Daniel T. Griffin (DE-54), and Loy (DE-160) to APD 37-38 and 56 23 Oct 44;
    Donnell (DE-56) to IX-182 10 Jul 44;
    Fogg (DE-57), Reuben James (DE-153), William T. Powell (DE-213), Spangenberg (DE-223), Alexander J. Luke (DE-577), and Robert I. Paine (DE-578) to DER 18 Mar 49; DE 28 Oct 54;
    Gantner (DE-60), George W. Ingram (DE-62), Ira Jeffery (DE-63), Lee Fox (DE-65), and Amesbury (DE-66) to APD 42-46 23 Feb 45;
    Bates (DE-68), Blessman (DE-69), Barr (DE-576), Bull (DE-693), and Bunch (DE-694) to APD 47-48, 39, and 78-79 31 Jul 44;
    Joseph E. Campbell (DE-70) and Chase (DE-158) to APD 49 and 54 24 Nov 44;
    Sims (DE-154), Hopping (DE-155), and Reeves (DE-156) to APD 50-52 25 Sep 44;
    Laning (DE-159) to APD-55 24 Nov 44; LPR-55 1 Jan 69;
    Barber (DE-161) to APD-57 23 Oct 44; LPR-57 1 Jan 69;
    Newman (DE-205), Liddle (DE-206), Kephart (DE-207), Cofer (DE-208), and Lloyd (DE-209) to APD 59-63 5 Jul 44;
    Hubbard (DE-211) and Hayter (DE-212) to APD 53 and 80 1 Jun 45;
    Scott (DE-214) and Jenks (DE-665) planned as APD 64 and 67, not converted or reclassified, conversion cancelled 28 Aug 45;
    Burke (DE-215), Enright (DE-216), Schmitt (DE-676), and Runels (DE-793) to APD 65-66, 76, and 85 24 Jan 45;
    Durik (DE-666), Borum (DE-790), and Maloy (DE-791) planned as APD 68 and 82-83, not converted or reclassified, DE 684-685 and 709 designated 9 Jun 45 for conversion to APD 137-139 instead.
    Yokes (DE-668), Pavlic (DE-669), Odum (DE-670), Jack C. Robinson (DE-671), Bassett (DE-672), and John P. Gray (DE-673) to APD 69-74 27 Jun 44;
    England (DE-635) to APD-41 10 Jul 45;
    Witter (DE-636) to APD-58 15 Aug 45;
    Bowers (DE-637) to APD-40 25 Jun 45;
    Weber (DE-675), Frament (DE-677), Tatum (DE-789), and Haines (DE-792) to APD-75, 77, 81, and 84 15 Dec 44;
    Raby (DE-698) to DEC-698 6 Oct 49; DE-698 27 Dec 57;
    Cronin (DE-704) and Frybarger (DE-705) to DEC 13 Sep 50; DE 27 Dec 57;
    Hollis (DE-794) to APD-86 24 Jan 45; LPR-86, 1 Jan 69.

RUDDEROW (TEV) class

Displacement: 1450 tons (standard)
Dimensions: 306'(oa.) x 36'10"(e) x 13'9"(max)
Armament: 2-5"/38AA 3-21"T; 2-5"AA (1950); 1-5"AA (APD
  conversions)

Machinery: 12,000 SHP; G. E. turbines
  with electric drive, 2 screws
Speed: 24 kts.
Complement: 186

No.		Hull	Laid down	Launched	Commiss'd	Disposition
224	RUDDEROW	Philadelphia	15 Jul 43	14 Oct 43	15 May 44	Stk. 1 Nov 69, sold Oct 70
225	DAY	Philadelphia	15 Jul 43	14 Oct 43	10 Jun 44	Stk. 30 Jun 68, sunk as target off California Mar 69
226	CROSLEY	Philadelphia	16 Oct 43	12 Feb 44	22 Oct 44	Stk. 1 Jun 60, to Ecuador as power hulk Jul 61
227	CREAD	Philadelphia	16 Oct 43	12 Feb 44	29 Jul 44	Stk. 1 Jun 60, sold 21 Feb 61
228	RUCHAMKIN	Philadelphia	14 Feb 44	15 Jun 44	16 Sep 45	To Colombia 24 Nov 69 as Cordoba, stk. 31 Oct 77
229	KIRWIN	Philadelphia	14 Feb 44	16 Jun 44	4 Nov 45	Stk. 15 Sep 74, sold 1 Jul 75
230	CHAFFEE	Charleston	26 Aug 43	27 Nov 43	9 May 44	Stk. 17 Apr 46, sold 29 Jun 48
231	HODGES	Charleston	9 Sep 43	9 Dec 43	27 May 44	Stk. 1 Dec 72, sold 12 Sep 73
232	KINZER	Charleston	9 Sep 43	9 Dec 43	1 Nov 44	Stk. 1 Mar 65, to Taiwan as Yu Shan 21 Apr 65
233	REGISTER	Charleston	27 Oct 43	20 Jan 44	11 Jan 45	Stk. 1 Sep 66, to Taiwan as Tai Shan Oct 66
234	BROCK	Charleston	27 Oct 43	20 Jan 44	9 Feb 45	Stk. 1 Jun 60, to Colombia as power hulk Jan 62
235	JOHN Q. ROBERTS	Charleston	15 Nov 43	11 Feb 44	8 Mar 45	Stk. 1 Jun 60, sold 19 Dec 61
236	WILLIAM M. HOBBY	Charleston	15 Nov 43	11 Feb 44	4 Apr 45	Stk. 1 May 67, to S. Korea as Chi Ju 23 Jul 67
237	RAY K. EDWARDS	Charleston	1 Dec 43	19 Feb 44	11 Jun 45	Stk. 1 Jun 60, sold 7 Jul 61
281	ARTHUR L. BRISTOL	Charleston	1 Dec 43	19 Feb 44	25 Jun 45	Stk. 1 Apr 64, sold Aug 65
282	TRUXTUN	Charleston	13 Dec 43	9 Mar 44	9 Jul 45	Stk. 15 Jan 66, to Taiwan as Fu Shan 22 Feb 66
283	UPHAM	Charleston	13 Dec 43	9 Mar 44	23 Jul 45	Stk. 1 Jun 60, to Colombia as power hulk Jan 62
284	VOGELGESANG	Charleston	No	No	No	Cancelled 10 Jun 44
285	WEEKS	Charleston	No	No	No	Cancelled 10 Jun 44
286	SUTTON	Hingham	No	No	No	Cancelled 12 Mar 44
287	WILLIAM M. WOOD	Hingham	No	No	No	Cancelled 12 Mar 44
288	WILLIAM R. RUSH	Hingham	No	No	No	Cancelled 12 Mar 44
289	Unnamed	Hingham	No	No	No	Cancelled 12 Mar 44
290	WILLIAMS	Hingham	No	No	No	Cancelled 12 Mar 44
291 -300	Unnamed	Hingham	No	No	No	Cancelled 12 Mar 44
579	RILEY	Hingham	20 Oct 43	29 Dec 43	13 Mar 44	To Taiwan 10 Jul 68 as Tai Yuan, stk. 25 Jan 74
580	LESLIE L. B. KNOX	Hingham	7 Nov 43	8 Jan 44	22 Mar 44	Stk. 15 Jan 72, sold 13 Jun 73
581	McNULTY	Hingham	17 Nov 43	8 Jan 44	31 Mar 44	Stk. 1 Mar 72, sunk as target off S. California 16 Nov 72
582	MERTIVIER	Hingham	24 Nov 43	12 Jan 44	7 Apr 44	Stk. 30 Jun 68, sold Jun 69
583	GEORGE A. JOHNSON	Hingham	24 Nov 43	12 Jan 44	15 Apr 44	Stk. 1 Nov 65, sold 19 Sep 66
584	CHARLES J. KIMMEL	Hingham	1 Dec 43	15 Jan 44	20 Apr 44	Stk. 30 Jun 68, sunk as target off S. California 13 Nov 69
585	DANIEL A. JOY	Hingham	1 Dec 43	15 Jan 44	28 Apr 44	Stk. 1 May 65, sold 11 Mar 66
586	LOUGH	Hingham	8 Dec 43	22 Jan 44	2 May 44	Stk. 1 Nov 69, sold Oct 70
587	THOMAS F. NICKEL	Hingham	15 Dec 43	22 Jan 44	9 Jun 44	Stk. 1 Dec 72, sold 6 Sep 73
588	PEIFFER	Hingham	21 Dec 43	26 Jan 44	15 Jun 44	Stk. 1 Dec 66, sunk as target off S. California 16 May 67
589	TINSMAN	Hingham	21 Dec 43	29 Jan 44	26 Jun 44	Stk. 15 May 72, sold 6 Sep 73
590	RINGNESS	Hingham	23 Dec 43	5 Feb 44	25 Oct 44	Stk. 15 Sep 74, sold 1 Jul 75
591	KNUDSON	Hingham	23 Dec 43	5 Feb 44	25 Nov 44	Stk. 15 Jul 72, sold 6 Dec 74
592	REDNOUR	Hingham	30 Dec 43	12 Feb 44	30 Dec 44	Stk. 1 Mar 67, to Mexico as Chihuahua Dec 69

No.		Hull	Laid down	Launched	Commiss'd	Disposition
593	TOLLBERG	Hingham	30 Dec 43	12 Feb 44	31 Jan 45	Stk. 1 Nov 64, to Colombia as Almirante Padilla 14 Aug 65
594	WILLIAM J. PATTISON	Hingham	4 Jan 44	15 Feb 44	27 Feb 45	Stk. 1 Jun 60, sold 18 Jan 62
595	MYERS	Hingham	15 Jan 44	15 Feb 44	26 Mar 45	Stk. 1 Jun 60, to Colombia as power hulk Jan 62
596	WALTER B. COBB	Hingham	15 Jan 44	23 Feb 44	25 Apr 45	Stk. 15 Jan 66, to Taiwan 22 Feb 66, sank enroute
597	EARLE B. HALL	Hingham	19 Jan 44	1 Mar 44	15 May 45	Stk. 1 Feb 65, sold 28 Jan 66
598	HARRY L. CORL	Hingham	19 Jan 44	1 Mar 44	5 Jun 45	Stk. 15 Jan 66, to S. Korea as Ah San 1 Jun 66
599	BELET	Hingham	26 Jan 44	3 Mar 44	15 Jun 45	Stk. 12 Dec 63, to Mexico as California 12 Dec 63
600	JULIUS A. RAVEN	Hingham	26 Jan 44	3 Mar 44	28 Jun 45	Stk. 15 Jan 66, to S. Korea as Ung Po 1 Jun 66
601	WALSH	Hingham	27 Feb 45	28 Apr 45	11 Jul 45	Stk. 1 May 66, sold 1 Jul 68
602	HUNTER MARSHALL	Hingham	9 Mar 45	5 May 45	17 Jul 45	Stk. 1 Jun 60, to Ecuador as power hulk Jul 61
603	EARHART	Hingham	20 Mar 45	12 May 45	26 Jul 45	Stk. 12 Dec 63, to Mexico as Papaloapan 12 Dec 63
604	WALTER S. GORKA	Hingham	3 Apr 45	26 May 45	7 Aug 45	Stk. 1 Jun 60, to Ecuador as power hulk Aug 61
605	ROGERS BLOOD	Hingham	12 Apr 45	2 Jun 45	22 Aug 45	Stk. 1 Jun 60, sold 19 Dec 61
606	FRANCOVICH	Hingham	19 Apr 45	5 Jun 45	6 Sep 45	Stk. 1 Apr 64, sold May 65
607 -616	Unnamed	Hingham	No	No	No	Cancelled 10 Jun 44
617 -632	Unnamed	Hingham	No	No	No	Cancelled 12 Mar 44
645 -646	Unnamed	Hingham	No	No	No	Cancelled 12 Mar 44
647 -664	Unnamed	Hingham	No	No	No	Cancelled 2 Oct 43
674	JOSEPH M. AUMAN	Orange	8 Nov 43	5 Feb 44	25 Apr 45	Stk. 12 Dec 63, to Mexico as Tehuantepec 12 Dec 63
684	DE LONG	Quincy	19 Oct 43	23 Nov 43	31 Dec 43	Stk. 8 Aug 69, sunk as target off Puerto Rico 19 Feb 70
685	COATES	Quincy	8 Nov 43	12 Dec 43	24 Jan 44	Stk. 30 Jan 70, sunk as target 19 Sep 71
686	EUGENE E. ELMORE	Quincy	27 Nov 43	23 Dec 43	4 Feb 44	Stk. 30 Jun 68, sold Jun 69
687	KLINE	Quincy	27 May 44	27 Jun 44	18 Oct 44	Stk. 15 Jan 66, to Taiwan as Shou Shan 22 Feb 66
688	RAYMON W. HERNDON	Quincy	12 Jun 44	15 Jul 44	3 Nov 44	Stk. 1 Sep 66, to Taiwan as Heng Shan Oct 66
689	SCRIBNER	Quincy	29 Jun 44	1 Aug 44	20 Nov 44	Stk. 1 Aug 66, sold 6 Sep 67
690	DIACHENKO	Quincy	18 Jul 44	15 Aug 44	8 Dec 44	Stk. 15 Sep 74, sold 1 Jul 75
691	HORACE A. BASS	Quincy	3 Aug 44	12 Sep 44	21 Dec 44	Stk. 15 Sep 74, sold 1 Jul 75
692	WANTUCK	Quincy	17 Aug 44	25 Sep 44	30 Dec 44	Stk. 4 Mar 58, sold 27 Oct 58
706	HOLT	Defoe	28 Nov 43	15 Feb 44	9 Jun 44	To S. Korea 19 Jun 63 as Chung Nam, stk. 15 Nov 74
707	JOBB	Defoe	20 Dec 43	4 Mar 44	4 Jul 44	Stk. 1 Nov 69, sold Oct 70
708	PARLE	Defoe	8 Jan 44	25 Mar 44	29 Jul 44	Stk. 1 Jul 70, sunk as target off NE Florida 27 Oct 70
709	BRAY	Defoe	27 Jan 44	15 Apr 44	4 Sep 44	Stk. 1 Jun 60, sunk as target 23 Mar 63
710	GOSSELIN	Defoe	17 Feb 44	4 May 44	31 Dec 44	Stk. 1 Apr 64, sold 23 Mar 65
711	BEGOR	Defoe	6 Mar 44	25 May 44	14 Mar 45	Stk. 15 May 75, sold 6 Dec 76
712	CAVALLARO	Defoe	28 Mar 44	15 Jun 44	13 Mar 45	To S. Korea 15 Oct 59 as Kyong Nam, stk. 15 Nov 74
713	DONALD W. WOLF	Defoe	17 Apr 44	22 Jul 44	14 Apr 45	Stk. 1 Mar 65, to Taiwan as Hua Shan 3 Apr 65
714	COOK	Defoe	7 May 44	26 Aug 44	25 Apr 45	Stk. 15 Nov 69, sold 6 Jul 70
715	WALTER X. YOUNG	Defoe	27 May 44	30 Sep 44	1 May 45	Stk. 1 May 62, sunk as target off S. California 11 Apr 67
716	BALDUCK	Defoe	17 Jun 44	27 Oct 44	7 May 45	Stk. 15 Jul 75, sold 6 Dec 76

No.		Hull	Laid down	Launched	Commiss'd	Disposition
717	BURDO	Defoe	26 Jul 44	25 Nov 44	2 Jun 45	Stk. 1 Apr 66, sold 30 Mar 67
718	KLEINSMITH	Defoe	30 Aug 44	27 Jan 45	12 Jun 45	To Taiwan 16 May 60 as Tien Shan
719	WEISS	Defoe	4 Oct 44	17 Feb 45	7 Jul 45	Stk. 15 Sep 74, sold 1 Jul 75
720	CARPELLOTTI	Defoe	31 Oct 44	10 Mar 45	30 Jul 45	Stk. 1 Dec 59, sold 31 May 60
721	DON O. WOODS	Orange	1 Dec 43	19 Feb 44	28 May 45	Stk. 12 Dec 63, to Mexico as Usumacinta 12 Dec 63
722	BEVERLY W. REID	Orange	5 Jan 44	4 Mar 44	25 Jun 45	Stk. 15 Sep 74, sold 1 Jul 75
723	WALTER X. YOUNG	Dravo, Pittsburgh	No	No	No	Cancelled 12 Mar 44
724	Unnamed	Dravo, Pittsburgh,	No	No	No	Cancelled 12 Mar 44
725 -738	Unnamed	Dravo, Pittsburgh	No	No	No	Cancelled 2 Oct 43
905 -959	Unnamed	Hingham	No	No	No	Cancelled 15 Sep 43
960 -995	Unnamed	Charleston	No	No	No	Cancelled 15 Sep 43
996 -1005	Unnamed	Defoe	No	No	No	Cancelled 15 Sep 43.

Notes: In December 1942 the Navy decided to shift to a main armament of 2-5"/38 in destroyer escorts that could be modified without causing construction delays. The revised design also included a new lower covered bridge. The Rudderow class consisted of modified units of the Buckley type and was called the Turbo Electric drive 5" (TEV) type. Contracts for some ships were reallocated before construction as follows: DE 224-29 from Newport News 3 Mar 42 and from James River Shipbuilding 8 Jun 42; DE 230-37 from Newport News 3 Mar 42, from James River Shipbuilding 11 Jun 42, and from Newport News 7 Aug 42; DE 286-300 from the Charleston Navy Yard 2 Oct 43; DE 645-64 from Bethlehem, Quincy, 14 Sep 42; DE-674 from the Charleston Navy Yard 2 Nov 42 and from Dravo, Pittsburgh 13 Jun 44; DE 684-87 from the Charleston Navy Yard 29 Oct 42; DE 688-92 from the Norfolk Navy Yard 29 Oct 42; DE 706-720 from the Philadelphia Navy Yard 9 Oct 42; and DE 721-22 from Dravo, Pittsburgh, 13 Jun 44.
   Fifty ships of the TEV type were designated for conversion to APD 87-136 in July 1944 and another three were selected to become APD 137-39 in 1945. These three TEVs replaced three TEs, DE-666 and 790-791 (to have been APD 68 and 82-83), in the APD conversion program.
Renamings: DE-286 ex William C. Cole 18 Sep 43; DE-688 ex Raymond W. Herndon 27 Dec 43; DE-690 ex Alex Diachenko 1 Mar 45. Truxtun (DE-282) dropped her name 24 Jun 63.
Reclassifications: DE 226-229, 232-237, 281-283, 590-606, 674, 687-692, 710-722 were reclassified APD 87-117, 120-136, 118-119 respectively 17 Jul 44. The Bray (DE-709) became APD-139 16 Jul 45. The De Long (DE 684) was reclassified APD 137 15 Aug 45 but was not converted and reverted to DE 10 Sep 45. The Coates (DE-685) was to have been reclassified APD-138 15 Sep 45 but her reclassification was cancelled 31 Aug 45. APD-89-90, 100-101, 119, 123-124, 127, 130, 132, and 135 became LPR (with the same numbers) on 1 Jan 69.

JOHN C. BUTLER (WGT) class

Displacement: 1350 tons (standard)
Dimensions: 306'(oa.) x 36'8"(e) x 13'4"(max)
Armament: 2-5"/38AA 3-21"T; 2-5"AA (DE 371-372, 436, 448, 450, 510 as built; others 1950); 2-5"AA 2-12.75"T (DE 539-540, 1968)

Machinery: 12,000 SHP; geared turbines, 2 screws
Speed: 24 kts.
Complement: 186

No.		Hull	Machinery	Laid down	Launched	Commiss'd	Disposition
339	JOHN C. BUTLER	Orange	Westinghouse	5 Oct 43	11 Dec 43	31 Mar 44	Stk. 1 Jun 70, sunk as target off S. California Dec 71
340	O'FLAHERTY	Orange	W'house	4 Oct 43	14 Dec 43	8 Apr 44	Stk. 1 Dec 72, sold 27 Nov 73
341	RAYMOND	Orange	Westinghouse	3 Nov 43	8 Jan 44	15 Apr 44	Stk. 1 Jul 72, sunk as target off NE Florida 22 Jan 74
342	RICHARD W. SUESENS	Orange	Westinghouse	1 Nov 43	11 Jan 44	26 Apr 44	Stk. 15 Mar 72, sold 13 Jun 73
343	ABERCROMBIE	Orange	Westinghouse	8 Nov 43	14 Jan 44	1 May 44	Stk. 1 May 67, sunk as target off S. California 7 Jan 68
344	OBERRENDER	Orange	G. E.	8 Nov 43	18 Jan 44	11 May 44	Stk. 25 Jul 45, sunk as target off Kerama Retto 6 Nov 45
345	ROBERT BRAZIER	Orange	G. E.	16 Nov 43	22 Jan 44	18 May 44	Stk. 1 Jan 68, sunk as target off S. California 9 Jan 69
346	EDWIN A. HOWARD	Orange	Westinghouse	15 Nov 43	25 Jan 44	25 May 44	Stk. 1 Dec 72, sold 12 Sep 73

No.		Hull		Laid down	Launched	Commiss'd	Disposition
347	JESSE RUTHERFORD	Orange	Westing-house	22 Nov 43	29 Jan 44	31 May 44	Stk. 1 Jan 68, sunk as target off S. California 8 Dec 68
348	KEY	Orange	G. E.	14 Dec 43	12 Feb 44	5 Jun 44	Stk. 1 Mar 72, sold 19 Dec 72
349	GENTRY	Orange	G. E.	13 Dec 43	15 Feb 44	14 Jun 44	Stk. 15 Jan 72, sold 15 Jan 73
350	TRAW	Orange	G. E.	19 Dec 43	12 Feb 44	20 Jun 44	Stk. 1 Aug 67, sunk as target off S. California 17 Aug 68
351	MAURICE J. MANUEL	Orange	G. E.	22 Dec 43	19 Feb 44	30 Jun 44	Stk. 1 May 66, sunk as target Aug 66
352	NAIFEH	Orange	G. E.	29 Dec 43	29 Feb 44	4 Jul 44	Stk. 1 Jan 66, sunk as target off S. California 11 Jul 66
353	DOYLE C. BARNES	Orange	G. E.	11 Jan 44	4 Mar 44	13 Jul 44	Stk. 1 Dec 72, sold 12 Sep 73
354	KENNETH M. WILLETT	Orange	Westing-house	10 Jan 44	7 Mar 44	19 Jul 44	Stk. 1 Jul 72, sunk as target off Puerto Rico 6 Mar 74
355	JACCARD	Orange	Westing-house	25 Jan 44	18 Mar 44	26 Jul 44	Stk. 1 Nov 67, sunk as target 4 Oct 68
356	LLOYD E. ACREE	Orange	W'house	24 Jan 44	21 Mar 44	1 Aug 44	Stk. 15 Jan 72, sold 13 Jun 73
357	GEORGE E. DAVIS	Orange	Westing-house	15 Feb 44	8 Apr 44	11 Aug 44	Stk. 1 Dec 72, sold 2 Jan 74
358	MACK	Orange	W'house	14 Feb 44	11 Apr 44	16 Aug 44	Stk. 15 Mar 72, sold 13 Jun 73
359	WOODSON	Orange	W'house	7 Mar 44	29 Apr 44	24 Aug 44	Stk. 1 Jul 65, sold 16 Aug 66
360	JOHNNIE HUTCHINS	Orange	Westing-house	6 Mar 44	2 May 44	28 Aug 44	Stk. 1 Jul 72, sold 5 Feb 74
361	WALTON	Orange	G. E.	21 Mar 44	20 May 44	4 Sep 44	Stk. 23 Sep 68, sunk as target off S. California 7 Aug 69
362	ROLF	Orange	W'house	20 Mar 44	23 May 44	7 Sep 44	Stk. 1 Dec 72, sold 11 Sep 73
363	PRATT	Orange	W'house	11 Apr 44	1 Jun 44	18 Sep 44	Stk. 15 Mar 72, sold 15 Jan 73
364	ROMBACH	Orange	G. E.	10 Apr 44	6 Jun 44	20 Sep 44	Stk. 1 Mar 72, sold 19 Dec 72
365	McGINTY	Orange	G. E.	3 May 44	5 Aug 44	25 Sep 44	Stk. 23 Sep 68, sold 27 Oct 69
366	ALVIN C. COCKRELL	Orange	G. E.	1 May 44	8 Aug 44	7 Oct 44	Stk. 23 Sep 68, sunk as target off S. California 19 Sep 69
367	FRENCH	Orange	G. E.	1 May 44	17 Jun 44	9 Oct 44	Stk. 15 May 72, sold 20 Sep 73
368	CECIL J. DOYLE	Orange	Westing-house	12 May 44	1 Jul 44	16 Oct 44	Stk. 1 Jul 67, sunk as target off S. California 2 Dec 67
369	THADDEUS PARKER	Orange	Westing-house	23 May 44	26 Aug 44	25 Oct 44	Stk. 1 Sep 67, sold 9 Jul 68
370	JOHN L. WILLIAMSON	Orange	Westing-house	22 May 44	29 Aug 44	31 Oct 44	Stk. 15 Sep 70, sold 13 Jun 73
371	PRESLEY	Orange	G. E.	6 Jun 44	19 Aug 44	7 Nov 44	Stk. 30 Jun 68, sold 2 Apr 70
372	WILLIAMS	Orange	G. E.	5 Jun 44	22 Aug 44	11 Nov 44	Stk. 1 Jul 67, sunk as target off S. California 29 Jun 68
373	WILLIAM C. LAWE	Orange	Unknown	No	No	No	Cancelled 6 Jun 44
374	LLOYD THOMAS	Orange	Unknown	No	No	No	Cancelled 6 Jun 44
375	KEPPLER	Orange	Unknown	No	No	No	Cancelled 6 Jun 44
376	KLEINSMITH	Orange	Unknown	No	No	No	Cancelled 6 Jun 44
377	HENRY W. TUCKER	Orange	Unknown	No	No	No	Cancelled 6 Jun 44
378	WEISS	Orange	Unknown	No	No	No	Cancelled 6 Jun 44
379	FRANCOVICH	Orange	Unknown	No	No	No	Cancelled 6 Jun 44
380	Unnamed	Orange	Unknown	No	No	No	Cancelled 6 Jun 44
381	Unnamed	Orange	Unknown	No	No	No	Cancelled 6 Jun 44
402	RICHARD S. BULL	Houston	Westing-house	18 Aug 43	16 Nov 43	26 Feb 44	Stk. 30 Jun 68, sunk as target off S. California 24 Jun 69
403	RICHARD M. ROWELL	Houston	Westing-house	18 Aug 43	17 Nov 43	9 Mar 44	Stk. 30 Jun 68, sold Jun 69
404	EVERSOLE	Houston	Westing-house	15 Sep 43	3 Dec 43	21 Mar 44	Sunk by HIJMS I-45 off Leyte 28 Oct 44
405	DENNIS	Houston	W'house	15 Sep 43	4 Dec 43	20 Mar 44	Stk. 1 Dec 72, sold 12 Sep 73
406	EDMONDS	Houston	W'house	1 Nov 43	17 Dec 43	3 Apr 44	Stk. 15 May 72, sold 20 Sep 73
407	SHELTON	Houston	Westing-house	1 Nov 43	18 Dec 43	4 Apr 44	Sunk by HIJMS RO-41 off Morotai 3 Oct 44
408	STRAUS	Houston	Westing-house	18 Nov 43	30 Dec 43	6 Apr 44	Stk. 1 May 66, sunk as target Aug 73

No.		Hull		Laid down	Launched	Commiss'd	Disposition
409	LA PARDE	Houston	W'house	18 Nov 43	31 Dec 43	20 Apr 44	Stk. 15 Jan 72, sold 15 Jan 73
410	JACK MILLER	Houston	W'house	29 Nov 43	10 Jan 44	13 Apr 44	Stk. 30 Jun 68, sold Jul 69
411	STAFFORD	Houston	W'house	29 Nov 43	11 Jan 44	19 Apr 44	Stk. 15 Mar 72, sold 13 Jun 73
412	WALTER C. WANN	Houston	Westing-house	6 Dec 43	19 Jan 44	2 May 44	Stk. 30 Jun 68, sold Jul 69
413	SAMUEL B. ROBERTS	Houston	Westing-house	6 Dec 43	20 Jan 44	28 Apr 44	Sunk by Japanese squadron off Samar 25 Oct 44
414	LERAY WILSON	Houston	W'house	20 Dec 43	28 Jan 44	10 May 44	Stk. 15 May 72, sold 14 Sep 73
415	LAWRENCE C. TAYLOR	Houston	Westing-house	20 Dec 43	29 Jan 44	13 May 44	Stk. 1 Dec 72, sold 12 Sep 73
416	MELVIN R. NAWMAN	Houston	Westing-house	3 Jan 44	7 Feb 44	16 May 44	Stk. 1 Jul 72, sold 3 Oct 73
417	OLIVER MITCHELL	Houston	Westing-house	3 Jan 44	8 Feb 44	14 Jun 44	Stk. 15 Mar 72, sold 15 Jan 73
418	TABBERER	Houston	W'house	12 Jan 44	18 Feb 44	23 May 44	Stk. 1 Jul 72, sold 3 Oct 73
419	ROBERT F. KELLER	Houston	Westing-house	12 Jan 44	19 Feb 44	17 Jun 44	Stk. 1 Jul 72, sold 5 Feb 74
420	LELAND E. THOMAS	Houston	Westing-house	21 Jan 44	28 Feb 44	19 Jun 44	Stk. 1 Dec 72, sold 11 Sep 73
421	CHESTER T. O'BRIEN	Houston	Westing-house	21 Jan 44	29 Feb 44	3 Jul 44	Stk. 1 Jul 72, sold 4 Apr 74
422	DOUGLAS A. MUNRO	Houston	Westing-house	31 Jan 44	8 Mar 44	11 Jul 44	Stk. 1 Dec 65, sunk as target
423	DUFILHO	Houston	W'house	31 Jan 44	9 Mar 44	21 Jul 44	Stk. 1 Dec 72, sold 12 Sep 73
424	HAAS	Houston	W'house	23 Feb 44	20 Mar 44	2 Aug 44	Stk. 1 Jul 66, sold 6 Sep 67
425 -437	Unnamed	Boston	Westing-house	No	No	No	Cancelled 13 Mar 44
438	CORBESIER	Port Newark	Westing-house	4 Nov 43	13 Feb 44	31 Mar 44	Stk. 1 Dec 72, sold 3 Dec 73
439	CONKLIN	Port Newark	Westing-house	4 Nov 43	13 Feb 44	21 Apr 44	Stk. 1 Oct 70, sold 12 May 72
440	McCOY REYNOLDS	Port Newark	G. E.	18 Nov 43	22 Feb 44	2 May 44	To Portugal 7 Feb 57 as Corte Real, stk. 1 Nov 68
441	WILLIAM SEIVERLING	Port Newark	Westing-house	2 Dec 43	7 Mar 44	1 Jun 44	Stk. 1 Dec 72, sold 20 Sep 73
442	ULVERT M. MOORE	Port Newark	G. E.	2 Dec 43	7 Mar 44	18 Jul 44	Stk. 1 Dec 65, sunk as target off S. California 13 Jul 66
443	KENDALL C. CAMPBELL	Port Newark	Westing-house	16 Dec 43	19 Mar 44	31 Jul 44	Stk. 15 Jan 72, sold 15 Jan 73
444	GOSS	Port Newark	Westing-house	16 Dec 43	19 Mar 44	26 Aug 44	Stk. 1 Mar 72, sold 20 Nov 72
445	GRADY	Port Newark	G. E.	3 Jan 44	2 Apr 44	11 Sep 44	Stk. 30 Jun 68, sold Jun 69
446	CHARLES E. BRANNON	Port Newark	G. E.	13 Jan 44	23 Apr 44	1 Nov 44	Stk. 23 Sep 68, sold 27 Oct 69
447	ALBERT T. HARRIS	Port Newark	G. E.	13 Jan 44	16 Apr 44	29 Nov 44	Stk. 23 Sep 68, sold 9 Apr 69
448	CROSS	Port Newark	G. E.	19 Mar 44	4 Jul 44	8 Jan 45	Stk. 1 Jul 66, sold 5 Mar 68
449	HANNA	Port Newark	G. E.	23 Mar 44	4 Jul 44	27 Jan 45	Stk. 1 Dec 72, sold 3 Dec 73
450	JOSEPH E. CONNOLLY	Port Newark	G. E.	6 Apr 44	6 Aug 44	28 Feb 45	Stk. 1 Jun 70, sunk as target 24 Feb 72
451	WOODROW R. THOMPSON	Port Newark	G. E.	No	No	No	Cancelled 6 Jun 44
452	STEINAKER	Port Newark	G. E.	No	No	No	Cancelled 6 Jun 44
453 -456	Unnamed	Port Newark	G. E.	No	No	No	Cancelled 6 Jun 44
457 -477	Unnamed	Port Newark	G. E.	No	No	No	Cancelled 12 Mar 44
478 -507	Unnamed	Port Newark	G. E.	No	No	No	Cancelled 2 Oct 43

No.		Hull		Laid down	Launched	Commiss'd	Disposition
508	GILLIGAN	Port Newark	G. E.	18 Nov 43	22 Feb 44	12 May 44	Stk. 1 Mar 72, sold 20 Nov 72
509	FORMOE	Port Newark	G. E.	3 Jan 44	2 Apr 44	5 Oct 44	To Portugal 7 Feb 57 as Diogo Cao, stk. 1 Oct 68
510	HEYLIGER	Port Newark	G. E.	27 Apr 44	6 Aug 44	24 Mar 45	Stk. 1 May 66, sunk as target 1969
511	Unnamed	Port Newark	G. E.	No	No	No	Cancelled 6 Jun 44
512 -515	Unnamed	Port Newark	G. E.	No	No	No	Cancelled 12 Mar 44
531	EDWARD H. ALLEN	Boston	Westinghouse	31 Aug 43	7 Oct 43	16 Dec 43	Stk. 1 Jul 72, sold 5 Feb 74
532	TWEEDY	Boston	Westinghouse	31 Aug 43	7 Oct 43	12 Feb 44	Stk. 30 Jun 69, sunk as target off Florida May 70
533	HOWARD F. CLARK	Boston	Westinghouse	8 Oct 43	8 Nov 43	25 May 44	Stk. 15 May 72, sold 6 Sep 73
534	SILVERSTEIN	Boston	W'house	8 Oct 43	8 Nov 43	14 Jul 44	Stk. 1 Dec 72, sold 3 Dec 73
535	LEWIS	Boston	Westinghouse	3 Nov 43	7 Dec 43	5 Sep 44	Stk. 1 Jan 66, sunk as target Apr 66
536	BIVIN	Boston	Westinghouse	3 Nov 43	7 Dec 43	31 Oct 44	Stk. 30 Jun 68, sunk as target off S. California 17 Jul 69
537	RIZZI	Boston	W'house	3 Nov 43	7 Dec 43	26 Jun 45	Stk. 1 Aug 72, sold 5 Feb 74
538	OSBERG	Boston	W'house	3 Nov 43	7 Dec 43	10 Dec 45	Stk. 1 Aug 72, sold 5 Feb 74
539	WAGNER	Boston	W'house	8 Nov 43	27 Dec 43	22 Nov 55	Stk. 1 Nov 74, sold 12 Sep 77
540	VANDIVIER	Boston	G. E.	8 Nov 43	27 Dec 43	11 Oct 55	Stk. 1 Nov 74, sunk as target off NE Florida 7 Feb 75
541	SHEEHAN	Boston	G. E.	18 Nov 43	17 Dec 43	No	Cancelled 7 Jan 46
542	OSWALD A. POWERS	Boston	G. E.	18 Nov 43	17 Dec 43	No	Cancelled 7 Jan 46
543	GROVES	Boston	Unknown	9 Dec 43	27 Jan 44	No	Cancelled 5 Sep 44
544	ALFRED WOLF	Boston	Unknown	9 Dec 43	27 Jan 44	No	Cancelled 5 Sep 44
545	HAROLD J. ELLISON	Boston	Unknown	No	No	No	Cancelled 10 Jun 44
546	MYLES C. FOX	Boston	Unknown	No	No	No	Cancelled 10 Jun 44
547	CHARLES R. WARE	Boston	Unknown	No	No	No	Cancelled 10 Jun 44
548	CARPELLOTTI	Boston	Unknown	No	No	No	Cancelled 10 Jun 44
549	EUGENE A. GREENE	Boston	Unknown	No	No	No	Cancelled 10 Jun 44
550	GYATT	Boston	Unknown	No	No	No	Cancelled 10 Jun 44
551	BENNER	Boston	Unknown	No	No	No	Cancelled 10 Jun 44
552	KENNETH D. BAILEY	Boston	Unknown	No	No	No	Cancelled 10 Jun 44
553	DENNIS J. BUCKLEY	Boston	Unknown	No	No	No	Cancelled 10 Jun 44
554	EVERETT F. LARSON	Boston	Unknown	No	No	No	Cancelled 10 Jun 44
555	ROGERS BLOOD	Boston	Unknown	No	No	No	Cancelled 10 Jun 44
556	WILLIAM R. RUSH	Boston	Unknown	No	No	No	Cancelled 10 Jun 44
557	WILLIAM M. WOOD	Boston	Unknown	No	No	No	Cancelled 10 Jun 44
558 -562	Unnamed	Boston	Unknown	No	No	No	Cancelled 10 Jun 44
801 -832	Unnamed	Boston	Unknown	No	No	No	Cancelled 15 Sep 43
833 -840	Unnamed	Mare I.	Unknown	No	No	No	Cancelled 15 Sep 43
841 -872	Unnamed	Houston	Unknown	No	No	No	Cancelled 15 Sep 43
873 -886	Unnamed	Dravo, Pittsburgh	Unknown	No	No	No	Cancelled 15 Sep 43
887 -898	Unnamed	Western Pipe	Unknown	No	No	No	Cancelled 15 Sep 43
899 -904	Unnamed	Port Newark	Unknown	No	No	No	Cancelled 15 Sep 43.

Notes: The final response to the shortage of reduction gears for the DE program was to develop a smaller, more easily produced, type of gear. The John C. Butler class featured a new pattern of geared turbine with double reduction gears designed by Westinghouse and also built by General Electric. Gibbs and Cox prepared the detailed plans for the class, which was called the Westinghouse Geared Turbine (WGT) type. In December 1942 the whole class was modified with a 5" main battery and a new, lower bridge. DE 425-437 were transferred from Houston 3 Oct 43 and DE 508-515 were transferred from the Puget Sound Navy Yard 3 Feb 43. The Oberrender (DE-344) was irreparably damaged by a suicide plane NW of Okinawa on 9 May 45. The Wagner (DE-539) and Vandivier (DE-540) were suspended incomplete on 17 Feb 47 and reinstated on 19 Oct 53 for completion as DERs. Three ships received major postwar ASW upgrades: LeRay Wilson (DE-414) in 1947, Tweedy (DE-532, SCB-63) in 1951, and Lewis (DE-535, SCB-63A), also in 1951.
Renaming: DE-508 ex Donaldson 28 Oct 43.
Reclassifications: DE 539-540 to DER 2 Sep 54.

1951

DEALEY class

Displacement: 1420 tons
Dimensions: 314'6"(oa.) x 36'9"(e) x 20'(max)
Armament: 4-3"/50AA 2-21"T (DE-1006); 4-3"/50AA (others); 4-3"AA 6-12.75"T (all c.1960); 2-3"AA 6-12.75"T (DE 1023-26, 1962-63; DE-1021, 1970); 2-3"AA 6-12.75"T DASH (DE-1015, 1022-30, 1964-68)

Machinery: 20,000 SHP; DeLaval geared turbines, 1 screw
Speed: 25 kts.
Complement: 170

No.	Hull	Laid down	Launched	Commiss'd	Disposition
1006 DEALEY	Bath	15 Oct 52	8 Nov 53	3 Jun 54	Stk. 28 Jul 72, to Uruguay as 18 de Julio 28 Jul 72
1014 CROMWELL	Bath	3 Aug 53	4 Jun 54	24 Nov 54	Stk. 5 Jul 72, sold 15 Jun 73
1015 HAMMERBERG	Bath	12 Nov 53	20 Aug 54	2 Mar 55	Stk. 14 Dec 73, sold 17 Jul 74
1021 COURTNEY	Defoe	2 Sep 54	2 Nov 55	24 Sep 56	Stk. 14 Dec 73, sold 17 Jul 74
1022 LESTER	Defoe	2 Sep 54	5 Jan 56	14 Jun 57	Stk. 14 Dec 73, sold 17 Jul 74
1023 EVANS	Puget Sd. Br.	8 Apr 55	14 Sep 55	14 Jun 57	Stk. 3 Dec 73, sold 16 Aug 74
1024 BRIDGET	Puget Sd. Br.	19 Sep 55	25 Apr 56	24 Oct 57	Stk. 12 Nov 73, sold 16 Aug 74
1025 BAUER	Alameda	1 Dec 55	4 Jun 57	21 Nov 57	Stk. 3 Dec 73, sold 22 Aug 74
1026 HOOPER	Alameda	4 Jan 56	1 Aug 57	18 Mar 58	Stk. 6 Jul 73, sold 20 Feb 74
1027 JOHN WILLIS	New York SB	5 Jul 55	4 Feb 56	21 Feb 57	Stk. 14 Jul 72, sold 18 May 73
1028 VAN VOORHIS	New York SB	29 Aug 55	26 Jul 56	22 Apr 57	Stk. 1 Jul 72, sold 15 Jun 73
1029 HARTLEY	New York SB	31 Oct 55	24 Nov 56	26 Jun 57	Stk. 8 Jul 72, to Colombia as Boyaca 8 Jul 72
1030 JOSEPH K. TAUSSIG	New York SB	3 Jan 56	9 Mar 57	10 Sep 57	Stk. 1 Jul 72, sold 15 Jun 73.

Notes: Fiscal years 1952 (DE-1006), 1953 (1014-15), 1954 (1021-22), and 1955 (1023-30). Built to the SCB-72 design as ocean escorts for merchant convoys, they were considered prototypes which would be reproduced in quantity in case of mobilization. They were extremely maneuverable despite the single screw. They had an all aluminum superstructure, twin rudders, and extensive electronics gear. Their main deficiencies were their relatively low endurance and high cost. All but DE-1006, 1014 and 1021 were modernized with DASH facilities and the SQS-23 sonar during the 1960s at the time of the FRAM modernization program.
Renaming: DE-1026 ex Gatch 19 Jul 56.

DE-1007 class

Displacement: 1295 tons
Dimensions: 327'6"(oa.) x 33'9"(e) x 10'
Armament: 6-57mmAA 12-12.75"T

Machinery: 20,000 SHP; geared turbines, 1 screw
Speed: 27 kts.
Complement: 200

No.	Hull	Laid down	Launched	Commiss'd	Disposition
1007 (LE NORMAND)	Ch. de la Med.	Jul 53	13 Feb 54	No	To France 10 Oct 56
1008 (LE LORRAIN)	Ch. de la Med.	Feb 54	19 Jun 54	No	To France 20 Dec 56
1009 (LE PICARD)	A. C. Loire	Nov 53	31 May 54	No	To France 31 Aug 56
1010 (LE GASCON)	A. C. Loire	Feb 54	23 Oct 54	No	To France 29 Mar 57
1011 (LE CHAMPENOIS)	A. C. Loire	May 54	12 Mar 55	No	To France 20 May 57
1012 (LE SAVOYARD)	Ch. de la Med.	Nov 53	7 May 55	No	To France 20 May 57
1013 (LE BOURGUIGNON)	Penhoet	Jan 54	28 Jan 56	No	To France 12 Jun 57.

Notes: Fiscal year 1952 (offshore procurement). A French design (E 52a type) built under MDAP, they were a modification of the Le Corse design. Seven later sisters were built without U.S. Navy funds.

DE-1016 class

Displacement: 1290 tons
Dimensions: 327'6"(oa.) x 33'9"(e) x 10'
Armament: 6-57mmAA 12-12.75"T

Machinery: 20,000 SHP; geared turbines, 1 screw
Speed: 27 kts.
Complement: 198

No.	Hull	Laid down	Launched	Commiss'd	Disposition
1016 (LE CORSE)	Lorient	Oct 51	5 Aug 52	No	To France 5 Aug 52
1017 (LE BRESTOIS)	Lorient	Nov 51	16 Aug 52	No	To France 16 Dec 52
1018 (LE BOULONNAIS)	A. C. Loire	Mar 52	12 May 53	No	To France 12 May 53
1019 (LE BORDELAIS)	Ch. de la Med.	Feb 52	11 Jul 53	No	To France 11 Jul 53.

Notes: Fiscal year 1952 (offshore procurement). They were French E-50 type Escorteurs Rapides Anti-Sousmarins which resembled the Dealey class. They were built under MDAP.

1952

DE-1031 class

Displacement: 1680 tons
Dimensions: 339'6"(oa.) x 38'(e) x 12'(max)
Armament: 4-3"/62AA 2-21"T

Machinery: 22,000 SHP; Tosi geared turbines, 2 screws
Speed: 25 kts.
Complement: 200

No.	Hull	Laid down	Launched	Commiss'd	Disposition
1020 (CIGNO)	Cant. Nav. di Taranto	10 Feb 54	20 Mar 55	No	To Italy 7 Mar 57
1031 (CASTORE)	Cant. Nav. de Taranto	14 Mar 55	8 Jul 56	No	To Italy 14 Jul 57.

Notes: Fiscal year 1953 and 1954 (offshore procurement). They were Italian Canopo class Fregate built under MDAP. Two sisters, Canopo and Centauro, were built without U.S. Navy funds.

1953

DE-1032

Displacement: 1250 tons
Dimensions: 321'6"(oa.) x 35'6"(e) x 10'
Armament: 2-3"/62AA 3-21"T

Machinery: 24,000 SHP; geared turbines, 2 screws
Speed: 32 kts.
Complement: 180

No.	Hull	Laid down	Launched	Commiss'd	Disposition
1032 (PERO ESCOBAR)	Navalmecc. Castellammare	7 Jan 55	25 Sep 55	No	To Portugal 30 Jun 57.

Notes: Fiscal year 1954 (offshore procurement). Built under MDAP to an Italian export design which was also used for six Venezuelan and two Indonesian ships.

1955

CLAUD JONES class

Displacement: 1285 tons (light)
Dimensions: 311'10"(oa.) x 38'11"(e) x 17'2"(max)
Armament: 2-3"/50AA 6-12.75"T

Machinery: 9200 BHP; 4 F. M. diesel engines, 1 screw
Speed: 22 kts.
Complement: 175

No.	Hull	Laid down	Launched	Commiss'd	Disposition
1033 CLAUD JONES	Avondale	1 Jun 57	27 May 58	10 Feb 59	To Indonesia 16 Dec 74 as Mongonsidi, stk. 16 Dec 74
1034 JOHN R. PERRY	Avondale	1 Oct 57	29 Jul 58	5 May 59	To Indonesia 20 Feb 73 as Samadikun, stk. 20 Feb 73
1035 CHARLES BERRY	Avondale	29 Oct 58	17 Mar 59	25 Nov 59	To Indonesia 31 Jan 74 as Martadinata, stk. 31 Jan 74
1036 McMORRIS	Avondale	5 Nov 58	26 May 59	4 Mar 60	To Indonesia 16 Dec 74 as Ngurah Rai, stk. 16 Dec 74.

Notes: Fiscal years 1956 (DE 1033-34) and 1957. The SCB-131 design combined the Dealey class hull with diesel engines in an attempt to get a simplified, austerity vessel capable of mass production. It had greater endurance than the Dealeys and was less expensive, but its designed speed of 21 knots proved too low and it lacked a long-range ASW weapon. The contracts for the Charles Berry and McMorris were originally let to American Shipbuilding Co., Lorain, Ohio, but were cancelled there in May 1958. Turkey built two similar ships, the Berk class, without U.S. Navy funds.

1959

BRONSTEIN class

Displacement: 2360 tons (light)
Dimensions: 371'6"(oa.) x 40'5"(e) x 23'(max)
Armament: 3-3"/50AA ASROC 6-12.75"T DASH; 2-3"AA ASROC
  6-12.75"T (1970)

Machinery: 23,000 SHP; DeLaval geared
  turbines, 1 screw
Speed: 25 kts.
Complement: 190

No.	Hull	Laid down	Launched	Commiss'd	Disposition
1037 BRONSTEIN	Avondale	16 May 61	31 Mar 62	15 Jun 63	USN
1038 McCLOY	Avondale	15 Sep 61	9 Jun 62	21 Oct 63	USN.

Notes: Fiscal year 1960. In 1958 Navy designers began efforts to adapt the relatively successful Dealey-class design to a new generation of ASW equipment: the SQS-26 sonar, ASROC, and DASH. They lengthened the hull and adopted a new hull form to maintain the designed speed at 24 knots. The result, the SCB-199 design, also featured an enclosed bridge and fin stabilizers.
Reclassifications: Both to FF 30 Jun 75.

DE-1039 class

Displacement: 1450 tons (standard)
Dimensions: 314'11"(oa.) x 36'9"(e) x 13'9"
Armament: 4-3"/50AA 6-12.75"T

Machinery: 20,000 SHP; DeLaval geared
  turbines, 1 screw
Speed: 25 kts.
Complement: 171

No.	Hull	Laid down	Launched	Commiss'd	Disposition
1039 (ALMIRANTE PEREIRA DA SILVA)	Lisnave	14 Jun 62	2 Dec 63	No	To Portugal 20 Dec 66
1042 (ALMIRANTE GAGO COUTINHO)	Lisnave	2 Dec 63	30 Aug 65	No	To Portugal 29 Nov 67
1046 (ALMIRANTE MAGALHAES CORREIA)	Viana	1 Sep 63	26 Apr 65	No	To Portugal 7 Nov 68.

Notes: Fiscal years 1960, 1961, and 1962 respectively (offshore procurement). MDAP vessels, they followed a modified Dealey class design. Norway also built five ships to a modified Dealey design in the 1960s, but without U.S. Navy funds.

1960

GARCIA class

Displacement: 2624 tons (light)
Dimensions: 414'6"(oa.) x 44'1"(e) x 13'(max)
Armament: 2-5"/38AA ASROC 2-21"T 6-12.75"T DASH; 2-5"AA ASROC
  6-12.75"T (1970)

Machinery: 35,000 SHP; G. E. geared
  turbines, 1 screw
Speed: 27 kts.
Complement: 220

No.	Hull	Laid down	Launched	Commiss'd	Disposition
1040 GARCIA	Beth-SF	16 Oct 62	3 Oct 63	21 Dec 64	To Pakistan 31 Jan 89 as Saif
1041 BRADLEY	Beth-SF	17 Jan 63	26 Mar 64	15 May 65	To Brazil 15 Apr 89 as Pernambuco
1043 EDWARD McDONNELL	Avondale	1 Apr 63	15 Feb 64	15 Feb 65	USN
1044 BRUMBY	Avondale	1 Aug 63	6 Jun 64	5 Aug 65	To Pakistan 31 Mar 89 as Harbah
1045 DAVIDSON	Avondale	30 Sep 63	2 Oct 64	7 Dec 65	To Brazil 15 Apr 89 as Paraiba
1047 VOGE	Defoe	21 Nov 63	4 Feb 65	25 Nov 66	USN
1048 SAMPLE	Puget Sd. Br.	19 Jul 63	28 Apr 64	23 Mar 68	To Brazil 15 Apr 89 as Parana
1049 KOELSCH	Defoe	19 Feb 65	8 Jun 65	10 Jun 67	To Pakistan 31 May 89 as Siqqat

The escort ship *Bradley* (DE-1041) in 1965. (NH 96714)

The escort ship *Gray* (DE-1054) ca. 1970. (USN 1143228)

No.		Hull	Laid down	Launched	Commiss'd	Disposition
1050 ALBERT DAVID		Puget Sd. Br.	29 Apr 64	19 Dec 64	19 Oct 68	To Brazil 18 Sep 89 as Para
1051 O'CALLAHAN		Defoe	19 Feb 64	20 Oct 65	13 Jul 68	To Pakistan 8 Feb 89 as Aslat.

Notes: Fiscal years 1961 (DE 1040-41), 1962 (1043-45), and 1963. Following studies of a 30-knot escort in 1959, the Navy concluded that a 27-knot type was feasible using the Bronstein class design, a 35,000 SHP DDG-2 class steam turbine, and two pressure fired boilers. These new boilers employed exhaust gases to power an air compressor which delivered pressurized air to the boilers. The increased power of the propulsion plant forced a redesign of the hull. The ships were also given 5" instead of 3" guns to permit their use as austerity destroyers. This design, SCB-199A, was the only postwar destroyer or destroyer escort design for which Bethlehem Steel instead of Gibbs and Cox prepared the detailed plans. DE-1040, 1041, 1044, and 1051 received LAMPS helicopter refits in 1972; 1043 and 1045 in 1973; 1049 in 1974; and 1047 in 1975.

Reclassifications: All to FF 30 Jun 75.

1963

KNOX class

Displacement: 3077 tons (standard)
Dimensions: 438'(oa.) x 46'9"x 25'
Armament: 1-5"/54AA ASROC 4-12.75"T

Machinery: 35,000 SHP; Westinghouse geared turbines, 1 screw
Speed: 27 kts.
Complement: 245

No.	Hull	Laid down	Launched	Commiss'd	Disposition
1052 KNOX	Todd, Seattle	5 Oct 65	19 Nov 66	12 Apr 69	USN
1053 ROARK	Todd, Seattle	2 Feb 66	24 Apr 67	22 Nov 69	USN
1054 GRAY	Todd, Seattle	19 Nov 66	3 Nov 67	4 Apr 70	USN
1055 HEPBURN	Todd, San Pedro	1 Jun 66	25 Mar 67	3 Jul 69	USN
1056 CONNOLE	Avondale	23 Mar 67	20 Jul 68	30 Aug 69	USN
1057 RATHBURNE	Lockheed	8 Jan 68	2 May 69	16 May 70	USN
1058 MEYERKORD	Todd, San Pedro	1 Sep 66	15 Jul 67	28 Nov 69	USN
1059 W. S. SIMS	Avondale	10 Apr 67	4 Jan 69	3 Jan 70	USN
1060 LANG	Todd, San Pedro	25 Mar 67	17 Feb 68	28 Mar 70	USN
1061 PATTERSON	Avondale	12 Oct 67	3 May 69	14 Mar 70	USN
1062 WHIPPLE	Todd, Seattle	24 Apr 67	12 Apr 68	22 Aug 70	USN
1063 REASONER	Lockheed	6 Jan 69	1 Aug 70	31 Jul 71	USN
1064 LOCKWOOD	Todd, Seattle	3 Nov 67	5 Sep 68	5 Dec 70	USN
1065 STEIN	Lockheed	1 Jun 70	19 Dec 70	8 Jan 72	USN
1066 MARVIN SHIELDS	Todd, Seattle	12 Apr 68	23 Oct 69	10 Apr 71	USN
1067 FRANCIS HAMMOND	Todd, San Pedro	15 Jul 67	11 May 68	25 Jul 70	USN
1068 VREELAND	Avondale	20 Mar 68	14 Jun 69	13 Jun 70	USN
1069 BAGLEY	Lockheed	22 Sep 70	24 Apr 71	6 May 72	USN
1070 DOWNES	Todd, Seattle	5 Sep 68	13 Dec 69	28 Aug 71	USN
1071 BADGER	Todd, San Pedro	17 Feb 68	7 Dec 68	1 Dec 70	USN
1072 BLAKELY	Avondale	3 Jun 68	23 Aug 69	18 Jul 70	USN
1073 ROBERT E. PEARY	Lockheed	20 Dec 70	23 Jun 71	23 Sep 72	USN
1074 HAROLD E. HOLT	Todd, San Pedro	11 May 68	3 May 69	26 Mar 71	USN
1075 TRIPPE	Avondale	29 Jul 68	1 Nov 69	19 Sep 70	USN
1076 FANNING	Todd, San Pedro	7 Dec 68	24 Jan 70	23 Jul 71	USN
1077 OUELLET	Avondale	15 Jan 69	17 Jan 70	12 Dec 70	USN
1078 JOSEPH HEWES	Avondale	15 May 69	7 Mar 70	24 Apr 71	USN
1079 BOWEN	Avondale	11 Jul 69	2 May 70	22 May 71	USN
1080 PAUL	Avondale	12 Sep 69	20 Jun 70	14 Aug 71	USN
1081 AYLWIN	Avondale	13 Nov 69	29 Aug 70	18 Sep 71	USN
1082 ELMER MONTGOMERY	Avondale	23 Jan 70	21 Nov 70	30 Oct 71	USN
1083 COOK	Avondale	20 Mar 70	23 Jan 71	18 Dec 71	USN
1084 McCANDLESS	Avondale	4 Jun 70	20 Mar 71	18 Mar 72	USN
1085 DONALD B. BEARY	Avondale	24 Jul 70	22 May 71	22 Jul 72	USN
1086 BREWTON	Avondale	2 Oct 70	24 Jul 71	8 Jul 72	USN
1087 KIRK	Avondale	4 Dec 70	25 Sep 71	9 Sep 72	USN
1088 BARBEY	Avondale	5 Feb 71	4 Dec 71	11 Nov 72	USN

No.	Hull	Laid down	Launched	Commiss'd	Disposition
1089 JESSE L. BROWN	Avondale	8 Apr 71	18 Mar 72	17 Feb 73	USN
1090 AINSWORTH	Avondale	11 Jun 71	15 Apr 72	31 Mar 73	USN
1091 MILLER	Avondale	6 Aug 71	3 Jun 72	30 Jun 73	USN
1092 THOMAS C. HART	Avondale	8 Oct 71	12 Aug 72	28 Jul 73	USN
1093 CAPODANNO	Avondale	25 Feb 72	21 Oct 72	17 Nov 73	USN
1094 PHARRIS	Avondale	22 Mar 72	16 Dec 72	26 Jan 74	USN
1095 TRUETT	Avondale	27 Apr 72	3 Feb 73	1 Jun 74	USN
1096 VALDEZ	Avondale	30 Jun 72	24 Mar 73	27 Jul 74	USN
1097 MOINESTER	Avondale	25 Aug 72	12 May 73	2 Nov 74	USN
1098 Unnamed -1100	Unknown	No	No	No	Cancelled 24 Feb 69
1102 Unnamed -1107	Unknown	No	No	No	Cancelled 1968.

Notes: Fiscal years 1964 (DE 1052-61), 1965 (1062-77), 1966 (1078-87), 1967 (1088-97), and 1968 (1098-1107). The plans for this class (SCB-199C) were the result of a complete redesign of the ocean escort type starting with the plans of the Brooke class missile escorts. The Tartar missile was deleted in 1962 and a 5"/54 gun substituted for the single 5"/38. In 1967 Gibbs and Cox recommended against using the relatively untested pressure fired boilers in such a large class, and the type was redesigned and lengthened 20 feet to accomodate conventional 1200-pound boilers. The ships were maneuverable and long ranged but proved wet as completed. Beginning in 1979, some received bulwarks forward to combat this problem. DE-1063, 1066, 1074, 1078-80 received LAMPS helicopter refits in 1972; 1055, 1057, 1069, 1071-73, 1075, 1081, 1083-88 in 1973; 1053-54, 1056-58, 1060, 1076, 1089-97 in 1974; 1062, 1064, 1067, 1077, 1082 in 1975; and 1052, 1061, 1068, and 1070 in 1976. DE 1102-1107 were deferred in 1968 to permit a shift to the Spruance class destroyers and DE-1098-1100 were later cancelled to cover cost overruns in nuclear submarines.
Renaming: DE-1073 ex Conolly 12 May 71.
Reclassifications: All to FF 30 Jun 75.

1967

DE-1101

Displacement: Unknown
Dimensions: Unknown
Armament: Unknown

Machinery: Gas turbine
Speed: Unknown
Complement: Unknown

No.	Hull	Laid down	Launched	Commiss'd	Disposition
1101 Unnamed	Unknown	No	No	No	Cancelled 9 Apr 69.

Notes: Fiscal year 1968. She was planned in 1968 as an experimental gas turbine ship, possibly with advanced features such as a regenerative cycle. In view of the extensive program of gas turbine ships that subsequently got underway (the Spruance class), the Navy decided in 1969 that this test ship was unnecessary.

Escort Research Ships (AGDE)

1960

GLOVER

Displacement: 2643 tons (light)
Dimensions: 414'6"(oa.) x 44'2"(e) x 14'6"
Armament: 1-5"/38AA ASROC 6-12.75"T; none (1990)

Machinery: 32,000 SHP; G. E. geared turbines, 1 screw
Speed: 27 kts.
Complement: 316

No.	Hull	Laid down	Launched	Commiss'd	Disposition
1 GLOVER	Bath	29 Jul 63	17 Apr 65	13 Nov 65	USN.

Notes: Originally planned as AGER-158 under fiscal year 1960, she was cancelled on 16 Dec 59 and reintroduced as AGER-163 in the fiscal year 1961 program. She was soon redesignated AGDE-1. She was essentially a DE-1040 class ship with a shrouded propellor and a raised stern to accomodate experimental sonar equipment. In 1979 she was reassigned to regular frigate duty in 1979 and was given the hull number of a cancelled Knox-class ship. On 15 Jun 90 she was transferred to MSC as a sonar trials ship without armament.
Reclassifications: Ex AGER-163; to AGFF-1 30 Jun 75; to FF-1098 1 Oct 79; to AGFF-1 15 Jun 90.

Guided Missile Escort Ships (DEG)

1961

BROOKE class

Displacement: 2643 tons (light)
Dimensions: 414'6"(oa.) x 44'1"(e) x 15'
Armament: 1-5"/38AA 1-Tartar-SAM ASROC 2-21"T 6-12.75"T DASH;
  1-5"/38AA 1-Tartar-SAM ASROC 6-12.75"T (1970)

Machinery: 35,000 SHP; G. E. geared
  turbines, 1 screw
Speed: 27 kts.
Complement: 258

No.		Hull	Laid down	Launched	Commiss'd	Disposition
1	BROOKE	Puget Sd. Br.	19 Dec 62	19 Jul 63	12 Mar 66	To Pakistan 8 Feb 89 as Khaiber
2	RAMSEY	Puget Sd. Br.	4 Feb 63	15 Oct 63	3 Jun 67	USN
3	SCHOFIELD	Puget Sd. Br.	15 Apr 63	7 Dec 63	11 May 68	USN
4	TALBOT	Bath	4 May 64	6 Jan 66	22 Apr 67	To Pakistan 31 May 89 as Hunain
5	RICHARD L. PAGE	Bath	4 Jan 65	4 Apr 66	5 Aug 67	To Pakistan 31 Mar 89 as Tabuk
6	JULIUS A. FURER	Bath	12 Jul 65	22 Jul 66	11 Nov 67	To Pakistan 31 Jan 89 as Badr.

Notes: Fiscal years 1962 (DEG 1-3) and 1963. The SCB-199B design duplicated the Garcia (DE-1040) class except for a Tartar missile launcher replacing the after 5-inch gun. (The Garcia design had included provisions for such a modification.) DEG-3 received a LAMPS helicopter refit in 1972; DEG-6 in 1973; and DEG 1, 2, and 5 in 1975.
Renaming: DEG-6 ex Furer 5 Apr 66.
Reclassifications: All to FFG 30 Jun 75.

1964

DEG-7 class

Displacement: 3015 tons
Dimensions: 438'(oa.) x 47' x 23'(max)
Armament: 1-5"/54AA 1-Tartar-SAM ASROC 2-21"T 4-12.75"T

Machinery: 35,000 SHP; geared
  turbines, 1 screw
Speed: 27 kts.
Complement: 250

No.		Hull	Laid down	Launched	Commiss'd	Disposition
7	(BALEARES)	Bazan	31 Oct 68	20 Aug 70	No	To Spain 24 Sep 73
8	(ANDALUCIA)	Bazan	2 Jul 69	30 Mar 71	No	To Spain 23 May 74
9	(CATALUNA)	Bazan	20 Aug 70	3 Nov 71	No	To Spain 16 Jan 75
10	(ASTURIAS)	Bazan	30 Mar 71	13 May 72	No	To Spain 2 Dec 75
11	(EXTREMADURA)	Bazan	3 Nov 71	21 Nov 72	No	To Spain 10 Nov 76.

Notes: Fiscal year 1965 (offshore procurement). Built for Spain under MDAP. They have most of the weapons of the original SCB-199C design (including the Tartar SAM and Mk-25 torpedo tubes). They lack DASH or helicopter facilities, however, and have the hull and conventional boilers of the final Knox class.

Corvettes (Twin Screw) (PG)

1942

ASHEVILLE class

Displacement: 1370 tons (standard)
Dimensions: 301'6"(oa.) x 36'6"(e) x 13'8"(max)
Armament: 3-3"/50AA

Machinery: 5500 IHP; vertical triple-
  expansion engines, 2 screws
Speed: 20 kts.
Complement: 194

No.		Hull	Laid down	Launched	Commiss'd	Disposition
101	ASHEVILLE	Canadian Vickers	10 Mar 42	22 Aug 42	1 Dec 42	Stk. 25 Feb 46, to Argentina as Hercules 13 Jun 46
102	NATCHEZ	Canadian Vickers	16 Mar 42	12 Sep 42	16 Dec 42	Stk. 1 Nov 45, to Dominican Rep. as J. P. Duarte 29 Jul 47

No.		Hull	Laid down	Launched	Commiss'd	Disposition
103	(BARLE)	Canadian Vickers	29 Apr 42	26 Sep 42	No	To Britain 30 Apr 43, stk. 17 Apr 46
104	(CUCKMERE)	Canadian Vickers	11 May 42	24 Oct 42	No	To Britain 14 May 43, stk. 7 Feb 47
105	(EVENLODE)	Canadian Vickers	28 May 42	9 Nov 42	No	To Britain 4 Jun 43 stk. 5 Jun 46
106	(FINDHORN)	Canadian Vickers	25 Aug 42	5 Dec 42	No	To Britain 20 Jun 43, stk. 8 May 46
107	(INVER)	Canadian Vickers	16 Sep 42	5 Dec 42	No	To Britain 17 Jul 43, stk. 8 May 46
108	(LOSSIE)	Canadian Vickers	2 Oct 42	29 Apr 43	No	To Britain 14 Aug 43, stk. 17 Apr 46
109	(PARRET)	Canadian Vickers	6 Nov 42	29 Apr 43	No	To Britain 31 Aug 43, stk. 17 Apr 46
110	(SHIEL)	Canadian Vickers	19 Nov 42	26 May 43	No	To Britain 29 Sep 43, stk. 8 May 46.

Notes: Under the Hyde Park agreement of February 1942, the British transferred to the U.S. some ships which they had ordered in Canada in October and December 1941. These included 15 Modified Flower class single-screw corvettes (PG 86-100), 10 River class twin-screw corvettes (PG 101-110), 15 Algerine class minesweepers (AM 325-39), and 8 Fairmile B class submarine chasers (SC 1466-73). Compared to the earlier Flowers, the River class ships had extra length and speed to make them suitable for mid-ocean service--the Flowers had been designed for coastal duty. River class ships were redesignated frigates by the British in 1942 and by the U.S. in 1943. Of the Hyde Park ships, seven Modified Flowers, eight Rivers, and all the Algerines were loaned back to Britain under Lend Lease allocation procedures. PG-104 was irreparably damaged in British service on 11 Dec 43.

Renamings: The U.S. name Danville was used at the launching of PG-105 but this name does not appear to have been formally approved in Washington. PG 101-102 were originally to have been the British Adur and Annan; subsequently PG-101 was to have been the Canadian Nadur.

Reclassifications: PG 101-102 to PF 1-2 (frigates) 15 Apr 43.

Frigates (PF)

1942

TACOMA class

Displacement: 1430 tons (standard)
Dimensions: 303'11"(oa.) x 37'6"(e) x 13'8"(max)
Armament: 3-3"/50AA; 2-3"/50AA (weather ships)

Machinery: 5500 IHP; vertical triple-expansion engines, 2 screws
Speed: 20 kts.
Complement: 190

No.		Hull	Machinery	Laid down	Launched	Commiss'd	Disposition
3	TACOMA	Kaiser	Hendry	10 Mar 43	7 Jul 43	6 Nov 43	To S. Korea 8 Oct 51 as Taetong, stk. 2 Apr 73
4	SAUSALITO	Kaiser	Hendry	7 Apr 43	20 Jul 43	4 Mar 44	Stk. 1 Sep 72, to S. Korea as Imchin 3 Sep 52
5	HOQUIAM	Kaiser	Hendry	10 Apr 43	31 Jul 43	8 May 44	To S. Korea 8 Oct 51 as Naktong, stk. 1 Aug 72
6	PASCO	Kaiser	Hendry	7 Jul 43	17 Aug 43	15 Apr 44	To Japan 14 Jan 53 as Kashi, stk. 1 Dec 61
7	ALBUQUERQUE	Kaiser	Hendry	20 Jul 43	14 Sep 43	20 Dec 43	To Japan 30 Nov 53 as Tochi, stk. 1 Dec 61
8	EVERETT	Kaiser	Hendry	31 Jul 43	29 Sep 43	22 Jan 44	To Japan 3 Sep 53 as Kiri, stk. 1 Dec 61
9	POCATELLO	Kaiser	Hendry	17 Aug 43	17 Oct 43	18 Feb 44	Stk. 5 Jun 46, sold 22 Sep 47
10	BROWNSVILLE	Kaiser	Hendry	14 Sep 43	14 Nov 43	6 May 44	Stk. 25 Sep 46, sold 30 Sep 47
11	GRAND FORKS	Kaiser	Hendry	29 Sep 43	27 Nov 43	18 Mar 44	Stk. 19 Jun 46, sold 20 May 47
12	CASPER	Kaiser	Hendry	17 Oct 43	27 Dec 43	31 Mar 44	Stk. 19 Jun 46, sold 20 May 47
13	PUEBLO	Kaiser	Hendry	14 Nov 43	20 Jan 44	27 May 44	Stk. 19 Jun 46, sold 22 Sep 47, to Dominican Republic as Presidente Troncoso
14	GRAND ISLAND	Kaiser	Hendry	27 Nov 43	19 Feb 44	27 May 44	Stk. 19 Jun 46, to Cuba as Maximo Gomez 16 Jun 47

No.	Hull	Machinery	Laid down	Launched	Commiss'd	Disposition
15 ANNAPOLIS	Lorain	Beloit	20 May 43	16 Oct 43	4 Jul 44	Stk. 19 Jun 46, to Mexico as Usumacinta 24 Nov 47
16 BANGOR	Lorain	Diamond	20 May 43	6 Nov 43	22 Aug 44	Stk. 23 Apr 47, to Mexico as Tehuantepec 24 Nov 47
17 KEY WEST	Lorain	Beloit	23 Jun 43	29 Dec 43	7 Aug 44	Stk. 3 Jul 46, sold 3 May 47
18 ALEXANDRIA	Lorain	Beloit	23 Jun 43	15 Jan 44	11 Mar 45	Stk. 21 May 46, sold 18 Apr 47
19 HURON	Cleveland	Koppers	1 Mar 43	3 Jul 43	7 Sep 44	Stk. 21 May 46, sold 15 Sep 47
20 GULFPORT	Cleveland	Koppers	5 May 43	21 Aug 43	16 Sep 44	Stk. 19 Jun 46, sold 13 Nov 47
21 BAYONNE	Cleveland	Koppers	6 May 43	11 Sep 43	14 Feb 45	To Japan 31 Oct 53 as Buna, stk. 1 Dec 61
22 GLOUCESTER	Butler	Hendry	4 Mar 43	12 Jul 43	10 Dec 43	To Japan 1 Oct 53 as Tsuge, stk. 1 Dec 61
23 SHREVEPORT	Butler	Diamond	8 Mar 43	15 Jul 43	24 Apr 44	Stk. 19 Jun 46, sold 15 Aug 47
24 MUSKEGON	Butler	Hendry	11 May 43	25 Jul 43	16 Dec 43	To France 26 Mar 47 as Mermoz, stk. 23 Apr 47
25 CHARLOTTESVILLE	Butler	Hendry	12 May 43	30 Jul 43	10 Apr 44	To Japan 14 Jan 53 as Matsu, stk. 1 Dec 61
26 POUGHKEEPSIE	Butler	Valley	3 Jun 43	12 Aug 43	6 Sep 44	To Japan 14 Jan 53 as Momi, stk. 1 Dec 61
27 NEWPORT	Butler	York Ice	8 Jun 43	15 Aug 43	8 Sep 44	To Japan 1 Oct 53 as Kaede, stk. 1 Dec 61
28 EMPORIA	Butler	Diamond	14 Jul 43	30 Aug 43	12 Jun 44	To France 26 Mar 47 as Le Verrier, stk. 23 Apr 47
29 GROTON	Butler	Valley	15 Jul 43	14 Sep 43	5 Sep 44	Stk. 20 Mar 47, to Colombia as Almirante Padilla 26 Mar 47
30 HINGHAM	Butler	Hendry	25 Jul 43	27 Aug 43	3 Nov 44	Stk. 3 Jul 46, sold 15 Aug 47
31 GRAND RAPIDS	Butler	Diamond	30 Jul 43	10 Sep 43	26 Oct 44	Stk. 21 May 46, sold 14 Apr 47
32 WOONSOCKET	Butler	Beloit	12 Aug 43	27 Sep 43	27 Jul 44	Stk. 14 Mar 47, to Peru as Galvez 4 Sep 47
33 DEARBORN	Butler	Diamond	15 Aug 43	27 Sep 43	17 Jul 44	Stk. 3 Jul 46, sold 8 Jul 47
34 LONG BEACH	Consolid.	Hendry	19 Mar 43	5 May 43	8 Sep 43	To Japan 30 Nov 53 as Shii, stk. 1 Dec 61
35 BELFAST	Consolid.	Hendry	26 Mar 43	20 May 43	24 Nov 43	Lost 17 Nov 48, stk. 31 Jan 50
36 GLENDALE	Consolid.	Hendry	6 Apr 43	28 May 43	1 Oct 43	To Thailand 29 Oct 51 as Tahchin, stk. 20 Nov 51
37 SAN PEDRO	Consolid.	Hendry	17 Apr 43	11 Jun 43	23 Oct 43	To Japan 2 Apr 53 as Kaya, stk. 1 Dec 61
38 CORONADO	Consolid.	Hendry	6 May 43	17 Jun 43	17 Nov 43	To Japan 14 Jan 53 as Sugi, stk. 1 Dec 61
39 OGDEN	Consolid.	Hendry	21 May 43	23 Jun 43	20 Dec 43	To Japan 14 Jan 53 as Kusu, stk. 1 Dec 61
40 EUGENE	Consolid.	Hendry	12 Jun 43	6 Jul 43	15 Jan 44	Stk. 19 Jul 46, to Cuba as Jose Marti 16 Jun 47
41 EL PASO	Consolid.	Hendry	18 Jun 43	16 Jul 43	1 Dec 43	Stk. 28 Aug 46, sold 14 Oct 47
42 VAN BUREN	Consolid.	Hendry	24 Jun 43	27 Jul 43	17 Dec 43	Stk. 19 Jun 46, sold 15 Aug 47
43 ORANGE	Consolid.	Hendry	7 Jul 43	6 Aug 43	1 Jan 44	Stk. 23 Apr 47, sold 17 Sep 47
44 CORPUS CHRISTI	Consolid.	Hendry	17 Jul 43	17 Aug 43	29 Jan 44	Stk. 8 Oct 46, sold 3 Oct 47
45 HUTCHINSON	Consolid.	Hendry	28 Jul 43	27 Aug 43	3 Feb 44	Stk. 29 Oct 46, to Mexico as California 24 Nov 47
46 BISBEE	Consolid.	Hendry	7 Aug 43	7 Sep 43	15 Feb 44	To Colombia 12 Feb 52 as Capitan Tono, stk. 25 Feb 52
47 GALLUP	Consolid.	Hendry	18 Aug 43	17 Sep 43	29 Feb 44	To Thailand 29 Oct 51 as Prasae, stk. 20 Nov 51
48 ROCKFORD	Consolid.	Hendry	28 Aug 43	27 Sep 43	6 Mar 44	To S. Korea 23 Oct 50 as Apnok, stk. 26 May 53
49 MUSKOGEE	Consolid.	Hendry	18 Sep 43	18 Oct 43	16 Mar 44	To S. Korea 23 Oct 50 as Duman, stk. 15 Sep 52
50 CARSON CITY	Consolid.	Hendry	28 Sep 43	13 Nov 43	24 Mar 44	To Japan 30 Apr 53 as Sakura, stk. 1 Dec 61
51 BURLINGTON	Consolid.	Hendry	19 Oct 43	7 Dec 43	3 Apr 44	Stk. 28 May 53, to Colombia as Almirante Brion 26 Jun 53
52 ALLENTOWN	Froemming	Hendry	23 Mar 43	3 Jul 43	24 Mar 44	To Japan 2 Apr 53 as Ume, stk. 1 Dec 61
53 MACHIAS	Froemming	Hendry	8 May 43	22 Aug 43	29 Mar 44	To Japan 14 Jan 53 as Nara, stk. 1 Dec 61

No.		Hull	Machinery	Laid down	Launched	Commiss'd	Disposition
54	SANDUSKY	Froemming	Hendry	8 Jul 43	5 Oct 43	18 Apr 44	To Japan 16 Feb 53 as Nire, stk. 1 Dec 61
55	BATH	Froemming	Hendry	23 Aug 43	14 Nov 43	1 Sep 44	To Japan 23 Dec 53 as Maki, stk. 1 Dec 61
56	COVINGTON	Globe SB	Hendry	1 Mar 43	15 Jul 43	7 Aug 44	Stk. 23 Apr 47, to Ecuador as Guayas 28 Aug 47
57	SHEBOYGAN	Globe SB	Valley	17 Apr 43	31 Jul 43	14 Oct 44	Stk. 8 Oct 46, to Belgium as Luitenant ter zee Victor Billet 19 Mar 47
58	ABILENE	Globe SB	Diamond	6 May 43	21 Aug 43	28 Oct 44	Stk. 13 Nov 46, to Netherlands as civilian Cirrus 7 May 47
59	BEAUFORT	Globe SB	Hendry	21 Jul 43	9 Oct 43	28 Aug 44	Stk. 21 May 46, sold 11 Apr 47
60	CHARLOTTE	Globe SB	Hendry	5 Aug 43	30 Oct 43	9 Oct 44	Stk. 21 May 46, sold 13 May 47
61	MANITOWOC	Globe SB	Diamond	26 Aug 43	30 Nov 43	5 Dec 44	To France 26 Mar 47 as Le Brix, stk. 23 Apr 47
62	GLADWYNE	Globe SB	Diamond	14 Oct 43	7 Jan 44	18 Aug 44	Stk. 8 Oct 46, to Mexico as Papaloapan 24 Nov 47
63	MOBERLY	Globe SB	Hendry	3 Nov 43	26 Jan 44	30 Aug 44	Stk. 23 Apr 47, sold 2 Dec 47
64	KNOXVILLE	L. Smith	Hendry	15 Apr 43	10 Jul 43	29 Apr 44	Stk. 19 Jul 46, sold 22 Sep 47, to Dominican Republic as Presidente Peynaldo
65	UNIONTOWN	L. Smith	Valley	21 Apr 43	7 Aug 43	15 Sep 44	Stk. 8 Jan 46, sold 19 Jun 46, to Argentina as Sarandi
66	READING	L. Smith	Koppers	25 May 43	28 Aug 43	19 Aug 44	Stk. 8 Jan 46, sold 23 Jun 46, to Argentina as Heroina
67	PEORIA	L. Smith	Valley	4 Jun 43	2 Oct 43	15 Oct 44	To Cuba 16 Jun 46 as Antonio Maceo, stk. 19 Jun 46
68	BRUNSWICK	L. Smith	Koppers	16 Jul 43	6 Nov 43	3 Oct 44	Stk. 19 Jun 46, sold 9 Apr 47
69	DAVENPORT	L. Smith	Diamond	7 Aug 43	8 Dec 43	15 Feb 45	Sold 6 Jun 46, stk. 29 Oct 46
70	EVANSVILLE	L. Smith	Diamond	28 Aug 43	27 Nov 43	4 Dec 44	To Japan 31 Oct 53 as Keyaki, stk. 1 Dec 61
71	NEW BEDFORD	L. Smith	Diamond	2 Oct 43	29 Dec 43	17 Jul 44	Stk. 3 Jul 46, sold 16 Nov 47
72	MACHIAS	Walsh	Unknown	1 Apr 43	14 Jul 43	No	To Britain 15 Oct 43 as Anguilla, stk. 29 Oct 46
73	(ANTIGUA)	Walsh	Unknown	3 Apr 43	26 Jul 43	No	To Britain 4 Nov 43, stk. 19 Jun 46
74	(ASCENSION)	Walsh	Unknown	30 Apr 43	6 Aug 43	No	To Britain 24 Nov 43, stk. 29 Oct 46
75	(BAHAMAS)	Walsh	Unknown	7 Apr 43	17 Aug 43	No	To Britain 6 Dec 43, stk. 19 Jul 46
76	(BARBADOS)	Walsh	Unknown	11 May 43	27 Aug 43	No	To Britain 18 Dec 43, stk. 19 Jul 46
77	(CAICOS)	Walsh	Unknown	23 Apr 43	6 Sep 43	No	To Britain 31 Dec 43, stk. 21 May 46, sold 2 Jul 46, to Argentina as Trinidad
78	(CAYMAN)	Walsh	Unknown	15 Jul 43	6 Sep 43	No	To Britain 20 Jan 44, stk. 19 Jun 46
79	(DOMINICA)	Walsh	Unknown	27 Jul 43	14 Sep 43	No	To Britain 25 Jan 44, stk. 19 Jun 46
80	(LABUAN)	Walsh	Unknown	7 Aug 43	21 Sep 43	No	To Britain 5 Feb 44, stk. 19 Jun 46
81	(TOBAGO)	Walsh	Unknown	17 Aug 43	27 Sep 43	No	To Britain 12 Aug 44, stk. 19 Jul 46
82	(MONTSERRAT)	Walsh	Unknown	28 Aug 43	27 Sep 43	No	To Britain 31 Aug 44, stk. 19 Jul 46
83	(NYASALAND)	Walsh	Unknown	7 Sep 43	6 Oct 43	No	To Britain 31 Jul 44, stk. 19 Jul 46
84	(PAPUA)	Walsh	Unknown	7 Sep 43	10 Oct 43	No	To Britain 25 Jul 44, stk. 19 Jul 46
85	(PITCAIRN)	Walsh	Unknown	14 Sep 43	15 Oct 43	No	To Britain 6 Jul 44, stk. 3 Jul 46
86	(ST. HELENA)	Walsh	Unknown	22 Sep 43	20 Oct 43	No	To Britain 19 Feb 44, stk. 19 Jun 46
87	(SARAWAK)	Walsh	Unknown	28 Sep 43	25 Oct 43	No	To Britain 18 Jul 44, stk. 19 Jul 46

The frigate *Albuquerque* (PF-7) ca. 1943. (NH 81377)

The guided missile frigate *Wadsworth* (FFG-9) on 1 January 1979. (DOD DN-SC-83-11901)

No.		Hull	Machinery	Laid down	Launched	Commiss'd	Disposition
88	(SEYCHELLES)	Walsh	Unknown	28 Sep 43	30 Oct 43	No	To Britain 27 Jun 44, stk. 3 Jul 46
89	(PERIM)	Walsh	Unknown	7 Oct 43	5 Nov 43	No	To Britain 16 Mar 44, stk. 3 Jul 46
90	(SOMALILAND)	Walsh	Unknown	11 Oct 43	11 Nov 43	No	To Britain 24 Jun 44, stk. 3 Jul 46
91	(TORTOLA)	Walsh	Unknown	16 Oct 43	16 Nov 43	No	To Britain 15 May 44, stk. 3 Jul 46
92	(ZANZIBAR)	Walsh	Unknown	20 Oct 43	21 Nov 43	No	To Britain 21 Jun 44, stk. 29 Oct 46
93	LORAIN	Lorain	Valley	25 Oct 43	18 Mar 44	15 Jan 45	To France 26 Mar 47 as Laplace, stk. 23 Apr 47
94	MILLEDGEVILLE	Lorain	Valley	9 Nov 43	5 Apr 44	18 Jan 45	Sold 9 Apr 47, stk. 23 Apr 47
95	STAMFORD	Lorain	Unknown	No	No	No	Cancelled 31 Dec 43
96	MACON	Lorain	Unknown	No	No	No	Cancelled 31 Dec 43
97	LORAIN	Lorain	Unknown	No	No	No	Cancelled 31 Dec 43
98	MILLEDGEVILLE	Lorain	Unknown	No	No	No	Cancelled 31 Dec 43
99	ORLANDO	Cleveland	Hendry	2 Aug 43	1 Dec 43	11 Nov 44	Stk. 19 Jul 46, sold 10 Nov 47
100	RACINE	Cleveland	Hendry	14 Sep 43	15 Mar 44	22 Jan 45	Stk. 19 Jul 46, sold 2 Dec 47
101	GREENSBORO	Cleveland	Hendry	23 Sep 43	9 Mar 44	29 Jan 45	Stk. 23 Apr 47, sold 28 Apr 48
102	FORSYTH	Cleveland	York Ice	6 Dec 43	20 May 44	11 Feb 45	Stk. 8 Oct 46, to Netherlands as civilian Cumulus 12 Jul 47.

Notes: Fiscal year 1943. Maritime Commission hulls 1421-32, 1481-87, 1433-62, 1477-80, 1463-68, 1475-76, 1488-95, 1654-74, and 1965-74 respectively. In October 1942, at the height of the U-boat war, President Roosevelt directed that 310 escorts be completed in 1943, including 260 under the existing Navy DE program and 50 by the Maritime Commission under a new program. The DEs had been designed to naval standards, and the Maritime Commission sought a simpler design more suited to its mass-production merchant ship yards. Gibbs and Cox modified the British River class design to suit American practice and Kaiser then produced the detailed plans. The changes included an additional foot of beam for stability and more length amidships to relieve congestion in the machinery spaces. The ships used reciprocating steam machinery. They had good seakeeping qualities but were excessively hot in warm climates. The following were used in 1944-45 as weather reporting ships with a balloon hangar replacing one 3" gun: PF-17, 18, 20, 23-24, 28-33, 40-41, 66-69, 71, 93-94, 99-102. Most of the others were on loan to the USSR between 1945 and 1949 as follows:

PF-3 to USSR 17 Aug 45 as EK-12, returned 16 Oct 49;
PF-4 to USSR 17 Aug 45 as EK-13, returned 1 Nov 49;
PF-5 to USSR 17 Aug 45 as EK-14, returned 1 Nov 49;
PF-6 to USSR 17 Aug 45 as EK-15, returned 2 Nov 49;
PF-7 to USSR 17 Aug 45 as EK-16, returned 15 Nov 49;
PF-8 to USSR 17 Aug 45 as EK-17, returned 15 Nov 49;
PF-21 to USSR 2 Sep 45 as EK-24, returned 14 Nov 49;
PF-22 to USSR 4 Sep 45 as EK-26, returned 31 Oct 49;
PF-25 to USSR 13 Jul 45 as EK-1, returned 17 Oct 49;
PF-26 to USSR 2 Sep 45 as EK-25, returned 31 Oct 49;
PF-27 to USSR 4 Sep 45 as EK-27, returned 14 Nov 49;
PF-34 to USSR 13 Jul 45 as EK-2, returned 17 Oct 49;
PF-35 to USSR 13 Jul 45 as EK-3, wrecked off Petropavlovsk;
PF-36 to USSR 13 Jul 45 as EK-4, returned 15 Nov 49;
PF-37 to USSR 13 Jul 45 as EK-5, returned 17 Oct 49;
PF-38 to USSR 13 Jul 45 as EK-6, returned 16 Oct 49;
PF-39 to USSR 13 Jul 45 as EK-7, returned 15 Oct 49;
PF-46 to USSR 27 Aug 45 as EK-18, returned 1 Nov 49;
PF-47 to USSR 27 Aug 45 as EK-19, returned 14 Nov 49;
PF-48 to USSR 27 Aug 45 as EK-20, returned 1 Nov 49;
PF-49 to USSR 27 Aug 45 as EK-21, returned 1 Nov 49;
PF-50 to USSR 27 Aug 45 as EK-22, returned 31 Oct 49;
PF-51 to USSR 27 Aug 45 as EK-23, returned 14 Nov 49;
PF-52 to USSR 13 Jul 45 as EK-8, returned 15 Oct 49;
PF-53 to USSR 13 Jul 45 as EK-9, returned 17 Oct 49;
PF-54 to USSR 13 Jul 45 as EK-10, returned 15 Oct 49;
PF-55 to USSR 13 Jul 45 as EK-11, returned 15 Nov 49;
PF-70 to USSR 4 Sep 45 as EK-28, returned 15 Nov 49.

After the war, many were loaned to the Coast Guard as weather ships: Brownsville (WPF-10) 15 Apr 46-2 Aug 46; Bangor (WPF-16) 15 Apr 46-16 Aug 46; Muskegon (WPF-24) 15 Mar 46-27 Aug 46; Emporia (WPF-28) 14 Mar 46-28 Aug 46; Groton (WPF-29) 13 Mar 46-25 Sep 46; Woonsocket (WPF-32) 16 Mar 46-18 Sep 46; Orange (WPF-43) 15 Apr 46-28 Oct 46; Corpus Christi (WPF-44) 15 Apr 46-2 Aug 46; Hutchinson (WPF-45) 15 Apr 46-23 Sep 46; Covington (WPF-56) 16 Mar 46-17 Sep 46; Sheboygan (WPF-57) 14 Mar 46-9 Aug 46; Abilene (WPF-58) 15 Mar 46-21 Aug 46; Manitiowoc (WPF-61) 14 Mar 46-3 Sep 46; Gladwyne (WPF-62) 15 Apr 46-31 Aug 46; Moberly (WPF-63) 15 Apr 46-12 Aug 46; and Forsyth (WPF-102) 14 Mar 46-2 Aug 46. The Lorain, Milledgeville, and Greensboro may also have been loaned to the Coast Guard between March and August 1946.
Renamings: PF-33 ex Toledo 18 Aug 43, PF-58 ex Bridgeport 28 Jun 44, PF-62 ex Worcester 18 Aug 44, PF-63 ex Scranton 28 Jun 44, PF-65 ex Chattanooga 18 Aug 44, PF-93 ex Roanoke 18 Mar 44, PF-94 ex Sitka 7 Feb 44, PF-97 ex Vallejo 19 Nov 43. Before receiving their "Colony" names, the British ships in this class had "Captain" names: Hallowell (PF-72), Hammond (73), Hargood (74), Hotham (75), Halsted (76), Hannam (77), Harland (78), Harnam (79), Harvey (80), Holmes (81), Hornby (82), Hoste (83), Howett (84), Pilford (85), Pasley (86), Patton (87), Peard (88), Phillimore (89), Popham (90), Peyton (91), and Prowse (92). Three original "Colony" names were replaced 3 Dec 43: Gold Coast (80), Hong Kong (81), and Sierra Leone (89).
Reclassifications: Ex PG 111-210 (corvettes) 15 Apr 43.

1960

PF-103 class

Displacement: 900 tons
Dimensions: 275' x 33' x 10'
Armament: 2-3"/50 (PF 103-6); 2-3"/50 6-12.75"T (PF 107-8)

Machinery: 5300 BHP, F. M. diesel engines, 2 screws
Speed: 20 kts.
Complement: 133 (PF 103-6); 150 (PF 107-8)

No.		Hull	Laid down	Launched	Commiss'd	Disposition
103	(BAYANDOR)	Levingston	20 Aug 62	7 Jul 63	No	To Iran 18 May 64
104	(NAGHDI)	Levingston	12 Sep 62	10 Oct 63	No	To Iran 22 Jul 64
105	(MILANIAN)	Levingston	1 May 67	4 Jan 68	No	To Iran 13 Feb 69
106	(KAHNAMUIE)	Levingston	12 Jun 67	4 Apr 68	No	To Iran 13 Feb 69
107	(TAPI)	Lorain	1 Sep 70	17 Oct 70	No	To Thailand 1 Nov 71
108	(KHIRIRAT)	Norfolk SB	31 Mar 72	2 Jun 73	No	To Thailand 10 Aug 74.

Notes: Fiscal years 1961, 1961, 1967, 1966, 1968, and 1970 respectively. Built under MDAP, the first four for Iran and the last two for Thailand. The design was based on the Italian Albatros type of 1953, eight of which were built for Italy, Denmark, and the Netherlands under the MDAP offshore procurement program as PC 1619-1626, and on an Italian improvement of that design which had been used to build two Indonesian Pattimura-class frigates in 1956-58.

Guided Missile Frigates (FFG)

1972

OLIVER HAZARD PERRY class

Displacement: 3700 tons
Dimensions: 445' x 45' x 24'6"
Armament: 1-3" 1-Standard-SAM Harpoon-SSM 6-12.75"T LAMPS

Machinery: 40,000 SHP, 2 G.E. LM-2500 gas turbines, 1 screw
Speed: 28.5 kts.
Complement: 180

No.		Hull		Laid down	Launched	Commiss'd	Disposition
7	OLIVER HAZARD PERRY	Bath		12 Jun 75	25 Sep 76	17 Dec 77	USN
8	McINERNEY	Bath		16 Jan 78	4 Nov 78	15 Dec 79	USN
9	WADSWORTH	Todd,	San Pedro	13 Jul 77	29 Jul 78	2 Apr 80	USN
10	DUNCAN	Todd,	Seattle	29 Apr 77	1 Mar 78	24 May 80	USN
11	CLARK	Bath		17 Jul 78	24 Mar 79	17 May 80	USN
12	GEORGE PHILIP	Todd,	San Pedro	14 Dec 77	16 Dec 78	15 Nov 80	USN
13	SAMUEL ELIOT MORISON	Bath		4 Dec 78	14 Jul 79	11 Oct 80	USN
14	SIDES	Todd,	San Pedro	7 Aug 78	19 May 79	30 May 81	USN
15	ESTOCIN	Bath		2 Apr 79	3 Nov 79	10 Jan 81	USN

No.		Hull	Laid down	Launched	Commiss'd	Disposition
16	CLIFTON SPRAGUE	Bath	30 Jul 79	16 Feb 80	21 Mar 81	USN
17	(ADELAIDE)	Todd, Seattle	29 Jul 77	21 Jun 78	No	To Australia 15 Nov 80
18	(CANBERRA)	Todd, Seattle	1 Mar 78	1 Dec 78	No	To Australia 21 Mar 81
19	JOHN A. MOORE	Todd, San Pedro	19 Dec 78	20 Oct 79	14 Nov 81	USN
20	ANTRIM	Todd, Seattle	21 Jun 78	27 Mar 79	26 Sep 81	USN
21	FLATLEY	Bath	13 Nov 79	15 May 80	20 Jun 81	USN
22	FAHRION	Todd, Seattle	1 Dec 78	24 Aug 79	16 Jan 82	USN
23	LEWIS B. PULLER	Todd, San Pedro	23 May 79	15 Mar 80	17 Apr 82	USN
24	JACK WILLIAMS	Bath	25 Feb 80	30 Aug 80	19 Sep 81	USN
25	COPELAND	Todd, San Pedro	24 Oct 79	26 Jul 80	7 Aug 82	USN
26	GALLERY	Bath	17 May 80	20 Dec 80	5 Dec 81	USN
27	MAHLON S. TISDALE	Todd, San Pedro	19 Mar 80	7 Feb 81	13 Nov 82	USN
28	BOONE	Todd, Seattle	27 Mar 79	16 Jan 80	15 May 82	USN
29	STEPHEN W. GROVES	Bath	16 Sep 80	4 Apr 81	17 Apr 82	USN
30	REID	Todd, San Pedro	8 Oct 80	27 Jun 81	19 Feb 83	USN
31	STARK	Todd, Seattle	24 Aug 79	30 May 80	23 Oct 82	USN
32	JOHN L. HALL	Bath	5 Jan 81	24 Jul 81	26 Jun 82	USN
33	JARRETT	Todd, San Pedro	11 Feb 81	17 Oct 81	2 Jul 83	USN
34	AUBREY FITCH	Bath	10 Apr 81	17 Oct 81	9 Oct 82	USN
35	(SYDNEY)	Todd, Seattle	16 Jan 80	26 Sep 80	No	To Australia 29 Jan 83
36	UNDERWOOD	Bath	30 Jul 81	6 Feb 82	29 Jan 83	USN
37	CROMMELIN	Todd, Seattle	30 May 80	1 Jul 81	18 Jun 83	USN
38	CURTS	Todd, San Pedro	1 Jul 81	6 Mar 82	8 Oct 83	USN
39	DOYLE	Bath	23 Oct 81	22 May 82	21 May 83	USN
40	HALYBURTON	Todd, Seattle	26 Sep 80	13 Oct 81	7 Jan 84	USN
41	McCLUSKY	Todd, San Pedro	21 Oct 81	18 Sep 82	10 Dec 83	USN
42	KLAKRING	Bath	19 Feb 82	18 Sep 82	20 Aug 83	USN
43	THATCH	Todd, San Pedro	6 Mar 82	18 Dec 82	17 Mar 84	USN
44	(DARWIN)	Todd, Seattle	2 Jul 81	26 Mar 82	No	To Australia 21 Jul 84
45	DE WERT	Bath	14 Jun 82	18 Dec 82	19 Nov 83	USN
46	RENTZ	Todd, San Pedro	18 Sep 82	16 Jul 83	30 Jun 84	USN
47	NICHOLAS	Bath	27 Sep 82	23 Apr 83	10 Mar 84	USN
48	VANDEGRIFT	Todd, Seattle	13 Oct 81	15 Oct 82	24 Nov 84	USN
49	ROBERT G. BRADLEY	Bath	28 Dec 82	13 Aug 83	11 Aug 84	USN
50	TAYLOR	Bath	5 May 83	5 Nov 83	1 Dec 84	USN
51	GARY	Todd, San Pedro	18 Dec 82	19 Nov 83	17 Nov 84	USN
52	CARR	Todd, Seattle	26 Mar 82	26 Feb 83	27 Jul 85	USN
53	HAWES	Bath	22 Aug 83	18 Feb 84	9 Feb 85	USN
54	FORD	Todd, San Pedro	16 Jul 83	23 Jun 84	29 Jun 85	USN
55	ELROD	Bath	21 Nov 83	12 May 84	6 Jul 85	USN
56	SIMPSON	Bath	27 Feb 84	31 Aug 84	9 Nov 85	USN
57	REUBEN JAMES	Todd, San Pedro	19 Nov 83	8 Feb 85	22 Mar 86	USN
58	SAMUEL B. ROBERTS	Bath	21 May 84	8 Dec 84	12 Apr 86	USN
59	KAUFFMAN	Bath	8 Apr 85	29 Mar 86	28 Feb 87	USN
60	RODNEY M. DAVIS	Todd, San Pedro	8 Feb 85	11 Jan 86	9 May 87	USN
61	INGRAHAM	Todd, San Pedro	30 Mar 87	25 Jun 88	5 Aug 89	USN.

Notes: Fiscal years 1973 (FFG-7), 1975 (8-10), 1976 (11-18), 1977 (19-26), 1978 (27-35), 1979 (36-43), 1980 (44-49), 1981 (50-55), 1982 (56-58), 1983 (59-60), and 1984 (61). Intended as relatively cheap, mass-production ships whose primary missions would be to escort fast (20-knot) transatlantic convoys and serve on mid-ocean ASW picket stations. Initially intended as single-mission ships, they ultimately received weapons and sensors for ASW, local air defense, and surface warfare. Their Harpoon SSMs are fired by the Standard SAM launcher. Early vessels (FFG-7 and FFG 9-35) have a narrower flight deck and were not fitted with the LAMPS III helicopter. Australia and Spain are building additional ships of this type locally without U.S. hull numbers.
Renaming: FFG-13 ex Samuel E. Morison 17 Aug 79; FFG-45 ex Dewert 2 Dec 82
Reclassification: FFG 7-10 ex PF 109-112 30 Jun 75; PF-109 ex PF-150 Mar 73.

Submarines (SS)

1893

PLUNGER

Displacement: 149/168 tons
Dimensions: 85'3" x 11'6" x 11'(mean)
Armament: 2-18"T
Complement: 7

Machinery: 1625 IHP, 2 triple-
expansion engines, 2 screws/ 70
BHP, E. D. electric motor, 1 screw
Speed: 15/10 kts. (designed)

	Hull	Machinery	Laid down	Launched	Commiss'd	Disposition
PLUNGER	Columbian		23 Jun 96	7 Aug 97	No	Cancelled Apr 00.

Notes: In March 1893 Congress appropriated funds for a competition for an experimental submarine. The Secretary of the Navy finally signed a contract for the boat with the inventor John P. Holland on 26 March 1895, and she was built in Baltimore under a sub-contract from the John P. Holland Torpedo Boat Co. The Navy's many design requirements included steam propulsion on the surface, which resulted in bulky machinery and an unshielded boiler which retained such tremendous amounts of heat as to make the boat nearly uninhabitable when submerged. Dock trials in 1898 and later trials underway confirmed that this installation would not work and also showed that the boat lacked stability. Under the legislation for fiscal year 1901 her contract was cancelled and the money paid by the government towards her purchase was credited towards the price of the new Plunger (SS-2).

1899

HOLLAND

Displacement: 64/74 tons
Dimensions: 53'10"(oa.) x 10'4"(e) x 8'6"
Armament: 1-18"T 1-8.4" dynamite gun; 1-18"T (1904)
Complement: 6

Machinery: 45 BHP Otto gasoline
engine/ 75 BHP, E. D. electric
motor, 1 screw
Speed: 8/5 kts.

No.		Hull	Laid down	Launched	Commiss'd	Disposition
1	HOLLAND	Crescent	Unknown	17 May 97	12 Oct 00	Stk. 21 Nov 10, sold 18 Jun 13.

Notes: Fiscal years 1897 and 1900. In June 1896 Congress authorized the Navy to order two more Holland-type submarines provided the Plunger fulfilled her contract. In late 1896 Holland became concerned that the Plunger would not succeed, and his company, the John P. Holland Torpedo Boat Co., authorized him to build a new boat to his own design as a private venture free of all external design requirements. His boat, the Holland, made her first dive on 11 March 1898, and in March 1899 Congress authorized her purchase under the 1896 authorization. The Navy purchased her on 11 Apr 00 after extensive trials. She was a milestone in submarine development because she combined internal combustion engines for surface propulsion with storage batteries and electric motors for submerged movement. She was underpowered, however, lacked longitudinal stability, and was difficult to steer. In addition, open battery cells prevented her from diving at an angle greater than 15 degrees. She was sold by the Navy in November 1910 but was reacquired and sold again in 1913.

PLUNGER class

Displacement: 107/123 tons
Dimensions: 63'10"(oa.) x 11'11"(e) x 12'
Armament: 1-18"T
Complement: 7

Machinery: 160 BHP Otto gasoline
engine/ 70 BHP, E. D. electric
motor, 1 screw
Speed: 9/7 kts.

No.		Hull	Laid down	Launched	Commiss'd	Disposition
2	PLUNGER	Crescent	21 May 01	1 Feb 02	19 Sep 03	Stk. 24 Feb 13, sold 26 Jan 22
3	ADDER	Crescent	3 Oct 00	22 Jul 01	12 Jan 03	Sunk as target in Manila Bay, stk. 16 Jan 22
4	GRAMPUS	Union	10 Dec 00	31 Jul 02	28 May 03	Sunk as target in Manila Bay, stk. 16 Jan 22
5	MOCCASIN	Crescent	8 Nov 00	20 Aug 01	17 Jan 03	Sunk as target in Manila Bay, stk. 16 Jan 22
6	PIKE	Union	10 Dec 00	14 Jan 03	28 May 03	Sunk as target in Manila Bay, stk. 16 Jan 22
7	PORPOISE	Crescent	13 Dec 00	23 Sep 01	19 Sep 03	Sunk as target in Manila Bay, stk. 16 Jan 22
8	SHARK	Crescent	11 Jan 00	19 Oct 01	19 Sep 03	Sunk as target in Manila Bay, stk. 16 Jan 22.

Notes: Fiscal years 1897 and 1900 (SS-2), 1901 (others). Enlarged Holland-type boats with increased horsepower, their hulls were built at Elizabethport, N.J., and San Francisco, Calif., under sub-contracts from the John P. Holland Torpedo Boat Co. Each cylinder of the gasoline engine could be used independently, but, as in the Holland, the engine could not be reversed. Their operating depth was 150'. Five of these boats were designated on 24 Sep 20 for use as targets and the other two, A-3 (ex Grampus) and A-5 (ex Pike), were similarly designated on 14 Jul 21. The A-1 (ex Plunger) was sold on the deck of the monitor Puritan as Target E.
Renamings: To A-1 through A-7 respectively on 17 Nov 11.

1904

VIPER class

Displacement: 145/173 tons
Dimensions: 82'5"(oa.) x 12'6" x 13
Armament: 2-18"T
Complement: 10

Machinery: 250 BHP Craig gasoline engine/ 150 BHP, E. D. electric motor, 1 screw
Speed: 9/8 kts.

No.		Hull	Laid down	Launched	Commiss'd	Disposition
10	VIPER	Fore River	5 Sep 05	30 Mar 07	18 Oct 07	Sunk as target in Manila Bay, stk. 16 Jan 22
11	CUTTLEFISH	Fore River	30 Aug 05	1 Sep 06	18 Oct 07	Sunk as target in Manila Bay, stk. 16 Jan 22
12	TARANTULA	Fore River	5 Sep 05	30 Mar 07	3 Dec 07	Sunk as target in Manila Bay, stk. 16 Jan 22.

Notes: Fiscal year 1905. A further enlargement of the Holland type with two torpedo tubes, their hulls were built at Quincy, Mass., under a sub-contract from the Electric Boat Co. Their operating depth was 150'. They were designated for use as targets on 24 Sep 20 (B-2), 14 Jul 21 (B-3), and in Aug 21 (B-1).
Renamings: To B-1 through B-3 respectively on 17 Nov 11.

OCTOPUS class

Displacement: 238/275 tons
Dimensions: 105'4"(oa.) x 13'11"(e) x 14'9"(max)
Armament: 2-18"T
Complement: 15

Machinery: 500 BHP, 2 Craig gasoline engines/ 300 (SS-9), 250 (others) BHP, 2 E. D. electric motors, 2 screws
Speed: 10/9 kts.

No.		Hull	Laid down	Launched	Commiss'd	Disposition
9	OCTOPUS	Fore River	3 Aug 05	4 Oct 06	30 Jun 08	To sale list 26 Dec 19, sold 13 Apr 20
13	STINGRAY	Fore River	4 Mar 08	8 Apr 09	23 Nov 09	To sale list 26 Dec 19, sold 13 Apr 20
14	TARPON	Fore River	17 Mar 08	8 Apr 09	23 Nov 09	To sale list 26 Dec 19, sold 13 Apr 20
15	BONITA	Fore River	17 Mar 08	17 Jun 09	23 Nov 09	To sale list 26 Dec 19, sold 13 Apr 20
16	SNAPPER	Fore River	17 Mar 08	16 Jun 09	2 Feb 10	To sale list 26 Dec 19, sold 13 Apr 20.

Notes: Fiscal years 1905 (SS-9) and 1908. These boats were built to a design of Lawrence Y. Spear, chief designer for Electric Boat, who preferred a lengthened and flattened hull shape to the streamlined form used by Holland. Like the earlier Holland-type boats, they were single-hulled submarines with the ballast tanks inside the pressure hull. Their operating depth was increased to 200 feet, a feature retained in all American submarines through the "S" class of World War I except the "AA" class fleet boats. The hulls were built under a sub-contract from the Electric Boat Co.
Renamings: To C-1 through C-5 respectively on 17 Nov 11.

1907

NARWHAL class

Displacement: 288/337 tons
Dimensions: 134'10"(oa.) x 13'11"(e) x 11'8"
Armament: 4-18"T
Complement: 15

Machinery: 600 BHP, 2 Nelseco gasoline engines/ 260 BHP, E. D. electric motors, 2 screws
Speed: 13/9.5 kts.

The submarine *Tarpon* (SS-14) in 1909. She was soon renamed *C-3*. (NH 43600)

The submarine *AA-1* (SS-52) off Provincetown, Mass., ca. 1920. She became the fleet submarine *T-1* (SF-1) later in 1920. (NH 43762)

No.		Hull	Laid down	Launched	Commiss'd	Disposition
17	NARWHAL	Fore River	16 Apr 08	8 Apr 09	23 Nov 09	Ordered sold 25 Mar 22, sold 5 Jun 22
18	GRAYLING	Fore River	16 Apr 08	16 Jun 09	23 Nov 09	Ordered sold 15 Dec 21, sold 25 Sep 22
19	SALMON	Fore River	16 Apr 08	12 Mar 10	8 Sep 10	Ordered sold 18 Apr 22, sold 31 Jul 22.

Notes: Fiscal year 1908. Much enlarged versions of the preceeding class, these were the earliest American submarines to be ocean-going. Their hulls were built under a sub-contract from Electric Boat.
Renamings: To D-1 through D-3 respectively on 17 Nov 11.

SEAL

Displacement: 400/516 tons
Dimensions: 161'(oa.) x 13'1"(e) x 12'6"
Armament: 6-18"T
Complement: 24

Machinery: 1200 BHP, 2 White & Middleton gasoline engines/ 520 BHP, Diehl electric motors, 2 screws
Speed: 14/10 kts.

	Hull	Laid down	Launched	Commiss'd	Disposition
SEAL	Newport News	2 Feb 09	8 Feb 11	28 Oct 12	Sunk as target 21 Jun 21 off Newport, R. I., stk. 29 Aug 21.

Notes: Fiscal year 1908. In 1907 competitive trials were held between Electric Boat's Octopus (SS-9) and the Lake, an experimental boat built by Holland's chief rival, Simon Lake. On 3 Feb 08 the Navy granted a contingent contract to Lake for a submarine of his design. The boat's hull was built at Newport News under a sub-contract from the Lake Torpedo Boat Co. Two of her torpedo tubes were mounted on the deck. The Navy granted final acceptance on 24 Oct 13. The G-1 was designated for target use on 19 Feb 20 and was sunk by USS Grebe (AM-43) in depth charge tests. Her hulk was sold 17 Aug 22.
Renaming: To G-1 17 Nov 11.
Reclassification: Initially without an official number because of the contingent nature of her contract, she was assigned the official number Submarine 19 1/2 on 12 Jun 16 and the hull number SS-20 on 17 Jul 20.

Subsurface Torpedo Boat

Displacement: Unknown
Dimensions: 140'(wl.) x 13'6" x 11'
Armament: 2-6# 1-21"T
Armor: 4 1/2" conning tower

Machinery: 3000 BHP; 2 Standard gasoline engines
Speed: 19 kts. (designed)
Complement: 16

Notes: Fiscal year 1907. This novel type, developed by W. I. Babcock, looked as if it had two hulls-- a torpedo boat hull on top of a submarine hull. An unspecified number of these semi-submerged torpedo boats was authorized by Congress on 29 Jun 06 under the condition that successful tests be conducted first on a prototype. The authorization act for the following year (1908) extended the deadline for the tests to 29 May 07 and increased the amount of money, but no boats were built. The specifications above refer to the prototype proposed by Babcock and Bath Iron Works in 1906.

1908

E-1 class

Displacement: 287/342 tons
Dimensions: 135'3"(oa.) x 14'7"(e) x 11'8"
Armament: 4-18"T
Complement: 20

Machinery: 550 BHP, 2 Nelseco diesel engines/ 300 BHP, E. D. electric motors, 2 screws
Speed: 13.5/11.5 kts.

No.		Hull	Laid down	Launched	Commiss'd	Disposition
24	E-1	Fore River	22 Dec 09	27 May 11	14 Feb 12	To sale list 22 Oct 21, sold 19 Apr 22
25	E-2	Fore River	22 Dec 09	15 Jun 11	14 Feb 12	To sale list 22 Oct 21, sold 19 Apr 22

Notes: Fiscal year 1909. These boats were generally similar to the "D" class except that they received diesel engines instead of the unsafe gasoline engines in the earlier boats. They were also the first American submarines to be fitted with diving planes and with radios. Their hulls were built under a sub-contract from Electric Boat. After an internal explosion in 1916, the E-2 was re-engined with 500 BHP McIntosh & Seymour diesels and 500 BHP Ridgeway electric motors.
Renamings: Ex Skipjack and Sturgeon respectively 17 Nov 11.

F-1 class

Displacement: 330/400 tons
Dimensions: 142'7"(oa.) x 15'5" x 12'2"
Armament: 4-18"T
Complement: 22

Machinery: 780 BHP, Nelseco (SS 20-
  21), 800 BHP, Craig (others)
  gasoline engines/ 620 BHP, E. D.
  electric motors, 2 screws
Speed: 14/11.5 kts.

No.	Hull	Laid down	Launched	Commiss'd	Disposition
20 F-1	Union	23 Aug 09	12 Mar 12	19 Jun 12	Sunk in collision with F-3 off Pt. Loma, Calif., 17 Dec 17
21 F-2	Union	23 Aug 09	19 Mar 12	25 Jun 12	Ordered sold 22 Apr 22, sold 17 Aug 22
22 F-3	Moran	17 Aug 09	6 Jan 12	5 Aug 12	Ordered sold 22 Apr 22, sold 17 Aug 22
23 F-4	Moran	21 Aug 09	6 Jan 12	3 May 13	Foundered off Pearl Harbor 25 Mar 15.

Notes: Fiscal year 1909. An Electric Boat design somewhat larger than the "E" class and with more powerful electric motors. All hulls were built under sub-contracts from the Electric Boat Co. The F-4 foundered because of acid corrosion in her hull. She was raised 29 Aug 15 and stricken from the Navy List two days later. In 1940 she was buried as fill in a trench off the Submarine Base, Pearl Harbor.
Renamings: Ex Carp, Barracuda, Pickerel, and Skate respectively 17 Nov 11.

G-4

Displacement: 360/457 tons
Dimensions: 157'6"(oa.) x 17'6" x 10'11"
Armament: 4-18"T
Complement: 24

Machinery: 1000 BHP, 2 Fiat gasoline
  engines/ 440 BHP, Diehl electric
  motors, 2 screws
Speed: 14/9.5 kts.

No.	Hull	Laid down	Launched	Commiss'd	Disposition
26 G-4	Cramp	9 Jul 10	15 Aug 12	22 Jan 14	Sold 15 Apr 20.

Notes: Fiscal year 1909. Built under a sub-contract from the American Laurenti Co. to a Fiat San Giorgio Co. design. She represented an attempt by the Navy to bring into the submarine program design features besides those used by Electric Boat and Lake. She lacked stability and proved to be generally unsatisfactory, however, and the Navy accorded final acceptance only on 7 Mar 16. Her pressure hull had a non-circular cross section, a feature repeated with equal lack of success in the V-1 (SF-4) class.
Renaming: Ex Thrasher 17 Nov 11.

G-2

Displacement: 400/516 tons
Dimensions: 161'(oa.) x 13'1" x 12'6"
Armament: 4-18"T
Complement: 24

Machinery: 1200 BHP, 2 White &
  Middleton gasoline engines/ 520
  BHP, Diehl electric motors, 2
  screws
Speed: 14/10.5 kts.

No.	Hull	Laid down	Launched	Commiss'd	Disposition
27 G-2	Newport News	20 Oct 09	10 Jan 12	6 Feb 15	Foundered near New London, Conn, 30 Jul 19.

Notes: Fiscal year 1909. The hull was built under sub-contract from the Lake Torpedo Boat Co. Her contract was declared forfeited on 6 Nov 13 following the failure of the Lake company and she was completed by New York Navy Yard. She sank off Niantic, Conn., while involved in depth charge tests with USCGC Acushnet. Her wreck was abandoned 9 Jun 23 as unsalable.
Renaming: Ex Tuna 17 Nov 11.

1909

G-3

Displacement: 393/460 tons
Dimensions: 161'(oa.) x 13'1"(e) x 12'10"
Armament: 6-18"T
Complement: 25

Machinery: 1200 BHP, 2 Busch-Sulzer
  diesel engines/ 600 BHP, Diehl
  electric motors, 2 screws
Speed: 14/9.5 kts.

No.	Hull	Laid down	Launched	Commiss'd	Disposition
31 G-3	Lake	30 Mar 11	27 Dec 13	22 Mar 15	Ordered sold 9 Sep 21, sold 19 Apr 22.

Notes: Fiscal year 1910. Another Lake design, she had bulges for added stability and a pair of deck mounted torpedo tubes. Her contract was declared forfeited on 6 Nov 13 following the closing of the Lake yard at Bridgeport, Conn, and she was completed by the New York Navy Yard.
Renaming: Ex Turbot 17 Nov 11.

H-1 class

Displacement: 358/467 tons
Dimensions: 150'4"(oa.) x 15'10"(e) x 12'5"(mean)
Armament: 4-18"T
Complement: 25

Machinery: 950 BHP, 2 Nelseco diesel engines/ 600 BHP, E. D. electric motors, 2 screws
Speed: 14/10.5 kts.

No.		Hull	Laid down	Launched	Commiss'd	Disposition
28	H-1	Union	22 Mar 11	6 May 13	1 Dec 13	Grounded in Magdalena Bay, Mex., 12 Mar 20
29	H-2	Union	23 Mar 11	4 Jun 13	1 Dec 13	Stk. 18 Dec 30, scrapped 1931
30	H-3	Moran	3 Apr 11	3 Jul 13	16 Jan 14	Stk. 18 Dec 30, scrapped 1931.

Notes: Fiscal year 1910. A highly successful Electric Boat design which was copied in boats for the British, Italian, Chilean, and Russian navies. They were the first American submarines to carry reload torpedoes. All three were built under sub-contracts from Electric Boat. The hulk of the H-1 sank 24 Mar 20 and was sold 25 Jun 20.
Renamings: Ex Seawolf, Nautilus, and Garfish respectively 17 Nov 11.

1909

Subsurface Torpedo Boats

Three "torpedo-boats (subsurface)" were authorized in fiscal year 1910 and re-authorized in fiscal year 1911. They were also described as destroyers or torpedo-boats whose vitals were located below the normal load water line. The 1910 act provided for one large vessel of 22 knots and two much smaller ones of 16 knots, while the 1911 act also allowed the Navy to purchase a small 19-knot type. Beyond the length of 150' for one and 115' for another of the 1910 vessels and their armament with 1-18"T, little is known of the designs. As in the case of the 1907 semi-submersible type, a prototype had to be tested before the Navy could spend the money. None was built.

1910

K-1 class

Displacement: 392/521 tons
Dimensions: 153'7"(oa.) x 16'9"(e) x 13'1"(mean)
Armament: 4-18"T
Complement: 28

Machinery: 960 BHP, 2 Nelseco diesel engines/ 680 BHP, E. D electric motors, 2 screws
Speed: 14/10.5 kts.

No.		Hull	Laid down	Launched	Commiss'd	Disposition
32	K-1	Fore River	20 Feb 12	3 Sep 13	17 Mar 14	Stk. 18 Dec 30, scrapped 1931
33	K-2	Fore River	20 Feb 12	4 Oct 13	31 Jan 14	Stk. 18 Dec 30, scrapped 1931
34	K-3	Union	15 Jan 12	14 Mar 14	30 Oct 14	Stk. 18 Dec 30, scrapped 1931
35	K-4	Moran	27 Jan 12	19 Mar 14	24 Oct 14	Stk. 18 Dec 30, scrapped 1931
36	K-5	Fore River	10 Jun 12	17 Mar 14	22 Aug 14	Stk. 18 Dec 30, scrapped 1931
37	K-6	Fore River	19 Jun 12	26 Mar 14	9 Sep 14	Stk. 18 Dec 30, scrapped 1931
38	K-7	Union	10 May 12	20 Jun 14	1 Dec 14	Stk. 18 Dec 30, scrapped 1931
39	K-8	Union	10 May 12	11 Jul 14	1 Dec 14	Stk. 18 Dec 30, scrapped 1931.

Notes: Fiscal year 1911 (SS 32-35) and 1912. An Electric Boat design built under sub-contracts from Electric Boat, they were similar to the "H" class but had greater fuel capacity and endurance. Four of them (K-1, K-2, K-5, and K-6) served in the Azores during World War I.
Renamings: SS 32-35 ex Haddock, Cachalot, Orca, and Walrus respectively 17 Nov 11.

1912

L-1 class

Displacement: 450/548 tons
Dimensions: 168'6"(oa.) x 17'5"(e) x 13'7"
Armament: 1-3"/23 4-18"T
Complement: 28

Machinery: 900 BHP, 2 Nelseco diesel engines/ 680 BHP, E. D. electric motors, 2 screws
Speed: 14/10.5 kts.

No.		Hull	Laid down	Launched	Commiss'd	Disposition
40	L-1	Fore River	13 Apr 14	20 Jan 15	11 Apr 16	Ordered sold 6 Feb 22,
						sold 31 Jul 22
41	L-2	Fore River	19 Mar 14	11 Feb 15	29 Sep 16	Stk. 18 Dec 30, scrapped 1933
42	L-3	Fore River	18 Apr 14	15 Mar 15	22 Apr 16	Stk. 18 Dec 30, scrapped 1933
43	L-4	Fore River	23 Mar 14	3 Apr 15	4 May 16	Ordered sold 6 Feb 22,
						sold 31 Jul 22
49	L-9	Fore River	2 Nov 14	27 Oct 15	4 Aug 16	Stk. 18 Dec 30, scrapped 1933
50	L-10	Fore River	17 Feb 15	16 Mar 16	2 Aug 16	Ordered sold 6 Feb 22,
						sold 31 Jul 22
51	L-11	Fore River	17 Feb 15	16 May 16	15 Aug 16	Stk. 18 Dec 30, scrapped 1933.

Notes: Fiscal years 1913 (SS 40-43) and 1914. Designed by Electric Boat and built under a sub-contract from the Electric Boat Co, they were the first U.S. submarine class with a deck gun. The gun lowered into a watertight trunk when the vessel submerged. All seven served during World War I in Irish waters, where they wore AL instead of L numbers to avoid confusion with the British L-class. L-3, L-9, and L-11 were re-engined in 1923 with the Busch-Sulzer diesels from the N-4, N-7, and N-5 respectively.

L-5 class

Displacement: 456/524 tons
Dimensions: 165'(oa.) x 14'9"(e) x 13'3"(mean)
Armament: 1-3"/23 4-18"T
Complement: 28

Machinery: 1200 BHP, 2 Busch-Sulzer diesel engines/ 800 BHP, Diehl electric motors, 2 screws
Speed: 14/10.5 kts.

No.		Hull	Laid down	Launched	Commiss'd	Disposition
44	L-5	Lake	14 May 14	1 May 16	17 Feb 18	Stk. 20 Mar 25, scrapped 1925
45	L-6	Craig	27 May 14	31 Aug 16	7 Dec 17	Stk. 20 Mar 25, scrapped 1925
46	L-7	Craig	2 Jun 14	28 Sep 16	7 Dec 17	Stk. 20 Mar 25, scrapped 1925
48	L-8	Portsmouth	24 Feb 15	23 Apr 17	30 Aug 17	Stk. 20 Mar 25, scrapped 1926.

Notes: Fiscal years 1913 (SS 44-46) and 1914. Lake-designed counterparts to the L-1 class, they suffered from engine problems which accounted for their short service. The two Craig-built hulls were sub-contracted from the Lake Torpedo Boat Co. The L-8 was ordered at Portsmouth to Lake plans in order to give a government yard experience in designing and building submarines.

M-1

Displacement: 488/676 tons
Dimensions: 196'3"(oa.) x 19'1"(e) x 11'
Armament: 1-3"/23 4-18"T
Complement: 28

Machinery: 840 BHP, 2 Nelseco diesel engines/ 680 BHP, E. D. electric motors, 2 screws
Speed: 14/10.5 kts.

No.		Hull	Laid down	Launched	Commiss'd	Disposition
47	M-1	Fore River	2 Jul 14	14 Sep 15	16 Feb 18	Ordered sold 5 Apr 22,
						sold 25 Sep 22.

Notes: Fiscal year 1913. In 1913 the Navy ordered a single experimental double-hulled submarine, in which the ballast and fuel tanks were located outside the pressure hull. The ballast tanks in this boat proved to be poorly arranged and she became unstable during the transition from submerged to surfaced operations. In addition, although she was larger than the other boats then building, she was too small to draw full benefit from the double-hull arrangement. She was designed by Electric Boat and built under a sub-contract from that company.

1914

AA class

Displacement: 1107/1482 tons
Dimensions: 268'9"(oa.) x 22'10"(e) x 14'2"(mean)
Armament: 2-3"/23 8-18"T (SS-52); 1-4"/50 4-18"T (others, SS-52 1920)
Complement: 38

Machinery: 4000 BHP, 4 Nelseco diesel engines/ 1350 BHP, 2 E. D. electric motors, 2 screws
Speed: 20/10.5 kts.

No.		Hull	Laid down	Launched	Commiss'd	Disposition
52	AA-1	Fore River	21 Jun 16	25 Jul 18	30 Jan 20	Stk. 19 Sep 30, scrapped 1931
60	AA-2	Fore River	31 May 17	6 Sep 19	7 Jan 22	Stk. 19 Sep 30, scrapped 1931
61	AA-3	Fore River	21 May 17	24 May 19	7 Dec 20	Stk. 19 Sep 30, scrapped 1931.

Notes: Fiscal years 1915 (SS-52) and 1916. A new type of seagoing submarine designed to keep up with the battle fleet and operate against the enemy during a fleet action. Electric Boat developed the design, which included a double-hulled configuration amidships, single-hull construction at the ends,

and an extra diesel engine on each shaft for increased speed. The operating depth was reduced to 150'
to allow increasing the size of the boat without thickening the hull structure. All were built under
a sub-contract from Electric Boat. Two pairs of torpedo tubes were mounted on the deck of AA-1 but
were soon removed. This first American effort to produce a fleet submarine failed because of chronic
vibrations in the paired diesels, difficulties maintaining depth control in a 268-foot submarine
within a 150-foot operating depth, poor seakeeping qualities with a low and narrow bow, and inadequate
striking power with the small warheads in the 18" torpedoes. By the time these boats were
commissioned they had also been rendered obsolete by large foreign boats designed with the benefit of
war experience. T-3 (ex AA-3) was re-engined in 1925 with 4700 BHP New York diesels.
Renamings: AA-1 ex Schley on 23 Aug 17. The three vessels became T 1 through T-3 on 22 Sep 20.
Reclassifications: To SF 1-3 (Fleet Submarines) on 17 Jul 20.

N-1 class

Displacement: 348/414 tons
Dimensions: 147'3"(oa.) x 15'9"(e) x 12'6"(mean)
Armament: 4-18"T
Complement: 25

Machinery: 480 BHP, 2 Nelseco diesel
engines/ 560 BHP, E. D. electric
motors, 2 screws
Speed: 13/11 kts.

No.		Hull	Laid down	Launched	Commiss'd	Disposition
53	N-1	Seattle	26 Jul 15	30 Dec 16	26 Sep 17	Stk. 18 Dec 30, scrapped 1931
54	N-2	Seattle	29 Jul 15	16 Jan 17	26 Sep 17	Stk. 18 Dec 30, scrapped 1931
55	N-3	Seattle	31 Jul 15	21 Feb 17	26 Sep 17	Stk. 18 Dec 30, scrapped 1931.

Notes: Fiscal year 1915. Authorized as a "coast and harbor defense type" in contrast to the
"seagoing" SS-52 in the same legislation, they were somewhat smaller than their predecessors. Their
horsepower was also reduced with the result that their engines were more reliable than those of
earlier submarines. The hulls were built under a sub-contract from the Electric Boat Co.

N-4 class

Displacement: 331/385 tons
Dimensions: 155'9"(oa.) x 14'6"(e) x 12'4"(mean)
Armament: 4-18"T
Complement: 29

Machinery: 600 BHP, 2 Busch-Sulzer
diesel engines/ 550 BHP, Diehl
electric motors, 2 screws
Speed: 13/11 kts.

No.		Hull	Laid down	Launched	Commiss'd	Disposition
56	N-4	Lake	24 Mar 15	27 Nov 16	15 Jun 18	Ordered sold 5 Apr 22, sold 25 Sep 22
57	N-5	Lake	10 Apr 15	22 Mar 17	13 Jun 18	Ordered sold 5 Apr 22, sold 25 Sep 22
58	N-6	Lake	15 Apr 15	21 Apr 17	9 Jul 18	Ordered sold 13 Mar 22, sold 31 Jul 22
59	N-7	Lake	20 Apr 15	19 May 17	15 Jun 18	Ordered sold 13 Mar 22, sold 5 Jun 22.

Notes: Fiscal year 1915. A Lake design developed to the same specifications as the N-1 class.

1915

O-1 class

Displacement: 521/624 tons
Dimensions: 172'4"(oa.) x 18'(e) x 16'5"(max)
Armament: 1-3"/23 4-18"T; 4-18"T (1942)
Complement: 29

Machinery: 880 BHP, 2 Nelseco diesel
engines/ 740 BHP, New York (SS 62-
63), E. D. (others) electric
motors, 2 screws
Speed: 14.5/11 kts.

No.		Hull	Laid down	Launched	Commiss'd	Disposition
62	O-1	Portsmouth	26 Mar 17	9 Jul 18	5 Nov 18	Stk. 14 May 38
63	O-2	Puget Sd.	27 Jul 17	24 May 18	19 Oct 18	Stk. 13 Aug 45, sold 16 Nov 45
64	O-3	Fore River	2 Dec 16	29 Sep 17	13 Jun 18	Stk. 11 Oct 45, sold 4 Sep 46
65	O-4	Fore River	4 Dec 16	20 Oct 17	28 May 18	Stk. 11 Oct 45, scrapped 1946
66	O-5	Fore River	5 Dec 16	11 Nov 17	8 Jun 18	Sunk in collision in Limon Bay, Panama, 28 Oct 23
67	O-6	Fore River	6 Dec 16	25 Nov 17	12 Jun 18	Stk. 11 Oct 45, sold 4 Sep 46
68	O-7	Fore River	14 Feb 17	16 Dec 17	4 Jul 18	Stk. 11 Jul 45, sold 22 Jan 46
69	O-8	Fore River	27 Feb 17	31 Dec 17	11 Jul 18	Stk. 11 Oct 45, sold 4 Sep 46
70	O-9	Fore River	15 Feb 17	27 Jan 18	27 Jul 18	Foundered off Isle of Shoals, Me., 20 Jun 41
71	O-10	Fore River	27 Feb 17	21 Feb 18	17 Aug 18	Stk. 11 Oct 45, sold 21 Aug 46.

Notes: Fiscal year 1916. Designed by Electric Boat as an improved version of the L-1 class. The first two were ordered from navy yards using Electric Boat plans and the others were built under a sub-contract from the Electric Boat Co. The wreck of the O-5 was raised in Nov 23, stricken 28 Apr 24, and sold 21 Dec 24. The O-1 was converted to an experimental vessel on 28 Dec 36 in accordance with the London Naval Treaty and served as such until stricken.

O-11 class

Displacement: 491/566 tons
Dimensions: 175'(oa.) x 16'4"(e) x 13'11"(mean)
Armament: 1-3"/23 4-18"T
Complement: 29

Machinery: 1000 BHP, 2 Busch-Sulzer
diesel engines/ 880 BHP, Diehl
electric motors, 2 screws
Speed: 14/11 kts.

No.		Hull	Laid down	Launched	Commiss'd	Disposition
72	O-11	Lake	6 Mar 16	29 Oct 17	19 Oct 18	Stk. 9 May 30, scrapped 1930
73	O-12	Lake	6 Mar 16	29 Sep 17	19 Oct 18	To Shipping Board 29 Jul 30, stk. 29 Jul 30
74	O-13	Lake	6 Mar 16	27 Dec 17	27 Nov 18	Stk. 9 May 30, scrapped 1930
75	O-14	California	6 Jul 16	6 May 18	1 Oct 18	Stk. 9 May 30, scrapped 1930
76	O-15	California	21 Sep 16	12 Feb 18	27 Aug 18	Stk. 9 May 30, scrapped 1930
77	O-16	California	7 Oct 16	9 Feb 18	1 Aug 18	Stk. 9 May 30, scrapped 1930.

Notes: Fiscal year 1916. Lake's counterpart to the O-1 class. The California boats went to Mare Island for completion. The O-12 was loaned by the Shipping Board to the Wilkes polar expedition under the name Nautilus and was scuttled in a Norwegian fjord on 20 Nov 31 after being returned to the Navy.

1916

R-1 class

Displacement: 569/680 tons
Dimensions: 186'2"(oa.) x 18'(e) x 14'6"(mean)
Armament: 1-3/50" 4-21"T
Complement: 29

Machinery: 880 BHP, 2 Nelseco diesel
engines/ 934 BHP, E. D. electric
motors, 2 screws
Speed: 13.5/10.5 kts.

No.		Hull	Laid down	Launched	Commiss'd	Disposition
78	R-1	Quincy	16 Oct 17	24 Aug 18	16 Dec 18	Stk. 11 Oct 45, sold 13 Mar 46
79	R-2	Quincy	16 Oct 17	23 Sep 18	24 Jan 19	Stk. 2 Jun 45, sold 28 Oct 45
80	R-3	Quincy	11 Dec 17	18 Jan 19	17 Apr 19	To Britain 4 Nov 41 as P-511, stk. 7 Nov 41
81	R-4	Quincy	16 Oct 17	26 Oct 18	28 Mar 19	Stk. 11 Jul 45, sold 22 Jan 46
82	R-5	Quincy	16 Oct 17	24 Nov 18	15 Apr 19	Stk. 11 Oct 45, sold 22 Aug 46
83	R-6	Quincy	17 Dec 17	1 Mar 19	1 May 19	Stk. 11 Oct 45, sold 13 Mar 46
84	R-7	Quincy	6 Dec 17	5 Apr 19	12 Jun 19	Stk. 11 Oct 45, sold 4 Sep 46
85	R-8	Quincy	4 Mar 18	17 Apr 19	21 Jul 19	Foundered 26 Feb 36
86	R-9	Quincy	6 Mar 18	24 May 19	30 Jul 19	Stk. 11 Oct 45, scrapped 1946
87	R-10	Quincy	21 Mar 18	28 Jun 19	20 Aug 19	Stk. 11 Jul 45, sold 22 Jan 46
88	R-11	Quincy	18 Mar 18	21 Jul 19	5 Sep 19	Stk. 11 Oct 45, sold 13 Mar 46
89	R-12	Quincy	28 Mar 18	15 Aug 19	23 Sep 19	Foundered off Key West, Fla., 12 Jun 43
90	R-13	Quincy	27 Mar 18	27 Aug 19	17 Oct 19	Stk. 11 Oct 45, sold 13 Mar 46
91	R-14	Quincy	6 Nov 18	10 Oct 19	24 Dec 19	Stk. 19 May 45, sold 28 Oct 45
92	R-15	Union	30 Apr 17	10 Dec 17	27 Jul 18	Stk. 11 Oct 45, sold 13 Mar 46
93	R-16	Union	26 Apr 17	15 Dec 17	5 Aug 18	Stk. 25 Jul 45, sold 22 Jan 46
94	R-17	Union	5 May 17	24 Dec 17	17 Aug 18	To Britain 9 Mar 42 as P-512, stk. 25 Mar 42
95	R-18	Union	16 Jun 17	8 Jan 18	11 Sep 18	Stk. 11 Oct 45, sold 4 Sep 46
96	R-19	Union	23 Jun 17	28 Jan 18	7 Oct 18	To Britain 9 Mar 42 as P-514, stk. 25 Mar 42
97	R-20	Union	4 Jun 17	21 Jan 18	26 Oct 18	Stk. 11 Oct 45, sold 13 Mar 46.

Notes: Fiscal year 1917. Designed by Electric Boat as an enlarged version of the O-1 class, they introduced the 21" torpedo tube and a more substantial 3" gun. The hulls were built under sub-contracts from the Electric Boat Co. The R-8 sank at her moorings in the Philadelphia reserve fleet; she was raised, stricken 12 May 36, and sunk as a bombing target off the Virginia Capes on 19 Aug 36. In 1945 the R-6 was fitted with an experimental snorkel, the first American submarine so equipped.

R-21 class

Displacement: 495/598 tons
Dimensions: 175'(oa.) x 16'8"(e) x 13'11"(mean)
Armament: 1-3"/50 4-18"T
Complement: 29

Machinery: 1000 BHP, 2 Busch-Sulzer
diesel engines/ 800 BHP, Diehl
electric motors, 2 screws
Speed: 14.5/11 kts.

No.		Hull	Laid down	Launched	Commiss'd	Disposition
98	R-21	Lake	19 Apr 17	10 Jul 18	17 Jun 19	Stk. 9 May 30, scrapped 1930
99	R-22	Lake	19 Apr 17	23 Sep 18	1 Aug 19	Stk. 9 May 30, scrapped 1930
100	R-23	Lake	25 Apr 17	5 Nov 18	23 Oct 19	Stk. 9 May 30, scrapped 1930
101	R-24	Lake	9 May 17	21 Aug 18	27 Jun 19	Stk. 9 May 30, scrapped 1930
102	R-25	Lake	26 Apr 17	15 May 19	23 Oct 19	Stk. 9 May 30, scrapped 1930
103	R-26	Lake	26 Apr 17	18 Jun 19	23 Oct 19	Stk. 9 May 30, scrapped 1930
104	R-27	Lake	16 May 17	23 Sep 18	3 Sep 19	Stk. 9 May 30, scrapped 1930.

Notes: Fiscal year 1917. They were Lake's counterpart to the R-1 class except that they reverted to the 18" torpedo tube.

Submarine No. 108

The Act of 29 Aug 16 (fiscal year 1917) authorized a submarine "equipped with the Neff system of...propulsion...of about one hundred and fifty tons displacement...." The Neff system involved operating diesel engines underwater by drawing oxygen from flasks and then exhausting the engines into empty flasks. The boat was assigned the official number 108 but was never built because the contract conditions could not be met.

S-3 class

Displacement: 876/1092 tons
Dimensions: 231'(oa.) x 21'10"(e) x 14'6"(max)
Armament: 1-4"/50 4-21"T (SS-107, 109-114); 1-4"/50 5-21"T (others)
Complement: 38

Machinery: 1400 BHP, 2 Nelseco (SS-107, 109-114), 2000 BHP, 2 New York (others) diesel engines / 1200 BHP, Westinghouse electric motors, 2 screws
Speed: 15/11 kts.

No.		Hull	Laid down	Launched	Commiss'd	Disposition
107	S-3	Portsmouth	29 Aug 17	21 Dec 18	30 Jan 19	Stk. 25 Jan 37, scrapped
109	S-4	Portsmouth	4 Dec 17	27 Aug 19	19 Nov 19	Stk. 15 Jan 36, scuttled off Hawaii 15 May 36
110	S-5	Portsmouth	5 Dec 17	10 Nov 19	6 Mar 20	Foundered off Delaware Capes 1 Sep 20
111	S-6	Portsmouth	29 Jan 18	23 Dec 19	17 May 20	Stk. 25 Jan 37, scrapped
112	S-7	Portsmouth	29 Jan 18	5 Feb 20	1 Jul 20	Stk. 25 Jan 37, scrapped
113	S-8	Portsmouth	9 Nov 18	21 Apr 20	1 Oct 20	Stk. 25 Jan 37, scrapped
114	S-9	Portsmouth	20 Jan 19	17 Jun 20	21 Feb 21	Stk. 25 Jan 37, scrapped
115	S-10	Portsmouth	11 Sep 19	9 Dec 20	21 Sep 22	Stk. 21 Jul 36, scrapped 1936
116	S-11	Portsmouth	2 Dec 19	7 Feb 21	11 Jan 23	Stk. 19 May 45, sold 28 Oct 45
117	S-12	Portsmouth	8 Jan 20	4 Aug 21	30 Apr 23	Stk. 22 Jun 45, sold 28 Oct 45
118	S-13	Portsmouth	14 Feb 20	20 Oct 21	14 Jul 23	Stk. 19 May 45, sold 28 Oct 45.

Notes: Fiscal years 1917 (SS-107) and 1918. At the time the "R" class was designed some officers pressed for the development of an 800-ton type which would be more capable than existing boats though smaller than the proposed fleet boats. Thanks to Portsmouth's experience in building the L-8 and O-1, the Navy was ready to undertake its own submarine design. Three 800-ton boats were funded in 1917 and were built to three competitive designs, Electric Boat's S-1, Lake's S-2, and the Navy's S-3. In the S-3 class, the S-5 was lost when she performed a crash dive with her main induction valve open. The S-4 was sunk in a collision with the Paulding (CG-17, ex DD-22) off Provincetown, Mass., on 17 Dec 27. She was raised on 17 Mar 28 and served thereafter as an experimental hulk. The S-3 and S-6 through S-9 were all reduced to hulks on 28 Dec 36.

S-1 class

Displacement: 854/1062 tons
Dimensions: 219'3"(oa.) x 20'8"(e) x 15'11"(mean)
Armament: 1-4"/50 4-21"T
Complement: 38

Machinery: 1200 BHP, 2 Nelseco diesel engines/ 1500 BHP, E. D. (SS-105, 135-140), G. E. (SS 141-146), Ridgeway (others) electric motors, 2 screws
Speed: 14.5/10.5 kts.

No.		Hull	Laid down	Launched	Commiss'd	Disposition
105	S-1	Quincy	11 Dec 17	26 Oct 18	5 Jun 20	To Britain 20 Apr 42 as P-552, stk. 24 Jun 42
123	S-18	Quincy	15 Aug 18	29 Apr 20	3 Apr 24	Stk. 13 Nov 45, sold 9 Nov 46
124	S-19	Quincy	15 Aug 18	21 Jun 20	24 Aug 21	Stk. 12 Dec 36, sunk off Pearl Harbor 18 Dec 38
125	S-20	Quincy	15 Aug 18	9 Jun 20	22 Nov 22	Stk. 25 Jul 45, sold 22 Jan 46
126	S-21	Quincy	19 Dec 18	18 Aug 20	24 Aug 21	To Britain 14 Sep 42 as P-553, stk. 2 Oct 42
127	S-22	Quincy	6 Jan 19	15 Jul 20	23 Jun 24	To Britain 19 Jun 42 as P-554, stk. 24 Jul 42
128	S-23	Quincy	18 Jan 19	27 Oct 20	30 Oct 23	Stk. 16 Nov 45, sold 9 Nov 46
129	S-24	Quincy	1 Nov 18	27 Jun 22	24 Aug 23	To Britain 10 Aug 42 as P-555, stk. 11 Sep 42
130	S-25	Quincy	26 Oct 18	29 May 22	9 Jul 23	To Britain 4 Nov 41 as P-551, stk. 7 Nov 41
131	S-26	Quincy	7 Nov 18	22 Aug 22	15 Oct 23	Sunk in collision with USS PC-460 off Panama 24 Jan 42
132	S-27	Quincy	11 Apr 19	18 Oct 22	22 Jan 24	Grounded off Amchitka Is., Aleutians, 19 Jun 42
133	S-28	Quincy	16 Apr 19	20 Sep 22	13 Dec 23	Foundered W of Oahu 4 Jul 44
134	S-29	Quincy	17 Apr 19	9 Nov 22	22 May 24	To Britain 5 Jun 42 as P-556, stk. 24 Jun 42
135	S-30	Beth-SF	1 Apr 18	21 Nov 18	29 Oct 20	Stk. 24 Oct 45, sold 5 Dec 46
136	S-31	Beth-SF	13 Apr 18	28 Dec 18	11 May 22	Stk. 1 Nov 45, sold 6 Dec 46
137	S-32	Beth-SF	12 Apr 18	11 Jan 19	15 Jun 22	Stk. 1 Nov 45, sold 19 Apr 46
138	S-33	Beth-SF	14 Jun 18	5 Dec 18	18 Apr 22	Stk. 1 Nov 45, sold 5 Dec 46
139	S-34	Beth-SF	28 May 18	13 Feb 19	12 Jul 22	Stk. 1 Nov 45, sold 23 Nov 46
140	S-35	Beth-SF	14 Jun 18	27 Feb 19	17 Aug 22	Stk. 21 Feb 46, sunk as target 4 Apr 46
141	S-36	Beth-SF	10 Dec 18	3 Jun 19	4 Apr 23	Grounded in Makassar Strait and scuttled 21 Jan 42
142	S-37	Beth-SF	12 Dec 18	20 Jun 19	16 Jul 23	Sunk as target off Imperial Beach, Cal., 20 Feb 45, stk. 23 Feb 45
143	S-38	Beth-SF	15 Jan 19	17 Jun 19	11 May 23	Stk. 20 Jan 45, sunk as target off S. California 20 Feb 45
144	S-39	Beth-SF	14 Jan 19	2 Jul 19	14 Sep 23	Grounded on Rossel I. 14 Aug 42
145	S-40	Beth-SF	5 Mar 19	5 Jan 21	20 Nov 23	Stk. 13 Nov 45, sold 19 Nov 46
146	S-41	Beth-SF	17 Apr 19	21 Feb 21	15 Jan 24	Stk. 25 Feb 46, sold 15 Nov 46.

Notes: Fiscal years 1917 (SS-105) and 1918. The hulls were built under sub-contracts from the Electric Boat Co. who was also the designer. The S-30 was built at the expense of the Philippine Government. S-1 was experimentally fitted with a hanger and a small plane in 1923. Three years later she experimented again with a small plane. During the 1920s the S-20 received external blisters to hold more fuel oil and a raised bow for better seakeeping. This attempt to increase her cruising range failed because of excessive speed reduction. In 1931 she received new diesel engines in one of the first full-scale tests of higher-speed diesels. The S-21 was sunk as an underwater target in Casco Bay, Me., 23 Mar 45 following her return by the British. The wreck of the S-37 was sold "as is, where is" on 30 Oct 59 and again on 11 Jul 74.

S-2

Displacement: 800/977 tons
Dimensions: 207'(oa.) x 19'7"(e) x 16'2"(mean)
Armament: 1-4"/50 4-21"T
Complement: 38

Machinery: 1800 BHP, 2 Busch-Sulzer diesel engines/ 1200 BHP, Diehl electric motors, 2 screws
Speed: 15/11 kts.

No.		Hull	Laid down	Launched	Commiss'd	Disposition
106	S-2	Lake	30 Jul 17	15 Feb 19	25 May 20	Stk. 26 Feb 31, scrapped 1931.

Notes: Fiscal year 1917. Lake's entry in the competition for an 800-ton submarine design. The Navy-designed S-3 proved to be superior to this Lake-designed vessel, and later boats constructed by Lake were built to government designs.

1917

S-14 class

Displacement: 876/1092 tons
Dimensions: 231'(oa.) x 21'10"(e) x 15'(max)
Armament: 1-4"/50 4-21"T
Complement: 38

Machinery: 1000 BHP, 2 Busch-Sulzer
  diesel engines/ 1200 BHP,
  Westinghouse electric motors, 2
  screws
Speed: 15/10.5 kts.

No.	Hull	Laid down	Launched	Commiss'd	Disposition
119 S-14	Lake	7 Dec 17	22 Oct 19	11 Feb 21	Stk. 22 Jun 45, sold 16 Nov 45
120 S-15	Lake	13 Dec 17	8 Mar 20	15 Jan 21	Stk. 3 Jul 46, sold 4 Dec 46
121 S-16	Lake	19 Mar 18	23 Dec 19	17 Dec 20	Stk. 13 Nov 44, sunk 3 Apr 45
122 S-17	Lake	19 Mar 18	22 May 20	1 Mar 21	Stk. 13 Nov 44, sunk 5 Apr 45.

Notes: Fiscal year 1918. Built by Lake to a government design. They were re-engined in 1925 with 2000 BHP MAN-type diesels built by the New York Navy Yard.

H-4 class

Displacement: 358/467 tons
Dimensions: 150'4"(oa.) x 15'10"(e) x 12'5"(mean)
Armament: 4-18"T
Complement: 25

Machinery: 480 BHP, 2 Nelseco diesel
  engines/ 600 BHP, E. D. electric
  motors, 2 screws
Speed: 14/10.5 kts.

No.	Hull	Laid down	Launched	Commiss'd	Disposition
147 H-4	Groton	12 May 18	9 Oct 18	24 Oct 18	Stk. 26 Feb 31, scrapped 1931
148 H-5	Groton	12 May 18	24 Sep 18	30 Sep 18	Stk. 26 Feb 31, scrapped 1933
149 H-6	Groton	14 May 18	26 Aug 18	9 Sep 18	Stk. 26 Feb 31, scrapped 1933
150 H-7	Groton	15 May 18	17 Oct 18	24 Oct 18	Stk. 26 Feb 31, scrapped 1933
151 H-8	Groton	25 May 18	14 Nov 18	18 Nov 18	Stk. 26 Feb 31, scrapped 1933
152 H-9	Groton	1 Jun 18	23 Nov 18	25 Nov 18	Stk. 26 Feb 31, scrapped 1933.

Notes: Fiscal year 1918. These boats were built under a contract from the Russian government but not delivered because of the Russian Revolution. They were to have been the Russian AG 17-20 and AG 27-28. They were purchased by the United States 20 May 18 while still in a knocked down condition and were assembled at the Puget Sound Navy Yard.

1918

S-42 class

Displacement: 906/1126 tons
Dimensions: 225'3"(oa.) x 20'8"(e) x 17'2"(max)
Armament: 1-4"/50 4-21"T
Complement: 38

Machinery: 1200 BHP, 2 Nelseco diesel
  engines/ 1500 BHP, E. D. electric
  motors, 2 screws
Speed: 14.5/11 kts.

No.	Hull	Laid down	Launched	Commiss'd	Disposition
153 S-42	Quincy	16 Dec 20	30 Apr 23	20 Nov 24	Stk. 13 Nov 45, sold 23 Nov 46
154 S-43	Quincy	13 Dec 20	31 Mar 23	31 Dec 24	Stk. 13 Nov 45, sold 7 Dec 46
155 S-44	Quincy	19 Feb 21	27 Oct 23	16 Feb 25	Sunk by a Japanese destroyer in Kurile Is. 7 Oct 43
156 S-45	Quincy	29 Dec 20	26 Jun 23	31 Mar 25	Stk. 13 Nov 45, sold 6 Dec 46
157 S-46	Quincy	23 Feb 21	11 Sep 23	5 Jun 25	Stk. 16 Nov 45, sold 19 Nov 46
158 S-47	Quincy	26 Feb 21	5 Jan 24	16 Sep 25	Stk. 13 Nov 45, sold 22 Nov 46.

Notes: Fiscal year 1919. Sixteen submarines with official numbers 153-68 and names S-42 through S-57 were ordered from Electric Boat on 1 Aug 18 in general accordance with the design for S-18 through S-41. Submarines 155-68 were to be built under emergency funds, the others under the regular fiscal year 1919 appropriation. Ten boats were cancelled on 4 Dec 18, numbers and names were reassigned to the remainder as above, and all were charged to the regular 1919 appropriation. The formal contract for them was signed on 1 Jul 19. The hulls were built under sub-contracts from the Electric Boat Co. They were the last U.S. submarines not designed by the Navy, although private builders continued to do much detail design work for the Navy.

S-48 class

Displacement: 993/1230 tons
Dimensions: 240'(oa.) x 21'10"(e) x 13'6"(mean)
Armament: 1-4"/50 5-21"T
Complement: 38

Machinery: 1800 BHP, 2 Busch-Sulzer
  diesel engines/ 1500 BHP, Ridgeway
  electric motors, 2 screws
Speed: 14.5/11 kts.

No.	Hull	Laid down	Launched	Commiss'd	Disposition
159 S-48	Lake	22 Oct 20	26 Feb 21	14 Oct 22	Stk. 17 Sep 45, sold 22 Jan 46
160 S-49	Lake	22 Oct 20	23 Apr 21	5 Jun 22	Stk. 21 Mar 31, sold 25 May 31
161 S-50	Lake	15 Mar 20	18 Jun 21	20 May 22	Stk. 21 Mar 31, scrapped 1931
162 S-51	Lake	22 Dec 19	20 Aug 21	24 Jun 22	Sunk in collision off Block Is. 25 Sep 25.

Notes: Fiscal year 1919. Eight submarines with official numbers 169-73 and names S-58 through S-65 were ordered from Lake on 1 Aug 18. They were to be generally similar to S-14 through S-17 but with more powerful engines. All were to be built under the regular fiscal year 1919 appropriation. Four boats were cancelled on 4 Dec 18 and numbers and names were reassigned to the remainder as above. The formal contract for them was signed on 23 Jul 19. Laid up after running aground in 1925, the S-48 was lengthened 27 feet in 1928 to increase her fuel capacity and was re-engined with 2000 BHP MAN-type diesels built by New York Navy Yard. This attempt to upgrade an "S" class boat to fleet submarine standards failed when she was found to be excessively wet in a seaway and too slow to operate with the fleet. The hulk of the S-51 was raised 5 Jul 26, stricken 27 Jan 30, and sold 4 Jun 30.

1920

V-1 (BARRACUDA) class

Displacement: 2000/2506 tons
Dimensions: 341'6"(oa.) x 27'7"(e) x 15'11"(max)
Armament: 1-5"/51 6-21"T; 1-3"/50 6-21"T (1928); none (1943)
Complement: 87; 54 (1943)

Machinery: 6200 BHP, 2 Busch-Sulzer diesel engines and 2 generator diesels/ 2400 BHP, 2 Elliott electric motors, 2 screws
Speed: 18/8 kts.

No.	Hull	Laid down	Launched	Commiss'd	Disposition
SF-4 V-1	Portsmouth	20 Oct 21	17 Jul 24	1 Oct 24	Stk. 10 Mar 45, sold 16 Nov 45
SF-5 V-2	Portsmouth	20 Oct 21	27 Dec 24	26 Sep 25	Stk. 10 Mar 45, scuttled off Block I., R. I., 12 Mar 45
SF-6 V-3	Portsmouth	16 Nov 21	9 Jun 25	22 May 26	Stk. 10 Mar 45, sold 28 Oct 45.

Notes: Fiscal year 1921. The first of nine fleet submarines authorized in 1916, they were designed with high speed and a bulbous bow so they could operate with battleship squadrons. They had composite-drive machinery, in which two diesels drove the shaft directly and two through electric generators and motors. Their operating depth was 200'. They proved unsatisfactory in service because their main engines and electric motors constantly required repairs and because they were overweight in the bows. They received new Ridgeway electric motors in 1940. In March-April 1943 they were converted to cargo carriers--their main engines and torpedo tubes were removed and their 2000 BHP generator engines were used to propel them at a maximum speed of 10 knots. This conversion also proved unsatisfactory. The Bass was scuttled as a sonar target; her hulk was sold in Jun 63.
Renamings: To Barracuda, Bass, and Bonita respectively on 19 Feb 31, with identification numbers B 1-3.
Reclassifications: Fleet submarines Nos. 1-9 were authorized in the 1916 building program but not ordered during the war. They were designated Submarines No. 163-171 after the orders for the coastal submarines with these numbers were cancelled on 4 Dec 18. When hull numbers were assigned on 17 Jul 20, however, they became SF 4-12 (Fleet Submarines). SF 4-6 were reclassified back to SS 163-165 on 1 Jul 31. They were to have become APS 2-4 in 1943 but were not reclassified.

1924

V-4 (ARGONAUT)

Displacement: 2710/4080 tons
Dimensions: 381'(oa.) x 33'10"(e) x 16'(max)
Armament: 2-6"/53 4-21"T 60m; 2-6" 6-21"T 60m (1942); 2-6" 6-21"T (1942)
Complement: 86

Machinery: 3175 BHP, 2 New York diesel engines and 1 generator diesel/ 2200 BHP, 2 Ridgeway electric motors, 2 screws
Speed: 13.6/7.4 kts. (trials)

No.	Hull	Laid down	Launched	Commiss'd	Disposition
SM-1 V-4	Portsmouth	1 May 25	10 Nov 27	2 Apr 28	Sunk by Japanese destroyers off Rabaul, New Britain, 10 Jan 43.

Notes: Fiscal year 1925. In the early 1920s the Navy, inspired by the large German World War I boats, decided to build long-range cruiser submarines in place of the remaining six fleet boats (SF 7-12) authorized in 1916. They were to have long range and endurance, a heavy gun armament, high freeboard for good seakeeping qualities on the surface, and engines designed for reliability rather than high speed. Their hull design was patterned after the German U-142 after that type was found to be superior to the V-1 design. The first of these boats became the Navy's only built-for-the-purpose

The cruiser submarine *V-6* (SC-2) on sea trials in San Francisco Bay on 8 October 1930. She became USS *Nautilus* (SS-168) in 1931. (NH 63446)

The submarine *Grampus* (SS-207) off Groton, Conn., on 26 March 1941. (NARA 19-N-23816)

minelaying submarine. Her hull classification of SM stood for Minelaying Submarine. Her operating depth was 300' and she had a full double hull and composite drive. She generally met her designers' expectations except that she was underpowered and failed to make her designed speed of 15/8 knots. She was modernized at Mare Is. in January-July 1942 and received 4300 BHP General Motors direct-drive diesels and two external torpedo tubes aft. She was then hastily converted at Pearl Harbor to a transport submarine for the August 1942 Makin Is. raid. Her minelaying equipment was removed and she was fitted to carry 120 troops.
Renaming: To Argonaut on 19 Feb 31, with identification number A-1.
Reclassifications: Ex SF-7, 24 Jul 24; to APS-1 (Transport Submarine), 22 Sep 42. She was never classified a straight submarine although the number SS-166 was reserved for her.

1925

V-5 (NARWHAL) class

Displacement: 2730/3960 tons
Dimensions: 370'7"(oa.) x 33'3"(e) x 17'8"(max)
Armament: 2-6"/53 6-21"T; 2-6" 10-21"T (6 hull, 4 deck, 1942)
Complement: 89

Machinery: 5633 BHP, 2 New York diesel engines and 2 generator diesels/ 1600 BHP, 2 Westinghouse electric motors, 2 screws
Speed: 14/8 kts.

No.		Hull	Laid down	Launched	Commiss'd	Disposition
SC-1	V-5	Portsmouth	10 May 27	17 Dec 29	15 May 30	Stk. 19 May 45, sold 16 Nov 45.
SC-2	V-6	Mare I.	2 Aug 27	15 Mar 30	1 Jul 30	Stk. 25 Jul 45, sold 16 Nov 45.

Notes: Fiscal year 1926. Designed by the Navy as commerce-raiding cruiser submarines, they were 10' shorter than the V-4 but had more powerful engines. Their hull classification of SC stood for Cruiser Submarines. They had an operating depth of 300', full double hulls, and composite drive. They made 17.4 knots on trials but could not manage over 14 knots in service. In 1942 they were re-engined with 6000 BHP General Motors direct-drive diesels and 2540 HP Westinghouse motors in an attempt to increase their speed. Four external torpedo tubes were also fitted. They were used as temporary transport submarines in 1942-43 but were not reclassified.
Renamings: To Narwhal and Nautilus respectively 19 Feb 31, with identification numbers N 1-2.
Reclassifications: Ex SF 8-9, 10 Mar 25; to SS 167-168, 1 Jul 31.

1929

DOLPHIN

Displacement: 1560/2215 tons
Dimensions: 319'1"(oa.) x 27'11"(e) x 16'6"(max)
Armament: 1-4"/50 6-21"T; 1-3"/50 6-21"T (ca. 1943)
Complement: 63

Machinery: 4086 BHP, 2 New York diesel engines and 2 generator diesels/ 1750 BHP, 2 E. D. electric motors, 2 screws
Speed: 17/8 kts.

No.	Hull	Laid down	Launched	Commiss'd	Disposition
169 DOLPHIN	Portsmouth	14 Jun 30	8 Mar 32	1 Jun 32	Stk. 24 Oct 45, sold 26 Aug 46.

Notes: Fiscal year 1930. In the mid-1920s, Navy opinion turned against the big fleet and cruiser submarine types in favor of a 1200-ton type in which maneuverability and habitability were emphasized instead of speed. The Navy designers were instructed to retain the performance characteristics of the V-5 class but in a much smaller hull with a reduced gun armament. The result was a boat optimized for offensive patrol operations in the Pacific. In concept and in many of her features, the Dolphin was the direct forerunner of the World War II fleet boats (a term commonly applied to SS 172-203 and 206-550), although the later boats had much better military qualities. Like the AA-1 and V-1 classes she had a double hull amidships and a single hull at the ends. She had the same composite-drive propulsion plant as the V-5. She had an operating depth of 250', which became the standard for U.S. submarines through the Tambor (SS-198) and Mackerel (SS-204) classes. She carried the identification number D-1 during the 1930s.
Renaming: Ex V-7 19 Feb 31.
Reclassifications: Ex SF-10, 2 Mar 29, ex SC-3, 1 Jul 31.

1930

CACHALOT class

Displacement: 1110/1650 (SS-170), 1130/1650 (SS-171) tons
Dimensions: 271'11"(oa.) x 24'11"(e) x 16'3"(max) (SS-170); 274'(oa.) x 24'9"(e) x 16'3"(max) (SS-171)
Armament: 1-3"/50 6-21"T
Complement: 43

Machinery: 3070 BHP, 2 New York diesel engines/ 1600 BHP, 2 E. D. (SS-170), Westinghouse (SS-171) electric motors, 2 screws
Speed: 17/8 kts.

No.	Hull	Laid down	Launched	Commiss'd	Disposition
170 CACHALOT	Portsmouth	21 Oct 31	19 Oct 33	1 Dec 33	Stk. 3 Jul 46, sold 26 Jan 47
171 CUTTLEFISH	Groton	7 Oct 31	21 Nov 33	8 Jun 34	Stk. 3 Jul 46, sold 12 Feb 47.

Notes: Fiscal year 1931. In this class, the Navy attempted to use a new lightweight diesel to achieve the performance of the Dolphin in a boat 400 tons lighter and 46 feet shorter. The hull design was a full double-hull type based on the German U-135. Propulsion was provided by two direct-drive diesels. The boats proved to be too small, and their diesels were a complete failure due to vibrations. Both were re-engined in 1938 with 3070 BHP General Motors direct-drive diesels. Prior to World War II they carried the identification numbers C 1-2. The Cuttlefish was awarded to Electric Boat to get that firm back into U.S. submarine construction; she was the first U.S. submarine to be air conditioned and also included a large amount of welded construction.
Renamings: Ex V-8 and V-9, 19 Feb 31.
Reclassifications: Ex SF 11-12, 2 Mar 29, ex SC 4-5, 1 Jul 31.

1933

PORPOISE class

Displacement: 1310/1934 tons
Dimensions: 301'(oa.) x 24'11"(e) x 13'1"(mean)
Armament: 1-3"/50 6-21"T; 1-3" 8-21"T (1942)
Complement: 50

Machinery: 4300 BHP, 4 Winton diesel engines/ 2085 BHP, 4 Elliott electric motors, 2 screws
Speed: 19/8 kts.

No.	Hull	Laid down	Launched	Commiss'd	Disposition
172 PORPOISE	Portsmouth	27 Oct 33	20 Jun 35	15 Aug 35	Stk. 13 Aug 56, sold 14 May 57
173 PIKE	Portsmouth	20 Dec 33	12 Sep 35	2 Dec 35	Stk. 17 Feb 56, sold 14 Jan 57.

Notes: Fiscal year 1934. In the four 1934 boats, the Navy returned to a larger design to relieve overcrowding. It also introduced a new type of propulsion plant consisting of four high-speed diesels and all-electric drive. The first two boats were designed by the Portsmouth Navy Yard as an enlargement of the Cachalot class with a longer engine room—they were the last U.S. submarines with a full double hull. Like other submarines before 1939, they carried special identification numbers painted on their conning towers. Theirs were P 1-2. A pair of deck mounted torpedo tubes was added in 1942, when they were reengined with 4300 BHP G. M. diesels.

SHARK class

Displacement: 1316/1958 tons
Dimensions: 298'1"(oa.) x 25'1"(e) x 13'10"(mean)
Armament: 1-3"/50 6-21"T; 1-4"/50 8-21"T (SS-175, 1942)
Complement: 50

Machinery: 4300 BHP, 4 Winton diesel engines/ 2085 BHP, 4 Elliott electric motors, 2 screws
Speed: 19.5/8 kts.

No.	Hull	Laid down	Launched	Commiss'd	Disposition
174 SHARK	Groton	24 Oct 33	21 May 35	25 Jan 36	Probably sunk by Japanese vessels E of Menado, Celebes I., 11 Feb 42
175 TARPON	Groton	22 Dec 33	4 Sep 35	12 Mar 36	Stk. 5 Sep 56, sold Jun 57.

Notes: Fiscal year 1934. Electric Boat designed these boats to the same specifications as the Porpoise class but used a partial double hull much like that of the Dolphin and, for the first time in a U.S. submarine, used all-welded construction. The identification numbers for these boats were P 3-4. Both boats were reengined in 1942 with 4300 BHP G. M. diesels and the Tarpon also received two deck mounted torpedo tubes. The Tarpon served as a training vessel after 1946. She foundered off Cape Hatteras 26 Aug 57 while in tow to the scrap yard.

1934

PERCH class

Displacement: 1330/1997 tons
Dimensions: 300'7"(oa.) x 25'1"(e) x 15'3"(max)
Armament: 1-3"/50 6-21"T; 1-4"/50 8-21"T (SS 177-178, 1942); 1-4" 6-21"T (SS 179-180, 1945)
Complement: 50

Machinery: 4300 BHP, 4 Winton (SS 176-178), F. M. (SS 179-180), H.O.R. (SS-181) diesel engines/ 2366 BHP, 8 G. E. (SS 176-178), 2285 BHP, 4 A. C. (SS-181), 4 Elliott (others) electric motors, 2 screws
Speed: 19/9 kts.

No.		Hull	Laid down	Launched	Commiss'd	Disposition
176	PERCH	Groton	25 Feb 35	9 May 36	19 Nov 36	Scuttled in Java Sea 3 Mar 42 after being damaged by Japanese destroyers
177	PICKEREL	Groton	25 Mar 35	7 Jul 36	26 Jan 37	Sunk by Japanese vessels N of Honshu 3 Apr 43
178	PERMIT	Groton	6 Jun 35	5 Oct 36	17 Mar 37	Stk. 26 Jul 56, sold 28 Jun 58
179	PLUNGER	Portsmouth	17 Jul 35	8 Jul 36	19 Nov 36	Stk. 6 Jul 56, sold 22 Apr 57
180	POLLACK	Portsmouth	1 Oct 35	15 Sep 36	15 Jan 37	Stk. 29 Oct 46, sold 2 Feb 47
181	POMPANO	Mare I.	14 Jan 36	11 Mar 37	12 Jun 37	Mined N of Honshu Sep 43.

Notes: Fiscal year 1935. This class duplicated the Electric Boat partial double-hull design of the Shark except that the engine room was lengthened two feet. The three Groton boats were all welded, the others were the Navy's last partly-riveted submarines. Their identification numbers were P 5-10. The class received three different types of main engines and had problems with all of them. Five boats were reengined in 1942-43 with 4 Fairbanks Morse diesels of 4300 BHP. During World War II Pickerel and Permit also had a pair of deck mounted torpedo tubes added. The Plunger was converted to a training vessel in 1946.
Renaming: Permit ex Pinna 13 Aug 35.

1935

SALMON class

Displacement: 1449/2198 tons
Dimensions: 308'(oa.) x 26'1"(e) x 17'6"(max)
Armament: 1-3"/50 8-21"T; 1-4"/50 8-21"T (1945, except SS-186)
Complement: 55

Machinery: 5500 BHP, 2 H. O. R. (SS 182-184), G. M. (others) diesel engines/ 2660 BHP, 4 Elliott electric motors, 2 screws
Speed: 21/9 kts.

No.		Hull	Laid down	Launched	Commiss'd	Disposition
182	SALMON	Groton	15 Apr 36	12 Jun 37	15 Mar 38	Stk. 11 Oct 45, scrapped 1946
183	SEAL	Groton	25 May 36	25 Aug 37	30 Apr 38	Stk. 1 May 56, sold 6 May 57
184	SKIPJACK	Groton	22 Jul 36	23 Oct 37	30 Jun 38	Sunk as target off S. California 11 Aug 48, stk. 13 Sep 48
185	SNAPPER	Portsmouth	23 Jul 36	24 Aug 37	15 Dec 37	Stk. 30 Apr 48, sold 18 May 48
186	STINGRAY	Portsmouth	1 Oct 36	6 Oct 37	15 Mar 38	Stk. 3 Jul 46, sold 6 Jan 47
187	STURGEON	Mare 1.	27 Oct 36	15 Mar 38	25 Jun 38	Stk. 30 Apr 48, sold 12 Jun 48.

Notes: Fiscal year 1936. In this class the Navy increased the number of torpedo tubes aft from two to four in response to complaints from the fleet. It also reverted to a composite-drive propulsion plant because of concern over the ability of all-electric installations to survive flooding. The boats' identification numbers were S 1-6. The Stingray carried a pair of deck mounted torpedo tubes for a short period in 1942-43. SS 182-184 were reengined in 1944 with 4 G.M. diesels of 5500 BHP. The Seal served as a training vessel 1946-57.

1936

SARGO class

Displacement: 1450/2350 tons
Dimensions: 310'6"(oa.) x 27'1"(e) x 17'3"(max)
Armament: 1-3"/50 8-21"T; 1-4"/50 8-21"T (1943); 1-5"/25 8-21"T (SS-188, 1945)
Complement: 55

Machinery: 5500 (SS 188-93), 5200 (SS 194-95), 5400 (others) BHP, 4 H.O.R. (SS 188-190, 194), G. M. (others) diesel engines/ 2740 BHP, 4 G. E. electric motors, 2 screws
Speed: 20/9 kts.

No.		Hull	Laid down	Launched	Commiss'd	Disposition
188	SARGO	Groton	12 May 37	6 Jun 38	7 Feb 39	Stk. 19 Jul 46, sold 19 May 47
189	SAURY	Groton	28 Jun 37	20 Aug 38	3 Apr 39	Stk. 19 Jul 46, sold 19 May 47
190	SPEARFISH	Groton	9 Sep 37	29 Oct 38	17 Jul 39	Stk. 19 Jul 46, sold 19 May 47
191	SCULPIN	Portsmouth	7 Sep 37	27 Jul 38	16 Jan 39	Scuttled off Truk 19 Nov 43 after being damaged by Japanese destroyers
192	SQUALUS	Portsmouth	18 Oct 37	14 Sep 38	1 Mar 39	Stk. 30 Apr 48, sold 18 Jun 48
193	SWORDFISH	Mare I.	27 Oct 37	1 Apr 39	22 Jul 39	Probably sunk by Japanese vessels in Ryukyu Is., 12 Jan 45

No.		Hull	Laid down	Launched	Commiss'd	Disposition
194	SEADRAGON	Groton	18 Apr 38	21 Apr 39	23 Oct 39	Stk. 30 Apr 48, sold 2 Jul 48
195	SEALION	Groton	20 Jun 38	25 May 39	27 Nov 39	Scuttled at Cavite 25 Dec 41 after being damaged by Japanese aircraft 10 Dec 41
196	SEARAVEN	Portsmouth	9 Aug 38	21 Jun 39	2 Oct 39	Sunk as target off S. Calif. 11 Sep 48, stk. 21 Oct 48
197	SEAWOLF	Portsmouth	27 Sep 38	15 Aug 39	1 Dec 39	Sunk by Richard M. Rowell (DE-403) off Morotai 3 Oct 44.

Notes: Fiscal years 1937 (SS 188-193) and 1938. This class essentially duplicated the Salmon class except that the distribution of the tanks was modified and the hull was lengthened two feet in the after engine room. The four 1938 boats duplicated the 1937 group except that they returned to all-electric drive, a feature retained in all later fleet boats. The boats were assigned identification numbers S 7-16 before this type of number was replaced on conning towers by hull numbers in 1939. The Squalus foundered off the Isle of Shoals, Me., on 23 May 39 but was raised on 13 Sep 39 and recommissioned on 15 May 40 under the name Sailfish. SS 188-190 and 194 were reengined in 1944 with 4 G.M. diesels of 5500 BHP.
Renaming: SS-192 to Sailfish 9 Feb 40.

1938

TAMBOR class

Displacement: 1475/2370 tons
Dimensions: 307'2"(oa.) x 27'3"(e) x 16'9"(max)
Armament: 1-3"/50 10-21"T; 1-5"/51 10-21"T (SS 198-200 1942);
  1-5"/25 10-21"T (198-200, 203, 206, 1944-45)
Complement: 59

Machinery: 5400 BHP, 4 G. M. (SS 198-200, 206-208), F. M. (others)
  diesel engines/ 2740 BHP, 4 G. E.
  electric motors, 2 screws
Speed: 20/9 kts.

No.		Hull	Laid down	Launched	Commiss'd	Disposition
198	TAMBOR	Groton	16 Jan 39	20 Dec 39	3 Jun 40	Stk. 1 Sep 59, sold 19 Nov 59
199	TAUTOG	Groton	1 Mar 39	27 Jan 40	3 Jul 40	Stk. 1 Sep 59, sold 13 Jul 60
200	THRESHER	Groton	27 Apr 39	27 Mar 40	27 Aug 40	Stk. 23 Dec 47, sold 18 Mar 48
201	TRITON	Portsmouth	5 Jul 39	25 Mar 40	15 Aug 40	Sunk by Japanese destroyers off Admiralty Is. 15 Mar 43
202	TROUT	Portsmouth	28 Aug 39	21 May 40	15 Nov 40	Lost NW of Philippines ca. 29 Feb 44
203	TUNA	Mare I.	19 Jul 39	2 Oct 40	2 Jan 41	Sunk as target off S. Calif. 24 Sep 48, stk. 21 Oct 48
206	GAR	Groton	27 Dec 39	7 Nov 40	14 Apr 41	Stk. 1 Aug 59, sold 23 Nov 59
207	GRAMPUS	Groton	14 Feb 40	23 Dec 40	23 May 41	Sunk by Japanese destroyers in Blackett Strait, Solomon Is., 5 Mar 43
208	GRAYBACK	Groton	3 Apr 40	31 Jan 41	30 Jun 41	Sunk by Japanese aircraft S of Okinawa 27 Feb 44
209	GRAYLING	Portsmouth	15 Dec 39	4 Sep 40	1 Mar 41	Sunk off Manila ca. 9 Sep 43
210	GRENADIER	Portsmouth	2 Apr 40	29 Nov 40	1 May 41	Scuttled off Penang, Malaya, 22 Apr 43 after damaged by Japanese aircraft
211	GUDGEON	Mare I.	22 Nov 39	25 Jan 41	21 Apr 41	Lost off Maug I., Mariana Is., 18 Apr 44.

Notes: Fiscal years 1939 (SS 198-203) and 1940. This class was designed following a major review of characteristics for an ideal, all-purpose fleet submarine. Improvements included two more torpedo tubes forward, a larger conning tower, more horsepower, and a refined and simplified hull design. The 3" gun of previous designs was retained, but its foundation was strengthened to take up to a 5"/51 gun. SS 206-211 are sometimes listed as the Gar class; they were exact repeats of the SS 198-205 group. The Tambor, Tautog, and Gar were converted to training vessels in 1946.

1939

MACKEREL class

Displacement: 825/1190 (SS-204), 800/1165 (SS-205) tons
Dimensions: 243'1"(oa.) x 22'1"(e) x 14'6"(max) (SS-204); 238'11"(oa.) x 21'8"(e) x 13'6"(max) (SS-205)
Armament: 1-3"/50 6-21"T; 1-5"/25 6-21"T (SS-205, 1945)
Complement: 38

Machinery: 1680 BHP, 2 Electric Boat (SS-204), 1700 BHP, 2 ALCO (SS-205) diesel engines/ 1500 BHP, 2 E. D. (SS-204), 2 G. E. (SS-205) electric motors, 2 screws
Speed: 16/11 kts.

No.	Hull	Laid down	Launched	Commiss'd	Disposition
204 MACKEREL	Groton	6 Oct 39	28 Sep 40	31 Mar 41	Stk. 28 Nov 45, sold 24 Apr 47
205 MARLIN	Portsmouth	28 May 40	29 Jan 41	1 Aug 41	Stk. 28 Nov 45, sold 29 Mar 46.

Notes: Fiscal year 1940. This class resulted from concern that the fleet boats were becoming too large and expensive to replace the many "S" class boats still in the fleet. The new type was intended to protect U.S. coasts but not conduct long-range patrol operations. Two experimental boats were authorized, and the builders were given considerable latitude in developing the designs. The Mackerel had direct-drive machinery and the Marlin had electric drive. The Navy quickly realized that the larger fleet boats were more cost effective and abandoned the smaller type.

1940

GATO class

Displacement: 1525/2424 tons
Dimensions: 311'8"(Portsmouth boats, oa.), 311'9"(Groton and Manitowoc boats, oa.), 311'10"(Mare I. boats, oa.) x 27'3"(e) x 17'(max)
Armament: 1-3"/50 10-21"T; 1-4"/50 10-21"T (late 1943); 1-5"/25 10-21"T (late 1944); 2-5"/25 10-21"T (SS 228, 231, 261, 1945); 8-21"T (SSK conversions); 6-21"T (SSR conversions); 2-21"T (SSO conversion)

Machinery: 5400 BHP, F. M. (SS 228-239, 269-271, 275-284), H.O.R. (SS 253-264), G. M. (others), 4 diesel engines/ 2740 BHP, 4 Elliott (SS 228-235), A. C. (SS 257-264), G. E. (others) electric motors, 2 screws
Speed: 20/10 kts.
Complement: 60

No.	Hull	Laid down	Launched	Commiss'd	Disposition
212 GATO	Groton	5 Oct 40	21 Aug 41	31 Dec 41	Stk. 1 Mar 60, sold 25 Jul 60
213 GREENLING	Groton	12 Nov 40	20 Sep 41	21 Jan 42	Stk. 1 Mar 60, sold 21 Jun 60
214 GROUPER	Groton	28 Dec 40	27 Oct 41	12 Feb 42	Stk. 2 Dec 68, sold 11 Aug 70
215 GROWLER	Groton	10 Feb 41	22 Nov 41	20 Mar 42	Sunk by Japanese vessels W of the Philippine Is. 8 Nov 44
216 GRUNION	Groton	1 Mar 41	22 Dec 41	11 Apr 42	Sunk off Kiska I. ca. 30 Jul 42, cause unknown
217 GUARDFISH	Groton	1 Apr 41	20 Jan 42	8 May 42	Stk. 1 Jun 60, sunk as target off Block Is. 10 Oct 61
218 ALBACORE	Groton	21 Apr 41	17 Feb 42	1 Jun 42	Mined off N Hokkaido 7 Nov 44
219 AMBERJACK	Groton	15 May 41	6 Mar 42	19 Jun 42	Sunk by HIJMS Hiyodori and SC-18 off Rabaul 16 Feb 43
220 BARB	Groton	7 Jun 41	2 Apr 42	8 Jul 42	To Italy 13 Dec 54 as Enrico Tazzoli, stk. 15 Oct 72
221 BLACKFISH	Groton	1 Jul 41	18 Apr 42	22 Jul 42	Stk. 1 Sep 58, sold 4 May 59
222 BLUEFISH	Groton	5 Jun 42	21 Feb 43	24 May 43	Stk. 1 Jun 59, sold 8 Jun 60
223 BONEFISH	Groton	25 Jun 42	7 Mar 43	31 May 43	Sunk by Japanese vessels in Toyama Wan, Honshu, 18 Jun 45
224 COD	Groton	21 Jul 42	21 Mar 43	21 Jun 43	Stk. 15 Dec 71, memorial at Cleveland 25 Jan 75
225 CERO	Groton	24 Aug 42	4 Apr 43	4 Jul 43	Stk. 30 Jun 67, sold Oct 70
226 CORVINA	Groton	21 Sep 42	9 May 43	6 Aug 43	Sunk by HIJMS I-176 S of Truk 16 Nov 43
227 DARTER	Groton	20 Oct 42	6 Jun 43	7 Sep 43	Grounded in Palawan Strait 24 Oct 44 and scuttled
228 DRUM	Portsmouth	11 Sep 40	12 May 41	1 Nov 41	Stk. 30 Jun 68, memorial at Mobile, Al., 14 Apr 69
229 FLYING FISH	Portsmouth	6 Dec 40	9 Jul 41	10 Dec 41	Stk. 1 Aug 58, sold Apr 59
230 FINBACK	Portsmouth	5 Feb 41	25 Aug 41	31 Jan 42	Stk. 1 Sep 58, sold Aug 59
231 HADDOCK	Portsmouth	31 Mar 41	20 Oct 41	14 Mar 42	Stk. 1 Jun 60, sold 29 Aug 60
232 HALIBUT	Portsmouth	16 May 41	3 Dec 41	10 Apr 42	Stk. 8 May 46, sold 10 Jan 47

No.		Hull	Laid down	Launched	Commiss'd	Disposition
233	HERRING	Portsmouth	14 Jul 41	15 Jan 42	4 May 42	Sunk by Japanese batteries on Matsuwa I., Kurile Is., 1 Jun 44
234	KINGFISH	Portsmouth	29 Aug 41	2 Mar 42	20 May 42	Stk. 1 Mar 60, sold 6 Oct 60
235	SHAD	Portsmouth	24 Oct 41	15 Apr 42	12 Jun 42	Stk. 1 Apr 60, sold 21 Jun 60
236	SILVERSIDES	Mare I.	4 Nov 40	26 Aug 41	15 Dec 41	Stk. 30 Jun 69, memorial at Chicago 24 May 73
237	TRIGGER	Mare I.	1 Feb 41	22 Oct 41	31 Jan 42	Sunk by Japanese vessels in E China Sea 28 Mar 45
238	WAHOO	Mare I.	28 Jun 41	14 Feb 42	15 May 42	Sunk by Japanese aircraft in La Perouse Strait 11 Oct 43
239	WHALE	Mare I.	28 Jun 41	14 Mar 42	1 Jun 42	Stk. 1 Mar 60, sold 29 Sep 60
240	ANGLER	Groton	9 Nov 42	4 Jul 43	1 Oct 43	Stk. 15 Dec 71, sold 1 Feb 74
241	BASHAW	Groton	4 Dec 42	25 Jul 43	25 Oct 43	Stk. 13 Sep 69, sold 19 Jul 72
242	BLUEGILL	Groton	17 Dec 42	8 Aug 43	11 Nov 43	Stk. 28 Jun 69, scuttled off Maui 3 Dec 70
243	BREAM	Groton	5 Feb 43	17 Oct 43	24 Jan 44	Stk. 28 Jun 69, sunk as target off California 7 Nov 69
244	CAVALLA	Groton	4 Mar 43	14 Nov 43	29 Feb 44	Stk. 30 Dec 69, memorial at Galveston, Tx., 21 Jan 71
245	COBIA	Groton	17 Mar 43	28 Nov 43	29 Mar 44	Stk. 1 Jul 70, memorial at Manitowoc, Wisc., 17 Aug 70
246	CROAKER	Groton	1 Apr 43	19 Dec 43	21 Apr 44	Stk. 20 Dec 71, memorial at Groton, Conn., 27 Jun 76
247	DACE	Groton	22 Jul 42	25 Apr 43	23 Jul 43	To Italy 31 Jan 55 as Leonardo da Vinci, stk. 15 Oct 72
248	DORADO	Groton	27 Aug 42	23 May 43	28 Aug 43	Sunk by United States aircraft off Panama 12 Oct 43
249	FLASHER	Groton	30 Sep 42	20 Jun 43	25 Sep 43	Stk. 1 Jun 59, sold 31 May 63
250	FLIER	Groton	30 Oct 42	11 Jul 43	18 Oct 43	Mined in Balabac Strait, P. I., 13 Aug 44
251	FLOUNDER	Groton	5 Dec 42	22 Aug 43	29 Nov 43	Stk. 1 Jun 59, sold 22 Dec 59
252	GABILAN	Groton	5 Jan 43	19 Sep 43	28 Dec 43	Stk. 1 Jun 59, sold Dec 59
253	GUNNEL	Groton	21 Jul 41	17 May 42	20 Aug 42	Stk. 1 Sep 58, sold Aug 59
254	GURNARD	Groton	2 Sep 41	1 Jun 42	18 Sep 42	Stk. 1 May 61, sold 27 Sep 61
255	HADDO	Groton	1 Oct 41	21 Jun 42	9 Oct 42	Stk. 1 Aug 58, sold 30 Apr 59
256	HAKE	Groton	1 Nov 41	17 Jul 42	30 Oct 42	Stk. 19 Apr 68, sold 5 Dec 72
257	HARDER	Groton	1 Dec 41	19 Aug 42	2 Dec 42	Sunk by Japanese minesweeper off Dazol Bay, Luzon, 24 Aug 44
258	HOE	Groton	2 Jan 42	17 Sep 42	16 Dec 42	Stk. 1 May 60, sold 23 Aug 60
259	JACK	Groton	2 Feb 42	16 Oct 42	6 Jan 43	To Greece 21 Apr 58 as Amfitriti, stk. 1 Sep 67
260	LAPON	Groton	21 Feb 42	27 Oct 42	23 Jan 43	To Greece 10 Aug 57 as Poseidon, stk. 31 Dec 75
261	MINGO	Groton	21 Mar 42	30 Nov 42	12 Feb 43	To Japan 15 Aug 55 as Kuroshio, stk. 20 Feb 71
262	MUSKALLUNGE	Groton	7 Apr 42	13 Dec 42	15 Mar 43	To Brazil 18 Jan 57 as Humaita, stk. 1 Dec 67
263	PADDLE	Groton	1 May 42	30 Dec 42	29 Mar 43	To Brazil 18 Jan 57 as Riachuelo, stk. 30 Jun 68
264	PARGO	Groton	21 May 42	24 Jan 43	26 Apr 43	Stk. 1 Jun 60, sold 17 Apr 61
265	PETO	Manitowoc	18 Jun 41	30 Apr 42	21 Nov 42	Stk. 1 Aug 60, sold 10 Nov 60
266	POGY	Manitowoc	15 Sep 41	23 Jun 42	10 Jan 43	Stk. 1 Sep 58, sold Apr 59
267	POMPON	Manitowoc	26 Nov 41	15 Aug 42	17 Mar 43	Stk. 1 Apr 60, sold 25 Nov 60
268	PUFFER	Manitowoc	16 Feb 42	22 Nov 42	27 Apr 43	Stk. 1 Jul 60, sold 4 Nov 60
269	RASHER	Manitowoc	4 May 42	20 Dec 42	8 Jun 43	Stk. 20 Dec 71, sold 7 Aug 74
270	RATON	Manitowoc	29 May 42	24 Jan 43	13 Jul 43	Stk. 28 Jun 69, sold 12 Oct 73
271	RAY	Manitowoc	20 Jul 42	28 Feb 43	27 Jul 43	Stk. 1 Apr 60, sold 25 Nov 60
272	REDFIN	Manitowoc	3 Sep 42	4 Apr 43	31 Aug 43	Stk. 1 Jul 70, sold Mar 71
273	ROBALO	Manitowoc	24 Oct 42	9 May 43	28 Sep 43	Mined W of Palawan 26 Jul 44
274	ROCK	Manitowoc	23 Dec 42	20 Jun 43	26 Oct 43	Stk. 13 Sep 69, sold 16 Aug 72
275	RUNNER	Portsmouth	8 Dec 41	30 May 42	30 Jul 42	Mined off Japan ca. Jun 43
276	SAWFISH	Portsmouth	20 Jan 42	23 Jun 42	26 Aug 42	Stk. 1 Apr 60, sold 14 Nov 60

No.		Hull	Laid down	Launched	Commiss'd	Disposition
277	SCAMP	Portsmouth	6 Mar 42	20 Jul 42	18 Sep 42	Probably sunk by Japanese vessels and aircraft S of Tokyo Bay 11 Nov 44
278	SCORPION	Portsmouth	20 Mar 42	20 Jul 42	1 Oct 42	Probably mined in Yellow Sea ca. 5 Jan 44
279	SNOOK	Portsmouth	17 Apr 42	15 Aug 42	24 Oct 42	Missing after 8 Apr 45 E of Formosa
280	STEELHEAD	Portsmouth	1 Jun 42	11 Sep 42	7 Dec 42	Stk. 1 Apr 60, sold 29 Jun 61
281	SUNFISH	Mare I.	25 Sep 41	2 May 42	15 Jul 42	Stk. 1 May 60, sold 29 Nov 60
282	TUNNY	Mare I.	10 Nov 41	30 Jun 42	1 Sep 42	Stk. 30 Jun 69, sunk as target 19 Jun 70
283	TINOSA	Mare I.	21 Feb 42	7 Oct 42	15 Jan 43	Stk. 1 Sep 58, scuttled off Hawaii Nov 60
284	TULLIBEE	Mare I.	1 Apr 42	11 Nov 42	15 Feb 43	Sunk by own torpedo N of Palau 26 Mar 44
361	GOLET	Manitowoc	27 Jan 43	1 Aug 43	30 Nov 43	Sunk by Japanese vessels NW of Honshu 14 Jun 44
362	GUAVINA	Manitowoc	3 Mar 43	29 Aug 43	23 Dec 43	Stk. 30 Jun 67, sunk as target off Cape Henry 14 Nov 67
363	GUITARRO	Manitowoc	7 Apr 43	26 Sep 43	26 Jan 44	To Turkey 7 Aug 54 as Preveze, stk. 1 Jan 72
364	HAMMERHEAD	Manitowoc	5 May 43	24 Oct 43	1 Mar 44	To Turkey 23 Oct 54 as Cerbe, stk. 1 Jan 72.

Notes: Fiscal years 1941 (SS 212-284) and 1942. The Gato design was a virtual repeat of the Tambor type except that a watertight bulkhead was added to subdivide the engine room. This required lengthening the hull 4'6". Its operating depth was increased to 300 feet, not because of any design change, but because the margin of safety built up in previous designs permitted it. The design was frozen for mass production in June 1940, and the Gato class along with their Balao class near sisters formed the bulk of the World War II submarine force. SS 253-264 had non-standard H.O.R. diesels, and Electric Boat built them ahead of SS 222-227 so it could standardize its production lines as soon as possible. The H.O.R. engines subsequently proved unsatisfactory and had to be replaced with G.M. diesels in 1943. SS 361-364 were built to the Gato design because Manitowoc built to Electric Boat plans and Electric Boat's Balao class plans were not ready when these boats were begun.

The postwar SSR conversions had a 30-foot mid-section inserted to house the additional electronics gear. The Tunny was fitted to fire the Regulus SSM. The Guavina was fitted with extra fuel tanks (increasing her beam to 38'3") as a submarine oiler. The Greenling (SS-213), Guardfish (SS-217), Gurnard (SS-254), Pargo (SS-264), Puffer (SS-268), Silversides (SS-236), Drum (SS-228), Kingfish (SS-234), Sawfish (SS-276), Shad (SS-235) and Steelhead (SS-280) were used as training vessels after 1946. The Hake (SS-256) began similar service in 1968. She and the Bluegill (SS-242) served as salvage training hulks after being stricken.

Renamings: The names of the Barb (SS-220), Dace (SS-247), and Jack (SS-259) were cancelled 28 Apr 59 and the names of the Lapon (SS-260), Guitarro (SS-363), and Hammerhead (SS-364) were cancelled on 22 Mar 65.

Reclassifications: Various boats were converted or reclassified as shown:
Grouper (SS-214) to SSK 2 Jan 51; AGSS 21 Jun 58;
Cod (SS-224) to AGSS 1 Dec 62; IXSS 30 Jun 71;
Cero (SS-225), Drum (SS-228), Silversides (SS-236), Cobia (SS-245), and Hake (SS-256) to AGSS 1 Dec 62;
Flying Fish (SS-229) to AGSS 29 Nov 50;
Angler (SS-240) to SSK 18 Feb 53; SS 15 Aug 59; AGSS 1 Jul 63; IXSS 30 Jun 71;
Bashaw (SS-241) to SSK 18 Feb 53; SS 15 Aug 59; AGSS 1 Sep 62;
Bluegill (SS-242) to SSK 18 Feb 53; SS 15 Aug 59; AGSS 1 Apr 66;
Bream (SS-243) to SSK 18 Feb 53; SS 15 Aug 59; AGSS 15 Apr 65;
Cavalla (SS-244) to SSK 18 Feb 53; SS 15 Aug 59; AGSS 1 Jul 63;
Croaker (SS-246) to SSK 9 Apr 53; SS 15 Aug 59; AGSS 1 May 67; IXSS 30 Jun 71;
Pompon (SS-267) to SSR 11 Dec 51;
Rasher (SS-269) to SSR 11 Dec 51; AGSS 1 Jul 60; IXSS 30 Jun 71;
Raton (SS-270) to SSR 18 Jul 52; AGSS 1 Jul 60;
Ray (SS-271) to SSR 2 Jan 51;
Redfin (SS-272) to SSR 2 Jan 51; SS 15 Aug 59; AGSS 28 Jun 63;
Rock (SS-274) to SSR 18 Jul 52; AGSS 31 Dec 59;
Tunny (SS-282) to SSG 18 Jul 52; SS 15 May 65; APSS 1 Oct 66; LPSS 1 Jan 69;
Guavina (SS-362) to SSO 13 Aug 48; AGSS 11 Dec 51; AOSS 22 Jun 57.

The *Gato*-class submarine *Croaker* (SS-246) on 16 July 1952, in a configuration typical of war-built submarines in 1945. (NARA 80-G-445899)

The submarine *Trout* (SS-566) on 13 May 1952. (NARA 80-G-443363)

1941

BALAO class

Displacement: 1526/2401 (SS 405-410), 2391 (SS 308-312, 381-
    404), 2414 (SS 285-291). 2424 (others) tons
Dimensions: 311'6"(SS 298-299, 308-312, 381-404), 311'8" (SS
    292-297, 300-303, 405-410), 311'10"(SS 304-307, 411-416),
    311'9"(others) (all oa.) x 27'4"(SS 304-307, 411-416, e),
    27'3"(others, e) x 16'10"(max)
Armament: 1-4"/50 10-21"T; 1-5"/25 10-21"T (late 1944); 2-
    5"/25 10-21"T (SS 285 and others, 1945); 10-21"T ("Guppy"
    conversions); Loon SSM 10-21"T (SS 337, 348, 1949); Regulus
    SSM 10-21"T (SSG conversions); 6-21"T (SSA conversion); 4-
    21"T (SSR-312); none (SSP conversions)
Complement: 66

Machinery: 5400 BHP, F. M. (SS 292-
    312, 381-416, 425-428, 431-434,
    530-536), H.O.R. (SS 429-430),
    G. M. (others), 4 diesel engines/
    2740 BHP, Elliott (SS 292-312, 381-
    410, 425-434), A.C. (SS 530-536),
    G.E. (others), 2 electric motors
    (SS 343-352, 405-410, 416, 425-
    426), 4 (others), 2 screws
Speed: 20/10 kts.

No.	Hull	Laid down	Launched	Commiss'd	Disposition
285 BALAO	Portsmouth	26 Jun 42	27 Oct 42	4 Feb 43	Stk. 1 Aug 63, sunk as target off Charleston, S.C., 6 Sep 63
286 BILLFISH	Portsmouth	23 Jul 42	12 Nov 42	20 Apr 43	Stk. 1 Apr 68, sold Jan 71
287 BOWFIN	Portsmouth	23 Jul 42	7 Dec 42	1 May 43	Stk. 1 Dec 71, memorial at Pearl Harbor 1 Aug 79
288 CABRILLA	Portsmouth	18 Aug 42	24 Dec 42	24 May 43	Stk. 30 Jun 68, memorial at Galveston 19 Oct 1968, sold 18 Apr 72
289 CAPELIN	Portsmouth	14 Sep 42	20 Jan 43	4 Jun 43	Missing N of Celebes I. after 2 Dec 43
290 CISCO	Portsmouth	29 Oct 42	24 Dec 42	10 May 43	Sunk by Japanese aircraft W of Mindanao 28 Sep 43
291 CREVALLE	Portsmouth	14 Nov 42	22 Feb 43	24 Jun 43	Stk. 15 Apr 68, sold Jan 71
292 DEVILFISH	Cramp	31 Mar 42	30 May 43	1 Sep 44	Stk. 1 Mar 67, sunk as target off San Francisco 14 Aug 68
293 DRAGONET	Cramp	28 Apr 42	18 Apr 43	6 Mar 44	Stk. 1 Jun 61, scuttled after tests in Chesapeake Bay 17 Sep 61
294 ESCOLAR	Cramp	10 Jun 42	18 Apr 43	2 Jun 44	Probably mined in Yellow Sea 17 Oct 44
295 HACKLEBACK	Cramp	15 Aug 42	30 May 43	7 Nov 44	Stk. 1 Mar 67, sold 4 Dec 68
296 LANCETFISH	Cramp	30 Sep 42	15 Aug 43	12 Feb 45	Stk. 9 Jun 58, sold 27 Aug 59
297 LING	Cramp	2 Nov 42	15 Aug 43	8 Jun 45	Stk. 1 Dec 71, memorial at Hackensack, N.J. 28 Jun 72
298 LIONFISH	Cramp	15 Dec 42	7 Nov 43	1 Nov 44	Stk. 20 Dec 71, memorial at Fall River, Mass., 30 Aug 72
299 MANTA	Cramp	15 Jan 43	7 Nov 43	18 Dec 44	Stk. 30 Jun 67, sunk as target off Norfolk 16 Jul 69
300 MORAY	Cramp	21 Apr 43	14 May 44	26 Jan 45	Stk. 1 Apr 67, sunk as target off S. California 18 Jun 70
301 RONCADOR	Cramp	21 Apr 43	14 May 44	27 Mar 45	Stk. 1 Dec 71, memorial at Redondo Beach, Cal., Feb 73
302 SABALO	Cramp	5 Jun 43	4 Jun 44	19 Jun 45	Stk. 1 Jul 71, disposed of ca. 1985
303 SABLEFISH	Cramp	5 Jun 43	4 Jun 44	18 Dec 45	Stk. 1 Nov 69, sold 29 Jul 71
304 SEAHORSE	Mare I.	1 Jul 42	9 Jan 43	31 Mar 43	Stk. 1 Mar 67, sold 4 Dec 68
305 SKATE	Mare I.	1 Aug 42	4 Mar 43	15 Apr 43	Sunk as target off S. Calif. 5 Oct 48, stk. 21 Oct 48
306 TANG	Mare I.	15 Jan 43	17 Aug 43	15 Oct 43	Sunk by own torpedo off Formosa 24 Oct 44
307 TILEFISH	Mare I.	10 Mar 43	25 Oct 43	15 Dec 43	To Venezuela 4 May 60 as Carite, stk. 1 Dec 60
308 APOGON	Portsmouth	9 Dec 42	10 Mar 43	16 Jul 43	Sunk in atomic bomb test at Bikini Atoll 25 Jul 46, stk. 25 Feb 47
309 ASPRO	Portsmouth	27 Dec 42	7 Apr 43	31 Jul 43	Stk. 1 Sep 62, sunk as target off San Diego 16 Nov 62
310 BATFISH	Portsmouth	27 Dec 42	5 May 43	21 Aug 43	Stk. 1 Nov 69, memorial at Muskogee, Okla., 18 Feb 72

No.	Hull	Laid down	Launched	Commiss'd	Disposition
311 ARCHERFISH	Portsmouth	22 Jan 43	28 May 43	4 Sep 43	Stk. 1 May 68, sunk as target off California 19 Oct 68
312 BURRFISH	Portsmouth	24 Feb 43	18 Jun 43	14 Sep 43	To Canada 11 May 61 as Grilse, stk. 31 Jul 69
313 PERCH	Groton	5 Jan 43	12 Sep 43	7 Jan 44	Stk. 1 Dec 71, sold 15 Jan 73
314 SHARK	Groton	28 Jan 43	17 Oct 43	14 Feb 44	Sunk by Japanese vessels off S Formosa 24 Oct 44
315 SEALION	Groton	25 Feb 43	31 Oct 43	8 Mar 44	Stk. 15 Mar 77, sunk as target off Newport 8 Jul 78
316 BARBEL	Groton	11 Mar 43	14 Nov 43	3 Apr 44	Sunk by Japanese aircraft off Palawan, P.I., 4 Feb 45
317 BARBERO	Groton	25 Mar 43	12 Dec 43	29 Apr 44	Stk. 1 Jul 64, sunk as target off Pearl Harbor 7 Oct 64
318 BAYA	Groton	8 Apr 43	2 Jan 44	20 May 44	Stk. 30 Oct 72, sold 12 Oct 73
319 BECUNA	Groton	29 Apr 43	30 Jan 44	27 May 44	Stk. 15 Aug 73, memorial at Philadelphia 21 Jun 76
320 BERGALL	Groton	13 May 43	16 Feb 44	12 Jun 44	To Turkey 18 Oct 58 as Turgut Reis, stk. 1 Feb 73
321 BESUGO	Groton	27 May 43	27 Feb 44	19 Jun 44	To Italy 31 Mar 66 as Francesco Morosini, stk. 15 Nov 75
322 BLACKFIN	Groton	10 Jun 43	12 Mar 44	4 Jul 44	Stk. 15 Sep 72, scuttled off San Diego 13 May 73
323 CAIMAN	Groton	24 Jun 43	30 Mar 44	17 Jul 44	To Turkey 30 Jun 72 as Dumlupinar, stk. 30 Jun 72
324 BLENNY	Groton	8 Jul 43	9 Apr 44	27 Jul 44	Stk. 15 Aug 73, scuttled off Ocean City, Md., 7 Jun 89
325 BLOWER	Groton	15 Jul 43	23 Apr 44	10 Aug 44	To Turkey 16 Nov 50 as Dumlupinar, stk. 20 Dec 50
326 BLUEBACK	Groton	29 Jul 43	7 May 44	28 Aug 44	To Turkey 23 May 48 as Ikinci Inonu, stk. 28 May 48
327 BOARFISH	Groton	12 Aug 43	21 May 44	23 Sep 44	To Turkey 23 May 48 as Sakarya, stk. 28 May 48
328 CHARR	Groton	26 Aug 43	28 May 44	23 Sep 44	Stk. 20 Dec 71, sold 16 Aug 72
329 CHUB	Groton	16 Sep 43	18 Jun 44	21 Oct 44	To Turkey 23 May 48 as Gur, stk. 28 May 48
330 BRILL	Groton	23 Sep 43	25 Jun 44	26 Oct 44	To Turkey 23 May 48 as Birinci Inonu, stk. 28 May 48
331 BUGARA	Groton	21 Oct 43	2 Jul 44	15 Nov 44	Stk. 1 Oct 70, foundered off Cape Flattery, Wash. 1 Jun 71
332 BULLHEAD	Groton	21 Oct 43	16 Jul 44	4 Dec 44	Sunk by Japanese aircraft in Java Sea 6 Aug 45
333 BUMPER	Groton	4 Nov 43	6 Aug 44	9 Dec 44	To Turkey 16 Nov 50 as Canakkale, stk. 20 Dec 50
334 CABEZON	Groton	18 Nov 43	27 Aug 44	30 Dec 44	Stk. 15 May 70, sold 28 Dec 71
335 DENTUDA	Groton	18 Nov 43	10 Sep 44	30 Dec 44	Stk. 30 Jun 67, sold 20 Jan 69
336 CAPITAINE	Groton	2 Dec 43	1 Oct 44	26 Jan 45	To Italy 5 Mar 66 as Alfredo Cappellini, stk. 5 Dec 77
337 CARBONERO	Groton	16 Dec 43	15 Oct 44	7 Feb 45	Stk. 1 Dec 70, sunk as target off Pearl Harbor 27 Apr 75
338 CARP	Groton	23 Dec 43	12 Nov 44	28 Feb 45	Stk. 20 Dec 71, sold 26 Jul 73
339 CATFISH	Groton	6 Jan 44	19 Nov 44	19 Mar 45	To Argentina 1 Jul 71 as Santa Fe, stk. 1 Jul 71
340 ENTEMEDOR	Groton	3 Feb 44	17 Dec 44	6 Apr 45	To Turkey 31 Jul 72 as Preveze, stk. 1 Aug 73
341 CHIVO	Groton	21 Feb 44	14 Jan 45	28 Apr 45	To Argentina 1 Jul 71 as Santiago del Estero, stk. 1 Jul 71
342 CHOPPER	Groton	2 Mar 44	4 Feb 45	25 May 45	Stk. 1 Oct 71, foundered off Cape Hatteras 21 Jul 76
343 CLAMAGORE	Groton	16 Mar 44	25 Feb 45	28 Jun 45	Stk. 27 Jun 75, memorial at Charleston, S.C., 1981
344 COBBLER	Groton	3 Apr 44	1 Apr 45	8 Aug 45	To Turkey 21 Nov 73 as Canakkale, stk. 21 Nov 73

No.	Hull	Laid down	Launched	Commiss'd	Disposition
345 COCHINO	Groton	13 Apr 44	20 Apr 45	25 Aug 45	Sunk by battery explosion and fire off Norway 26 Aug 49
346 CORPORAL	Groton	27 Apr 44	10 Jun 45	9 Nov 45	To Turkey 21 Nov 73 as Ikinci Inonu, stk. 21 Nov 73
347 CUBERA	Groton	11 May 44	17 Jun 45	19 Dec 45	To Venezuela 5 Jan 72 as Tiburon, stk. 5 Jan 72
348 CUSK	Groton	25 May 44	28 Jul 45	5 Feb 46	Stk. 24 Sep 69, sold 13 Jun 72
349 DIODON	Groton	1 Jun 44	10 Sep 45	18 Mar 46	Stk. 15 Jan 71, sold 18 Apr 72
350 DOGFISH	Groton	22 Jun 44	27 Oct 45	29 Apr 46	To Brazil 28 Jul 72 as Guanabara, stk. 28 Jul 72
351 GREENFISH	Groton	29 Jun 44	21 Dec 45	7 Jun 46	To Brazil 19 Dec 73 as Amazonas, stk. 19 Dec 73
352 HALFBEAK	Groton	6 Jul 44	19 Feb 46	22 Jul 46	Stk. 1 Jul 71, sold 13 Jun 72
353 DUGONG	Groton	No?	No	No	Cancelled 23 Oct 44 as of 29 Jul 44
354 EEL	Groton	No?	No	No	Cancelled 23 Oct 44 as of 29 Jul 44
355 ESPADA	Groton	No?	No	No	Cancelled 23 Oct 44 as of 29 Jul 44
356 JAWFISH	Groton	No	No	No	Cancelled 29 Jul 44
357 ONO	Groton	No	No	No	Cancelled 29 Jul 44
358 GARLOPA	Groton	No	No	No	Cancelled 29 Jul 44
359 GARRUPA	Groton	No	No	No	Cancelled 29 Jul 44
360 GOLDRING	Groton	No	No	No	Cancelled 29 Jul 44
365 HARDHEAD	Manitowoc	7 Jul 43	12 Dec 43	18 Apr 44	To Greece 26 Jul 72 as Papanikolis, stk. 26 Jul 72
366 HAWKBILL	Manitowoc	7 Aug 43	9 Jan 44	17 May 44	To Netherlands 21 Apr 53 as Zeeleeuw, stk. 20 Feb 70
367 ICEFISH	Manitowoc	4 Sep 43	20 Feb 44	10 Jun 44	To Netherlands 21 Feb 53 as Walrus, stk. 15 Jul 71
368 JALLAO	Manitowoc	29 Sep 43	12 Mar 44	8 Jul 44	To Spain 26 Jun 74 as Narciso Monturiol, stk. 26 Jun 74
369 KETE	Manitowoc	25 Oct 43	9 Apr 44	31 Jul 44	Probably sunk by Japanese submarine off Nansei Shoto ca. 20 Mar 45
370 KRAKEN	Manitowoc	13 Dec 43	30 Apr 44	8 Sep 44	To Spain 24 Oct 59 as Almirante Garcia de los Reyes, stk. 18 Nov 74
371 LAGARTO	Manitowoc	12 Jan 44	28 May 44	14 Oct 44	Sunk by Japanese minelayer Hatsutaka in Gulf of Siam 4 May 45
372 LAMPREY	Manitowoc	22 Feb 44	18 Jun 44	17 Nov 44	To Argentina 21 Aug 60 as Santiago del Estero, stk. 1 Sep 71
373 LIZARDFISH	Manitowoc	14 Mar 44	16 Jul 44	30 Dec 44	To Italy 9 Jan 60 as Evangelista Torricelli, stk. 15 Jul 78
374 LOGGERHEAD	Manitowoc	1 Apr 44	13 Aug 44	9 Feb 45	Stk. 30 Jun 67, sold Aug 69
375 MACABI	Manitowoc	1 May 44	19 Sep 44	29 Mar 45	To Argentina 11 Aug 60 as Santa Fe, stk. 1 Sep 71
376 MAPIRO	Manitowoc	30 May 44	9 Nov 44	30 Apr 45	To Turkey 18 Mar 60 as Piri Reis, stk. 1 Aug 73
377 MENHADEN	Manitowoc	21 Jun 44	20 Dec 44	22 Jun 45	Stk. 15 Aug 73, submerged hulk at Keyport, Wash., 1976
378 MERO	Manitowoc	22 Jul 44	17 Jan 45	17 Aug 45	To Turkey 20 Apr 60 as Hizir Reis, stk. 1 Aug 73
379 NEEDLEFISH	Manitowoc	No	No	No	Cancelled 29 Jul 44
380 NERKA	Manitowoc	No	No	No	Cancelled 29 Jul 44
381 SAND LANCE	Portsmouth	12 Mar 43	25 Jun 43	9 Oct 43	To Brazil 7 Sep 63 as Rio Grande do Sul, stk. 1 Sep 72
382 PICUDA	Portsmouth	15 Mar 43	12 Jul 43	16 Oct 43	To Spain 1 Oct 72 as Narciso Monturiol, stk. 18 Nov 74
383 PAMPANITO	Portsmouth	15 Mar 43	12 Jul 43	6 Nov 43	Stk. 20 Dec 71, memorial at San Francisco 21 Nov 75

No.		Hull	Laid down	Launched	Commiss'd	Disposition
384	PARCHE	Portsmouth	9 Apr 43	24 Jul 43	20 Nov 43	Stk. 8 Nov 69, sold Jul 70
385	BANG	Portsmouth	30 Apr 43	30 Aug 43	4 Dec 43	To Spain 1 Oct 72 as Cosme Garcia, stk. 18 Nov 74
386	PILOTFISH	Portsmouth	15 May 43	30 Aug 43	16 Dec 43	Damaged in atomic bomb test, Bikini, 25 Jul 46, stk. 25 Feb 47, sunk as target off Eniwetok 16 Oct 48.
387	PINTADO	Portsmouth	7 May 43	15 Sep 43	1 Jan 44	Stk. 1 Mar 67, sold 20 Jan 69
388	PIPEFISH	Portsmouth	31 May 43	12 Oct 43	22 Jan 44	Stk. 1 Mar 67, sold 20 Jan 69
389	PIRANHA	Portsmouth	21 Jun 43	27 Oct 43	5 Feb 44	Stk. 1 Mar 67, sold 11 Aug 70
390	PLAICE	Portsmouth	28 Jun 43	15 Nov 43	12 Feb 44	To Brazil 7 Sep 63 as Bahia, stk. 1 Apr 73
391	POMFRET	Portsmouth	14 Jul 43	27 Oct 43	19 Feb 44	To Turkey 1 Jul 71 as Oruc Reis, stk. 1 Aug 73
392	STERLET	Portsmouth	14 Jul 43	27 Oct 43	4 Mar 44	Stk. 1 Oct 68, sunk as target 31 Jan 69
393	QUEENFISH	Portsmouth	27 Jul 43	30 Nov 43	11 Mar 44	Stk. 1 Mar 63, sunk as target 14 Aug 63
394	RAZORBACK	Portsmouth	9 Sep 43	27 Jan 44	3 Apr 44	To Turkey 30 Nov 70 as Murat Reis, stk. 30 Nov 70,
395	REDFISH	Portsmouth	9 Sep 43	27 Jan 44	12 Apr 44	Stk. 30 Jun 68, sunk as target off San Diego 6 Feb 69
396	RONQUIL	Portsmouth	9 Sep 43	27 Jan 44	22 Apr 44	To Spain 1 Jul 71 as Isaac Peral, stk. 1 Jul 71
397	SCABBARDFISH	Portsmouth	27 Sep 43	27 Jan 44	29 Apr 44	To Greece 26 Feb 65 as Triaina, stk. 31 Jan 76
398	SEGUNDO	Portsmouth	14 Oct 43	5 Feb 44	9 May 44	Stk. 8 Aug 70, sunk as target
399	SEA CAT	Portsmouth	30 Oct 43	21 Feb 44	16 May 44	Stk. 2 Dec 68, sold 18 May 73
400	SEA DEVIL	Portsmouth	18 Nov 43	28 Feb 44	24 May 44	Stk. 1 Apr 64, sunk as target off S. California 24 Nov 64
401	SEA DOG	Portsmouth	1 Nov 43	28 Mar 44	3 Jun 44	Stk. 2 Dec 68, sold 18 May 73
402	SEA FOX	Portsmouth	2 Nov 43	28 Mar 44	13 Jun 44	To Turkey 14 Dec 70 as Burak Reis, stk. 14 Dec 70
403	ATULE	Portsmouth	2 Dec 43	6 Mar 44	21 Jun 44	Stk. 15 Aug 73, to Peru as Pacocha 31 Jul 74
404	SPIKEFISH	Portsmouth	29 Jan 44	26 Apr 44	30 Jun 44	Stk. 1 May 63, sunk as target off Long Island 4 Aug 64
405	SEA OWL	Portsmouth	7 Feb 44	7 May 44	17 Jul 44	Stk. 15 Nov 69, sold 3 Jun 71
406	SEA POACHER	Portsmouth	23 Feb 44	20 May 44	31 Jul 44	Stk. 15 Aug 73, to Peru as La Pedrera 1 Jul 74
407	SEA ROBIN	Portsmouth	1 Mar 44	25 May 44	7 Aug 44	Stk. 1 Oct 70, sold 3 Jun 71
408	SENNET	Portsmouth	8 Mar 44	6 Jun 44	22 Aug 44	Stk. 2 Dec 68, sold 18 May 73
409	PIPER	Portsmouth	15 Mar 44	26 Jun 44	23 Aug 44	Stk. 1 Jul 70, sold Jun 71
410	THREADFIN	Portsmouth	18 Mar 44	26 Jun 44	30 Aug 44	To Turkey 18 Aug 72 as Birinci Inonu, stk. 1 Aug 73
411	SPADEFISH	Mare I.	27 May 43	8 Jan 44	9 Mar 44	Stk. 1 Apr 67, sold 17 Oct 69
412	TREPANG	Mare I.	25 Jun 43	23 Mar 44	22 May 44	Stk. 30 Jun 67, sunk as target off S. California 16 Sep 69
413	SPOT	Mare I.	24 Aug 43	19 May 44	3 Aug 44	To Chile 12 Jan 62 as Simpson, stk. 1 Aug 75
414	SPRINGER	Mare I.	30 Oct 43	3 Aug 44	18 Oct 44	To Chile 23 Jan 61 as Thomson, stk. 1 Sep 72
415	STICKLEBACK	Mare I.	1 Mar 44	1 Jan 45	29 Mar 45	Sunk in collision with USS Silverstein (DE-534) off Oahu 29 May 58
416	TIRU	Mare I.	17 Apr 44	16 Sep 47	1 Sep 48	Stk. 1 Jul 75, sunk as target off Norfolk 19 Jul 79.
425	TRUMPETFISH	Cramp	23 Aug 43	13 May 45	29 Jan 46	To Brazil 15 Oct 73 as Goias, stk. 15 Oct 73
426	TUSK	Cramp	23 Aug 43	8 Jul 45	11 Apr 46	To Taiwan 18 Oct 73 as Hai Pao, stk. 18 Oct 73
427	TURBOT	Cramp	13 Nov 43	12 Apr 46	No	Cancelled 12 Aug 45, test hulk, scrapped 1986
428	ULUA	Cramp	13 Nov 43	23 Apr 46	No	Cancelled 12 Aug 45, test hulk, stk. 12 Jun 58, sold 30 Sep 58

No.		Hull	Laid down	Launched	Commiss'd	Disposition
429	UNICORN	Cramp	No	No	No	Cancelled 29 Jul 44
430	VENDACE	Cramp	No	No	No	Cancelled 29 Jul 44
431	WALRUS	Cramp	No	No	No	Cancelled 29 Jul 44
432	WHITEFISH	Cramp	No	No	No	Cancelled 29 Jul 44
433	WHITING	Cramp	No	No	No	Cancelled 29 Jul 44
434	WOLFFISH	Cramp	No	No	No	Cancelled 29 Jul 44
438 -457	Unnamed	Groton	No	No	No	Cancelled 29 Jul 44
458 -463	Unnamed	Manitowoc	No	No	No	Cancelled 29 Jul 44
464	CHICOLAR	Manitowoc	No	No	No	Cancelled 29 Jul 44
465 -474	Unnamed	Manitowoc	No	No	No	Cancelled 29 Jul 44
530 -536	Unnamed	Cramp	No	No	No	Cancelled 29 Jul 44.

Notes: Fiscal years 1942 (SS 285-434) and 1943. In this class the material of the pressure hull was changed from mild steel to high-tensile steel and the plating was thickened to increase the operating depth to 400 feet. The boats were otherwise almost identical to the Gato class. Groton boats beginning with SS-343 and Portsmouth boats beginning with SS-405 had a new type of large, slow-speed electric main propulsion motor which could be connected directly to the propellor shaft, making them the first boats since the Cuttlefish (SS-171) without reduction gears. SS 458-463 were shifted from Groton 4 Apr 44. SS 353-55 were cancelled in connection with the reordering of SS 435-37 as Tench class boats, below. The Lionfish (SS-298) and Manta (SS-299) were towed to the Boston Navy Yard for completion in February 1944 and were shifted again to the Portsmouth Navy Yard in April 1944. The Lancetfish (SS-296) and Ling (SS-297) were towed to Boston for completion in May 1944. The Lancetfish sank at her pier at Boston while fitting out on 15 Mar 45; she was raised on 23 Mar 45 and delivered incomplete on 14 Jul 47. The unfinished hulls of Turbot (SS-427) and Ulua (SS-428) were used respectively as a machinery silencing test platform and an underwater shock test hulk.
After the war many received Greater Underwater Propulsive Power (Guppy) conversions, which involved streamlining the hull and sail as well as adding snorkel and larger batteries. Two Tench class boats received the prototype "Guppy I" modification, which lacked a snorkel, in 1947. In 1948-49, SS-339, 343-347, 349-352, 416, and 425-426 got "Guppy II" conversions, which combined the Guppy I features with the snorkel and made them 1870/2420 tons; 307'6"(oa.) x 27'4"(e) x 15'(max). SS-319, 322-324, 341-342, 403, and 406-407 received less elaborate "Guppy IA" alterations during 1950-52 becoming: 1870 (normal)/2440 tons; 308'(oa.) x 27'(e) x 17'. SS-340, 365, 368, 377, 382, 385, 391, 394, 396, 402, 410, and 415 were given "Guppy IIA" treatment in 1952-54: 1840/2445 tons; 306'(oa.) x 27'(e) x 17'(max). They resembled the Guppy IA type but had one main engine removed and a sonar room added. The SS-302, 303, 320, 328, 331, 337, 338, 348, 392, 398, 399, 405, 408, and 409 had less extensive non-Guppy modifications which did, however, include the addition of a snorkel. They came out 1820/2400 tons; 312'(oa.) x 27'4"(e) x 17'. Under the FRAM program, the Tiru (SS-416) in 1959 received a prototype Guppy III reconstruction which included lengthening by 12'6", and five other boats (SS 343, 344, 346, 351, and 425) were lengthened 15' in similar refits in 1961-62. The Baya was lengthened 23' as an AGSS in 1959. The Carbonero (SS-337) was involved in trials of the Loon and Regulus I missiles from 1949 to 1961 but was never reclassified SSG.
Renamings: SS-308 ex Abadejo, SS-309 ex Acedia, SS-310 ex Acoupa, SS-312 ex Arnillo, SS-323 ex Blanquillo, SS-328 ex Bocaccio, SS-329 ex Bonaci, SS-335 ex Capidoli, SS-340 ex Chickwick, SS-351 ex Doncella, SS-352 ex Dory, SS-356 ex Fanegal, SS-357 ex Friar, SS-382 ex Obispo, SS-392 ex Pudiano, SS-404 ex Shiner, SS-410 ex Sole, and SS-412 ex Senorita, all on 24 Sep 42; SS-409 ex Awa on 31 Jan 44. The Orca (SS-381) became the Ojanca on 5 Sep 42 and the Sand Lance on 24 Sep 42. The Chubb (ex Bonaci, SS-329) became the Chub 24 May 44; the Logger-Head (SS-374) became the Loggerhead on 12 Jan 44; and the Archer-Fish (SS-311) became the Archerfish. The following names were cancelled: Bergall (SS-320), Hawkbill (SS-365), and Sand Lance (SS-381) on 22 Mar 65; Seahorse (AGSS-304) and Spadefish (AGSS-411) on 4 Aug 66; and Pintado (AGSS-387) on 25 Oct 66.
Reclassifications: The following have been reclassified and converted as shown:
Balao (SS-285) and Crevalle (SS-291) to AGSS 1 Apr 60;
Aspro (SS-309), Capitaine (SS-336), Queenfish (SS-393), Redfish (SS-395), and Sea Devil (SS-400) to AGSS 1 Jul 60;
Billfish (SS-286), Cabrilla (SS-288), Devilfish (SS-292), Hackleback (SS-295), Moray (SS-300), Seahorse (SS-304), Batfish (SS-310), Besugo (SS-321), Cabezon (SS-334), Dentuda (SS-335), Loggerhead (SS-374), Parche (SS-384), Pintado (SS-387), Pipefish (SS-388), Piranha (SS-389), Sea Dog (SS-401), Spadefish (SS-411), and Trepang (SS-412) to AGSS 1 Dec 62;
Bowfin (SS-287), Ling (SS-297), Lionfish (SS-298), Roncador (SS-301) and Pampanito (SS-383) to AGSS 1 Dec 62; to IXSS 30 Jun 71;
Spikefish (SS-404) to AGSS 1 Jul 62;
Sablefish (SS-303) and Sea Owl (SS-405) to AGSS 30 Jun 69;

Manta (SS-299), Baya (SS-318) to AGSS 16 Aug 49;
Archerfish (SS-311) to AGSS 22 Feb 60;
Burrfish (SS-312) to SSR 27 Jan 49; SS 15 Jan 61;
Perch (SS-313) to SSP 19 Jan 48; ASSP 31 Jan 50; APSS 24 Oct 56; LPSS 1 Jan 69; IXSS 30 Jun 71;
Sealion (SS-315) to SSP 31 Mar 48; ASSP 31 Jan 50; APSS 24 Oct 56; LPSS 1 Jan 69;
Barbero (SS-317) to SSA 31 Mar 48; ASSA 31 Jan 50; SSG 25 Oct 55;
Becuna (SS-319), Blenny (SS-324), and Atule (SS-403) to AGSS 1 Oct 69; SS 30 Jun 71;
Charr (SS-328) to AGSS 1 Jul 66; IXSS 30 Jun 71;
Bugara (SS-331) and Carbonero (SS-337) to AGSS 30 Jun 69; SS 1 Oct 69;
Carp (SS-338) to AGSS 1 May 68; IXSS 30 Jun 71;
Chopper (SS-342) to AGSS 15 Sep 69; IXSS 30 Jun 71;
Cusk (SS-348) to SSG 19 Jan 48; SS 1 Jul 54; AGSS 30 Jun 69;
Sea Cat (SS-399) to AGSS 30 Sep 49; SS 11 Dec 51; AGSS 29 Jun 68;
Sea Poacher (SS-406) to AGSS 1 Nov 69; SS 30 Jun 71;
Piper (SS-409) to AGSS 15 Jun 67.

TENCH class

Displacement: 1570/2414 (SS 475-490), 2416 (SS 417-424), 2428 (SS 435, 522-525) tons

Dimensions: 311'9"(Groton boats, oa.), 311'8"(others, oa.) x 27'3"(Groton & Boston boats, e), 27'4" (Portsmouth boats, e) x 17'(max)

Armament: 1-5"/25 10-21"T; 2-5"/25 10-21"T (SS-476, 481, 1945); 10-21"T (Guppy conversions)

Complement: 66

Machinery: 5400 BHP, G. M. (SS 435-437), F. M. (others), 4 diesel engines/ 2740 BHP, 2 G. E. (SS 417-424, 435-437), Elliott (SS 475-515), Westinghouse (SS 516-529), A. C. (SS 537-544) electric motors, 2 screws

Speed: 20/10 kts.

No.	Hull	Laid down	Launched	Commiss'd	Disposition
417 TENCH	Portsmouth	1 Apr 44	7 Jul 44	6 Oct 44	Stk. 15 Aug 73, sold 16 Sep 76 to Peru for spare parts
418 THORNBACK	Portsmouth	5 Apr 44	7 Jul 44	13 Oct 44	To Turkey 1 Jul 71 as Uluc Ali Reis, stk. 1 Aug 73
419 TIGRONE	Portsmouth	8 May 44	20 Jul 44	25 Oct 44	Stk. 27 Jun 75, sunk as target off Cape Hatteras 25 Oct 76
420 TIRANTE	Portsmouth	28 Apr 44	9 Aug 44	6 Nov 44	Stk. 1 Oct 73, sold 21 Mar 74
421 TRUTTA	Portsmouth	22 May 44	18 Aug 44	16 Nov 44	To Turkey 1 Jul 72 as Cerbe, stk. 1 Jul 72
422 TORO	Portsmouth	27 May 44	23 Aug 44	8 Dec 44	Stk. 1 Apr 63, sold Apr 65
423 TORSK	Portsmouth	7 Jun 44	6 Sep 44	16 Dec 44	Stk. 15 Dec 71, memorial at Baltimore, Md., 26 Sep 72
424 QUILLBACK	Portsmouth	27 Jun 44	1 Oct 44	29 Dec 44	Stk. 23 Mar 73, sold 21 Mar 74
435 CORSAIR	Groton	1 Mar 45	3 May 46	8 Nov 46	Stk. 1 Feb 63, sold 21 Oct 63
436 UNICORN	Groton	25 Apr 45	1 Aug 46	No	Stk. 9 Jun 58, sold 27 Aug 59
437 WALRUS	Groton	21 Jun 45	20 Sep 46	No	Stk. 9 Jun 58, sold 27 Aug 59
475 ARGONAUT	Portsmouth	28 Jun 44	1 Oct 44	15 Jan 45	To Canada 2 Dec 68 as Rainbow, stk. 2 Dec 68
476 RUNNER	Portsmouth	10 Jul 44	17 Oct 44	6 Feb 45	Stk. 15 Dec 71, sold 19 Jun 73
477 CONGER	Portsmouth	11 Jul 44	17 Oct 44	14 Feb 45	Stk. 1 Aug 63, sold Jun 64
478 CUTLASS	Portsmouth	22 Jul 44	5 Nov 44	17 Mar 45	To Taiwan 12 Apr 73 as Hai Shih, stk. 12 Apr 73
479 DIABLO	Portsmouth	11 Aug 44	1 Dec 44	31 Mar 45	To Pakistan 1 Jun 64 as Ghazi, stk. 4 Dec 71
480 MEDREGAL	Portsmouth	21 Aug 44	15 Dec 44	14 Apr 45	Stk. 1 Aug 70, sold 13 Jun 72
481 REQUIN	Portsmouth	24 Aug 44	1 Jan 45	28 Apr 45	Stk. 20 Dec 71, memorial at Tampa, Fla., 17 Jul 72
482 IREX	Portsmouth	2 Oct 44	26 Jan 45	14 May 45	Stk. 17 Nov 69, sold 13 Sep 71
483 SEA LEOPARD	Portsmouth	7 Nov 44	2 Mar 45	11 Jun 45	To Brazil 27 Mar 73 as Bahia, stk. 27 Mar 73
484 ODAX	Portsmouth	4 Dec 44	10 Apr 45	11 Jul 45	To Brazil 8 Jul 72 as Rio de Janeiro, stk. 8 Jul 72
485 SIRAGO	Portsmouth	3 Jan 45	11 May 45	13 Aug 45	Stk. 1 Jun 72, sold 2 May 73
486 POMODON	Portsmouth	29 Jan 45	12 Jun 45	11 Sep 45	Stk. 1 Aug 70, sold 28 Dec 71
487 REMORA	Portsmouth	5 Mar 45	12 Jul 45	3 Jan 46	To Greece 29 Oct 73 as Katsonis, stk. 29 Oct 73
488 SARDA	Portsmouth	12 Apr 45	24 Aug 45	19 Apr 46	Stk. 1 Jun 64, sold Mar 65
489 SPINAX	Portsmouth	14 May 45	20 Nov 45	20 Sep 46	Stk. 11 Oct 69, sold 13 Jun 72

No.	Hull	Laid down	Launched	Commiss'd	Disposition
490 VOLADOR	Portsmouth	15 Jun 45	21 May 48	1 Oct 48	To Italy 18 Aug 72 as Gianfranco Gazzana Priaroggia, stk. 5 Dec 77
491 POMPANO	Portsmouth	16 Jul 45	No	No	Cancelled 12 Aug 45
492 GRAYLING	Portsmouth	No	No	No	Cancelled 12 Aug 45
493 NEEDLEFISH	Portsmouth	No	No	No	Cancelled 12 Aug 45
494 SCULPIN	Portsmouth	No	No	No	Cancelled 12 Aug 45
495 Unnamed -515	Portsmouth	No	No	No	Cancelled 29 Jul 44
516 WAHOO	Mare I.	15 May 44	No	No	Cancelled 7 Jan 46
517 Unnamed	Mare I.	29 Jun 44	No	No	Cancelled 29 Jul 44
518 WAHOO	Mare I.	No	No	No	Cancelled 29 Jul 44
519 Unnamed -521	Mare I.	No	No	No	Cancelled 29 Jul 44
522 AMBERJACK	Boston	8 Feb 44	15 Dec 44	4 Mar 46	To Brazil 17 Oct 73 as Ceara, stk. 17 Oct 73
523 GRAMPUS	Boston	8 Feb 44	15 Dec 44	26 Oct 49	To Brazil 13 May 72 as Rio Grande do Sul, stk. 13 May 72
524 PICKEREL	Boston	8 Feb 44	15 Dec 44	4 Apr 49	To Italy 18 Aug 72 as Primo Longobardo, stk. 5 Dec 77
525 GRENADIER	Boston	8 Feb 44	15 Dec 44	10 Feb 51	To Venezuela 15 May 73 as Picua, stk. 15 May 73
526 DORADO	Boston	No	No	No	Cancelled 29 Jul 44
527 COMBER	Boston	No	No	No	Cancelled 29 Jul 44
528 SEA PANTHER	Boston	No	No	No	Cancelled 29 Jul 44
529 TIBURON	Boston	No	No	No	Cancelled 29 Jul 44
537 Unnamed -544	Boston	No	No	No	Cancelled 29 Jul 44
545 Unnamed -547	Groton	No	No	No	Cancelled 28 Mar 45
548 Unnamed -550	Portsmouth	No	No	No	Cancelled 27 Mar 45.

Notes: Fiscal years 1942 (SS 417-424), 1943 (435/544), and 1945 (545-550). In 1944 the Portsmouth Navy Yard prepared plans for a Balao class submarine in which the ballast and fuel tanks were rearranged to eliminate vulnerable points. The operating depth was 450'. Torpedo stowage was increased by four, and other wartime improvements were incorporated including the new type of main propulsion electric motor first fitted in late Balao class boats. SS 537-44 were transferred from Cramp to Boston 6 Apr 44. On 29 Jun 44, 63 boats which had been ordered from navy yards as Balao class units, including the Boston boats, were reordered to the new design. In addition, Portsmouth applied the new plans to SS 417-424, which had been transferred to it from Mare Island on 22 Feb 43. On 23 Oct 44 three more boats of the new type, SS 435-437, were ordered from Electric Boat to give that firm a chance to develop its own design with the same improvements. SS 435-437 had been cancelled as Balao class units at Groton on 29 Jul 44, and when they were reordered the earlier cancellation was shifted to SS 353-355. The Corsair (SS-435) was the only Tench class boat completed to other than Portsmouth plans. SS 545-550 were part of a fiscal year 1945 program which was disapproved by the President. The Unicorn (SS-436) and Walrus (SS-437) were delivered incomplete.
     Many boats were given "Guppy" conversions 1947-54 which increased their subsurface speed and endurance. SS 484 and 486 received the prototype Guppy I modification and were later upgraded to Guppy IIs. SS-478, 483-487, 490, and 522-525 received the Guppy II modification, SS-417 became a Guppy IA, and SS-418, 420, 421, and 424 received the Guppy IIA refit. As modified their dimensions were: 318'10" x 27'2"(e) x 17'(max). SS-423, 475, 476, 480, and 482 received the fleet snorkel conversion. SS-487, 490, and 524 later received the Guppy III upgrade and were lengthened 15'.
Renamings: SS-421 ex Tomtate 24 Sep 42; SS-424 ex Trembler 7 Dec 43. The name Wahoo was assigned to SS-518 on 17 Jun 44 and shifted to SS-516 on 29 Aug 44. The following names were proposed for SS 545-550 respectively but were probably not assigned: Banta, Charoca, Lucifer, Makaira, Narcine, and Texgon.
Reclassifications: The following were reclassified as shown:
    Tench (SS-417) to AGSS 1 Oct 69; SS 30 Jun 71;
    Tigrone (SS-419) to SSR 31 Mar 48; SS 3 Feb 61; AGSS 1 Dec 63;
    Toro (SS-422), Cutlass (SS-478), and Sarda (SS-488) to AGSS 1 Jul 62;
    Torsk (SS-423) to AGSS 1 May 68; IXSS 30 Jun 71;
    Corsair (SS-435) to AGSS 1 Apr 60;
    Runner (SS-476) to AGSS 1 Feb 69; IXSS 30 Jun 71;
    Conger (SS-477) to AGSS 9 Mar 62;

Medregal (SS-480) to AGSS 1 May 67; to SS 1 Oct 69;
Requin (SS-481) to SSR 19 Jan 48; SS 15 Aug 59; AGSS 29 Jun 68; IXSS 30 Jun 71;
Irex (SS-482) to AGSS 30 Jun 69;
Spinax (SS-489) to SSR 19 Jan 48; SS 15 Aug 59; AGSS 30 Jun 69.

1945

SS-551 class

Displacement: 1960/2990 tons
Dimensions: 336'(oa.) x 29'2"
Armament: 1-5"/25 12-21"T 6-21"T (deck)
Complement: Unknown

Machinery: 9500 BHP, F. M. 12-cylinder diesel engines with supercharging/ 2745 BHP, 2 electric motors, 2 screws
Speed: 22.5/9 kts.

No.	Hull	Laid down	Launched	Commiss'd	Disposition
551 Unnamed -562	Not Awarded	No	No	No	Cancelled 26 Mar 45.

Notes: Fiscal year 1945. SS 551-55 were to have been awarded to Groton, 556-560 to Portsmouth, and 561-562 to Mare Is., but the authorization for all was cancelled after the President disapproved most of the 1945 combatant shipbuilding program on 22 Mar 45. The data above are for a preliminary design (Study B) prepared in May 1945 for an enlarged Tench type boat with higher speed on the surface, two more torpedo tubes aft, and two fixed sets of triple torpedo tubes under the deck to fire a new short anti-escort torpedo. Its operating depth was 450'. This design was not final, and it was dropped when the full potential of the German Type XXI submarine became apparent.

1946

TANG class

Displacement: 1560/2260 tons
Dimensions: 269'2"(oa.) x 27'2"(SS-563, 565, 567, e), 27'3" (others, e) x 17'
Armament: 8-21"T
Complement: 83
Speed: 15.5/18.3

Machinery: 4500 BHP, G. M. (SS 563-566), F. M. (others), 4 diesel engines/ 3200 BHP, 2 Elliott (SS 563-564), G. E. (SS 565-566), Westinghouse (SS 567-568) electric motors, 2 screws

No.	Hull	Laid down	Launched	Commiss'd	Disposition
563 TANG	Portsmouth	18 Apr 49	19 Jun 51	25 Oct 51	To Turkey 8 Feb 80 as Piri Reis, stk. 6 Aug 87
564 TRIGGER	Groton	24 Feb 49	14 Jun 51	31 Mar 52	To Italy 10 Jul 73 as Livio Piomarta, stk. 10 Jul 73
565 WAHOO	Portsmouth	24 Oct 49	16 Oct 51	30 May 52	Stk. 15 Jul 83
566 TROUT	Groton	1 Dec 49	21 Aug 51	27 Jun 52	Stk. 19 Dec 78
567 GUDGEON	Portsmouth	20 May 50	11 Jun 52	21 Nov 52	To Turkey 30 Sep 83 as Hizir Reis, stk. 6 Aug 87
568 HARDER	Groton	30 Jun 50	3 Dec 51	19 Aug 52	To Italy 20 Feb 74 as Romeo Romei, stk. 20 Feb 74.

Notes: Fiscal year 1948 (SS 563-564, deferred from 1947), 1948 (SS 565-56), and 1949. These boats were built to the SCB-2A design following competitive plans prepared by the Portsmouth Navy Yard and Electric Boat. They introduced into the U.S. navy the key features of the German Type XXI boats: high sustained underwater speed and the snorkel. They were shorter than the wartime fleet boats and therefore more maneuverable underwater, but they retained a hull form consistent with good surface performance. Their design featured a new type of lightweight, high-powered diesel engine. Their operating depth was 700'. The two torpedo tubes aft were for short anti-escort torpedoes only. The radial diesels installed in SS 563-566 proved unsuccessful and were replaced in 1957 with three Fairbanks Morse engines similar to those in the Tench class. The four re-engined boats were enlarged to 278' and 1650/2380 tons. All six were modernized and lengthened to 287' in 1965-69, at which time the Gudgeon and Harder were re-engined as their sisters. The Trout was transferred to Iran on 19 Dec 78 as Kousseh but was abandoned by her crew at New London in March 1979 following the Iranian revolution. Planned transfers of the Tang and Wahoo to Iran under the names Dolfin and Nahang were cancelled on 3 Feb 79 and 31 Mar 79 respectively. The Wahoo was in overhaul at the time and was laid up partly dismantled.
Reclassifications: Tang (SS-563) to AGSS 30 Jun 75; SS 15 Aug 78; Gudgeon (SS-567) to AGSS 1 Apr 79; SSAG 5 Nov 79.

1953

DARTER

Displacement: 1622/2388 tons
Dimensions: 268'7"(oa.) x 27'2"(e) x 19'(max)
Armament: 8-21"T
Complement: 83

Machinery: 4500 BHP F. M. diesel
engines/ 3100 BHP, 2 Elliott
electric motors, 2 screws
Speed: 15.5/16 kts.

No.	Hull	Laid down	Launched	Commiss'd	Disposition
576 DARTER	Groton	10 Nov 54	28 May 56	20 Oct 56	Stk. 17 Jan 90.

Notes: Fiscal year 1954, SCB-116 design. She was an improved Tang with console controls and a sound-proof engine room. She was modernized in 1965.

1955

BARBEL class

Displacement: 1750 (light)/2637 tons
Dimensions: 219'6"(oa.) x 29'(e) x 25'(max)
Armament: 6-21"T
Complement: 75

Machinery: 4800 BHP F. M. diesel
engines/ 3150 BHP, 2 G. E. electric
motors, 1 screw
Speed: 12/25 kts.

No.	Hull	Laid down	Launched	Commiss'd	Disposition
580 BARBEL	Portsmouth	18 May 56	19 Jul 58	17 Jan 59	Stk. 17 Jan 90
581 BLUEBACK	Ingalls	15 Apr 57	16 May 59	15 Oct 59	Stk. 30 Oct 90
582 BONEFISH	New York SB	3 Jun 57	22 Nov 58	9 Jul 59	Stk. 28 Feb 89, sold 17 Aug 89.

Notes: Fiscal year 1956, SCB-150 design. They combined the highly maneuverable teardrop hull form pioneered by the Albacore with the power plant of earlier diesel submarines. Their bow planes were moved to the sail soon after completion. The Bonefish was gutted by fire at sea on 24 Apr 88.

1959

SS-553 class

Displacement: 350/472 tons
Dimensions: 149' x 15' x 14'
Armament: 8-21"T
Complement: 18

Machinery: 1200 BHP, 2 MB-820 diesel
engines/ 1200 BHP, 1 electric
motor, 1 screw
Speed: 13.5/17 kts.

Notes: Fiscal years 1960 (SS-553) and 1961 (SS-556, both offshore procurement). U.S participation in the Norwegian submarine program which ultimately produced 15 German-designed boats of the Kobben class was announced in July 1959. A U.S. contract for SS-553 was concluded on 26 May 60 and SS-556 appeared in the U.S. building program in April 1961. Their Norwegian names are unknown. Both disappeared from the U.S. program in May 1961 and the U.S. contracts were cancelled on 29 Aug 61. Ultimately the U.S. provided assistance for all 15 boats, but without assigning them U.S. hull numbers. These were part of a series of miscellaneous diesel boats which reused hull numbers of cancelled World War II submarines. Other reused numbers included 551-552 (ex SSK 2-3), 554 (below), and 555 (the AGSS Dolphin).

SS-554

Displacement: 550/643 tons
Dimensions: 117'2" x 15'4" x 13'1"
Armament: 4-21"T
Complement: 33

Machinery: 1200 BHP, Burmeister &
Wain diesel engines/ 1200 BHP, 2
electric motors, 2 screws
Speed: 15/15 kts.

No.	Hull	Laid down	Launched	Commiss'd	Disposition
554 (SPRINGEREN)	Royal Dockyard, Copenhagen	3 Jan 61	26 Apr 63	22 Oct 64	To Denmark 22 Oct 64.

Notes: Fiscal year 1960 (offshore procurement). A U.S. contract for financial assistance in building this boat, the fourth and last of the Danish-designed Delfinen class, was concluded on 20 May 60.

Anti-Submarine Submarines (SSK)

1947

K class

Displacement: 765/1160 tons
Dimensions: 196'1"(oa.) x 24'7"(e) x 14'5"(mean)
Armament: 4-21"T
Complement: 37

Machinery: 1050 BHP, 3 G. M. diesel
engines/unknown BHP, 2 G. E.
electric motors, 2 screws
Speed: 13/8.5 kts.

No.		Hull	Laid down	Launched	Commiss'd	Disposition
1	K-1	Groton	1 Jul 49	2 Mar 51	10 Nov 51	Stk. 1 Oct 73, sold 21 Mar 74
2	K-2	Mare I.	23 Feb 50	2 May 51	16 Nov 51	Stk. 1 Apr 65, sold 17 Nov 66
3	K-3	Mare I.	19 May 50	21 Jun 51	11 Jan 52	Stk. 1 Apr 65, sold 17 Nov 66.

Notes: Fiscal year 1949 (SSK-1 deferred from 1948). This class (SCB-35 design) was the Navy's first response to a requirement for specialized hunter-killer submarines to counter increasingly capable enemy diesel submarines. The SSKs were to lie in wait off enemy bases, using large passive sonars to listen for submarines snorkelling or transiting on the surface and killing them with long-range homing torpedoes. It was initially believed that large numbers of these boats would be needed, and they were made as small as possible. Full speed and depth capabilities were also thought to be unnecessary—the operating depth of the class was only 400'. They were soon found to be too small and too slow, and the Navy turned to conversions of World War II fleet boats for additional SSKs. The K-3 was initially assigned to New York Shipbuilding and was transferred to Mare Is. on 21 Apr 49.
Renamings: To Barracuda, Bass, and Bonita respectively on 15 Dec 55.
Reclassifications: On 15 Aug 59 the Barracuda (ex K-1) was reclassified SST-3 while her two sisters became SS 551-552. The latter were reissued numbers originally assigned to projected submarines cancelled in 1945. In a force-level adjustment, the Barracuda (SST-3) was reclassified SS-T3 on 1 Aug 72 to allow her to be listed as an attack submarine.

Nuclear Powered Submarines (SSN)

1951

NAUTILUS

Displacement: 2975/3747 tons
Dimensions: 323'9"(oa.) x 27'8"(e) x 22'(mean)
Armament: 6-21"T
Complement: 94

Machinery: 13,400 SHP; Westinghouse
(S2W) nuclear reactor driving
geared turbines, 2 screws
Speed: 18/23.3 kts.

No.		Hull	Laid down	Launched	Commiss'd	Disposition
571	NAUTILUS	Groton	14 Jun 52	21 Jan 54	30 Sep 54	Memorial at Groton, Conn., 1985, stk. ca. 1988.

Notes: Fiscal year 1952, SCB-64 design. The world's first nuclear-powered vessel, she revolutionized undersea warfare with her ability to operate at maximum submerged speed practically indefinitely. Her reactor used pressurized water for heat transfer and her turbines used relatively low-temperature (saturated) steam. She was primarily an experimental vessel but was fully armed. Her reactor was removed in 1979-80 and she was decommissioned on 3 Mar 80 and towed to Groton, Conn., in 1985.

1952

SEAWOLF

Displacement: 3260/4110 tons
Dimensions: 337'6"(oa.) x 27'8"(e) x 21'6"
Armament: 6-21"T
Complement: 94

Machinery: ca. 13,000 SHP; G. E.
(S2G) nuclear reactor driving
geared turbines, 2 screws
Speed: 19/23 kts.

No.		Hull	Laid down	Launched	Commiss'd	Disposition
575	SEAWOLF	Groton	15 Sep 53	21 Jul 55	30 Mar 57	Stk. 10 Jul 87.

Notes: Fiscal year 1953. A modified Nautilus (SCB-64A), she was a testbed for an alternative type of propulsion plant. Her reactor used liquid sodium as the heat transfer agent and her turbines used high-temperature (superheated) steam. The sodium reactor developed corrosion problems and had to be replaced in 1958-60 with a Nautilus-type S2W. Like the Nautilus, the Seawolf was fully armed but was primarily an experimental vessel.

The nuclear powered submarine *Skate* (SSN-578) on 6 December 1957. (NARA 80-G-1037389)

The nuclear powered submarine *San Francisco* (SSN-711) on sea trials in the James River on 31 March 1981. (USN 1180787)

1954

SKATE class

Displacement: 2370 (SSN-578, 583), 2376 (SSN-579, 584) (all
  light)/2850 (SSN-578, 583), 2851 (SSN-579, 584) tons
Dimensions: 267'8"(oa.) x 25'(e) x 20'3"
Armament: 8-21"T
Complement: 95

Machinery: 6600 BHP; Westinghouse
(S3W in SSN-578, 583; S4W in SSN-
579, 584) nuclear reactor driving
Westinghouse geared turbines, 2
screws
Speed: 15/18 kts.

No.	Hull	Laid down	Launched	Commiss'd	Disposition
578 SKATE	Groton	21 Jul 55	16 May 57	23 Dec 57	Stk. 30 Oct 86
579 SWORDFISH	Portsmouth	25 Jan 56	27 Aug 57	15 Sep 58	Stk. 2 Jun 89
583 SARGO	Mare I.	21 Feb 56	10 Oct 57	1 Oct 58	Stk. 21 Apr 88
584 SEADRAGON	Portsmouth	20 Jun 56	16 Aug 58	5 Dec 59	Stk. 30 Apr 86.

Notes: Fiscal years 1955 (SSN 578-579) and 1956, SCB-121 design. In this class, the Navy produced a submarine roughly the size of the Tang class with the nearly unlimited underwater endurance provided by nuclear propulsion. Extremely high speed was not sought, and these boats had compact reactors of the same type as the Nautilus plant but of about half the power.

1955

SKIPJACK class

Displacement: 2859 (light)/3500 tons
Dimensions: 251'9"(oa.) x 31'7"(e) x 25'
Armament: 6-21"T
Complement: 94

Machinery: 15,000 SHP; Westinghouse
(S5W) nuclear reactor driving
Westinghouse (SSN-585), G. E.
(others) geared turbines, 1 screw
Speed: 15/30+ kts.

No.	Hull	Laid down	Launched	Commiss'd	Disposition
585 SKIPJACK	Groton	29 May 56	26 May 58	15 Apr 59	Stk. 19 Apr 90
588 SCAMP	Mare I.	23 Jan 59	8 Oct 60	5 Jun 61	Stk. 28 Apr 88
589 SCORPION	Groton	20 Aug 58	19 Dec 59	29 Jul 60	Foundered SW of the Azores 21 May 68
590 SCULPIN	Ingalls	3 Feb 58	31 Mar 60	1 Jun 61	Stk. 3 Aug 90
591 SHARK	Newport News	24 Feb 58	16 Mar 60	9 Feb 61	Stk. 15 Sep 90
592 SNOOK	Ingalls	7 Apr 58	31 Oct 60	24 Oct 61	Stk. 14 Nov 86.

Notes: Fiscal years 1956 (SSN-585) and 1957, SCB-154 design. Designed as specialized attack boats with very high submerged speed for attacking fast surface ships. The design combined the Albacore teardrop hull form and a new reactor, similar to the Skate reactor but of twice the power. It also introduced sail-mounted diving planes into the nuclear submarine force. The Scorpion was originally laid down 1 Nov 57 but this hull was ordered completed as the George Washington (SSBN-598) on 31 Dec 57. Materials collected for the Scamp and Sculpin were used in SSBN 599 and 600.

1956

THRESHER class

Displacement: 3526 (light)/4310 tons
Dimensions: 278'6"(oa.) x 31'8"(e) x 26'
Armament: 4-21"T Subroc-UUM
Complement: 95

Machinery: 15,000 SHP; Westinghouse
(S5W) nuclear reactor driving
geared turbines, 1 screw
Speed: 15/30 kts.

No.	Hull	Laid down	Launched	Commiss'd	Disposition
593 THRESHER	Portsmouth	28 May 58	9 Jul 60	3 Aug 61	Foundered off Boston 10 Apr 63
594 PERMIT	Mare I.	16 Jul 59	1 Jul 61	29 May 62	USN
595 PLUNGER	Mare I.	2 Mar 60	9 Dec 61	21 Nov 62	Stk. 2 Feb 90
596 BARB	Ingalls	9 Nov 59	12 Feb 62	24 Aug 63	Stk. 20 Dec 89
603 POLLACK	New York SB	14 Mar 60	17 Mar 62	26 May 64	Stk. 1 Mar 89
604 HADDO	New York SB	9 Sep 60	18 Aug 62	16 Dec 64	USN
605 JACK	Portsmouth	16 Sep 60	24 Apr 63	31 Mar 67	Stk. 11 Jul 90
606 TINOSA	Portsmouth	24 Nov 59	9 Dec 61	17 Oct 64	USN
607 DACE	Ingalls	6 Jun 60	18 Aug 62	4 Apr 64	Stk. Dec 88
612 GUARDFISH	New York SB	28 Feb 61	15 May 65	20 Dec 66	USN
621 HADDOCK	Ingalls	24 Apr 61	21 May 66	22 Dec 67	USN.

Notes: Fiscal years 1957 (SSN-593), 1958 (594-96), 1959 (603-7), 1960 (612), and 1961 (621); SCB-188 design. This class combined the features of two specialized types, the Skipjack attack submarine (above) and the Tullibee ASW submarine (below), into a single highly-successful multipurpose type. The design included the large BQQ-2 bow sonar of the Tullibee, the long-range Subroc anti-submarine missile, and elaborate measures to silence the geared turbines of the high-speed propulsion plant. The new features made the boat considerably larger than the Skipjack, and since the two used the same reactor some loss in speed was inevitable. This was also the first class designed to be built of the new HY80 high-yield steel, allowing it to dive deeper than earlier classes. The construction of the later vessels was delayed following the loss of the Thresher. The Permit, Plunger, Barb, and Dace were ordered as SSGN: 3500/4000 tons; 360' x 33' with 4 Regulus II SSM. They were built as Thresher class attack submarines after the Regulus II program was cancelled. The Jack was built with an experimental direct-drive plant with counter-rotating propellers on a single shaft; her length was 297'4".
Renamings: SSN-595 ex Pollack 28 Apr 59; SSN-596 ex Pollack 23 Jul 59 and ex Plunger 28 Apr 59; SSN-603 ex Barb 23 Jul 59.
Reclassifications: SSN 594, 595, 596, and 607 ex SSGN when the Regulus II program was cancelled on 18 Dec 58.

1957

TULLIBEE

Displacement: 2177 (light)/2607 tons
Dimensions: 272'9"(oa.) x 23'4"(e) x 19'
Armament: 4-21"T Subroc-UUM
Complement: 52

Machinery: 2500 SHP; Combustion Engineering (S2C) nuclear reactor driving Westinghouse turbo-electric machinery, 1 screw
Speed: 15/20 kts.

No.	Hull	Laid down	Launched	Commiss'd	Disposition
597 TULLIBEE	Groton	26 May 58	27 Apr 60	9 Nov 60	Stk. 18 Jun 88.

Notes: Fiscal year 1958, SCB-178 design. This boat was a specialized ASW submarine (originally SSKN) with the same mission as the diesel SSK types. She was designed around the new long-range BQQ-2 sonar which filled her entire bow area and displaced her torpedo tubes to a position amidships. She also had turbo-electric drive, which eliminated noisy reduction gears and made her the first truly quiet nuclear submarine.
Reclassification: Ex SSKN-597 15 Aug 59.

1959

FLASHER class

Displacement: 4103/4634 tons
Dimensions: 292'3"(oa.) x 32' x 28'9"
Armament: 4-21"T Subroc-UUM
Complement: 95

Machinery: 15,000 SHP; Westinghouse (S5W) nuclear reactor driving geared turbines, 1 screw
Speed: 15/30 kts.

No.	Hull	Laid down	Launched	Commiss'd	Disposition
613 FLASHER	Groton	14 Apr 61	22 Jun 63	22 Jul 66	USN
614 GREENLING	Groton	15 Aug 61	4 Apr 64	3 Nov 67	USN
615 GATO	Groton	15 Dec 61	14 May 64	25 Jan 68	USN.

Notes: Fiscal year 1960. These three boats are modifications (SCB-188M design) of the Thresher class with a longer hull, a taller sail, and heavier machinery. SSN 613-14 were completed at Bethlehem, Quincy.

1961

STURGEON class

Displacement: 4250 (std.)/4780 (SSN 637/677), 4460 (std.)/4960 (others) tons
Dimensions: 292'(oa., SSN 637/677), 302' (oa., others) x 31'7"(e) x 28'10"
Armament: 4-21"T Subroc-UUM
Complement: 129

Machinery: 15,000 SHP; Westinghouse (S5W) nuclear reactor driving G. E. geared turbines, 1 screw
Speed: 15/30 kts.

No.		Hull	Laid down	Launched	Commiss'd	Disposition
637	STURGEON	Groton	10 Aug 63	26 Feb 66	3 Mar 67	USN
638	WHALE	EB-Quincy	27 May 64	14 Oct 66	12 Oct 68	USN
639	TAUTOG	Ingalls	27 Jan 64	15 Apr 67	17 Aug 68	USN
646	GRAYLING	Portsmouth	12 May 64	22 Jun 67	11 Oct 69	USN
647	POGY	New York SB	5 May 64	3 Jun 67	15 May 71	USN
648	ASPRO	Ingalls	23 Nov 64	29 Nov 67	20 Feb 69	USN
649	SUNFISH	EB-Quincy	15 Jan 65	14 Oct 66	15 Mar 69	USN
650	PARGO	Groton	3 Jun 64	17 Sep 66	5 Jan 68	USN
651	QUEENFISH	Newport News	11 May 64	25 Feb 66	6 Dec 66	USN
652	PUFFER	Ingalls	8 Feb 65	30 Mar 68	9 Aug 69	USN
653	RAY	Newport News	4 Jan 65	21 Jun 66	12 Apr 67	USN
660	SAND LANCE	Portsmouth	15 Jan 65	11 Nov 69	25 Sep 71	USN
661	LAPON	Newport News	26 Jul 65	16 Dec 66	14 Dec 67	USN
662	GURNARD	Mare I.	22 Dec 64	20 May 67	6 Dec 68	USN
663	HAMMERHEAD	Newport News	29 Nov 65	14 Apr 67	28 Jun 68	USN
664	SEA DEVIL	Newport News	12 Apr 66	5 Oct 67	30 Jan 69	USN
665	GUITARRO	Mare I.	9 Dec 65	27 Jul 68	9 Sep 72	USN
666	HAWKBILL	Mare I.	12 Sep 66	12 Apr 69	4 Feb 71	USN
667	BERGALL	Groton	16 Apr 66	17 Feb 68	13 Jun 69	USN
668	SPADEFISH	Newport News	21 Dec 66	15 May 68	14 Aug 69	USN
669	SEAHORSE	Groton	13 Aug 66	15 Jun 68	19 Sep 69	USN
670	FINBACK	Newport News	26 Jun 67	7 Dec 68	4 Feb 70	USN
672	PINTADO	Mare I.	27 Oct 67	16 Aug 69	11 Sep 71	USN
673	FLYING FISH	Groton	30 Jun 67	17 May 69	29 Apr 70	USN
674	TREPANG	Groton	28 Oct 67	27 Sep 69	14 Aug 70	USN
675	BLUEFISH	Groton	13 Mar 68	10 Jan 70	8 Jan 71	USN
676	BILLFISH	Groton	20 Sep 68	1 May 70	12 Mar 71	USN
677	DRUM	Mare I.	20 Aug 68	23 May 70	15 Apr 72	USN
678	ARCHERFISH	Groton	19 Jun 69	16 Jan 71	17 Dec 71	USN
679	SILVERSIDES	Groton	13 Oct 69	4 Jun 71	5 May 72	USN
680	WILLIAM H. BATES	Ingalls	4 Aug 69	11 Dec 71	5 May 73	USN
681	BATFISH	Groton	9 Feb 70	9 Oct 71	1 Sep 72	USN
682	TUNNY	Ingalls	22 May 70	10 Jun 72	26 Jan 74	USN
683	PARCHE	Ingalls	10 Dec 70	13 Jan 73	17 Aug 74	USN
684	CAVALLA	Groton	4 Jun 70	19 Feb 72	9 Feb 73	USN
686	L. MENDEL RIVERS	Newport News	26 Jun 71	2 Jun 73	1 Feb 75	USN
687	RICHARD B. RUSSELL	Newport News	19 Oct 71	12 Jan 74	16 Aug 75	USN.

Notes: Fiscal years 1962 (SSN 637-39), 1963 (646-53), 1964 (660-64), 1965 (665-70), 1966 (672-77), 1967 (678-82), 1968 (683-84), and 1969 (686-87). This class was built to an improved Thresher-class design (SCB-188A). The Pogy was cancelled at New York Shipbuilding on 5 Jun 67 and transferred to the Ingalls yard for completion. The Whale and Sunfish were completed at Groton. The Guitarro sank while fitting out on 15 May 69 and was raised on 19 May 69. The Archerfish and later boats were built to a modified long-hull design.
Renaming: SSN-680 ex Redfish 25 Jun 71.

1963

NARWHAL

Displacement: 5284 (std.)/5830 tons
Dimensions: 314'11"(oa.) x 37'9" x 25'11"
Armament: 4-21"T Subroc-UUM
Complement: 129

Machinery: 17,000 SHP; G. E. (S5G) nuclear reactor driving geared turbines, 1 screw
Speed: 20/25 kts.

No.		Hull	Laid down	Launched	Commiss'd	Disposition
671	NARWHAL	Groton	17 Jan 66	9 Sep 67	28 Jun 69	USN.

Notes: Fiscal year 1964, SCB-245 design. She was built to evaluate the S5G natural circulation reactor, which used the internal heat gradient instead of noisy pumps to circulate water within the plant. She was larger and heavier than the Sturgeon class but had the same combat systems.

1969

GLENARD P. LIPSCOMB

Displacement: 5800 (std.)/6480 tons
Dimensions: 365'(oa.) x 31'9" x 28'10"
Armament: 4-21"T Subroc-UUM
Complement: 129

Machinery: ca.15,000 SHP;
    Westinghouse (S5Wa) nuclear reactor
    with G. E. turbo-electric drive, 1
    screw
Speed: 18/25 kts.

No.	Hull	Laid down	Launched	Commiss'd	Disposition
685 GLENARD P. LIPSCOMB	Groton	5 Jun 71	4 Aug 73	21 Dec 74	Stk. 11 Jul 90.

Notes: Fiscal year 1968. She was built as a prototype turbo-electric submarine for ASW missions in which ultra-quiet operation was more important than speed. This plant made her substantially larger than the Sturgeon class, which she otherwise resembled. The experiment was not repeated because the faster Los Angeles class also proved to be sufficiently quiet for most ASW roles.

1969

LOS ANGELES class

Displacement: 6080 (std.)/6927 tons
Dimensions: 360'(oa.) x 33' x 32'
Armament: 4-21"T Subroc-USM (SSN 688-699); 4-21"T (SSN 700-
    718); 4-21"T 12-Tomahawk-SSM (SSN 719 and later)
Complement: 133

Machinery: ca.30,000 SHP; G. E. (S6G)
    nuclear reactor driving geared
    turbines, 1 screw
Speed: Unknown/30+ kts.

No.	Hull		Laid down	Launched	Commiss'd	Disposition
688 LOS ANGELES	Newport News		8 Jan 72	6 Apr 74	13 Nov 76	USN
689 BATON ROUGE	Newport News		18 Nov 72	26 Apr 75	25 Jun 77	USN
690 PHILADELPHIA	Groton		12 Aug 72	19 Oct 74	25 Jun 77	USN
691 MEMPHIS	Newport News		23 Jun 73	3 Apr 76	17 Dec 77	USN
692 OMAHA	Groton		27 Jan 73	21 Feb 76	11 Mar 78	USN
693 CINCINNATI	Newport News		6 Apr 74	19 Feb 77	10 Jun 78	USN
694 GROTON	Groton		3 Aug 73	9 Oct 76	8 Jul 78	USN
695 BIRMINGHAM	Newport News		26 Apr 75	29 Oct 77	16 Dec 78	USN
696 NEW YORK CITY	Groton		15 Dec 73	18 Jun 77	3 Mar 79	USN
697 INDIANAPOLIS	Groton		19 Oct 74	30 Jul 77	5 Jan 80	USN
698 BREMERTON	Groton		8 May 76	22 Jul 78	28 Mar 81	USN
699 JACKSONVILLE	Groton		21 Feb 76	18 Nov 78	16 May 81	USN
700 DALLAS	Groton		9 Oct 76	28 Apr 79	18 Jul 81	USN
701 LA JOLLA	Groton		16 Oct 76	11 Aug 79	24 Oct 81	USN
702 PHOENIX	Groton		30 Jul 77	8 Dec 79	19 Dec 81	USN
703 BOSTON	Groton		11 Aug 78	19 Apr 80	30 Jan 82	USN
704 BALTIMORE	Groton		21 May 79	13 Dec 80	24 Jul 82	USN
705 CITY OF CORPUS CHRISTI	Groton		4 Sep 79	25 Apr 81	8 Jan 83	USN
706 ALBUQUERQUE	Groton		27 Dec 79	13 Mar 82	21 May 83	USN
707 PORTSMOUTH	Groton		8 May 80	18 Sep 82	1 Oct 83	USN
708 MINNEAPOLIS-SAINT PAUL	Groton		20 Jan 81	19 Mar 83	10 Mar 84	USN
709 HYMAN G. RICKOVER	Groton		23 Jul 81	27 Aug 83	21 Jul 84	USN
710 AUGUSTA	Groton		1 Apr 82	21 Jan 84	19 Jan 85	USN
711 SAN FRANCISCO	Newport News		26 May 77	27 Oct 79	24 Apr 81	USN
712 ATLANTA	Newport News		17 Aug 78	16 Aug 80	6 Mar 82	USN
713 HOUSTON	Newport News		29 Jan 79	21 Mar 81	25 Sep 82	USN
714 NORFOLK	Newport News		1 Aug 79	31 Oct 81	21 May 83	USN
715 BUFFALO	Newport News		25 Jan 80	8 May 82	5 Nov 83	USN
716 SALT LAKE CITY	Newport News		26 Aug 80	16 Oct 82	12 May 84	USN
717 OLYMPIA	Newport News		31 Mar 81	30 Apr 83	17 Nov 84	USN
718 HONOLULU	Newport News		10 Nov 81	24 Sep 83	6 Jul 85	USN
719 PROVIDENCE	Groton		14 Oct 82	4 Aug 84	27 Jul 85	USN
720 PITTSBURGH	Groton		15 Apr 83	8 Dec 84	23 Nov 85	USN
721 CHICAGO	Newport News		5 Jan 83	13 Oct 84	27 Sep 86	USN
722 KEY WEST	Newport News		6 Jul 83	20 Jul 85	12 Sep 87	USN

No.		Hull	Laid down	Launched	Commiss'd	Disposition
723	OKLAHOMA CITY	Newport News	4 Jan 84	2 Nov 85	9 Jul 88	USN
724	LOUISVILLE	Groton	16 Sep 84	14 Dec 85	8 Nov 86	USN
725	HELENA	Groton	28 Mar 85	28 Jun 86	11 Jul 87	USN
750	NEWPORT NEWS	Newport News	3 Mar 84	15 Mar 86	3 Jun 89	USN
751	SAN JUAN	Groton	16 Aug 85	6 Dec 86	6 Aug 88	USN
752	PASADENA	Groton	20 Dec 85	12 Sep 87	11 Feb 89	USN
753	ALBANY	Newport News	22 Apr 85	13 Jun 87	7 Apr 90	USN
754	TOPEKA	Groton	13 May 86	23 Jan 88	21 Oct 89	USN
755	MIAMI	Groton	24 Oct 86	12 Nov 88	30 Jun 90	USN
756	SCRANTON	Newport News	29 Aug 86	3 Jul 89		USN
757	ALEXANDRIA	Groton	19 Jun 87	23 Jun 90		USN
758	ASHEVILLE	Newport News	9 Jan 87	24 Feb 90		USN
759	JEFFERSON CITY	Newport News	21 Sep 87	17 Aug 90		USN
760	ANNAPOLIS	Groton	15 Jun 88			USN
761	SPRINGFIELD	Groton	29 Jan 90			USN
762	COLUMBUS	Groton				USN
763	SANTA FE	Groton				USN
764	BOISE	Newport News	25 Aug 88			USN
765	MONTPELIER	Newport News	19 May 89			USN
766	CHARLOTTE	Newport News				USN
767	HAMPTON	Newport News	2 Mar 90			USN
768	HARTFORD	Groton				USN
769	TOLEDO	Newport News				USN
770	TUCSON	Newport News				USN
771	COLUMBIA	Groton				USN
772	GREENEVILLE	Newport News				USN
773	CHEYENNE	Newport News				USN.

Notes: Fiscal years 1970 (SSN 688-90), 1971 (691-94), 1972 (695-99), 1973 (700-5), 1974 (706-10), 1975 (711-13), 1976 (714-15), 1977 (716-18), 1978 (719), 1979 (720), 1980 (721-22), 1981 (723-24), 1982 (725 and 750), 1983 (751-52), 1984 (753-55), 1985 (756-59), 1986 (760-63), 1987 (764-67), 1988 (768-70), 1989 (771-72) and 1990 (773). In this class, the Navy returned to the idea of a specialized fast attack submarine which would also be able to carry out a new mission, providing direct anti-submarine support to a carrier battle group. According to official statements, with this class "the speed threshold which had been established by Skipjack 18 years earlier was finally surpassed." The reactor in the new class was essentially a submarine version of the D2G destroyer reactor with about twice the power of the S5W. This, plus the retention of a large, long-range sonar for direct-support operations, caused the boats to be considerably larger than their predecessors. The Providence (SSN-719) and later boats are built to an improved design with numerous changes, including 12 vertical launch Tomahawk tubes forward. These and some earlier boats can also fire Tomahawk and Harpoon SSM from their torpedo tubes. Beginning with the San Juan (SSN-751) the diving planes were moved from the sail to the bow to permit under-ice operations. The submarine hull numbers 726-49 were reserved for the Ohio SSBN class.
Renaming: SSN-705 ex Corpus Christi 10 May 82, SSN-757 ex Asheville 27 Feb 87.

1988

SEAWOLF class

Displacement: Unknown/9150 tons
Dimensions: 326'(oa.) x 40' x 35'11"
Armament: 8-30"T
Complement: 130

Machinery: 60,000 SHP; nuclear reactor driving geared turbines, 1 screw
Speed: Unknown/35 kts.

No.		Hull	Laid down	Launched	Commiss'd	Disposition
21	SEAWOLF	Groton				USN.

Notes: Fiscal year 1989. The result of the "SSN-21" program, intended to produce an attack submarine for the 21st century. She is to be the lead boat of a new class whose missions, according to the Chief of Naval Operations, include land attack with Tomahawk/Excalibur missiles, anti-SSBN patrol under the Arctic ice, and ASW against increasingly modern Soviet submarines. The design emphasizes improved machinery, quieting, and combat systems. The new boats will be slightly faster than the Los Angeles class. They will not have special Tomahawk SSM tubes but will fire SSMs from their enlarged torpedo tubes. The lead boat, ordered on 9 Jan 89, received the program designation as her hull number instead of the next number in the normal sequence, SSN-774.

Radar Picket Submarines (SSR)

1951

SAILFISH class

Displacement: 1990/3168 tons
Dimensions: 350'6"(oa.) x 29'1"(e) x 16'4"(mean)
Armament: 6-21"T
Complement: 95

Machinery: 6000 BHP, 4 F. M. diesel
engines/8200 BHP, 2 Elliott
electric motors, 2 screws
Speed: 20.5/10 kts.

No.		Hull	Laid down	Launched	Commiss'd	Disposition
572	SAILFISH	Portsmouth	8 Dec 53	7 Sep 55	14 Apr 56	Stk. 30 Sep 78
573	SALMON	Portsmouth	10 Mar 54	25 Feb 56	25 Aug 56	Stk. 1 Oct 77.

Notes: Fiscal year 1952, SCB-84 design. Unlike most submarines, radar picket submarines carried out their primary mission on the surface. The Navy's first radar picket subs were ten wartime fleet boats converted between 1946 and 1953. The design for this class, the Navy's only diesel-powered submarines built expressly for radar picket service, was based on the World War II fleet boats (which had good qualities on the surface) with space added for the cumbersome radars and a combat information center. Carrier-based early warning aircraft took over the radar picket mission in the late 1950s, and these two boats had their radars removed in 1959 and shifted to general-purpose submarine duties in 1961. They were rebuilt as attack subs (to the SCB 242 design) under the FRAM program in 1964-65. The Salmon became a DSRV test ship in 1968 but reverted to regular service in 1969 when the DSRV program was delayed. These were the largest diesel powered submarines ever built for the U.S. Navy
Reclassifications: Both to SS 1 Mar 61. Salmon (SS-573) to AGSS 29 Jun 68; SS 30 Jun 69.

Nuclear Powered Radar Picket Submarines (SSRN)

1955

TRITON

Displacement: 5948 (light)/7781 tons
Dimensions: 447'5"(oa.) x 36'11"(e) x 24'(max)
Armament: 6-21"T
Complement: 148

Machinery: 34,000 SHP; 2 G. E. (S4G)
nuclear reactors driving G. E.
geared turbines, 2 screws
Speed: 27/20+ kts.

No.	Hull	Laid down	Launched	Commiss'd	Disposition
586 TRITON	Groton	29 May 56	19 Aug 58	10 Nov 59	Stk. 30 Apr 86.

Notes: Fiscal year 1956, SCB-132 design. This boat was designed with a characteristic unattainable in diesel-powered radar picket submarines--enough speed to accompany carrier forces. To achieve it, she was given an advanced, high-power plant which also tested features for surface ship plants. She was the only U.S. nuclear submarine designed for higher speeds on the surface than submerged and the only one with two reactors. When built she was the largest submarine ever constructed, exceeding the Lafayette class in length, if not in displacement. She was converted to an attack submarine in 1962-64 and decommissioned in 1969.
Reclassification: To SSN-586 on 1 Mar 61.

Guided Missile Submarines (SSG)

1952

GRAYBACK

Displacement: 2287 (light)/3638 tons
Dimensions: 322'4"(oa.) x 30'(e) x 19'(max)
Armament: 8-21"T Regulus-SSM; 8-21"T (1968)
Complement: 84

Machinery: 4500 BHP, 3 F. M. diesel
engines/ 5500 SHP, 2 Elliott
electric motors, 2 screws
Speed: 15/12 kts.

No.	Hull	Laid down	Launched	Commiss'd	Disposition
574 GRAYBACK	Mare I.	1 Jul 54	2 Jul 57	7 Mar 58	Stk. 16 Jan 84.

Notes: Fiscal year 1953. Originally intended as a half sister to the Darter (SS-576) with dimensions of 274' x 30' and a light displacement of 1740 tons, she was converted during construction to fire the Regulus II missile (SCB-161 design). She was a successor to four fleet boats (the Cusk, Carbonero, Barbero and Tunny) converted to carry the Loon and Regulus I missiles between 1948 and 1956. After the cancellation of the Regulus II program, the Grayback carried Regulus I missiles on strategic patrols until Polaris submarines replaced her in 1964. In 1967-69 she was converted to a transport submarine for commandos at Mare Island and was lengthened to 334'(oa.).
Reclassification: Ex SS-574 26 Jul 56; to LPSS-574 30 Aug 68; SS-574 30 Jun 75.

1954

GROWLER

Displacement: 2174 (light)/3387 tons
Dimensions: 317'7"(oa.) x 27'2"(e) x 19'(max)
Armament: 6-21"T Regulus-SSM
Complement: 84

Machinery: 4600 BHP, 3 F. M. diesel
  engines/ 5500 BHP, 2 Elliott
  electric motors, 2 screws
Speed: 15/12 kts.

No.	Hull	Laid down	Launched	Commiss'd	Disposition
577 GROWLER	Portsmouth	15 Feb 55	5 Apr 58	30 Aug 58	Stk. 30 Sep 80, memorial at New York City 29 Sep 88.

Notes: Fiscal year 1955, SCB-161 design. She began life as an exact sister of the Darter and was converted in the same way as the Grayback. Her career was similar to that of the Grayback except that her conversion to a transport submarine was dropped because of cost overruns with the Grayback conversion.
Reclassification: Ex SS-577 26 Jul 56.

Nuclear Powered Guided Missile Submarines (SSGN)

1955

HALIBUT

Displacement: 3602 (light)/4895 tons
Dimensions: 350'(oa.) x 29'7"(e) x 20'(max)
Armament: 6-21"T Regulus-SSM; 6-21"T (1965)
Complement: 119

Machinery: 6600 SHP; Westinghouse
  (S3W) nuclear reactor driving
  Westinghouse geared turbines, 2
  screws
Speed: 15.5/15+ kts.

No.	Hull	Laid down	Launched	Commiss'd	Disposition
587 HALIBUT	Mare I.	11 Apr 57	9 Jan 59	4 Jan 60	Stk. 30 Apr 86.

Notes: Fiscal year 1956. She was the prototype (SCB-237A design) of the projected Regulus II carriers which were washed out when the Polaris proved successful. She had the same type of compact reactor as the Skate (SSN-578). Four later boats ordered as Regulus II carriers (SSGN 594-96, 607) were built as Thresher class attack subs.
Reclassification: To SSN-587 15 Aug 65.

Nuclear Powered Fleet Ballistic Missile Submarines (SSBN)

1957

GEORGE WASHINGTON class

Displacement: 5900 (normal)/6700 tons
Dimensions: 381'8"(oa.) x 33'(e) x 26'8"(max)
Armament: 6-21"T 16-Polaris-USM
Complement: 110

Machinery: 15,000 SHP; Westinghouse
  (S5W) nuclear reactor driving
  geared turbines, 1 screw
Speed: 15/20 kts.

No.		Hull	Laid down	Launched	Commiss'd	Disposition
598	GEORGE WASHINGTON	Groton	1 Nov 57	9 Jun 59	30 Dec 59	Stk. 30 Apr 86
599	PATRICK HENRY	Groton	27 May 58	22 Sep 59	9 Apr 60	Stk. 25 May 85
600	THEODORE ROOSEVELT	Mare I.	20 May 58	3 Oct 59	13 Feb 61	Stk. 1 Dec 82
601	ROBERT E. LEE	Newport News	25 Aug 58	18 Dec 59	16 Sep 60	Stk. 30 Apr 86
602	ABRAHAM LINCOLN	Portsmouth	1 Nov 58	14 May 60	11 Mar 61	Stk. 1 Dec 82

Notes: Fiscal year 1958. Designed around the Polaris missile, their plans (SCB-180A design) called for a Skipjack hull lengthened 130' to accommodate the missiles. The George Washington, indeed, had been laid down as the Scorpion (SSN-589). They carried the shorter range Polaris A1 missiles when commissioned but were refitted with the longer range A3 type during 1964-67.
Renaming: The name Scorpion was cancelled when SSN-589 was reclassified SSGN-598 8 Apr 58.
Reclassifications: SSN 589-590 to SSGN 598-599 (and the number SSGN 600 assigned) 8 Apr 58; SSGN 598-600 to SSBN 26 Jun 58. SSBN 598, 599, and 601 to SSN 20 Nov 81, 24 Oct 81, and 1 Mar 82 respectively.

1958

ETHAN ALLEN class

Displacement: 6900 (normal)/7900 tons
Dimensions: 410'5"(oa.) x 33'(e) x 30'9"(max)
Armament: 4-21"T 16-Polaris-USM
Complement: 112

Machinery: 15,000 SHP; Westinghouse (S5W) nuclear reactor driving Westinghouse (SSBN 610-611), G. E. (others) geared turbines, 1 screw
Speed: 15/20 kts.

No.		Hull	Laid down	Launched	Commiss'd	Disposition
608	ETHAN ALLEN	Groton	14 Sep 59	22 Nov 60	8 Aug 61	Stk. 31 Mar 83
609	SAM HOUSTON	Newport News	28 Dec 59	2 Feb 61	6 Mar 62	USN
610	THOMAS A. EDISON	Groton	15 Mar 60	15 Jun 61	10 Mar 62	Stk. 30 Apr 86
611	JOHN MARSHALL	Newport News	4 Apr 60	15 Jul 61	21 May 62	USN
618	THOMAS JEFFERSON	Newport News	3 Feb 61	24 Feb 62	4 Jan 63	Stk. 30 Apr 86.

Notes: Fiscal years 1959 (SSBN 608-11) and 1961. The SCB-180 design, unlike the George Washington class, was planned from the keel up as an SSBN. The ships were designed to be built of HY80 steel and could dive deeper than the earlier class. They originally carried the Polaris A2 missile but were reequipped with the A3 beginning in 1966. The Sam Houston and John Marshall were converted in 1984-86 to carry frogmen or commandos.
Reclassifications: To SSN on 1 Sep 80, 10 Nov 80, 6 Oct 80, 1 May 81, and 11 Mar 81 respectively.

1960

LAFAYETTE class

Displacement: 7320 (normal)/8250 tons
Dimensions: 425'(oa.) x 33'(e) x 31'5"(max)
Armament: 4-21"T 16-Polaris-USM
Complement: 140

Machinery: 15,000 SHP; Westinghouse (S5W) nuclear reactor driving geared turbines, 1 screw
Speed: 15/25 kts.

No.		Hull	Laid down	Launched	Commiss'd	Disposition
616	LAFAYETTE	Groton	17 Jan 61	8 May 62	23 Apr 63	USN
617	ALEXANDER HAMILTON	Groton	26 Jun 61	18 Aug 62	27 Jun 63	USN
619	ANDREW JACKSON	Mare I.	26 Apr 61	15 Sep 62	3 Jul 63	Stk. 31 Aug 89
620	JOHN ADAMS	Portsmouth	19 May 61	12 Jan 63	12 May 64	Stk. 24 Mar 89
622	JAMES MONROE	Newport News	31 Jul 61	4 Aug 62	7 Dec 63	Stk. 25 Sep 90
623	NATHAN HALE	Groton	2 Oct 61	12 Jan 63	23 Nov 63	Stk. 31 Dec 86
624	WOODROW WILSON	Mare I.	13 Sep 61	22 Feb 63	27 Dec 63	USN
625	HENRY CLAY	Newport News	23 Oct 61	30 Nov 62	20 Feb 64	Stk. 5 Nov 90
626	DANIEL WEBSTER	Groton	28 Dec 61	27 Apr 63	9 Apr 64	USN
627	JAMES MADISON	Newport News	5 Mar 62	15 Mar 63	28 Jul 64	USN
628	TECUMSEH	Groton	1 Jun 62	22 Jun 63	29 May 64	USN
629	DANIEL BOONE	Mare I.	6 Feb 62	22 Jun 63	23 Apr 64	USN
630	JOHN C. CALHOUN	Newport News	4 Jun 62	22 Jun 63	15 Sep 64	USN
631	ULYSSES S. GRANT	Groton	18 Aug 62	2 Nov 63	17 Jul 64	USN

The nuclear powered guided missile submarine *Halibut* (SSGN-587) in early 1960. (USN 1046796)

The nuclear powered fleet ballistic missile submarine *Henry L. Stimson* (SSBN-655) on 14 August 1966. (USN 1117530)

No.		Hull	Laid down	Launched	Commiss'd	Disposition
632	VON STEUBEN	Newport News	4 Sep 62	18 Oct 63	30 Sep 64	USN
633	CASIMIR PULASKI	Groton	12 Jan 63	1 Feb 64	14 Aug 64	USN
634	STONEWALL JACKSON	Mare I.	4 Jul 62	30 Nov 63	26 Aug 64	USN
635	SAM RAYBURN	Newport News	3 Dec 62	20 Dec 63	2 Dec 64	Stk. 28 Aug 89
636	NATHANIEL GREENE	Portsmouth	21 May 62	12 May 64	19 Dec 64	Stk. 31 Jan 87
640	BENJAMIN FRANKLIN	Groton	25 May 63	5 Dec 64	22 Oct 65	USN
641	SIMON BOLIVAR	Newport News	17 Apr 63	22 Aug 64	29 Oct 65	USN
642	KAMEHAMEHA	Mare I.	2 May 63	16 Jan 65	10 Dec 65	USN
643	GEORGE BANCROFT	Groton	24 Aug 63	20 Mar 65	22 Jan 66	USN
644	LEWIS AND CLARK	Newport News	29 Jul 63	21 Nov 64	22 Dec 65	USN
645	JAMES K. POLK	Groton	23 Nov 63	22 May 65	16 Apr 66	USN
654	GEORGE C. MARSHALL	Newport News	2 Mar 64	21 May 65	29 Apr 66	USN
655	HENRY L. STIMSON	Groton	4 Apr 64	13 Nov 65	20 Aug 66	USN
656	GEORGE WASH- INGTON CARVER	Newport News	24 Aug 64	14 Aug 65	15 Jun 66	USN
657	FRANCIS SCOTT KEY	Groton	5 Dec 64	23 Apr 66	3 Dec 66	USN
658	MARIANO G. VALLEJO	Mare I.	7 Jul 64	23 Oct 65	16 Dec 66	USN
659	WILL ROGERS	Groton	20 Mar 65	21 Jul 66	1 Apr 67	USN.

Notes: Fiscal years 1961 (SSBN 616/26), 1962 (627-36), 1963 (640-45), and 1964. A new design (SCB-216) lengthened 15 feet to increase habitability during the long 60-day patrols. The Daniel Webster was completed with experimental bow diving planes. Later units had various refinements in living arrangements, simplified construction, and (beginning with SSBN-640) quieter machinery. The first eight were built with the Polaris A2 missile, and the Daniel Webster and later boats were completed with the 2500-mile range Polaris A3. SSBN 620 and 622-25 received the Polaris A3 in 1968-70 and the entire class was refitted with the Poseidon missile between 1969-78. In 1979-82 12 boats received the Trident I missile: SSBN 627, 629-30, 632-34, 640-41, 643, 655, and 657-58. After being dismantled, the hull of the Sam Rayburn was classified as floating equipment and retained as a machinery training hulk.

Renaming: SSBN-628 ex William Penn 11 Apr 62.

1973

OHIO class

Displacement: 16,764(std.)/18,750 tons
Dimensions: 560'(oa.) x 42' x 36'3"
Armament: 4-21"T 24-Trident-USM
Complement: 156

Machinery: 60,000 SHP (design); G. E. (S8G) nuclear reactor driving geared turbines, 1 screw
Speed: 18/30 kts.

No.		Hull	Laid down	Launched	Commiss'd	Disposition
726	OHIO	Groton	10 Apr 76	7 Apr 79	11 Nov 81	USN
727	MICHIGAN	Groton	4 Apr 77	26 Apr 80	11 Sep 82	USN
728	FLORIDA	Groton	9 Jun 77	14 Nov 81	18 Jun 83	USN
729	GEORGIA	Groton	7 Apr 79	6 Nov 82	11 Feb 84	USN
730	HENRY M. JACKSON	Groton	19 Jan 81	15 Oct 83	6 Oct 84	USN
731	ALABAMA	Groton	27 Aug 81	19 May 84	25 May 85	USN
732	ALASKA	Groton	9 Mar 83	12 Jan 85	25 Jan 86	USN
733	NEVADA	Groton	8 Aug 83	14 Sep 85	16 Aug 86	USN
734	TENNESSEE	Groton	9 Jun 86	13 Dec 86	17 Dec 88	USN
735	PENNSYLVANIA	Groton	2 Mar 87	23 Apr 88	9 Sep 89	USN
736	WEST VIRGINIA	Groton	18 Dec 87	14 Oct 89	20 Oct 90	USN
737	KENTUCKY	Groton	18 Dec 87	11 Aug 90		USN
738	MARYLAND	Groton	18 Dec 87			USN
739	NEBRASKA	Groton	18 Dec 87			USN
740	RHODE ISLAND	Groton				USN
741	MAINE	Groton				USN
742		Groton				USN.

Notes: Fiscal years (respectively): 1974, 1975, 1975, 1976, 1977, 1978, 1978, 1980, 1981, and one per year 1983-1990. These are the largest submarines yet built in the U.S., their size being due to their large natural-circulation S8G reactor and their 24 ballistic missile tubes. Their reactor is an ultra-quiet type derived from the S5G in the Narwhal (SSN-671). The first eight boats were fitted with the Trident I (C4) missile and the others were built with the Trident II (D5).
Renaming: SSBN-730 ex Rhode Island 27 Sep 83.
Reclassifications: SSBN-726 ex SSBN-1 10 Apr 74, ex SSBN-711 21 Feb 74.

Auxiliary Submarines (AGSS)

1949

ALBACORE

Displacement: 1242/1847 tons
Dimensions: 203'10"(oa.) x 27'4"(e) x 18'7"(mean)
Armament: None
Complement: 40

Machinery: 1700 BHP, 2 G. M. diesel engines/ 1500 BHP, 1 Westinghouse electric motor, 1 screw
Speed: 15/25 kts.

No.	Hull	Laid down	Launched	Commiss'd	Disposition
569 ALBACORE	Portsmouth	15 Mar 52	1 Aug 53	5 Dec 53	Stk. 1 May 1980.

Notes: Fiscal year 1951 (deferred from 1950). She was built to the SCB-56 design as a purely experimental submarine to investigate control problems associated with very high speed submerged operations. She demonstrated that her revolutionary teardrop hull form, based in part on airship designs, was capable of overcoming these problems. She was modified frequently during her career to test additional submarine design concepts. In 1964 new batteries and a new 15,000 BHP motor with counterrotating screws were fitted in Phase IV of this program, increasing her submerged speed to 33 knots.

1960

DOLPHIN

Displacement: 750/930 tons
Dimensions: 152' x 19'4" x 18'1"
Armament: 1-21"T; none (1970)
Complement: 27

Machinery: Unknown BHP, 2 Detroit diesel engines/1650 BHP, 1 electric motor, 1 screw
Speed: 7.5/15 kts.

No.	Hull	Laid down	Launched	Commiss'd	Disposition
555 DOLPHIN	Portsmouth	9 Nov 62	8 Jun 68	17 Aug 68	USN.

Notes: Fiscal year 1961, SCB-207 design. She was designed to dive deeper than any submarine afloat in order to provide deep diving engineering data needed for future submarine designs. Her hull has a constant diameter and is closed at each end by hemispheric caps.

Target and Training Submarines (SST)

1950

T class

Displacement: 303/347 tons
Dimensions: 131'3"(oa.) x 13'7"(e) x 12'2"(mean)
Armament: 1-21"T
Complement: 14

Machinery: 250 BHP, 2 G. M. diesel engines/Unknown BHP, 1 Elliott electric motor, 1 screw
Speed: 10/10.5 kts.

No.		Hull	Laid down	Launched	Commiss'd	Disposition
1	T-1	Groton	1 Apr 52	17 Jul 53	9 Oct 53	Stk. 31 Jan 73, sunk as target off Puerto Rico 18 Oct 78
2	T-2	Groton	12 May 52	14 Oct 53	20 Nov 53	Stk. 31 Jan 73, memorial at Omaha, Neb., Apr 74.

Notes: Fiscal years 1951 (SST-1) and 1952, SCB-68 design. Built specifically for target and training duty, they were the smallest U.S. submarines since the "E" class of 1908.
Renaming: To Mackerel and Marlin respectively on 15 Jul 56.
Reclassifications: The T-1 was originally AGSS-570 and was reclassified SST-1 before May 1951.

Armed Merchantmen (New Navy)

1. Auxiliary Cruisers

1898

BADGER (ex-Yumuri). 4784 tons. 329'9" x 48'3"(e) x 18'6". Armament: 6-5"; none (1899); 2-4" (1902). Machinery: 3200 IHP, triple-expansion engine, 1 screw. Speed: 16 kts. Complement: 424. Built by Delaware River, launched 12 Oct 89. Purchased 19 Apr 98. Converted by New York. Commissioned 25 Apr 98. Stk. 23 Mar 00. Transferred to War Dept. 7 Apr 00. Returned by the Army 13 Nov 02 as the transport Lawton. Ordered sold 24 Apr 07. Sold 5 Jun 07.

BUFFALO (ex-Brazilian Nictheroy, ex-El Cid). 6114 tons. 406'1"(oa.) x 48'3"(e) x 19'5". Armament: 2-5" 4-4"; 2-5" (1899); 6-4" (1910). Machinery duplicates the Yankee. Built by Newport News, launched 31 May 93. Purchased from Brazil 11 Jul 98. Fitted out by New York. Commissioned 18 Jul 98. Used as a transport 1907-16 and then as a destroyer tender. Designated AD-8 17 Jul 20. Stk. 27 May 27. Sold 28 Sep 27. Sister to the Yankee, Yosemite, and Dixie.

DIXIE (ex-El Rio). 6114 tons. 405'10"(oa.) x 48'3"(e) x 19'11". Armament: 10-6; none (1899); 8-5" (1899); 10-3" (1909); 4-3" 1-3"AA (1919). Machinery duplicates the Yankee. Built by Newport News, launched 20 Oct 92. Purchased 15 Apr 98. Converted by Newport News. Commissioned 19 Apr 98. Used as a transport 1907-9 and a destroyer tender after 1911. Designated AD-1 17 Jul 20. Stk. 5 Aug 22. Sold 25 Sep 22. Sister to the Yankee, Yosemite, and Buffalo.

HARVARD (ex-New York, ex-City of New York). 15,390 tons. 560'(oa.) x 63'2" x 23'. Armament: 8-5". Machinery: 20,600 IHP, triple-expansion engines, 1 screw. Speed: 14.5 kts. Complement: 286. Built by Thomson 1888. Chartered 1898. Converted by New York and Newport News. Commissioned 26 Apr 98. Returned to owners 1899. Reacquired 9 May 18 as the transport Plattsburg, ID-1645 (ex-SS New York, renamed 18 Apr 18). Commissioned 24 May 18. Returned to owners 7 Oct 19. Sister to the Yale.

PANTHER (ex-Venezuela). 3380 tons. 324'4"(oa.) x 40'8"(e) x 15'9"(mean). Armament: 6-5" 6-3"; 6-5" 4-3" (1898); 6-5" 3-3" (1899); 3-3" (1900); 2-6# (1910); 4-3" (1919). Machinery: 3200 IHP, triple-expansion engine, 1 screw. Speed: 13.5 kts. Complement: 198. Built by Cramp 1889. Purchased 19 Apr 98. Converted by Morgan and New York. Commissioned 22 Apr 98. Served as a training vessel 1900-01, transport 1907, repair vessel 1907-14, and destroyer tender 1914-23. Designated AD-6 17 Jul 20. Stk. 5 Aug 22. Sold 24 Mar 23.

PRAIRIE (ex-El Sol). 6620 tons. 404'9"(oa.) x 48'3"(e) x 20'9". Armament: 10-6"; 8-6" (1899); 7-6" (1903); 8-6" (1905); 10-3"(1909); 4-5" (1917); 8-3"(1918); 8-3" 1-3"AA (1919). Machinery: 3800 IHP, vertical triple-expansion engine, 1 screw. Speed: 14.5 kts. Complement: 286. Built by Cramp 1890. Purchased 6 Apr 98. Converted by New York. Commissioned 14 Apr 98. Used as a training vessel 1900-17 and thereafter as a destroyer tender. Designated AD-5 17 Jul 20. Stk 22 Nov 22. Sold 22 Jun 23.

ST. LOUIS (ex-St. Louis). 16,275 tons. 554'2"(oa.) x 62'9" x 25'. Armament: 4-5". Machinery: 20,000 IHP, quadruple-expansion engines, 2 screws. Speed: 22 kts. Complement: 381. Built by Cramp 1895. Chartered 1898. Converted by New York and Philadelphia. Commissioned 24 Apr 98. Returned to owners 2 Sep 98. Reacquired 26 Apr 18 as the transport Louisville, ID-1644 (ex-SS St. Louis, renamed 18 Apr 18). Commissioned 27 Apr 18. Returned to owners 12 Sep 19. Sister to the St. Paul.

ST. PAUL (ex-St. Paul). Hull and machinery duplicate the St. Louis. Armament: 6-5". Built by Cramp, launched 10 Apr 95. Chartered 1898. Converted by Philadelphia and Cramp. Commissioned 20 Apr 98. Returned to owners 2 Sep 98. Capsized at New York 28 Apr 18 while being prepared for Navy service in World War I. Commissioned as St. Paul, ID-1643, when salvaged 13 May 18. Spent the rest of the war under repair. Returned to owners 24 Mar 19. Sister to the St. Louis.

YALE (ex-Paris, ex-City of Paris). Hull and machinery duplicate the Harvard. Armament: 8-5". Built by Thomson 1889. Chartered 1898. Converted by New York and Newport News. Commissioned 2 May 98. Returned to owners 1899. Recommissioned 29 May 18 as the transport Harrisburg, ID-1663 (ex-SS Philadelphia, renamed 18 Apr 18). Returned to owners 25 Sep 19. Sister to the Harvard.

YANKEE (ex-El Norte). 6225 tons. 406'(oa.) x 48'4" x 20'11". Armament: 10-5"; none (1899); 8-5" (1902); 10-3" (1909). Machinery: 3800 IHP, vertical triple-expansion engine, 1 screw. Speed: 14.5 kts. Complement: 302. Built by Newport News, launched 14 Jun 92. Purchased 6 Apr 98. Converted by New York. Commissioned 14 Apr 98. Used as a training vessel 1903-4 and a transport 1906-8. Foundered under tow in Buzzards Bay, Mass., 4 Dec 08 after running aground. Sister to the Yosemite, Buffalo, and Dixie.

YOSEMITE (ex-El Sud). 6179 tons. 405'9"(oa.) x 48'3"(e) x 19'5". Machinery duplicates the Yankee. Armament: 10-5". Built by Newport News, launched 16 Mar 92. Purchased 6 Apr 98. Converted by Newport News. Commissioned 13 Apr 98. Scuttled off Guam 13 Nov 00 after being damaged in a typhoon. Sister to the Yankee, Buffalo, and Dixie.

2. Gunboat

1917

WILMETTE (ex-Eastland). 1820 tons. 275'3"(oa.) x 38'2"(e) x 19'6"(h). Armament: 4-4" 2-3"AA; 2-4"/50 (1941); 2-4" 1-3"AA (1943); 1-3"/50AA (1945). Machinery: 4000 IHP, vertical triple-expasion engines, 2 screws. Speed: 12 kts. Complement: 181. Built by Jenks, launched 6 May 03. As a merchant ship, she capsized at Chicago on 24 Jul 15 with the loss of 812 lives. Purchased by the Navy at Chicago 21 Nov 17. Converted to a gunboat by Ship Owners. Renamed 20 Feb 18. Commissioned 25 Sep 18. Spent her entire career as a training ship on the Great Lakes. Designated "unclassified" (IX-29) 17 Jul 20. Stk. 19 Dec 45, sold Chicago 31 Oct 46.

3. Torpedo Boat

1887

STILETTO (ex-Stiletto). 31 tons. 94'(b.p.) x 11' x 4'10". Armament: none; 2-18"T (1898). Machinery: 359 IHP, 1 vertical inverted compound engine, 1 screw. Speed: 18.22 kts (trials). Complement: 6. Built by Herreshoff 1885 for his own use as a fast wooden-hulled yacht and experimental torpedo boat. Purchased 1887. Commissioned Jul 87. Stk. 28 Jan 11. Sold Newport, R. I., 18 Jul 11.

4. Destroyer

1917

ISABEL (ex-Isabel). 710 tons. 245'3"(oa.) x 26'8"(e) x 11'(max). Armament: 4-3/50" 4-18"T; 4-3"(1920); 4-3"/50 2-3"/23AA (1921); 2-3" 2-3"AA (1924); 2-3"/50AA (1945). Machinery: 8400 SHP, geared turbines, 2 screws. Speed: 29 kts. Complement: 103. Built as a private yacht by Bath, launched 7 Jun 17. Purchased 3 Jul 17 before completion and numbered SP-521. Commissioned 28 Dec 17. As large and fast as the Navy's earlier destroyers, she was classified as a destroyer and was converted for this role by her builder. Her torpedo tubes were later removed and she was designated as an armed yacht (PY-10) on 17 Jul 20. Stk. 26 Feb 46. Scrapped at Mare Is. 25 Mar 46.

Bibliography

This list is intended as a guide to the more productive sources of information available to students interested in the vessels of the United States Navy. It is not a complete list of all the sources used in the preparation of this work although it does include all major ones.

Official Sources

Clark, William Bell, and Morgan, William James (Eds.). Naval Documents of the American Revolution. 15 vols. Washington, 1964-.

...Construction of Naval Vessels, 31 Jan. 1859. 35th Cong., 2d Sess., Senate Report 363.

...Cost of Building and Repairing Certain Vessels, 1 March 1841. 26th Cong., 2d Sess., Senate Document 223.

Documents...in Relation to Building an Additional Number of Sloops of War, 13 Jan. 1824. 18th Cong., 1st Sess., Senate Document 12.

...Information Upon Various Subjects Pertaining to the Naval Establishment, 30 Jan. 1861. 36th Cong., 2d Sess., Senate Executive Document 4.

Knox, Dudley W. (Ed.). Quasi-War Between United States and France. 7 vols. Washington, 1935-1938.

_____ (Ed.). Register of Officer Personnel...and Ships Data, 1801-1807. Washington, 1945.

_____ (Ed.). United States Wars with the Barbary Pirates. 6 vols. Washington, 1939-1941.

Lincoln, Charles Henry (Ed.). Naval Records of the American Revolution, 1775-1788. Washington, 1906.

List of Merchant Vessels of the United States. Washington, 1868-1967. Issued annually by various offices with some changes in title.

"List of Vessels United States Navy, 1795-1850." Manuscript in Record Group 45, National Archives.

Lowrie, Walter, et al. (Eds.). American State Papers...Naval Affairs. 4 vols. Washington, 1834-1861.

Naval History Division, Department of the Navy. Dictionary of American Naval Fighting Ships. 8 vols. Washington, 1959-1981.

_____. Civil War Chronology, 1861-1865. 5 vols. Washington, 1961-1965.

_____. United States Naval Chronology, World War II. Washington, 1955.

Navy Yearbook: Compilation of Annual Naval Appropriation Laws.... Washington, 1911-1921. Issued annually.

Paullin, Charles Oscar (Ed.). Out Letters of the Continental Marine Committee and Board of Admiralty, August 1776-September 1780. 2 vols. New York, 1914.

Register of...Officers of the Navy...and of the Marine Corps. Washington, 1816- . Issued annually.

"Register of Union and Confederate Vessels." Manuscript in Record Group 45, National Archives.

Report of the Chief of Naval Operations, October 1945. Washington, 1945.

Report of the Secretary of the Navy. Washington, 1815-1949. Issued annually.

Ships, Bureau of (later Naval Ship Systems Command). Monthly Progress Report. Washington, 1942-

Ships' Data, U. S. Naval Vessels. Washington, 1911. Issued periodically.

"Ships' Histories," Washington, 1946- Short histories of individual vessels prepared in the Ships' Histories Branch, Naval Historical Center, Navy Department.

...Statement of Vessels Built by the United States Navy Since the Year 1826..., 11 Jan. 1843. 27th Cong. 3d Sess., House Executive Document 49.

...Steam Navy of the United States, 24 Feb. 1854. 33d Cong., 1st Sess., House Executive Document 65.

Stewart, Charles W. (Ed.). Official Records of the Union and Confederate Navies in the War of the Rebellion. 28 vols. Washington, 1895-1921.

...Vessels of the Navy of the United States Which Have Been Captured, Lost, or Destroyed, 2 March 1859. 35th Cong., 2d Sess., Senate Document 38.

Unofficial Sources

Adams, Henry. War of 1812. Washington, 1944.

Alden, John D. "A New Fleet Emerges: Combat Ships." Naval Review, 1964. Fiscal year programs, 1946-1964.

_____. The Fleet Submarine in the U. S. Navy. Annapolis, 1979.

_____. Flush Decks and Four Pipes. Annapolis, 1965.

Allen, Gardiner Weld. A Naval History of the American Revolution. 2 vols. Boston, 1913.

_____. Our Naval War with France. Boston, 1909.

_____. Our Navy and the Barbary Pirates. Boston, 1905.

Babcock, W. I. "The Subsurface Torpedo-Boat." Transactions, Society Naval Architects and Marine Engineers, vol. 15 (1907), pp. 243-47. See also Marine Review, 7 June 1906, pp. 21-24.

Barnes, Robert Hatfield. United States Submarines. New Haven, 1944.

Bauer, K. Jack. Surfboats and Horse Marines. Annapolis, 1969.

Bauer, K. Jack. "Naval Shipbuilding Programs 1794-1860." Military Affairs, vol 29 (1965), pp. 29-40.

Bauer, K. Jack. "United States Naval Shipbuilding Programs, 1775-1860." Masters Thesis. Indiana
   University, 1949.   Copy in the Archives at Rensselaer Polytechnic Institute.
Baxter, James Phinney, 3d. The Introduction of the Ironclad Warship. Cambridge, 1933.
Benham, Edith Wallace, and Hall, Anne M. Ships of the United States Navy and Their Sponsors, 1797-
   1913. n. p., 1913.
Bennett, Frank M. The Steam Navy of the United States. Pittsburgh, 1897.
Boynton, Charles B. The History of the Navy During the Rebellion. 2 vols. New York, 1867.
Brassey's Naval Annual, 1886-1945. Annual with varying title and publisher.
Canney, Donald L. The Old Steam Navy. Volume One: Frigates, Sloops, and Gunboats, 1815-1885.
   Annapolis, 1990.   A second volume on ironclads is in preparation.
Chapelle, Howard Irving. History of the American Sailing Navy. New York, 1949.
_____. History of American Sailing Ships. New York, 1935.
Chesneau, Roger. Aircraft Carriers of the World, 1914 to the Present. Annapolis, 1984.
Clark, William Bell. Captain Dauntless. Baton Rouge, 1949.
_____. The First Saratoga. Baton Rouge, 1953.
_____. Gallant John Barry, 1745-1803. New York, 1940.
_____. Lambert Wickes, Sea Raider and Diplomat. New Haven, 1932.
Combat Fleets of the World. Annapolis, 1978/79-1990/91. English language edition of the French Flottes
   de Combat prepared by A. D. Baker III.
Conway's All the World's Fighting Ships. 5 vols., 1860-1982. London and Annapolis, 1979-1985.
Cooling, Benjamin Franklin. Gray Steel and Blue Water Navy: The Formative Years of America's Military-
   Industrial Complex. Hamden, Conn., 1979.
Cooper, James Fenimore. The History of the Navy of the United States of America. 2 vols. Philadelphia,
   1839.
Donko, Wilhelm M. Die Atomkreuzer der U.S. Navy. Koblenz, 1987.
Dulin, Robert O, Jr., and William H. Garzke, Jr. Battleships: United States Battleships in World War
   II. Annapolis, 1976.
Elliott, Peter. Allied Escort Ships of World War II. Annapolis, 1977.
Emmons, George F. The Navy of the United States. Washington, 1853.
Fahey, James C. Ships and Aircraft of the U. S. Fleet. 1st through 8th eds. Various places, 1939-1965.
Friedman, Norman. Submarine Design and Development. Annapolis, 1984.
_____. U. S. Aircraft Carriers. Annapolis, 1983.
_____. U. S. Battleships. Annapolis, 1985.
_____. U. S. Cruisers. Annapolis, 1984.
_____. U. S. Destroyers. Annapolis, 1982.
_____. U. S. Small Combatants. Annapolis, 1987.
Heyl, Erik. Early American Steamers. 3 vols. Buffalo, 1953-1960.
Hibben, Henry B. Navy Yard, Washington. Washington, 1890. (51st Cong., 1st Sess.. Senate Executive
   Document 22).
Holdcamper, Forrest R. (Ed.). Merchant Steam Vessels of the United States, 1807-1868. Mystic, 1952.
Jane's Fighting Ships. London, 1898- . Annual with some gaps and variations in title.
Johnson, Robert V., and Buel, C. C. (Eds.). Battles and Leaders of the Civil War. 4 vols. New York,
   1884-1888.
Kafka, Roger, and Pepperburg, Roy L. Warships of the World. New York, 1944-1946. 2 editions.
Kern, Florence. The United States Revenue Cutters in the Civil War. Washington, s.d.
Knox, Dudley W. A History of the United States Navy. New York, 1946.
Lewis, Charles Lee. Admiral Franklin Buchanan. Baltimore, 1929.
_____. David Glasgow Farragut. 2 vols. Annapolis, 1941-1943.
Lott, Arnold. A Long Line of Ships. Annapolis, 1954.
Lull, Edward P. History of the Gosport Navy Yard. Washington, 1874.
Maclay, Edgar Stanton. A History of the United States Navy From 1776 to 1893. 2 vols. New York, 1894.
Milligan, John D. Gunboats Down the Mississippi. Annapolis, 1965.
Mitchell, Donald W. History of the Modern American Navy. New York, 1946.
Morison, Samuel Eliot. United States Naval Operations In World War II. 15 vols., Boston, 1947-1961.
Morison, Samuel L. Warships of the U. S. Navy. London, 1983.
Morris, Richard K. John P. Holland, 1841-1914: Inventor of the Modern Submarine. Annapolis, 1966.
Musicant, Ivan. U. S. Armored Cruisers: A Design and Operational History. Annapolis, 1985.
Neeser, Robert W. Statistical and Chronological History of the United States Navy 1775-1907. 2 vols.
   New York, 1909.
Osbon, B. S. Hand Book of the United States Navy. New York, 1864.
Paullin, Charles Oscar. The Navy of the American Revolution. Chicago, 1906.
Peck, Taylor. Round-Shot to Rockets. Annapolis, 1949.
Polmar, Norman. The Ships and Aircraft of the U. S. Fleet. 11th through 14th eds. Annapolis, 1978-
   1987.
Pratt, Fletcher. Civil War on Western Waters. New York, 1956.
_____. The Navy, A History. Garden City, 1941.

Preble, George Henry. _A Complete List of Vessels of the United States Navy from 1797 to 1874._
    Washington, 1874.
_____. _History of U. S. Navy Yard, Portsmouth, N. H._ Washington, 1892.
Reilly, John C., Jr. _United States Navy Destroyers of World War II._ Poole, Dorset, 1983.
_____ and Robert L. Scheina. _American Battleships, 1886-1923._ Annapolis, 1980.
Rickover, H. G. _How the Battleship Maine Was Destroyed._ Washington, 1976.
Roberts, Stephen S. "U.S. Navy Building Programs During World War II." _Warship International,_ no. 3,
    1981, pp. 218-261. Program and contract data for all Navy-built ships.
Roosevelt, Theodore. _The Naval War of 1812._ New York, 1902.
Roscoe, Theodore. _United States Destroyer Operations in World War II._ Annapolis, 1953.
_____. _United States Submarine Operations in World War II._ Annapolis, 1949.
Rosenberg, Max. _The Building of Perry's Fleet on Lake Erie, 1812-1813._ Harrisburg, 1950.
Rowe, John S. and Samuel L. Morison. _The Ships and Aircraft of the U. S. Fleet._ 9th and 10th eds.
    Annapolis, 1972-1975.
Silverstone, Paul H. _U. S. Warships Since 1945._ Annapolis, 1987.
_____. _Warships of the Civil War Navies._ Annapolis, 1989.
Sloan, Edward William, III. _Benjamin Franklin Isherwood, Naval Engineer._ Annapolis, 1965.
Society of Naval Architects and Marine Engineers. _Historical Transactions, 1893-1943._ New York, 1945.
Soley, James Russell. _The Blockade and the Cruisers._ New York, 1883.
Somerville, Keith Frazier, and Smith, Harriotte W. B. _Ships of the United States Navy and Their
    Sponsors, 1924-1950._ Annapolis, 1952.
Stuart, Charles B. _Naval and Mail Steamers of the United States._ New York, 1853.
Sumrall, Robert F. _Iowa Class Battleships: Their Design, Weapons, and Equipment._ Annapolis, 1988.
Swann, Leonard Alexander, Jr. _John Roach, Maritime Entrepreneur._ Annapolis, 1965.
Terzibaschitsch, Stefan. _Aircraft Carriers of the US Navy._ Annapolis, 1980.
_____. _Battleships of the U.S. Navy in World War II._ New York, 1977.
_____. _Cruisers of the US Navy, 1922-1962._ Annapolis, 1984.
_____. _Escort Carriers and Aviation Support Ships of the US Navy._ Annapolis, 1981.
_____. _Der FRAM-Modernisierungs-programm der US-Navy._ Munich, 1975.
Turnbull, Archibald Douglas. _John Stevens, An American Record._ New York, 1928.
U. S. Submarine Losses, World War II. Washington, 1949. Reissued 1963.
Weyers Taschenbuch der Kriegsflotten. Munich, 1904-   . Annual with some gaps and changes in title.
    Published in 1967 in an English language edition by the U. S. Naval Institute as _Weyers Warships of
    the World._
Whitley, M. J. _Destroyers of World War Two._ Annapolis, 1988.
Wilson, Henry W. _Ironclads in Action._ 2 vols. Boston, 1898.

Periodicals

The American Neptune.
Army Navy Journal (later _Army Navy Air Force Journal_ and _Journal of the Armed Forces_).
Army Navy Register (later _Army Navy Air Force Register_).
Bureau of Ships Journal (later _Naval Ships Systems Command Technical Notes_).
Harper's Monthly Magazine.
Historical Collections of the Essex Institute.
Inland Seas.
Journal of the American Society of Naval Engineers.
Marine Digest.
Marine Engineering (later _Marine Engineering/Log_).
Marine Journal.
Military Affairs.
The Naval Magazine.
Nautical Gazette.
Navy Times.
New England Historical and Genealogical Register.
The New York Times.
Niles Weekly Register.
Our Navy.
Pennsylvania Magazine of History and Biography.
Scientific American.
Transactions of the Society of Naval Architects and Marine Engineers.
United Service Magazine.
United States Naval Institute Proceedings. Annual updates on the U.S. Navy building program are in
    the issues for January (1981-83 and 1985), February (1984), and May (1986-). Annual updates on
    changes in status of ships (including dispositions) are in the issues for October (1977-79),
    January (1981-82), February (1983-84) and May (1985-).
Warship International.

Hull Number Index

This index covers all of the hull numbers contained in this volume. It is designed to be used with the primary (tabular) listings of the ships and the reclassification paragraphs for the ship classes.
-- Entries with nothing but page numbers following hull types or numbers indicate that the designations are the primary ones under which the ships are listed. For example, the listing "ACV 6-25 ... Page 128" indicates that ACV 6-25 may be found listed in the ACV section on page 128.
-- Entries which cross-reference hull numbers to other hull numbers refer to reclassifications. For example, the listing "AG 83 ... Ex DD 138, page 175" indicates that the primary listing for the ship that became AG 83 is under the designation DD 138 and that the reclassification is referred to on page 175.
-- Entries which cross-reference hull types to other hull types refer to reclassifications in which hull types were changed but numbers were not. For example, the listing "CVS ... Ex CV, pages 115-120" indicates that the primary listings for all ships reclassified CVS are under the CV designation, that the original CV hull numbers were retained and should be used to locate the ships, and that the reclassifications are described in the reclassification paragraphs in the CV section between pages 115 and 120.

AB 1	Ex BB 5, page 103		AG 120	Ex DD 230, page 182
			AG 126-127	Ex DD 358-359, page 184
ACV 1	Ex AVG 1, page 126		AG 128	Ex BB 41, page 111
ACV 6-25	Page 128		AG 151	Ex DD 849, page 206
ACV 26-29	Page 126		AG 152	Ex DD 828, page 206
ACV 30	Ex BAVG 4, page 126		AG 191	Ex CL 120, page 152
ACV 31-104	Pages 128-130			
ACV 105-119	To CVE 105-119, page 132		AGDE 1	Page 244
AG 6-7	Ex PG 17-18, page 160		AGER 163	To AGDE 1, page 244
AG 16-17	Ex BB 31-32, page 108			
AG 18	Ex DD 302, page 183		AGFF 1	Ex AGDE 1, page 244
AG 19-20	Ex DD 136-137, page 175			
AG 21-22	Ex DD 119-120, page 177		AGMR 1	Ex CVE 107, page 132
AG 24	Ex DD 189, page 182		AGMR 2	Ex CVL 48, page 121
AG 28	Ex DD 74, page 172			
AG 80	Ex DD 152, page 175		AGSS 555	Page 296
AG 81	Ex DD 156, page 175		AGSS 569	Page 296
AG 82	Ex DD 159, page 178		AGSS 570	To SST 1, page 296
AG 83	Ex DD 138, page 175		AGSS (others)	Ex SS, pages 271-283
AG 84	Ex DD 231, page 182			
AG 85	Ex DD 234, page 182		AKV 8-23	Ex CVE 108-123, page 132
AG 86	Ex DD 222, page 182		AKV 24-28	Ex ACV 74-78, page 131
AG 87	Ex DD 220, page 182		AKV 29	Ex ACV 81, page 131
AG 91	Ex DD 187, page 182		AKV 30	Ex ACV 86, page 131
AG 95	Ex DD 336, page 183		AKV 31	Ex ACV 89, page 131
AG 96	Ex DD 210, page 182		AKV 32	Ex ACV 94, page 131
AG 97	Ex DD 221, page 182		AKV 33-34	Ex ACV 97-98, page 131
AG 98	Ex DD 124, page 177		AKV 35-36	Ex ACV 100-101, page 131
AG 99-101	Ex DD 345-347, page 183		AKV 37-39	Ex CVE 105-107, page 132
AG 102	Ex DD 128, page 178		AKV 40	Ex ACV 11, page 129
AG 103	Ex DD 144, page 175		AKV 41	Ex ACV 13, page 129
AG 104	Ex DD 146, page 175		AKV 42	Ex ACV 23, page 129
AG 105-107	Ex DD 178-180, page 176		AKV 43	Ex ACV 25, page 129
AG 108	Ex DD 206, page 182			
AG 109	Ex DD 337, page 182		AOSS	Ex SS, pages 271-283
AG 110	Ex DD 339, page 182			
AG 111	Ex DD 141, page 175		APD 1	Ex DD 74, page 172
AG 112-113	Ex DD 148-149, page 175		APD 2	Ex DD 85, page 176
AG 114	Ex DD 151, page 175		APD 3	Ex DD 82, page 176
AG 115-116	Ex DD 154-155, page 175		APD 4	Ex DD 79, page 176
AG 117	Ex DD 217, page 182		APD 5	Ex DD 90, page 176
AG 118	Ex DD 223, page 182		APD 6	Ex DD 83, page 176
AG 119	Ex DD 228, page 182		APD 7-9	Ex DD 114-116, page 175

APD	10-11	Ex DD 232-233, page 182	ASSA		Ex SS, pages 271-283
APD	12	Ex DD 236, page 182			
APD	13	Ex DD 243, page 182	ASSP		Ex SS, pages 271-283
APD	14	Ex DD 103, page 176			
APD	15	Ex DD 137, page 175	AV 3		Ex CV 1, page 115
APD	16	Ex DD 139, page 175			
APD	17	Ex DD 164, page 176	AVD	1	Ex DD 241, page 182
APD	18	Ex DD 235, page 182	AVD	2	Ex DD 244, page 183
APD	19	Ex DD 125, page 178	AVD	3	Ex DD 196, page 182
APD	20	Ex DD 147, page 175	AVD	4	Ex DD 186, page 182
APD	21	Ex DD 157, page 178	AVD	5	Ex DD 188, page 182
APD	22	Ex DD 160, page 178	AVD	6	Ex DD 342, page 183
APD	23	Ex DD 239, page 182	AVD	7	Ex DD 344, page 183
APD	24	Ex DD 343, page 183	AVD	8	Ex DD 251, page 183
APD	25	Ex DD 113, page 175	AVD	9	Ex DD 255, page 183
APD	26	Ex DD 237, page 182	AVD	10	Ex DD 267, page 183
APD	27	Ex DD 244, page 183	AVD	11	Ex DD 270, page 183
APD	28	Ex DD 342, page 183	AVD	12	Ex DD 260, page 183
APD	29	Ex DD 248, page 183	AVD	13	Ex DD 266, page 183
APD	30	Ex DD 341, page 183	AVD	14	Ex DD 237, page 182
APD	31	Ex DD 186, page 182			
APD	32	Ex DD 188, page 182	AVG	1-5	Pages 125-126
APD	33	Ex DD 196, page 182	AVG	6-25	To ACV 6-25, page 129
APD	34	Ex DD 251, page 183	AVG	26-29	To ACV 26-29, page 126
APD	35	Ex DD 255, page 183	AVG	30	Ex BAVG 4, page 126
APD	36	Ex DD 266, page 183	AVG	31-104	To ACV 31-104, pages 129, 131
APD	37-38	Ex DE 53-54, page 232			
APD	39	Ex DE 576, page 232	AVP	14	Ex DD 241, page 182
APD	40	Ex DE 637, page 232	AVP	15	Ex DD 244, page 183
APD	41	Ex DE 635, page 232	AVP	16	Ex DD 196, page 182
APD	42	Ex DE 60, page 232	AVP	17	Ex DD 186, page 182
APD	43-44	Ex DE 62-63, page 232	AVP	18	Ex DD 188, page 182
APD	45-46	Ex DE 65-66, page 232	AVP	19	Ex DD 342, page 183
APD	47-48	Ex DE 68-69, page 232	AVP	20	Ex DD 344, page 183
APD	49	Ex DE 70, page 232			
APD	50-52	Ex DE 154-156, page 232	AVT	1-2	Ex CV 25-26, page 120
APD	53	Ex DE 211, page 232	AVT	3-5	Ex CV 28-30, page 120
APD	54-57	Ex DE 158-161, page 232	AVT	6-7	Ex CVL 48-49, page 121
APD	58	Ex DE 636, page 232	AVT	8	Ex CV 13, page 118
APD	59-63	Ex DE 205-209, page 232	AVT	9	Ex CV 17, page 118
APD	64-66	Ex DE 214-216, page 232	AVT	10	Ex CV 32, page 119
APD	67-68	Ex DE 665-666, page 232	AVT	11	Ex CV 47, page 119
APD	69-74	Ex DE 668-673, page 232	AVT	12	Ex CV 40, page 119
APD	75-77	Ex DE 675-677, page 232	AVT	16	Ex CV 16, page 118
APD	78-79	Ex DE 693-694, page 232			
APD	80	Ex DE 212, page 232	BAVG	1-6	Pages 125, 128
APD	81-86	Ex DE 789-794, page 232			
APD	87-90	Ex DE 226-229, page 235	BACV	1-3	Ex BAVG 1-3, page 126
APD	91-96	Ex DE 232-237, page 235	BACV	5-6	Ex BAVG 5-6, pages 126, 128
APD	97-99	Ex DE 281-283, page 235			
APD	100-116	Ex DE 590-606, page 235	BB 1-71		Pages 102-114
APD	117	Ex DE 674, page 235			
APD	118-119	Ex DE 721-722, page 235	BDE 1-50		To DE 1-50, page 221
APD	120-125	Ex DE 687-692, page 235			
APD	126-136	Ex DE 710-720, page 235	BM 1-10		Pages 99-101
APD	137-138	Ex DE 684-685, page 235			
APD	139	Ex DE 709, page 235	CA	1	Maine, page 102
			CA	2-13	Pages 133-135
APS	1	Ex SM 1, page 267	CA	14	Chicago, page 141
APS	2-4	Ex SS 163-165, page 265	CA	15	Ex Cruiser 6, page 144
			CA	16-17	Ex Cruisers 12-13, page 145
APSS		Ex SS, pages 271-283	CA	18-19	Ex Cruisers 20 & 22, page 146
			CA	24-39	Pages 136-138
AS 4		Alert, page 78	CA	44-45	Page 138

CA 68-75	Page 139		CV 44	Page 121
CA 122-143	Pages 139-140		CV 45-47	Page 119
CA 148-153	Page 140		CV 50-55	Page 119
			CV 59-64	Ex CVA 59-64, pages 123-124
CAG 1-2	Page 153		CV 66-67	Ex CVA 66-67, page 124
CB 1-6	Page 135		CVA 41-43	Ex CVB 41-43, page 121
			CVA 58-64	Pages 123-124
CBC 1	Ex CB 3, page 135		CVA 66-67	Page 124
			CVA (others)	Ex CV, pages 115-120
CC 1-6	Page 114			
			CVAN 65	Page 124
CC 1	Ex CLC 1, page 153		CVAN 68-69	Page 125
CC 2	Ex CVL 49, page 121			
CC 3	Ex CVL 48, page 121		CVB 41-43	Page 122
			CVB 56-57	Page 122
CG 10-12	Page 155		CVB 59	To CVA 59, page 123
CG 16-24	Ex DLG 16-24, page 214			
CG 26-34	Ex DLG 26-34, page 215		CVE 1	Ex AVG 1, page 126
CG 47-73	Page 218		CVE 6-25	Ex ACV 6-25, page 129
			CVE 26-29	Ex AVG 26-29, page 126
CGN 9	Page 154		CVE 30	Ex BAVG 4, page 126
CGN 25	Ex DLGN 25, page 215		CVE 31-104	Ex ACV 31-104, pages 129, 131
CGN 35-37	Ex DLGN 35-37, pages 215-216		CVE 105-139	Pages 131-132
CGN 38-41	Page 217			
CGN 160	To CGN 9, page 155		CVHA 1	Ex ACV 90, page 131
CL 1-3	Ex Scout Cruisers 1-3, page 147		CVHE	Ex AVG/ACV/CVE, pages 125-132
CL 4-13	Page 148			
CL 14	Chicago, page 141		CVL 22-30	Ex CV 22-30, page 120
CL 15	Ex Cruiser 6, page 144		CVL 48-49	Page 121
CL 16-21	Ex Cruisers 14-19, page 146			
CL 22	New Orleans, page 145		CVN 65	Ex CVAN 65, page 124
CL 23	Albany, page 145		CVN 68-69	Ex CVAN 68-69, page 125
CL 24-39	To CA 24-39, pages 136-138		CVN 70-75	Page 125
CL 40-43	Page 148			
CL 44-45	To CA 44-45, page 138		CVS	Ex CV, pages 115-120
CL 46-67	Pages 148-151			
CL 76-121	Pages 150-152		CVT 16	Ex CV 16, page 118
CL 144-147	Page 152			
CL 154-159	Page 153		CVU	Ex ACV/CVE, pages 126-132
CLAA 53-54	Ex CL 53-54, page 150		DD 1-926	Pages 168-205
CLAA 95-98	Ex CL 95-98, page 150		DD 927-930	To DL 2-5, page 213
CLAA 119-21	Ex CL 119-121, page 152		DD 931-951	Pages 206-208
			DD 952-959	To DDG 2-9, page 211
CLC 1	Page 153		DD 960-992	Pages 208-210
			DD 993-996	To DDG 993-996, page 212
CLG 3-8	Page 154		DD 997	Page 210
CLG 93	To CLG 3, page 154			
			DDE	Ex DD, pages 183-210
CLGN 160	To CGN 9, page 155			
			DDG 1	Ex DD 712, page 206
CLK 1	To DL 1, page 213		DDG 2-30	Page 211
CLK 2	New Haven, page 213		DDG 31	Ex DD 936, page 207
			DDG 32	Ex DD 932, page 207
CM 1	Ex Cruiser 3, page 143		DDG 33	Ex DD 949, page 208
CM 2	Ex Cruiser 5, page 144		DDG 34	Ex DD 947, page 208
			DDG 35-36	Ex DL 2-3, page 213
Cruisers 1-22	Pages 141-146		DDG 37-46	Ex DLG 6-15, page 214
			DDG 47-48	To CG 47-48, page 218
CV 1-40	Pages 115-120		DDG 51-63	Page 212
CV 41-43	Ex CVB 41-43, page 121		DDG 712	Ex DD 712, page 206
			DDG 993-996	Page 212

DDK	Ex DD, pages 183–210	
DDR	Ex DD, pages 183–210	
DE 1–1107	Pages 219–244	
DEC	Ex DE, pages 219–244	
DEG 1–11	Page 245	
DER	Ex DE, pages 219–244	
DL 1–5	Page 213	
DL 6–8	To DLG 6–8, page 214	
DLG 1–3	To DLG 9–11, page 214	
DLG 6–24	Page 214	
DLG 26–34	Page 215	
DLGN 25	Page 215	
DLGN 35–37	Pages 215–217	
DLGN 38–41	To CGN 38–41, page 217	
DM 1–7	Ex DD 96–102, page 176	
DM 8–10	Ex DD 110–112, page 176	
DM 11–14	Ex DD 171–174, page 176	
DM 15–16	Ex DD 123–124, page 177	
DM 17–18	Ex DD 121–122, page 177	
DM 19	Ex DD 214, page 182	
DM 20–22	Ex DD 345–347, page 183	
DM 23–28	Ex DD 735–740, page 201	
DM 29–31	Ex DD 749–751, page 201	
DM 32–34	Ex DD 771–773, page 201	
DMS 1	Ex DD 117, page 175	
DMS 2	Ex DD 119, page 177	
DMS 3	Ex DD 136, page 175	
DMS 4	Ex DD 146, page 175	
DMS 5	Ex DD 161, page 176	
DMS 6–8	Ex DD 178–180, page 176	
DMS 9–12	Ex DD 206–209, page 182	
DMS 13	Ex DD 249, page 182	
DMS 14–17	Ex DD 337–340, page 182	
DMS 18	Ex DD 141, page 175	
DMS 19–23	Ex DD 454–458, page 191	
DMS 24–25	Ex DD 461–462, page 191	
DMS 26	Ex DD 464, page 191	
DMS 27	Ex DD 621, page 191	
DMS 28	Ex DD 625, page 191	
DMS 29–30	Ex DD 636–637, page 191	
DMS 31–32	Ex DD 489–490, page 191	
DMS 33–36	Ex DD 493–496, page 191	
DMS 37	Ex DD 618, page 191	
DMS 38	Ex DD 627, page 191	
DMS 39–42	Ex DD 632–635, page 191	
FF 1098	Ex AGDE 1, page 244	
FF (others)	Ex DE, pages 219–244	
FFG 1–6	Ex DEG 1–6, page 245	
FFG 7–61	Pages 251–252	
FFR	Ex DER, ex DE, pages 219–244	
IX 1	Ex PG 10, page 158	
IX 2	Boston, page 141	
IX 4	Ex BM 10, page 101	
IX 5	Chicago, page 141	
IX 6	Ex BB 4, page 103	
IX 9	Ex PG 17, page 160	
IX 10	Essex, page 77	
IX 13	Hartford, page 63	
IX 15	Ex BB 7, page 104	
IX 16	Ex BB 5, page 103	
IX 17	Ex BM 3, page 99	
IX 18	Ranger, page 78	
IX 19	Ex PG 12, page 158	
IX 20	Constellation, page 23	
IX 21	Constitution, page 9	
IX 22	Ex BB 3, page 103	
IX 23	Ex PG 18, page 160	
IX 24	Ex Cruiser 4, page 143	
IX 25	Reina Mercedes, page 145	
IX 28	Ex PG 14, page 159	
IX 30	Ex PG 8, page 158	
IX 31	Michigan, page 82	
IX 32	Yantic, page 76	
IX 35	Ex DD 302, page 183	
IX 36 (1)	Ex DD 107, page 176	
IX 36 (2)	Ex DD 136, page 175	
IX 37 (1)	Ex DD 275, page 183	
IX 37 (2)	Ex DD 137, page 175	
IX 39	Ex CA 11, page 135	
IX 40	Ex Cruiser 6, page 144	
IX 44	Ex DD 163, page 176	
IX 98	Ex DD 259, page 183	
IX 182	Ex DE 56, page 232	
IX 300	Page 140	
IX 304	Ex CL 104, page 151	
IXSS	Ex SS, pages 271–283	
LPH 1	Ex CVE 106, page 132	
LPH 4	Ex CV 21, page 119	
LPH 5	Ex CV 37, page 119	
LPH 6	Ex ACV 90, page 131	
LPH 8	Ex CV 45, page 119	
LPR	Ex APD (see above)	
LPSS	Ex SS, pages 271–283	
MMD	Ex DM (see above)	
PF 1–2	Ex PG 101–102, page 246	
PF 3–108	Pages 246–251	
PF 109–112	Ex FFG 7–10, page 252	
PF 150	Ex FFG 7, page 252	
PG 1–15	Pages 155–158	
PG 17–19	Page 160	
PG 21–22	Page 160	
PG 23	Ranger, page 78	
PG 24	Dolphin, page 161	
PG 25–26	Ex Cruisers 7–8, page 144	
PG 27	Ex Cruiser 11, page 144	
PG 28–33	Ex Cruisers 14–19, page 146	

PG 34	New Orleans, page 145
PG 35	Topeka, page 159
PG 36	Albany, page 145
PG 38	Elcano, page 160
PG 50-51	Page 161
PG 101-110	Pages 245-246
PG 111-210	To PF 3-102, page 251
SC 1-2	Page 267
SC 3	To SS 169, page 267
SC 4-5	To SS 170-171, page 268
Scout Cruisers 1-3	Page 147
Scout Cruisers 4-13	To CL 4-13, page 148
SF 1	Ex SS 52, page 260
SF 2-3	Ex SS 60-61, page 260
SF 4-6	Page 265
SF 7	To SM 1, page 267
SF 8-9	To SC 1-2, page 267
SF 10	To SS 169, page 267
SF 11-12	To SS 170-171, page 268
SM 1	Page 265
SS 1-19	Pages 253-256
SS 19 1/2	Seal, page 256
SS 20 (1)	Page 257
SS 20 (2)	Seal, page 256
SS 21-162	Pages 257-265
SS 163-165	To SF 4-6, page 265
SS 166	To SM 1, pages 265, 267
SS 167-168	To SC 1-2, pages 265, 267
SS 169-550	Pages 267-281
SS 551-556 (1)	Page 282
SS 551-552 (2)	Ex SSK 2-3, page 284
SS 553-554 (2)	Page 283
SS 555-556 (2)	Page 283
SS 557-568	Page 282
SS 572-573	Ex SSR 572-573, page 291
SS 574	To SSG 574, page 292
SS 576	Page 283
SS 577	To SSG 577, page 292
SS 580-582	Page 283
SS-T3	Ex SSK 1, page 284
SSA	Ex SS, pages 271-283
SSAG 567	Ex SS 567, page 282
SSBN 1	To SSBN 726, page 296
SSBN 598-602	Page 293
SSBN 608-611	Page 293
SSBN 616-620	Page 293
SSBN 622-636	Page 293-295
SSBN 640-645	Page 295
SSBN 654-659	Page 295
SSBN 711	To SSBN 726, page 296
SSBN 726-742	Page 295
SSG 574	Page 291
SSG 577	Page 292
SSG (others)	Ex SS, pages 271-283
SSGN 587	Page 292
SSGN 594-96	To SSN 594-96, page 287
SSGN 598-600	To SSBN 598-600, page 293
SSGN 607	To SSN 607, page 287
SSK 1-3	Page 284
SSK (others)	Ex SS, pages 271-283
SSKN 597	To SSN 597, page 287
SSN 571	Page 284
SSN 575	Page 284
SSN 578-579	Page 286
SSN 583-585	Page 286
SSN 586	Ex SSRN 586, page 291
SSN 587	Ex SSGN 587, page 292
SSN 588-597	Pages 286-287
SSN 598-599	Ex SSBN 598-599, page 293
SSN 601	Ex SSBN 601, page 293
SSN 603-607	Page 286
SSN 608-611	Ex SSBN 608-611, page 293
SSN 612-615	Pages 286-287
SSN 618	Ex SSBN 618, page 293
SSN 621	Page 286
SSN 637-639	Page 288
SSN 646-653	Page 288
SSN 660-725	Pages 288-290
SSN 750-773	Page 290
SSO	Ex SS, pages 271-283
SSP	Ex SS, pages 271-283
SSR 572-573	Page 291
SSR (others)	Ex SS, pages 271-283
SSRN 586	Page 291
SST 1-2	Page 296
SST 3	Ex SSK 1, page 284
Torpedo Boats 1-35	Pages 162-167
YFB 3-4	Ex Torpedo Boats 15-16, page 165
YW 56	Ex DD 259, page 183
YW 57	Ex DD 163, page 183

Index

Ship names in ALL CAPS have primary entries in the tables; others are only mentioned elsewhere. Hull numbers and dates refer to the main listings for the ships and their classes. Non-standard abbreviations: C = Protected or Unprotected Cruiser, CS = Scout Cruiser, TB = Torpedo Boat.

9 de Julio, 148
17 de Octubre, 148
18 de Julio, 239
25 de Julio, 230
A-1 (SS-2), 254
A-2 (SS-3), 254
A-3 (SS-4), 254
A-4 (SS-5), 254
A-5 (SS-6), 254
A-6 (SS-7), 254
A-7 (SS-8), 254
A. D. Vance, 93
A. O. Tyler, 96
AA-1 (SS-52), 255 (photo), 259, 267
AA-2 (SS-60), 259
AA-3 (SS-61), 259
AARON WARD (DD-132), 174
AARON WARD (DD-483), 190
AARON WARD (DD-773), 201
Abadejo (SS-308), 279
ABBOT (DD-184), 177
ABBOT (DD-629), 195
ABEL P. UPSHUR (DD-193), 178
ABERCROMBIE (DE-343), 235
ABILENE (PF-58), 248
ABNER READ (DD-526), 193
ABNER READ (DD-769), 202
ABRAHAM LINCOLN (CVN-72), 125
ABRAHAM LINCOLN (SSBN-602), 293
Acedia (SS-309), 279
Achilles (1863), 45
Acoupa (SS-310), 279
ACREE (DE-167), 222
Acushnet, 257
ADAMS (1798), 10, 17
ADAMS (1812), 17
ADAMS (1873), 74 (photo), 77
ADAMS (DD-739), 200
Adatepe, 204
ADDER (SS-3), 253
ADELA (1863), 92
(ADELAIDE) (FFG-17), 252
ADIRONDACK (1861), 67
ADMIRALTY ISLANDS (ACV-99), 130
Adriana, 33
Adur, 246
ADVANCE (1864), 93
Aetna (1863), 45
Aetos, 224
Affleck, 227
AG 17-20, 264
AG-27-28, 264
AGAMENTICUS (1862), 41 (photo), 43
AGAWAM (1862), 80
AGERHOLM (DD-826), 203
Agua Prieta, 157

Aguirre, 223
Ah San, 234
AHRENS (DE-575), 230
AINSWORTH (DE-1090), 244
Ajax (1862), 44
(AKIZUKI) (DD-961), 208
Alabama (1816), 4
ALABAMA (1861), 86
ALABAMA (BB-8), 104
ALABAMA (BB-60), 113
Alabama (CSS), 86
ALABAMA (SSBN-731), 295
Alagoas, 200
Alamgir, 204
ALARM (1874), 83, 84 (photo)
ALASKA (1867), 70
ALASKA (CB-1), 135, 152
ALASKA (SSBN-732), 295
Alava Bay (ACV-103), 131
Alazan Bay (ACV-94), 131
Alazon Bay (ACV-55), 131
Alazon Bay (ACV-94), 131
ALBACORE (AGSS-569), 283, 286, 296
ALBACORE (SS-218), 271
ALBANY (1843), 20
Albany (1863), 69
ALBANY (1898), 145
Albany (CA-72), 139
ALBANY (CA-123), 139; (CG-10), 155
ALBANY (SSN-753), 290
Albatros, 251
ALBATROSS (1861), 90
Albatross (PG-7), 157
ALBEMARLE (1865), 47, 85, 95
ALBERT DAVID (DE-1050), 243
ALBERT T. HARRIS (DE-447), 237
ALBERT W. GRANT (DD-649), 195
ALBUQUERQUE (PF-7), 246, 249 (photo)
ALBUQUERQUE (SSN-706), 289
Alcala Galiano, 196
Alcitepe, 203
Aldebaran, 223
ALDEN (DD-211), 179
ALERT (1812), 33
ALERT (1864), 76
ALERT (1873), 78
Alert (HMS), 34
Alex Diachenko (DE-690), 235
Alexander Dallas (DD-199), 182
ALEXANDER HAMILTON (SSBN-617), 293
Alexander Hamilton (ex PG-11), 158
ALEXANDER J. LUKE (DE-577), 230
Alexandre Petion, 88
ALEXANDRIA (PF-18), 247
ALEXANDRIA (SSN-757), 290
ALFRED (1775), 33

ALFRED A. CUNNINGHAM (DD-752), 200
ALFRED WOLF (DE-544), 238
Alfredo Cappellini, 276
ALGER (DE-101), 222
Algerien, 222
Algoma (1863), 45
ALGOMA (1864), 69, 71
ALGOMA (1867), 70
ALGONQUIN (1862), 80
Alick Scott, 50
Alikula Bay (ACV-57), 131
Alikula Bay (ACV-95), 131
ALLEGHANY (1844), 61
ALLEN (DD-66), 172
ALLEN M. SUMNER (DD-692), 199, 205
ALLENTOWN (PF-52), 247
ALLIANCE (1776), 7
ALLIANCE (1873), 77
Alliance, later HURON (1873), 78
ALLIGATOR (1820), 31
ALLIGATOR (1862), 83
Almirante Abreu, 145
Almirante Brion (ex DE-215), 230
Almirante Brion (ex PF-51), 247
Almirante Brown, 193
Almirante Domecq Garcia, 195
Almirante Ferrandiz, 194
(ALMIRANTE GAGO COUTINHO) (DE-1042), 241
Almirante Garcia de los Reyes, 277
Almirante Guise, 193
(ALMIRANTE MAGALHAES CORREIA) (DE-1046),
    241
Almirante Padilla (ex DE-593), 234
Almirante Padilla (ex PF-29), 247
(ALMIRANTE PEREIRA DA SILVA) (DE-1039),
    241
Almirante Storni, 194
Almirante Tono, 231
Almirante Valdes, 193
Alonzo Child, 46
Altair, 224
ALTAMAHA (ACV-6), 128
ALTAMAHA (ACV-18), 127 (photo), 128
Alton (IX-5), 141
ALVIN C. COCKRELL (DE-366), 236
Amatsukaze, 189
Amazonas, later NEW ORLEANS (1898), 145
Amazonas (ex SS-351), 277
Amazone, 16
AMBERJACK (SS-219), 271
AMBERJACK (SS-522), 281
Ameer (ex ACV-35), 128
Ameer (ex ACV-55), 131
Ameer (ex ACV-56), 131
AMERICA (1776), 1
AMERICA (CVA-66), 124
AMESBURY (DE-66), 227
Amfitriti, 272
AMICK (DE-168), 222
AMMEN (DD-35), 170
AMMEN (DD-527), 193
AMMONOOSUC (1863), 58
Amphitrite (1862), 43
AMPHITRITE (BM-2), 99

AMSTERDAM (CL-59), 120, 151
AMSTERDAM (CL-101), 151
An Yang, 193
Ancud, 94
(ANDALUCIA) (DEG-8), 245
ANDERSON (DD-411), 185 (photo), 188
ANDRES (DE-45), 220
ANDREW DORIA (1775), 34, 37
ANDREW JACKSON (SSBN-619), 293
Andromeda, 223
ANGLER (SS-240), 272
Anguilla Bay (ACV-58), 131
Anguilla Bay (ACV-96), 131
Anguilla, 248
Anittepe, 203
Annan, 246
Annapolis (AGMR-1), 132
ANNAPOLIS (PF-15), 247
ANNAPOLIS (PG-10), 158, 159
ANNAPOLIS (SSN-760), 290
Annapolis (ex DD-175), 176
Annie, 94
Anniston (C-9), 144
Anoushirvan, 212
ANTHONY (DD-172), 176
Anthony (DD-266), 182
ANTHONY (DD-515), 193, 197 (photo)
ANTIETAM (1863), 59, 62
ANTIETAM (CG-54), 218
ANTIETAM (CV-36), 119
(ANTIGUA) (PF-73), 248
Antioquia, 195
ANTONA (1863), 92
Antonio Maceo, 248
ANTRIM (FFG-20), 252
Anzio (ACV-57), 131
ANZIO (CG-68), 218
Apnok, 247
APOGON (SS-308), 275
Apostolis, 203
Arabe, 223
Arago, 92
ARAPAHO (1863), 69
Arbiter, 129
ARCHER (1846), 27
(ARCHER) (BAVG-1), 125
Archer-Fish (SS-311), 279
ARCHERFISH (SS-311), 276
ARCHERFISH (SSN-678), 288
Ardeshir, 212
Argonaut (SM-1), 267
ARGONAUT (SS-475), 280
ARGUS (1803), 25
ARGUS (1813), 17
Argus (1863), 45
Ariadne, 33
Ariake, 195
ARIEL (1780), 16
ARIES (1863), 88
Arizona, ex NESHAMINY (1863), 58
ARIZONA (1863), 88
ARIZONA (BB-39), 109, 110 (photo)
ARKANSAS (1863), 88
ARKANSAS (BB-33), 108

ARKANSAS (BM-7), 101
ARKANSAS (CGN-41), 217
ARLEIGH BURKE (DDG-51), 212
Arlington (AGMR-2), 121
Arnillo (SS-312), 279
ARNOLD J. ISBELL (DD-869), 204
AROOSTOOK (1861), 73
ARTHUR L. BRISTOL (DE-281), 233
ARTHUR W. RADFORD (DD-968), 210
Artigas, 223
Artigliere, 188
Asahi, 222
Asakaze, 190
(ASCENSION) (PF-74), 248
ASCUTNEY (1862), 80
ASHEVILLE (PG-21), 160
ASHEVILLE (PG-101), 245
Asheville (SSN-757), 290
ASHEVILLE (SSN-758), 290
ASHUELOT (1863), 82
Aslat, 243
Aspis, 195
ASPRO (SS-309), 275
ASPRO (SSN-648), 288
Astoria (1867), 70
ASTORIA (CA-34), 138
ASTORIA (CL-90), 151
Astrolabe Bay (ACV-60), 131
Astrolabe Bay (ACV-97), 131
(ASTURIAS) (DEG-10), 245
Atahualpa, 44
Atalanta (1858), 90
Atheling (ex ACV-33), 128
Atheling (ex ACV-58), 131
Atheling (ex ACV-59), 131
ATHERTON (DE-169), 222
ATLANTA (1863), 46
ATLANTA (1883), 141, 142 (photo)
ATLANTA (CL-51), 139, 150, 152, 213
ATLANTA (CL-104), 151
ATLANTA (SSN-712), 289
Atlantic, later ESSEX JUNIOR (1813), 34
Atlantic, later COMMODORE READ (1863), 96
Atlas (1862), 42
Attacker, 128
ATTU (ACV-102), 130
ATULE (SS-403), 278
AUBREY FITCH (FFG-34), 252
Augusta (1798), 35
AUGUSTA (1799), 35
AUGUSTA (1861), 86
AUGUSTA (CA-31), 136
AUGUSTA (SSN-710), 289
AUGUSTA DINSMORE (1863), 88
AULICK (DD-258), 180
AULICK (DD-569), 194
AULT (DD-698), 199
Ausburn (DD-294), 182
AUSTIN (1846), 23
AUSTIN (DE-15), 219
AVENGER (1864), 97
(AVENGER) (BAVG-2), 125
Aviere, 190
Awa (SS-409), 279

Aylmer, 227
AYLWIN (DD-47), 170
AYLWIN (DD-355), 183
AYLWIN (DE-1081), 243
Azuma, 47
B-1 (SS-10), 254
B-2 (SS-11), 254
B-3 (SS-12), 254
BABBITT (DD-128), 178
Babitonga, 222
Babr, 201
BACHE (DD-470), 192
BADGER (1898), 297
BADGER (DD-126), 178
BADGER (DE-1071), 243
BADOENG STRAIT (CVE-116), 127 (photo),
    131
Badr, 245
Baependi, 222
BAFFINS (ACV-35), 128
BAGLEY (DD-185), 177
BAGLEY (DD-386), 186, 187
BAGLEY (DE-1069), 243
BAGLEY (TB-24), 167
(BAHAMAS) (PF-75), 248
Bahia (ex SS-390), 278
Bahia (ex SS-483), 280
BAILEY (DD-269), 180
BAILEY (DD-492), 188
BAILEY (TB-21), 166
BAINBRIDGE (1841), 27
BAINBRIDGE (DD-1), 168
BAINBRIDGE (DD-246), 179
BAINBRIDGE (DLGN-25), 215
BAIROKO (CVE-115), 131
BAKER (DE-190), 223
BALAO (SS-285), 273, 275, 281
BALCH (DD-50), 170
BALCH (DD-363), 183
BALDUCK (DE-716), 234
BALDWIN (DD-624), 191
(BALEARES) (DEG-7), 245
Balfour, 227
Balinas (AVG-36), 129
Balize, 97
BALLARD (DD-267), 180
BALTIMORE (1798), 33
BALTIMORE (C-3), 143
BALTIMORE (CA-68), 121, 139, 140, 155
BALTIMORE (SSN-704), 289
Bambara, 223
BANCROFT (1888), 157
BANCROFT (DD-256), 180
BANCROFT (DD-598), 189
BANG (SS-385), 278
BANGOR (PF-16), 247
BANGUST (DE-739), 223
BANSHEE (1864), 93
Banta (SS-545), 281
BARATARIA (1863), 52
BARB (SS-220), 271
BARB (SSN-596), 286
Barb (SSN-603), 287
(BARBADOS) (PF-76), 248

BARBEL (SS-316), 276
BARBEL (SS-580), 283
BARBER (DE-161), 228
BARBERO (SS-317), 276
BARBEY (DE-1088), 243
BARKER (DD-213), 179
(BARLE) (PG-103), 246
BARNES (ACV-7), 128
BARNES (ACV-20), 128
BARNEY (DD-149), 174
BARNEY (DDG-6), 211
BARNEY (TB-25), 167
BARON (DE-166), 222
Baron de Kalb (1861), 48 (photo), 49
BARR (DE-576), 230
Barracuda (SS-21), 257
Barracuda (SS-163), 265
Barracuda (SSK-1), 284
Barroso, 148
BARRY (DD-2), 168
BARRY (DD-248), 179
BARRY (DD-933), 207
BARRY (DDG-52), 212
BARTON (DD-599), 189
BARTON (DD-722), 199
BASHAW (SS-241), 272
BASILONE (DD-824), 203
Bass (SS-164), 265
Bass (SSK-2), 284
BASSETT (DE-672), 231
BASTIAN (ACV-37), 128
BASTOGNE (CVE-124), 132
BAT (1864), 93
BATAAN (CV-29), 120
BATES (DE-68), 227
BATFISH (SS-310), 275
BATFISH (SSN-681), 288
BATH (PF-55), 248
Bath (ex DD-181), 177
BATON ROUGE (SSN-689), 289
Battler, 128
BAUER (DE-1025), 239
Bauru, 223
BAUSELL (DD-845), 203
BAYA (SS-318), 276
(BAYANDOR) (PF-103), 251
(BAYNTUN) (BDE-1), 219
BAYONNE (PF-21), 247
(BAZELY) (BDE-2), 219
BEALE (DD-40), 170
BEALE (DD-471), 192
BEARSS (DD-654), 195
Beatty (DD-528), 198
BEATTY (DD-640), 191
BEATTY (DD-756), 200
Beatty (DD-873), 206
BEAUFORT (PF-59), 248
BEBAS (DE-10), 219
Beberibe, 223
BECUNA (SS-319), 276
BEGOR (DE-711), 234
Begum (ex ACV-36), 128
Begum (ex ACV-62), 131
BELET (DE-599), 234

BELFAST (PF-35), 247
BELKNAP (DD-251), 179
BELKNAP (DLG-26), 215
BELL (DD-95), 175
BELL (DD-587), 195
BELLEAU WOOD (CV-24), 120
Belmont, 178
Belvidera, 35
Benevente, 222
BENHAM (DD-49), 170
BENHAM (DD-397), 184, 186, 187, 188
BENHAM (DD-796), 196
Benicia (1867), 63, 70
BENJAMIN FRANKLIN (SSBN-640), 295
BENJAMIN STODDERT (DDG-22), 211
BENNER (DD-807), 203
BENNER (DE-551), 238
BENNETT (DD-473), 192
BENNINGTON (CV-20), 118
BENNINGTON (PG-4), 155, 156 (photo)
BENNION (DD-662), 195
BENSON (DD-421), 188, 191, 198
Bentinck (ex DE-13), 221
Bentinck (ex DE-52), 227
Bentley, 227
BENTON (1861), 49
Berbere, 222
BERCEAU (1800), 17
Berceau (ferry), 165
BERGALL (SS-320), 276
BERGALL (SSN-667), 288
Berk, 241
BERKELEY (DDG-15), 211
BERNADOU (DD-153), 174
Berry (ex DE-14), 221
(BERRY) (BDE-3), 219
Bertioga, 223
BESUGO (SS-321), 276
Beta, 158
BEVERLY W. REID (DE-722), 235
Beverly, 178
Bickerton, 227
BIDDLE (DD-151), 174
BIDDLE (DDG-5), 211
BIDDLE (DLG-34), 215
BIDDLE (TB-26), 167
BIENVILLE (1861), 86, 92
BIGELOW (DD-942), 207
BILLFISH (SS-286), 275
BILLFISH (SSN-676), 288
BILLINGSLEY (DD-293), 180
BILOXI (CL-80), 151
Birinci Inonu (ex SS-330), 276
Birinci Inonu (ex SS-410), 278
BIRMINGHAM (CL-62), 151
BIRMINGHAM (CS-2), 147
BIRMINGHAM (SSN-695), 289
BISBEE (PF-46), 247
BISMARCK SEA (ACV-95), 130
(BITER) (BAVG-3), 125
BIVIN (DE-536), 238
BLACK (DD-666), 196
BLACK HAWK (1862), 97
Black Prince, 33

BLACKFIN (SS-322), 276
BLACKFISH (SS-221), 271
Blackwood (ex DE-15), 221
(BLACKWOOD) (BDE-4), 219
BLAIR (DE-147), 225
BLAKELEY (DD-150), 174
BLAKELY (DE-1072), 243
BLAKELY (TB-27), 167
Blanco Encalada, 196
BLANDY (DD-943), 207
Blanquillo (SS-323), 279
Blas de Lezo, 203
BLENNY (SS-324), 276
BLESSMAN (DE-69), 227
Bligh, 227
BLOCK ISLAND (ACV-8), 128
BLOCK ISLAND (ACV-21), 128
Block Island (AVG-19), 129
BLOCK ISLAND (CVE-106), 131
BLOWER (SS-325), 276
BLUE (DD-387), 186
BLUE (DD-744), 200
BLUEBACK (SS-326), 276
BLUEBACK (SS-581), 283
BLUEFISH (SS-222), 271
BLUEFISH (SSN-675), 288
BLUEGILL (SS-242), 272
BOARFISH (SS-327), 276
Bocaccio (SS-328), 279
Bocaina, 222
BOGGS (DD-136), 174
BOGUE (ACV-9), 128
Bois Belleau, 120
BOISE (CL-47), 148
BOISE (SSN-764), 290
BOLINAS (ACV-36), 128
BON HOMME RICHARD (1779), 8, 33
BON HOMME RICHARD (1863), 58
Bon Homme Richard (CV-10), 118
BON HOMME RICHARD (CV-31), 118
Bonaci (SS-329), 279
BONEFISH (SS-223), 271
BONEFISH (SS-582), 283
BONITA (SS-15), 254
Bonita (SS-165), 265
Bonita (SSK-3), 284
BOONE (FFG-28), 252
BOOTH (DE-170), 222
BORDELON (DD-881), 204
Boreas, 34
BORIE (DD-215), 179
BORIE (DD-704), 199
BORUM (DE-790), 231
BOSTON (1775), 6, 8
BOSTON (1798), 10, 17
BOSTON (1825), 19
BOSTON (1883), 141
BOSTON (CA-69), 139; (CAG-1), 153
BOSTON (SSN-703), 289
BOSTWICK (DE-103), 222
BOUGAINVILLE (ACV-100), 130
BOURBON (1777), 8
BOWEN (DE-1079), 243
BOWERS (DE-637), 230

BOWFIN (SS-287), 275
BOXER (1814), 26
BOXER (1831), 31
Boxer (1864), 95
BOXER (CV-21), 119
Boyaca, 239
BOYD (DD-544), 193
BOYLE (DD-600), 189
BRACKETT (DE-41), 219
Bracui, 223
BRADFORD (DD-545), 193
Bradford, 180
BRADLEY (DE-1041), 241, 242 (photo)
BRAINE (DD-630), 195
Braithwaite, 227
BRANCH (DD-197), 178
Branch (DD-310), 182
BRANDYWINE (1816), 14
BRAY (DE-709), 234
BREAM (SS-243), 272
BRECK (DD-283), 180
BRECKINRIDGE (DD-148), 174
BREEMAN (DE-104), 222
BREESE (DD-122), 177
BREMERTON (CA-130), 139, 155
BREMERTON (SSN-698), 289
BRENNAN (DE-13), 219
BRETON (ACV-10), 128
BRETON (ACV-23), 128
BREWTON (DE-1086), 243
BRIDGEPORT (CA-127), 139
Bridgeport (PF-58), 251
BRIDGET (DE-1024), 239
BRIGHT (DE-747), 223
Brighton, 176
BRILL (SS-330), 276
BRINKLEY BASS (DD-887), 205
(BRISBANE) (DDG-27), 211
BRISCOE (DD-977), 210
BRISTER (DE-327), 225
BRISTOL (DD-453), 190
BRISTOL (DD-857), 201
BRITANNIA (1863), 92
Broadwater, 178
Broadway, 178
BROCK (DE-234), 233
BRONSTEIN (DE-189), 223
BRONSTEIN (DE-1037), 241, 243
BROOKE (DEG-1), 245, 244
BROOKLYN (1857), 63, 92
BROOKLYN (CA-3), 133, 134 (photo)
BROOKLYN (CL-40), 138, 148, 150
BROOKS (DD-232), 179
BROOME (DD-210), 179
BROUGH (DE-148), 225
BROWN (DD-546), 193
BROWNSON (DD-518), 193
BROWNSON (DD-868), 204
BROWNSVILLE (PF-10), 246
BRUCE (DD-329), 181
BRUMBY (DE-1044), 241
BRUNSWICK (PF-68), 248
BRUSH (DD-745), 200
BRYANT (DD-665), 196

Bucareli Bay (ACV-61), 131
Bucareli Bay (ACV-98), 131
BUCHANAN (DD-131), 174
BUCHANAN (DD-484), 190
BUCHANAN (DDG-14), 211
BUCK (DD-420), 188
BUCK (DD-761), 200
BUCKLEY (DE-51), 224, 226, 227, 229, 235
BUFFALO (1898), 297, 298
BUFFALO (CL-84), 151
BUFFALO (CL-99), 120, 151
BUFFALO (CL-110), 152
BUFFALO (SSN-715), 289
BUGARA (SS-331), 276
BULL (DE-52), 227
BULL (DE-693), 231
Bull Dog, 37
BULLARD (DD-660), 195
(BULLEN) (DE-78), 227
BULLHEAD (SS-332), 276
BULMER (DD-222), 179
BUMPER (SS-333), 276
Buna, 247
BUNCH (DE-694), 231
BUNKER HILL (CG-52), 218
BUNKER HILL (CV-17), 118
Burak Reis, 278
BURDEN R. HASTINGS (DE-19), 219
BURDO (DE-717), 235
Burges (ex DE-16), 221
(BURGES) (BDE-12), 219
BURKE (DE-215), 230
BURLINGTON (PF-51), 247
Burnham, 180
BURNS (DD-171), 176
BURNS (DD-588), 195
BURRFISH (SS-312), 276
BURROWS (DD-29), 169
BURROWS (DE-105), 222
Burwell, 180
BUSH (DD-166), 176
BUSH (DD-529), 193
BUTLER (DD-636), 191
Buxton, 180
Byard (ex DE-17), 221
Byard (ex DE-55), 227
(BYRON) (DE-79), 227
C-1 (SS-9), 254
C-2 (SS-13), 254
C-3 (SS-14), 254, 255 (photo)
C-4 (SS-15), 254
C-5 (SS-16), 254
C.E. Hillman, 50
CABANA (DE-260), 220
CABEZON (SS-334), 276
CABOT (1775), 34
Cabot (CV-16), 118
CABOT (CV-28), 120
CABRILLA (SS-288), 275
Cachalot (SS-33), 258
CACHALOT (SS-170), 268
Cadmus, 62
(CAICOS) (PF-77), 248
CAIMAN (SS-323), 276

CAIRO (1861), 49
CALCATERRA (DE-390), 226
Caldas, 201
Calder (ex DE-18), 221
Calder (ex DE-58), 227
Calder (ex DE-307), 221
CALDWELL (DD-69), 172
CALDWELL (DD-605), 189
Caldwell (ex DD-133), 174
Caledonia (1858), 90
CALHOUN (1862), 91
California (1863), 59
California (BB-40), 111
CALIFORNIA (BB-44), 111
CALIFORNIA (CA-6), 133
CALIFORNIA (DLGN-36), 217
California (ex DE-599), 234
California (ex PF-45), 247
CALLAGHAN (DD-792), 196
CALLAGHAN (DDG-994), 212
Callao, 159
CALYPSO (1863), 92, 94
CAMANCHE (1862), 42
CAMBRIDGE (1861), 86
Cambridge (1863), 69
CAMBRIDGE (CA-126), 139
Camden (AOE-2), 113
Cameron, 180
CAMP (DE-251), 225
Campbell (DE-70), 232
Campbeltown, 174
Canakkale (ex SS-333), 276
Canakkale (ex SS-344), 276
CANANDAIGUA (1861), 68, 94
CANBERRA (CA-70), 139; (CAG-2), 153
(CANBERRA) (FFG-18), 252
CANFIELD (DE-262), 220
CANNON (DE-99), 222, 231
CANONICUS (1862), 44
Canopo, 240
CAPE ESPERANCE (ACV-88), 130
CAPE GLOUCESTER (CVE-109), 131
CAPE ST. GEORGE (CG-71), 218
Capel (ex DE-45), 221
Capel (ex DE-266), 220
CAPELIN (SS-289), 275
CAPERTON (DD-650), 195
Capidoli (SS-325), 279
CAPITAINE (SS-336), 276
Capitan Prat, 148
Capitan Tono, 247
CAPODANNO (DE-1093), 244
CAPPS (DD-550), 194
Carabobo, 200
CARBONERO (SS-337), 276
CARD (ACV-11), 128
Carite, 275
CARL VINSON (CVN-70), 125
CARLSON (DE-9), 219
CARMICK (DD-493), 190
CARNEGIE (ACV-38), 128
CAROLINA (1812), 36
Caroline, 88
CARON (DD-970), 210

CARONDELET (1861), 49
Carp (SS-20), 257
CARP (SS-338), 276
CARPELLOTTI (DE-548), 238
CARPELLOTTI (DE-720), 235
CARPENTER (DD-825), 203
CARR (FFG-52), 252
CARROLL (DE-171), 222
CARSON CITY (PF-50), 247
CARTER (DE-112), 222
CASABLANCA (ACV-55), 130, 132
CASCO (1863), 45
CASE (DD-285), 180
CASE (DD-370), 184
CASIMIR PULASKI (SSBN-633), 295
CASPER (PF-12), 246
CASSIN (DD-43), 170
CASSIN (DD-372), 184, 185 (photo)
CASSIN YOUNG (DD-793), 196
Castilla, 223
CASTINE (PG-6), 157
CASTLE (DD-720), 202
Castleton, 174
Castor (1862), 44
(CASTORE) (DE-1031), 240
(CATALUNA) (DEG-9), 245
CATAWBA (1862), 44
CATES (DE-763), 224
CATFISH (SS-339), 276
CATSKILL (1862), 42
CAVALLA (SS-244), 272
CAVALLA (SSN-684), 288
CAVALLARO (DE-712), 234
(CAYMAN) (PF-78), 248
CAYUGA (1861), 73
Ceara, 281
CECIL J. DOYLE (DE-368), 236
Centaur (1862), 44
Centauro, 240
Cerbe (ex SS-364), 273
Cerbe (ex SS-421), 280
Ceres, 33
CERO (SS-225), 271
CHAFFEE (DE-230), 233
CHAMBERS (DE-391), 226
CHAMPLIN (DD-104), 175
CHAMPLIN (DD-601), 189
CHANCELLORSVILLE (CG-62), 218
CHANDLER (DD-206), 179
CHANDLER (DDG-996), 212
Chao Yang (ex DD-718), 202
Chao Yang (ex DD-782), 202
Chapin Bay (ACV-63), 131
Chapin Bay (ACV-99), 131
CHARETTE (DD-581), 195
CHARGER (BAVG-4), 125
Charger (ex ACV-24), 128
Charity, 208
CHARLES AUSBURN (DD-294), 180
CHARLES AUSBURNE (DD-570), 194
CHARLES BERRY (DE-1035), 240
CHARLES E. BRANNON (DE-446), 237
CHARLES F. ADAMS (DDG-2), 211
CHARLES F. HUGHES (DD-428), 188

CHARLES H. ROAN (DD-815), 203
CHARLES H. ROAN (DD-853), 204
CHARLES J. BADGER (DD-657), 195
CHARLES J. KIMMEL (DE-584), 233
CHARLES LAWRENCE (DE-53), 227
CHARLES P. CECIL (DD-835), 203
Charles P. Cecil (FFG-850), 206
CHARLES R. GREER (DE-23), 219
CHARLES R. WARE (DD-865), 204
CHARLES R. WARE (DE-547), 238
CHARLES S. SPERRY (DD-697), 199
CHARLESTON (C-2), 143
CHARLESTON (C-22), 142 (photo), 146
CHARLESTON (PG-51), 161
Charlestown, 177
Charlotte (CA-12), 135
CHARLOTTE (PF-60), 248
CHARLOTTE (SSN-766), 290
CHARLOTTESVILLE (PF-25), 247
Charoca (SS-546), 281
CHARR (SS-328), 276
Charybdis (1863), 45
CHASE (DD-323), 181
CHASE (DE-158), 228
Chaser, 128
CHATELAIN (DE-149), 225
CHATHAM (ACV-32), 128
CHATTANOOGA (1863), 59
CHATTANOOGA (C-16), 146
CHATTANOOGA (CL-118), 152
Chattanooga (PF-65), 251
CHAUNCEY (DD-3), 168
CHAUNCEY (DD-296), 180
CHAUNCEY (DD-667), 196
Chelsea, 174
Chemung (AO-30/AVG-29), 126
Chen Yang, 202
CHENANGO (1862), 80
CHENANGO (ACV-28), 126
CHEROKEE (1864), 94, 95
Cherub, 10
CHESAPEAKE (1794), 9
Chesapeake (1798), 17
CHESTER (CA-27), 136
CHESTER (CS-1), 13 (photo), 147
CHESTER T. O'BRIEN (DE-421), 237
Chesterfield, 178
CHEVALIER (DD-451), 192
CHEVALIER (DD-805), 202
CHEW (DD-106), 175
Cheyenne (BM-10), 101
Cheyenne (CL-86), 151
CHEYENNE (CL-117), 152
CHEYENNE (SSN-773), 290
Chi Ju, 233
Chiang Yang, 193
CHICAGO (1883), 141
CHICAGO (CA-29), 136
Chicago (CA-127), 140
CHICAGO (CA-136), 139; (CG-11), 155
CHICAGO (SSN-721), 289
CHICKASAW (1862), 52
Chickwick (SS-340), 279
CHICOLAR (SS-464), 279

CHICOPEE (1862), 80
Chien Yang, 202
Chihuahua, 233
CHILDS (DD-241), 179
CHILLICOTHE (1862), 50
CHIMO (1863), 45
CHIPPEWA (1813), 4
CHIPPEWA (1814), 26
CHIPPEWA (1861), 73
Chippeway (1814), 26
CHIVO (SS-341), 276
CHOCTAW (1862), 50
CHOCURA (1861), 73
CHOPPER (SS-342), 276
CHOSIN (CG-65), 218
CHRISTOPHER (DE-100), 222
CHUB (SS-329), 276
Chubb (SS-329), 279
Chubb, 37
Chung Bok, 202
Chung Mu, 195
Chung Nam, 234
Chung Shan, 227
Churchill, 178
Churruca, 202
(CIGNO) (DE-1020), 240
CIMARRON (1861), 79
Cimmerone (1861), 79
CINCINNATI (1861), 47, 48 (photo), 49
CINCINNATI (C-7), 144
CINCINNATI (CL-6), 148
CINCINNATI (SSN-693), 289
Cinemaugh (1861), 79
Circe (1862), 51
Cirrus, 248
CISCO (SS-290), 275
City of Boston, 89
CITY OF CORPUS CHRISTI (SSN-705), 289
City of New York, 297
City of Paris, 297
City of Philadelphia (1798), 10
CLAMAGORE (SS-343), 276
Clare, 178
CLARENCE K. BRONSON (DD-668), 196
CLARENCE L. EVANS (DE-113), 222
CLARK (DD-361), 183
CLARK (FFG-11), 251
CLAUD JONES (DE-1033), 240
Claude V. Ricketts (DDG-5), 211
CLAXTON (DD-140), 174
CLAXTON (DD-571), 194
CLEMSON (DD-186), 178
CLEVELAND (C-19), 146
CLEVELAND (CL-55), 120, 121, 139, 151, 152, 154
CLIFTON (1861), 95
Clifton, later SHOKOKON (1863), 96
CLIFTON SPRAGUE (FFG-16), 252
Clinton, 96
CLOUES (DE-265), 220
CLYDE (1863), 92
Coahuila, 228
Coast Battleship No. 1 (BB-1), 103
Coast Battleship No. 2 (BB-2), 103

Coast Battleship No. 4 (BB-4), 103
Coast Torpedo Boat No. 1 (TB-3), 164
Coast Torpedo Boat No. 2 (TB-4), 164
Coast Torpedo Boat No. 3 (TB-7), 164
Coast Torpedo Boat No. 4 (TB-9), 164
Coast Torpedo Boat No. 5 (TB-11), 165
Coast Torpedo Boat No. 6 (TB-14), 165
Coast Torpedo Boat No. 7 (TB-20), 166
Coast Torpedo Boat No. 8 (TB-21), 166
Coast Torpedo Boat No. 9 (TB-22), 166
Coast Torpedo Boat No. 10 (TB-24), 167
Coast Torpedo Boat No. 11 (TB-25), 167
Coast Torpedo Boat No. 12 (TB-26), 167
Coast Torpedo Boat No. 13 (TB-27), 167
Coast Torpedo Boat No. 14 (TB-28), 167
Coast Torpedo Boat No. 15 (TB-31), 167
Coast Torpedo Boat No. 16 (TB-33), 167
Coast Torpedo Boat No. 17 (TB-34), 167
COATES (DE-685), 234
COBBLER (SS-344), 276
COBIA (SS-245), 272
COCHINO (SS-345), 277
COCHRANE (DDG-21), 211
Cochrane (ex DD-804), 196
Cockburn, 221
COCKRILL (DE-398), 226
COD (SS-224), 271
COFER (DE-208), 228
COFFMAN (DE-191), 223
COGHLAN (DD-326), 181
COGHLAN (DD-606), 189
COGSWELL (DD-651), 195
COHOES (1863), 45
COLAHAN (DD-658), 195
COLE (DD-155), 174
COLHOUN (DD-85), 175
COLHOUN (DD-801), 196
COLLETT (DD-730), 200
COLORADO (1854), 55
COLORADO (BB-45), 112
COLORADO (CA-7), 106, 133
Colorado, later WHARTON (1846), 27
Colossus (1863), 46
COLUMBIA (1813), 12
COLUMBIA (1816), 14
COLUMBIA (1862), 91
COLUMBIA (1865), 46
COLUMBIA (C-12), 145
COLUMBIA (CL-56), 151
COLUMBIA (SSN-771), 290
Columbia (ex DD-183), 177
Columbine, 12
COLUMBUS (1775), 33
COLUMBUS (1799), 1, 17
COLUMBUS (1816), 4
COLUMBUS (CA-74), 139; (CG-12), 155
COLUMBUS (SSN-762), 290
COMBER (SS-527), 281
COMET (1813), 36
COMMENCEMENT BAY (CVE-105), 131
Commodore, 89
COMMODORE BARNEY (1861), 95
COMMODORE HULL (1862), 96
COMMODORE JONES (1863), 96

COMMODORE McDONOUGH (1862), 96
COMMODORE MORRIS (1862), 96
COMMODORE PERRY (1861), 95
COMMODORE READ (1863), 96
Comodoro Manuel Azueta, 225
Comodoro Py, 204
COMPTON (DD-705), 199
COMTE DE GRASSE (DD-974), 210
Concepcion, 89
CONCORD (1825), 19
CONCORD (CL-10), 148
CONCORD (PG-3), 155
CONE (DD-866), 204
CONEMAUGH (1861), 79, 84 (photo)
CONESTOGA (1861), 50, 96
Conestoga (1862), 42
CONFEDERACY (1777), 8
Confederate, 8
CONFIANCE (1814), 15
CONFIANCE (1864), 69
CONGER (SS-477), 280
CONGRESS (1775), 6
CONGRESS (1794), 9, 15
CONGRESS (1834), 15, 55
Congress (1863), 69
Congress, later GENERAL WASHINGTON
   (1782), 33
CONKLIN (DE-439), 237
(CONN) (DE-80), 227
CONNECTICUT (1798), 11, 35
CONNECTICUT (1861), 86
Connecticut (1863), 58
CONNECTICUT (BB-18), 106
Connecticut (BM-8), 101
CONNER (DD-72), 172
CONNER (DD-582), 195
CONNOLE (DE-1056), 243
CONNOLLY (DE-306), 220
CONOLLY (DD-979), 210
Conolly (DE-1073), 244
CONQUEST OF ITALY (1799), 35
CONSTELLATION (1794), 9, 11, 23
CONSTELLATION (1853), 23, 62
CONSTELLATION (CC-2), 114
CONSTELLATION (CVA-64), 124
CONSTITUTION (1794), 9, 12, 13 (photo)
Constitution (CC-1), 114
CONSTITUTION (CC-5), 114
Continental (1813), 12
CONTOOCOOK (1863), 57, 59, 69
CONVERSE (DD-291), 180
CONVERSE (DD-509), 193
Conway (DD-70), 172
CONWAY (DD-507), 192
CONY (DD-508), 193
CONYNGHAM (DD-58), 171
CONYNGHAM (DD-371), 184
CONYNGHAM (DDG-17), 211
COOK (DE-714), 234
COOK (DE-1083), 243
Cooke (ex DE-47), 221
Cooke (ex DE-267), 220
COOLBAUGH (DE-217), 230
COONER (DE-172), 222

COONTZ (DLG-9), 214
COOPER (DD-695), 199
COPAHEE (ACV-12), 128
COPELAND (FFG-25), 252
CORAL SEA (ACV-57), 130
Coral Sea (CVB-42), 123
CORAL SEA (CVB-43), 121
CORBESIER (DE-106), 222
CORBESIER (DE-438), 237
Cordoba, 233
CORDOVA (ACV-39), 128
CORE (ACV-13), 128
CORNUBIA (1863), 92
CORONADO (PF-38), 247
CORPORAL (SS-346), 277
CORPUS CHRISTI (PF-44), 247
Corpus Christi (SSN-705), 290
CORREGIDOR (ACV-58), 130
CORRY (DD-334), 181
CORRY (DD-463), 190
CORRY (DD-817), 203
CORSAIR (SS-435), 280
Corte Real, 237
CORVINA (SS-226), 271
(COSBY) (DE-94), 228
Cosme Garcia, 278
COTTEN (DD-669), 196
(COTTON) (DE-81), 227
COURTNEY (DE-1021), 239
COVINGTON (PF-56), 248
Cowell (DD-139), 175
COWELL (DD-167), 176
COWELL (DD-547), 194
COWIE (DD-632), 191
COWPENS (CG-63), 218
COWPENS (CV-25), 120
CRANE (DD-109), 175
Crane Ship No. 1 (AB-1), 103
(CRANSTOUN) (DE-82), 227
CRAVEN (DD-70), 172
CRAVEN (DD-382), 186
Craven (TB-10), 164
CREAD (DE-227), 233
CREAMER (DE-308), 220
CREVALLE (SS-291), 275
CROAKER (SS-246), 272, 274 (photo)
CROATAN (ACV-14), 128
CROATAN (ACV-25), 128
CROMMELIN (FFG-37), 252
CROMWELL (DE-1014), 239
CRONIN (DE-107), 222
CRONIN (DE-704), 231
CROSBY (DD-164), 176
CROSLEY (DE-108), 222
CROSLEY (DE-226), 233
CROSS (DE-448), 237
CROUTER (DE-11), 219
CROWLEY (DE-303), 220
Crown Point (CV-27), 120
Crown Point (CV-32), 119
CROWNINSHIELD (DD-134), 174
CRUSADER (1858), 90
Cuauhtemoc, 194
Cuba, 91

CUBERA (SS-347), 277
(CUBITT) (DE-83), 228
(CUCKMERE) (PG-104), 246
Cuitlahuac, 194
CUMBERLAND (1816), 14, 62
CUMMINGS (DD-44), 170
CUMMINGS (DD-365), 184
Cumulus, 250
CURRIER (DE-700), 231
CURTIS W. HOWARD (DE-752), 223
CURTIS WILBUR (DDG-54), 212
CURTS (FFG-38), 252
(CURZON) (DE-84), 228
CUSHING (DD-55), 171
CUSHING (DD-376), 184
CUSHING (DD-797), 196
CUSHING (DD-985), 210
CUSHING (TB-1), 162, 163 (photo)
CUSK (SS-348), 277
CUTLASS (SS-478), 280
CUTTLEFISH (SS-11), 254
CUTTLEFISH (SS-171), 268, 279
CYANE (1815), 12
CYANE (1837), 19, 20
Cyane (ferry), 165
Cyclops (1862), 52
D-1 (SS-17), 256
D-2 (SS-18), 256
D-3 (SS-19), 256
DACE (SS-247), 272
DACE (SSN-607), 286
DACOTAH (1858), 66
Dacres (ex DE-48), 221
Dacres (ex DE-268), 220
Daegu, 199
DAHLGREN (DD-187), 178, 198
DAHLGREN (DLG-12), 214
DAHLGREN (TB-9), 164
DAI CHING (1863), 92
(DAKINS) (DE-85), 228
Dakota (1858), 66
Dakotah (1858), 66
DALE (1837), 20, 61
DALE (DD-4), 168
DALE (DD-290), 180
DALE (DD-353), 183
DALE (DLG-19), 214
DALE W. PETERSON (DE-337), 226
DALLAS (CA-140), 140
DALLAS (CA-150), 140
DALLAS (DD-199), 178
DALLAS (SSN-700), 289
DALY (DD-519), 193
Damage Control Hulk No. 40, 174
DAMATO (DD-871), 204
DAMON CUMMINGS (DE-756), 224
DAMON M. CUMMINGS (DE-643), 230
Dang Yang, 202
DANIEL (DE-335), 225
DANIEL A. JOY (DE-585), 233
DANIEL BOONE (SSBN-629), 293
DANIEL T. GRIFFIN (DE-54), 227
DANIEL WEBSTER (SSBN-626), 293
Danville (PG-105), 246

DARBY (DE-218), 230
DARTER (SS-227), 271
DARTER (SS-576), 283, 292
(DARWIN) (FFG-44), 252
Daryush, 212
(DASHER) (BAVG-5), 125
DASHIELL (DD-659), 195
Datu Kalantiaw, 222
Datu Siratuna, 222
DAVENPORT (PF-69), 248
DAVID R. RAY (DD-971), 209 (photo), 210
DAVID W. TAYLOR (DD-551), 194
DAVIDSON (DD-618), 191
DAVIDSON (DE-1045), 241
DAVIS (DD-65), 172
DAVIS (DD-395), 187
DAVIS (DD-937), 207
DAVIS (TB-12), 165
DAWN (1861), 90
DAY (DE-225), 233
DAYLIGHT (1861), 90
DAYTON (CL-78), 120, 151
DAYTON (CL-105), 151
DCH-1 (IX-44), 176
DD-224 (ex Stewart), 182
De Bitter, 223
DE HAVEN (DD-469), 192
DE HAVEN (DD-727), 200
DE LONG (DD-129), 178
DE LONG (DE-684), 234
DE LONG (TB-28), 167
DE SOTO (1861), 86
DE WERT (FFG-45), 252
De Zeeuw, 223
DEALEY (DE-1006), 239, 240, 241
DEANE (1776), 7
(DEANE) (DE-86), 228
DEARBORN (PF-33), 247
DECATUR (1837), 20
DECATUR (DD-5), 168
DECATUR (DD-341), 181
DECATUR (DD-936), 207
DECKER (DE-47), 220
Dedalo, 120
DEEDE (DE-263), 220
Defiance, 34
DELAWARE (1775), 6
DELAWARE (1798), 33, 35
DELAWARE (1816), 2
DELAWARE (1861), 90
Delaware (1863), 59
DELAWARE (BB-28), 107, 108
DELBERT W. HALSEY (DE-310), 220
Delfinen, 283
DELGADA (ACV-40), 128
DELPHY (DD-261), 180
Demologos (1814), 53
DEMPSEY (DE-26), 219
DEMPSEY (DE-267), 220
DENNIS (DE-405), 236
DENNIS J. BUCKLEY (DD-808), 203
DENNIS J. BUCKLEY (DE-553), 238
DENT (DD-116), 174
DENTUDA (SS-335), 276

DENVER (C-14), 146, 160
DENVER (CL-58), 151
DES MOINES (C-15), 146
Des Moines (CA-75), 139
DES MOINES (CA-134), 140
DESPATCH (1855), 72, 89
Despatch (IX-2), 141
DETROIT (1813), 24
Detroit (1861), 68
DETROIT (1864), 69
DETROIT (C-10), 144
DETROIT (CL-8), 148
DEVILFISH (SS-292), 275
Dewert (FFG-45), 252
DEWEY (DD-349), 183
Dewey (DLG-7), 214
DEWEY (DLG-14), 214
Dewey, ex DON JUAN DE AUSTRIA (1899), 159
DEYO (DD-989), 210
DIABLO (SS-479), 280
DIACHENKO (DE-690), 234
DICKERSON (DD-157), 178
DICTATOR (1862), 43, 58
Didrickson Bay (ACV-64), 131
Didrickson Bay (ACV-100), 131
DILIGENCE (1798), 25, 29
DILIGENT (1779), 24
DIODON (SS-349), 277
Diogenes, 159
Diogo Cao, 238
DIONNE (DE-261), 220
Ditter (DD-751), 201
DIXIE (1898), 297, 298
Dixmude, 125
DOBLER (DE-48), 220
DOGFISH (SS-350), 277
DOHERTY (DE-14), 219
Dolfin, 282
Dolomi Bay (ACV-65), 131
Dolomi Bay (ACV-101), 131
DOLPHIN (1777), 37
DOLPHIN (1820), 31
DOLPHIN (1834), 26
DOLPHIN (1883), 141, 161
DOLPHIN (AGSS-555), 283, 296
DOLPHIN (SS-169), 267, 268
Domett (ex DE-49), 221
Domett (ex DE-269), 220
(DOMINICA) (PF-79), 248
DON (1864), 94
DON JUAN DE AUSTRIA (1899), 159
DON O. WOODS (DE-721), 235
DONALD B. BEARY (DE-1085), 243
DONALD W. WOLF (DE-713), 234
DONALDSON (DE-44), 220
DONALDSON (DE-55), 227
Donaldson (DE-508), 239
Doncella (SS-351), 279
DONEFF (DE-49), 220
DONNELL (DE-56), 227
DORADO (SS-248), 272
DORADO (SS-526), 281
Doran (DD-185), 177
DORAN (DD-634), 191

DORSEY (DD-117), 174
DORTCH (DD-670), 196
Dory (SS-352), 279
Douglas, 93
DOUGLAS A. MUNRO (DE-422), 237
DOUGLAS H. FOX (DD-779), 201
DOUGLAS L. HOWARD (DE-138), 224
Dover (IX-30), 158
DOWNES (DD-45), 170
DOWNES (DD-375), 184
DOWNES (DE-1070), 243
Doxa, 190
DOYEN (DD-280), 180
DOYLE (DD-494), 190
DOYLE (FFG-39), 252
DOYLE C. BARNES (DE-353), 236
DRAGONET (SS-293), 275
DRAYTON (DD-23), 169
DRAYTON (DD-366), 184
Dreadnought, 107
DREXLER (DD-741), 200
DRUM (SS-228), 271
DRUM (SSN-677), 288
Drury (ex DE-50), 221
(DRURY) (BDE-46), 220
DU PONT (DD-152), 174
DU PONT (DD-941), 207
Dubois, 223
DUBUQUE (PG-17), 160
Duc de Duras, 33
DUC DE LAUZUN (1782), 33
Duckworth (ex DE-19), 221
Duckworth (ex DE-61), 227
Duff (ex DE-20), 221
Duff (ex DE-64), 227
DUFFY (DE-27), 219
DUFFY (DE-268), 220
DUFILHO (DE-423), 237
DUGONG (SS-353), 277
DULUTH (CL-87), 151
Duman, 247
DUMBARTON (1864), 94
Dumlupinar (ex SS-323), 276
Dumlupinar (ex SS-325), 276
DUNCAN (DD-46), 170
DUNCAN (DD-485), 190
DUNCAN (DD-874), 204
DUNCAN (FFG-10), 251
DUNDERBERG (1862), 42
DUNLAP (DD-384), 186
DUPONT (TB-7), 164
DURANT (DE-389), 226
DURIK (DE-666), 231
DWIGHT D. EISENHOWER (CVAN-69), 122
   (photo), 125
DYER (DD-84), 175
DYESS (DD-880), 204
DYSON (DD-572), 194
E-1 (SS-24), 256
E-2 (SS-25), 256
E. A. Stevens, 39
EAGLE (1798), 29
EAGLE (1812), 37
EAGLE (brig, 1814), 28

EAGLE (schooner, 1814), 36
Eagle, later WASHINGTON (1775), 34
Eagle, later RHODE ISLAND (1861), 87
EARHART (DE-603), 234
EARL K. OLSEN (DE-765), 224
EARL V. JOHNSON (DE-702), 231
EARLE (DD-635), 191
EARLE B. HALL (DE-597), 234
Eastland, 298
EASTPORT (1862), 50
EATON (DD-510), 193
EBERLE (DD-430), 189
EBERT (DE-74), 227
EBERT (DE-768), 224
EDGAR G. CHASE (DE-16), 219
EDISON (DD-439), 190
EDISTO (ACV-41), 128
EDMONDS (DE-406), 236
EDSALL (DD-219), 179
EDSALL (DE-129), 224, 231
EDSON (DD-946), 208
Edward, 37
EDWARD C. DALY (DE-17), 219
EDWARD H. ALLEN (DE-531), 238
EDWARD McDONNELL (DE-1043), 241
EDWARDS (DD-265), 180
EDWARDS (DD-619), 191
EDWIN A. HOWARD (DE-346), 235
EEL (SS-354), 277
EFFINGHAM (1775), 6
EICHENBERGER (DE-202), 228
EISELE (DE-34), 219
EISELE (DE-75), 227
Eisner (DE-28), 221
EISNER (DE-192), 223
EISNER (DE-269), 220
EK-1 through EK-28, 250
(EKINS) (DE-87), 228
El Cid, 297
El Norte, 297
EL PASO (PF-41), 247
El Rayo, 87
El Rio, 297
El Sol, 297
El Sud, 298
Elbour Bay (ACV-66), 131
Elbour Bay (ACV-102), 131
Elbow Bay (ACV-102), 131
ELCANO (1899), 159
ELDON (DE-264), 220
ELDRIDGE (DE-173), 222
Ella and Annie, 93
ELLEN (1861), 95
ELLET (DD-398), 187
ELLIOT (DD-146), 174
ELLIOT (DD-967), 210
ELLIS (DD-154), 174
ELLYSON (DD-454), 190
ELMER MONTGOMERY (DE-1082), 243
ELROD (FFG-55), 252
ELY (DE-309), 220
EMERY (DE-28), 219
Emery Rice, 78
EMMA (1863), 92

Emma Duncan, 97
EMMA HENRY (1865), 95
EMMONS (DD-457), 190
Emperor (ex ACV-34), 128
Emperor (ex ACV-67), 131
EMPORIA (PF-28), 247
Empress (ex ACV-38), 128
Empress (ex ACV-71), 131
Endeavour, 34
ENDICOTT (DD-495), 190
ENGLAND (DE-635), 229 (photo), 230
ENGLAND (DLG-22), 214
ENGLISH (DD-696), 199
ENGSTROM (DE-50), 220
ENIWETOK (CVE-125), 132
Enrico Tazzoli, 271
ENRIGHT (DE-216), 230
ENTEMEDOR (SS-340), 276
ENTERPRISE (1775), 37
ENTERPRISE (1798), 29, 30 (photo)
ENTERPRISE (1831), 31
ENTERPRISE (1873), 77
ENTERPRISE (CV-6), 117
ENTERPRISE (CVAN-65), 124, 125, 154
Eolus (1863), 45
Eolus (small steamer, 1864), 94
EPERVIER (1814), 26
EPERVIER (1864), 76
EPPERSON (DD-719), 202
ERBEN (DD-631), 195
Erebus (1863), 45
ERICSSON (DD-56), 171
ERICSSON (DD-440), 190
ERICSSON (TB-2), 162, 164
ERIE (1813), 17, 18
ERIE (1821), 18
ERIE (PG-50), 156 (photo), 161
ERNEST G. SMALL (DD-838), 203
Escape, 36
ESCOLAR (SS-294), 275
ESPADA (SS-355), 277
Espirito Santo, 200
Espora, 196
ESSEX (1798), 10, 33, 34
Essex (1813), 12
ESSEX (1861), 49
ESSEX (1873), 77
ESSEX (CV-9), 116, 118, 119, 120, 121,
  123, 135
ESSEX JUNIOR (1813), 34
ESSINGTON (DE-67), 227
Essington (ex DE-21), 221
Essington (ex DE-67), 227
Esso New Orleans, 126
Esso Trenton, 126
ESTERO (ACV-42), 128
ESTOCIN (FFG-15), 251
ESTRELLA (1862), 91
ETHAN ALLEN (SSBN-608), 293
Ethan Allen, later COMMODORE BARNEY, 95
ETLAH (1863), 45
EUGENE (PF-40), 247
EUGENE A. GREENE (DD-711), 202
EUGENE A. GREENE (DE-549), 238

EUGENE E. ELMORE (DE-686), 234
EUTAW (1862), 80
Evangelista Torricelli, 277
EVANS (DD-78), 174
EVANS (DD-552), 194
EVANS (DE-1023), 239
EVANSVILLE (PF-70), 248
EVARTS (DE-5), 219, 221, 224
(EVENLODE) (PG-105), 246
EVERETT (PF-8), 246
EVERETT F. LARSON (DD-830), 203
EVERETT F. LARSON (DE-554), 238
EVERSOLE (DD-789), 202
EVERSOLE (DE-404), 236
EXPERIMENT (1798), 29
EXPERIMENT (1831), 31
(EXTREMADURA) (DEG-11), 245
F-1 (SS-20), 257
F-2 (SS-21), 257
F-3 (SS-22), 257
F-4 (SS-23), 257
FAHRION (FFG-22), 252
FAIR (DE-35), 219
FAIRFAX (DD-93), 174
FAIRFIELD (1825), 19
Falcon, later HORNET (1775), 36
Falcon (ex DD-781), 201
FALGOUT (DE-324), 225
FALL RIVER (CA-131), 139, 155
FALMOUTH (1825), 18
Fanegal (SS-356), 279
FANNING (DD-37), 170
FANNING (DD-385), 186
FANNING (DE-1076), 243
FANSHAW BAY (ACV-70), 130
Fante, 193
FARENHOLT (DD-332), 181
FARENHOLT (DD-491), 188
FARGO (CL-85), 120, 151
FARGO (CL-106), 139, 140, 152
Farley (DD-496), 191
FARQUHAR (DD-304), 181
FARQUHAR (DE-139), 224
FARRAGUT (DD-300), 181
FARRAGUT (DD-348), 183, 184, 186
FARRAGUT (DLG-6), 214
FARRAGUT (TB-11), 164
Farralones (1849), 86
FECHTELER (DD-870), 204
FECHTELER (DE-157), 228
Fencer, 128
FERRET (1804), 31
FESSENDEN (DE-142), 224
FIEBERLING (DE-640), 230
FIFE (DD-991), 210
FINBACK (SS-230), 271
FINBACK (SSN-670), 288
FINCH (DE-328), 225
Finch, ex GROWLER (1812), 37
(FINDHORN) (PG-106), 246
Fingal, 46
FINNEGAN (DE-307), 220
FIREFLY (1814), 35
FISKE (DD-842), 203

FISKE (DE-143), 225
FITCH (DD-462), 190
FITZGERALD (DDG-62), 212
(FITZROY) (DE-88), 228
FLAHERTY (DE-135), 224
FLAMBEAU (1814), 35
FLAMBEAU (1861), 86
FLASHER (SS-249), 272
FLASHER (SSN-613), 287
FLATLEY (FFG-21), 252
FLEMING (DE-32), 219
FLEMING (DE-271), 220
FLETCHER (DD-445), 192, 197, 198, 201,
    207, 208
FLETCHER (DD-992), 210
FLIER (SS-250), 272
Flint (CL-64), 151
FLINT (CL-97), 150
Flora, 8
Florida, ex WAMPANOAG (1863), 56 (photo),
    58
FLORIDA (BB-30), 105 (photo), 107, 108
FLORIDA (BM-9), 101
FLORIDA (SSBN-728), 295
Florida, ex FROLIC (1813), 18
Florida, later HENDRICK HUDSON (1862), 91
Florida, later SELMA (1864), 94
Florida (merchant), 161
FLOUNDER (SS-251), 272
FLOYD B. PARKS (DD-884), 205
FLUSSER (DD-20), 169
FLUSSER (DD-289), 180
FLUSSER (DD-368), 184
FLYING FISH (SS-229), 271
FLYING FISH (SSN-673), 288
FOGG (DE-57), 227
Foley (ex DE-22), 221
Foley (ex DE-270), 220
FOOTE (DD-169), 176
FOOTE (DD-511), 193
FOOTE (TB-3), 147, 164
Forban, 164, 167
FORD (DD-228), 179
FORD (FFG-54), 252
FOREMAN (DE-633), 230
FORMOE (DE-58), 227
FORMOE (DE-509), 238
FORREST (DD-461), 190
Forrest B. Royal (DD-872), 206
FORREST ROYAL (DD-872), 204
FORREST SHERMAN (DD-931), 207, 208, 211
FORRESTAL (CVA-59), 118, 123, 124
FORSTER (DE-334), 225
FORSYTH (PF-102), 250
FORT DONELSON (1864), 89
FORT HENRY (1862), 96
Fort Henry, later LAFAYETTE (1862), 50
Fort Hindman (river steamer, 1863), 97
FORT JACKSON (1863), 88, 94, 95
Fortaleza Bay (ACV-72), 131
Fortazela Bay (ACV-72), 131
FOSS (DE-59), 227
FOWLER (DE-222), 230

Fowley, 34
FOX (1777), 8
FOX (DD-234), 179
FOX (DLG-33), 215
FOX (TB-13), 165
FRAMENT (DE-677), 231
Francesco Morosini, 276
FRANCIS HAMMOND (DE-1067), 243
FRANCIS M. ROBINSON (DE-220), 230
FRANCIS SCOTT KEY (SSBN-657), 295
FRANCOVICH (DE-379), 236
FRANCOVICH (DE-606), 234
FRANK E. EVANS (DD-754), 200
FRANK KNOX (DD-742), 202
FRANKFORD (DD-497), 190
Frankfurt, 140
FRANKLIN (1799), 1
FRANKLIN (1813), 2, 54
FRANKLIN (1853), 54
FRANKLIN (CV-13), 118
FRANKLIN D. ROOSEVELT (CVB-42), 121
FRANKS (DD-554), 194
FRAZIER (DD-607), 189
FRED T. BERRY (DD-858), 204
Frederick (CA-8), 135
FREDERICK C. DAVIS (DE-136), 224
FRENCH (DE-367), 236
FRESNO (CL-121), 152
Friar (SS-357), 279
FROLIC (1813), 18
Frolic (1864), 93
FROST (DE-144), 225
Frosty Bay (CVE-112), 132
FRYBARGER (DE-705), 231
Fu Shan, 233
Fu Yang, 203
FULLAM (DD-474), 192
FULLER (DD-297), 180
FULTON (1814), 53
FULTON (1835), 60
Fulton the First (1814), 53
Fulton (USAT), 93
Furer (DEG-6), 245
FURSE (DD-882), 204
Fury (1863), 45
G-1 (SS-19 1/2), 256
G-2 (SS-27), 257
G-3 (SS-31), 257
G-4 (SS-26), 257
GABILAN (SS-252), 272
GAINARD (DD-706), 199
Gainard (DD-734), 201
GALATEA (1863), 88, 89
GALENA (1861), 40, 71
GALENA (1872), 70, 71
GALLERY (FFG-26), 252
GALLUP (PF-47), 247
GALVESTON (C-17), 146
GALVESTON (CL-93), 151; (CLG-3), 154
Galveston, later ARCHER (1846), 27
Galvez, 247
GAMBIER BAY (ACV-73), 130
GAMBLE (DD-123), 177
GANDY (DE-764), 224

GANGES (1798), 33
GANSEVOORT (DD-608), 189
GANTNER (DE-60), 227
GAR (SS-206), 270
GARCIA (DE-1040), 241, 245
Gardiner, 220
GARFIELD THOMAS (DE-193), 223
Garfish (SS-30), 258
Garlies, 220
GARLOPA (SS-358), 277
GARRUPA (SS-359), 277
GARY (CL-147), 152
Gary (DE-326), 226
GARY (FFG-51), 252
Gatch (DE-1026), 239
GATLING (DD-671), 196
GATO (SS-212), 271, 274, 279
GATO (SSN-615), 287
GAYNIER (DE-751), 223
Gayret, 202
Gaziantep, 190
GEARING (DD-710), 184, 197, 202
Geier, 161
Gelibolu, 190
Gemlik, 190
GENDREAU (DE-639), 230
General Admiral, 59
General Belgrano, 150
GENERAL BRAGG (1862), 97
GENERAL GATES (1777), 34
GENERAL GREENE (frigate, 1798), 9
GENERAL GREENE (sloop, 1798), 32
General Meigs, 90
General Monk, 6, 33
GENERAL PIKE (1813), 23
GENERAL PRICE (1862), 96, 97
General Sedgwick, 91
General Sterling Price, 97
General Sumter, 97
GENERAL WASHINGTON (1782), 33
GENESEE (1861), 79
Geniere, 194
GENTRY (DE-349), 236
GEORGE (DE-276), 220
GEORGE (DE-697), 231
George, later ENTERPRISE (1775), 37
GEORGE A. JOHNSON (DE-583), 233
GEORGE BANCROFT (SSBN-643), 295
GEORGE C. MARSHALL (SSBN-654), 295
GEORGE E. BADGER (DD-196), 178
GEORGE E. DAVIS (DE-357), 236
GEORGE K. MACKENZIE (DD-836), 203
GEORGE M. CAMPBELL (DE-773), 224
GEORGE PHILIP (FFG-12), 251
GEORGE W. INGRAM (DE-62), 227
GEORGE WASHINGTON (1798), 33
GEORGE WASHINGTON (CVN-73), 125
GEORGE WASHINGTON (SSBN-598), 286, 293
GEORGE WASHINGTON CARVER (SSBN-656), 295
Georgetown, 176
GEORGIA (BB-15), 104, 105 (photo)
GEORGIA (SSBN-729), 295
Georgia, later TROUP (1812), 35
GEORGIANA (1813), 34

GERMANTOWN (1843), 21
GERTRUDE (1863), 92
GETTYSBURG (1863), 93, 94
GETTYSBURG (CG-64), 218
Ghazi, 280
GHERARDI (DD-637), 191
Gianfranco Gazzana Priaroggia, 281
GILBERT ISLANDS (CVE-107), 131
GILLESPIE (DD-609), 189
Gillette (DE-31), 221
GILLETTE (DE-270), 220
GILLETTE (DE-681), 231
GILLIGAN (DE-508), 238
GILLIS (DD-260), 180
GILMER (DD-233), 173 (photo), 179
GILMORE (DE-18), 219
Giraffe, 89
Giresun, 190
GLACIER (ACV-33), 128
GLADWYNE (PF-62), 248
GLAUCUS (1863), 88, 89
GLEAVES (DD-423), 189, 199
GLENARD P. LIPSCOMB (SSN-685), 289
GLENDALE (PF-36), 247
GLENNON (DD-620), 191
GLENNON (DD-840), 203
GLOUCESTER (PF-22), 247
GLOVER (AGDE-1), 244
GOFF (DD-247), 179
Goias, 278
Gold Coast, 251
GOLDRING (SS-360), 277
GOLDSBOROUGH (DD-188), 178
GOLDSBOROUGH (DDG-20), 211
GOLDSBOROUGH (TB-20), 166
GOLET (SS-361), 273
Goliath (1862), 42
Goodall, 220
GOODRICH (DD-831), 203
Goodson, 220
Gore, 220
Gorgon (1863), 45
GOSS (DE-444), 237
GOSSELIN (DE-710), 234
Gould, 220
GOVERNOR BUCKINGHAM (1863), 89
GOVERNOR JAY (1798), 29
Governor Moore, 88
GRADY (DE-445), 237
GRAHAM (DD-192), 178
GRAMPUS (1820), 31
GRAMPUS (SS-4), 253
GRAMPUS (SS-207), 266 (photo), 270
GRAMPUS (SS-523), 281
Grampus, later SPITFIRE (1814), 36
GRAND FORKS (PF-11), 246
GRAND GULF (1863), 89, 93
GRAND ISLAND (PF-14), 246
GRAND RAPIDS (PF-31), 247
GRANITE CITY (1863), 93
Granite State (1816), 4
Gravina, 204
GRAY (DE-1054), 242 (photo), 243
GRAYBACK (SS-208), 270

GRAYBACK (SSG-574), 291
GRAYLING (SS-18), 256
GRAYLING (SS-209), 270
GRAYLING (SS-492), 281
GRAYLING (SSN-646), 288
Grayson (DD-429), 191
GRAYSON (DD-435), 190
Grebe (AM-43), 256
GREENE (DD-266), 180
GREENEVILLE (SSN-772), 290
GREENFISH (SS-351), 277
GREENLING (SS-213), 271
GREENLING (SSN-614), 287
GREENSBORO (PF-101), 250
GREENWICH (1813), 34
GREENWOOD (DE-679), 231
GREER (DD-145), 174
GREGORY (DD-82), 175
GREGORY (DD-802), 196
GREINER (DE-37), 219
GRENADIER (SS-210), 270
GRENADIER (SS-525), 281
Greyhound, 37
GRIDLEY (DD-92), 175
GRIDLEY (DD-380), 186
GRIDLEY (DLG-21), 214
Grilse, 276
Grindall, 220
GRISWOLD (DE-7), 219
GROTON (PF-29), 247
GROTON (SSN-694), 289
GROUPER (SS-214), 271
GROVES (DE-543), 238
GROWLER (1812), 37
GROWLER (SS-215), 271
GROWLER (SSG-577), 292
GRUNION (SS-216), 271
GUADALCANAL (ACV-60), 130
GUAM (CB-2), 134 (photo), 135
Guanabara, 277
GUARDFISH (SS-217), 271
GUARDFISH (SSN-612), 286
GUAVINA (SS-362), 273
Guayas, 248
GUDGEON (SS-211), 270
GUDGEON (SS-567), 282
GUERRIERE (1813), 12
GUERRIERE (1863), 57, 59, 60, 69
GUEST (DD-472), 192
GUITARRO (SS-363), 273
GUITARRO (SSN-665), 288
GULFPORT (PF-20), 247
GUNASON (DE-795), 231
GUNNEL (SS-253), 272
Gur, 276
GURKE (DD-783), 202
GURNARD (SS-254), 272
GURNARD (SSN-662), 288
GUSTAFSON (DE-182), 223
GWIN (DD-71), 172
GWIN (DD-433), 190
GWIN (DD-772), 201
GWIN (TB-16), 165
GYATT (DD-712), 202

GYATT (DE-550), 238
H-1 (SS-28), 258
H-2 (SS-29), 258
H-3 (SS-30), 146, 258
H-4 (SS-147), 264
H-5 (SS-148), 264
H-6 (SS-149), 264
H-7 (SS-150), 264
H-8 (SS-151), 264
H-9 (SS-152), 264
H. L. Hunley, 67
HAAS (DE-424), 237
HACKLEBACK (SS-295), 275
HADDO (SS-255), 272
HADDO (SSN-604), 286
Haddock (SS-32), 258
HADDOCK (SS-231), 271
HADDOCK (SSN-621), 286
HAGGARD (DD-555), 194
Hague (1776), 7
Hai Pao, 278
Hai Shih, 280
HAILEY (DD-556), 194
HAINES (DE-792), 231
HAKE (SS-256), 272
HALE (DD-133), 174
HALE (DD-642), 195
HALFBEAK (SS-352), 277
HALFORD (DD-480), 192
HALIBUT (SS-232), 271
HALIBUT (SSGN-587), 292, 294 (photo)
Halifax, 16
HALL (DD-583), 195
HALLIGAN (DD-584), 195
HALLORAN (DE-305), 220
Hallowell, 251
HALSEY (DLG-23), 214
HALSEY POWELL (DD-686), 196
Halsted, 251
HALYBURTON (FFG-40), 252
HAMBLETON (DD-455), 190
Hamburg Packet, 33
HAMILTON (DD-141), 174
Hamilton (DD-307), 182
Hamilton (ex DD-170), 176
HAMLIN (ACV-15), 128
HAMMANN (DD-412), 188
HAMMANN (DE-131), 224
HAMMERBERG (DE-1015), 239
HAMMERHEAD (SS-364), 273
HAMMERHEAD (SSN-663), 288
Hammond, 251
HAMNER (DD-718), 202
HAMPDEN (1776), 34
Hampshire (1776), 16
HAMPTON (SSN-767), 290
Han Yang (ex DD-427), 188
Han Yang (ex DD-833), 203
(HANATSUKI) (DD-934), 206
HANCOCK (1775), 5, 8
Hancock (1776), 7
Hancock (CV-14), 119
HANCOCK (CV-19), 119
HANK (DD-702), 199

HANNA (DE-449), 237
Hannam, 251
HANSON (DD-832), 203
HARADEN (DD-183), 177
HARADEN (DD-585), 195
Harbah, 241
HARDER (SS-257), 272
HARDER (SS-568), 282
HARDHEAD (SS-365), 277
HARDING (DD-91), 175
HARDING (DD-625), 191
Hargood (ex PF-74), 251
(HARGOOD) (DE-573), 230
HARLAN R. DICKSON (DD-708), 199
Harland, 251
HARMON (DE-72), 227
HARMON (DE-678), 231
Harnam, 251
HAROLD C. THOMAS (DE-21), 219
HAROLD E. HOLT (DE-1074), 243
HAROLD J. ELLISON (DD-864), 204
HAROLD J. ELLISON (DE-545), 238
Harpy (1863), 45
HARRIET LANE (1861), 73
Harrisburg, 297
HARRISON (DD-573), 194
Harry B. Bass (DD-887), 206
HARRY E. HUBBARD (DD-748), 200
HARRY E. YARNELL (DLG-17), 214
HARRY F. BAUER (DD-738), 200
HARRY L. CORL (DE-598), 234
HARRY W. HILL (DD-986), 210
HART (DD-110), 176
HART (DD-594), 195
HARTFORD (1857), 63, 141
HARTFORD (SSN-768), 290
HARTLEY (DE-1029), 239
HARVARD (1898), 297
HARVESON (DE-316), 225
HARVEST MOON (1863), 93
Harvey, 251
HARWOOD (DD-861), 204
HASSALO (1863), 59, 60
HASTINGS (1863), 97
Hatakaze, 190
HATFIELD (DD-231), 179
Hatsuhi, 222
Hatsutaka, 277
HATTERAS (1861), 86
HAVERFIELD (DE-393), 226
HAWAII (CB-3), 135
HAWES (FFG-53), 252
HAWKBILL (SS-366), 277
HAWKBILL (SSN-666), 288
HAWKINS (DD-873), 204
HAYLER (DD-997), 210
HAYNSWORTH (DD-700), 199
HAYTER (DE-212), 230
HAZELWOOD (DD-107), 175
HAZELWOOD (DD-531), 193
HEALY (DD-672), 196
Hecate (1863), 45
Hecla (1863), 46
HEERMAN (DD-532), 193

HELENA (CA-75), 139
HELENA (CL-50), 150, 151
HELENA (CL-113), 152
HELENA (PG-9), 158
HELENA (SSN-725), 290
Hellas, 14
HELM (DD-388), 186
HEMMINGER (DE-746), 223
HENDERSON (DD-785), 202
HENDRICK HUDSON (1862), 91
Heng Shan, 234
Heng Yang, 200
HENLEY (DD-39), 170
HENLEY (DD-391), 186
HENLEY (DD-762), 200
HENRY A. WILEY (DD-749), 200
HENRY B. WILSON (DDG-7), 209 (photo), 211
HENRY CLAY (SSBN-625), 293
HENRY L. STIMSON (SSBN-655), 294 (photo), 295
HENRY M. JACKSON (SSBN-730), 295
HENRY R. KENYON (DE-683), 231
HENRY W. TUCKER (DD-875), 204
HENRY W. TUCKER (DE-377), 236
HENSHAW (DD-278), 180
HEPBURN (DE-1055), 243
HERALD (1798), 33
HERBERT (DD-160), 178
HERBERT C. JONES (DE-137), 224
HERBERT J. THOMAS (DD-833), 203
Hercules (1863), 46
Hercules (ex PG-101), 245
HERNDON (DD-198), 178
HERNDON (DD-638), 191
Hero (1863), 45
Heroina, 248
HERRING (SS-233), 272
HERZOG (DE-178), 223
HERZOG (DE-277), 220
HEWITT (DD-966), 210
HEYLIGER (DE-510), 238
HEYWOOD L. EDWARDS (DD-663), 195
HIBISCUS (1864), 94
HICKOX (DD-673), 196
Hiei, 188
HIGBEE (DD-806), 202
HILARY P. JONES (DD-427), 188
HILBERT (DE-742), 223
HILL (DE-141), 224
HINGHAM (PF-30), 247
Hipolito Bouchard, 199
HISSEM (DE-400), 226
Hiyodori, 271
Hizir Reis (ex SS-378), 277
Hizir Reis (ex SS-567), 282
(HOBART) (DDG-26), 211
Hobart Bay (CVE-113), 132
HOBBY (DD-610), 189
HOBSON (DD-464), 190
HODGES (DE-231), 233
HOE (SS-258), 272
HOEL (DD-533), 193
HOEL (DD-768), 202
HOEL (DDG-13), 211

HOGAN (DD-178), 176
HOGGATT BAY (ACV-75), 130
HOLDER (DD-819), 203
HOLDER (DE-401), 226
HOLLAND (SS-1), 253, 254
HOLLANDIA (ACV-97), 130
HOLLIS (DE-794), 231
HOLLISTER (DD-788), 202
Holmes (ex PF-81), 251
(HOLMES) (DE-572), 230
HOLT (DE-706), 234
HOLTON (DE-703), 231
Hong Kong, 251
HONOLULU (CL-48), 148
HONOLULU (SSN-718), 289
Hood (DD-655), 198
Hood, 114
HOOPER (DE-1026), 239
HOPEWELL (DD-181), 177
HOPEWELL (DD-681), 196
HOPKINS (DD-6), 168
HOPKINS (DD-249), 179
HOPPING (DE-155), 228
HOQUIAM (PF-5), 246
HORACE A. BASS (DE-691), 234
Hornby, 251
HORNE (DLG-30), 215
HORNET (1775), 36
HORNET (1804), 25
HORNET (1804), ex Traveler, 37
Hornet (1864), 94
HORNET (CV-8), 117, 118, 120
HORNET (CV-12), 118
Hoste (ex PF-83), 251
(HOSTE) (DE-521), 221
Hotham (ex PF-75), 251
(HOTHAM) (DE-574), 230
HOUSATONIC (1861), 67
HOUSTON (CA-30), 136
HOUSTON (CL-81), 151
HOUSTON (SSN-713), 289
(HOVA) (DE-110), 222
HOVEY (DD-208), 179
HOWARD (DD-179), 176
HOWARD D. CROW (DE-252), 225
HOWARD F. CLARK (DE-533), 238
Howett, 251
HOWORTH (DD-592), 195
Howquah (small steamer, 1863), 93
Hsiang Yang, 200
Hsuen Yang (ex DD-456), 190
Hsuen Yang (ex DD-458), 190
Hua Shan, 234
Hua Yang, 201
HUBBARD (DE-211), 228
HUDSON (1825), 14
HUDSON (DD-475), 192
HUE CITY (CG-66), 218
Huei Yang, 199
HUGH PURVIS (DD-709), 199
HUGH W. HADLEY (DD-774), 201
HUGHES (DD-410), 188
HULBERT (DD-342), 181
HULL (DD-7), 168

HULL (DD-330), 181
HULL (DD-350), 183
HULL (DD-945), 208
Humaita, 272
HUMPHREYS (DD-236), 179
Hunain, 245
HUNCHBACK (1861), 95
HUNT (DD-194), 178
HUNT (DD-674), 196
HUNTER (1813), 28
Hunter, later GROWLER (1812), 37
Hunter (ex ACV-8), 128
HUNTER MARSHALL (DE-602), 234
Huntington (CA-5), 135
HUNTINGTON (CL-77), 120, 151
HUNTINGTON (CL-107), 152
HUNTSVILLE (1861), 87, 92
HURON (1861), 73
HURON (1873), 78
Huron (CA-9), 135
HURON (PF-19), 247
Huron, later ALLIANCE (1873), 77
HURST (DE-250), 225
HUSE (DE-145), 225
HUTCHINS (DD-476), 192
HUTCHINSON (PF-45), 247
Hyder Ally, 33
Hydra (1863), 45
HYMAN (DD-732), 200
HYMAN G. RICKOVER (SSN-709), 289
I-12, 183
I-15, 188
I-19, 117
I-26, 150
I-45, 236
I-58, 138
I-168, 117, 188
I-175, 130
I-176, 271
ICEFISH (SS-367), 277
Icel, 196
IDAHO (1863), 59
IDAHO (BB-24), 106
IDAHO (BB-42), 111
Ierax, 224
Ikinci Inonu (ex SS-326), 276
Ikinci Inonu (ex SS-346), 277
ILLINOIS (1863), 59, 69
ILLINOIS (BB-7), 104
ILLINOIS (BB-65), 113
Imchin, 246
INCH (DE-146), 225
Inchon, 200
INDEPENDENCE (1775), 36
INDEPENDENCE (1777), 37
INDEPENDENCE (1813), 2
INDEPENDENCE (CV-22), 117, 120, 121
INDEPENDENCE (CVA-62), 123
INDIANA (BB-1), 102, 103
INDIANA (BB-50), 112
INDIANA (BB-58), 113
INDIANAPOLIS (CA-35), 138
INDIANAPOLIS (SSN-697), 289
INDIANOLA (1862), 51

Indoctrinator (ex DD-802), 198
Industrious Bee, 34
Infanta Maria Teresa, 145
INGERSOLL (DD-652), 195
INGERSOLL (DD-990), 210
(INGLIS) (DE-525), 221
INGRAHAM (DD-111), 176
INGRAHAM (DD-444), 190
INGRAHAM (DD-694), 199
INGRAHAM (FFG-61), 252
INGRAM (DD-255), 180
(INMAN) (DE-526), 221
INSURGENTE (1799), 11
INTREPID (1874), 83
INTREPID (CV-11), 118
(INVER) (PG-107), 246
Ionie (1858), 64
IOSCO (1862), 80
Iowa (1863), 58
IOWA (BB-4), 103, 104
IOWA (BB-53), 112
IOWA (BB-61), 109, 113, 114, 117, 123, 198
IRA JEFFERY (DE-63), 227
IREX (SS-482), 280
Iris (1863), 45
Iris, ex HANCOCK (1775), 5, 6
IRON AGE (1863), 89, 93
IROQUOIS (1858), 64, 66, 67, 94
IRWIN (DD-794), 196
ISAAC HULL (1813), 36
Isaac Peral, 278
ISAAC SMITH (1861), 90
ISABEL (1917), 298
ISHERWOOD (DD-284), 180
ISHERWOOD (DD-520), 193
Iskenderun, 193
ISLA DE CUBA (1899), 159
ISLA DE LUZON (1899), 159
ISONOMIA (1864), 94
ISRAEL (DD-98), 175
Istanbul, 196
ITASCA (1861), 73
Itasca, ex BANCROFT (1888), 157
IUKA (1864), 89
IWO JIMA (CV-46), 119
IZARD (DD-589), 195
Izmir, 195
Izmit, 195
J. DOUGLAS BLACKWOOD (DE-219), 230
J. FRED TALBOTT (DD-156), 174
J. P. Duarte, 245
J. R. Y. BLAKELY (DE-140), 224
J. RICHARD WARD (DE-243), 225
J. WILLIAM DITTER (DD-751), 200
JACCARD (DE-355), 236
JACK (SS-259), 272
JACK (SSN-605), 286
JACK C. ROBINSON (DE-671), 231
JACK MILLER (DE-410), 237
JACK W. WILKE (DE-800), 231
JACK WILLIAMS (FFG-24), 252
JACKSONVILLE (SSN-699), 289
JACOB JONES (DD-61), 171

JACOB JONES (DD-130), 178
JACOB JONES (DE-130), 224
JALLAO (SS-368), 277
JAMAICA (ACV-43), 128
JAMES ADGER (1861), 87, 89, 92
JAMES B. KYES (DD-787), 202
JAMES C. OWENS (DD-776), 201
James D. Blackwood (DE-219), 232
JAMES E. CRAIG (DE-201), 228
James F. Freeborn, 93
JAMES K. PAULDING (DD-238), 179
JAMES K. POLK (SSBN-645), 295
JAMES MADISON (SSBN-627), 293
James Miller (DD-535), 198
JAMES MONROE (SSBN-622), 293
James R. Ward (DE-243), 226
JAMESTOWN (1843), 21
JANSSEN (DE-396), 226
JARRETT (FFG-33), 252
JARVIS (DD-38), 170
JARVIS (DD-393), 186
JARVIS (DD-799), 196
Jason (1862), 42
JAVA (1813), 12, 14
JAVA (1863), 59, 69
JAWFISH (SS-356), 277
JEFFERS (DD-621), 191
JEFFERSON (1813), 28
JEFFERSON CITY (SSN-759), 290
Jeffery (DE-63), 232
JENKINS (DD-42), 170
JENKINS (DD-447), 192
JENKS (DE-665), 231
Jeong Buk, 203
Jeong Ju, 204
JESSE L. BROWN (DE-1089), 244
JESSE RUTHERFORD (DE-347), 236
JOBB (DE-707), 234
JOHN A. BOLE (DD-755), 200
John A. Bole (DD-783), 206
JOHN A. MOORE (FFG-19), 252
JOHN ADAMS (1798), 11
JOHN ADAMS (1825), 19
JOHN ADAMS (SSBN-620), 293
John Barry (DDG-52), 212
JOHN C. BUTLER (DE-339), 229, 235, 239
JOHN C. CALHOUN (SSBN-630), 293
JOHN C. STENNIS (CVN-74), 125
JOHN D. EDWARDS (DD-216), 179
John D. Ford (DD-228), 182
JOHN D. HENLEY (DD-553), 194
JOHN F. KENNEDY (CVA-67), 124, 215
JOHN FRANCIS BURNS (DD-299), 181
JOHN HANCOCK (DD-981), 210
JOHN HOOD (DD-655), 195
JOHN J. POWERS (DE-528), 221
JOHN J. VANBUREN (DE-753), 224
JOHN KING (DDG-3), 211
JOHN L. HALL (FFG-32), 252
JOHN L. WILLIAMSON (DE-370), 236
JOHN M. BERMINGHAM (DE-530), 221
JOHN MARSHALL (SSBN-611), 293
JOHN P. GRAY (DE-673), 231
JOHN P. JACKSON (1861), 95

John P. King, 87
JOHN PAUL JONES (DD-932), 207
JOHN PAUL JONES (DDG-53), 212
JOHN Q. ROBERTS (DE-235), 233
JOHN R. CRAIG (DD-885), 205
JOHN R. PERRY (DE-1034), 240
JOHN R. PIERCE (DD-753), 200
JOHN RODGERS (DD-574), 194
JOHN RODGERS (DD-983), 210
JOHN S. McCAIN (DDG-56), 212
JOHN S. McCAIN (DL-3), 213
JOHN W. THOMASON (DD-760), 200
JOHN W. WEEKS (DD-701), 199
JOHN WILLIS (DE-1027), 239
JOHN YOUNG (DD-973), 210
JOHNNIE HUTCHINS (DE-360), 236
JOHNSTON (DD-557), 194
JOHNSTON (DD-821), 203
Jon Nam, 230
JONAS INGRAM (DD-938), 207
JONES (1813), 28
JORDAN (DE-204), 228
Jorge Juan, 196
Jose Marti, 247
JOSEPH E. CAMPBELL (DE-70), 227
JOSEPH E. CONNOLLY (DE-450), 237
JOSEPH HEWES (DE-1078), 243
JOSEPH K. TAUSSIG (DE-1030), 239
JOSEPH M. AUMAN (DE-674), 234
JOSEPH P. KENNEDY, JR. (DD-850), 204
JOSEPH STRAUSS (DDG-16), 211
JOSEPHUS DANIELS (DLG-27), 215
JOUETT (DD-41), 170
JOUETT (DD-396), 187
JOUETT (DLG-29), 215
Joy (DD-951), 208
JOYCE (DE-317), 225
JULIUS A. FURER (DEG-6), 245
JULIUS A. RAVEN (DE-600), 234
JUNEAU (CL-52), 150
JUNEAU (CL-119), 139, 152, 153
JUNIATA (1861), 67
Junius Beebe, 97
Jupiter (AC-3), 115
K-1 (SS-32), 258
K-1 (SSK-1), 284
K-2 (SS-33), 258
K-2 (SSK-2), 284
K-3 (SS-34), 258
K-3 (SSK-3), 284
K-4 (SS-35), 258
K-5 (SS-36), 258
K-6 (SS-37), 258
K-7 (SS-38), 258
K-8 (SS-39), 258
Kabyle, 223
KADASHAN BAY (ACV-76), 130
Kaede, 247
(KAHNAMUIE) (PF-106), 251
Kai Yang, 202
Kaita Bay (ACV-78), 131
KALAMAZOO (1863), 46
KALININ BAY (ACV-68), 130
KALK (DD-170), 176

Kalk (DD-254), 182
KALK (DD-611), 189
KAMEHAMEHA (SSBN-642), 295
Kanalku Bay (ACV-77), 131
Kanaris, 205
KANAWHA (1861), 73
KANE (DD-235), 173 (photo), 179
Kang Shan, 227
Kang Won (ex DD-714), 202
Kang Won (ex DE-771), 224
KANSAS (1862), 75, 94
KANSAS (BB-21), 106
KANSAS CITY (CA-128), 139
KASAAN BAY (ACV-69), 130
Kashi, 246
KATAHDIN (1861), 73
KATAHDIN (1889), 162
Katsonis, 280
Katy, 34
KAUFFMAN (FFG-59), 252
Kawakaze, 186
Kaya, 247
KEARNY (DD-432), 189
KEARSARGE (1858), 64
KEARSARGE (BB-5), 103
Kearsarge (CV-12), 118
KEARSARGE (CV-33), 119
Keats, 220
KEITH (DE-241), 225
Kempthorne, 220
KENDALL C. CAMPBELL (DE-443), 237
KENDRICK (DD-612), 189
KENNEBEC (1861), 73
KENNEDY (DD-306), 181
KENNETH D. BAILEY (DD-713), 202
KENNETH D. BAILEY (DE-552), 238
KENNETH M. WILLETT (DE-354), 236
KENNISON (DD-138), 174
KENOSHA (1867), 70
KENTUCKY (BB-6), 100 (photo), 103
KENTUCKY (BB-66), 113
KENTUCKY (SSBN-737), 295
KEOKUK (1862), 40
KEOSAUQUA (1863), 69
KEPHART (DE-207), 228
KEPPLER (DD-765), 202
KEPPLER (DE-311), 220
KEPPLER (DE-375), 236
KETE (SS-369), 277
Kewaydin (1862), 52
KEWAYDIN (1863), 59, 63
KEWEENAW (ACV-44), 128
KEY (DE-348), 236
KEY WEST (PF-17), 247
KEY WEST (SSN-722), 289
Keyaki, 248
Keystone State (1825), 19
KEYSTONE STATE (1861), 87, 93, 94
Keystone State (ex PG-10), 158
Khaiber, 245
Khedive (ex ACV-39), 128
Khedive (ex ACV-74), 131
(KHIRIRAT) (PF-108), 251
KICKAPOO (1862), 52

KIDD (DD-661), 195
KIDD (DDG-993), 210, 212
KIDDER (DD-319), 181
Kilic Ali Pasa, 203
Kilkis, 106
KILLEN (DD-593), 195
KILTY (DD-137), 174
KIMBERLY (DD-80), 175
KIMBERLY (DD-521), 193
KINEO (1861), 73
KING (DD-242), 179
KING (DLG-10), 214
KINGFISH (SS-234), 272
(KINGSMILL) (DE-280), 220
KINKAID (DD-965), 210
KINZER (DE-232), 233
Kiri, 246
KIRK (DE-1087), 243
KIRKPATRICK (DE-318), 225
KIRWIN (DE-229), 233
KITKUN BAY (ACV-71), 130
KITTY HAWK (CVA-63), 124, 216
KLAKRING (FFG-42), 252
KLAMATH (1863), 45
KLEINSMITH (DE-376), 236
KLEINSMITH (DE-718), 235
KLINE (DE-687), 234
KNAPP (DD-653), 195
KNIGHT (DD-633), 191
KNOX (DE-1052), 243, 244, 245
KNOXVILLE (PF-64), 248
KNUDSON (DE-591), 233
Kobben, 283
Kocatepe (ex DD-859), 204
Kocatepe (ex DD-861), 204
KOELSCH (DE-1049), 241
KOINER (DE-331), 225
KOKA (1863), 45
Kongo, 113
Kotetsu, 47
Kountouriotis, 204
Kouroosh, 212
Kousseh, 282
KRAKEN (SS-370), 277
KRETCHMER (DE-329), 225
Kriezis, 203
KULA GULF (CVE-108), 131
Kun Yang, 193
Kungsholm (AVG-5), 126
Kuroshio, 272
Kusu, 247
KWAJALEIN (ACV-98), 130
Kwang Ju, 204
Kwei Yang, 193
KYNE (DE-744), 223
Kyong Ki (ex DD-883), 205
Kyong Ki (ex DE-770), 224
Kyong Nam, 234
Kyong Puk, 228
L'INDIEN (1776), 7
L'Insurgente, 11, 35
L'Italie Conquise, 35
L-1 (SS-40), 259, 261
L-2 (SS-41), 259

L-3 (SS-42), 259
L-4 (SS-43), 259
L-5 (SS-44), 259
L-6 (SS-45), 259
L-7 (SS-46), 259
L-8 (SS-48), 259, 262
L-9 (SS-49), 259
L-10 (SS-50), 259
L-11 (SS-51), 259
L. MENDEL RIVERS (SSN-686), 288
La Brune, 33
LA JOLLA (SSN-701), 289
LA PARDE (DE-409), 237
La Pedrera, 278
LABOON (DDG-58), 212
(LABUAN) (PF-80), 248
LACKAWANNA (1861), 67, 92
Lady Davis, 92
LADY PREVOST (1813), 32
LADY STERLING (1864), 94
LAFAYETTE (1862), 50
LAFAYETTE (SSBN-616), 291, 293
Lafayette (ex CV-27), 120
LAFFEY (DD-459), 188
LAFFEY (DD-724), 199
LAGARTO (SS-371), 277
Lai Yang, 204
LAKE (DE-301), 220
Lake (submarine), 256
LAKE CHAMPLAIN (CG-57), 218
LAKE CHAMPLAIN (CV-39), 119
LAKE ERIE (CG-70), 218
LAMBERTON (DD-119), 174, 177
LAMONS (DE-64), 227
LAMONS (DE-743), 223
LAMPREY (SS-372), 277
LAMSON (DD-18), 169
LAMSON (DD-328), 181
LAMSON (DD-367), 184
LANCASTER (1857), 59, 62, 71, 85
Lancaster (ex DD-76), 172
LANCETFISH (SS-296), 275
Lanciere, 192
LANG (DD-399), 187
LANG (DE-1060), 243
Langara, 204
LANGLEY (CV-1), 115
LANGLEY (CV-27), 120
Langley (DE-131), 226
LANING (DE-159), 228
LANSDALE (DD-101), 175
LANSDALE (DD-426), 188
LANSDALE (DD-766), 202
LANSDOWNE (DD-486), 190
LANSING (DE-388), 226
Lao Yang, 202
Laplace, 250
LAPON (SS-260), 272
LAPON (SSN-661), 288
LARDNER (DD-286), 180
LARDNER (DD-487), 190
LAUB (DD-263), 180
LAUB (DD-613), 189
Laurent Millaudon, 97

LA VALLETTE (DD-315), 181
LA VALLETTE (DD-448), 192
(LAWFORD) (DE-516), 221
LAWRENCE (1813), 28
LAWRENCE (1843), 27
LAWRENCE (DD-8), 168
LAWRENCE (DD-250), 179
LAWRENCE (DDG-4), 211
LAWRENCE C. TAYLOR (DE-415), 237
LAWS (DD-558), 194
(LAWSON) (DE-518), 221
Lawton, 297
Le Berceau, 17
(LE BORDELAIS) (DE-1019), 240
(LE BOULONNAIS) (DE-1018), 240
(LE BOURGUIGNON) (DE-1013), 239
(LE BRESTOIS) (DE-1017), 240
Le Brix, 248
(LE CHAMPENOIS) (DE-1011), 239
(LE CORSE) (DE-1016), 240
Le Croyable, 35
(LE GASCON) (DE-1010), 239
(LE LORRAIN) (DE-1008), 239
(LE NORMAND) (DE-1007), 239
(LE PICARD) (DE-1009), 239
(LE SAVOYARD) (DE-1012), 239
Le Verrier, 247
LEA (DD-118), 174
Leader, 35
LEAHY (DLG-16), 214, 215
Leamington, 178
Leander, 35
LEARY (DD-158), 178
LEARY (DD-879), 204
Lee (small schooner, 1775), 34
LEE FOX (DE-65), 227
Leeds, 172
LEFTWICH (DD-984), 210
LEHARDY (DE-20), 219
LEHIGH (1862), 42
LELAND E. THOMAS (DE-420), 237
Lemnos, 106
LENAPEE (1862), 80
Leon, 222
LEONARD F. MASON (DD-852), 204
Leonardo da Vinci, 272
LEOPOLD (DE-319), 225
Lepanto, 194
LERAY WILSON (DE-414), 237
LESLIE L. B. KNOX (DE-580), 233
LESTER (DE-1022), 239
Let Her Rip, 95
LEUTZE (DD-481), 192
LEVANT (1837), 19
Levant (ferry), 167
LEVY (DE-162), 222
Lewes, 172
LEWIS (DE-535), 238
LEWIS AND CLARK (SSBN-644), 295
LEWIS B. PULLER (FFG-23), 252
LEWIS HANCOCK (DD-675), 196
LEXINGTON (1776), 34, 37
LEXINGTON (1825), 19
LEXINGTON (1861), 50, 96

LEXINGTON (CC-1), 114, 174
Lexington (CC-4), 114
LEXINGTON (CV-2), 115, 116 (photo)
LEXINGTON (CV-16), 118
LEYTE (CV-32), 119
LEYTE GULF (CG-55), 218
Liao Yang, 203
Liberator, 14
LIDDLE (DE-76), 227
LIDDLE (DE-206), 228
Light Target No. 1 (AG-21, ex DD-119), 177
Light Target No. 1 (IX-35, ex DD-302), 182
Light Target No. 2 (IX-36, ex DD-107), 176
Light Target No. 2 (IX-36, ex DD-136), 174
Light Target No. 3 (AG-22, ex DD-120), 177
Light Target No. 3 (IX-37, ex DD-137), 174
Light Target No. 3 (IX-37, ex DD-275), 182
LIGHTNING (1876), 85
LILIAN (1864), 94
Lima, 159
Lincoln, 174
Lindsay, 221
LINDSEY (DD-771), 201
LING (SS-297), 275
LINGAYEN (CVE-126), 132
LINNET (1814), 28
LIONFISH (SS-298), 275
LISCOME BAY (ACV-56), 130
LITCHFIELD (DD-336), 181
LITTLE (DD-79), 174, 175
LITTLE (DD-803), 196
LITTLE ROCK (CL-92), 151; (CLG-4), 154
LIVERMORE (DD-429), 189
Livermore (DD-435), 191
Livio Piomarta, 282
LIZARDFISH (SS-373), 277
LLOYD (DE-209), 228
LLOYD E. ACREE (DE-356), 236
LLOYD THOMAS (DD-764), 202
LLOYD THOMAS (DE-312), 220
LLOYD THOMAS (DE-374), 236
Lo Yang (ex DD-421), 188
Lo Yang (ex DD-746), 200
LOCKWOOD (DE-1064), 243
LODONA (1862), 88
LOESER (DE-680), 231
LOFBERG (DD-759), 200
Logger-Head (SS-374), 279
LOGGERHEAD (SS-374), 277
Lonchi, 195
LONG (DD-209), 179
LONG BEACH (CGN-9), 149 (photo), 154
LONG BEACH (PF-34), 247
LONG ISLAND (AVG-1), 125, 129
LONGSHAW (DD-559), 194
LORAIN (PF-93), 250
LORAIN (PF-97), 250

Lord Clyde, 93
(LORING) (DE-520), 221
LOS ANGELES (CA-135), 139
LOS ANGELES (SSN-688), 289, 290
(LOSSIE) (PG-108), 246
LOUGH (DE-586), 233
(LOUIS) (DE-517), 221
LOUISIANA (1812), 34
LOUISIANA (BB-19), 106
LOUISIANA (BB-71), 114
LOUISVILLE (1861), 49
LOUISVILLE (CA-28), 136, 137 (photo)
LOUISVILLE (SSN-724), 290
Louisville, later OUACHITA (1863), 97
Louisville, ex ST. LOUIS (1898), 297
LOVELACE (DE-198), 228
LOVERING (DE-39), 219
LOVERING (DE-272), 220
LOWE (DE-325), 225
LOWRY (DD-770), 200
LOY (DE-160), 228
Lu Shan, 231
LUCE (DD-99), 175
LUCE (DD-522), 193
LUCE (DLG-7), 214
Lucifer (SS-547), 281
Lucifer (ex ACV-37), 128
LUDLOW (DD-112), 176
LUDLOW (DD-438), 190
Ludlow (ex DD-73), 172
Luitenant ter zee Victor Billet, 248
Lung Shan, 231
LUNGA POINT (ACV-94), 130
(LUTJENS) (DDG-28), 211
LYMAN (DE-302), 220
LYMAN K. SWENSON (DD-729), 200
LYNDE McCORMICK (DDG-8), 211
M-1 (SS-47), 259
MACABI (SS-375), 277
MACDONOUGH (DD-9), 168
MACDONOUGH (DD-331), 181
MACDONOUGH (DD-351), 183
MACDONOUGH (DLG-8), 214
MACEDONIAN (1812), 11, 14
MACEDONIAN (1832), 14, 62
MACHIAS (PF-53), 247
MACHIAS (PF-72), 248
MACHIAS (PG-5), 157
MACK (DE-358), 236
MACKENZIE (DD-175), 176
MACKENZIE (DD-614), 189
MACKENZIE (TB-17), 165
MACKEREL (SS-204), 267, 271
Mackerel (SST-1), 296
MACKINAW (1862), 80
MACLEISH (DD-220), 179
MACOMB (DD-458), 190
MACON (CA-132), 139
MACON (PF-96), 250
MADAWASKA (1863), 57
MADDOX (DD-168), 176
MADDOX (DD-622), 191
MADDOX (DD-731), 200
MADISON (1813), 23

MADISON (DD-425), 188
Magnifique, 1
MAGNOLIA (1862), 88, 92
MAHAN (DD-102), 175
MAHAN (DD-364), 184, 186
MAHAN (DLG-11), 214, 216 (photo)
MAHASKA (1861), 79
MAHLON S. TISDALE (FFG-27), 252
MAHOPAC (1862), 44
MAINE (1886), 102, 133
MAINE (BB-10), 104
MAINE (BB-69), 114
MAINE (SSBN-741), 295
MAJOR (DE-796), 231
Makaira (SS-548), 281
MAKASSAR STRAIT (ACV-91), 130
Maki, 248
MAKIN ISLAND (ACV-93), 130
MALEK ADHEL (1846), 35
Malgache, 223
MALOY (DE-791), 231
MALVERN (1863), 93
MANAYUNK (1862), 44
MANCHESTER (CL-83), 151
Manco Capac, 44
MANHATTAN (1862), 44
MANILA BAY (ACV-61), 130
MANITOU (1863), 69
Manitou (river steamer, 1863), 97
MANITOWOC (PF-61), 248
MANLEY (DD-74), 172
MANLEY (DD-940), 207
MANLEY (TB-23), 167
MANLOVE (DE-36), 219
Manly (TB-23), 167
(MANNERS) (DE-523), 221
MANNERT L. ABELE (DD-733), 200
MANNING (DE-199), 228
Mansfield (DD-594), 198
MANSFIELD (DD-728), 200
Mansfield (ex DD-78), 174
MANTA (SS-299), 275
MAPIRO (SS-376), 277
Maranhao, 195
MARATANZA (1861), 80
MARBLEHEAD (1861), 73, 74 (photo)
MARBLEHEAD (C-11), 144
MARBLEHEAD (CL-12), 148
MARCHAND (DE-249), 225
Marcilio Dias, 204
MARCUS (DD-321), 181
MARCUS ISLAND (ACV-77), 130
Maresal Fevzi Cakmak, 204
Margaret & Jessie, 93
MARIANO G. VALLEJO (SSBN-658), 295
MARIETTA (1862), 51
MARIETTA (PG-15), 158
MARION (1837), 20, 71
MARION (1872), 71
Marion, later MORSE (1861), 95
Mariscal Sucre, 159
Mariz e Barros, 205
Markay, 126
MARLIN (SS-205), 271

Marlin (SST-2), 296
(MAROCAIN) (DE-109), 222
MARSH (DE-699), 231
MARSHALL (DD-676), 196
Martadinata, 240
MARTIN (DE-30), 219
MARTIN H. RAY (DE-338), 226
MARTS (DE-174), 222
MARVIN SHIELDS (DE-1066), 243
MARYLAND (1798), 17
MARYLAND (BB-46), 112
MARYLAND (CA-8), 133
MARYLAND (SSBN-738), 295
MASON (DD-191), 178
MASON (DE-529), 221
Massachusetts (1816), 4
MASSACHUSETTS (1849), 86
Massachusetts (1863), 46
MASSACHUSETTS (BB-2), 102
MASSACHUSETTS (BB-54), 112
MASSACHUSETTS (BB-59), 113
MASSASOIT (1862), 81
MASSEY (DD-778), 201
MATANIKAU (ACV-101), 130
Matsu, 247
MATTABESETT (1862), 81
Matto Grosso, 199
MAUMEE (1862), 76
MAURICE J. MANUEL (DE-351), 236
MAURY (DD-100), 175
MAURY (DD-401), 186
Maximo Gomez, 246
MAYO (DD-422), 188
MAYRANT (DD-31), 169
MAYRANT (DD-402), 187
McANN (DE-73), 227
McANN (DE-179), 223
McCAFFERY (DD-860), 204
McCALL (DD-28), 169
McCALL (DD-400), 186
McCALLA (DD-253), 179
McCALLA (DD-488), 190
McCANDLESS (DE-1084), 243
McCAWLEY (DD-276), 180
McCLELLAND (DE-750), 223
McCLOY (DE-1038), 241
McClure (AVG-45), 129
McCLUSKY (FFG-41), 252
McCONNELL (DE-163), 222
McCOOK (DD-252), 179
McCOOK (DD-496), 190
McCORD (DD-534), 193
McCORMICK (DD-223), 179
McCOY REYNOLDS (DE-440), 237
McDERMUT (DD-262), 180
McDERMUT (DD-677), 196
McDOUGAL (DD-54), 171
McDOUGAL (DD-358), 183
McFARLAND (DD-237), 179
McGINTY (DE-365), 236
McGOWAN (DD-678), 196
McINERNEY (FFG-8), 251
McKEAN (DD-90), 175
McKEAN (DD-784), 202

McKEE (DD-87), 175
McKEE (DD-575), 194
McKEE (TB-18), 165
McLANAHAN (DD-264), 180
McLANAHAN (DD-615), 189
McMORRIS (DE-1036), 240
McNAIR (DD-679), 196
McNULTY (DE-581), 233
MEADE (DD-274), 180
MEADE (DD-602), 189
MEDREGAL (SS-480), 280
Medusa (1862), 42
Medway, 25
Melbourne, 201
MELVIN (DD-335), 181
MELVIN (DD-680), 196
MELVIN R. NAWMAN (DE-416), 237
Memphis (1858), 90
MEMPHIS (1862), 88
Memphis (CA-10), 135
MEMPHIS (CL-13), 148
MEMPHIS (SSN-691), 289
Mendez Nunez, 205
MENDOTA (1862), 81
MENGES (DE-320), 225
MENHADEN (SS-377), 277
MERCEDITA (1861), 87
MEREDITH (DD-165), 176
MEREDITH (DD-434), 190
MEREDITH (DD-726), 199
MEREDITH (DD-890), 205
MEREDOSIA (1864), 69
Mermoz, 247
MERO (SS-378), 277
MERRILL (DD-976), 210
MERRILL (DE-392), 226
Merrimac (1854), 57
MERRIMAC (1864), 94
MERRIMACK (1798), 11, 35
Merrimack (1803), 25
MERRIMACK (1854), 57, 83
MERTIVIER (DE-582), 233
MERTZ (DD-691), 196
MERVINE (DD-322), 181
MERVINE (DD-489), 190
METACOMET (1862), 81, 94
Metacomet, later PULASKI (1858), 90
METCALF (DD-595), 195
Mexico, 97
MEYER (DD-279), 180
MEYERKORD (DE-1058), 243
MIAMI (1861), 78, 80
MIAMI (CL-89), 151
MIAMI (SSN-755), 290
MIANTONOMOH (1862), 43
MIANTONOMOH (BM-5), 45, 99, 100 (photo)
Miaoulis, 199
MICHIGAN (1841), 72, 82
MICHIGAN (BB-27), 107
MICHIGAN (SSBN-727), 295
MICKA (DE-176), 223
MIDWAY (ACV-63), 130
MIDWAY (CVB-41), 121, 122 (photo)
Mikuma, 136

(MILANIAN) (PF-105), 251
Miles (DE-183), 224
Milford, 34
MILLEDGEVILLE (PF-94), 250
MILLEDGEVILLE (PF-98), 250
MILLER (DD-535), 193
MILLER (DE-1091), 244
MILLS (DE-383), 226
MILTON LEWIS (DE-772), 224
MILWAUKEE (1862), 52
MILWAUKEE (C-21), 146
MILWAUKEE (CL-5), 148
MINDORO (CVE-120), 132
Minerva (1862), 51
MINGO (SS-261), 272
MINGOE (1862), 81
Ministro Portales, 201
Ministro Zenteno, 199
MINNEAPOLIS (C-13), 145
MINNEAPOLIS (CA-36), 138
MINNEAPOLIS-SAINT PAUL (SSN-708), 289
MINNESOTA (1854), 55, 56 (photo)
MINNESOTA (BB-22), 106
MINNETONKA (monitor, 1863), 45
MINNETONKA (sloop, 1863), 59
MISSION BAY (ACV-59), 130
MISSISSIPPI (1839), 53
MISSISSIPPI (BB-23), 106
MISSISSIPPI (BB-41), 103, 111
MISSISSIPPI (CGN-40), 216 (photo), 217
Mississippi, later CONNECTICUT (1861), 86
Missoula (CA-13), 135
MISSOURI (1839), 54
MISSOURI (1865), 52
MISSOURI (BB-11), 104
MISSOURI (BB-63), 113
MITCHELL (DE-43), 219
Mitchell (ex DE-521), 221
MITSCHER (DDG-57), 212
MITSCHER (DL-2), 207, 213, 214, 215
MOALE (DD-693), 199
MOBERLY (PF-63), 248
Mobile (1862), 88
MOBILE (CL-63), 151
MOBILE BAY (CG-53), 218
MOCCASIN (SS-5), 253
MODOC (1863), 45
MOFFETT (DD-362), 183
Mogami, 136, 150
MOHAWK (1813), 15
MOHAWK (1858), 90
MOHICAN (1858), 64, 67, 71
MOHICAN (1872), 71
MOHONGO (1863), 82
MOINESTER (DE-1097), 244
(MOLDERS) (DDG-29), 211
Molly, 34
Momi, 247
MONADNOCK (1862), 43
MONADNOCK (BM-3), 99
MONAGHAN (DD-32), 170
MONAGHAN (DD-354), 183
MONDAMIN (1863), 69
Mongonsidi, 240

MONITOR (1861), 39
MONOCACY (1863), 82
MONONGAHELA (1861), 68
MONSSEN (DD-436), 190
MONSSEN (DD-798), 196
Mont Organise, 87
MONTANA (BB-51), 112
MONTANA (BB-67), 114, 135, 153
MONTANA (CA-13), 135
MONTAUK (1862), 42
MONTEREY (BM-6), 101
MONTEREY (CG-61), 218
MONTEREY (CV-26), 120
MONTEZUMA (1798), 33
MONTGOMERY (1775), 7
MONTGOMERY (1861), 87, 88, 93
MONTGOMERY (C-9), 144, 146
MONTGOMERY (DD-121), 177
Montgomery (ex DD-75), 172
MONTICELLO (1861), 89, 90
MONTPELIER (CL-57), 151
MONTPELIER (SSN-765), 290
(MONTSERRAT) (PF-82), 248
Moodna (1862), 40
MOODY (DD-277), 180
MOORE (DE-240), 225
(MOORSOM) (DE-522), 221
MOOSBRUGGER (DD-980), 210
Moosehead (IX-98), 182
MORAY (SS-300), 275
Mormacland (later BAVG-1), 126
Mormacland (later AVG-17), 129
Mormacmail (later AVG-1), 126
Mormacmail (later BAVG-6), 129
Mormacpenn, 129
MORRIS (1778), 37
MORRIS (DD-271), 180
MORRIS (DD-417), 188
MORRIS (TB-14), 165
MORRISON (DD-560), 194
MORSE (1861), 95
MORTON (DD-948), 208
Moser Bay (CVE-114), 131
MOSHOLU (1863), 69
MOSLEY (DE-321), 225
Mosser Bay (CVE-114), 132
MOUND CITY (1861), 48 (photo), 49
(MOUNSEY) (DE-524), 221
Mount Savage, 90
MOUNT VERNON (1861), 91
Mount Vernon (AVG-3), 126
Mount Vernon, later MOUNT WASHINGTON
    (1861), 91
MOUNT WASHINGTON (1861), 91
Muavenet, 201
MUGFORD (DD-105), 175
MUGFORD (DD-389), 186
MUIR (DE-770), 224
MULLANY (DD-325), 181
MULLANY (DD-528), 193
MULLINIX (DD-944), 207
MUNDA (ACV-104), 130
Murat Reis, 278
Murmansk, 148

MURPHY (DD-603), 189
MURRAY (DD-97), 175
MURRAY (DD-576), 194
MUSCOOTA (1863), 82
MUSKALLUNGE (SS-262), 272
MUSKEGON (PF-24), 247
MUSKOGEE (PF-49), 247
MUSTIN (DD-413), 188
MYERS (DE-595), 234
MYLES C. FOX (DD-829), 203
MYLES C. FOX (DE-546), 238
MYSTIC (1858), 90
N-1 (SS-53), 260
N-2 (SS-54), 260
N-3 (SS-55), 260
N-4 (SS-56), 259, 260
N-5 (SS-57), 259, 260
N-6 (SS-58), 260
N-7 (SS-59), 259, 260
Nabob (ex ACV-41), 128
Nabob (ex ACV-79), 131
Nader, 212
Nadur, 246
Nagara, 184
(NAGHDI) (PF-104), 251
Nahang, 282
NAHANT (1862), 41 (photo), 42, 46
NAIFEH (DE-352), 236
Naktong, 246
Nan Yang (ex DD-431), 189
Nan Yang (ex DD-760), 200
NANSEMOND (1863), 93
NANTASKET (1864), 64, 76, 77
NANTUCKET (1862), 42
Nantucket (1873), 78
NAPA (1863), 45
Nara, 247
(NARBROUGH) (DE-569), 230
Narcine (SS-549), 281
Narciso Monturiol (ex SS-368), 277
Narciso Monturiol (ex SS-382), 277
Narcissus, 31
NARRAGANSETT (1858), 66
NARWHAL (SS-17), 256
Narwhal (SS-167), 267
NARWHAL (SSN-671), 288, 296
NASHVILLE (1865), 47
NASHVILLE (CL-43), 148
NASHVILLE (PG-7), 157
NASSAU (ACV-16), 128
Nassuk Bay (ACV-67), 131
NATCHEZ (1825), 19
NATCHEZ (PG-102), 245
NATHAN HALE (SSBN-623), 293
NATHANIEL GREENE (SSBN-636), 295
NATOMA BAY (ACV-62), 130
NAUBUC (1863), 45
Naugatuck, 39
NAUSETT (1863), 45
NAUTILUS (1803), 35
Nautilus (SS-29), 258
Nautilus (SS-168), 266 (photo), 267
NAUTILUS (SSN-571), 284, 286
Nautilus (ex SS-73), 261

Navarinon, 193
NEAL A. SCOTT (DE-769), 224
Nebraska (1863), 46
NEBRASKA (BB-14), 104
Nebraska (CA-4), 135
NEBRASKA (SSBN-739), 295
NEEDLEFISH (SS-379), 277
NEEDLEFISH (SS-493), 281
NEHENTA BAY (ACV-74), 130
NELSON (DD-623), 191
Nemesis (1863), 45
NEOSHO (1862), 52
Neptune (1862), 44
NEPTUNE (1863), 88, 89
Neptune, later CLYDE (1863), 92
NEREUS (1863), 88, 89
NERKA (SS-380), 277
Neshaming (1863), 58
NESHAMINY (1863), 58
Netzahualcoyotl, 204
NEUENDORF (DE-200), 228
NEUNZER (DE-150), 225
Nevada (1863), 58
NEVADA (BB-36), 107, 109, 111
NEVADA (BM-8), 101
NEVADA (SSBN-733), 295
NEW (DD-818), 203
NEW BEDFORD (PF-71), 248
New Era, 49
New Hampshire (1775), 5
NEW HAMPSHIRE (1816), 2
NEW HAMPSHIRE (BB-25), 102, 106
NEW HAMPSHIRE (BB-70), 114
NEW HAVEN (CL-76), 120, 151
NEW HAVEN (CL-109), 152
NEW HAVEN (CLK-2), 213
NEW IRONSIDES (1861), 39
New Jersey (BB-13), 106
NEW JERSEY (BB-16), 104
NEW JERSEY (BB-62), 113
NEW MEXICO (BB-40), 111
NEW ORLEANS (1813), 4
NEW ORLEANS (1898), 145
NEW ORLEANS (CA-32), 138, 150
New Uncle Sam (1862), 97
NEW YORK (1798), 10
NEW YORK (1816), 2
New York (1863), 60
NEW YORK (BB-34), 108
NEW YORK (CA-2), 133
NEW YORK CITY (SSN-696), 289
New York, later HARVARD (1898), 297
NEWARK (C-1), 141, 143
NEWARK (CL-88), 151
NEWARK (CL-100), 120, 151
NEWARK (CL-108), 152
Newark (ex DD-89), 175
NEWCOMB (DD-586), 195
NEWELL (DE-322), 225
NEWMAN (DE-205), 228
NEWMAN K. PERRY (DD-883), 205
Newmarket, 175
NEWPORT (PF-27), 247
NEWPORT (PG-12), 158

Newport (ex DD-81), 175
NEWPORT NEWS (CA-148), 140
NEWPORT NEWS (SSN-750), 290
Ngurah Rai, 240
NIAGARA (1813), 28
NIAGARA (1854), 57, 59
Niagara (DD-162), 176
Niagara, later LINNET (1814), 28
NIANTIC (ACV-46), 128
NIBLACK (DD-424), 189
NICHOLAS (DD-311), 181
NICHOLAS (DD-449), 192
NICHOLAS (FFG-47), 252
NICHOLSON (DD-52), 171
NICHOLSON (DD-442), 190
NICHOLSON (DD-982), 210
NICHOLSON (TB-29), 167
Nictheroy, 297
NIELDS (DD-616), 189
Niki, 189
NIMITZ (CVAN-68), 125
Niobe (1863), 45
NIPHON (1863), 92, 93, 94
NIPSIC (1862), 57, 75, 76, 77
NIPSIC (1873), 77
Nire, 248
NOA (DD-343), 181
NOA (DD-841), 203
Noe-Daquy, 93
NONSUCH (1812), 36
NORFOLK (1798), 34
NORFOLK (CA-137), 139
Norfolk (CL-118), 152
NORFOLK (DL-1), 213
NORFOLK (SSN-714), 289
NORMAN SCOTT (DD-690), 196
NORMANDY (CG-60), 218
NORRIS (DD-859), 204
NORTH CAROLINA (1816), 2
NORTH CAROLINA (BB-52), 112
NORTH CAROLINA (BB-55), 112, 113
NORTH CAROLINA (CA-12), 135
NORTH DAKOTA (BB-29), 107, 108, 109
NORTHAMPTON (CA-26), 136, 138
NORTHAMPTON (CA-125), 139; (CLC-1), 153
NORWICH (1861), 91
Nossuk Bay (ACV-67), 131
Nuestra Senora de Regla, 96
NYACK (1862), 75
(NYASALAND) (PF-83), 248
O'BANNON (DD-177), 176
O'BANNON (DD-450), 192
O'BANNON (DD-987), 210
O'BRIEN (DD-51), 171
O'BRIEN (DD-415), 188
O'BRIEN (DD-725), 199
O'BRIEN (DD-975), 210
O'BRIEN (TB-30), 167
O'CALLAHAN (DE-1051), 243
O'FLAHERTY (DE-340), 235
O'HARE (DD-889), 205
O'Higgins, 148
O'NEILL (DE-188), 223
O'REILLY (DE-330), 225

O'TOOLE (DE-274), 220
O'Toole (DE-327), 226
O'TOOLE (DE-527), 221
O-1 (SS-62), 260, 261, 262
O-2 (SS-63), 260
O-3 (SS-64), 260
O-4 (SS-65), 260
O-5 (SS-66), 260
O-6 (SS-67), 260
O-7 (SS-68), 260
O-8 (SS-69), 260
O-9 (SS-70), 260
O-10 (SS-71), 260
O-11 (SS-72), 261
O-12 (SS-73), 261
O-13 (SS-74), 261
O-14 (SS-75), 261
O-15 (SS-76), 261
O-16 (SS-77), 261
OAKLAND (CL-95), 150
OBERRENDER (DE-344), 235
Obispo (SS-382), 279
OCTOPUS (SS-9), 254, 256
OCTORARA (1861), 79
ODAX (SS-484), 280
ODUM (DE-670), 231
OGDEN (PF-39), 247
OHIO (1816), 4
OHIO (BB-12), 104
OHIO (BB-68), 114
OHIO (SSBN-726), 290, 295
Ojanca (SS-381), 279
OKINAWA (CVE-127), 132
OKLAHOMA (BB-37), 109, 110 (photo)
OKLAHOMA CITY (CL-91), 151; (CLG-5), 154
OKLAHOMA CITY (SSN-723), 290
Old Columbia (CA-16), 145
Old Constellation (1853), 23
Old Constitution (1794), 9
OLDENDORF (DD-972), 210
Olinde, 47
OLIVER HAZARD PERRY (FFG-7), 251
OLIVER MITCHELL (DE-417), 237
Olsen (DE-765), 224
OLYMPIA (C-6), 144, 146
OLYMPIA (SSN-717), 289
OMAHA (1867), 70, 141
OMAHA (CL-4), 148, 174
OMAHA (SSN-692), 289
OMMANEY BAY (ACV-79), 130
ONEIDA (1807), 27
ONEIDA (1858), 64
ONEOTA (1862), 44
ONO (SS-357), 277
ONONDAGA (1862), 42
ONTARIO (1813), 17, 18
ONTARIO (1863), 59, 69
Onward, 89
ORANGE (PF-43), 247
Orca (SS-34), 258
Orca (SS-381), 279
ORDRONAUX (DD-617), 189
Oregon (1863), 46
OREGON (BB-3), 102

OREGON CITY (CA-122), 139, 140, 153, 155
Orella, 231
Oriole (1837), 20
Orion (1863), 45
Oriskany (CV-18), 118
ORISKANY (CV-34), 118, 120
ORLANDO (PF-99), 250
ORLECK (DD-886), 205
Orpheus (HMS, 1780), 8
Orpheus (HMS, 1809), 18
Oruc Reis, 278
OSAGE (1862), 52
OSBERG (DE-538), 238
OSBORNE (DD-295), 180
Osceola, ex NEOSHO (1862), 52
OSCEOLA (1862), 81
Osmond Ingram (DD-255), 182
OSMUS (DE-701), 231
OSSIPEE (1861), 67, 68
OSTERHAUS (DE-164), 222
Ostfriesland, 140
OSWALD (DE-71), 227
OSWALD (DE-767), 224
OSWALD A. POWERS (DE-542), 238
OTSEGO (1862), 81
Otsego (1863), 45
OTTAWA (1861), 73
OTTER (DE-210), 228
OTTERSTETTER (DE-244), 225
OUACHITA (1863), 97
OUELLET (DE-1077), 243
OVERTON (DD-239), 179
OWASCO (1861), 73
OWEN (DD-536), 193
Oxford, 33
Oyashio, 136
OZARK (1862), 51
Ozark (BM-7), 101
OZBOURN (DD-846), 203
P-511, 261
P-512, 261
P-514, 261
P-551, 263
P-552, 263
P-553, 263
P-554, 263
P-555, 263
P-556, 263
Pacocha, 278
PADDLE (SS-263), 272
PADUCAH (PG-18), 160
Palang, 201
PALAU (CVE-122), 132
PALMER (DD-161), 176
PAMPANITO (SS-383), 277
PANTHER (1898), 297
Panthir, 223
Papaloapan (ex DD-603), 234
Papaloapan (ex PF-62), 248
Papanikolis, 277
(PAPUA) (PF-84), 248
Para (ex DD-472), 192
Para (ex DE-1050), 243
Paraiba (ex DD-473), 192

Paraiba (ex DE-1045), 241
Parana (ex DD-797), 196
Parana (ex DE-1048), 241
PARCHE (SS-384), 278
PARCHE (SSN-683), 288
PARGO (SS-264), 272
PARGO (SSN-650), 288
Paris, 297
PARKER (DD-48), 170
PARKER (DD-604), 189
Parker Vein, 90
PARKS (DE-165), 222
PARLE (DE-708), 234
(PARRET) (PG-109), 246
PARROTT (DD-218), 179
PARSONS (DD-949), 208
PASADENA (CL-65), 151, 154
PASADENA (SSN-752), 290
PASCO (PF-6), 246
Pasley (ex PF-86), 251
(PASLEY) (DE-519), 221
PASSACONAWAY (1863), 46
PASSAIC (1862), 42, 44
PATAPSCO (1798), 17
PATAPSCO (1813), 36
PATAPSCO (1862), 42
PATRICK HENRY (SSBN-599), 293
Patrol Boat No. 102, 182
Patroller, 128
PATTERSON (DD-36), 170
PATTERSON (DD-392), 186
PATTERSON (DE-1061), 243
Pattimura, 251
Patton, 251
PAUL (DE-1080), 243
PAUL F. FOSTER (DD-964), 210
PAUL G. BAKER (DE-642), 230
PAUL G. BAKER (DE-755), 224
PAUL HAMILTON (DD-307), 181
PAUL HAMILTON (DD-590), 195
PAUL HAMILTON (DDG-60), 212
PAUL JONES (1834), 15
PAUL JONES (1861), 78
PAUL JONES (DD-10), 168
PAUL JONES (DD-230), 179
PAULDING (DD-22), 169, 262
PAVLIC (DE-669), 231
PAWNEE (1858), 66
PAWTUXET (1862), 81
PC-460, 263
PEACOCK (1813), 18, 19, 26, 28
PEACOCK (1828), 19, 20
PEACOCK (1864), 69
Peacock, ex WASP, 25
Peard, 251
Pearl, 62
PEARY (DD-226), 179
PEIFFER (DE-588), 233
Pelican, 25
PEMBINA (1861), 73
PENGUIN (1861), 91
Penguin (PG-8), 158
PENNEWELL (DE-175), 223
PENNSYLVANIA (1816), 2

Pennsylvania (1863), 59
Pennsylvania (BB-14), 106
PENNSYLVANIA (BB-38), 109, 111
PENNSYLVANIA (CA-4), 133
PENNSYLVANIA (SSBN-735), 295
PENOBSCOT (1861), 73
PENSACOLA (1857), 59, 63
PENSACOLA (CA-24), 136
PEORIA (1862), 81
PEORIA (PF-67), 248
PEQUOT (1862), 76, 94
PERCH (SS-176), 269
PERCH (SS-313), 276
PERCIVAL (DD-298), 180
PERCIVAL (DD-452), 198
PERDIDO (ACV-47), 129
(PERIM) (PF-89), 250
PERKINS (DD-26), 169
PERKINS (DD-377), 184
PERKINS (DD-877), 204
PERMIT (SS-178), 269
PERMIT (SSN-594), 286
Pernambuco (ex DD-556), 194
Pernambuco (ex DE-1041), 241
(PERO ESCOBAR) (DE-1032), 240
PERRY (1843), 27
PERRY (DD-11), 168
PERRY (DD-340), 181
PERRY (DD-844), 203
(PERTH) (DDG-25), 211
Pet, 93
PETERHOFF (1863), 89
PETERSON (DD-969), 210
PETERSON (DE-152), 225
PETO (SS-265), 272
PETREL (PG-2), 157
PETROF BAY (ACV-80), 130
PETTIT (DE-253), 225
Peyton, 251
PHARRIS (DE-1094), 244
Phelps (DD-349), 183
PHELPS (DD-360), 183
PHILADELPHIA (1798), 10
PHILADELPHIA (C-4), 142 (photo), 143
PHILADELPHIA (CL-41), 148
PHILADELPHIA (SSN-690), 289
Philadelphia, ex YALE (1898), 297
PHILIP (DD-76), 172
PHILIP (DD-498), 192
PHILIPPINE SEA (CG-58), 218
PHILIPPINE SEA (CV-47), 119
PHILIPPINES (CB-4), 135
Phillimore, 251
Phineas Sprague, 86
Phoebe, 10
PHOENIX (CL-46), 148
PHOENIX (SSN-702), 289
Piaui, 196
Pickerel (SS-22), 257
PICKEREL (SS-177), 269
PICKEREL (SS-524), 281
PICKERING (1798), 25
Picket Boats Nos. 1-6 (1864), 85
PICKING (DD-685), 196

Picua, 281
PICUDA (SS-382), 277
Piedra Buena, 200
PIKE (SS-6), 253
PIKE (SS-173), 268
Pilford, 251
PILLSBURY (DD-227), 179
PILLSBURY (DE-133), 224
PILOTFISH (SS-386), 278
Pin Klao, 223
PINCKNEY (1798), 25
Pinna (SS-178), 269
PINOLA (1861), 73
PINTADO (SS-387), 278
PINTADO (SSN-672), 288
PIPEFISH (SS-388), 278
PIPER (SS-409), 278
PIRANHA (SS-389), 278
Piri Reis (ex SS-376), 277
Piri Reis (ex SS-563), 282
PISCATAQUA (monitor, 1863), 45
PISCATAQUA (sloop, 1863), 59
(PITCAIRN) (PF-85), 248
PITTSBURGH (1861), 49
Pittsburgh (CA-4), 135
Pittsburgh (CA-70), 139
PITTSBURGH (CA-72), 139
PITTSBURGH (SSN-720), 289
Piyale Pasa, 203
PLAICE (SS-390), 278
Plan de Guadalupe, 161
PLATTSBURG (1813), 15
Plattsburg, ex HARVARD (1898), 297
PLUNGER (1893), 253
PLUNGER (SS-2), 253
PLUNGER (SS-179), 269
PLUNGER (SSN-595), 286
Plunger (SSN-596), 287
PLUNKET (DD-431), 189
PLYMOUTH (1843), 21
Plymouth (1867), 70
Po Yang, 200
POCAHONTAS (1859), 72, 75, 89, 92
POCATELLO (PF-9), 246
POGY (SS-266), 272
POGY (SSN-647), 288
Poictiers, 25
POINT CRUZ (CVE-119), 131
POLLACK (SS-180), 269
Pollack (SSN-595), 287
Pollack (SSN-596), 287
POLLACK (SSN-603), 286
POMFRET (SS-391), 278
POMODON (SS-486), 280
POMPANO (SS-181), 269
POMPANO (SS-491), 281
POMPON (SS-267), 272
POMPONOOSUC (1863), 58
PONTIAC (1862), 81
PONTOOSUC (1862), 81
POOLE (DE-151), 225
POPE (DD-225), 179
POPE (DE-134), 224
Popham, 251

Porcupine, 36
PORPOISE (1820), 31
PORPOISE (1834), 26
Porpoise (PG-9), 158
PORPOISE (SS-7), 253
PORPOISE (SS-172), 268
PORT ROYAL (1861), 78
Port Royal (CG-69), 218
PORT ROYAL (CG-73), 218
Portage Bay (CVE-115), 132
PORTER (DD-59), 171
PORTER (DD-356), 183, 187
PORTER (DD-800), 196
PORTER (TB-6), 164
PORTERFIELD (DD-682), 196
PORTLAND (CA-33), 138
PORTSMOUTH (1798), 11
PORTSMOUTH (1843), 21
PORTSMOUTH (CL-102), 151
PORTSMOUTH (SSN-707), 289
Poseidon, 272
POTOMAC (1816), 14
POUGHKEEPSIE (PF-26), 247
Powell (DD-686), 198
POWER (DD-839), 203
POWHATAN (1847), 48 (photo), 54
PRAIRIE (1898), 297
Prairie State (IX-15), 103, 104
Prasae, 247
PRATT (DE-363), 236
PREBLE (1837), 20
PREBLE (DD-12), 163 (photo), 168
PREBLE (DD-345), 181
PREBLE (DLG-15), 214
Premier (ex ACV-42), 128
Premier (ex ACV-83), 131
PRESIDENT (1794), 9
President Bourguiba, 225
Presidente Eloy Alfaro, 203
Presidente Peynaldo, 248
Presidente Troncoso, 246
PRESLEY (DE-371), 236
PRESTON (1864), 94
PRESTON (DD-19), 169, 173 (photo)
PRESTON (DD-327), 181
PRESTON (DD-379), 184
PRESTON (DD-795), 196
Preveze (ex SS-363), 273
Preveze (ex SS-340), 276
PRICE (DE-332), 225
PRIDE (DE-323), 225
Primo Longobardo, 281
PRINCE (ACV-45), 128
PRINCE WILLIAM (ACV-31), 128
Princess Amelia, 35
PRINCESS ROYAL (1863), 75, 89
PRINCETON (1837), 60, 62
PRINCETON (1851), 62
PRINCETON (CG-59), 218
PRINCETON (CV-23), 120
PRINCETON (CV-37), 119
PRINCETON (PG-13), 158
Pringle (DD-451), 198
PRINGLE (DD-477), 192

PRINZ EUGEN (1945), 140
PRITCHETT (DD-561), 194
PROMETHEUS (1814), 36
PROTEUS (1863), 88, 89
PROVIDENCE (brig, 1775), 24, 34
PROVIDENCE (frigate, 1775), 6
PROVIDENCE (CL-82), 151; (CLG-6), 154
PROVIDENCE (SSN-719), 289
Prowse, 251
PRUITT (DD-347), 181
Pudiano (SS-392), 279
Pueblo (CA-7), 135
PUEBLO (PF-13), 246
PUERTO RICO (CB-5), 135
PUFFER (SS-268), 272
PUFFER (SSN-652), 288
PUGET SOUND (CVE-113), 131
PULASKI (1858), 90
Puncher, 129
PURDY (DD-734), 200
PURITAN (1862), 44
PURITAN (BM-1), 45, 99, 254
Pursuer, 128
Pursuit (bark, 1861), 91
PURVIS (DD-709), 201
Pusan, 196
PUSHMATAHA (1863), 69
PUTNAM (DD-287), 180
Putnam (DD-537), 198
PUTNAM (DD-757), 200
PYBUS (ACV-34), 128
QUAKER CITY (1861), 87, 92
Queen (ex ACV-49), 129
Queen (ex ACV-90), 131
QUEEN CHARLOTTE (1813), 24
QUEEN OF FRANCE (1777), 33
QUEENFISH (SS-393), 278
QUEENFISH (SSN-651), 288
Quetzalcoatl, 204
QUICK (DD-490), 190
QUILLBACK (SS-424), 280
QUINCY (CA-39), 138
QUINCY (CA-71), 139
QUINNEBAUG (1864), 71, 76
QUINNEBAUG (1872), 71
QUINSIGAMOND (1863), 46
R-1 (SS-78), 261, 262
R-2 (SS-79), 261
R-3 (SS-80), 261
R-4 (SS-81), 261
R-5 (SS-82), 261
R-6 (SS-83), 261
R-7 (SS-84), 261
R-8 (SS-85), 261
R-9 (SS-86), 261
R-10 (SS-87), 261
R-11 (SS-88), 261
R-12 (SS-89), 261
R-13 (SS-90), 261
R-14 (SS-91), 261
R-15 (SS-92), 261
R-16 (SS-93), 261
R-17 (SS-94), 261
R-18 (SS-95), 261

R-19 (SS-96), 261
R-20 (SS-97), 261
R-21 (SS-98), 262
R-22 (SS-99), 262
R-23 (SS-100), 262
R-24 (SS-101), 262
R-25 (SS-102), 262
R-26 (SS-103), 262
R-27 (SS-104), 262
R. R. CUYLER (1861), 87
RABAUL (CVE-121), 132
Raby (DE-190), 224
RABY (DE-698), 231
RACEHORSE (1776), 37
RACINE (PF-100), 250
RADFORD (DD-120), 177
RADFORD (DD-446), 192
Rainbow (HMS), 5
Rainbow (ex SS-475), 280
Rajah (ex ACV-45), 128
Rajah (ex ACV-94), 131
Rajah Humabon, 222
Rajah Lakandula, 225
Rajah Soliman, 230
RALEIGH (1775), 5
RALEIGH (C-8), 144
RALEIGH (CL-7), 148
RALL (DE-304), 220
RALPH TALBOT (DD-390), 186
RAMAGE (DDG-61), 212
Rambler, 35
RAMSAY (DD-124), 177
RAMSDEN (DE-382), 226
RAMSEY (DEG-2), 245
Ramsey (ex DD-274), 180
RANDOLPH (1775), 5
RANDOLPH (CV-15), 119
Ranee (ex ACV-46), 128
Ranee (ex ACV-99), 131
RANGER (1776), 16
RANGER (1873), 78
RANGER (CC-4), 114
Ranger (CC-5), 114
RANGER (CV-4), 115, 117
RANGER (CVA-61), 123
RARITAN (1816), 14
RASHER (SS-269), 272
RATHBURNE (DD-113), 174
RATHBURNE (DE-1057), 243
RATON (SS-270), 272
Rattler (river steamer, 1862), 97
RATTLESNAKE (1813), 35
Rattletrap (armed rowboat), 37
(RAVAGER) (ACV-24), 128
RAY (SS-271), 272
RAY (SSN-653), 288
RAY K. EDWARDS (DE-237), 233
RAYMON W. HERNDON (DE-688), 234
RAYMOND (DE-341), 235
Raymond W. Herndon (DE-688), 235
RAZORBACK (SS-394), 278
READING (PF-66), 248
Reading (ex DD-269), 180
Reaper, 129

REASONER (DE-1063), 243
Rebecca, 37
REDFIN (SS-272), 272
REDFISH (SS-395), 278
Redfish (SSN-680), 288
(REDMILL) (DE-89), 228
REDNOUR (DE-592), 233
REEVES (DE-156), 228
REEVES (DLG-24), 214
Reeves (ex DE-94), 232
REGISTER (DE-233), 233
Register (DE-308), 221
REID (DD-21), 169
REID (DD-292), 180
REID (DD-369), 184
REID (FFG-30), 252
REINA MERCEDES (1898), 145
REMEY (DD-688), 196
Remittance, 34
REMORA (SS-487), 280
RENDOVA (CVE-114), 131
RENO (CL-96), 150
Reno (CL-98), 150
RENO (DD-303), 181
RENSHAW (DD-176), 176
RENSHAW (DD-499), 192
RENTZ (FFG-46), 252
REPRISAL (1776), 34
Reprisal (CV-30), 120
REPRISAL (CV-35), 119
Republique, 86
REQUIN (SS-481), 280
RESACA (1864), 70, 76, 77
RESISTENCE (1777), 34
RETALIATION (1798), 35
(RETALICK) (DE-90), 228
REUBEN JAMES (DD-245), 179
REUBEN JAMES (DE-153), 228
REUBEN JAMES (FFG-57), 252
REVENGE (1777), 37
REVENGE (1806), 36
REVENGE (1813), 36
Reviver, 159
REYBOLD (DE-177), 223
REYBOLD (DE-275), 220
REYNOLDS (DE-42), 219
(REYNOLDS) (DE-91), 228
RHIND (DD-404), 187
RHODE ISLAND (1861), 87
RHODE ISLAND (BB-17), 104
Rhode Island (SSBN-730), 296
RHODE ISLAND (SSBN-740), 295
RHODES (DE-384), 226
Riachuelo (ironclad), 102
Riachuelo (ex SS-263), 272
RICH (DD-820), 197 (photo), 203
RICH (DE-695), 231
RICHARD B. ANDERSON (DD-786), 202
RICHARD B. RUSSELL (SSN-687), 288
RICHARD E. BYRD (DDG-23), 211
RICHARD E. KRAUS (DD-849), 204
RICHARD L. PAGE (DEG-5), 245
RICHARD M. ROWELL (DE-403), 236, 269
RICHARD P. LEARY (DD-664), 195

RICHARD S. BULL (DE-402), 236
RICHARD S. EDWARDS (DD-950), 208
RICHARD W. SUESENS (DE-342), 235
RICHEY (DE-385), 226
RICHMOND (1798), 35
RICHMOND (1857), 63
RICHMOND (CL-9), 148
RICHMOND K. TURNER (DLG-20), 214
Richmond (ex DD-93), 174
RICKETTS (DE-254), 225
RIDDLE (DE-185), 223
RILEY (DE-579), 233
RINEHART (DE-196), 223
RINGGOLD (DD-89), 175
RINGGOLD (DD-500), 192
RINGNESS (DE-590), 233
Rio de Janeiro (later BAVG-5), 126
Rio de Janeiro (ex SS-484), 280
Rio de la Plata, 126
Rio Grande do Norte, 200
Rio Grande do Sul (ex SS-381), 277
Rio Grande do Sul (ex SS-523), 281
Rio Hudson, 126
Rio Parana, 126
(RIOU) (DE-92), 228
Ripley, 180
Riquelme, 227
RIZAL (DD-174), 176
RIZZI (DE-537), 238
RO-41, 236
RO-108, 186
ROANOKE (1854), 55; (monitor, 1862), 40
ROANOKE (CL-114), 152
ROANOKE (CL-145), 152
Roanoke (PF-93), 251
ROARK (DE-1053), 243
ROBALO (SS-273), 272
ROBERT A. OWENS (DD-827), 203
ROBERT A. OWENS (DD-854), 204
ROBERT BRAZIER (DE-345), 235
ROBERT E. LEE (SSBN-601), 293
Robert E. Lee, later FORT DONELSON
  (1864), 89
ROBERT E. PEARY (DE-132), 224
ROBERT E. PEARY (DE-1073), 243
ROBERT F. KELLER (DE-419), 237
ROBERT G. BRADLEY (FFG-49), 252
ROBERT H. McCARD (DD-822), 203
ROBERT H. SMITH (DD-735), 200
ROBERT I. PAINE (DE-578), 230
ROBERT K. HUNTINGTON (DD-781), 201
ROBERT L. WILSON (DD-847), 204
ROBERT SMITH (DD-324), 181
ROBERTS (DE-749), 223
ROBINSON (DD-88), 175
ROBINSON (DD-562), 194
ROBISON (DDG-12), 211
Rochambeau, 42
ROCHE (DE-197), 223
Rochester (CA-2), 133
Rochester (CA-73), 139
ROCHESTER (CA-124), 137 (photo), 139, 155
ROCK (SS-274), 272
ROCKFORD (PF-48), 247

Rockingham, 180
Rockport (1873), 78
Rodgers (DD-170), 176
RODGERS (DD-254), 180
RODGERS (DD-876), 204
RODGERS (TB-4), 164
RODMAN (DD-456), 190
RODNEY M. DAVIS (FFG-60), 252
Rodriguez, 223
ROE (DD-24), 169
ROE (DD-418), 188
Roebuck, 8
Rogers (DE-772), 224
ROGERS BLOOD (DE-555), 238
ROGERS BLOOD (DE-605), 234
ROI (ACV-103), 130
ROLF (DE-362), 236
ROMBACH (DE-364), 236
Romeo Romei, 282
(ROMMEL) (DDG-30), 211
RONCADOR (SS-301), 275
RONQUIL (SS-396), 278
ROOKS (DD-804), 196
ROPER (DD-147), 174
Rosales, 195
ROSS (DD-563), 194
Rossie, 35
ROWAN (DD-64), 171
ROWAN (DD-405), 187
ROWAN (DD-782), 202
ROWAN (TB-8), 164
ROWE (DD-564), 194
(ROWLEY) (DE-95), 228
Roxborough, 176
ROY O. HALE (DE-336), 225
ROYAL SAVAGE (1775), 36
RUCHAMKIN (DE-228), 233
RUDDEROW (DE-224), 233, 235
RUDYERD BAY (ACV-81), 130
Ruler (ex ACV-50), 129
Ruler (ex ACV-103), 131
RUNELS (DE-793), 231
RUNNER (SS-275), 272
RUNNER (SS-476), 280
(RUPERT) (DE-96), 228
RUPERTUS (DD-851), 204
RUSSELL (DD-414), 188
RUSSELL (DDG-59), 212
RUSSELL M. COX (DE-774), 224
(RUTHERFORD) (DE-93), 228
S-1 (SS-105), 262, 263
S-2 (SS-106), 262, 263
S-3 (SS-107), 262, 263
S-4 (SS-109), 262
S-5 (SS-110), 262
S-6 (SS-111), 262
S-7 (SS-112), 262
S-8 (SS-113), 262
S-9 (SS-114), 262
S-10 (SS-115), 262
S-11 (SS-116), 262
S-12 (SS-117), 262
S-13 (SS-118), 262
S-14 (SS-119), 264, 265

S-15 (SS-120), 264
S-16 (SS-121), 264
S-17 (SS-122), 264
S-18 (SS-123), 263, 264
S-19 (SS-124), 263
S-20 (SS-125), 263
S-21 (SS-126), 263
S-22 (SS-127), 263
S-23 (SS-128), 263
S-24 (SS-129), 263
S-25 (SS-130), 263
S-26 (SS-131), 263
S-27 (SS-132), 263
S-28 (SS-133), 263
S-29 (SS-134), 263
S-30 (SS-135), 263
S-31 (SS-136), 263
S-32 (SS-137), 263
S-33 (SS-138), 263
S-34 (SS-139), 263
S-35 (SS-140), 263
S-36 (SS-141), 263
S-37 (SS-142), 263
S-38 (SS-143), 263
S-39 (SS-144), 263
S-40 (SS-145), 263
S-41 (SS-146), 263
S-42 (SS-153), 264
S-42 thru S-57 (SS 153-168), 264
S-43 (SS-154), 264
S-44 (SS-155), 264
S-45 (SS-156), 264
S-46 (SS-157), 264
S-47 (SS-158), 264
S-48 (SS-159), 265
S-49 (SS-160), 265
S-50 (SS-161), 265
S-51 (SS-162), 265
S-58 thru S-65 (SS 169-173), 265
S. P. LEE (DD-310), 181
SABALO (SS-302), 275
SABINE (1816), 13 (photo), 14
SABLEFISH (SS-303), 275
SACHEM (1776), 37
Sachtouris, 204
SACO (1862), 75
SACRAMENTO (1861), 68
Sacramento (AOE-1), 113
SACRAMENTO (PG-19), 160
SAGAMORE (1861), 73
SAGINAW (1858), 64, 72
SAGINAW BAY (ACV-82), 130
SAIDOR (CVE-117), 131
Saif, 241
Sailfish (SS-192), 270
SAILFISH (SSR-572), 291
SAIPAN (CVL-48), 121
Sakalave, 223
Sakarya, 276
Sakura, 247
SALAMAUA (ACV-96), 130
SALEM (CA-139), 140
SALEM (CS-3), 147
SALERNO BAY (CVE-110), 131

Salisbury, 174
Sally, later COLUMBUS (1775), 33
Sally, later CABOT (1775), 34
SALMON (SS-19), 256
SALMON (SS-182), 269
Salmon (SS-269), 270
SALMON (SSR-573), 291
Salnave, 80
SALT LAKE CITY (CA-25), 136
SALT LAKE CITY (SSN-716), 289
Saltery Bay (CVE-117), 132
SAM HOUSTON (SSBN-609), 293
SAM RAYBURN (SSBN-635), 295
Samadikun, 240
SAMOA (CB-6), 135
SAMPLE (DE-1048), 241
SAMPSON (DD-63), 171
SAMPSON (DD-394), 187
SAMPSON (DDG-10), 211
Samson (1862), 52
SAMUEL B. ROBERTS (DD-823), 203
SAMUEL B. ROBERTS (DE-413), 237
SAMUEL B. ROBERTS (FFG-58), 252
Samuel E. Morison (FFG-13), 252
SAMUEL ELIOT MORISON (FFG-13), 251
SAMUEL N. MOORE (DD-747), 200
Samuel Rotan (schooner, 1861), 91
SAMUEL S. MILES (DE-183), 223
San Alberto Bay (CVE-116), 132
San Diego (CA-6), 135
SAN DIEGO (CL-53), 150
SAN FRANCISCO (C-5), 143
SAN FRANCISCO (CA-38), 138
SAN FRANCISCO (SSN-711), 285 (photo), 289
SAN JACINTO (1847), 62
SAN JACINTO (CG-56), 218
SAN JACINTO (CV-30), 120
SAN JUAN (CL-54), 150
SAN JUAN (SSN-751), 290
San Marcos (1886), 102
SAN PEDRO (PF-37), 247
SAND LANCE (SS-381), 277
SAND LANCE (SSN-660), 288
SANDERS (DE-40), 219
SANDERS (DE-273), 220
SANDS (DD-243), 179
SANDUSKY (1862), 51
SANDUSKY (PF-54), 248
Sandy Bay (CVE-118), 132
SANGAMON (1862), 42
SANGAMON (ACV-26), 126, 132
Santa Catarina, 196
SANTA FE (CL-60), 151
SANTA FE (SSN-763), 290
Santa Fe (ex SS-339), 276
Santa Fe (ex SS-375), 277
Santander, 199
SANTEE (1816), 14
SANTEE (ACV-29), 126
SANTIAGO DE CUBA (1861), 87, 91, 92, 93
Santiago del Estero (ex SS-341), 276
Santiago del Estero (ex SS-372), 277
Sarah S. B. Cary, 93
SARANAC (1814), 26

SARANAC (1847), 61, 62
Sarandi, 248
SARATOGA (1776), 16
SARATOGA (1814), 24
SARATOGA (1841), 20
Saratoga (CA-2), 133
SARATOGA (CC-3), 114
SARATOGA (CV-3), 115
SARATOGA (CVA-60), 123
(SARAWAK) (PF-87), 248
SARDA (SS-488), 280
SARGENT BAY (ACV-83), 130
SARGO (SS-188), 269
SARGO (SSN-583), 286
SARSFIELD (DD-837), 203
SASSACUS (1862), 78, 81, 82
SATTERLEE (DD-190), 178
SATTERLEE (DD-626), 191
SAUFLEY (DD-465), 192
SAUGUS (1862), 44
SAURY (SS-189), 269
SAUSALITO (PF-4), 246
SAVAGE (DE-386), 226
SAVANNAH (1816), 14
SAVANNAH (CL-42), 148
Savastepe, 205
SAVO ISLAND (ACV-78), 130
SAWFISH (SS-276), 272
SC-18, 271
SCABBARDFISH (SS-397), 278
SCAMMEL (1798), 29
SCAMP (SS-277), 273
SCAMP (SSN-588), 286
SCHENCK (DD-159), 178
Schley (DD-99), 176
SCHLEY (DD-103), 175
Schley (SS-52), 260
SCHMITT (DE-676), 231
SCHOFIELD (DEG-3), 245
SCHROEDER (DD-501), 192
SCHURZ (1917), 161
SCIOTA (1861), 75
SCORPION (SS-278), 273
SCORPION (SSN-589), 286, 293
SCOTT (DDG-995), 212
SCOTT (DE-214), 230
Scott (DE-241), 226
SCOURGE (1804), 35
SCRANTON (CA-138), 139
Scranton (PF-63), 251
SCRANTON (SSN-756), 290
SCRIBNER (DE-689), 234
SCROGGINS (DE-799), 231
SCULPIN (SS-191), 269
SCULPIN (SS-494), 281
SCULPIN (SSN-590), 286
Scylla (1862), 44
SEA CAT (SS-399), 278
SEA DEVIL (SS-400), 278
SEA DEVIL (SSN-664), 288
SEA DOG (SS-401), 278
SEA FOX (SS-402), 278
SEA LEOPARD (SS-483), 280
SEA OWL (SS-405), 278

SEA PANTHER (SS-528), 281
SEA POACHER (SS-406), 278
SEA ROBIN (SS-407), 278
SEADRAGON (SS-194), 270
SEADRAGON (SSN-584), 286
SEAHORSE (SS-304), 275
SEAHORSE (SSN-669), 288
Seakay, 126
SEAL (1907), 256
SEAL (SS-183), 269
SEALION (SS-195), 270
SEALION (SS-315), 276
SEAMAN (DD-791), 202
SEARAVEN (SS-196), 270
(SEARCHER) (ACV-22), 128
Seattle (CA-11), 135
Seawolf (SS-28), 258
SEAWOLF (SS-197), 270
SEAWOLF (SSN-21), 290
SEAWOLF (SSN-575), 284
SEBAGO (1861), 79
SEDERSTROM (DE-31), 219
Segui, 199
SEGUNDO (SS-398), 278
SEID (DE-256), 220
SELFRIDGE (DD-320), 181
SELFRIDGE (DD-357), 183
SELLERS (DDG-11), 211
SELLSTROM (DE-255), 225
SELMA (1864), 94
Selma (CSS), 94
SEMINOLE (1858), 64, 67
SEMMES (DD-189), 178
SEMMES (DDG-18), 211
SENECA (1861), 75
Senegalais, 222
SENNET (SS-408), 278
Senorita (SS-412), 279
Seoul, 196
SERAPIS (1779), 8
SERAPIS (1864), 69
Sergipe, 201
Serrano, 231
Severn (1863), 69
(SEYCHELLES) (PF-88), 250
(SEYMOUR) (DE-98), 228
SEYMOUR D. OWENS (DD-767), 202
Sfendoni, 194
SHACKAMAXON (1863), 46
SHAD (SS-235), 272
Shah (ex ACV-43), 128
Shah (ex ACV-86), 131
(SHAH JAHAN) (DD-962), 208
Shah Jahan (ex DD-864), 204
SHAMOKIN (1863), 82
SHAMROCK (1862), 81
Shamrock, later ISONOMIA (1864), 94
SHAMROCK BAY (ACV-84), 130
SHANGRI LA (CV-38), 119
SHANNON (DD-737), 200
Shannon (HMS), 9
Shao Yang, 204
Shapour, 212
SHARK (1820), 31

SHARK (SS-8), 253
SHARK (SS-174), 268, 269
SHARK (SS-314), 276
SHARK (SSN-591), 286
SHARKEY (DD-281), 180
SHAW (DD-68), 172
SHAW (DD-373), 184
SHAWMUT (1862), 75
SHAWNEE (1863), 45
SHEA (DD-750), 200
SHEBOYGAN (PF-57), 248
SHEEHAN (DE-541), 238
SHELTON (DD-790), 202
SHELTON (DE-407), 236
Shen Yang, 203
SHENANDOAH (1861), 68, 70
Sherwood, 180
(SHIEL) (PG-110), 246
SHIELDS (DD-596), 195
Shii, 247
SHILOH (1863), 45
SHILOH (CG-67), 218
Shiner (SS-404), 279
SHIPLEY BAY (ACV-85), 130
SHIRK (DD-318), 181
SHOKOKON (1863), 96
Shou Shan, 234
SHREVEPORT (PF-23), 247
SHUBRICK (DD-268), 180
SHUBRICK (DD-639), 191
SHUBRICK (TB-31), 167
SIBONEY (CVE-112), 131
SICARD (DD-346), 181
SICILY (CVE-118), 131
SIDES (FFG-14), 251
Sierra Leone, 251
SIGOURNEY (DD-81), 175
SIGOURNEY (DD-643), 195
SIGSBEE (DD-502), 192
SILVERSIDES (SS-236), 272
SILVERSIDES (SSN-679), 288
SILVERSTEIN (DE-534), 238, 278
SIMON BOLIVAR (SSBN-641), 295
SIMPSON (DD-221), 179
SIMPSON (FFG-56), 252
Simpson (ex SS-413), 278
SIMS (DD-409), 188, 189
SIMS (DE-154), 228
SINCLAIR (DD-275), 180
Siqqat, 241
SIRAGO (SS-485), 280
Siren (1803), 25
Sitka (PF-94), 251
SITKOH BAY (ACV-86), 130
Skate (SS-23), 257
SKATE (SS-305), 275
SKATE (SSN-578), 285 (photo), 286, 292
Skipjack (SS-24), 256
SKIPJACK (SS-184), 269
SKIPJACK (SSN-585), 286, 287, 290, 293
SLATER (DE-766), 224
Slinger (ex ACV-32), 128
Slinger (ex ACV-39), 128
SLOAT (DD-316), 181

SLOAT (DE-245), 225
SMALLEY (DD-565), 194
SMARTT (DE-257), 220
Smiter (ex ACV-52), 129
Smiter (ex ACV-54), 129
SMITH (DD-17), 169
Smith (DD-348), 183
SMITH (DD-378), 184
SMITH THOMPSON (DD-212), 179
SNAPPER (SS-16), 254
SNAPPER (SS-185), 269
SNOOK (SS-279), 273
SNOOK (SSN-592), 286
SNOWDEN (DE-246), 225
SNYDER (DE-745), 223
Socrates, 159
SOLAR (DE-221), 230
Sole (SS-410), 279
SOLEY (DD-707), 199
SOLOMONS (ACV-67), 130
(SOMALI) (DE-111), 222
(SOMALILAND) (PF-90), 250
SOMERS (1841), 27
SOMERS (DD-301), 181
SOMERS (DD-381), 187
SOMERS (DD-947), 208
SOMERS (TB-22), 166
SOMERSET (1862), 96
SONOMA (1861), 79, 93
Soudanais, 224
SOUTH CAROLINA (1798), 29
SOUTH CAROLINA (1861), 87, 92
SOUTH CAROLINA (BB-26), 107
SOUTH CAROLINA (DLGN-37), 217
South Carolina, ex L'INDIEN (1776), 7
SOUTH DAKOTA (BB-49), 112
SOUTH DAKOTA (BB-57), 113
SOUTH DAKOTA (CA-9), 133
SOUTHAMPTON (1841), 71
Southampton (HMS), 29
SOUTHARD (DD-207), 179
SOUTHERLAND (DD-743), 202
Southern Star, 90
SOUTHFIELD (1861), 95
SPADEFISH (SS-411), 278
SPADEFISH (SSN-668), 288
SPANGENBERG (DE-223), 230
SPANGLER (DE-696), 231
SPARK (1814), 35
Speaker (ex ACV-40), 128
Speaker (ex ACV-42), 128
SPEARFISH (SS-190), 269
SPENCE (DD-512), 193
Sphinx, 47
SPIKEFISH (SS-404), 278
SPINAX (SS-489), 280
SPIREA (1864), 94
SPITFIRE (1814), 36
Spitfire (1863), 45
Spokane (CL-97), 150
SPOKANE (CL-120), 152
SPOT (SS-413), 278
(SPRAGGE) (DE-563), 230
SPRINGER (SS-414), 278

(SPRINGEREN) (SS-554), 283
SPRINGFIELD (CL-66), 151; (CLG-7), 154
SPRINGFIELD (SSN-761), 290
SPROSTON (DD-173), 176
SPROSTON (DD-577), 194
SPRUANCE (DD-963), 210, 211, 217, 218, 244
SPUYTEN DUYVIL (1864), 83
SQUALUS (SS-192), 269
SQUANDO (1863), 45
SS-553, 283
SS-556, 283
SSBN-742, 295
St. Albans, 177
ST. ANDREWS (ACV-49), 129
St. Andrews Bay (CVE-107), 132
St. Clair, 175
St. Croix, 179
St. Francis, 180
ST. GEORGE (ACV-17), 128
(ST. HELENA) (PF-86), 248
ST. JOSEPH (ACV-50), 129
St. Joseph Bay (CVE-105), 132
ST. LAWRENCE (1816), 14
St. Lo (ACV-63), 131
ST. LOUIS (1825), 19
ST. LOUIS (1861), 49
ST. LOUIS (1898), 297
ST. LOUIS (C-20), 146
ST. LOUIS (CL-49), 149 (photo), 150
ST. MARY'S (1843), 21, 22 (photo)
St. Mary's, later HATTERAS (1861), 86
St. Marys (ex DD-185), 177
ST. PAUL (1898), 297
St. Paul (CA-71), 139
ST. PAUL (CA-73), 139
ST. SIMON (ACV-51), 129
STACK (DD-406), 187
STADTFELD (DE-29), 219
Staerkodder, 47
STAFFORD (DE-411), 237
Stalker, 128
STAMFORD (PF-95), 250
Stanley, 179
STANLY (DD-478), 192
STANSBURY (DD-180), 176
STANTON (DE-247), 225
Star (1861), 90
STARK (FFG-31), 252
STARS AND STRIPES (1861), 91
STATE OF GEORGIA (1861), 87
(STAYNER) (DE-564), 230
Steam Launches Nos. 1-6 (1876), 85
STEAMER BAY (ACV-87), 130
Steel Architect, 129
Steel Artisan, 129
STEELE (DE-8), 219
STEELHEAD (SS-280), 273
STEIN (DE-1065), 243
STEINAKER (DD-863), 204
STEINAKER (DE-452), 237
STEMBEL (DD-644), 195
STEPHEN POTTER (DD-538), 193
STEPHEN W. GROVES (FFG-29), 252

STERETT (DD-27), 169
STERETT (DD-407), 187
STERETT (DLG-31), 215
STERLET (SS-392), 278
STERN (DE-187), 223
STETHEM (DDG-63), 212
STETTIN (1862), 88, 92
STEVENS (DD-86), 175
STEVENS (DD-479), 192
STEVENS BATTERY (1842), 39
STEVENSON (DD-503), 198
STEVENSON (DD-645), 191
STEWART (DD-13), 163 (photo), 168
Stewart (DD-216), 182
STEWART (DD-224), 179
Stewart (DD-291), 182
Stewart (DD-292), 182
STEWART (DE-238), 225
STICKELL (DD-888), 205
STICKLEBACK (SS-415), 278
STILETTO (1887), 298
STINGRAY (SS-13), 254
STINGRAY (SS-186), 269
STOCKDALE (DE-399), 226
STOCKHAM (DD-683), 196
(STOCKHAM) (DE-97), 228
STOCKTON (DD-73), 172
STOCKTON (DD-504), 198
STOCKTON (DD-646), 191
STOCKTON (TB-32), 167
STODDARD (DD-566), 194
STODDERT (DD-302), 181
STONEWALL (1865), 47
STONEWALL JACKSON (SSBN-634), 295
STORMES (DD-780), 201
STOUT (DDG-55), 212
STRAUB (DE-77), 227
STRAUB (DE-181), 223
STRAUS (DE-408), 236
STRIBLING (DD-96), 175
STRIBLING (DD-867), 204
STRICKLAND (DE-333), 225
(STRIKER) (ACV-19), 128
STRINGHAM (DD-83), 175
STRINGHAM (TB-19), 166
Stromboli (1863), 45
Stromboli (1864), 83
STRONG (DD-467), 192
STRONG (DD-758), 200
STUMP (DD-978), 210
Sturgeon (SS-25), 256
STURGEON (SS-187), 269
STURGEON (SSN-637), 288, 289
STURTEVANT (DD-240), 179
STURTEVANT (DE-239), 225
Submarine No. 7, 49
Sugi, 247
SUMNER (DD-333), 181
Sumpter (1858), 90
SUMTER (1858), 90
SUMTER (1862), 97
SUNCOOK (1863), 45
SUNFISH (SS-281), 273
SUNFISH (SSN-649), 288

SUNSET (ACV-48), 129
Sunset (CVE-106), 132
SUPERIOR (1813), 15
Surprize (1814), 28
SUSQUEHANNA (1847), 54, 61
Susquehannah (1816), 14
SUTTON (DE-286), 233
SUTTON (DE-771), 224
SUWANEE (1863), 82
Suwanee (ACV-27), 126
SUWANNEE (ACV-27), 126
SWANSON (DD-443), 190
SWASEY (DD-273), 180
Swasey (DD-299), 182
SWASEY (DE-248), 225
SWATARA (1864), 57, 70, 71, 76
SWATARA (1872), 71
SWEARER (DE-186), 223
SWENNING (DE-394), 226
SWORDFISH (SS-193), 269
SWORDFISH (SSN-579), 286
(SYDNEY) (FFG-35), 252
SYLPH (1813), 32
SYREN (1803), 25, 35
T 1 (SS-52), 255 (photo), 260
T-1 (SST-1), 296
T-2 (SS-60), 260
T-2 (SST-2), 296
T-3 (SS-61), 260
T-4, 207
T-14, 207
T-19, 207
(T-35) (DD-935), 207
T.A.M. CRAVEN (TB-10), 164
TABBERER (DE-418), 237
Tabuk, 245
Tacloban (PG-22), 160
TACOMA (C-18), 146
TACOMA (PF-3), 246
TACONY (1862), 81
Taejon, 203
Taetong, 246
TAGHKANIC (1864), 69
Tahchin, 247
TAHGAYUTA (1863), 69
Tahoe (CM-2), 144
TAHOMA (1861), 75
Tai Chao, 222
Tai Chong, 222
Tai Ho, 222
Tai Hu, 222
Tai Kang, 219
Tai Ping, 220
Tai Shan, 233
Tai Yuan, 233
Taimur, 202
TAKANIS BAY (ACV-89), 130
Take, 199
TALBOT (DD-114), 174
TALBOT (DEG-4), 245
TALBOT (TB-15), 165
TALLADEGA (1864), 69
Tallahassee (BM-9), 101
TALLAHASSEE (CL-61), 120, 151

TALLAHASSEE (CL-116), 152
TALLAHOMA (1862), 81
TALLAPOOSA (1862), 81
Tamandare, 150
TAMBOR (SS-198), 267, 270, 273
Tananek Bay (ACV-88), 131
TANG (SS-306), 275
TANG (SS-563), 282, 283, 286
(TAPI) (PF-107), 251
TARANTULA (SS-12), 254
TARAWA (CV-40), 116 (photo), 119
TARBELL (DD-142), 174
Target A, 162
Target B, 99
Target C, 99
Target D, 99
Target E, 254
Tariq, 202
TARPON (SS-14), 254, 255 (photo)
TARPON (SS-175), 268
Tartar (1863), 45
TATTNALL (DD-125), 174, 178
TATTNALL (DDG-19), 211
TATUM (DE-789), 231
TAUSSIG (DD-746), 200
TAUTOG (SS-199), 270
TAUTOG (SSN-639), 288
Taylor (1861), 96
TAYLOR (DD-94), 174
TAYLOR (DD-468), 192
TAYLOR (FFG-50), 252
TCHIFONTA (1814), 32
Te Yang, 203
TECUMSEH (1862), 44
TECUMSEH (SSBN-628), 293
Tehuantepec (ex DE-674), 234
Tehuantepec (ex PF-16), 247
Tempest (1863), 45
TENCH (SS-417), 279, 280, 282
TENNESSEE (1862), 88
Tennessee (1863), 58, 141
TENNESSEE (1864), 46
TENNESSEE (BB-43), 111, 112
TENNESSEE (CA-10), 135
TENNESSEE (SSBN-734), 295
Teratsuki, 188
Terreur, 76
Terror (1862), 43
TERROR (BM-4), 99
TERRY (DD-25), 169
TERRY (DD-513), 193
(TERUZUKI) (DD-960), 208
TEXAS (1865), 46
TEXAS (1886), 102
TEXAS (BB-35), 108, 112
TEXAS (CGN-39), 217
Texgon (SS-550), 281
THADDEUS PARKER (DE-369), 236
Thane (ex ACV-48), 129
Thane (ex ACV-104), 131
THATCH (FFG-43), 252
THATCHER (DD-162), 176
THATCHER (DD-514), 193
THE SULLIVANS (DD-537), 193

Themistocles, 202
THEODORE E. CHANDLER (DD-717), 202
THEODORE ROOSEVELT (CVN-71), 125
THEODORE ROOSEVELT (SSBN-600), 293
THETIS BAY (ACV-90), 130
Thistle, later CHEROKEE (1864), 94
Thistle, later DUMBARTON (1864), 94
THOMAS (DD-182), 177
THOMAS (DE-102), 222
THOMAS A. EDISON (SSBN-610), 293
THOMAS C. HART (DE-1092), 244
THOMAS E. FRASER (DD-736), 200
THOMAS F. NICKEL (DE-587), 233
THOMAS J. GARY (DE-61), 227
THOMAS J. GRAY (DE-326), 225
THOMAS JEFFERSON (SSBN-618), 293
THOMAS S. GATES (CG-51), 218
THOMASON (DE-203), 228
THOMPSON (DD-305), 181
THOMPSON (DD-627), 191
Thomson, 278
THORN (DD-505), 198
THORN (DD-647), 191
THORN (DD-988), 210
THORNBACK (SS-418), 280
(THORNBOROUGH) (DE-565), 230
THORNHILL (DE-195), 223
THORNTON (DD-270), 180
THORNTON (TB-33), 167
Thrasher (SS-26), 257
THREADFIN (SS-410), 278
THRESHER (SS-200), 270
THRESHER (SSN-593), 286, 287, 288, 292
Thunderer (1863), 46
Thyella, 193
TIBURON (SS-529), 281
Tiburon (ex SS-347), 277
TICONDEROGA (1814), 36
TICONDEROGA (1861), 65 (photo), 67
TICONDEROGA (CG-47), 212, 218
TICONDEROGA (CV-14), 119, 120
Ticonderoga (CV-19), 119
Tien Shan, 235
TIGRONE (SS-419), 280
TILEFISH (SS-307), 275
TILLMAN (DD-135), 174
TILLMAN (DD-641), 191
TILLS (DE-748), 223
TIMMERMAN (DD-816), 203
TIMMERMAN (DD-828), 198, 203
Tinaztepe, 202
TINGEY (DD-272), 180
TINGEY (DD-539), 193
TINGEY (TB-34), 167
TINIAN (CVE-123), 132
TINOSA (SS-283), 273
TINOSA (SSN-606), 286
TINSMAN (DE-589), 233
TIOGA (1861), 79, 93
TIPPECANOE (1862), 44
Tippu Sultan, 204
TIRANTE (SS-420), 280
TIRU (SS-416), 278
TISDALE (DE-33), 219

TISDALE (DE-278), 220
(TOBAGO) (PF-81), 248
Tochi, 246
TOLEDO (CA-133), 139
Toledo (PF-33), 251
TOLEDO (SSN-769), 290
TOLLBERG (DE-593), 234
TOLMAN (DD-740), 200
Tombazis, 202
TOMICH (DE-242), 225
Tomtate (SS-421), 281
TONAWANDA (1862), 43
Tonawanda, later ARKANSAS (1863), 88
Tonopah (BM-8), 101
Tonowek Bay (ACV-104), 131
TOPEKA (1898), 159
TOPEKA (CL-67), 151; (CLG-8), 154
TOPEKA (SSN-754), 290
TORCH (1814), 36
Tornado (1862), 52
TORO (SS-422), 280
(TORRINGTON) (DE-568), 230
TORSK (SS-423), 280
(TORTOLA) (PF-91), 250
Totem Bay (CVE-111), 132
Touareg, 223
Toucey (1858), 72
TOUCEY (DD-282), 180
TOWERS (DDG-9), 211
TRACKER (BAVG-6), 128
TRACY (DD-214), 179
Trailer, 128
Tran Hung Dao, 225
Tran Khanh Du, 225
Transfer, 35
TRATHEN (DD-530), 193
Traveller, 37
TRAW (DE-350), 236
Trembler (SS-424), 281
TRENTON (?) (1841), 71
TRENTON (1873), 62, 71, 141
TRENTON (CL-11), 148
TREPANG (SS-412), 278
TREPANG (SSN-674), 288
TREVER (DD-339), 181
Triaina, 278
TRIGGER (SS-237), 272
TRIGGER (SS-564), 282
Trinidad, 248
TRIPOLI (ACV-64), 130
TRIPPE (DD-33), 170
TRIPPE (DD-403), 187
TRIPPE (DE-1075), 243
TRISTAM SHANDY (1864), 94
TRITON (SS-201), 270
TRITON (SSRN-586), 291
TRITONIA (1863), 93
Triumph, 46
Trocadero Bay (CVE-119), 132
(TROLLOPE) (DE-566), 230
Trouncer (ex ACV-47), 129
Trouncer (ex ACV-49), 129
Trouncer (ex ACV-50), 129
TROUP (1812), 35

TROUT (SS-202), 270
TROUT (SS-566), 274 (photo), 282
TRUETT (DE-1095), 244
TRUMBULL (1775), 6
TRUMBULL (1798), 16
TRUMPETER (DE-180), 223
TRUMPETER (DE-279), 220
Trumpeter (ex AVG-37), 128
TRUMPETFISH (SS-425), 278
TRUTTA (SS-421), 280
TRUXTUN (1841), 26
TRUXTUN (DD-14), 169
TRUXTUN (DD-229), 179
TRUXTUN (DE-282), 233
TRUXTUN (DLGN-35), 215
Tsuge, 247
TUCKER (DD-57), 171, 172
TUCKER (DD-374), 184
Tucson (CL-96), 150
TUCSON (CL-98), 150
TUCSON (SSN-770), 290
Tughril, 202
TULAGI (ACV-72), 130
TULLIBEE (SS-284), 273
TULLIBEE (SSN-597), 287
TULSA (CA-129), 139
TULSA (PG-22), 160
Tuna (SS-27), 257
TUNA (SS-203), 270
Tunisien, 222
TUNNY (SS-282), 273
TUNNY (SSN-682), 288
TUNXIS (1863), 45
Turbot (SS-31), 258
TURBOT (SS-427), 278
Turgut Reis, 276
TURNER (DD-259), 180
TURNER (DD-506), 198
TURNER (DD-648), 191
TURNER (DD-834), 203
TURNER JOY (DD-951), 208
TUSCALOOSA (CA-37), 138
TUSCARORA (1858), 66
TUSCUMBIA (1862), 51
TUSK (SS-426), 278
TWEEDY (DE-532), 238
TWIGGS (DD-127), 178
TWIGGS (DD-591), 195
TWINING (DD-540), 193
TYLER (1861), 50, 96
(TYLER) (DE-567), 230
U-53, 171
U-135, 268
U-142, 265
U-163, 161
U-255, 225
U-275, 178
U-371, 190
U-405, 179
U-546, 224
U-549, 128
U-562, 179
U-578, 178
U-616, 188

U-804, 225
U-967, 228
UHLMANN (DD-687), 196
Ulitka Bay (ACV-91), 131
ULUA (SS-428), 278
Uluc Ali Reis, 280
ULVERT M. MOORE (DE-442), 237
ULYSSES S. GRANT (SSBN-631), 293
Ume, 247
UMPQUA (1863), 45
UNADILLA (1861), 75, 88, 89
UNDERHILL (DE-682), 231
UNDERWOOD (FFG-36), 252
UNDERWRITER (1861), 91
Ung Po, 234
UNICORN (SS-429), 279
UNICORN (SS-436), 280
UNION (1839), 61
UNION (1861), 91
Union (transport, 1862), 91
Union, ex MARATANZA (1861), 80
Union, later FORT JACKSON (1863), 88
UNIONTOWN (PF-65), 248
UNITED STATES (1794), 9, 11
UNITED STATES (CC-6), 114
UNITED STATES (CVA-58), 123
UNITED STATES (CVN-75), 125
Unknown name (SS-553), 283
Unknown name (SS-556), 283
Unknown names, brigs (1798), 24
Unknown names, ships of the line (1776),
    1; (1799), 1
Unknown names, sloops of war (1799), 17
Unnamed (CA 141-143, 149, 151-153), 140
Unnamed (CL-115), 152
Unnamed (CL 154-159), 153
Unnamed (CV 50-55), 119
Unnamed (CVB-44, 56-57), 121
Unnamed (CVE 128-139), 132
Unnamed (DD 200-205), 178
Unnamed (DD 523-525), 193
Unnamed (DD 542-543), 193
Unnamed (DD 548-549), 194
Unnamed (DD 809-814), 203
Unnamed (DD 855-856), 204
Unnamed (DD 891-926), 205
Unnamed (DE 114-128), 222
Unnamed (DE-289), 233
Unnamed (DE 291-300), 233
Unnamed (DE-315), 221
Unnamed (DE 380-381), 236
Unnamed (DE 425-437), 237
Unnamed (DE 453-507), 237
Unnamed (DE 511-515), 238
Unnamed (DE 558-562), 238
Unnamed (DE 607-632), 234
Unnamed (DE 645-664), 234
Unnamed (DE 724-738), 235
Unnamed (DE 757-762), 224
Unnamed (DE 775-788), 224
Unnamed (DE 801-904), 238
Unnamed (DE 905-1005), 235
Unnamed (DE 1098-1107), 244
Unnamed (SS 438-463), 279

Unnamed (SS 465-474), 279
Unnamed (SS 495-515), 281
Unnamed (SS-517), 281
Unnamed (SS 519-521), 281
Unnamed (SS 530-536), 279
Unnamed (SS 537-550), 281
Unnamed (SS 551-562), 282
Unnamed dynamite cruiser (1890), 147
Unnamed floating batteries (1814), 53;
    (1816), 53
Unnamed frigates (1776), 7
Unnamed monitor (1889), 101
Unnamed Neff submarine (SS-108), 262
Unnamed schooners (1777), 31
Unnamed steam sloop (1841), 71
Unnamed subsurface boat (1907), 256
Unnamed subsurface boats (1909), 258
Unnamed torpedo cruiser (1890), 147
UPHAM (DE-283), 233
UPSHUR (DD-144), 174
Uribe, 227
Uruguay, 222
Usumacinta (ex DE-721), 235
Usumacinta (ex PF-15), 247
UTAH (BB-31), 107
V-1 (SF-4), 257, 265, 267
V-2 (SF-5), 265
V-3 (SF-6), 265
V-4 (SM-1), 265, 267
V-5 (SC-1), 267
V-6 (SC-2), 266 (photo), 267
V-7 (SC-3), 267
V-8 (SC-4), 268
V-9 (SC-5), 268
VALDEZ (DE-1096), 244
VALLEJO (CL-112), 152
VALLEJO (CL-146), 152
Vallejo (PF-97), 251
VALLEY FORGE (CG-50), 218
Valley Forge (CV-37), 119
VALLEY FORGE (CV-45), 119
VAMMEN (DE-644), 231
Van Amstel, 222
VAN BUREN (PF-42), 247
Van Ewijck, 223
VAN VALKENBURGH (DD-656), 195
VAN VOORHIS (DE-1028), 239
Van Zijll, 223
VANCE (DE-387), 226
VANDALIA (1825), 19, 22 (photo), 70
VANDALIA (1872), 70
VANDEGRIFT (FFG-48), 252
VANDERBILT (1862), 88, 89, 92
VANDIVIER (DE-540), 238
VARIAN (DE-798), 231
VARUNA (1861), 88
VELLA GULF (CG-72), 218
VELLA GULF (CVE-111), 131
Velos, 195
VENDACE (SS-430), 279
Venezuela, 297
VENGEANCE (1779), 34
Ventura, 76
VERMILLION (ACV-52), 129

Vermillion Bay (CVE-108), 132
VERMONT (1816), 2, 3 (photo)
VERMONT (BB-20), 106
Vermont, later VIRGINIA (1816), 4
VESOLE (DD-878), 204
Vesuvius (1862), 44
VESUVIUS (1886), 146, 147
VICKSBURG (1863), 89
VICKSBURG (CG-69), 218
Vicksburg (CL-81), 151
VICKSBURG (CL-86), 151
VICKSBURG (PG-11), 158
Victoria de los Tunas, 94
Villar, 196
VINCENNES (1825), 19
VINCENNES (CA-44), 138
VINCENNES (CG-49), 218
VINCENNES (CL-64), 151
VINDICATOR (1864), 97
Viper (1804), 31
VIPER (SS-10), 254
VIRGINIA (1775), 5
VIRGINIA (1798), 29
VIRGINIA (1816), 2
VIRGINIA (1863), 93
VIRGINIA (BB-13), 104, 106
Virginia (BB-16), 106
VIRGINIA (CGN-38), 217
Virginia (CSS), 14, 15, 57, 83
Virginia, later VERMONT (1816), 4
Virginia II (CSS), 83
Virginia Dare, 90
VIXEN (1803), 29
VIXEN (1813), 35
Vixen (1862), 52
VOGE (DE-1047), 241
VOGELGESANG (DD-862), 204
VOGELGESANG (DE-284), 233
VOLADOR (SS-490), 281
Volent, 35
Volontaire, 35
VON STEUBEN (SSBN-632), 295
VREELAND (DE-1068), 243
W. S. SIMS (DE-1059), 243
WABASH (1854), 55, 141
WACHUSETT (1858), 64, 93
WADDELL (DDG-24), 211
WADLEIGH (DD-689), 196
WADSWORTH (DD-60), 171
WADSWORTH (DD-516), 193
WADSWORTH (FFG-9), 249 (photo), 251
WAGNER (DE-539), 238
WAHOO (SS-238), 272
WAHOO (SS-516), 281
WAHOO (SS-518), 281
WAHOO (SS-565), 282
WAINWRIGHT (DD-62), 171
WAINWRIGHT (DD-419), 188
WAINWRIGHT (DLG-28), 215
WAKE ISLAND (ACV-65), 130
Wakefield (AVG-2), 126
(WALDEGRAVE) (DE-570), 230
WALDRON (DD-699), 199
WALKE (DD-34), 170

WALKE (DD-416), 188
WALKE (DD-723), 199
WALKER (DD-163), 176
WALKER (DD-517), 193
WALLACE L. LIND (DD-703), 199
WALLER (DD-466), 192
Walrus (SS-35), 258
WALRUS (SS-431), 279
WALRUS (SS-437), 280
Walrus (ex SS-367), 277
WALSH (DE-601), 234
WALTER B. COBB (DE-596), 234
WALTER C. WANN (DE-412), 229 (photo), 237
WALTER S. BROWN (DE-258), 220
WALTER S. GORKA (DE-604), 234
WALTER X. YOUNG (DE-715), 234
WALTER X. YOUNG (DE-723), 235
WALTON (DE-361), 236
WAMPANOAG (1863), 56 (photo), 57, 58, 59, 69
WANALOSET (1863), 63, 69
WANDO (1864), 95
WANTUCK (DE-692), 234
WARD (DD-139), 174
WARREN (1775), 5
WARREN (1798), 16
WARREN (1825), 19, 35
WARRINGTON (DD-30), 169
WARRINGTON (DD-383), 187
WARRINGTON (DD-843), 203
WASHINGTON (brig, 1775), 34
WASHINGTON (frigate, 1775), 5
WASHINGTON (1813), 2
WASHINGTON (BB-47), 109, 112
WASHINGTON (BB-56), 112
WASHINGTON (CA-11), 135
WASMUTH (DD-338), 181
WASP (1804), 25
WASP (1813), 18
Wasp (1865), 95
WASP (CV-7), 115, 117
WASP (CV-18), 118, 190
WASSUC (1863), 45
WATAUGA (1863), 60
Water Witch (1843), 72
WATER WITCH (1852), 72
WATEREE (1862), 81
WATERMAN (DE-740), 223
WATERS (DD-115), 174
WATSON (DD-482), 198
WATTS (DD-567), 194
WAXSAW (1863), 45
WEAVER (DE-741), 223
WEBER (DE-675), 231
WEDDERBURN (DD-684), 196
WEEDEN (DE-797), 231
WEEHAWKEN (1862), 42, 46
WEEKS (DE-285), 233
WEISS (DE-378), 236
WEISS (DE-719), 235
WELBORN C. WOOD (DD-195), 178
WELLES (DD-257), 180
WELLES (DD-628), 191
Wells, 174

Wen Shan, 227
WESSON (DE-184), 223
West Point (AVG-4), 126
WEST VIRGINIA (BB-48), 112
WEST VIRGINIA (CA-5), 133
WEST VIRGINIA (SSBN-736), 295
Western Port (1858), 90
WESTERN WORLD (1861), 91
WESTFIELD (1861), 95
WHALE (SS-239), 272
WHALE (SSN-638), 288
WHARTON (1846), 27
WHEELING (PG-14), 158
WHIPPLE (DD-15), 169
WHIPPLE (DD-217), 179
WHIPPLE (DE-1062), 243
(WHITAKER) (DE-571), 230
WHITE PLAINS (ACV-66), 130
WHITEFISH (SS-432), 279
WHITEHALL (1861), 96
WHITEHURST (DE-634), 230
WHITING (SS-433), 279
WHITMAN (DE-24), 219
WICHITA (CA-45), 138, 139
WICKES (DD-75), 172, 176, 177, 178
WICKES (DD-578), 194
Wild Duck, 34
Wilderness (small steamer, 1864), 94
WILEMAN (DE-22), 219
WILEY (DD-597), 195
WILHOITE (DE-397), 226
WILKES (DD-67), 172
WILKES (DD-441), 190
WILKES (TB-35), 167
Wilkes Barre (CL-90), 151
WILKES BARRE (CL-103), 151
WILKINSON (DL-5), 213
WILL ROGERS (SSBN-659), 295
WILLAMETTE (1863), 69
WILLAPA (ACV-53), 129
Willapa Bay (CVE-109), 132
WILLARD KEITH (DD-775), 201
WILLARD KEITH (DE-314), 221
WILLARD KEITH (DE-754), 224
WILLIAM B. PRESTON (DD-344), 181
William C. Cole (DE-286), 235
WILLIAM C. COLE (DE-641), 230
WILLIAM C. LAWE (DD-763), 202
WILLIAM C. LAWE (DE-313), 220
WILLIAM C. LAWE (DE-373), 236
WILLIAM C. MILLER (DE-259), 220
WILLIAM D. PORTER (DD-579), 194
William Ditter (DD-751), 201
William G. Hewes, 93
William G. Thomas (DE-193), 224
WILLIAM H. BATES (SSN-680), 288
WILLIAM H. STANDLEY (DLG-32), 215
WILLIAM J. PATTISON (DE-594), 234
WILLIAM JONES (DD-308), 181
WILLIAM M. HOBBY (DE-236), 233
WILLIAM M. WOOD (DD-715), 202
WILLIAM M. WOOD (DE-287), 233
WILLIAM M. WOOD (DE-557), 238
William Penn (SSBN-628), 295

WILLIAM R. RUSH (DD-714), 202
WILLIAM R. RUSH (DE-288), 233
WILLIAM R. RUSH (DE-556), 238
WILLIAM SEIVERLING (DE-441), 237
WILLIAM T. POWELL (DE-213), 230
WILLIAM V. PRATT (DLG-13), 214
WILLIAMS (DD-108), 175
WILLIAMS (DE-290), 233
WILLIAMS (DE-372), 236
WILLIAMSON (DD-244), 179
WILLIS (DE-395), 226
WILLIS A. LEE (DL-4), 213
WILLMARTH (DE-638), 230
WILMETTE (1917), 298
WILMINGTON (CL-79), 120, 151
WILMINGTON (CL-111), 152
WILMINGTON (PG-8), 158
WILSON (DD-408), 187
WILTSIE (DD-716), 202
WINDHAM BAY (ACV-92), 130
WINGFIELD (DE-194), 223
WINJAH (ACV-54), 129
Winjah Bay (CVE-110), 132
WINNEBAGO (1862), 52
WINNIPEC (1863), 82
WINONA (1861), 75
WINOOSKI (1862), 81
WINSLOW (DD-53), 171
WINSLOW (DD-359), 183
WINSLOW (TB-5), 164
WINTLE (DE-25), 219
WINTLE (DE-266), 220
WISCONSIN (BB-9), 104
WISCONSIN (BB-64), 110 (photo), 113
WISEMAN (DE-667), 231
WISSAHICKON (1861), 75
WITEK (DD-848), 204
WITTER (DE-636), 230
WOLFFISH (SS-434), 279
Wolverine (1841), 82
WOOD (DD-317), 181
WOODBURY (DD-309), 181
Woodcliff Bay (ACV-93), 131
WOODROW R. THOMPSON (DD-721), 202
WOODROW R. THOMPSON (DE-451), 237
WOODROW WILSON (SSBN-624), 293
WOODSON (DE-359), 236
WOODWORTH (DD-460), 188
WOOLSEY (DD-77), 172
WOOLSEY (DD-437), 190
WOONSOCKET (PF-32), 247
Worcester (1863), 69
WORCESTER (CL-144), 140, 152
Worcester (PF-62), 251
WORDEN (DD-16), 169
WORDEN (DD-288), 180
WORDEN (DD-352), 183
WORDEN (DLG-18), 214
WREN (DD-568), 194
Wright (CV-47), 119
WRIGHT (CVL-49), 121
WYALUSING (1862), 81
WYANDOTTE (1858), 90
Wyandotte (1862), 44

WYFFELS (DE-6), 219
WYMAN (DE-38), 219
WYOMING (1858), 65 (photo), 66, 67
WYOMING (BB-32), 108
WYOMING (BM-10), 101
YALE (1898), 297
YANKEE (1898), 297, 298
YANTIC (1862), 75
YARBOROUGH (DD-314), 181
Yarmouth, 5
YARNALL (DD-143), 174
YARNALL (DD-541), 193
YAZOO (1863), 45
YOKES (DE-668), 231
York (CL-1), 147
YORKTOWN (1837), 20
YORKTOWN (CG-48), 218
YORKTOWN (CV-5), 117, 198
YORKTOWN (CV-10), 118
YORKTOWN (PG-1), 155
YOSEMITE (1898), 297, 298
Yosemite (CM-2), 144
Yoshun, 75
YOUNG (DD-312), 181

YOUNG (DD-580), 194
YOUNG ROVER (1861), 91
YOUNGSTOWN (CL-94), 151
Yu Shan, 233
Yucetepe, 205
Yuen Yang, 199
Yugumo, 192
Yugure, 195
YUMA (1863), 45
Yumuri, 297
Yung Yang, 203
Z-1, 193
Z-2, 192
Z-3, 193
Z-4, 194
Z-5, 194
Z-6, 194
(Z-39) (DD-939), 207
Zafer, 199
ZANE (DD-337), 181
(ZANZIBAR) (PF-92), 250
Zeeleeuw, 277
ZEILIN (DD-313), 181
ZELLARS (DD-777), 201

About the Authors

K. JACK BAUER was a noted historian, long associated with Rensselaer Polytechnic Institute. He is the author of the *Ships of the Navy, 1775-1969* (1969) and *A Maritime History of the United States* (1988), co-editor of *United States Navy and Marine Corps Bases* (Greenwood, 1985) with Paolo Coletta, and editor of *The New American State Papers: Naval Affairs, 1789-1860* (1981), among others.

STEPHEN S. ROBERTS received his Ph.D. in History at the University of Chicago in 1976. He is currently a naval historian concerned especially with the history of naval technology since the eighteenth century and editor of *The Development of a Modern Navy: French Naval Policy, 1871-1904* by Theodore Ropp (1987).